Ukrainian Futurism, 1914–1930

UKRAINIAN RESEARCH INSTITUTE
HARVARD UNIVERSITY

HARVARD SERIES IN UKRAINIAN STUDIES

Cambridge, Massachusetts

Ukrainian Futurism, 1914–1930

A Historical and Critical Study

Oleh S. Ilnytzkyj

Distributed by Harvard University Press
for the
Ukrainian Research Institute, Harvard University

Publication of this volume has been made possible by the Dr. Evhen Omelsky and the Vladimir Jurkowsky publication funds in Ukrainian Studies at Harvard University.

ISBN 0-916458-56-3 (cl.)
ISBN 0-916458-59-8 (pb.)

∞ *This book has been printed on acid-free paper .*

The Ukrainian Research Institute was established in 1973 as an integral part of Harvard University. It supports research associates and visiting scholars who are engaged in projects concerned with all aspects of Ukrainian studies. The Institute also works in close cooperation with the Committee on Ukrainian Studies, which supervises and coordinates the teaching of Ukrainian history, language, and literature at Harvard University.

For My Mother and Father,
Nina and Roman Ilnytzkyj

Contents

List of Illustrations

Preface

Мене не знає історія.
History does not know me.

Поети не обминайте Семенка.
Poets, don't sidestep Semenko.

Mykhail' Semenko

With the realities of the post-Soviet world upon us, there is reason to believe that the magnificent modernist and avant-garde movements of late Imperial Russia and the early Soviet period—commonly recognized only as "Russian"—may be on the threshold of acquiring less exclusive national appellations and recognition. As one researcher recently noted, "many of the modern artists and designers who are generally categorized as Russian were, in fact, Ukrainian, Georgian, Armenian, Lithuanian, Latvian, Polish, etc." (Van Norman Baer 1991, 54). Of course, the issue is not so much the ethnic origin of individuals as the problem of what type of cultural system shaped both this art and this period and how it relates to the national cultures of Russians and non-Russians alike. The current practice of viewing this illustrious artistic revolution of the early twentieth century solely from a Russian national perspective will, no doubt, face serious challenge, for already some successor states to the Soviet Union are beginning to interpret the cultural contribution of their native sons and daughters to the former empire as an aspect of their own national heritage. It seems likely therefore that the art of this period gradually will be seen less in terms of a single nationality and culture—even one as predominant as the Russian—and more as an "imperial" (and therefore multinational) phenomenon, the historical and cultural "rights" to which belong to many peoples.

In this respect, the role of Ukraine—which has aptly been called "the cradle of the artistic revolution" (Marcadé 1980, 46)—is particularly relevant. Although its cultural identity has been entirely eclipsed and, often, usurped by Russia,[1] it was in Ukraine (in such cities as Kharkiv,

[1] A recent Moscow publication includes several Ukrainian painters (for example, Aleksandr K. Bogomazov [Oleksander A. Bohomazov], Aleksei V. Grishchenko [Oleksa V. Hryshchenko], Vasilii D. Ermilov [Vasyl' D. Iermilov/Iermylov], and Viktor N. Pal'mov) as members of the "unknown Russian avant-garde." See Sarab'ianov 1992.

Kherson, Odesa, and Kyiv) that many of the seminal artistic activities in publishing and painting took place and whence a number of outstanding artists hailed. Unfortunately, the idea of a Ukrainian contribution to the imperial artistic ferment remains, for now, a relatively vague and controversial notion.

Many students of this period may be even more surprised to discover that alongside the vanguard so celebrated in the heart of the empire (that is, in Moscow and St. Petersburg [Leningrad]), there existed in Ukraine a separate and parallel avant-garde which consciously guarded its national distinctiveness. Centered primarily in Kyiv and Kharkiv, this movement never succeeded in capturing the imagination of the West the way the imperial movement did—and, even when it was noticed, it was apprehended mostly as "Russian" or "Soviet," rather than specifically Ukrainian.[2]

The story of that little-known vanguard, as manifested in literature, is the subject of this book. Ukrainian Futurism—as it came to be known—sprang from, and was a reaction to, early Ukrainian modernist trends of the 1900s and 1910s. The fact that this vanguard was advanced in 1914 within the parameters of Ukrainian society (and demonstratively refused to merge with imperial currents) was just one of many indicators confirming that Ukraine's long process of withdrawal and disengagement from the imperial cultural mainstream was now nearly complete. In 1917 this development received political attestation in the form of Ukraine's declaration of independence from Russia.

Ukrainian Futurism made its debut at a time when Ukrainian society was reaching a consensus on a new national cultural norm, the main principle of which rested on a denial of populism and provincialism (stigmas of Ukraine's colonial position in the empire) and the recognition of Europe—primarily in its traditional and classical guise—as the preeminent cultural model. Understandably, the intelligentsia of the day reacted with dismay when a radical artistic strain suddenly appeared, renouncing tradition (including the father of modern Ukrainian literature, Taras Shevchenko) and the idea of a "national" art, while simultaneously displaying indiscriminate fascination for everything exotic, extreme, and innovative. Ukrainian polite society immediately dubbed Futurism a foreign intrusion and proceeded to purge it—in the name of good taste and high art—from the national cultural system.

[2] To cite just one example, in *Art et poésie russes* (1979, 219), the premier Ukrainian avant-garde journal and the official organ of Ukrainian Futurists, *Nova generatsiia* (Kharkiv, 1927–1930), figures as a "Russian" publication.

This work represents the first effort not only to describe the conflict between the Ukrainian avant-garde and the public, but to provide a comprehensive account of Ukrainian Futurism as a literary movement. This is a work of history and criticism that endeavors to recover, reconstruct, and elucidate a large body of forgotten writings. It traces Futurism's historical, theoretical, and literary development from its origins (1914) to its demise (1931). To illustrate the need for such an undertaking, it may be useful to review briefly how the movement has fared in recent history.

In 1930—just months before Ukrainian Futurism ceased to exist—a critic tried to assess what exactly was known about the sixteen-year-old phenomenon. His conclusions were sobering:

> Today we still lack a single study, nay, a single serious article that would objectively describe the role of Futurism in the literary process of Soviet Ukraine. In addition, various literary facts remain unexplained and many materials are inaccessible. Of these some are, even today, bibliographical rarities (e.g., *Katafalk mystetstva* [*iskusstva*]) and others are in manuscript, held by those comrades who in one way or another were affiliated with the Futurist movement. Naturally, much of this material has already been lost... (Kachaniuk 1930, 186).

Today, more than sixty years later, this statement continues to ring distressingly true. Very little of what has been written since 1930 can be regarded as genuinely "serious" or "objective." "Various literary facts" still "remain unexplained" and access to materials is problematic at best. The corpus remains essentially unknown and ill-defined; the movement's adherents are mostly mysterious names. Even famous—or, as some would have it, infamous—individuals evoke few literary associations either in the critic or reader.

The reasons behind this state of affairs are complex. Ukrainian Futurism's initial appearance on the eve of the First World War was a shock to the collective literary and national sensibility. Critical energies were directed not at understanding or explaining the new artistic presence but at expunging all traces of it from the body politic. In 1918 a critic advanced what turned out to be a rather popular opinion, namely that Futurism was inherently antipathetic to Ukrainian culture: "For some reason, Futurism has not been able to sink deep roots into the Ukrainian soil: the stable and durable traditions of Ukrainian literature have not given this literary 'movement' [an opportunity] to develop fully" (O. Hrushevs'kyi 1918). Others concluded that Futurism was not suited to the Ukrainian temperament. One noted figure of Ukrainian scholarship maintained that while Symbolism had "somewhat of a tradition" and a "natural foundation" in Ukraine, Futurism had absolutely none. Futurism, he reasoned, "cannot naturally assume a place in Ukrainian poetry, which is tied to a nation whose psychology is constructive, not destructive, since, after all, there really is nothing to destroy" (Mezhenko 1919).[3] Whether true or not, these views were convenient rationalizations to avoid dealing seriously with the new movement, both then and later.[4]

During the 1920s, as the movement flowered, politicians and intellectuals alike continued to eye Futurism with suspicion, as something ideologically, aesthetically, and nationally alien. Again, the problem was aggravated by the near total absence of critics and scholars prepared to champion the avant-garde (a sharp contrast to Russia, for example, where Futurism was embraced by the Formalists). Marxist and sociological schools of criticism had no sympathy for the movement. More traditional critics continued to view it as a national disgrace. In his influential literary history, the populist scholar Serhii Iefremov—a foe of Modernism since the early 1900s—maintained that the founder of Futurism (Mykhail' Semenko) "is not a writer [...] and his writings are not poetry, but simple and quite ordinary trickery" (Iefremov 1924, 2: 388; see also 2: 386–89). Largely through him such jaundiced and one-sided positions took deep root, resurfacing years later in derivative histories.[5]

If objective discussion of Ukrainian Futurism was difficult in the twenties, it became literally impossible by the thirties. Following the dissolution of literary organizations and the centralization of Soviet letters in 1932, Futurism became a favorite target of the Party's apparatus. Under Stalin, Futurists came to share in the tragic fate of all the "unorthodox," suffering incarceration and execution. Understandably, those who survived the Great Terror were loath to recall, much less write about, their so-called youthful "follies." Under such circumstances, the

3 Quoted from Rod'ko (1971, 177).

4 Subsequent writings betrayed similar ideas as well. For instance, an émigré historian maintained that the poetry of one Futurist (Geo Shkurupii) "is proof of the unnaturalness and irrelevance [*nedoladnist'*] of Ukrainian Futurism" (see Radzykevych 1952, 91). A Soviet scholar insisted that "in general, for Ukrainian literature Futurism was an inorganic phenomenon and enthusiasm for it was short-lived" (Trostianets'kyi 1968a, 5). The noted Western critic Iurii Sherekh claimed that Futurism "was not organic in Ukrainian literature." He suggested further that a rural Ukraine was not an ideal place for the flowering of a movement that "as a rule was connected with urbanism" (1955, 262). Ironically, Vladimir Markov has observed that "[Russian] Futurist literature was mainly created on the periphery of Russia" (1968, 381). Of course, one major "periphery" for the movement was Ukraine. Among Western critics, I am aware only of Ivan Koshelivets' objection (in passing) to the "organicity" argument (1964, 81).

5 For example, Radzykevych (1955–1956, 3: 88).

study of Ukrainian Futurism came to a halt. Were it not for the occasional invective, memory of the phenomenon in the Soviet Union might have faded completely.[6]

During the post-Stalinist thaw, when the exterminated and silenced were partially rehabilitated in the public's eye, Futurists benefited much less than adherents of other literary groups.[7] Nonetheless, through the sixties and seventies, Futurism became gradually a topic that could be broached.[8] A handful of articles appeared, cautiously deploring its long consignment to oblivion. Unfortunately, this attenuated rehabilitation never really overcame the deeply ingrained Soviet biases against the avant-garde.[9] Moreover, allowing for a few exceptions, it did not lead to the republication of Futurist works.[10]

Western and, in particular, émigré scholars proved to be equally reluctant to champion the movement. While they were instrumental in filling many gaps in Soviet Ukrainian scholarship, their contribution to the documentation and exegesis of Futurism was relatively meager.[11] In

[6] The following will give an impression how Futurism was treated between the 1930s and early 1950s. At the First All-Ukrainian Congress of Soviet Writers, Ivan Kulyk stated: "The reconstruction of former Futurists, the so-called New Generationists, is transpiring very feebly. [Take] for example, M. Semenko. We have heard presentations in which he cultivated vulgarity, calculated awkwardness [and] defended the publicistic form and language of his own works and those of others" (Kulyk 1934, 226). A history of Ukrainian literature published in 1945 by the Ukrainian Academy of Sciences had only nine lines about Futurism and mentioned Semenko alone by name. The movement was characterized as "a serious threat to Soviet culture" (Maslov and Kyryliuk 1945, 239). In 1954 a publication of the Academy of Sciences of the USSR called Ukrainian Futurism (together with VAPLITE and the Neoclassicists) a leading anti-Soviet literary group. The movement was attacked for nihilism, nationalism, and cosmopolitanism (Bilets'kyi et al. 1954, 69–70).

[7] When the rehabilitation process in Ukraine began with the publication of *Antolohiia ukraïns'koï poeziï* (Kyiv, 3 vols., 1957), the leader of the Futurist movement, Mykhail' Semenko, was not represented by any works. The anthology included three poems by another prominent poet of the group, Geo Shkurupii, but did not mention that he had been a Futurist.

[8] *Istoriia ukraïns'koï literatury* (see vol. 2; Kyiv, 1957 [Bilets'kyi et al. 1954–1957]); *Istoriia ukraïns'koï radians'koï literatury* (Kyiv, 1964 [Kryzhanivs'kyi et al. 1964]); *Istoriia ukraïns'koï literatury u vos'my tomakh* (see vols. 5 and 6; Kyiv, 1968, 1970 [Buriak 1967–1971]).

[9] See Korsuns'ka 1968, Poltorats'kyi 1966, Rod'ko 1970, Rod'ko 1971, Levchenko 1971, Kostenko 1971, Trostianets'kyi 1968b, and Pivtoradni 1968. See Nevrli 1966 for an interesting article published in Czechoslovakia.

[10] Geo Shkurupii's *Dveri v den': Vybrane* (Kyiv, 1968) is one of these exceptions. It represents only a fraction of his total work. As a rule, former Futurists—if republished—appeared in sanitized form.

[11] Brief but useful references can be found in Lavrynenko 1959, Kravtsiv 1955 and 1973. See also the earlier work by Iaroslav Hordyns'kyi (1939, 10–12).

their eyes, Futurism remained reprehensible for its purported political conformism and acquiescence to the Soviet regime.[12] Declaring it an aesthetic failure, critics maintained that it was "hopeless to search [in Futurist] journals and works for any special depth, poetic flight, or political thought" (e.g., Shevchuk 1947, 14; Sherekh 1955, 264–65).[13] The major poet of the movement was presumed to have "little" or "no" talent (Koshelivets' 1964, 181).[14] Some condemned Futurism for "disturbing the socially (ethically) conditioned system of language," citing this as a "negative" instance of creativity (Chaplenko 1947, 28).

Paradoxically, Soviet scholarship entertained almost identical views. Common notions included: "Futurism had a generally negative influence on Ukrainian poetry," "slowing down" its development (A. Kostenko 1959) by being a "far cry from real creativity" (Trostianets'kyi 1968a, 8).[15] Futurism was considered a "sad episode" in the career of any number of poets, because it had a "tendency to destroy the poem's form" (Ishchuk 1966, 5). One highly respected poet wrote the following: "The notorious Futurists [...] conducted harmful, destructive work in our language, trying their very best to separate the language from the living, folk roots.... We will say nothing about the foolishness, the antisocial blasphemy of the 'left formation of art,' as this little group called itself" (Ryl's'kyi 1956, 65).

More recently, in Ukraine and in the West, attitudes toward Futurism have been changing for the better and several encouraging steps have been taken to redress the long neglect. Especially during Mikhail Gorbachev's perestroika interest in Ukrainian Futurism—as in all forbidden subjects—flared anew. Since Ukrainian independence in 1991, the subject has been raised with increasing frequency, both there and abroad. Although these developments are promising and very useful, serious scholarship on the movement still remains in its infancy.[16]

[12] "For years Soviet Ukrainian Futurism exposed VAPLITE's and Neoclassicism's nationalism" (Lavrynenko 1959, 111). See also Lavrynenko (1955, 1).

[13] In the latter, Sherekh was slightly more generous to Futurism than he had been in 1947.

[14] The reference is to Mykhail' Semenko.

[15] In the late 1960s, some critics continued to maintain that "Futurism caused a lot of harm to Ukrainian art" (Korsuns'ka 1967, 177).

[16] The following are among the noteworthy contributions of the recent past: Semenko 1979–1982 (this has an excellent introduction by the editor, see Krigor 1979); Semenko 1985 (an extended version of the editor's introduction to this volume appears in Adel'heim [1987, 47–135]); Chernysh 1989a; Chernysh 1989b; Sulyma 1989. The visual arts of this period are discussed in Mudrak 1986. See also the exhibition catalogue, Susovski 1991. In 1990 an All-Union conference on the Russian and Ukrainian avant-garde was held in Kherson. For abstracts of the papers, see *Poeziia russkogo* 1990.

This study begins in the year 1914 with a detailed description and analysis of Ukrainian Futurism's scandalous and complex genesis. The narrative resumes after the Bolshevik Revolution, when the movement sprang back to life following a prolonged hiatus, forced by the war. I trace the history and fate of various Futurist organizations, showing how such external factors as politics and conservative cultural attitudes affected their course. Futurism's conflicts with the Neoclassicists, various literary groups (for example, Hart, Pluh, VAPLITE, VUSPP), Russian Futurists, and writers like Mykola Khvyl'ovyi are discussed in detail.

A separate section is devoted to a reconstruction of Panfuturism, the theory that guided literary practice and justified the avant-garde's existence under the Soviets. This is followed by a discussion of Futurist poetics and aesthetics. Moving from these generalizations to specific works and authors, I provide a selective but representative survey of Futurist poetry and prose. A concluding chapter places Ukrainian Futurism in the context of other avant-gardes and summarizes its achievements.

Throughout this book my focus is on a movement. I devote little attention to biographical detail and make no attempt to provide complete portraits or career summaries for individual writers. Mykhail' Semenko, the founder and central figure of the Futurist movement, represents a partial departure from this rule. I justify such limitations largely by the paucity of requisite material (biographies, autobiographies, eyewitness reports, memoirs, and so forth) and partly by a desire not to stray far afield from my main theme.

Ukrainian Futurism developed in a complex political and social environment. In the twenties especially, Ukrainian and All-Soviet politics impinged heavily on its progress. This book hints at these realities and provides an essential context for purposes of orientation, but it deliberately eschews tangents (literary and political) that are either well-known or have been treated in detail by others (Luckyj 1956; Shkandrij 1992; Mace 1983; Ermolaev 1963; Liber 1992; and so forth).

As will become apparent, Ukrainian Futurism was a constituent member of the international avant-garde. It was keenly self-conscious of all forerunners and contemporaries, and its history and artistic practice resonate with this rich intertextual atmosphere. While some reference is made to the broader context, the details of how Ukrainian Futurism intersects with the avant-gardes of Europe and Russia have been left for another work. Here the comparative aspect remains largely implicit. To have done justice to that theme would have required a work of considerably greater scope. I can only hope that this book will serve as a basis for a true comparative study in the future. My major concern has been to prepare the way for such an interdisciplinary discussion by documenting and reconstituting a subject which through years of neglect, ignorance, and ill-will has virtually ceased to exist as a coherent historical reality.

I have provided my own translations for the poetry and prose cited in this book. They do not aspire toward artistry but are offered, with apologies, as a purely practical matter for readers unfamiliar with Ukrainian.

A word about transliteration. With respect to Ukrainian place-names, the contemporary Ukrainian spelling is used throughout the book. However, personal names, journal titles, publishers, and the like may appear in forms other than those prescribed by current Ukrainian orthography. This is due to the fact that during the periods covered in this study, Ukrainian orthographic conventions were in flux. Rather than standardize on the current practice, I have chosen to cite the sources in their original. This is especially true for the references. Relevant variations in spelling are indicated in brackets. In the narrative proper, I tended to embrace a single, most commonly used form for a title or name, in order to avoid confusion.

I owe several people my sincere gratitude. Professor George G. Grabowicz supervised my doctoral dissertation many years ago: that work (Ilnytzkyj 1983), substantially revised and enlarged, forms the heart of this book. Edward Kasinec, Myroslova Mudrak, John Muchin, the late Iryna Semenko (who wrote under the pseudonym Leo Kriger), and Halyna Chernysh helped me obtain rare publications. I also wish to thank the kind staff of the Stefanyk Library in Lviv for their patient help at a time when this subject was still relatively taboo. Special thanks go to my wife and colleague, Natalia Pylypiuk; she came to my assistance morally and intellectually throughout this long process. Most importantly, I am immeasurably grateful and indebted to my mother and father, Nina and Roman Ilnytzkyj: without their fine example, encouragement, and many years of unfailing love and support, this book would never have seen the light of day. It is to them that I dedicate my effort.

OSI
Edmonton, Alberta
September 1993

Ukrainian Futurism, 1914–1930

I

The History of a Movement

CHAPTER 1

Anatomy of a Literary Scandal: Mykhail' Semenko and the Origins of Ukrainian Futurism

> В українській поезії счинився тарарам. І вчинив його—Михайль Семенко.
> *A great hullabaloo broke out in Ukrainian poetry. And it was created by Mykhail' Semenko.*
>
> Volodymyr Koriak

Ukrainian Futurism has been frequently associated with a single writer—the poet Mykhail' (Mykhailo) Semenko (1892–1937). Although inaccurate, this impression rests on the fact that he was the movement's founder and, initially, its sole literary representative. Without his initiative, possibly, the movement might not have existed at all. Certainly, it would not have materialized in 1914, nor have survived as long as it did. Nothing, however, in Semenko's early career hinted that he would become the "bad boy" of Ukrainian letters (Poltorats'kyi 1966, 194). On the contrary, his beginnings were thoroughly traditional, modest, and circumspect.

Semenko stepped into the public limelight at the age of twenty-one in Kyiv, as a member of the then fashionable Modernists. Several of his poems appeared in the leading Modernist journal, *Ukraïns'ka khata* (The Ukrainian House, 1909–1914).[1] His first collection *Prélude* (Kyiv, 1913) was undistinguished but very much in the literary mainstream. The poems therein—written between 1910 and 1912—were melancholy meditations, chiefly on love, loneliness, personal dreams, and aspirations. Discontent with earthly life and yearning for spiritual tranquillity were dominant motifs. The poet sought solace in nature and music. He perceived the city as a threat: "This city is huge and fearful" [місто це, велике і страшне].* Thematically and formally, he echoed Modernist

[1] Semenko's poems "Darunok" [Gift]; "Hrikh" [Sin]; "Moia kvitka" [My Flower] appeared, respectively, in *Ukraïns'ka khata* 12 (1913): 757; 2, 3 (1914): 167 and 357.

* Within the text, poetry citations are given in their original Cyrillic form, while explanatory references to Ukrainian words are given in italicized transliteration.

poets like Oleksander Oles', Hryts'ko Chuprynka, and Mykola Voronyi. The influence of Taras Shevchenko and folk poetry was also evident [І линуть дні, і линуть роки *or* лютує буря, серце стогне]. A characteristic Modernist ambivalence persecutes him: should he serve Beauty or Country? In one instance Semenko declares, "I want to live, smile at life and beauty" [Я хочу жить, життю і красі всміхатись]. But in another, he confesses: "I want to weep for our shackled freedom" [Хочеться плакать за волю закутую]; and yet further, "It is hard to sing in bondage" [Тяжко в неволі співати].

Prélude was accorded critical attention by three leading literary figures: the poets Voronyi and Chuprynka, as well as the critic M. Sriblians'kyi (pseudonym of Mykyta Shapoval, 1882–1932). Of the three, Voronyi—who in 1901 decidedly launched the Modernist transformation of Ukrainian literature with his programmatic letters and declarations to fellow writers—was most skeptical of the collection. He could not resolve whether to call Semenko a genuine poet or a "poetaster" [*virshomaz*] (Voronyi 1913). He tempered his exasperation by trying to attribute *Prélude*'s faults to the naiveté of an overzealous beginner. Sriblians'kyi and Chuprynka, on the other hand, were more forbearing. The latter wrote, "*Prélude* is weak, but it testifies to an undeniable literary talent, although one that is uncultivated and rough. Obviously, Mr. Semenko is a young poet...He has many mistakes, inharmonious expressions, Russianisms, but he also has genuine lyrics, successful images, genuine poetic feeling" (Chuprynka 1913a, 381). He was, in short, a person to be encouraged. Sriblians'kyi took a similar tack, anticipating that, with a little refinement, some poems in *Prélude* could become real gems [*brylianty*] (Sriblians'kyi 1913c). In short, while Semenko's appearance as a Modernist was not greeted with hosannas, his poetic potential was recognized. The judiciousness of this evaluation vanished entirely, however, with the appearance of his next collections.

Toward the end of 1913 Mykhailo Semenko had united with two painters, his brother Vasyl' (d. 1915) and Pavlo Kovzhun (1896-1939), to form the first Ukrainian Futurist group. All three adapted eccentric names (Mykhail', Bazyl', Pavl') and established the publishing enterprise, "Kvero" (from the Latin *quaero*, 'to seek, search'), which in 1914 released two small books by Semenko, thereby officially inaugurating Ukrainian Futurism and setting the stage for an unprecedented scandal in Ukrainian letters (Tsebro [Semenko] 1922, 40).

The Scandal

It started in February with the eight-page publication *Derzannia* [Bravado] (Semenko 1914a). Shortly afterwards, in March, *Kvero-futuryzm* [Quaero-futurism] appeared, boasting twenty-four pages (Semenko 1914b). Both were designed to be a severe jolt to the prevailing Modernist sensibility. Instead of being quietly introspective, these collections were gleefully extroverted; instead of assuming a dreamy "poetic" stance, they were prosaic and coarse; instead of dealing with eternal verities, they tended toward the routine and banal. Semenko revealed on these pages a new-found irony and self-mockery ("My life has no meaning" [В моїм житті немає змісту]), which only slightly tempered his theatrical egotism—as in the following poem, where he publicly struggles with the artists who purportedly inspired him:

> Ще нижче поклонись! Ще кланяйсь, кланяйсь
> Вони здобутки всі зараз тобі дали—
> І Ігорь, і Бальмонт, і Білий, і Чурляніс—
> Всі хором, і ретельно так, гули:
> Семенко—кланяйсь, кланяйсь!
> —Ні, не схилюсь...
> ("Prytysnutyi"; Semenko 1925a, 76)[2]

> *Bow lower still! Ever lower, lower*
> *They gave you all your present acquisitions—*
> *And Igor' and Bal'mont and Belyi and Čiurlionis—*
> *In chorus, so flawlessly, all bellowed:*
> *Semenko, bow, bow!*
> *"No, I will not kowtow..."*

Among other requisite avant-garde trappings, the collections sported incomprehensible trans-sense verse along the lines of "вн с ті к / пі к к / нуп..."[3] and violated word-boundaries by merging separate lexemes into single strings of letters.

Clearly, such poems were intended to offend any audience accustomed to the mellifluous and dignified tones of the Modernists. But nothing enraged readers more than the pronouncements that introduced these two publications. Especially obnoxious was Semenko's manifesto in *Derzannia*, which bore the title "Alone":

2 This poem (dated 1 April 1914), like others written that year, was not originally published in either *Derzannia* or *Kvero-futuryzm*, but appeared in later editions under these headings.

3 See "V stepu" (Semenko 1914a), quoted here from Semenko (1925a, 79).

> Hey, man, listen here! Listen here, I say. You're really strange, man. I'd like to tell you a few things about art and about the things that relate to it, just a few words. Nothing can be better than talking with you about art, man. I clutch my sides and laugh. I reel with laughter. Your appearance is strange, man! Oh, you're funny as hell. Ah, it's terribly boring to be with you...I don't want to talk to you. You raise your greasy *Kobzar* and say: here is my art. Man, I'm embarrassed for you....You bring me debased 'ideas' about art and it makes me sick. Man, art is something you haven't even dreamt of. I want to tell you, that where there is a cult, there is no art. And most importantly, it [art] doesn't fear attack. Quite the contrary. It is strengthened when attacked. But you've latched onto your *Kobzar*, which smells of wagon grease and lard, and you think that your reverence will protect it. Your reverence has killed it and there is no way to resurrect it. Who is enthusiastic about it [the *Kobzar*] now? Primitive men, precisely of your type, who read [the newspaper] *Rada* [Council]. Man, time turns Titans into worthless Lilliputians, and their place now is in the annals of scholarly institutions. Living among you, one falls decades behind the times. I don't accept that type of art. How can I respect Shevchenko [the author of the *Kobzar*], when I see that he is under my feet? I can't pull veins of reverence from my body for months at a time the way you do for a man who, because he is a contemporary factor, is [therefore] a deeply repulsive phenomenon. Man, I want to tell you that right now, as I write this, I find it loathsome to pick up our papers. If I don't tell you what's on my mind, then I'll suffocate in the atmosphere of your "sincere" Ukrainian art. I wish it would die. Such is your jubilee celebration.[4] That's all there is left of Shevchenko. But, neither can I avoid my own celebration. I burn my *Kobzar*.[5]

A less strident but equally provocative declaration appeared in *Kvero-futuryzm*, where Semenko expounded a theory of art based on the idea of perpetual exploration and change: "The absence of permanence in art—this is the premise of Kvero-futurism...In art, everything that has been discovered and experienced is of no interest..." (Semenko 1914b, 1–2). Further into the manifesto, he offered a diagnosis of what ailed Ukrainian art and a program for its regeneration. Once again he condemned parochialism while trumpeting the contemporary:

> We desire, by artificial means [*shtuchnym rukhom*], to bring our art closer to those frontiers of universal art where a new era is beginning.

4 In 1914 Ukrainians were marking the hundredth anniversary of Taras Shevchenko's (1814–1861) birth.

5 The original is quoted in Ievshan (1914b, 272–73). My citation comes from this source.

> At the very least, art should be in step with Life, but now it is falling behind. And our Ukrainian art is so shamefully retrograde in its vulgar routine and slavish mustiness that it is not deserving of the name...[Art] can neither be Ukrainian nor anything else...National traits in art are a sign of its backwardness. The Kvero-futuristic art must be an expression of universal feelings [because] art has already shed its thin national veneer...Before the advent of futurism, art was primitive and its only way out lies through Kvero-futurism. Today, as we enter an entirely new world, we cannot feel at home inside a Ukrainian or some other dwelling. Only the universal, to which the spirit of man strives, has value. The things we call our very own, those "native" things which have become repugnant in our time but which might be necessary for the establishment of universal human values, will—don't fret—manifest themselves of their own accord, even if we consciously try to stop them. Should they prove to be vital and indispensable, they will survive; but we will not fall under their influence because then we will not move beyond popular art. We have outlived the national period in art...and our temperament will now express itself to the extent necessary. We must overtake the present. Therefore, let us leap ahead....Let our fathers (who have left us nothing to inherit) take pleasure in their own "native" art, dying along with it; we, the young, will not stretch out our hands to them. Let us overtake the present! (ibid., 2-3).

Reaction to these statements was extremely negative. At first, newspapers declined to accept reviews and bookstores refused to stock Semenko's publications. One critic wrote that Semenko was treated like a leper [*stav prokazhenym*] (Ia. Savchenko 1918a, 28), another that "some sincere Ukrainian" threatened to "punch Semenko in the snout" (Bohats'kyi 1923, 35). But the real offensive against him began when *Ukraïns'ka khata*, the journal that previously published Semenko's poems (the last, in February 1914), ran two scathing articles, "'Suprema Lex'," (Ievshan 1914b) and "An Étude on Futurism" (Sriblians'kyi 1914)[6] authored by the eminent young critics Mykola Ievshan (pseudonym of Mykola Fediushka, 1889–1919) and M. Sriblians'kyi. "Even from the point of view of the most elementary ethics, one cannot imagine a more shameful and unacceptable criticism than Sriblians'kyi's," a critic would write some four years later (Ia. Savchenko 1918a, 28).

6 This essay was republished again more than ten years later (Sriblians'kyi 1924). The appearance of the booklet prompted Oleksa Slisarenko, then a Futurist, to declare that just as an old maid, "[who] loses hope of ever getting married, rereads old love letters, so Sriblians'kyi delights in articles whose 'earthly time has passed.'" See *Chervonyi shliakh* 11–12 (1924): 306–307. Sriblians'kyi also wrote a significantly less vitriolic review of *Kvero-futuryzm* (*Ukraïns'ka khata* 6 [1914]: 471).

Ievshan and Sriblians'kyi had utter contempt for Semenko. Both called him an "idiot" and characterized the verse as "idiotic stuttering." Ievshan compared Semenko's poetry and theories to spitting in a reader's face (Ievshan 1914b, 272) and scorned him as an *inteligent* who, "having failed to produce something himself, mocks his native language, national music, poetry, literature" (ibid., 274). Sriblians'kyi proclaimed Semenko's writings "brigandage—not literature" and described his style as the ravings of a "degenerate" (ibid., 464). "Impudence, not boldness" is how he deciphered the title *Derzannia*. Particularly reprehensible, in the opinion of both critics, was the insolent tone in which Semenko treated Ukraine's greatest poet, Taras Shevchenko. The phrases "Shevchenko is under my feet" and "I burn my *Kobzar*" were vehemently condemned.[7] "The greatest hypocrisy...a lie," cried Sriblians'kyi: "The burning of the *Kobzar* is not the valor of a warrior, but the villainy of a brigand" (ibid., 464). Sriblians'kyi's wrath culminated with this frenetic onslaught:

> Presumably, one could remain calm [in the face of this futuristic poetry] but the point is that this [man] Semenko is a symbol of Ukrainian reality. He protests against that which will not land him in prison. He is a typical Ukrainian: he does not know Ukrainian, he stutters *vn tk,*[8] presenting this as the future language. He is a symbol of Ukrainian disintegration and cynicism. He is a product of that patriotic villainy [*khamstvo*] that latches on to the newest slogans, without knowing their content; he fingers and defiles them. . . . He does not understand that this poem "V stepu" [In the Steppe] is his soul. He is just like the famous painter-artist who boasted about the strength of his imagination by saying that he paints dung not from nature, but from memory (ibid., 464).

Semenko emerged from under Sriblians'kyi's pen as the archetype of chaos, an antagonist of all that is natural, freedom-loving, and beautiful. The tirade culminated with the hope that good might triumph over this evil. Borrowing heavily from the Modernist repertoire of images, Sriblians'kyi portrayed his own ideals thus:

> The future language will be a language of free people, not the limited scale of sounds [produced] by a degenerate. Let us become free people—

7 Subsequently, this aspect of Semenko's manifesto was mentioned in almost every article and history; it is one of the few universally known facts about Semenko and Futurism. Leonid Novychenko's statement can serve as an example: "M. Semenko [. . .] in one of his poems [*sic*] blasphemously called for the [. . .] burning of the *Kobzar* of T. H. Shevchenko" (*Antolohiia . . . v 4-kh tomakh* 1958, 3:8).

8 This refers to Semenko's trans-sense poem "V stepu" [In the Steppe].

> then we will have a free, musical, and supple language which will ring forth in a symphony of magical sounds. This language will shine and blaze in one's eyes, will astound by the beauty of its gestures, will enthrall the body with bliss. The future language is Beauty. The future life is Beauty. This will be a language that will echo from the mouths of free people and not from contemporary impertinent scatterbrains, ignoramuses, savages with yellow shoes and protruding collars.... Free people will not scurry about, provoking, burning books, will not stand like simpletons on spread-eagled legs lolling out their tongues.... There will only be silence, filled with the sun's luster, the breathing of flowers, the sounds of unspoken poems, the beauty of rays crisscrossing the air...(ibid., 464–65).

Conspicuously, no dissenting voices were heard refuting the views of Ievshan and Sriblians'kyi. Semenko was compelled to mount his own defense privately and in poetry that would appear (for reasons beyond his control) only years later. His single contemporaneous dialogue with opponents was contained in *Kvero-futuryzm.* But inasmuch as it came out before *Ukraïns'ka khata*'s verbal paroxysm, it was more of an extension of Semenko's own vituperations than an actual riposte. *Kvero-futuryzm* included a poem that poked fun at Mykola Voronyi ("K drugu stikhotvortsu"; Semenko 1914b, 18) and a brief prose note ("Pro domo sua") that contained several sarcastic remarks. One was aimed at Social Democrats in *Dzvin* [The Bell, Kyiv, 1913–14], a journal that published many of the same Modernists writers that *Ukraïns'ka khata* did. Semenko addressed these "Marxists" (as he called them), urging them not to meddle in art since they knew less about it than a cow trampling flowers. Simultaneously, he reserved the right for artists to explore Marxism, on the grounds that they were individuals both "more profound and intelligent." Another barb was leveled at Mykola Sadovs'kyi, the popular director of the Ukrainian ethnographic theater. Noting Sadovs'kyi's success among farmers in Uman', Semenko urged him to remain in that milieu, for in Kyiv, he made a "worn and poor" impression ("Pro domo sua"; Semenko 1914b, 4). He also offered a tongue-in-cheek characterization of the appearance of his own *Derzannia*: "...In the year of Our Lord 1914, in the month of February, Ukraine for the first time revealed the treasure she carried within her." The refusal of booksellers to handle his first Futurist book elicited these mock-heroic lines: "Glory to Ukraine! There is no way we can perish [as a nation] with sons like these! Father Taras [Shevchenko] spoke the truth when he said: 'Our thoughts, our glory will not die, will not perish'—or something like that."

As for Sriblians'kyi, Semenko's most caustic counterattack was written only on 11 July 1914 (but published much later):

Я зіпсував собі настрій
Прочитавши статтю Сріблянського.
Так гарно коли він про інших пише
Читаючи ж про себе—розчарувався.
Та і змагатися не варт з людиною
Що Бальмонтом зіпсувала собі смак
І цього добродія куди треба і не треба тиче.
Ах безнадійна робота—від сріблянських чогось сподіватися,
Буду чекати, поки він подавиться за обідом
("Prykryi stan"; Semenko 1925a, 112).

I spoiled my mood
Reading Sriblians'kyi's article.
It's so nice when he writes about others
But having read about myself—I felt disappointed.
Heck, there's no sense in arguing with a man
Who's had his taste ruined by Bal'mont
And shoves this fellow in all sorts of appropriate and inappropriate places.
Oh, it's hopeless to expect anything from the Sriblians'kyis of this world,
I'll have to wait until he chokes on his lunch.

Three years later, while stationed in Vladivostok as a soldier, Semenko ironically invoked Sriblians'kyi again in the poem "Aesthete" [Estet] (Semenko 1925a, 251). On several later occasions, he also fired versified barbs at Oles', Voronyi, and Chuprynka.[9]

Futurism and the Ukrainian Modernist Context

> Литературные скандалы закономерно сопровождают литературные революции.
> *Literary scandals inevitably accompany literary revolutions.*
>
> Iurii Tynianov

Examined dispassionately, the invectives of the two critics boiled down to three basic arguments. The first held that Futurism—as represented by Semenko—was not literature but some kind of verbal abomination, threatening the very existence of Ukrainian literature and language. Hence, the aspersion that the movement was "brigandage," "idiocy," and a "defilement" of the Ukrainian "word." The second suggested that by attacking Shevchenko and rejecting "national" art, Semenko undermined more than letters—he threatened Ukrainian nationhood.

[9] See, for example, the poems "Bilia Volodymyra" and "Parykmakher" (Semenko 1925a, 77, 209).

Sriblians'kyi openly implied that the movement was treacherous, putting Semenko in one camp with Russian monarchists and chauvinists (Sriblians'kyi 1914, 459). To be sure, matters were made worse for Semenko by the reactionary policies of the Russian government. On the eve of Semenko's Futurist debut, Russian authorities had forbidden the commemoration of the centennial of Shevchenko's birth—an action that triggered bitter resentment in Ukraine. Under these tense circumstances, Semenko's swipe at the "national" principle in art and his symbolic burning of Shevchenko's *Kobzar* were gestures waiting to be misinterpreted. And Sriblians'kyi willingly obliged: "Representatives of the two-headed eagle [monarchists] burned the portrait of Shevchenko on the street, and Semenko burned the *Kobzar*" (ibid., 457).

The third line of argument challenged Semenko's originality. Sriblians'kyi went as far as to charge Semenko with "plagiarism" (ibid., 457, 458), calling his poems "stolen rags" whose worthlessness was compounded by their origin in Russia, the country "where every new human thought or movement is distorted" (ibid., 461–62). As a "Muscovite Ukrainianism" [*moskovs'ka ukraïnshchyna;* ibid., 462], the reasoning went, Semenko's Futurism had no place in an authentically Ukrainian cultural milieu.[10]

This overwrought effort to declare Futurism an alien danger in Ukrainian culture was not without its ironies. The critics were so agitated by Semenko that they totally missed the perfectly good Ukrainian motivations for proclaiming his movement. They were equally blind to the fact that they and their journal were in several instances the stimulus to and progenitors of key Futurist ideas.

As we shall presently see, the perception of Futurism as a national threat totally obscured a much more fundamental fact—namely, that Ukraine's own intellectual and artistic environment had set the stage for Futurism. Contrary to what Sriblians'kyi and Ievshan believed, the Russian influence—in the guise of the imperial avant-garde flowering in Ukraine—while relevant, was not necessarily the preeminent factor among the philosophical, social, and literary stimuli that inspired Semenko.

[10] Such sentiments survived in later Soviet and émigré writings. Mykola D. Rod'ko, a Soviet critic, wrote that "all these Kvero-futuristic innovations were nothing but the most common modifications of Russian Futurism" (1971, 143). And, in the West, Sherekh [Shevelov] maintained that "Ukrainian Futurism was basically an imitation of foreign, primarily Russian, models, and was incapable of forming some kind of school" (1955, 262). See also Strikha (1955, 262). Only rarely were voices raised against this tendency to reduce Ukrainian Futurism wholly to a Russian "influence." In the 1920s Borys Iakubs'kyi said: "Russian influences...do not exhaust the content of Semenko's poetry: he is much more interesting, rich, and sincere [than that]" (1925a, 247).

In the waning years of the nineteenth century, Ukrainian literature had taken its first tentative but irrevocable steps on a road that would dramatically alter it as an institution and as an art.[11] This was a time of growing national self-assertiveness (even nationalism), when judgments about Ukrainian literature tended to be made increasingly against the background of West European (rather than Imperial Russian) developments. Although the Populist, Realist, and ethnographic orientations remained alive and well, a new generation of writers began looking toward more "universal" horizons. With the appearance of the first Modernists—poets like Mykola Voronyi and the West Ukrainian Moloda muza [The Young Muse] group—attacks on tradition, particularly on "utilitarian" and narrowly "patriotic" literature, increased. The positivist and civilizing function attributed to literature by the previous generation began giving way to an understanding that Art was both a value and an institution worthy of cultivation in its own right. Art, which previously was fostered in the name of the "people," became more and more the exclusive domain of a small class of acolytes (the intelligentsia) who now defined its social mission as the creation of a genuine national institution—a national but universal art—which might eventually rival the best achievements of Europe. This attitude so distressed Populists-Realists like Ivan Franko, Serhii Iefremov, and Ivan Nechui-Levyts'kyi that it led to some of the sharpest literary polemics hitherto known in Ukrainian literature. Although Ukrainian Modernism did not attain European or Russian levels of "aestheticism" or "decadence," the new generation managed to loosen the fabric of tradition and, to an extent, legitimize non-conformity. By the 1900s, in short, there were already inherent radicalizing forces at work in the Ukrainian literary process. These indirectly paved the way for Futurism.

Without question the most radical index of cultural change in Ukraine was *Ukraïns'ka khata*—a journal that delighted in doing battle with the "old generation," especially with the venerable *Literaturno-naukovyi vistnyk* [The Literary-Scientific Herald, founded in 1898] and the newspaper *Rada* [Council, 1906–1914].[12] Sriblians'kyi's circle designated their Realist-Populist opponents, with their Ukrainophile (as opposed to

[11] For a detailed discussion of these issues, see Ilnytzkyi 1991 and 1992a. Compare also the interesting and related discussion in Hundorova 1992.

[12] Critics have noted that *Ukraïns'ka khata* "parted ways much more radically" with the ideas of the Realists and Populists "than [did] the 'Moloda muza' poets..." (Rubchak 1968, 40) and that its members "carried forward the work of the 'Moloda muza' group, developing their ideological-aesthetic program to the extreme..." (*Istoriia ukraïns'koï literatury* 1967–1971, 5:343).

a true "national") consciousness, as "mammoths" (Zhurba 1934, 2). In the sphere of art, there is evidence that "Marinetti and his Futurism" constituted for *Ukraïns'ka khata* one of the "burning issues" (Zhurba 1962, 440). Some of the journal's contributors—for instance, the writers Hnat Khotkevych and Hryts'ko Chuprynka—cultivated a "bohemian" image and life-style not unlike the one later associated with the Futurists. A portrait of Chuprynka helps to illustrate the point:

> Hryts'ko Chuprynka sat in the corner, stiff and silent. He was tall, lean, and bald, with two tufts of hair on his temples. The face was gray, mute, without any mustache; the lips were narrow, tight, the eyes—gray and cold. Probably, he felt ill at ease in this company without drinking, without scandalous activity. Nevertheless, he survived till the end, without engaging in some extravagance. He was an anarchic type, who had grown up on a wild, steppe-like, and poorly cultivated soil. He walked about in a long black cape, a black brimmed hat from beneath which he stared like Rinaldo Rinaldini. He liked to give himself airs. Nevertheless, later, during the liberation struggle, he showed character and patriotism and knew how to die for Ukraine with rifle in hand (ibid., 445).[13]

The last sentence is significant. As we shall see below, this group's radicalism and bohemianism was very much intertwined with—and, in the opinion of some, redeemed by—its strong sense of patriotism.

The intellectual dialogue in *Ukraïns'ka khata* had its very own inflection. As a contemporary noted, the journal was imbued with the spirit of avant-gardism and revolt:

> *Ukraïns'ka khata* was at that time the most progressive revolutionary platform for the young, a platform for their protest, revolt against all types of stagnation [*zaskoruzlist'*], lack of principle, political opportunism. It consisted of an uncompromising politico-literary group.... Its belligerent style occasionally took on a very sharp tone in the war with the conservative camp of [Ievhen] Chykalenko [and Serhii] Iefremov (ibid., 437–38).[14]

No one in the group was more belligerent than Sriblians'kyi and Ievshan. These young critics delighted in the works of Ol'ha Kobylians'ka and subscribed to her form of individualism and Nietzscheanism. Fondness for a "higher order of men" caused them to belittle earlier Ukrainian culture, which they construed as a feeble ethnographic product

[13] For a sense of how Semenko was described, see Smolych 1968 and 1969. See also Klym Polishchuk (1923, 12, 14).

[14] Ievhen Chykalenko (1861–1929) bankrolled the newspaper *Rada*.

of a poorly crystallized national spirit. Their antagonism to this "Ukrainophile" past was expressed in ways that rivaled some of Futurism's most extreme pronouncements. In 1913 Sriblians'kyi affirmed:

> There is no culture in our past.... We shall not bow, the way the patriots demand, to our forefathers, who have left us only one inheritance—their stupidity, lack of principle, barbarism, and darkness. We shall not honor their "uncultured culture," we shall not bow in front of their art. This is something we do not need, while that which we do need our forefathers have not created and have not given us.... We have no forefathers worthy of honor and those who are unworthy of honor are useless to us (Bohats'kyi et al. 1955, 14).[15]

Ievshan was capable of similar passion. Commenting on the contemporary literary situation, he ridiculed typically "Ukrainian" art in terms not unlike those later used by Semenko:

> And thus the drunken mob of buffoons rushes onward somewhere and bursts into insane laughter, [all] under the banner of "Ukrainian" art.... And one is convinced for the nth time, that in all these works there is often no sign of creative thought, [nor] even of the intensity that would indicate some kind of broader interests; there is absolutely no desire to venture out from one's own warm corner where everything takes place easily, of its own accord (Ievshan 1912, 10, 12).

Both critics despaired over Ukrainian literature's legacy of narrowness, provincialism, and superficiality. They were offended by its effeteness as art. They resented its portrayal of suffering, meekness, and helplessness. They emphasized that literature must heal the "maimed" human soul, must "enter [life] boldly."[16] Characteristically, Ievshan deplored the absence of "protest" and "struggle" in contemporary writing (Ievshan 1912, 31). He was pleased by Chuprynka's poem "To My Countrymen" [*Do svoïkh*, 1910], mainly because it contained the line "revolt for the sake of revolt" [*bunt dlia buntu*].[17]

Inarguably, this vigor of spirit had an effect on Semenko's own development. His Futurism gives every indication of being a logical

[15] Sriblians'kyi was reacting to the appearance of Mykhailo Hrushevs'kyi's *Kul'turno-national'nyi rukh v XVII st. na Ukraïni.*

[16] This is a leitmotif that recurs constantly in *Ukraïns'ka khata*. It is especially evident in Sriblians'kyi (1909, 413–31) and Ievshan (1910b, 24–31).

[17] Chuprynka's poem contained an epigraph from Panteleimon Kulish (1819–1897) which read: "З громадського багна, багно літературне зробили ви" [From civic garbage, you have created literary garbage] (Chuprynka 1926, 71). Ievshan refers to Chuprynka's poem in his (1912, 50–51).

extension of such attitudes. Clearly, there is more than a casual resemblance between his manifestoes and the views prevailing in *Ukraïns'ka khata.* Consider Semenko's attack on the newspaper *Rada,* his rejection of the "fathers" and their art, and his mockery of "sincere" Ukrainian art. Even more telling is that his writings after *Prélude* betrayed a temperament remarkably similar to the one cherished by critics of *Ukraïns'ka khata.* During the last months of 1913 his poetry began replacing Modernist melancholy and timidity with a new kind of assertiveness and rebellion.[18] Interestingly, Semenko's formal experimentation grew in direct proportion to his defiance of the traditional cultural milieu—a transformation that can be traced precisely.

On 9 October 1913 he wrote a poem still permeated with Modernist commonplaces. Dejection and sadness were rendered in the movement's characteristic "mellifluous" manner ("Sleep, Sleep My Dear World" [*Oi liuli liuli liubyi svit*]; Semenko 1925a, 53). But the poem "Ia idu" [I am leaving], written on 24 November, heralded a much different attitude, expressed in a rather novel and prose-like manner:

Я іду від вас—ланцюг скидаю,
....
В майбутнє я пішов—стежками
Якими звірі у свій час ішли.
....
Ми різні, ми розійшлись.

Дякую за історію і за хліб.
Також за кохання й млу ночей.
Від світла нового я осліп—
Я не бачу своїх очей.

Я кидаю вас—ланцюг скидаю,
До своїх залізних спішу.
Беріте попіл все, що маю.
Я світ новий оголошу
("Ia idu"; Semenko 1925a, 55).

I'm leaving you—taking off my shackles.
....
I go into the future, along paths
That beasts traversed one time...
....
We're different, you and I, our ways have parted.

[18] These poems are grouped in the *Kobzar* under the heading "Naïvni poeziiky" [Naive little poems].

Thanks for the memory and for the bread…
And also for the love and the evening haze.
I am made blind by a new light—
I cannot see my own eyes.

I'm leaving you—taking off my shackles,
I'm off to see my iron friends.
You take the cinders, everything I have.
I shall announce a new world.

Another poem, "Zaklyk" [Call to Arms], written on 25 November, echoed Sriblians'kyi's irreverent denial of all "forefathers": "We will not be frightened by the shadows of our ancestors / Let the forgotten geniuses sleep" [Нас тіні предків не злякають / Забуті генії хай сплять] (Semenko 1925a, 57). Two days later, Semenko hailed the "kingdom of eternal change" in verse whose very title ("Poezosong" [*Poezopisnia*]) (ibid., 59) alluded to Futurism (specifically, Igor' Severianin). By 8 December, in "Pochatok" [Beginning], there appears an awkward but even more pronounced combination of Modernist images, Futurist neologisms, and the ideology of *Ukraïns'ka khata:*

Живущосмілими екстазами
Ми ваші душі враз напоємо
Безмежнодивними фантазами
Всі виразки на вас загоємо.
Ми не прийшли з мозками хорими—
Наші чуття життям наповнені,
А наші думи світозорими
Новими темами оздоблені.
Співожиття прожить дуезами—
Це наші маріння загадні,
І сміло, сміло йдем з поезами,
Як ваші сни ясні, негадані.
І не страшні нам ваші накрики
І осуд рабського обурення,—
……………………………………………………
І прийде час—свої фантази ми
У храм прекрасний перетворимо,
А потім соняшноекстазами
Щось на руїнах знов утворимо
("Pochatok"; Semenko 1925a, 64).

With vitabold ecstasies
We will fill your souls abruptly
With fantasies endlesslymarvelous
And heal your every abscess.

We have not come with minds diseased—
Our senses brim with life
Our thoughts with dawn-eyed
New themes adorned.
To live life's melodies in harmonies—
These are our secret visions,
And boldly, boldly we go forth with poesies
As clear, precocious as your dreams.
And we fear not your clamor,
Your judgment born of slavish indignation,—
....
And the time will come: we will transform
our fantasies into an alluring temple
And then in sunny ecstasies
We will erect on ruins something new.

These quasi-Futurist exercises were far from masterful, but they did show that Semenko's embrace of the avant-garde was an extension—rather "organic" to all appearances—of Ukrainian Modernism. Everything pointed to a gradual transition rather than any sudden break with his own literary milieu.

Similar precedents and analogies can be found for Semenko's "shocking" broadside against Shevchenko. Long before Semenko, several figures in Ukrainian life (for example, Panteleimon Kulish, Mykhailo Drahomanov, and Ivan Franko) had, in their own way, attempted to divest Shevchenko of his absolute social, national, and poetic authority.[19] No one did this more "scientifically" than Drahomanov in *Shevchenko, ukraïnofily i sotsiializm* [Shevchenko, Ukrainophiles, and Socialism, 1879], a work which, significantly, saw its third printing in 1914 (Drahomanov 1914).[20] This is how Drahomanov characterized Shevchenko's great book of poetry:

> The *Kobzar* has already outlived its time—"ein überwundener Standpunkt," as the Germans say. And moreover the *Kobzar* is, in many respects, a seed which has been left lying in the storehouse and did not perform the service it ought to have while it was yet fresh, and today it is of little use (Drahomanov 1970, 100).

At another point, he added:

[19] In 1901 Franko scoffed at those who identified Ukrainian literature exclusively with Shevchenko, as if nothing had been written after him (1950–1956, 16:333–34).

[20] This edition contains a foreword by Andrii Nikovs'kyi and inspires speculation that it could have influenced Semenko's manifestos. There are actually many parallels between Drahomanov and Semenko—more than can be cited or discussed here.

> Litanies, particularly litanies said after the death of a saint, bring little benefit and much harm to people. And perhaps no one is harmed more by litanies than we, the semi-barbarians of Eastern Europe. Let us remember that Russian literature began to grow in earnest only after Belinskii pointed out that Russia has no real literature, that Pushkin by himself does not constitute a literature and that there is no real need as yet to pray to him. It is time that someone did a similar favor for Ukrainian literature in respect to Shevchenko, particularly because the Ukrainophiles for a long time now have exalted him as a writer and as a leader in social endeavors. But from all this exaltation the Ukrainian cause, whether literary or social, has not progressed very far (ibid., 97).[21]

In 1911 Ievshan also addressed this problem, warning that uncritical adoration of Shevchenko was dangerous both for the great poet and for Ukrainian society (note the similarity to Semenko's manifesto):

> Every year we organize all kinds of concerts and evenings; we pronounce that "Ukraine lives on" and think that in doing so we honor the memory of Shevchenko. Such official celebration of Shevchenko has not advanced us one step forward, has not brought us closer to the poet and his ideas; it has only taught us lies!!...We have not yet learned anything from Shevchenko, we only deceive ourselves. We systematically insult not only his memory, but everything that is beautiful, good, and holy, everything that governs the life of nobler souls (Ievshan 1911b, 6–7).

Sriblians'kyi, too, wrote a scathing attack against cult-mongers, charging that "Nowhere does the mob show its hypocrisy and villainy more than in a cult [devoted to] its 'prophet' and martyr" (Sriblians'kyi 1910, 28).

A close parallel between Semenko's manifesto "Alone" and his contemporaries can be found in an article by another Young Turk from this group, the critic Andrii Tovkachevs'kyi (1886-?). His "Literature and Our 'Populists'" contained this passage:

> When I take the *Kobzar* into my hands, I cannot rid myself of a feeling of revulsion. I see before me that entire heinous crowd which has smeared a great name with its own filth; I see gaping black mouths and I feel the breath of these monstrous beings, who have turned a great prophet into their very own prophet....They have dared to raise voices, from which only lately came foul expletives, in praise of Shevchenko. Such voices could blacken any diamond, even Shevchenko's poetry (Tovkachevs'kyi 1911b, 421).

[21] For the scandalous effect these words had, see Franko (1906, iii–iv).

It is in this spirit and context that Semenko's own pronouncements must be seen. He obviously was following a certain convention when he assailed those whose ignorance had made Shevchenko repulsive to "nobler souls." (Recall that Semenko paints Shevchenko's apologist as a conservative and "primitive man.") *Derzannia*'s manifesto was not so much aimed against Shevchenko, as it was a statement "about art and about those things that pertain to it."[22] Like his forerunners, Semenko criticized a cult ("...your jubilee celebrations. That's all that is left of Shevchenko") that trivialized Shevchenko and thwarted the revitalization of literature. His attitude toward Shevchenko remained fundamentally positive—after all, he still counted him among the "Titans" of art. By observing that great art had nothing to fear, he plainly implied that Shevchenko, as any great poet, would not suffer from being "burned," especially since this fire had a cleansing and liberating purpose. In Semenko's view, the idealization of the *Kobzar* was a form of artistic embalming. Shevchenko had become a "repulsive phenomenon" because the Philistine cult-mongers had turned his poetry into a "greasy" object of worship and then proffered it as a contemporary model for literature—thereby condemning Ukrainian art to fall "decades behind the times."

Modernism vs. Futurism

Given the many conspicuous parallels between *Ukraïns'ka khata* and Semenko, one must ask why Sriblians'kyi and Ievshan reacted as negatively as they did to his debut. After all, both with respect to content and manner, Semenko said little that had not already been said by them or others. Semenko did not even attack *Ukraïns'ka khata* directly (although there may have been a veiled criticism in *Kvero-futuryzm:* "Today, as we enter an entirely new world, we cannot feel *at home* inside a *Ukrainian* or some other *dwelling*"), choosing instead as his target the journal's traditional enemies (*Rada, Dzvin*). Part of the answer may lie in the fact that Semenko expressed familiar concepts not in the name of the journal but rather in the name of a new literary movement. At the same time he assumed the stance of an outsider (note well the title "Alone") and gave the impression he was distancing himself from the "national-patriotic"

[22] Consider with what consistency Semenko emphasized art: "Nothing can be better than talking with you about art....You raise your greasy *Kobzar* and say: here is my art....You bring me debased 'ideas' about art....Art is something you haven't even dreamt of....Where there is a cult, there is no art....[Art] doesn't fear attack....I don't accept that type of art.... [I'd] suffocate in the atmosphere of your 'sincere' Ukrainian art" (1914b, 2–3).

camp. This, in Sribliansʹkyi's eyes, stripped Semenko of all moral authority to protest against Shevchenko's cult, in particular since Semenko himself seemed to be less than a fully "conscious Ukrainian" (what with his Russianisms and Russian influence). Moreover, it must be noted that Sribliansʹkyi and Ievshan never condemned the idea of the cult itself: they objected primarily against its "Ukrainophile" character. Sribliansʹkyi proved on several occasions that he was willing to defend the cult when it unequivocally served the Ukrainian national cause.[23] In the case of Semenko, Sribliansʹkyi obviously felt that this vulgarian was doing much more than just attacking a Ukrainophile syndrome: he gave every impression of questioning the national idea itself. This misunderstanding came about because Semenko took the national factor in art for granted, as a given. ("The things we call our very own, those 'native' things which have become repugnant in our time but which might be necessary for the establishment of universal human values, will—don't fret—manifest themselves of their own accord, even if we consciously try to stop them.") Sribliansʹkyi and Ievshan, on the other hand, always invoked it as an active and constructive element of their theories. The furor over Shevchenko, therefore, had deeper implications. Similarities notwithstanding, Semenko and *Ukraïnsʹka khata* had radically different visions of the course Ukrainian literature should take.

We have seen above that, in comparison to its contemporaries and immediate predecessors, *Ukraïnsʹka khata* was extremely radical in its assessment of Ukrainian society and in setting an agenda for its transformation. However, its literary and aesthetic position showed less originality and did not diverge much from the mainstream. Many of Modernism's basic themes, stylistic features, values and assumptions—for example, the cult of Beauty, the notion that art is autonomous and that the artist is always preeminent over the "mob"—were embraced almost wholesale by the journal. Its contribution to Modernism was not

[23] In "Etiud pro futuryzm" Sribliansʹkyi described Shevchenko as "the productive stimulus for the rebirth of man in Ukraine." A few years earlier he had rejoiced at the thought that "Shevchenko's name is everywhere surrounded by a joyous cult, wherever there are conscious Ukrainians [. . . .] And no wonder! His name is the very content of the Ukrainian idea [*ukraïnstvo*]. [...] The *Kobzar* has primarily an organizing [...], educational meaning." (See *Ukraïnsʹka khata* 1 [1909]: 4; *emphasis in the original*). Sribliansʹkyi's view is surprisingly like Franko's. Compare what Franko said in 1905 when defending Shevchenko from the so-called Muscophiles (Russophiles): "For a long time now our Muscophiles have considered undermining Shevchenko's cult in our society. By doing so they hope to deprive this society of its major source of idealism, which gives it the zeal to work and raises its members from simple consumers of bread to the dignity of men" (1950–1956, 16: 344).

in the introduction of any obvious innovations but in the ability to elaborate commonly held premises with intense forthrightness and sophistication. *Ukraïns'ka khata* was remarkable for raising the Modernist discourse to new intellectual and polemical heights. It is also true that its major critics had much less sympathy for Modernism's subjectivism and inwardness, its world-weariness and mysticism. But this disagreement was easier to articulate in theory than to implement as an editorial policy. As a result, the actual literature published in the journal differed little from prevailing Modernist currents.

What really distinguished *Ukraïns'ka khata* was its unabashed nationalist ideology. It drove Sriblians'kyi, Ievshan, and Tovkachevs'kyi to stress the development of an elite "national" literature—their answer to the populist and provincial writings of the previous century. In effect, *Ukraïns'ka khata* not only confirmed and accelerated the trends begun by the intelligentsia of the 1890s, when it claimed art as its very own institution and made the idea of "high culture" the centerpiece of what defined Ukrainian nationhood, but it took that premise to its very limits.

It was this elitism and national self-consciousness that placed the journal in direct conflict with the tepid "Ukrainophilism"[24] of the older generation, which, as we have seen, was faulted for not creating a full-fledged nation and culture. The "new literature," said Sriblians'kyi, "is the answer to a fundamental problem of Ukrainian culture: its [lack of] cultural emancipation, its tragic dependence [on Russia], its historically determined [but] unfortunate slavishness" (Sriblians'kyi 1955, 104).[25] Ievshan saw the relationship between literature and nation in this way: "Literature is not in itself the struggle for liberation, but a great force, which helps liberation. [Literature] is the beauty of protest, the beauty of rebellion against enslavement and the most awful type of slavery that can possibly exist: spiritual slavery" (Ievshan 1911a, 564). *Ukraïns'ka khata* saw art as something that was fundamentally good *for* society, even as it recognized that it was not meant to be used explicitly *for* social or political goals. Art was a social good in its own right (and, of course, a necessity for the intelligentsia) because it was at once an embodiment of human individualism, spiritual freedom, and the essential ingredient of culture which alone endowed a nation with an identity.

24 *Ukraïns'ka khata* "came out with a sharp critique of traditional petty actions and of the psychological remnants of so-called Ukrainophilism with its moderate liberalism, superficial democracy, loyalty [to the Russian Empire], compromises, and orientation on alien social forces in the national liberation struggle" (Bohats'kyi et al. 1955, 52).

25 Elsewhere he says: "The spiritual slavishness [*rabstvo*] of our 'creative' elite was and is the reason for our national wretchedness. Because where there is slavishness, there is no creative initiative, action, development of life's potential" (1913a, 564).

While Sriblians'kyi and Ievshan were known on occasion to lambaste their fellow Modernists for manifestations of extreme aestheticism and passivity, on the whole they felt quite comfortable with Modernism as an artistic orthodoxy and had relatively few quarrels with its formal and stylistic direction. (Sriblians'kyi even wrote fairly typical Modernist poetry and prose under his real name, Shapoval, and the initials "M. S.") As much can be inferred even from Sriblians'kyi's "Étude on Futurism," which sanctioned writings that were mellow and musical (1914, 451), decent and elegant (ibid., 455). Neither Sriblians'kyi's nor Ievshan's literary agenda called for experimentation as such; they always maintained that literature was a dignified activity, replete with high moral, intellectual, and national responsibility.

It is clear that there were certain artistic limits beyond which *Ukraïns'ka khata* was not prepared to go. The journal, much like Ukrainian Modernism in general, adhered to a fairly monolithic concept of art as Beauty. The "beautiful" also subsumed the notion of "cultured." Art, essentially, was a universal medium of communion for educated individuals ("sensitive souls"); it was not a formalist object. Ievshan said: "Beauty is the same for everyone. Literature is the same for everyone" [*Krasa iest' til'ky odna dlia vsikh. Literatura iest' til'ky odna dlia vsikh*] (Ievshan 1914a, 39). For him, partisan or ideological art was not art: "Of course, there is populist, proletarian, Catholic and Ukrainophile literature; but that is the point: this is 'literature,' it is not art" (ibid., 40). The same argument held true when art betrayed a *formal* preoccupation or narrowness; then it became nothing but empty play. Not surprisingly, Ievshan lamented the first signs of "differentiation" (ideological and formal) in the Ukrainian literary process:

> Ukrainian literary life is moving in the direction of "decentralization," it is fanning out; some kind of stupid "differentiation" is beginning. Various party groupings are spawning, *family interests take precedent over the noble emulation of individual servants of art.* [We face] group particularism, all kinds of "borders".... As a consequence, even among us a literary industry is springing up, even among us literary movements and all manner of self-interest set the pace, *rather than the talented individual* (ibid., 49; *emphasis added*).

Ievshan reacted with equal skepticism to those literary works and writers in Galicia who enjoyed "rising above the 'gray masses' with the aid of effective poses and even more effective appearances." A writer of this ilk, "in order to rise above the 'mob,'...acts like a comedian who demonstrates his 'tricks' before the public...All this is loud, unpalatable, and an offense to dignity..."

> Consequently, we have a very sad situation: Coming out in the defense of art, its rights and rules, we have *genuinely creative individuals of high intellect* as well as—*comedians,* all kinds of word *fetishists,* people who are irresponsible for their actions. They join the warriors who struggle for art, they operate with identical words, promote the same slogans and propagate the same values, but they do more harm to art than [art's] enemies: they compromise it, they soil high ideals with low instincts, they bring them into the marketplace, and are even capable of destroying a genius, if he comes into conflict with them, trying to rid himself of them (Ievshan 1913, 698–99; *emphasis added*).

Such statements make it plain that *Ukraïns'ka khata* conceived art in terms of great individuals and geniuses—not in terms of movements and styles, which were construed as petty pursuits.[26] Content (cultured, noble, idealistic, philosophical) and the dignity of the artist remained the journal's chief values. Buffoonery or any obvious focus on the medium itself was an affront to art's intellectual, sacred, and high calling ("I eternally create ideals for sacred poetry"—Для поезії святої, Вік творю я ідеали—said the poet Chuprynka) (Chuprynka 1913b, 324). Ievshan avowed that self-conscious play with form was a sign of intellectual poverty and warned against a Ukrainian art that might be "without ideas" [*bezideine*]. "Bereft of content, [writers] take form for content and get pleasure from it," he said with disapproval (Ievshan 1910a, 119).[27]

When Semenko elected Futurism as a new way for Ukrainian letters, he was surely going beyond the aesthetics of *Ukraïns'ka khata* and Modernism; he was proposing a self-consciously formalist approach in which novelty became the bellwether. The strange and irreverent tonal, attitudinal, and linguistic shift that his work effected stood in complete opposition to what both Sriblians'kyi and Ievshan identified as "art."

The issue that divided Semenko most from the critics of *Ukraïns'ka khata* was the question of a "national" literature. As was pointed out above, one of Ukrainian Modernism's most characteristic features was its conscious West European bias. Voronyi had called on Ukrainian writers to create a literature that would "in content and in form at least approximate the new currents and directions in contemporary European

26 The following is a typical pronouncement by Ievshan: "In turning now to Shevchenko's aesthetics, I again do not wish to focus on narrow and dry formal issues; I again take the creative individuality of Shevchenko as my point of departure..." (1911b, 154). See also his attack on "pointless play with words and form" (1910a, 120).

27 Tovkachevs'kyi suggests that one of the definitions of "decadence" is "a stylization of form [and] the neglect of content" (1911a, 571).

culture" (Bilets'kyi 1929, 25).[28] Ostap Luts'kyi's (1883–1941) manifesto, "Moloda Muza," had referred to Nietzsche, Ibsen, Maeterlinck, and Baudelaire as examples of what literature should be. When Semenko proclaimed his Kvero-futurism, he was, unquestionably, following this European reflex.

Ukraïns'ka khata, too, can hardly be considered anti-European. Both Sriblians'kyi and Ievshan were well-read in Western literatures, which they admired and frequently favored over traditional Ukrainian writings. Their formulation of a national Ukrainian culture was modeled entirely on European national cultures, and served as a major argument for rejecting the All-Russian (Imperial) ideal, promoted for Ukraine by Russians like Peter Struve.[29] Nevertheless, it is impossible not to see that, as the critics elaborated the notion of a "national" literature, they grew increasingly more suspicious of outside influences, primarily because of their potential to undermine the development of uniquely "Ukrainian" letters. Apprehension about the "Europeanization" of Ukrainian literature—a major achievement of the Modernist movement—grew in direct proportion to the success of European trends on Ukrainian soil. When Futurism appeared, this festering issue came to a head. The dilemma facing Ukrainian literature was succinctly stated by Ievshan: "A new creativity, well and good. But on what foundation [*na iakomu hrunti*]?" (Ievshan 1914b, 271).

Ievshan and Sriblians'kyi answered the question by a resounding affirmation of the "national" orientation. Both critics maintained that little was gained by following "European fashions." Lamented Sriblians'kyi: "We had all the most fashionable products of Europe, we discussed [her] wisest words, but our Ukrainian cause 'weeps like an orphan by the Dnipro'" (1914, 463). Ievshan looked around at the newfangled writings and sighed: "It is a pity that there is no one who might defend the Ukrainian creative idea" (Ievshan 1914b, 272). The problem with Ukrainian letters, he argued, was that its writers had never established a "real" national literature. He accused nineteenth-century writers—whom he called "eunuch-Ukrainophiles"—of killing Ukrainian national literature at its birth (ibid., 270). Literature's current predicament, according to Ievshan, stemmed from its failure to follow the example of Mykhailo Kotsiubyns'kyi's *Fata Morgana,* Ol'ha Kobylians'ka's *Zemlia* [The Earth], and Lesia Ukraïnka's *Lisova pisnia* [The Forest Song], that is, the example of works that were deeply rooted in native Ukrainian

[28] For further details, see also Doroshkevych 1925.
[29] *Ukraïns'ka khata* frequently criticized the "All-Russian" idea and also polemicized with Peter Struve. See especially Tovkachevs'kyi 1912 and Sriblians'kyi 1913b.

reality and thus suited as prototypes for a true national literature. Instead, writers were training their gaze on Europe and writing about "nerves, coffeehouses, night life, and trolley cars," ignoring Ukrainian topics completely. For Ievshan, Semenko was the very embodiment of this betrayal, but he also implied that this unseasoned Futurist was symptomatic of a much larger problem: "Tens of thousands [*sic*] from among the Ukrainian intelligentsia in Galicia and Bukovyna mock the Ukrainian temperament [*stykhiia*]" (ibid., 274). He elaborated:

> This then is precisely the problem: the Ukrainian creative idea has begun to chase electric lamps, not having learned to examine life properly in the light of a gas lamp. The blinding light has had a bad effect on the eyes and they squint and cannot see the "nearest of objects." The "nearest of objects" in literature is the culture of the native word, that natural soil without which every creative work must emerge stunted and useless....Let us reach for that beauty which contains the soul and thoughts of the Ukrainian people!! (ibid., 277).

And Sriblians'kyi was so exasperated by Semenko's new variety of Europeanism that he called out: "My dear people, leave the latest words of Europe, and speak Ukrainian freely and loudly in your own home" (Sriblians'kyi 1914, 463).

The gulf between Semenko and the two critics was, clearly, enormous. His development had taken him through Modernism's genteel, "cultured" European orientation (his *Prélude* invoked Villon, Musset, and Baudelaire) and brought him to an aggressive, "ill-bred" style that refused to acknowledge in art any overt sign of "nationality." While things foreign and exotic triggered angst and alarm in the souls of Sriblians'kyi and Ievshan, Semenko derived pleasure from ridiculing "sincere" Ukrainian art in the name of modernity and progress. The strong desire to escape his native tradition, which he equated with insularity and conservatism, is captured remarkably well in a mature poem from 1914:

> ...Немає нічого більш прекрасного
> Як сьогоднішній день.
> І не дожену його тут.
> Кожного дня зостаюсь з-заду
> Тут між своїми.
> Геть *родичів*—у серці моєму
> Місця немає рідному всьому—
> Рідним жити буду після 40 літ.
> Геть усе що спиняє мене
> Що шкодить моєму бігові
> Що душу мою елястичну старить!
> Лагідність тягне мене під рельси

Благополучіє мене вбиває
Не хочу слави тут
Між своїми де за мішок
Сміття та козацького вуса славу дадуть.
Що мені за діло до Києва та *родичів*
Коли про Семенка мусять марсіяне знать
("Duzhe shchyra poeziika"; Semenko 1925a, 101–102; *emphasis added*).

...There is nothing more beautiful
Than the present day.
I will not catch up to it here.
Every day I fall behind
Here among my own brethren.
Off with the family—there is no room
In my heart for anything kindred.
I will live my heritage once I reach 40.
Off with everything that slows me down,
that hinders my motion
that ages my supple soul!
Tenderness drags me under the rails
Contentment kills me.
I don't want to be famous here
Among my brethren, where for a bag of
Garbage and a Cossack's mustache they'll make me a celebrity.
What is Kyiv to me or family
When the Martians must be made aware of Semenko.

There is no question that Sriblians'kyi and Ievshan lost all intellectual composure when confronted by Semenko's Futurism. Their generally high and sophisticated discourse degenerated into atavistic cries, turning their pursuit of a universal but "national" literature into the promotion of writings "with national characteristics."[30] Their paradigm for the new Ukrainian literature was now increasingly being shaped by elements both familiar and from the past. In the heat of the polemic, Sriblians'kyi held up Shevchenko as the only light of the future: "We have *only one* great, phenomenal, insanely brave, pathetic, tearful Shevchenko, who was buried with his fists clenched. We have *only one* futurist, *only one* promising, blameless Ukrainian" (Sriblians'kyi 1914, 463; *emphasis added*). Despite his elitism and disdain for the "mob," Sriblians'kyi suddenly revealed a marked preference for peasants over literary innovators: "You understand that every one of our peasants is a thousand times more of a Ukrainian than you [Semenko], a Muscovite product" (ibid.).

30 See, for example, Sriblians'kyi 1910a and 1911.

Ievshan also managed to talk himself into an intellectual *cul-de-sac.* Having rejected writers of Semenko's ilk, he turned to Mariia Proskurivna, a contemporary epigone of the dying ethnographic tradition (and, ironically, Semenko's mother!), hailing this decidedly minor and anachronistic writer virtually as a literary reformer: "The soul rejoices, as if someone had brought into the stifling *city atmosphere* a bouquet of *wild* flowers" (Ievshan 1914b, 274–75; *emphasis added*). Ievshan found the Ukrainian elements so appealing that he was ready to suspend critical judgment: "The fresh, pleasant gust coming from this little book is so strong that one could even *overestimate* its literary qualities. That, after all, would not be a sin" (ibid., 275; *emphasis added*).

The purely literary achievements of Semenko's first two Futurist collections were modest, to be sure, but the challenge they posed to the prevailing literary and cultural ethos was formidable. In tone, style, theme, and social function, *Derzannia* and *Kvero-futuryzm* went counter to everything that the society cherished as good, beautiful and sensible. It dethroned the Poet, along with his cherished themes, and brought high language down to earth. No recent literary debut had struck at the very quick of the literary process as had Semenko's. The scandal laid bare the often unspoken principles on which literature was made in Ukraine. It drove home the essence of the social and stylistic parameters by which writing functioned and the grave seriousness with which it took itself.

Unfortunately, the scandal yielded no instructive lessons for literary criticism—nor for society. Critics and patriots alike considered their job accomplished once they had beaten back, to all appearances, Semenko's threat. No effort was made to assimilate further his intentions or speculate on the implications it had for the literary process. In part, this was due to the impending World War and the Russian government's accompanying repression of Ukrainian activities. Only months after the literary scandal broke, *Ukraïns'ka khata* and other Ukrainian publications were banned. One of the journal's editors was exiled to Siberia (Doroshenko 1969, 21). But the political situation did not account for everything. The fact is that neither Ukrainian society nor literary scholarship was equipped to deal with the revolutionary significance of the avant-garde, the transformation it wrought in the role of the writer, the change of attitude it brought toward language, elite culture, and the creative act itself. For this reason, Semenko's battle for Futurism had only begun.

Збожеволів.
Збожеволі
Збожевол
Збожево
Збожев
Збоже
Збож
Збо
Зб
З
Я
Ще
Не
!

Кобзарі

Михайло Васильович Семенко:
— Одступіться трохи, Тарасе Григоровичу, а то нас переплутають.

Мал. Б. Фрідкіна

Top: Portrait of M. Semenko by M. Simashkevych. Cover art for M. Semenko, *Kobzar* (Kyiv: Hol'fshtrom, 1924). *Bottom:* B. Fridkin. "Kobzari." Reproduced from H. A. Nud'ha, comp. and ed., *Ukraïns'ki parodiï* (Kyiv, 1963), p. 231. The anagram above reads: "I have gone mad…not yet." The text below reads: "Mykhailo Vasyl'ovych Semenko: 'Step back a bit, Taras Hryhorovych [i.e., Shevchenko], or else they might confuse us.'"

CHAPTER 2

The Lean Years, 1914–1921

> Майбутній історик скаже в яких умовах робилося те все, як важко приходилося те, що належить по праву, як напружено працювала в ті дні горстка голодних і молодих мисців...
> *A future historian will reveal under what conditions all this was done, how difficult it was to achieve that which belonged to us by right, and how intensely a small group of starving young artists worked during those days...*
>
> Klym Polishchuk

Mykhail' Semenko, his brother Bazyl', and Pavl' Kovzhun were proud of their scandal. Reflecting on the events of 1914 several years later, Semenko declared, "[Our] success was total" (Tsebro [Semenko] 1922, 41). He and his colleagues were convinced that "everything indicated that [our] work would proceed energetically and in an interesting manner" (ibid.). To his father, Semenko wrote somewhat apologetically but firmly, "Right now I wish one thing: may God grant you many years of life so that I can justify myself and atone for all the grief I brought you...." He continued:

> I consider myself a member of the community of artists, and if I did not feel my own strength, then I would not, of course, contradict you and would not be doing so many disagreeable things. The problem is that you do not understand the seriousness of our task and do not consider it important. You think all this is nonsense and leisure games....You are worried about how we are going to earn our daily bread and think that we can only get our bread at some job.... In a few years I will find my place in life. It is hard to be successful immediately. As long as I was not a Futurist, the foremost Ukrainian poet, Hryts'ko Chuprynka, and the foremost Ukrainian critic, M. Sriblians'kyi wrote nice things about me in journals. When I became a Futurist, everyone jumped on me. That is a guarantee of success.[1]

[1] This letter (written in Russian) appears in Sulyma (1989, 291).

By mid-year the three Futurists had embarked on a second edition of *Derzannia*, augmenting it with articles by Mykhail' and Bazyl' Semenko, as well as Futurist graphics by Pavl' Kovzhun (Semenko 1918e, 95).[2] They planned "Futurist activities," public appearances, exhibits, new publications, and "confrontations" [*boiovyshcha*]. Provisions were made to stage a Futurist drama [*futurodrama*] entitled *Trahediia onuch* [Tragedy of the Bootlegs], complete with "Futurist music and Futurist decorations" (ibid.). Mykhail' Semenko prepared a booklet on "Kvero-futurism in philosophy," entitled *Limityvnyi futuryzm* [Open-ended Futurism] (Sulyma 1989, 289n2).[3] Frustrating all these efforts—including an almanac, *Mertvopetliuiu* [I Do the Death Spiral] that contained "extremely leftist" material—was the outbreak of the First World War and the simultaneous repressions against Ukrainian cultural activities by the Russian government (Tsebro [Semenko] 1922, 41).[4] All three Futurists were conscripted. As Semenko wrote his father: "The war ruined everything. My latest work got held up in the printing house just before I was taken into the army.... Our journal and all our newspapers were shut down" (Sulyma 1989, 291).

The military dispatched Semenko to Vladivostok. His brother ended up on the Western front where he died in 1915 (ibid.). Pavl' Kovzhun (later known simply as "Pavlo") was sent to the Carpathian front in 1915 where he was wounded. He returned to Kyiv and was again mobilized, this time by the Ukrainian Central Rada. After his demobilization in 1918, he rejoined Semenko on Kyiv's cultural scene for about a year. He emigrated to Western Ukraine after that (Hordyns'kyi 1943, 8–9, 12).[5]

2 Semenko recreated the contents of the second edition in a later publication. It was described thus: "*Derzannia. Poezy*. Second edition, enlarged: Pavlo Kovzhun—graphics ("City" No. 1 and No. 2, "Street," "Tango"). Mykh. Semenko, "Concerning two realities" [*Pro dvi real'nosty*], Pav. Kovzhun, "Notes on Art (Cubo-Futurism). Kyiv, 1914, Kvero (Destroyed by military censors)."

3 An announcement to that effect appeared in Semenko (1914b, 25). Semenko attributes the term *limityvnyi* to K. F. Zhakov, a professor in the Psychoneurological Institute (St. Petersburg), where he studied. It is used to suggest an indefinite approaching or nearing.

4 The title, *Mertvopetliuiu,* may have been inspired by the first death spiral performed in Kyiv by the pilot P. M. Nesterov on 9 September 1913. Semenko indicated in a later publication that this almanac was destroyed by military censors in 1914. See Semenko (1918e, 95). Semenko used the verb *mertvopetliuvaty* [to do the death spiral] to title some of his later collections, and as a pseudonym (Mertvopetliuiko). See below.

5 See also Fediuk (1924, 3–8). Semenko made this ironic comment on Kovzhun's emigration: He "settled down comfortably with Symon Petliura (not a Futurist)." See Tsebro [Semenko] (1922, 41). In the late 1920s Kovzhun had some contact with Semenko; for example, *Nova generatsiia* 7 (1929) lists him as a representative of the journal for Lviv. He designed the cover for *Nova generatsiia* 6 (1929).

Semenko left Kyiv around the middle of October 1914.[6] By the end of November he was already in the far eastern part of the Russian Empire. From 24 March 1915 to 26 September 1917 he lived in Vladivostok.

There is virtually no information available about his life in the Far East. Rumor had it he tried to emigrate to America (Leites and Iashek 1930, 1: 432; *Ukraïns'ki pys'mennyky* 1960–65, 5: 417; Plevako 1923–26, 2: 157). It is known that he worked as a telegraph operator and that in 1916 he joined the Russian Social-Democratic Revolutionary Party (RSDRP) (Leites and Iashek, 1930, 1: 432).[7] In Vladivostok he also met his future wife, Lidiia Ivanivna Horenko, whose surname he would later use as a pseudonym (Kriger 1979, 114).[8] One other aspect stands out about the Vladivostok period—his literary output was prolific. In 1924 when the first edition of his *Kobzar* was published—a collection of more than six hundred pages containing works written between 1910 and 1922—some forty percent of the poems dated from the war years.

In the last days of September 1917, Semenko was in Suchan, then in Harbin, suggesting that he was either traveling in connection with military duties, or else had begun his return journey to Ukraine, which he made in a convoy composed primarily of Ukrainians and of which he was second-in-command (Kriger, 1979, 65). By December 1917 he arrived in his native village of Kybyntsi (Poltava region) where he remained secluded through the first few months of 1918. In April he traveled to Kyiv to resume public literary life. It was here that the first Futurist organizations and publications would make their appearance.

Semenko returned from the Far East at a time of unprecedented political and military chaos. On 7 November 1917 the Russian Provisional Government collapsed. With its collapse, the Empire began to disintegrate. As Viktor Shklovskii cleverly phrased it, "the show 'Russia' was over; everyone was hurrying to get his coat and hat" (Shklovskii 1970, 122). For the non-Russian nationalities this was an opportunity to bid for statehood and independence. In no region were these goals pursued more earnestly than in Ukraine, where immediately after the fall of the Tsarist regime bitter and bloody conflicts ensued for political power among various indigenous and foreign forces.

6 The chronology that follows is reconstructed on the basis of information contained in Semenko's volume of collected verse, *Kobzar* (Semenko 1925a). Every poem here is dated and the place of composition indicated, allowing for a rough reconstruction of his whereabouts.

7 This source literally says that he joined the "Communist Party." He was not a party member after 1922.

8 In 1927 he and Horenko separated, and Semenko began a relationship with the famous actress Nataliia Mykhailivna Uzhvii.

Semenko's homecoming coincided with the Central Rada's formation of the Ukrainian National Republic (20 [7] November 1917).[9] At first merely autonomous, the Rada declared the Republic independent on 22 [9] January 1918 after the Bolsheviks seized power in Russia. Within the span of a few months the inhabitants of Kyiv lived through a succession of astounding military and political reversals. In February 1918 the Rada was driven out of Kyiv by the Bolsheviks. By 1 March, backed by German troops, it was again in Kyiv only to fall victim to these same forces when its policies went counter to German interests. The Rada was dissolved at the end of April and the Germans installed a government headed by Hetman Pavlo Skoropads'kyi.

War and unceasing political unrest were not conducive to a flourishing culture. A witness, who lived in Kyiv during these turbulent months, remarked: "Those who might express interest in the literary activities during the years of our national revolution and wars can simply be told, 'there was none.' These were years subsumed by a drive to create a [Ukrainian] state....People...fought with arms and words, but no one wrote. Only publicists wrote. Writers and poets were silent. *Inter arma silent musae*" (Zhurba 1962, 461).

In fact, the muses were not entirely silent.[10] As inhospitable as the climate was, Kyiv did evince signs of creative life in 1918–1919. Journals such as *Shliakh* [The Way], *Literaturno-naukovyi visnyk* [The Literary-Scientific Herald], and *Knyhar* [Bookseller] kept appearing, as did quite a few newspapers. Despite shortages of paper and printing facilities some poets even succeeded in having their collections published.[11] But from the point of view of the recently arrived Semenko, the political and literary situation was discouraging at best because both "fronts" (that is, the literary and political) were dominated by his opponents. Semenko's leftist sympathies alienated him from the moderate Rada and, especially, from the rightist Hetmanate. In strictly literary terms, he found himself in a luckless situation because Kyiv was under the sway of the ascending Symbolists and the still active Modernists. In short, both politics and poetry simply were too conservative. Looking back at this period, he said that "Parliamentarism, the Central Rada, the Ukrainian National Republic, the Western model of an officer's uniform—this new and

9 Dates given first are according to the Gregorian calendar (i.e., "New Style"). "Old Style" (Julian) dates, which were still standard in the Russian Empire at this time, are given in brackets.

10 For details about literature in Kyiv in 1918, see Rod'ko 1971.

11 Among these were: Iaroshenko 1918; Ryl's'kyi 1918; Savchenko 1918b; Slisarenko 1918; Tychyna 1918; Zahul 1918.

attractive 'civilized' background agreed with contemporary Ukrainian Modernism, with Symbolism in poetry and the Young Theater and its 'European' repertoire..." (Tsebro [Semenko] 1922, 41).[12] He was unhappy with the cultural climate and exasperated by the Symbolists:

> "Young Ukrainian poetry" (Tychyna, Iakiv Savchenko, Zahul) took as the latest word, and as the "new form" in art such innovations as capital letters (Ia. Savchenko), while "learned" Ukrainian critics noted this as a great progressive step. Iakiv Savchenko cackled along this line (this crow of Ukrainian poetry, [this] Symbolist from the most remote provincial steppe [was] full of enthusiasm and bellicose energy). Pavlo Tychyna [meanwhile] sat quietly in his little den, content with onanism, translating "beautiful Ukrainian folk songs" into the language of poetry, stylizing Ukrainian rugs, restoring ancient *dumy* and other useless things, preparing to become "father's" (or, "mother's") little boy and the successor to Voronyi, Lesia Ukraïnka, and Oles'. Dmytro Zahul was no better. He rehashed and translated Bal'mont while stumbling around Kyiv's cafes (ibid.).

This rude caricature, written several years later, hints at the disdain Semenko had for the state of literature in 1918. His friends and supporters were primarily artists like Anatolii Petryts'kyi and Robert Lisovs'kyi (ibid.). Pavlo Kovzhun continued to side with him. But as Semenko himself acknowledged, it was precisely a *literary* following that he could not muster—thus, he had to postpone the creation of a Futurist organization. This did not prevent him, however, from immersing himself in what literary life there was in Kyiv. His estrangement notwithstanding, the year 1918 proved to be surprisingly productive for him both as a poet and as a literary organizer.

The earliest sign of Semenko's return to literary activity is a negative review he published in June 1918 of Iakiv Savchenko's Symbolist collection, *Poeziï* [Poetry] (Rod'ko 1971, 99).[13] Toward the latter part of that year Semenko managed to release three of his own collections.[14] The reaction of critics was beggarly and unenthusiastic at best (Fylypovych 1919b,

[12] The Young Theater (*Molodyi Teatr*) was founded in Kyiv by the brilliant director Les' Kurbas. Initially, i.e., from June 1916 to September 1917, it was known as The Studio (*Studiia*). It was highly experimental and anti-realistic. It was forced to cease activities in April 1919. In 1920 it was revived as The Berezil' [March] Theater.

[13] *Vidrodzhennia* (Kyiv) 5 June 1918. *Vidrodzhennia* was described as "a daily non-partisan democratic newspaper," edited by Petro Pevnyi first in Moscow, then in Kyiv (see *Knyhar* 16 [December 1918]). This newspaper ceased publication on 31 December 1918 after 223 issues. See *Knyhar* 17 (January 1919): 1078.

[14] *Devi'at' poem* (Semenko 1918a); *P'iero zadaiet'sia. Fragmenty. Intymni poeziï. Knyzhka 1-a* (Semenko 1918e); *P'iero kokhaie. Misteriï (1916–1917). Intymni poeziï. Knyzhka 2-a* (Semenko 1918d).

1147; Burchak 1919; Fylypovych 1918, 858). The notable exception, ironically, was Iakiv Savchenko who, in reviewing the collection *P'iero zadaiet'sia* [Pierrot Brags], came to unexpected conclusions: "At the present moment, Semenko is living through a period of symbolism, and no matter where he might end up in the future, he will not arrive at futurism, because futurism is organically alien to him. But regardless of who Semenko may be, he is an interesting phenomenon...and deserves a certain standing among poets of the youngest generation" (Savchenko 1918a, 45).

In 1918 Semenko became actively involved with the publishing house Grunt [Foundation], established by Mykhailo Lebedynets', I. Nemolovs'kyi, and O. Solodub. These were Borot'bists and Semenko apparently felt comfortable in their midst.[15] The group included Vasyl' Ellan-Blakytnyi, Volodymyr Kobylians'kyi, and O. Hrudnyts'kyi, all of whom were contributors to *Universal'nyi zhurnal* [The Universal Magazine], a fortnightly published by Grunt.[16] Nemolovs'kyi was the official editor but some contend that Semenko was the actual power behind the throne.[17]

Universal'nyi zhurnal prevailed for only two issues (the first was dated October 1918), yet was remembered as "interesting not only in content but in appearance" (K. Polishchuk 1923, 1), probably because Pavlo Kovzhun was involved.[18] The publisher called *Universal'nyi zhurnal* "an example of a family journal" whose goal was to "defend...Ukrainian statehood..., fortify this idea among wide circles of society...defend universal progress...and promote the peaceful development of

[15] The Borot'bists, or the Ukrainian Party of Socialist Revolutionaries-Borot'bists (Communists), was the left faction of the Ukrainian Party of Socialists-Revolutionaries (UPSR). In May 1918 this faction gained control of the UPSR and collaborated with the Bolsheviks. For a history of the Borot'bist movement see Majstrenko (1954). Lebedynets' and Nemolovs'kyi are mentioned briefly in this study (see ibid., 177, 179, 253). No mention is made of O. Solodub. Dr. Janusz Radziejowski stated in a private communication to me that Solodub was a member of this party. In the 1920s he held official positions in the Soviet Ukrainian government and wrote political fiction. His name appears in Radziejowski 1983. Semenko, apparently, appeared in print in the Borot'bist party organ, *Borot'ba* 1920 (55) under the cryptonym "Tr. M." See Dei (1969, 363).

[16] Ellan-Blakytnyi's participation in *Universal'nyi zhurnal* is mentioned by Rod'ko (1971, 212). Kobylians'kyi is mentioned ibid., 117, 195. For Hrudnyts'kyi's publications in *Universal'nyi zhurnal* see Leites and Iashek (1930, 1: 120).

[17] In his short memoir, Klym Polishchuk clearly states that the journal appeared under the "editorship of M. Semenko" (1923, 1).

[18] Kovzhun: "After being demobilized, I was one of the organizers of the publishing house 'Grunt,' secretary of *Universal'nyi zhurnal*, the first issue of which I published [*vydav*]" See Hordyns'kyi (1943, 12). Another source identifies Kovzhun as the head of the art section in Grunt. See Fediuk (1924, 7).

democratic ideals among the Ukrainian people." Its policy was to depict "Ukrainian life...through a prism of statehood, nationality, and democratism" ("Vid redaktsiï" 1918). In terms of literary works, the journal differed little from others of this period, reflecting for the most part Modernist and Symbolist styles. With contributors like Mykola Tereshchenko, Klym Polishchuk, Iakiv Savchenko, Pavlo Tychyna, and Mykola Voronyi, it could hardly have a different profile.[19] It seems significant that although Semenko was intimately connected with this journal, he published none of his poetic works here. He did, however, edit for Grunt the so-called Universal Library, a series devoted mostly to translations.[20] Semenko appended brief introductions to these volumes under the pseudonym Les' Horenko. A reviewer called "Horenko's" characterizations "simply wonderful," saying that they "greatly increased the value of the Universal Library" (Dykyi 1919).

Semenko's association with Grunt was not without its ironies. The first issue of *Universal'nyi zhurnal* published Mykyta Sriblians'kyi; Semenko (as "Horenko") also served with him on a jury selecting "original" works for the Universal Library (*Universal'nyi zhurnal* 1 [October 1918]: 16).

Because Grunt published Semenko's collection (Semenko 1918), and he was an important member of the organization, one critic has contended that this publishing house was a Futurist stronghold (Pivtoradni 1968, 11). That seems an exaggeration, but there is no doubt that Semenko's presence in Grunt was keenly felt. Kovzhun recalls explicitly that during this time two orientations developed: one Futurist (led, naturally, by Semenko), the other Symbolist (led by Iakiv Savchenko). In the Futurist faction—described as the more active—Kovzhun included himself, Oleksa Slisarenko, Volodymyr Iaroshenko, and the artists Obidnyi and Robert Lisovs'kyi (Kovzhun 1934; Pivtoradni 1968, 26–27; Hordyns'kyi 1943, 21). It was probably no coincidence that in 1918 Grunt published a small pamphlet by Viktor Obiurten, *Mystetstvo vmyraie* [Art is Dying], translated from the German by the theater director Les' Kurbas, who, too, was beginning to edge closer to Semenko (Obiurten 1918).[21] The death of art was to became a major theme in Semenko's movement.

[19] I have not had the opportunity to examine the second issue; these writers are enumerated in a review that appeared in *Knyhar* 16 (December 1918): 1014.

[20] Among the authors published were Valerii Briusov, Knut Hamsun, Oscar Wilde, Maurice Maeterlinck, John August Strindberg, Gabriele D'Annunzio, Sir Rabindranath Tagore, Henri de Regnier, Obstfelder Sigbjørn, Kazimierz Przerwa-Tetmajer, Hugo von Hofmannsthal, Guy de Maupassant, Konstantin Bal'mont, and Jack London. See the back cover of *Universal'nyi zhurnal* (October 1918).

[21] See also the review by Serhii Iefremov in *Knyhar* 22 (June 1919): 1489–92.

Apparently encouraged by this support and taking advantage of his editorial position, Semenko tried (probably in November 1918) to publish through Grunt a journal with a "leftist orientation" that he decided to call *Studiia* [Studio] (Tsebro [Semenko] 1922, 41). An announcement to this effect appeared on the back cover of *Universal'nyi zhurnal*'s first issue: "A new book will appear soon: 'Studio,' an almanac of young writers." In the course of preparing this publication, Semenko realized that there "were no 'leftist' poets in Kyiv yet" and the project was abandoned (ibid.). Instead, in December 1918, Grunt published *Literaturno-krytychnyi al'manakh* [The Literary-Critical Almanac] to which Semenko contributed a long poem, "Vinok tremtiachyi" [Trembling Wreath] (Semenko 1918f),[22] but which otherwise was dominated by the Symbolists.

This aborted effort at a Futurist publication raises an interesting question about the relationship between Semenko's *Studiia* and the equally unsuccessful and unrealized Symbolist organization and almanac *Bila studiia* [White Studio] to which there are references in the historical literature (Pavliuk 1922, 98; Bilets'kyi 1965–66, 3: 96). It would appear that despite the discrepancy in names, the Symbolist almanac and the Futurist journal may really have been one and the same fruitless effort; their apparent separateness was the result of two opposing camps trying to claim or control Semenko's initiative. Chronology tends to lend credence to this argument, for in both cases there is a consensus that the project was an unsuccessful predecessor of *Literaturno-krytychnyi al'manakh* (Pavliuk 1922, 97–98; Pivtoradni 1968, 26–27). The sources betray uncertainty and variations only about the exact title of the project. Klym Polishchuk, who implies that there was some kind of link between the Symbolist journal *Muzahet* (Musagetes; 1919) and *Bila studiia*, formulates his connection in a most uncertain and vague manner, stating: "They say that before [*Muzahet*] there was some kind of *Bila studiia*" (K. Polishchuk 1923, 1). Semenko betrays no such indecisiveness when he calls his project a journal and titles it *Studiia*. But, curiously, he is contradicted by a source that should have known better. Kovzhun states that "the Futurists [N.B.] wanted to publish an almanac [*sic*], *Bila studiia* [*sic*]," and then adds the following confusing bit of information: "But the Symbolists took advantage of the title and published it themselves under the name *Studiia*, which [ended up] pleasing no one, not even the Symbolists" (Kovzhun 1934). Kovzhun is probably wrong when he states that the Symbolists published *Studiia*, for as far as one can tell no such journal

22 Klym Polishchuk refers to it as "Tremtiachyi vinok" (1923, 1).

appeared.[23] He undoubtedly had in mind *Literaturno-krytychnyi al'manakh,* which did appear in December 1918.[24]

In light of these inconsistencies, it seems plausible that there was in fact only one project (probably Semenko's) over which Futurists and Symbolists quarreled. When it finally died, it left behind only befuddled memories among the discussants.[25] The divergence of opinion in Grunt on this subject was so great that when time came to compromise on a publication that would satisfy both factions, the original title or titles were probably abandoned. That is when *Literaturno-krytychnyi al'manakh* was born, a journal designed to appeal to (and, quite likely, to appease) both factions. This may account for the substantial exposure given here to Semenko (it contained the above-mentioned poem and Savchenko's long review of *P'iero zadaiet'sia*) alongside works of Tychyna, Zahul, Savchenko, and Slisarenko. This heterogeneity—a characteristic noted even by a contemporary reviewer—ended up pleasing no one.[26] One source refers to the almanac as "abridged," contending that some writers had refused to compromise, and did not submit their works for publication (Pavliuk 1922, 98).

It is obvious from the short life-span of *Universal'nyi zhurnal,* the failure of *Studiia* (or *Bila studiia*), and even from the limited success of *Literaturno-krytychnyi al'manakh* that differences among the participants made cooperation difficult if not impossible. Writers who had come together partially out of economic necessity, partially out of a desire to oppose the older generation, found themselves driven apart by the inherent contradictions of their literary views.[27] Thus, no sooner did

23 Since initially writing this section, I have discovered a potentially strong argument for the existence of *Studiia.* A recent edition of Pavlo Tychyna's works makes reference to an almanac *Studiia* 1 (1918), identifying it as representing "a group of young poets" in Kyiv, and gives it as the initial place of publication of Tychyna's poem "Enharmoniine." See Tychyna (1983–90, 1: 587). Unfortunately, efforts, my own and those of my colleagues in Kyiv, to track down this publication have been futile thus far.

24 This date is corroborated by Klym Polishchuk (1923, 1) who states that the almanac came out "during the entry of the armies of the Directory into Kyiv."

25 The subsequent confusion surrounding the title was probably exacerbated by the fact that the name "Studiia" and "Bila studiia" were common and popular during 1918–1919. Polishchuk mentions that a literary artistic "Studiia" (N.B., *not* "Bila studiia") was formed during the planning stages of *Muzahet.* There was also a "Studiia" mentioned after the appearance of *Muzahet* (See *Mystetstvo* 3: 33). One of Semenko's cycles of poems from 1918 bore the title "Bila studiia" (see 1925a, 641).

26 Borys Iakubs'kyi (1919b, 1413) observed that in this single publication there were "different approach[es] to themes and problems."

27 There can be little doubt that, despite their differences, Semenko and the Symbolist-Modernists also shared certain general goals. Literary reform and novelty, and opposition to the older generation of writers (especially those represented in *Literaturno-naukovyi*

Literaturno-krytychnyi al'manakh appear, when Grunt, finding itself in an "unclear" position because of the frequent literary conflicts, suspended operations (K. Polishchuk 1923, 2). The brief alliance between Semenko and the Symbolists-Modernists unraveled as both groups set out in opposite directions.

In January 1919 the Symbolists mobilized their resources to prepare *Muzahet*. Semenko categorically refused to participate in this venture, even though all his so-called Futurist supporters from Grunt (that is, Kovzhun, Slisarenko, Iaroshenko) did so (ibid., 4). He and a small minority of Borot'bist writers—Hnat Mykhailychenko, Ellan-Blakytnyi, and Vasyl' Chumak—went their own way, creating, along with the painter Anatolii Petryts'kyi, the "art group Flamingo" (ibid., 6). Its short existence and limited activity probably qualifies "Flamingo" only as an ostentatious declaration of independence from the Symbolists rather than as a true Futurist organization. It seems to have served only one practical purpose: under this trademark Semenko issued three books of poetry (Petryts'kyi designed two covers, Robert Lisovs'kyi one).[28] This was a considerable feat at a time when printing anything was extremely difficult. As one journal noted: "Writers are writing, but they publish little because there is no one and nowhere to publish" (*Mystetstvo* 4 [1919]: 42).

The year 1919 began with a new series of military and political upheavals. In late December 1918, the eight-month-old government of Hetman Skoropads'kyi was overthrown in an uprising engineered by the Directory of the Ukrainian National Republic. In Kyiv, hopes for an independent Ukrainian state soared once again, especially in January when the Ukrainian National Republic and the Western Ukrainian National Republic (established in November 1918) merged into a single

---

visnyk), were certainly among them. It is probably no accident, for example, that Pavliuk (1922, 98) spoke of *Bila studiia* not in any partisan literary terms but rather as an undertaking of the "young" generation. *Literaturno-krytychnyi al'manakh* was certainly an example of this "generational" solidarity. The reaction to the almanac was slightly reminiscent of Semenko's Futurist debut in 1914. The critic Borys Iakubovs'kyi noted in his review that "each page [of *Literaturno-krytychnyi al'manakh*] is a protest against the old ways: against the old poetry, against the old criticism, against the old theater." And he added: "this protest would lose none of its strength, if it tried to stay within the bounds of decency...Insults have never served as a substitute for proof" (see *Knyhar* 22 [May 1919]: 1415). The struggle against the older generation and its ways was also the goal of *Muzahet*. Klym Polishchuk noted that one of *Muzahet*'s "programmatic goals" was to "drive the old *[Literaturno-naukovyi]* *visnyk* into a corner" (1923, 3).

28 *P'iero mertvopetliuie. Futuryzy. 1914–1918. Poezii̋. Knyha 3-a* (Semenko 1919e); *Bloc-Notes. Poezii̋ 1919 roku. Knyha 4-a* (Semenko 1919a). These two collections were designed by Petryts'kyi. *V sadakh bezroznykh. Saturnalii̋. Poezii̋. Knyzhka 5-a* (Semenko 1919k) was published with a cover by Lisovs'kyi.

state. The euphoria inspired by these events quickly vanished, however, when the Bolsheviks took Kyiv on 5 February 1919.

The sudden change in regimes brought into play a completely new set of political factors which did not portend well for Ukrainians. The Bolsheviks showed little understanding and even less sympathy for the situation in Ukraine, and their approach to cultural questions betrayed some of the same unsavory and chauvinistic attitudes that had characterized the Old Regime. One historian writes that the Bolsheviks

> simply refused to recognize Ukraine as a nation, not only politically but even culturally.... The Soviet administration requisitioned buildings of Ukrainian cultural institutions for state purposes and excluded the Ukrainian language from public use. In practice, the administration was even more anti-Ukrainian than the government (Majstrenko 1954, 122).

Richard Pipes states that this "contempt and hostility toward the Ukrainian language on the part of the government also alienated the Ukrainian intelligentsia, who for two years had grown accustomed to free activity" (1954, 143).[29]

In the wake of the Bolsheviks' rise to power, literary controls in Kyiv fell into the hands of the "Proletkul'ts." These, according to a Soviet source, "not only failed to acknowledge Ukrainian national art, culture, or language, but referred to the Soviet Republic as a 'region' [*krai*]" (Zolotoverkhyi 1961, 249). The Proletkul'ts exercised their influence over literature through the All-Ukrainian Literary Committee (headed by Grigorii Petnikov, Aleksei Gastev, and M. Levchenko), created in February 1919 as an arm of the Arts Council, which itself was a division of the People's Commissariat of Education. The Literary Committee "ignored the development of Ukrainian literature at first because Ukrainian literature was, supposedly, a literature of the village, which the Proletkul'ts considered bourgeois" (ibid., 270).[30] Eventually, the Committee did create a Ukrainian section (headed by Volodymyr Koriak, a Borot'bist), which however was relegated to the humiliating position of being recognized as just one of several sections established for "national minorities" (ibid.). Klym Polishchuk, a witness to these events, described the attitudes of Valentin Rozhitsin, head of the Literary Committee in Kyiv and one of its members, Natan Vengrov, a Russian poet:

> The first appearances of these "emissaries" in Kyiv were not a success. Rozhitsin was quick to declare that "there is no Ukrainian culture and

[29] See also Zolotoverkhyi (1961, 176–77).
[30] See also Ostashko (1987, 64).

> none can exist," as a result of which he had to disappear later from Kyiv's horizon. The poet Natan Vengrov, on the occasion of Shevchenko's anniversary, expressed [the thought] that "the best way that one can honor the memory of this chauvinist is to construct near his grave a row of gallows." There was a decisive protest against [this] not only from the members of *Muzahet* but from the Jewish writers' group "Bailika." [Consequently], Koriak found himself in a difficult position....It may be that Koriak's efforts were completely sincere, but they had no success—if only because in almost all government cultural institutions unscrupulous Russification was taking place (K. Polishchuk 1923, 5).[31]

With attitudes like these, links between the Proletkul'ts and Ukrainian writers were virtually impossible to establish. The Proletkul'ts never attracted any meaningful number of Ukrainian writers precisely because their leadership did not take into account specific Ukrainian needs and cultural aspirations. This remained true for the duration of the life of the Proletkul'ts in Ukraine despite several attempts on the part of men like Mykhailychenko, Ellan-Blakytnyi, and later Serhii Pylypenko to establish a *modus vivendi*.[32]

Under such circumstances, the situation for Ukrainian letters would have been disastrous were it not for the fact that the old-time, non-Soviet Ukrainian journals (for example, *Literaturno-naukovyi visnyk*, *Shliakh*, *Knyhar*, *Hromada*, and so on) continued to appear through most of 1919, thus cushioning the initial blow of the Soviet regime. Primarily because the new Soviet institutions ignored Ukrainian cultural needs and partly because the new government found it impossible to extend immediate control over the bureaucracies of previous governments, matters that related to Ukrainian culture continued to fall under the control of the Ministry of Arts, a body of the defeated Directory. This ministry, which had a "sharp [Ukrainian] national profile" and whose "every activity was directed at a stubborn and decisive Ukrainization of art" (*Mystetsvo* 1 [1919]: 36) continued its work into March of 1919, when it was finally subordinated to the Art Council of the Commissariat of Education (Zolotoverkhyi 1961, 248–49). This development may have had a catastrophic effect had it not been for the fact that soon afterwards, in early May, the Borot'bists, who were the only Ukrainian party at this time with any leverage with the Bolsheviks, wrested control of the Commissariat of Education from the Proletkul'ts (ibid., 177, 249). Hnat

31 His statement finds corroboration in many other sources. See Shklovskii (1970, 163); Pipes (1954, 143); Rod'ko (1971, 198); Pavliuk (1922, 99); Zhurba (1962, 464); and Pivtoradni (1968, 21, 24, 32–33, 67).

32 On this subject, see Trostianets'kyi (1968b, 74–75). See also Rod'ko (1971, 207).

Mykhailychenko became its new head. Accusing Rozhitsin of "Ukrainophobia," he had him removed as head of the Literary Committee (Hadzins'kyi 1928, 140; Hadzins'kyi 1929a, 55). This led to a slight improvement for Ukrainian letters. In May, the first Soviet-sponsored literary journal, *Mystetstvo* [Art], made its appearance; just a few days later the long overdue Symbolist journal *Muzahet* was published. The month of May saw the establishment of the Art Guild [*Mystets'kyi tsekh*], a "general organization of Ukrainian literati, poets and actors." (*Mystetstvo* 1 [1919]: 37; see also Polishchuk 1923, 13–15). In June, certainly with Borot'bist encouragement, a broad coalition of Ukrainian literary forces established the so-called Literary-Artistic Studio [*Literaturno-mystets'ka studiia*]. This body was composed primarily of *Muzahet* members, but significantly it also included "some" Borot'bist writers; it even welcomed associates of *Literaturno-naukovyi visnyk*. This organization failed to publish a planned biweekly journal, *Studiia*, which was to have been a forum for "all" writers (*Mystetstvo* 3 [1919]: 33).

The rise of the Bolsheviks to power in February 1919 was particularly detrimental to the Symbolists. The most immediate consequence for them was the loss of a loan promised by the Directory for the publication of *Muzahet*.[33] This delayed the appearance of their journal for several months (when it appeared in May it was backdated for the months of January, February, and March). Not only were the Symbolists handicapped financially, but their entire political and cultural world view stood in glaring contrast to the new "proletarian" orientation. Their position was both awkward and precarious:

> The open, clear and uncompromising policy of *Muzahet* in the area of national art caused sharp conflicts with the emissaries of official 'proletarian art'....As a result the situation was very difficult, so much so that all the members of *Muzahet* found themselves in a semi-legal position which curtailed their work (K. Polishchuk 1923, 4–5).

Clearly, the political reversals suffered by the Ukrainian National Republic had dire consequences for the Symbolists. Klym Polishchuk even claimed that some of them narrowly escaped mobilization into the Red Army. As a result, the group that had virtually set the tone for Ukrainian literature during the national renascence found itself disenfranchised. The problem, however, was not limited to the Symbolists; it confronted Ukrainian culture as a whole, inasmuch as the new political order afforded few legal or institutional channels through which it could

[33] Iakiv Savchenko followed the Directory out of Kyiv in an attempt to secure the funds. His efforts proved futile. See K. Polishchuk (1923, 3).

be practiced. The Borot'bists tried hard to change this "semi-legal" position of Ukrainian culture. As a close associate of the Borot'bists, Semenko came to play an increasingly important part. Polishchuk attributes to him quite a central role, stating that "the solution to this [dilemma] was found by M. Semenko" (ibid., 5).

The solution in question took the form of an organization known as the Kyiv Professional Union of Writers [*Profesiina spilka mystsiv slova mista Kyieva*]. The idea for the Union, according to Polishchuk, came from Semenko, and was quickly "co-opted" by the Russians. This, however, did not prevent Ukrainians from benefitting from this new body, for they were invited to send representatives. Among them were members of *Muzahet* who, Polishchuk claims, accepted the invitation "readily" (ibid.). Besides Ukrainians and Russians, the Professional Union was composed of Jews and Poles. Each nationality had its own section. Cooperation among the groups was limited, but it did lead to joint literary evenings, public debates, and a "tournament of poets," the winner of which was Volodymyr Iaroshenko (ibid., 7). The Professional Union tried to publish a collective journal with separate sections for each nationality, but the venture never went beyond the planning stage (*Mystetstvo* 3 [1919]: 33). In May, when the Professional Union opened a Literature Workshop [*Maisternia mystets'koho slova*] to study "the theoretical and practical aspects of literature," the Ukrainian section was completely dominated by members of *Muzahet* (Dmytro Zahul, Mykhailo Ivchenko, Iurii Ivanov-Mezhenko, O. Mikul's'kyi, Klym Polishchuk, Pavlo Tychyna, Artym Khomyk, Volodymyr Iaroshenko) (*Mystetstvo* 1 [1919]: 35).

Through their activities in the Professional Union, Ukrainians were gradually able to attain access to other officially sponsored cultural institutions. When the Universal Publishing House [*Vsevydav*] was established in May 1919, its head became Ivan Klochka (Ivan Lyven'), while Tychyna led the special Ukrainian section (Pivtoradni 1968, 23). Halyna Zhurba indicates that quite a few Ukrainian writers were able to establish themselves in this organization (Zhurba 1962, 462–63). Thus, in a relatively short period the desperate situation of Ukrainian writers was alleviated slightly. Despite economic hardships and bitter memories of political defeat, there were signs of guarded optimism, a sense of achievement among some writers. Klym Polishchuk, for example, suggests that had the writers been more forward-looking and less nostalgic for the Ukrainian National Republic, even more could have been accomplished:

> It soon turned out that the Ukrainian sections in almost all the committees of the "Art Department," and also all the sections of the

> Universal Publishing House [*Vsevydav*] became the most important and creative ones. The latter was so evident that some officials considered it suspicious and they began demanding that each department or section have an obligatory communist as chief. But because these "communist chiefs" were in fact "chiefs," productivity did not decrease, in fact, it increased. And who knows whether this was not the best time for true cultural work on behalf of the Ukrainian people? To our great misfortune, however, the majority (I included) did not realize this then....The first attempt at a cultural "federation" in Kyiv under the banner of the Professional Writers' Union, doubtlessly, yielded and could have yielded, incomparably more, if only we had not believed in our dreams and looked back at Kam'ianets' [the seat of government of the Ukrainian National Republic after it was forced out of Kyiv by the Bolsheviks] (1923, 8–9).[34]

Although Polishchuk attributes the idea for the Professional Union to Semenko, it is difficult to say just how involved he was in the Union. In general Semenko's participation in literary-organizational matters was extensive. He, it must be understood, had unique qualifications for this. In contrast to his literary competitors, the Symbolists, Semenko's relative standing improved after the Soviets came to power. His leftist political and literary leanings, especially his proximity to the Borot'bists, lent him an air of legitimacy at a time when most other Ukrainian writers were suspect. Moreover, as a Futurist, Semenko was more acceptable to the leadership of the Proletkul'ts: no doubt, their common antagonism toward classical and traditional forms of culture was a point in Semenko's favor. While it is true that certain Borot'bists (especially Ellan-Blakytnyi and Mykhailychenko) played important roles as arbiters and intermediaries between Ukrainian writers and the new Soviet regime, none of them could claim as intimate a relationship with the majority of young Ukrainian writers, as did Semenko. Since 1913 he had associated with a wide spectrum of writers. In addition, he was not a political activist or party functionary as were Ellan-Blakytnyi and Mykhailychenko. Consequently he was freer to devote time to purely literary matters. Nothing speaks more forcefully of Semenko's unique qualifications for literary leadership in 1919 than the fact that of all the possible writers, he specifically was entrusted with the editorship of *Mystetstvo,* the first Soviet Ukrainian-language literary journal.[35]

[34] See also Zhurba 1962.

[35] Semenko shared the editorship with Mykhailychenko for a single issue. From the second issue on, editorial responsibility shifted solely to Semenko. Mykhailychenko's departure from the editorial board is easily explained by the fact that at the end of May 1919 he was sent as an emissary to the Western front. He returned sick and wounded in

The appearance of *Mystetstvo* was made possible, as stated above, in mid-May because the Borot'bists won the struggle against Russian chauvinism in the All-Ukrainian Literary Committee. This not only made the journal a reality but gave them control over editorial policy: with Semenko as editor and Chumak as secretary this was easy to accomplish (Kryzhanivs'kyi 1956, 9). Ideologically, of course, the journal espoused the revolution and shunned all overt theoretical statements that might suggest Modernism or Symbolism. In this respect it was significantly different from *Muzahet,* which appeared shortly after the first issue of *Mystetstvo*.[36] The latter tried to reflect the new political situation and had a decisively proletarian bent; the former remained quite true to the principles that dominated Ukrainian literature before the advent of Soviet power. *Muzahet* went as far as to assert a writer's individualism and to disparage the masses and the Proletkul't's notion of collective creativity (Ivanov-Mezhenko 1919).[37] Naturally, *Mystetstvo* disassociated itself from such ideas ("Vahr" [Chumak] 1919).

When it came to actual literary practice, however, the two journals were not that far apart; both resembled their predecessors *Universal'nyi zhurnal* and *Literaturno-krytychnyi al'manakh*. This was, of course, inevitable because virtually the same contributors appeared again and again in all these publications. *Mystetstvo*, in short, did not deviate radically from the literary norm, although it did sound the first "proletarian" notes. Its significance lies in the fact that it directed existing or, as was the case with Futurism, nascent literary tendencies into acceptable political channels. As such, it was the crowning organizational achievement in the Borot'bists' drive to legitimize, consolidate, and strengthen the position of Ukrainian culture under the new circumstances.

Part of the credit for this early success of Ukrainian letters goes directly to Semenko who, despite his partisan literary views, played a statesman-like role in fostering the growth and unity of Ukrainian literature. He is known not only to have helped in the publication of the Symbolist journal *Muzahet* (Pivtoradni 1968, 28), but through his balanced and tolerant editorial policy in *Mystetstvo* managed to embrace a large circle of Ukrainian writers. Klym Polishchuk, who was an ardent supporter of *Muzahet* and never associated with Futurism, went out of his way to praise Semenko's political and literary balancing act of 1919:

July. Between his illness and other literary and political commitments, he was obviously in no position to return to *Mystetstvo*. See Hadzins'kyi (1928, 141) and (1929a, 56–57).

36 In *Mystetstvo* 1 (1919): 34 it is clearly stated that the first issue of *Muzahet* "is being printed and will soon be on sale."

37 Reprinted in Leites and Iashek (1930, 2: 3–15).

> Mykhailo Semenko was engaged in his own business, which—there is no denying the fact—was useful.... Within a short period, he managed to win an appropriate position in almost every official cultural department...and thus became *the only sure contact between us, "Muzahet," and the representatives of official art* who had come to Kyiv...to "implant universal culture on the peripheries of 'Little Russia'" (Polishchuk 1923, 4; *emphasis added*).

While expressing dismay at the "leftist" drift of art among certain young people, Polishchuk admitted that Semenko's and Petryts'kyi's "Flamingo" "was for the moment advantageous for *Muzahet*" (ibid., 6). About *Mystetstvo* and specifically Semenko's role in it, he said:

> It will be easy for some "critics" to degrade Semenko's Futurist poems...which appeared time and again in *Mystetstvo*, but let [these critics] try to create something similarly unifying which might embrace [both] the "right" and the "left" while at the same time preserving the integrity [...] of all the creative groups (ibid., 9).

Polishchuk summarized his views about Semenko, saying, "Those 'ludicrous futuristic Semenkos' know how to love their country and people. [They might] have the [bad] habit of not always eating [well] but they always, everywhere and under every condition continued to do [their] work" (ibid., 10).

Mystetstvo's non-sectarian profile was as much the result of necessity as design.[38] Under the prevailing circumstances, no one group (Futurist, Borot'bist, or Symbolist) could alone sustain a journal. But Futurist tendencies were well represented here. In sacrificing "Flamingo" for *Mystetstvo*,[39] Semenko achieved more for Futurism than by any other action. The editorship did something very important for him: it enhanced his standing in the literary community, transforming him from an outcast ("idiot") into one of Ukrainian letters' important leaders. This, naturally, also reflected well on his movement. As editor, Semenko was in a position to ensure that "the bacilli of Futurism" would multiply (Tsebro [Semenko] 1922, 42). And they did, not only on account of his own numerous literary and theoretical works published in *Mystetstvo*,[40] but also due to

[38] For a characterization and overview of *Mystetstvo,* see Volodymyr Mel'nyk 1987.

[39] In 1922 Anatol' Tsebro [Semenko] wrote: "Having lost hope in organizing a Futurist group [i.e. 'Flamingo'] he [i.e., Semenko] assumed the editorship of [...] *Mystetstvo*." See Tsebro (1922, 42).

[40] Among Semenko's works that appeared in *Mystetstvo* are the following: M. Mertvopetliuiko, "Mystetstvo perekhodovoï doby" (2 [1919]: 33); M. Tryroh, "Prozopisni (Spirali)" (4 [1919]: 15); "Tov. Sontse. Revfutpoema" (1 [1919], 6); "Vesna. Poezofil'ma" (2 [1919]: 6); "Step. Poezofil'ma" (3 [1919]: 7); "Poezy" [Two poems: 1. "Zupynys'!—

the Futurist works of other writers (for example, Oleksa Slisarenko). The very fact that Futurist literature now appeared alongside other writings enhanced the prestige and visibility of the phenomenon.

Semenko's star rose especially high in relation to the Symbolists. While he gained control of a relatively successful journal, they struggled in vain to sustain *Muzahet.*[41] This contrast was symptomatic of how political realities affected both movements. Symbolism as a coherent movement was receding; Futurism, on the other hand, had begun its gradual ascent. The signs of this may not have been numerous or all that clear in 1919, but they were unmistakably there. In the provinces, for example, a student journal reacted favorably to Semenko's poetry.[42] Writers with whom Semenko had worked earlier in Grunt (for example, Lebedynets'), as well as some Symbolists (Iaroshenko) showed evidence of edging closer to Semenko's camp.[43] Particularly telling was the conversion to Futurism of the Symbolist Oleksa Slisarenko in 1919. During the years that followed he became one of the movement's most ardent supporters.[44]

Semenko's influence extended briefly to the Borot'bists as well. In November 1919 he laid plans—along with Mykhailychenko, Chumak, and Ellan-Blakytnyi—for the creation of a group that was to have embodied the "healthy" side of Futurism. The initiative for the group (according to Semenko) came from Mykhailychenko, a writer who until then had vacillated between Impressionism, Symbolism (see his "Blakytnyi roman" [The Azure Novel]), and the Proletkul't (Mykhailychenko 1919). Mykhailychenko's initiative led to two meetings in November during which it was resolved to embark under the old name

---

Khtos' kazav z-zadu"; 2. "Nich pokhniupylas'"] (4 [1919]: 6); Three poems appeared under the pseudonym Iakiv Moshek: "Sviatyi metronom," "Navzdohin," "Ne plakaly i ne prosyly" (3 [1919]: 5).

41 In June a second issue of *Muzahet* was in preparation but it never came out. See *Mystetstvo* 3 (1919): 33.

42 *Haslo* (Pryluky) published a favorable review of his revolutionary poems. See Pivtoradni (1968, 47).

43 M. Lebedynets' published futurist-like prose poems in *Mystetstvo*: "Spolokh" (1 [1919], 14), "Zemkolo" (4 [1919], 11). Iaroshenko released a collection of poems in 1919 entitled *Luny* (Kyiv), which, in contrast to his first Symbolist collection, *Svitotin'*, was said to have definite Futurist traits. Rod'ko, for example, states that "the central place in [this] collection was devoted to poems with a self-aggrandizing theme, written not without the influence of I. Severianin and M. Semenko" (1971, 112).

44 Slisarenko's first Futurist poems appeared in *Mystetstvo*: "Tsarivna ostann'oho (prohnozy)" (5-6 [1919]: 5); "Poema znevahy" (1 [1920]: 6). Slisarenko participated in *Al'manakh tr'okh* (1920), a Futurist publication, and later contributed to *Semafor u Maibutnie*. He also published a Futurist collection of poems, *Poemy* (Slisarenko 1923b). For more details see the following chapters.

"Flamingo" and publish an almanac with the same title (Tsebro [Semenko] 1922, 42).[45]

Nothing came of these plans because in the fall of 1919 the political and military situation in Ukraine suddenly deteriorated. In late August Kyiv fell to General Denikin. Those who had been closely associated with the Soviet order withdrew or went underground. The latter course was taken by Semenko and the Borot'bists. Most cultural activity came to an end, since the Whites had no sympathy at all for Ukrainian ambitions. Just before their arrival Semenko did succeed in publishing the July issue (the year's last) of *Mystetstvo*. He was less fortunate with a number of his own works which became casualties of war. Among them was his drama *Lilit* [Lilith] which was to have been staged by Les' Kurbas.[46]

The occupation of Kyiv placed Semenko and the Borot'bists in physical danger. Their clandestine activities took place at a secret dacha outside Kyiv where some of them also lived. It was there that "Flamingo" was discussed. Semenko's sense of insecurity during this period is conveyed by Polishchuk. He recalled that with the approach of the White Army, this "funny Futurist" recited for him his short biography, and "just in case" handed over a packet of his unpublished works (K. Polishchuk 1923, 10). Semenko's precautions proved to be justified, for he was arrested (Sulyma 1989, 295). Although he survived, his friends did not. Vasyl' Chumak and Hnat Mykhailychenko were apprehended by Denikin's forces at the dacha and subsequently executed.[47]

The Denikin regime was short-lived. By the end of December 1919 the Whites were in total disarray, pursued southward by the Red Army. The Soviet order began to re-establish itself in Ukraine. The ceaseless conflicts, however, had already taken their toll. The country was scarred and in total desolation. Sporadic armed resistance continued. There was no question of life returning to normal. For two years following the defeat of Denikin, Ukrainian literary activities, like almost everything else, came

[45] For corroboration see Hadzins'kyi (1928, 142) and (1929a, 61). The influence of Futurism on certain Borot'bists is also suggested by Antin Pavliuk. He wrote that Ellan-Blakytnyi and Mykola Liubchenko "have in recent times leaned toward programmatic work in accordance with the dogmas of Futurism" (1922, 113). Semenko insisted, perhaps too strongly, that Ellan-Blakytnyi showed a "clear Futurist physiognomy" and called him a "specialist in the destruction of form and content" (Tsebro [Semenko] 1922, 42).

[46] The cycles *Poezofiry*, *Naïvni poeziiky*, and the Futurist drama *Trahediia onuch* and *Lilit* had been scheduled for publication (See *Mystetstvo* 1 [1919]: 36–37). Pivtoradni (1968, 24), citing Soviet archival sources, says that the State Publishing House had planned to release some of Semenko's works, but he does not identify any titles.

[47] Hadzins'kyi (1928, 143) and (1929a, 62–63). See Majstrenko (1954, 136–57, especially 149).

virtually to a standstill. In Kyiv, as in Kharkiv—which had become the capital of the new Soviet Ukraine—there were widespread shortages of paper, printing facilities, and a disruption of electrical power. There also was outright famine.

Ukrainian culture was dealt a heavy blow during 1920–1921 by large-scale emigration, as well. Toward the end of 1919 the respected journals of the non-Soviet establishment such as *Literaturno-naukovyi visnyk*, *Shliakh*, *Knyhar* and many others folded. Ukrainian cultural and political activities shifted to Galicia, Vienna, Warsaw, and Prague. Meanwhile, the Soviet regime was neither able nor inclined to sponsor Ukrainian cultural pursuits. What publications appeared (almanacs, miscellanies) were very irregular. Some writers were fortunate to have their own works published, but these were few and far between.[48]

Semenko's activities in 1920 were, naturally, also severely circumscribed. In that year Soviet authority was challenged briefly for the last time by Polish and Ukrainian forces, which launched an offensive in April, scoring some impressive, but fleeting, victories against the Bolsheviks, including a short occupation of Kyiv (7 May). In April, just before this offensive, Semenko succeeded in publishing the final issue of *Mystetstvo*—for a total of six. Sometime after that he nursed to life the first collective Futurist publication, *Al'manakh tr'okh* [Almanac of the Three], which besides himself featured Oleksa Slisarenko and Mykola Liubchenko (Kost' Kotko).[49] In July he received permission from the Universal Publishing House to print his collection *Preriia zir* [A Prairie of Stars], but under the prevailing conditions actually printing it proved impossible. Semenko's subsequent book of poems, *Prominnia pohroz*

[48] Amidst the meager literary production of 1920 a disproportionate amount was in some way linked to the Borot'bists. In Kyiv, they published the almanac *Zshytky borot'by* (1920) and Vasyl' Chumak's posthumous collection *Zaspiv* (1920). Ellan-Blakytnyi issued a small but popular collection, *Udarom molota i sertsia* (1920). In October, Valeriian Polishchuk (not a Borot'bist) published the almanac *Grono* (Kyiv). The only other notable sign of literary life came from the Kyiv newspaper *Bil'shovyk,* which devoted a small section to literature and the arts, publishing feuilletons, poems, impressionistic prose and literary announcements. The bleak year's single most memorable event was the appearance of Tychyna's collection *Pluh*.

[49] The almanac was sixty-two pages long. It was divided into three parts, according to author. Slisarenko's poems opened the volume with two short cycles: "Prahnennia" [Desire] and "Zakokhannia" [Love]. This was followed by Liubchenko's cycle of lyrics: one, fairly long, was untitled; another (two poems) had the heading, "Frahmenty mynuloho" [Fragments of the Past]. The last twenty-five pages were devoted to Semenko's "Himny sv. Terezi" [Hymns to St. Theresa]. The almanac was reviewed in *Nash shliakh* (Kam'ianets'-Podil's'kyi) on 16 June 1920 by Valeriian Polishchuk, and again by him (under the pseudonym M. Volok) in *Grono* (1920: 91–93).

[Rays of Peril; Semenko 1921b], appeared only because he and his friends resorted to manual operation of the printing press when electrical power failed (Pivtoradni 1968, 51; Trostianets'kyi 1968b, 89).

Due to the invasion of Kyiv, Semenko established residence in Kharkiv for brief periods during the months of May and June 1920.[50] He returned to Kyiv after military conflicts subsided, only to return again to Kharkiv in December, where he remained until the end of February 1921. Kharkiv represented a slightly more hospitable environment, hence a number of Kyiv writers moved to the new capital. During his few months there, Semenko attempted to organize a Futurist group. His efforts led to the formation of The Poet-Futurists' Shock Brigade [*Udarna hrupa poetiv-futurystiv*] (Kachaniuk 1930, 312), with Iuliian Shpol (Mykola Ialovyi), Vasyl' Aleshko, and Vasyl' Ellan-Blakytnyi. Of the two newcomers, Shpol had virtually no literary experience, while Aleshko's credentials were those of a Modernist-Symbolist. In 1920, however, Aleshko published three collections, one of which—*Dymari v kvitkakh* [Smokestacks among the Flowers]—purportedly betrayed a Futurist influence (Rod'ko 1971, 276).

The Poet-Futurists' Shock Brigade, as Semenko readily admitted, accomplished nothing besides demonstrating that there was among its members a certain literary consensus. But even this proved fleeting. Ellan-Blakytnyi eventually balked at the word "Futurist" in the organization's name and withdrew. The remaining writers began preparing an almanac, *Povstannia* [Uprising], but before it was completed the group disintegrated, circumstances having forced each individual to migrate to a different city (Tsebro [Semenko] 1922, 43).

Although this incipient Futurist group failed to establish a practical working alliance, the members did advance the cause of Futurism slightly by publishing their works in the new Kharkiv monthly *Shliakhy mystetstva* [Pathways of Art], which began appearing irregularly in February 1921.[51] Thanks to a liberal editorial policy formulated by Ellan-Blakytnyi, which permitted every literary "school" and "direction" access to its pages (Pivtoradni 1968, 68; Trostianets'kyi 1968b, 25–33),[52] Futurism acquired a high profile there. This was especially true of the first two issues, where organizers of The Poet-Futurists' Shock Brigade were well represented. Not only did Semenko, Shpol, and Aleshko publish works here, but so

50 The chronology is based on his *Kobzar* (1925a).

51 Five issues appeared between February 1921 and April 1923.

52 Besides Ellan-Blakytnyi, the editorial board consisted of the Borot'bists Volodymyr Koriak and Hordii Kotsiuba. Valeriian Polishchuk and Mykola Khvyl'ovyi were also on the board.

did the reluctant Futurist Ellan-Blakytnyi. He appeared in the first issue with a fragment from a long poem entitled "Elektra" [Electra], subtitled futuristically "Radio-poema" [radio-poem]. The works of Mykhailo Lebedynets' and Geo Shkurupii (known then simply as "Heorhii"), Mykola Tereshchenko and, to some degree, O. Korzh, testified to a Futurist influence. In time, these individuals would become Semenko's official associates.

Besides Futurist poems, *Shliakhy mystetstva* published reviews and articles that gave further impetus to the movement. While these, to be sure, ranged from the ambivalent to the negative, they did help to keep Futurism in the limelight and constituted a grudging acknowledgment that it was prospering. It can be said that Ukrainian Futurism first assumed the character of a real *movement* on the pages of this journal. It became obvious here that Futurism was no longer the crusade of just a single individual.

In Kyiv, on 25 June 1921, Oleksa Slisarenko, Geo Shkurupii, and Mykola Tereshchenko, together with a painter, Oleh Shymkov, founded the organization "Komkosmos" [The Communist Cosmos] (Kachaniuk 1930, 312–13).[53] The foundations of this "scientific-artistic" group were laid without Semenko who was in Kharkiv, having recently returned from a trip to Riga as part of a delegation (headed by Iu. Kotsiubyns'kyi and E. Kviring) that signed a peace treaty between Poland, Russia, and Ukraine (Kriger 1979, 75; Sulyma 1989, 297). The "Komkosmos" declaration reflected the then-popular Proletkul'tist and Constructivist phraseology (Kachaniuk 1930, 313–14). The declaration read more like a political than an artistic document, and, curiously, made no mention of the word "futurism," although it was avant-gardist in tone.

"Komkosmos" never got off the ground, having been immediately suppressed by political authorities. On 5 July 1921 a body of the People's Commissariat of Education [*Kolehiia holovpolitosvity*] denied the group permission to organize. It declared that the "program of the communist-futurists [*komfuty*] contradicts the principle for Party organizations; they will hardly be useful from the point of view of cultural construction" (Pryhodii 1972, 91).[54] A few days later the Organizational Bureau [*Orhbiuro*] of the Central Committee of the KP(b)U resolved that "the communist-futurist organization does not suit the spirit of the party; approval [to organize] denied; communists who joined should be called to order" (ibid.).

53 Their announcement appeared in the press on 26 June 1921 (see Pryhodii 1972, 90).
54 He quotes from Soviet archival sources.

In November 1921 Semenko was back in Kyiv and, thanks to his stature and influence, succeeded in doing what the above writers failed. By the end of the year, he had created an organization called "Aspanfut," that is, The Association of Panfuturists, and convinced the founders of "Komkosmos" to join him in this venture.

The consolidation of "Aspanfut" in the early months of 1922 marked a new stage in the development of Ukrainian Futurism. This was to be a real organization, the culmination of Semenko's many false starts. It had a program, a variety of activities, its own publications, all of which left a tangible mark on the sands of time. The "bacilli" that Semenko conscientiously nurtured had finally infected the seemingly immune body of Ukrainian culture and began multiplying of their own accord.

The defenses erected against Futurism had begun showing cracks throughout these turbulent years. In 1919 Pavlo Fylypovych observed that "a few years ago Futurism elicited from many critics—as well as from the 'general public'—only smiles [scowls would have been more precise—O.I.]; now it is taken into account, and some people even note that the Futurists are somewhat 'classical'" (Fylypovych 1919c, 1361–62). In 1920, Valeriian Polishchuk, while distancing himself from Semenko and his movement, admitted that Futurism, along with Impressionism, was one of the "most outstanding artistic forms" of the day (V. Polishchuk 1921). Similarly, Ivan Kulyk, while advancing the cause of Impressionism, noted that Futurism was superior to Realism, which he characterized as "superfluous and harmful" (Kulyk 1921, 35).

Credit for statements like these goes almost entirely to Semenko not only because of his tireless organizational efforts on behalf of Futurism, but because of his own publishing record. Remarkably, during 1918–1919 he released nine separate books of poetry.[55] Another was brought out in 1921.[56] If nothing else, this stream of work compelled critics to take note of Semenko's creativity. As they did, they no longer betrayed the strong outrage of yesteryear, even if in many essentials their judgment was reminiscent of the past.[57] Pavlo Fylypovych, for example, espied little

[55] They were: 1) *Dev'iat' poem* (Semenko 1918a); 2) *P'iero zadaiet'sia. Fragmenty. Intymni poeziï. Knyzhka 1-a* (Semenko 1918e); 3) *P'iero kokhaie. Misterii (1916–1917). Intymni poeziï. Knyzhka 2-a* (Semenko 1918d); 4) *P'iero mertvopetliuie. Futuryzy. 1914–1918. Poeziï. Knyzhka 3-ia* (Semenko 1919e); 5) *Bloc-Notes. Poeziï 1919 roku. Knyzhka 4-a* (Semenko 1919a); 6) *V sadakh bezroznykh. Saturnaliï. Poeziï. Knyzhka 5-a* (Semenko 1919k); 7) *Dvi poezofil'my* (1919b); 8) *Lilit. Scènes pathétiques* (1919c); 9) *Tov. Sontse. Revfutpoema* (1919j).

[56] *Prominnia pohroz. 8-ma kn. poezii. 1919–1920* (Semenko 1921b).

[57] For a brief sampling of the critical reaction, see Rod'ko (1971, 176–79).

beyond the influence of Russian Futurism in the new collections, dismissing them as "negative phenomena" (Fylypovych 1918, 860). Inasmuch as Semenko failed to manifest "internal depth and serious ideas" and did not deal with life's "tragic contradictions," Fylypovych concluded that his work was neither "valuable nor necessary today" (1919, 1147–48). Another critic looked at Semenko's "queer capers" and asked, "But is this poetry?" (Burchak 1919).

Among these perfunctory readings of Semenko, there was one essay from 1919 that deserves special mention—Andrii Nikovs'kyi's long and witty appraisal in his book *Vita Nova* (Nikovs'kyi 1919, 59–74 and 75–114).[58] Like other critics, Nikovs'kyi tended to look upon Semenko with condescension and sarcasm; he continued to have reservations about Futurism, maintaining that the rustic character of Ukraine militated against the success of this movement. Echoing Sriblians'kyi, Nikovs'kyi said it was "most terrible" that this foreign "fashion" had been borrowed from Russia (ibid., 72). Yet in trying to "explain the boundary between [Semenko's] pretensions and natural abilities," Nikovs'kyi was ready to concede that he was "interesting" and had "a very explicit poetic talent" (ibid., 74, 87, 93). The critic was attracted to the "rather sincere and candid" tone of the verse; he took cognizance of its foreign, prosaic properties and admitted that in some instances "it sounded good" (ibid., 84, 88, 90). He urged the reader to accept Semenko's "stupid capers" calmly because "his stridency, escapades and indecencies—both literary and cultural—attest, if not [necessarily] to the birth of a new literature, [then at least] to a sharp reaction against traditional directions..." (ibid, 91). About the traces of Whitman, Strindberg, Hamsun and other poets that he detected in his verse, Nikovs'kyi said the following:

> What could I prove by [pointing out these parallels]? That Semenko is not an independent poet, that his is a borrowed muse? Yes, undoubtedly, Semenko does have many borrowed (but not stolen) motifs, rhythms, words; they obstruct the poet's own personality, but there are times when Semenko's own character comes through.... [T]he reader should not be very surprised by Semenko's external originality... [for] behind him stands...a very strong, cultural tradition. This tradition stems from the *new* literature, specifically the *European*.... [His poetry] reveals the rather fine sources of this [literary] current, [and attests to] a literary education and a peculiar taste in the selection of literary models.... (ibid., 96).

[58] "Poeziia buduchyny" and "Mykhailo Semenko" respectively.

Nikovs'kyi reserved some of his harshest words for Semenko's language which he called "slovenly" and deprived of traditional Ukrainian "mellifluousness." He charged the poet with striking a "non-Ukrainian chord" that reverberated with alien timbres, redolent of the Russian intelligentsia. As far as Nikovs'kyi was concerned, this Futurist belonged in the same notorious company as Volodymyr Vynnychenko and Dmytro Dontsov both of whom, he alleged, violated the spirit of the Ukrainian language. He took Semenko to task for modeling his neologisms on Severianin's Russian morphology instead of exploiting analogous Ukrainian forms (ibid., 106). In short, Nikovs'kyi found everything from the "feeble" to the "unusually dazzling, talented" (ibid., 112). He concluded that "Semenko is essential [in Ukrainian literature] if only because the defects of his works and psyche reflect the cultural decay of the city." It would be preferable, however, if "Semenko were able to move someone emotionally now and in the future....[Unfortunately], the Ukrainian public is not moved. Why? Because Semenko has surrendered to his organic defects and errors..." (ibid., 112–13).

The essay, unexpectedly, terminated on a charitable note: "One feels and sees that this is a creative person....And it will not take much to turn [his] work into genuine art...." Interrupting at this point his own summation, Nikovs'kyi turns figuratively to his reader and fields from him an imaginary question: "Well, what if this happens, Mr. Critic, will all these ingenious words [by Semenko] really have been uttered by a great artist?" And Nikovs'kyi responds: "I answer you in all sincerity: Yes. Then all of them, even in hindsight, will be considered brilliant" (ibid, 114).

From such remarks it may be concluded that although Semenko and the movement continued to encounter opposition, it was, nonetheless, gradually developing into an independent presence that even opponents and skeptics were forced to acknowledge. Clearly, by late 1921, Futurism had been transformed from just a potential force in Ukrainian literature into an actual one.

Cover art from the journal *Nova generatsiia* 1929, no. 6

CHAPTER 3

Aspanfut: The Association of Panfuturists

In the inchoate literary environment of 1921–1922 no group had a clearer self-image than the Futurists. They constituted the first cohesive movement of the 1920s, predating by several months the appearance of organizations such as the Union of Village Writers, *Pluh* [The Plow; 1922] and the Union of Proletarian Writers, *Hart* [Tempering; 1923].

The Association of Panfuturists (Aspanfut) insinuated itself into the public's consciousness as a company of rebels bent on wrecking art. For better or for worse, its complex and controversial existence was exemplified by a set of publications issued in 1922: *Semafor u Maibutnie* [Semaphore into the Future] and *Katafalk iskusstva* [Catafalque of Art]. These titles were emblematic of the group's objectives, namely, to bury art as it was traditionally practiced and to erect on its grave a new system—a "meta-art" of the future. As the prefix in their name implied, the Panfuturists embraced the entire spectrum of the avant-garde, advocating not some specific movement but rather the vanguard as a whole, which they interpreted as a unique turning point in the history of art. Marinetti's Futurism, Dada, and German Expressionism were held in special esteem; this was less true, however, of Russian Futurism.

When Semenko founded Aspanfut in November 1921, his former allies—the Borot'bists and in particular Vasyl' Ellan-Blakytnyi—refused to participate. The once close relationship unraveled as the Borot'bists moved into key positions in the Communist Party and state apparatus, simultaneously distancing themselves from the Proletkul'ts and Futurism, with which they previously associated. Semenko reported in 1922 that "Vasyl' Ellan-Blakytnyi is in Kharkiv with V. Koriak and the Proletkul't. It is not known what he is working on as a poet (he conceals this well) but he continues to straddle the fence." Wistfully, he added, "perhaps in about five years he will join the Panfuturists" (Semenko 1922b, 46).

In 1920 the Borot'bists were pressured by Moscow to disband as an independent Ukrainian Communist Party and merge with the KP(b)U. Once part of the political establishment, they played an important and beneficial role in the "Ukrainianization" process (Mace 1983), but were also compelled to toe the Party's line in literary matters. The Russian Communist Party had attacked the Proletkul'ts in 1920 for their ambition to remain independent of the Party and for falling under the sway of "petty bourgeois elements," among which the "senseless and corrupted tastes" of the Futurists were singled out ("Pro proletkul'ty" 1959, 79). By September 1921 the KP(b)U was echoing these same sentiments, criticizing the Proletkul'ts for rejecting the artistic heritage of the past and warning them against inculcating workers with Futurism (*Kommunist* 1 September 1921).[1] For the Borot'bists the message was obvious: avoid the radical left. Ellan-Blakytnyi, who went on to become a member of the Central Committee of the KP(b)U and editor of the newspaper *Visti VUTsVK*, embraced a middle-of-the-road position acceptable to the Party. This was exemplified by the establishment of Hart in 1923, an organization he led, and one which, among other things, was vehemently anti-Futurist.

One former Borot'bist, however, did join Aspanfut. He was Iuliian Shpol (Mykola Ialovyi), who from the very first was a highly profiled member of the organization.[2] With this one exception, the other constituents of Aspanfut came primarily from the ranks of former Modernists and Symbolists. These were Oleksa Slisarenko, Mykola Tereshchenko, and Vasyl' Aleshko (the latter was described in November 1921 as "living in the provinces and writing Futurist poems"; *Zhovten'* 1921, 152).[3] The other participants were young writers—practically unknown and untested—like Geo Shkurupii and Andrii Chuzhyi. Somewhat later, they were joined by Mykola (Nik) Bazhan who arrived in Kyiv in 1921, having, apparently, shown sympathy for the Futurist cause while still living in Uman' (Kostenko 1971, 12). Of these, only Shkurupii could claim a modest literary reputation: he had been published in Valeriian Polishchuk's (later the leader of the Constructivists) *Hrono* (also spelled *Grono*) [Cluster; Kyiv, 1920] and *Vyr revoliutsiï* [The Vortex of the Revolution; Katerynoslav, 1921]. Chuzhyi, on the other hand, made his debut only in 1922 in *Semafor u Maibutnie*. Bazhan's first literary works would appear a year later in the newspaper *Bil'shovyk*.[4]

In the early months, Aspanfut enjoyed the support of two other men, the critic Feliks Iakubovs'kyi and the writer Myroslav Irchan. Iakubovs'kyi's

1 Cited in Trostianets'kyi (1968b, 86–89).
2 Majstrenko (1954, 262) identifies him as a Borot'bist.
3 Aleshko later joined Pluh.
4 Most of these poems have not been republished. For a recent compilation see Ilnytzkyj (1979, 20–23).

association with the Futurists was episodic and is best explained by his quasi-formalist leanings. Myroslav Irchan's brief relationship with the Futurists was viewed by contemporaries as a misunderstanding (Kulyk 1922).[5] He made contact with the Futurists sometime before he left for Prague where he was a student in 1922–1923. From there he wrote a boisterous letter to *Katafalk iskusstva*, in which he alluded to himself as a Futurist and espoused the group's destructive principles (Irchan and Shkurupii 1922, 2). However, later when Aspanfut described him as an "old Panfuturist" and boasted that he was organizing branches of the organization in Winnipeg, Canada (*Bil'shovyk* 287 [18 December 1923]: 4), where he had settled in 1923, Irchan angrily denied this.[6]

To this list of problematic and peripheral supporters of Aspanfut one must add the names of Varvara Bazas and Iakiv Saval'iev—about whom we now know nothing—and the marginally meaningful name of Iosyp Stril'chuk. Their names appeared in Futurist publications of 1922, but with the exception of Stril'chuk's, none were ever heard of again in any literary context.[7] Varvara Bazas' claim to fame is a poem Geo Shkurupii dedicated to her in 1921 (Shkurupii 1921).

In light of the Communist Party's negative attitude toward Futurism, there is some irony in the fact that Aspanfut's first steps were taken with the help of the bilingual Ukrainian-Russian newspaper *Izvestiia/Visti*, an official organ of the Kyiv District Committee of the KP(b)U. From the sparse information available both about this newspaper and Aspanfut's affiliation with it, the one thing certain is that the Futurists exercised considerable influence over its literary section, a fact that disquieted Valeriian Polishchuk. In November he registered a violent protest with the editors of the Kharkiv miscellany *Zhovten'* [October]:

> Futurism's bourgeois rot, in the persons of M. Semenko, Iu. Shpol, F. Iakubovs'kyi and others, rules over the editorial policy of the newspaper *Visti* [and is destroying] every creative undertaking in the field of proletarian culture. Free discussion is forbidden in the columns of this newspaper; artists are being gagged by a small group of literary specialists who are too old for life and who by [mere] accident have [gained]

5 Reprinted in Leites and Iashek (1930, 2: 47).

6 See "Zaiava M. Irchana" (*Bil'shovyk* 43 [21 February 1924]). On Irchan in Canada, see Kolasky 1990.

7 Iosyp Stril'chuk was active in the Futurist organizaion during the years 1923 to 1925. Semenko described him as a medical doctor and member of the Ukrainian Communist Party (UKP). He is reported to have lectured to the Futurists on "The Psychophysiology of Art" (*Chervonyi shliakh* 4–5 [1924]: 278). Later, he was also elected Secretary of the Futurist organization in Kyiv (see *Bil'shovyk* 210 [18 September 1924]: 4).

> control over the technical resources of Soviet printing. I expect that everyone who holds dear [the ideal] of experimentation in art will raise their voice against this galvanization of Futurism's corpse at government expense, so that the culturally corrupting activity that is being carried out [by the Futurists] among various groups of workers, through the agency of the Soviet press, might be brought to a halt (*Zhovten'* 1921, 157).

Polishchuk's display of social conscience had no effect. When *Izvestiia/Visti* was closed in June 1922 and reappeared in July as the newspaper *Bil'shovyk* (still under the jurisdiction of the same provincial committee of the KP[b]U), Aspanfut's members received immediate access to its pages, and Semenko was even for a time made Secretary.[8] In 1923, when *Bil'shovyk* began publishing a supplement, *Hlobus* [The Globe] the Futurists established near total mastery over it. An observer noted that "*Hlobus* is under the complete control of Aspanfut, which also has in its hands *Bil'shovyk*. Attempts by a wider circle of writers to work with *Hlobus* ended in failure, producing only unpleasant scenes; the Panfuturists use every occasion to mock those who do not belong [to their organization]" ("Literaturne zhyttia" 1924). Confirmation of this comes from the editor of *Bil'shovyk*, Samiilo Shchupak, who admitted treating the Futurists with favoritism, even though their relationship was frequently quite inimical.[9] Both sides, no doubt, needed each other. Under the dire social circumstances prevailing in Ukraine, the Futurists were happy to have access to any newspaper, even one that dealt mostly with agricultural, economic, and political matters. Shchupak, on the other hand, needed more or less ideologically acceptable coworkers. In Kyiv, practically speaking, this narrowed down his choice to the Futurists because most other alternatives (for example, the Neoclassicists) were ideologically even more wanting.

Bil'shovyk proved to be an important instrument for the Futurists. From 1922 to 1923 it carried short but frequent announcements and reports of their activities, and served as an outlet for certain agitprop poems, reviews, and articles. Although a priceless promotional vehicle, *Bil'shovyk* fell far short of being an adequate medium for their more ambitious work. It could not be expected, nor would it have been allowed,

8 A few years later, in what appears to have been an echo of Valeriian Polishchuk's statement, Semenko was accused of refusing to accept for publication in *Bil'shovyk* submissions by his literary competitors (Ellan-Blakytnyi 1930b, 107n1).

9 "On several occasions, I expressed my attitude toward Aspanfut [referring to it] as a revolutionary organization.... I [also] published in the newspaper *Bil'shovyk* rather large quantities of materials that belonged to members of Aspanfut" (Shchupak 1924b, 4).

to become an exponent of Aspanfut's radical literary and theoretical writings. For this reason, one of the first actions taken by the group was the creation of the independent publishing house Gulf Stream, known under both a German and Ukrainian name: "Golfstrom" and "Hol'fshtrom," respectively. By July 1922 several items had been released.[10]

An overriding concern of the Futurists in 1922 was to put their movement on a firm theoretical footing. *Semafor u Maibutnie* and the newspaper *Katafalk iskusstva* (subtitled "a Daily Journal of the Panfuturists-Destructivists") devoted the bulk of its pages to explaining and promoting the Panfuturist theory of art, that is, the "destruction" of old art and the "construction" of a new "system." Declared *Semafor*, "The liquidation of art is our art." Its manifestoes were published in French, English and German (for example, "Du panfuturisme special," "What Panfuturism Wants," "Die Kunst ist tot"). Literary works were included here as well. *Semafor u Maibutnie* contained poems by Semenko, Shkurupii, Slisarenko, Shpol, Mykola Tereshchenko, Vasyl' Desniak, Zoia Chaikivs'ka, and prose by Irchan. The title of Andrii Chuzhyi's poem suggests the extravagance and provocation toward which the publication leaned: "Semenko and I on the Garbage Heap" ["My z Semenkom na smitnyku"]. With its stunning color cover and layout, *Semafor* made a strong visual impression as well. Throughout its fifty-five pages there was a constant tension between text printed traditionally in Cyrillic and text realized in an odd Latin system of transliteration (Shkurupii [Шкурупій], for example, became "Wkurupij;" Irchan [Ірчан]—"Irxan"). There was an especially strong promotion of Dada through translations from *Dada Almanach* (Berlin, 1920). Tristan Tzara's "Negerlieder" were featured, as was Richard Huelsenbeck's 1918 "First Dada Speech in Germany" (*Semafor u Maibutnie* 1922, 50–51). Myroslav Irchan favored the Expressionists, providing small poetic samples of Austrians Georg Trakl (1887–1914) and Albert Ehrenstein (1886–1950). Geo Shkurupii promoted Futurism in articles about Marinetti and noise-music (Shkurupii 1922b and Shkurupii 1922c). Semenko contributed an article on visual poetry (Semenko 1922c, 34–36), while Mark (Marko) Tereshchenko discussed performance art in the theater.[11] True to its

[10] Geo Shkurupii's collection of poetry, *Psykhetozy. Vitryna tretia* (Shkurupii 1922e); Marko Tereshchenko's theoretical writings on the theater, *Budova i metody roboty mystetstva diistva* (Tereshchenko 1922c); and the Futurist organ, *Semafor u Maibutnie.* A few months later, in December, Gulf Stream released Aspanfut's *Katafalk iskusstva.* Although not especially prolific, the publishing house issued a steady flow of titles into 1925.

[11] Tereshchenko (1922b) and (1922a). The former was later reprinted, with minor changes, in *Chervonyi shliakh* 3 (1923) as "Teatr mystetstva diistva."

pan-avantgardism, *Semafor* offered an extensive survey of the latest artistic trends in Germany, France, Italy, England, America, Poland, Switzerland, and Czechoslovakia. Russian developments were ignored, except for a few aggressively sarcastic attacks. Semenko, for example, sent Maiakovskii a Russian-language telegram telling him he could either become a "Panfuturist or a corpse" (Semenko 1922e). Shkurupii engaged in exuberant verbal harassment of "Volod'ka" Maiakovskii, "Vas'ka" Kamenskii, and "Igugu" Esenin (Shkurupii 1922d, 46). The three were challenged to "an unprecedented duel" of words in which fists were optional. "Evasion [of this challenge] will not save you," said Shkurupii. "I am a very adroit Comanche who inhabits the prairies of Futurism and I possess an endless lasso of wit with which I shall rope you in like a buffalo" (ibid.). The article "Stuck in Place (A Letter from Moscow)" was an apt summary of the Panfuturists' attitude toward Russian practices. The author, Vasyl' Desniak, argued that Moscow needed to be revived with "a strong dose" of influence from the "South" (that is, Ukraine; Desniak 1922a, 45). In general, the polemic as a literary form was finely tuned in *Semafor*. It was used with deadliest effect against home-grown critics and writers, as in Desniak's assault on Valeriian Polishchuk and the critics Volodymyr Koriak and M. Trostianets'kyi (Desniak 1922b).

During December 1922 and in the first few months of 1923 Aspanfut kept intriguing the public with a steady stream of announcements about the activities of its members.[12] In particular, there was a lot of information on Aspanfut's publishing plans. These were ambitious projects, but, except for the journals already mentioned, none actually bore fruit. Nonetheless, the plans themselves are worthy of attention, for they reveal much about the nature of Aspanfut as an organization.

[12] See for example *Bil'shovyk* 64 (22 December 1922): 3 and 66 (30 December 1922): 3. The announcements of 1922 referred specifically to Geo Shkurupii and Andrii Chuzhyi. None of the Futurists, however, received as much attention as did Mykhail' Semenko, whose productivity at this time was really quite extraordinary. The announcements spoke of the imminent appearance of his two collections, "Moia Mozaika" [My Mosaic] and "Proiekt" [Project]. The first represented a genre he called "poetry-painting" [*poezomaliarstvo*], the second contained "suprematist poems" [*suprepoezii*]. Semenko was also finishing two narrative poems, one entitled "Meredian" [Meridian], the other, "Sifilis" [Syphilis]. There was also a "cosmic drama" entitled "Kontynenty. Poema heokosmichynykh katastrof" [Continents. A Narrative Poem of Geo-Cosmic Catastrophes]. It was also announced that he was working on a novel based on contemporary revolutionary life which was referred to by the title "Holod" [Famine]. However, not all of these works appeared at that time. As for theory, Semenko was putting the finishing touches to his conception of the theater. Entitled "Mystetstvo ihryshch" [The Art of Games], this art form was to take the place of the traditional theater; it was to ignore the common boundaries between actors and spectators, making everyone a participant.

One of the earliest news items concerned *Semafor u Maibutnie.* Apparently on 7 December 1922 a second issue of the journal had been sent to the printer ("Panfuturysty pratsiuiut'" 1922). The contents included a lead article by Semenko entitled "A Study of Facture [Texture]" [*Nauka pro fakturu*], and others on the concept of "meta-art." This theoretical material was prepared in five languages. The issue also contained a collective work under the title, "The Siege of the Earth's Globe" [*Obloha zemnoï kuli*]. The authors were identified as the "Panfuturists-Destructivists" Semenko, Shkurupii, Slisarenko, Irchan, and Shpol. The announcement went on to explain that *Semafor u Maibutnie* was being developed into a theoretical non-periodic publication with a limited press-run for the purpose of promoting questions of destruction, construction and meta-art—in other words, all aspects of the Panfuturist theory.

There was also news about *Katafalk mystetstv*, "an organ of the Panfuturists-Destructivists," which first appeared on 13 December 1922 in a bilingual (Ukrainian and Russian) format as *Katafalk iskusstva*. On 30 December Aspanfut announced a second issue, which was to appear that very week—this time in Russian, Ukrainian, and Yiddish (*Bil'shovyk* 66 [30 December 1922]: 3). One of the avowed goals of this publication was to explain the "boundaries" between Panfuturism and Constructivism.

As an antidote to the "destructive" side of their program, the Futurists announced *Smoloskyp* [Torch], "a journal of the Panfuturists-Constructivists," scheduled for appearance in mid-January 1923.[13] Its purpose was to develop theories of meta-art and advocate slogans along the lines of: "Away with Science in the Academies and Universities. Long Live Science and Life" (*Bil'shovyk* 64 [22 December 1922]: 3). In keeping with this program, the very first issue was to contain some unspecified translation of Albert Einstein by Semenko.

Almost simultaneously with *Smoloskyp*, Aspanfut promised *Kermo* [Helm] in December 1922. The inaugural issue of this journal was set to appear in January 1923. Unlike *Smoloskyp*, however, which was announced twice and then forgotten, *Kermo* was doggedly pursued and, by all indications, came closest to being realized.[14] Advertised as a literary and artistic biweekly from the publisher Gulf Stream, its editorial board

[13] *Smoloskyp* was first advertised in *Katafalk iskusstva* 13 December 1922.

[14] Repeated announcements about *Kermo* appeared in the following issues of *Bil'shovyk*: 64 (22 December 1922): 3; 66 (30 December 1922): 3; 36 (15 February 1923): 4; 39 (18 February 1923): 4; 59 (16 March 1923): 3; 117 (30 May 1923): 2. Announcements also appeared in *Chervonyi shliakh* 1 (1923): 260, and in left-wing West Ukrainian journals.

included Semenko, Les' Kurbas, and Iakiv Savchenko. Separate sections were to be devoted to poetry, prose, theater, music, film, choreography, theory, and translation. Plans called for the publication of the German Expressionist Georg Kaiser (his plays *Gas* and *Die Koralle*), Ernst Toller, Carl Sternheim, and Jules Romains. The actual completed first issue featured Les' Kurbas, Semenko, Shkurupii, Savchenko, Chuzhyi, Slisarenko, Vadym Meller, Jules Romains, and Georg Kaiser. Time went by, but the journal failed to materialize. In May 1923 an explanation finally appeared:

> To the subscribers of *Kermo*:
> The editorial board of the journal *Kermo* announces that the appearance of the journal has been delayed for the following reasons:
> 1. The reorganization of the editorial board.
> 2. The departure of key personnel from the editorial board.
> 3. The current, technically inopportune, time for publishing a journal.
> Publication of the journal is being delayed for yet some time but its appearance is guaranteed and subscribers will receive their due (*Bil'shovyk* 117 [30 May 1923]: 2).[15]

Despite these encouraging words, the publication never saw the light of day.

Gulf Stream also planned a series of almanacs under the common title, *Tvorcha Ukraïna* [Creative Ukraine] (*Bil'shovyk* 30 [8 February 1923]: 4; *Chervonyi shliakh* 1 [1923]: 260). Like *Kermo*, these advances were to highlight poetry, prose, drama, music, and art, with the important difference that they would be open to writers of "all movements." The first issue was to have been released simultaneously in Kyiv and New York at the end of April 1923 (*Nova kul'tura* 1 [1923] May: 45–46). The announced editorial board included Vasyl' Atamaniuk, Semenko, and Shkurupii.

One can only speculate why these publishing plans met with failure. Clearly, it was not for a lack of trying. A plausible reason is that they ran into trouble with authorities, whose resistance to the movement was keen. Given also the paralysis that gripped publishing, a problem to which the Futurists alluded, the journals seem to have been doomed from the start. The difficulty of surmounting economic problems, especially by political and cultural outsiders, was made clear by a contemporary:

> The unusually harsh economic conditions force people to think only about bread....At present, art is a luxury, especially for that category

[15] Earlier, on 16 March 1923, an announcement declared: "For reasons beyond our control, printing [of *Kermo*] is being further delayed. [The journal] has been sent to the printer" (*Bil'shovyk* 59 [16 March 1923]: 3).

> [of writer] who does not carry the honorable title of "state" [*kaz'onnyi*]. ([Only] the latter, after all, are ensured work in state institutions.) I know of exceptional (and famous) poets who work in slaughterhouses all year, far from any kind of cultural life (e.g., O. Slisarenko). Some of those who live in the cities must work as day-laborers: G. Shkurupii, Mykola Tereshchenko,[16] M. Semenko, M. Irchan. In the winter they clear snow off roofs, railroad tracks, [and] chop firewood in the forest. Others make shoes or teach in obscure villages (e.g., M. Ryl's'kyi, M. Filians'kyi, D. Zahul, and V. Pidmohyl'nyi) (Donets' 1922, 30–31).

Another source from 1922 made this laconic remark: "In this terrible hour of need people are losing even the barest cultural consciousness, they are becoming wild beasts, because hunger destroys everything and forces people to such horrors as cannibalism" (Ellan-Blakytnyi 1930d, 73).

Cultural life was made especially difficult in Kyiv where publishing enterprises had come to a virtual standstill.[17] The former capital of the "bourgeois" Ukrainian National Republic was steadily being provincialized as power (both political and cultural) flowed to Kharkiv, which by the mid-twenties became the undisputed center of literary life. A majority of literary organizations eventually established their headquarters in Kharkiv and did most of their publishing there. Even as early as 1921–1922, Kharkiv was out-producing Kyiv in literary publications. The journal *Shliakhy mystetstva* and the majority of the leading miscellanies and almanacs appeared there. As late as May 1923 the bibliographer and critic Iurii Mezhenko wrote that "Kyiv, at first glance, gives the impression of being a total vacuum" (Mezhenko 1923b, 263). Explaining why Kyiv's "significant potential" was not being realized, Mezhenko identified "material want" as the major reason for the city's cultural deprivation. He indicated that because of economic hardships, all attempts at creating a literary journal in Kyiv met with failure. As one such example he mentioned Pavlo Tychyna's and Anatolii Petryts'kyi's undertaking in 1922 to establish *Mystets'ka trybuna* [The Artistic Rostrum].[18] Even in the fall of 1923 people still pointed to the economy

[16] Elsewhere it is stated that Tereshchenko worked as a chemist in a sugar factory (*Chervonyi shliakh* 1 [1923]: 250).

[17] Publishing figures for the first six months of 1923 show that fourteen publishing houses in Kyiv (including Gulf Stream) published a total of only 55 titles. Just how difficult conditions were is demonstrated by the fact that out of this number the Ukrainian Academy of Sciences published only six titles, while the Kyiv branch of the state-run publishing house (DVU) managed 20 titles (Ozerians'kyi 1923).

[18] Mezhenko also mentioned the failure of another projected journal, *Honh* [Gong]. This may have been another Futurist effort since they traditionally liked to revive their unsuccessful titles. In 1924 they published *Honh Komunkul'ta* [Gong of the Komunkul't].

as the main stumbling block to a normal literary life in Kyiv.[19]

In light of this situation, the Futurists were, even with their failures, the most vigorous of all groups. Mezhenko explicitly called them "the strongest [group], ideologically and organizationally" (Mezhenko 1923b, 265). In fact, they had no serious competition in Kyiv. The Neoclassicists, as Mezhenko states, had an ideological profile but no organizational base and so could not be compared to the Panfuturists.[20] Pluh was equally uncompetitive. Attempts at creating a chapter of this "peasant writers' union" in Kyiv had begun in April 1922. Hryhorii Kosynka, Teodosii (Todos') Os'machka, and Iakiv Savchenko were mentioned as members at that time (ibid., 264). However, nothing came of it, as witnessed by the fact that a few months later a fresh effort got under way (*Chervonyi shliakh* 6–7 [1923]: 214). Success came only in January 1924 when Samiilo Shchupak became head of Kyiv-Pluh.

Although Kharkiv was better off than Kyiv, even there the achievements of the proletarians were rather speckled. Consider that the officially sanctioned journal, the flagship of Ukrainian literature during this period, *Shliakhy mystetstva*, appeared with great irregularity. Comparatively speaking, therefore, Aspanfut was a prominent and thriving organization, enjoying high visibility and critical attention[21]—so much so that it even left a mark beyond the borders of the Soviet state. Irchan, writing to Semenko and Shkurupii from Prague on 6 October 1922 stated that:

19 "Without doubt, only technical roadblocks prevent the creation of mutual, friendly work [conditions]." See "Kyïv. Kul'turne zhyttia" 1923. As late as November 1925 one author observed that "the economic state, the working conditions for a writer, and to a certain extent the moral conditions (I have in mind [the writer's] relationship to the publishing houses) is simply horrendous...There is hardly a writer among us who is exclusively engaged in his literary work" (see Ivanenko 1925).

20 A few months later another source stated the following: "In Kyiv, besides the Futurists [...] there are no other poetic groups. Much was said about the so-called Neoclassicists, several reports and speeches were devoted to them, but in reality the Neoclassicists do not form any organization [ob'iednannia]. At present there is not a single Neoclassicist in Kyiv" (*Chervonyi shliakh* 4–5 [1923]: 255). In the September–October issue of *Chervonyi shliakh* another author writes that besides the Panfuturists "there are no other [literary] organizations in Kyiv. The literary forces are pulverized: not only are they not unified, they are not even differentiated into various movements" (*Chervonyi shliakh* 6–7 [1923]: 218).

21 Among the Futurist publications reviewed at this time were M. Semenko, *Prominnia pohroz* (reviewed in *Shliakhy mystetstva* 1 [1921]: 57–58); *Psykhotezy* by Geo Shkurupii, (reviewed by Vasyl' Rolenko in *Shliakhy mystetstva* 2[4] 1922: 62) and *Semafor u Maibutnie* (reviewed by Maik Iohansen in *Shliakhy mystetstva*. See Rolenko 1922 and Iohansen 1922, respectively.

> No sooner did I arrive in Prague when even here I heard moans and cries. Obviously [Panfuturism] is having a bad effect not only on the 'repenting intellectuals'...but also on the real émigré bourgeoisie and Petliurite counter-revolutionaries. Our term 'destruction' affects them just as the genuine proletarian revolution [has]. They are shriveling up and moaning in anger, cursing us as 'Communists.' Ha! As if that were an insult to us!...Klym Polishchuk approached me with his 'criticism' but I laid him flat on his back with one finger. It's very easy to deal with such chameleons....Not too long ago an article appeared in the journal *Nova Ukraïna* written by R. Donets....[22] It speaks very favorably about Mykhail' and Geo. Much is also said [about Futurism] at meetings here....(Irchan and Shkurupii 1922, 1, 2).

Earlier, in July 1922, the Prague journal *Sterni* [Stalks] showed both awareness and respect for Semenko and his movement. Antin Pavliuk, in an article surveying recent Ukrainian poetry, made the bold statement that "the really talented figure of Mykhail' Semenko is not widely recognized simply because the theory of Futurism and city life, both of which sustain him and dominate his works, are so alien and inharmonic in the chaos [which is witnessing] the rebirth of the Ukrainian village as the creative force of [our] nation" (Pavliuk 1922).

In February 1922, the Lviv journal *Mytusa* [Mytusa] (where Semenko's old ally Pavlo Kovzhun sat on the editorial board) published one poem by Semenko ("Osinni skrypky" [Autumn Violins] and two by Slisarenko ("Tryvoha" [Alarm]; "Obiimy shybenyts'" [The Embrace of Gallows]). A reviewer in the Kharkiv journal *Shliakhy mystetstva* noted ironically that *Mytusa* considered Futurism the latest vogue in literature and argued (not very persuasively, one might add) that some of *Mytusa*'s contributors betrayed Semenko's influence (Sontsvit [Polishchuk] 1922, 56). This issue of *Mytusa* also reported that Semenko, Slisarenko, Shkurupii, and Shpol "had united on a platform of Futurist slogans and formed a group that was to publish a 'Futurist Miscellany,'" a reference, clearly, to the impending appearance of *Semafor u Maibutnie*" ("Khronika. Kyievs'ki [*sic*] futurysty" 1922).[23]

Perhaps the best measure of Aspanfut's success was the criticism it received. The movement, naturally, invited intellectual confrontations and thrived on them. Fortunately or not, there were plenty of people willing to oblige. We have already seen with what alarm Valeriian Polishchuk wrote of the Futurists to *Zhovten'*. He, of course, was not

[22] See Donets' 1922.

[23] A notice about the appearance of *Semafor u Maibutnie* is included in *Mytusa* 4 (April 1922): 124.

speaking for himself alone, but was expressing the views of *Zhovten*'s three editors—Mykola Khvyl'ovyi, Volodymyr Sosiura, and Mykhailo (Maik) Iohansen. This quartet of writers was on intimate terms at this time, and spoke in the name of "proletarian" art.[24] In its editorial, *Zhovten'* took a strong stand against "feudal and bourgeois aesthetics" criticizing especially the "futureless Futurists who present naked destruction as creativity" (Khvyl'ovyi et al. 1928, 67). What is ironic is that *Zhovten'* not only carried a long, informative, and actually not unfriendly article on Futurism (Koriak 1921), but counted among its major contributors Shkurupii, Slisarenko, and Shpol, all of whom by this time had gone over to Semenko.

Valeriian Polishchuk and Mykola Khvyl'ovyi (now joined by Volodymyr Hadzins'kyi and three Russian writers) repeated their attack on Futurism almost verbatim in "The Declaration of the All-Ukrainian Federation of Proletarian Writers and Artists," dated January 1922. This Federation (head by Khvyl'ovyi) was an altogether inauspicious attempt to unite Ukrainian and Russian "proletarian" writers. Its only success was the single issue of *Arena*, published in March 1922, which also carried the Declaration. Among other things, the Federation espoused the principle of "free discussion among proletarian writers of all artistic currents," arguing that a proletarian writer should be allowed to write "as he pleases, in other words, to choose his own methods of creativity." Futurism, however, was one method that was disallowed. In fact, members of this movement were excluded from the "proletarian writer" category. Anyone who dared to emulate Futurism could expect unpleasant consequences: "If a proletarian writer should forget that he has burned the bridges of feudal and bourgeois aesthetics and should follow in the footsteps of the futureless Futurists or other formalist schools... then this type of 'comrade' will have to be dismissed from our group" ("Deklaratsiia Vseukraïns'koï" 1922).[25] Remarkably, censure of this type did not prevent

24 Iohansen and Khvyl'ovyi appeared together in the almanac *Shtabel'* (1921). Polishchuk and Khvyl'ovyi shared the same pages in the collection *2* (1922).

25 It is rather ironic to note in retrospect that although Valeriian Polishchuk, Mykola Khvyl'ovyi, and Maik Iohansen attacked Futurism and formalism at the beginning of the decade, all three writers were keenly influenced by Formalist, if not specifically Futurist, theories and their writings certainly reflect this fact. A few cases in point: back in 1920, as was noted earlier, Polishchuk had called Futurism and Impressionism "the most outstanding artistic forms of the day" and advocated a synthesis of these two currents (see "Manifest 'Hrono,'" Leites and Iashek 1930, 2: 31). Soon after his attacks on formalism and Futurism, Khvyl'ovyi became identified with what was called "Red Formalism." And Maik Iohansen began one of his books by justifying the similarities between his methods and those of Futurism (1928, 3).

Aspanfut from prospering or releasing publications like *Semafor* and *Katafalk*. In the short term, the fate of Semenko's Futurist organization certainly proved more auspicious than that of Khvyl'ovyi's proletarian Federation.

Still, exponents of proletarian art continued hammering at Futurism. When *Semafor u Maibutnie* rolled off the press, Ivan Kulyk said it "was designed to derail the locomotive of the proletarian revolution." Shkurupii's writings were characterized as the subterfuge of a "cretin-individualist." His conclusion was that "We might as well just give up on Semenko and Shkurupii. They are hopelessly lost [to proletarian literature]. There is no sense also in regretting the loss of Slisarenko and Mykola Tereshchenko" (Kulyk 1922, 32).

The proletarian camp headquartered in Kharkiv was not Futurism's only foe. Local opposition came also from the more sophisticated Kyiv Neoclassicists, who heaped scorn on Futurists for their undisciplined form and politicized content. With poor access to the media, their own aesthetic and ideological positions open to question, the Neoclassicists were never able to mount as public or as strong opposition to the Futurists as did the proletarians. But as Maksym Ryl's'kyi, the foremost member of this group pointed out, the *raison d'être* and identity of Neoclassicism was at least partially based on rivalry with Futurism. Writing about these events many years later, he said:

> Ukrainian Neoclassicism was to a significant degree an expression of the struggle against the Panfuturists, the destructivists, and other representatives of art who groundlessly called themselves the 'left.'...In [the Neoclassicists'] struggle against Futurism and other formalist currents, in their call to honor literary tradition, in their love for Greek and Roman classics...there was, without doubt, a healthy seed (Ryl's'kyi 1966, 6–7).

Contemporary observers also saw Neoclassicism and Futurism as antipodes. Valeriian Polishchuk, for example, called the Neoclassicists simply a "reaction" to Futurism (V. Polishchuk 1922, 36).

Doubtless, such a view does not do justice to Neoclassicism. It does, however, say something about the polemical bond between these groups.[26] Sometimes their tug-of-war expressed itself ironically in poetry and at

[26] Leo Kriger points out that Maksym Ryl's'kyi was actually a close personal friend of Semenko; in the early thirties, when the fortunes of Futurism had completely sunk, he had some positive words for Semenko, although obviously not for the movement he represented (Kriger 1979, 118).

other times through hostile reviews.[27] As early as 1919 the Neoclassicist Pavlo Fylypovych, writing in the journal *Knyhar*, had criticized Semenko's collection *Dev'iat' poem* for not being mellifluous (Fylypovych 1919b, 1148–49).[28] For their part, the Futurists accused the "toothless Zerovs and Fylypovychs" for being "frightened to death" by the present and took them to task for desperately restoring "old, dusty, familiar forms" (Shkurupii 1922b, 9; Semenko 1922c, 32). When an anthology of contemporary poetry edited by Mykola Zerov appeared, Semenko (writing under the pseudonym M. Tryroh) charged that the editor's outmoded tastes and standards were impediments to an accurate portrayal of the new poetry (Tryroh [Semenko] 1922b). Semenko was incensed that Vasyl' Ellan-Blakytnyi, Mykola Khvyl'ovyi, and Maik Iohansen were represented in Zerov's collection by just a single poem each, while others (for example, Geo Shkurupii) were overlooked altogether. Zerov's "perfectly bad taste," claimed Tryroh, extended even to his choice of Semenko's works: four of the five poems were completely uncharacteristic and worthless, he said. Ultimately, Semenko's review was not so much a defense of himself and his friends as an exposé of what he termed a "sterile academic mind" and "academic conservatism." This type of vociferous antagonism to the Neoclassicists garnered the Futurists an occasional and grudging compliment from the proletarian camp. Volodymyr Koriak, for example, noted that "under the conditions [prevailing] in Kyiv, where Ukrainian literary traditions dating to the period of the Ukrainian National Republic still survive, the Futurist group is an outpost of the October literature. Their usefulness lies precisely in their destruction, liquidation of old traditions" (Koriak 1923a, 204).

Despite—or perhaps because of—their controversial temperament, the Futurists continued to win friends and influence people. A case in point was the defection to their side of two former Symbolists in late 1923. For the Futurists, this was an especially satisfying event, because it occurred in a public manner and resulted in no slight embarrassment to their proletarian detractors.

The first to come over was Volodymyr Iaroshenko. He did so in August with a ringing endorsement of the Futurists' "destructive" program: "Just as in the proletarian movement the Communist Party [gave] the impulse for the struggle with capital, so Panfuturism—which

[27] See, for example, Ryl's'kyi's poem "Druhe rybal'ske poslannia" or Mykola Zerov's "Kyïv. Tradytsiia." See also Zerov (1989, 104–109).

[28] The journal was edited by the Neoclassicist Zerov. See my comments about this episode (1980, 110).

is, so to speak, the Communist Party in art—[will act as the impulse] in the struggle for the eventual demise of art."[29] That same month Aspanfut netted an even more sensational catch in the person of Iakiv Savchenko, who had been fraternizing informally with the Futurists for nearly a year. In December 1922 he acquiesced to serving on *Kermo*'s editorial board. In April 1923 he and Semenko agreed to co-author a history of contemporary Ukrainian literature (*Chervonyi shliakh* 1 [1923]: 219). Officially, however, he kept his distance from Aspanfut. In the months prior to taking this decision, Savchenko had been described alternately as a member of Pluh's Kyiv chapter (*Chervonyi shliakh* 2 [1923]: 264), as a person with no affiliation at all (*Chervonyi shliakh* 4–5 [1923]: 255), and finally it was rumored that he was considering membership in Hart, founded in January 1923. On 5 September he quelled all speculation, revealing in *Bil'shovyk* that he had joined the Panfuturists. His open letter, however, was more than a simple announcement—it was a way to disparage Hart for being an organization "uncharacteristic of a proletarian ideology":

> These (rather acute) deviations give me reason to believe that Hart is proletarian [only] in theory; in fact its world view has become stranded elsewhere and, consequently, it cannot forge an organization with a strict Marxist ideology and a proper understanding of the literary process.... A consistent theoretical and practical answer to the demands [of our time] is being provided by the Panfuturists, an organization of writers that is most in touch with those who are presently creating a communist culture. It is by way of these facts that I explain my entry into the [ranks] of the Panfuturists (quoted from Ellan-Blakytnyi et al. 1923, 5).

This declaration brought an angry reply from the presidium of Hart. On 14 September 1923, speaking for the organization, Vasyl' Ellan-Blakytnyi, Mykola Khvyl'ovyi, and Ivan Dniprovs'kyi took delight in divulging that only a few months earlier Savchenko harbored very different feelings for the Futurists (Ellan-Blakytnyi et al. 1923). They said he had written—on 17 March of that year—the following to Ellan-Blakytnyi:

> I definitely do not belong to the Panfuturists [organization]. My attitude toward them is hostile; I do not acknowledge their artistic "science."

[29] Quoted in *Bil'shovyk* 18 August 1923 (cited in Trostianets'kyi 1968b, 96). The literary historian Mykola Sulyma defined Iaroshenko as a Futurist much earlier. But M. T. [Mykola Tereshchenko?] in reviewing Sulyma's *Istoriia ukraïns'koho pys'menstva* (1923), where this claim was made, stated in January 1923 that to include Iaroshenko among the Futurists so early was "arbitrary." See M.T. 1923.

> All this Panfuturism is nonsense....However, I am treating them in a "scholarly" fashion; right now, I am writing an article.... I would like to finish with this affliction once and for all, trace all the sources from which this Panfuturist stream is trickling and expose the social nature of Ukrainian Futurism. This is the only association I have with the Panfuturists (ibid., 5).

Having thus humiliated Savchenko, the Hart members made this point:

> Regardless of betrayals by the weak in spirit and attacks by enemies and unfaithful friends, Hart will continue to wage a merciless struggle with bourgeois ideology, with anarchistic mediocrity as well as deviations and errors in proletarian cultural work, [all of] which can be explained as the influence of petty-bourgeois "fellow travelers" (ibid.).

The very next day *Bil'shovyk* ran a response from Savchenko. He called Hart's letter "hysterical," characterizing the publication of his private correspondence as the prurient act of a rejected "old maid." Savchenko countered Hart's moralizing tone by pointing out that the organization was not an "infallible communist pope," but rather an "ideological cripple" stumbling over its own two feet. He denied his letter had been an overture to Hart, explaining that it was merely a private response to Ellan-Blakytnyi's request to clarify where he stood in the literary conflicts. Hart, he charged, was so heterogeneous that "one could not guess how many [literary] currents and sub-currents" were present in the organization. "I must acknowledge that there was in Hart a healthy proletarian seed, but for some reason it has given off very sickly shoots." The Panfuturists, in his estimation, possessed much more vitality and coherence in their program (Ia. Savchenko 1923f).

Aspanfut also received strong support from two theatrical groups, one headed by Marko Tereshchenko, the other by Les' Kurbas. These "heroes of contemporary Ukrainian theater" ("'Karnaval.' Kompozytsiia" 1923), as one anonymous observer called them, directed, respectively, the Hnat Mykhailychenko and the Berezil' Theaters, both with a well-deserved reputation for radical innovations. Marko Tereshchenko's association with Semenko dated back at least to 1920, when he staged a performance based on Semenko's verse (Petryts'kyi 1929, 36). As was noted, he was a contributor to *Semafor u Maibutnie*, and Gulf Stream published his book on performance art. Tereshchenko recounted that when he first began his trials in the theater, Semenko was one of few people to lend him moral support by calling his work "one of the most interesting" experiments anywhere. Although Tereshchenko's first encounters with the Futurists had a private character, involving only Semenko and Slisarenko, by 1922 he was able to declare that he had found "complete contact with the

Panfuturists...We have common artistic goals and are uniting in a common front to break new ground. We look forward to many fresh, interesting, and essential experiments" (Tereshchenko 1922a, 45).

Kurbas, it will be recalled, had planned to stage Semenko's *Lilit* as early as 1919. According to reliable accounts, the two men were close personal friends (Hirniak 1982, 217). In December 1922 Kurbas joined Semenko and Savchenko as co-editor of the ill-fated *Kermo*.[30] The clearest evidence of a more formal partnership between Berezil' and Aspanfut appeared in November 1923 when Berezil' began putting out its organ, *Barykady teatru* [Barricades of the Theater]. From the onset Panfuturists had access to this journal and in each of the three issues that ultimately appeared they were represented with either articles or reviews.[31] Perhaps the most indulgent of these was one entitled "Mykhail' Semenko, Panfuturist," penned by an unknown member of Aspanfut under the initials O. B. It was an unreserved encomium to the Futurist leader, paying tribute to him as a "genuine revolutionary" who, through his Panfuturist system of art, had transformed himself into an individual of world stature. The conclusion struck a querulous note: "This assertion may elicit a scowl from Ukrainian Philistines, but, then, that is [to be expected from] a lackey's psychology, especially from a Ukrainian one" (O.B. 1923, 5). Other articles by Bazhan, Semenko, and Slisarenko were only slightly less tendentious (N. B. 1923; Slisarenko 1923a; Semenko 1924e).

Tereshchenko's and Kurbas' alliance with Semenko was a genuine meeting of minds on a number of theoretical issues. To a greater or lesser degree, all three opposed aestheticism, academism, emotionalism (psychologism), and traditionalism in art. None minced words about the propriety of utilizing art for promoting Communist ideals and culture. Berezil's avowed interest in innovation (what was called a commitment to "tomorrow's day") was reminiscent of Semenko's earlier pronouncements about "overtaking the present" and his dithyrambs to contemporaneity (recall: "There is nothing more beautiful than the present" [Немає нічого більш прекрасного/як сьогоднішній день]). By conceding that "Berezil' simply does not know whether there will be a theater in the future," Kurbas came close to Semenko's dictum about the eventual demise of art in a communist society. Significantly, when Kurbas

30 The planned publication in *Kermo* of Kaiser's *Gas* was undoubtedly linked to the fact that it was part of Berezil's repertoire.

31 *Barykady teatru* ceased publication in January 1924. Attempts at resuscitating the journal in October 1924 failed. See *Bil'shovyk* 246 (28 October 1924): 4.

wrote about the obligation to "de-aestheticize" art, he pointed first of all to the practice of Semenko and the Panfuturists.[32]

Although Futurists were inherently a censorious *équipe*, Aspanfut, amazingly, meted out generous praise to its theatrical allies. Iakiv Savchenko, who was one of the more regular commentators and reviewers of Berezil's activities in Kyiv, described Kurbas' direction as the work of a genius and his theater "a brilliant step" forward for proletarian art in Ukraine.[33] In 1924, when a small group of disaffected Berezil' members tried to besmirch the organization's good name by saying it was anti-revolutionary, intellectualist, and guilty of idealism, Savchenko published a scorching denunciation of these individuals, accusing them of lies, intrigues, and provocations against "the greatest civic and revolutionary organization in Ukraine" (Ia. Savchenko 1924a). Semenko apparently thought so much of the director's talent that he even worked to promote a career for him in the cinema. In a bold public gesture, he took to task those "members of the Party" who dealt with matters of film, urging them "to show more responsibility" by ousting "dilettantes, fellow-travelers [and] unemployed 'deserving specialists'" from the industry, and entrusting it instead to Kurbas (Semenko 1923a). In fact, Kurbas did eventually make several films, but this medium was not his forte.[34]

The young Nik Bazhan was also a great admirer of the director. Following performances in Kyiv and Kharkiv by troupes of Kurbas and Meyerhold, Bazhan (writing under the pseudonym "Panfuturyst-ekstruktor") stated that the Kurbas theater had "stunned" audiences, while Meyerhold's performance, in contrast, only "made the impression of a fly buzzing against an autumn window." Bazhan acknowledged Meyerhold's talent for "destroying" the traditional theater, but argued that he relied too much on old Futurist techniques, and, unlike Kurbas, was ideologically retrograde. Bazhan asked rhetorically: "What is the purpose of such pretty words and slogans as 'epoch,' 'socialist revolution,' 'the Red Army,' 'The First Red Army Soldier, Comrade Trotsky'? This

32 For Tereshchenko's views, see the articles in *Semafor u Maibutnie* mentioned above and the anonymous article "'Karnaval.' Kompozytsiia" 1923. For Kurbas' views, see his 1923a, 1923b, 1923c. See also the theater's statement of purpose entitled "Berezil'" in *Barykady teatru* 1 (1923): 1. For a concise discussion of Berezil', see Tkacz 1988.

33 See his review of Kaiser's *Gas* (Savchenko 1923d). Refer also to his 1923e and 1924c.

34 Kurbas directed the following films: *Vendetta* [Vendetta, VUFKU, Odesa, 1924], *Makdonal'd* [Macdonald, VUFKU, Odesa, 1924], *Son Tovstopuzenka* [The Dream of Tovstopuzenko, VUFKU, Odesa, 1924], and *Arsenal'tsi* [The Arsenal Workers, VUFKU, Odesa, 1924]. On the making of these films, see Perehuda 1970. The Russian-language publication *Iugo-lef* noted that while Kurbas was in Odesa, Favst Lopatyns'kyi took his place in Kyiv. See "Berezil'" 1924.

primitive intellectualist 'consonance with the revolution' sets one's teeth on edge...." His obvious preference for Kurbas did not, however, deter Bazhan from identifying his weaknesses. As an example of a notably "great sin," Bazhan pointed to Kurbas' occasional tendency toward "aestheticism" and "symbolism." But despite such reservations, he concluded that the "champion of Kyiv (Kurbas) has knocked out the champion of Moscow (Meyerhold)" (Panfuturyst-ekstruktor 1923).[35] Berezil' never reciprocated with such profuse praise, but it was known to defend the Futurists ("Z redzhurnalu" 1923). At one time, twenty-five members of Berezil' expressed their collective gratitude for the aid they received from Aspanfut, and voiced the hope that the two organizations would continue to work together ("Kalendar AsPF" 1924).

Through Berezil', Aspanfut found a common language with Vadym Meller, a set and costume designer who presided (together with his wife Henke Meller) over an avant-garde (that is, "leftist") artistic studio in Kyiv. Henke Meller designed the cover for a Futurist miscellany (*Zhovtnevyi zbirnyk panfuturystiv* 1923) and Vadym Meller's students—those who, it was said, had not been "corrupted by the old school"—were working "on a portrait of the Panfuturist Mykhail' Semenko which will soon be finished" ("Maliars'ka maisternia" 1923).[36]

Aspanfut's expanding membership and alliances were made possible in part because the organization retreated slightly from some of its more extravagant positions. Savchenko brought this up when he declared himself a Panfuturist, saying that Aspanfut acknowledged to him certain "tactical mistakes," rejected its "destructive program" (toward which his own attitude was "negative" and "antagonistic") and committed itself to the "new principles" of "construction" (*Bil'shovyk* 208 [15 September 1923]: 4). This change did not occur at Savchenko's urging alone but was a response to the ceaseless pressures coming from the Party and various literary adversaries. Under the influences of these forces, the organization began to divide into two factions. A Kyiv observer reported the following in August 1923:

> Among the Panfuturists there are arguments about destructivism (Semenko and Co.) and constructivism (Shkurupii and Co.). The young

[35] I should point out that while it has been established that Bazhan wrote under the pseudonym "Panfuturyst," it is not completely certain that "Panfuturyst-ekstruktor" refers to him. While circumstantial evidence strongly suggests that Bazhan was indeed the author of this article, prudence compels me to acknowledge that there is an element of doubt here.

[36] For details on Meller's biography, see Bazhan (1973, 148).

> Panfuturists are losing faith in their leadership (Semenko, Slisarenko, and Shkurupii). Panfuturism is struggling in a mass of contradictory ideologies and cannot find a way out. Shkurupii is printing a new "platform" that is supposed to unite the splintering forces but it is doubtful whether this will succeed (Iu.S. 1923, 255).[37]

To save the organization from a potential rupture Semenko made a major public concession to the "constructivist" camp in Aspanfut. On 12 September 1923, just days after Savchenko proclaimed himself a Futurist, he released an article in which he condemned early forms of Futurism and raised the prospect of a "scientific aesthetic" based on Marxism and Leninism.

> The Futurists imagined themselves a "proletarian" movement in art, had ambitions of attaining national importance, and [hoped their principles] would become universally binding [on all]. But that was a mistake. Futurism could not be a proletarian art because it is a continuation of...bourgeois revolutionary "Great Art." Futurism did not originate from a proletarian ideology; it denied bourgeois art but stood on its ideological positions....It is important to note that Futurism in Russia and here [in Ukraine] was in fact "Bolshevism"...but it has no future. The Dadaists, [after all], also eagerly proclaim themselves "Bolsheviks" in art....Futurism is approaching a crisis and a reevaluation of its values. What then is the further course of art? In our view, the moment approaches when the dreams Plekhanov and other Marxists had about creating a "scientific aesthetic" will be realized. We are on the eve of formulating a universally obligatory, a universally significant formula of art that will become the criterion for a national artistic policy...Marxism plus Leninism, applied specifically to art, provides this formula (Semenko 1923b).[38]

Aspanfut's retreat from its "destructivist" emphasis was underscored in a short report that appeared in the September-October issue of *Chervonyi shliakh*. It showed that the pro-destructivist forces had indeed compromised their militant stance: "In view of the fact that the destructivists have already expressed themselves adequately, [and] whereas constructive work has barely been outlined, the last [few] plenary assemblies of Panfuturists have resolved to focus special attention on Panfuturist *construction*. This task will absorb the Panfuturists during the entire 1923–1924 season" ("Asotsiiatsiia panfuturystiv" 1923; *emphasis*

[37] The journal *Nova hromada* (Kyiv) also reported that the Futurists "are undergoing a crisis." See the citation in Trostianets'kyi (1968b, 94).

[38] Reprinted in *Nova kul'tura* (Lviv) 7–8 (1923): 50–53. My citation is from the latter source.

in the original). As if to prove this, the November issue of *Chervonyi shliakh* carried brief announcements about the activities of several Panfuturists and, almost to a man, they were described as engaging in either "constructivist" or "exstructivist" (i.e., the opposite of "*de*-structivist") work. Semenko was "developing the program of the constructive front"; Mykola Tereshchenko was working on his "exstructivist prose"; Volodymyr Iaroshenko was writing "exstructivist fables" and Shkurupii a "large exstructivist novel" (*Chervonyi shliakh* 8 [1923]: 291).[39]

Aspanfut's endeavor to project a positive public image was again reflected at the organization's plenary assembly that took place on 10 and 11 December. Semenko, who, despite the crisis, was still the undisputed leader, presided over a session attended by all Kyiv Panfuturists. Outlining Aspanfut's plans and activities for the near term, Semenko called for "practical work" involving public demonstrations, talks at factories, plants, and workshops. The plenum ratified that "public appearances of the Panfuturists will have a mass character and emphasis will be placed mainly on village and proletarian youth, with the goal of attracting them into cultural construction" ("Cherhovyi plenum Aspanfutu" 1923). Aspanfut was also to offer its services to the Agitprop division of the KP(b)U so that it might be used by the government for cultural work. With such changes taking place in the organization, Savchenko was able to describe Aspanfut in November 1923 in the following way:

> Standing on the foundations of revolutionary Marxism, slowly but firmly absorbing the psychology of the proletarian collective, this organization is directing its activities toward a complete utilitarianization of art and every manifestation of the [human] "spirit," subordinating them to the practical every-day needs of the workers and making them part of the normal order of current Soviet construction. Along with this, [Aspanfut] seeks, through the medium of "artistic" methods and devices, to rebuild every-day life [*pobut*], to bring it closer to the hypothetical collective "ideal." Simultaneously, the Panfuturists are discrediting and criticizing every manifestation of bourgeois narrow-mindedness in art, leading a struggle against all that is directed at weakening the proletarian world view (Ia. Savchenko 1923b).[40]

The affirmative and civic temper sweeping through Aspanfut did not mean it had totally forsaken "destructivism." At the same time as it wrestled with this metamorphosis and trumpeted its constructive

[39] By "exstructivism" the Futurists meant the *temporary* exploitation of art for immediate social needs. See below, chapter 6.

[40] Reprinted in *Nova kul'tura* (Lviv) 1923 [7–8], 44. My citation is from the latter source.

programs, the organization announced that by 1 October 1923 it would publish a regular, biweekly "Panfuturist bulletin" and revive *Semafor u Maibutnie* as a monthly. It also planned to publish special almanacs devoted to individual aspects of Panfuturist theory (obstructivism,[41] exstructivism, constructivism), including destructivism (*Chervonyi shliakh* 6–7 [1923]: 224). However, realizing this program proved impossible. None of the publications announced for October were issued. In November, Andrii Chuzhyi is known to have prepared for publication a typically "destructivist" collection of poems under the title *Pid zdokhlym nebom. Pisni smitnyka* [Under the Putrid Sky. Songs of the Rubbish Heap], but it was never printed (*Chervonyi shliakh* 8 [1923]: 291).[42] On the other hand—and this is quite significant—Aspanfut did release in early November *Zhovtnevyi zbirnyk panfuturystiv* [The Panfuturists' October Collection],[43] an unabashed exercise in "positive" Futurism, a tribute to the October Revolution that featured such slogans as "Proletarians of the World—Unite!," "The Red Army and the Red Fleet is Our Sword and Our Defense!" and "The Sixth Anniversary of the Liberation of Nations—Lives!" Themes ranged from Lenin, to the struggle of the working class in the West, to machines ("The Machine Is Our Path towards Victory"). Contributors to this effort included new members of Aspanfut (Iaroshenko, Ia. Savchenko, Bazhan, and Mykhailo Shcherbak) and such regulars as Semenko, Slisarenko, and Shkurupii.

In early November 1923 Aspanfut and Berezil' set in motion the Initiative Bureau for the October Coalition of Arts [*Initsiiatyvne biuro zhovtnevoho bloku mystetstv*]. On 7 November an appeal was published to "all proletarian literary-artistic organizations" urging them to join a common front against "bourgeois traditions" and those who fostered them ("Vidozva Initsiiatyvnoho" 1923). Signing for Aspanfut were Mykhail' Semenko, Oleksa Slisarenko, and Geo Shkurupii; the signatories for Berezil' were Les' Kurbas, Favst Lopatyns'kyi, and Hnat Ihnatovych. These men argued that at a time when "the cultural and artistic counter-revolution" was engaged in an offensive to influence Soviet culture, the groups that stood under the banner of the October Revolution were plagued by dangerous divisiveness, enmity, and "sectarian narrow-mindedness." They called on everyone who adhered to the principles of "revolutionary Marxism" to abandon their "personal ambitions" and become members of the October Coalition of Arts, which was being

[41] Meaning, the tactic of obstructing, compromising, and directly combating any phenomenon of culture inimical to Futurists.
[42] Chuzhyi's poems in *Semafor u Maibutnie* were from this series.
[43] Its appearance was announced in *Bil'shovyk* 250 (3 November 1923): 4.

proposed as a "voluntary union" of proletarian groups whose aim would be to combat the influence of bourgeois ideology, coordinate cultural work among the masses and develop, in an atmosphere of camaraderie and equality, the question of communist culture. The appeal ended with a request that all appropriate organizations consider this issue at their meetings and delegate members to a convention that would draw up a constitution and plan of action (ibid., 8).

Considering the negative attitude toward the Futurists, this proposal met with a surprisingly positive reception and led to a dialogue among the major artistic organizations of Kyiv and Kharkiv.[44] The discussants were Aspanfut, Berezil', Hart, H.A.R.T.,[45] Pluh, and the Hnat Mykhailychenko Theater. In early December, members of Hart came to Kyiv to consult with Aspanfut, Berezil', and the Hnat Mykhailychenko Theater. A report on their meeting stated that "all representatives agreed on one thing: regardless of certain differences among the groups, the coalition is necessary" (*Chervonyi shliakh* 9 [1923]: 225–26). The participating organizations formed a commission to examine several proposals and one, which was adopted, foresaw, in the words of Ellan-Blakytnyi, "the creation of a coalition (at the moment without any organizational structures), amicable discussions, and a single front against counter-revolutionary, anti-Marxist elements in [our] culture." Ellan-Blakytnyi added that "the issue [of the October Coalition] is entering a new stage of development, namely, friendly discussions, explanation of positions and attitudes among various groups" (Ellan-Blakytnyi 1930a, 103).[46] The Panfuturists made an effort to promote the Coalition even in the provinces by sending Bazhan and Slisarenko with speeches to Uman' and Cherkasy.[47] But as participants outlined their views on art and culture,

[44] A note following this appeal from the editorial board of *Bil'shovyk* stated: "*Bil'shovyk* considers an organization of all revolutionary artistic groups a completely timely proposal and therefore completely supports the idea expressed in the appeal of the Panfuturists and Berezil'" (*Bil'shovyk* 253 [7 November 1923]: 9).

[45] The initials stand for "Hart Amatoriv Robitnychoho Teatru," a rather insignificant theatrical offshoot of Hart (Bondarchuk 1923, 11–12). See also Ellan-Blakytnyi (1958, 2: 171–73).

[46] This appeared originally in *Literatura, nauka, mystetstvo* (supplement to *Visti VUTsVK)* 1923 [13].

[47] Slisarenko spoke in Cherkasy on 18 December 1923. His lecture was entitled, "The Literary Organizations, Panfuturism and the October Coalition of Arts" ("Lektsiï pro panfuturyzm" 1923). Bazhan spoke in Uman' on 20 February 1924. The title was "The October Coalition of Art and Contemporary Literary Organizations"(see *Chervonyi shliakh* 3 [1924]: 273).

it soon became obvious that despite some conciliatory gestures, the differences among them were virtually insurmountable. Consequently, what was supposed to have led toward consolidation deteriorated into acrimonious divisiveness.[48]

Plans for the Coalition remained alive well into February 1924, but as early as 30 December 1923 it was obvious to Berezil' that the idea "had turned out to be premature. The trip from Kharkiv to Kyiv by representatives of Hart and Pluh has in fact brought nothing for the proposed coalition" (*Barkyady teatru* 2–3 [1923]: 1). It seemed that the longer the discussions lasted, the more strain and disillusionment set in among the negotiating groups, so much so that even allies began wrangling among themselves. Pluh and Hart, for example, which at first formed a common negotiating front against Aspanfut and Berezil', entered into conflicts over the definition of their respective spheres of influence. (Hart felt that Pluh was trying to extend its influence to the proletariat rather than limiting itself to the peasantry [Ellan-Blakytnyi 1930b, 108–112].) Berezil' began to view the negotiations with a certain alarm as well, feeling excluded by Aspanfut, which was dominating the process. Berezil' also distrusted Hart and Pluh, expressing the view that both these organizations had entered negotiations in bad faith: when they came to Kyiv, "all their attention seemed to be directed at another possible coalition." Rather than concentrating on Aspanfut and Berezil', they gave the impression of making overtures to "the Neoclassicists, Aspys, VUAN, N. Romanovych-Tkachenko, the Hnat Mykhailychenko Theater, L. Ianovs'ka, [and] the Leontovych Society."[49] Moreover, Berezil' took issue with the "hostile tone" that was emanating from Pluh's public meetings in Kharkiv against Kyiv organizations in general and Aspanfut in particular ("Z redzhurnalu" 1923).

48 The proposal for the October Coalition spawned a fairly sizable literature. Some of the more significant articles relating to this issue are as follows: M.K. (1923, 5); Koriak 1923b; Shevchenko 1923; Semenko 1923c; Semenko 1923d; Doroshkevych 1924a; Semenko 1924a; Pylypenko 1924. Late echoes of the discussion include: "Vede" (1924, 6) and Doroshkevych (1924b).

49 Aspys stands for the "Asotsiiatsiia pys'mennykiv" [Association of Writers], founded in 1923 in Kyiv. Among its members were Valeriian Pidmohyl'nyi, Hryhorii Kosynka, Borys Antonenko-Davydovych, Teodosii Os'machka, Ievhen Pluzhnyk, and M. Halych. VUAN is the acronym for the "Vseukraïns'ka Akademiia nauk" [All-Ukrainian Academy of Sciences]. The Leontovych Society was a music association, publisher of the monthly *Muzyka*. Natalia Romanovych-Tkachenko and Liubov Ianovs'ka were writers of the older generation. The implication here is that Pluh and Hart were ready to form a coalition with "reactionary" forces. Whether this was indeed the case is not certain, but there is evidence that the above organizations and individuals had been contacted (see *Chervonyi shliakh* 1923 [9]: 226).

The sharpest disagreements, and probably the ultimate reason for the failure of the proposed coalition, stemmed from the polarity of views between Hart and Aspanfut, the primary antagonists in this drama. Although the leader of Hart, Vasyl' Ellan-Blakytnyi, tried to be diplomatic, his criticism of the Futurists was so far-reaching and fundamental that it gives the impression of being designed to preclude any possibility of cooperation. While acknowledging that Aspanfut had positive features (for example, it was revolutionary and showed appropriate enmity toward old bourgeois art), he at the same time accused it of "anarchic individualism" and, what was worse, of being "a group of artists and not civic workers."

> While building complex systems (in thin air) for uniting various branches of the arts and sciences, [the Futurists] are, at the same time, categorically refusing to take part in propaganda...or study meetings,...arguing that writers, actors and other artists can obviously find everything they need...for creating "new living conditions [and] a new society" in their own brilliant souls....Aspanfut looks down much too much at the dirty work of agitation, at the work of educating the young, at the work of spreading ideas among common workers and underprivileged people. [This], after all, is the basis on which the new society and its new culture will be formed (Ellan-Blakytnyi 1930b, 106).

Furthermore, said Ellan-Blakytnyi, the "Panfuturists continue to exaggerate the role of artistic and cultural organizations" in Soviet society, refusing to see that they must all be subordinated to the Communist Party, which alone can be the major force in building a communist culture. He took Aspanfut to task for raising its voice against "the Soviet front of culture" (meaning, of course, Hart and Pluh) and for stubbornly insisting that the headquarters of the October Coalition be located in Kyiv ("the center of artistic achievement," according to the Futurists) rather than in Kharkiv, the seat of political power.

Ellan-Blakytnyi's main contentions, namely, that the Futurists were interested in art more than they were in social and ideological work, was driven home in a second article, in which he insisted that the Coalition must be built on ideological grounds and on the premise of social activism, not on artistic or formalist principles. As an example of what it should *not* be, he pointed to several "revolutionary" theaters, among them Berezil' and the Hnat Mykhailychenko Theater. He expressed dismay at the fact that these "artistic organizations" were governed by formal and aesthetic criteria but displayed a poor "social consciousness." On the basis of such reasoning, Ellan-Blakytnyi concluded that although amicable discussions and informal contacts might be feasible, no unity could be expected and no organization could be formed between Hart and such groups.

> The essence,...the foundation [of this Coalition] lies in work among the masses and for the masses; it lies in...those "meetings" that the Panfuturists so resolutely reject; it lies in the crystallization of the world view of the workers of culture, in education,...in dirty, daily work. [This] may not be as impressive as drumming the "rediscovery" of America or of some kind of confounded "system" that supposedly equals Marxism. When all those who call themselves revolutionaries understand this [truth], then the case of the October Coalition of Arts will take off from the point at which it has become stuck (Ellan-Blakytnyi 1930b, 111).[50]

The October Coalition never did off the ground. By the end of February 1924 it was a dead issue, a casualty of the literary wars. For Futurism it had important consequences. Failure of the October Coalition was in effect a vote of no-confidence in Aspanfut, an expression of misgiving about the purportedly new direction it espoused since the August crisis and the acceptance of Iakiv Savchenko. Despite Aspanfut's new pronouncements, critics continued to view it primarily as an artistic organization, one guilty of formalistic sins, of promoting a radical and incomprehensible aesthetic program under the facade of Marxist rhetoric. As Ellan-Blakytnyi maintained, Aspanfut was alienated from life and stood apart from the worker and peasant. It was moving against the tide, against prevailing organizational trends which were epitomized by Pluh and Hart, associations espousing the cause of the "masses" for whom art was first of all a vehicle toward literacy and basic culture. The times required that Aspanfut unambiguously demonstrate that it too was committed to these broad cultural and social goals.

Under these increasingly trying circumstances, the Futurists unveiled to the public a new image. In early 1924 they established an organization modeled on the opposition (that is, Hart and Pluh), an organization with grass-roots appeal, with chapters in outlying cities, and a program, both literary and social, that set out to promote the cause of communist culture.

[50] The reference to "drumming" is clearly an allusion to Geo Shkurupii's collection of poems, *Baraban* [Drum; Shkurupii 1923e].

На літературному фронті.

(Дружні шаржі Е. Мандельберга).

"Druzhni sharzhi E. Mandel'berha: Na literaturnomy fronti." ["Friendly Caricatures by E. Mandel'berh: On the Literary Front." Internal captions have been lost in reproduction: *Top:* "Head of the Kyiv Chapter of 'Pluh' [The Plow] S. Shchupak." *Bottom:* "The Founder of Komunkul't (Aspanfut) Mykhail' Semenko." *Lettering on carriage:* "The Catafalque of Art." *Lettering on gong:* "Gong of the Komunkul't." *Lettering on roadsign:* "Semaphore into the Future."] From *Hlobus* 13–14 (1924): 31.

"'A meeting of the three at a crossing station' —or Semenko, Shkurupii, and Bazhan signal into the future." From *Hlobus* 8 (April 1927): 128.

CHAPTER 4

AsKK: Futurists Among the Masses

Following the fiasco with the October Coalition, the issue for Aspanfut was no longer whether to change but how. While there were individuals in the organization (most notably Iakiv Savchenko) who would have preferred to see the Futurists reject their past completely, it became apparent almost immediately that Aspanfut was not willing to sever its ties with previous theories and practices. One expression of this was the name chosen for the reformed organization: "Aspanfut-Komunkul't."[1] Between January and April 1924 this became the formal designation under which the Futurists were known. On 23 April the hyphenated name gave way to "AsKK" or "Komunkul't," an acronym that stood for "The Association of Communist Culture" (F—l' 1924, 13). Notwithstanding this change, the older terminology remained popular both in and outside the organization.[2]

If there was some vacillation with respect to the organization's name, there was absolute certainty on the theory that was to guide it. Panfuturism, expanded and reinterpreted to accommodate AsKK's new sociocultural orientation, became the official creed. By resorting to revisionist interpretations of their past, Futurists began to claim that their system had always implied more than just a preoccupation with art, that only the "difficult working conditions in Kyiv" had prevented a more balanced presentation of their program (M.S. 1924). To lend legitimacy to their past, the Futurists even resorted to using the new name and concepts when referring to an earlier period of their history.[3] Futurism's foes,

[1] The printed sources are not consistent when referring to this organization. Some of the more frequent versions of the name are "Aspanfut (K)," "Komunkul't (Aspanfut)," "Aspanfut (AsKK)," and "AsKK (Panfuturysty)."

[2] Although the term "Komunkul'tist" (i.e., member of Komunkul't) came into vogue at this time, "Panfuturist" remained equally popular as a synonym. The term "Komunkul't" or "AsKK" was used more frequently toward the end of 1924 and in early 1925. At that time Futurists came under increasing criticism and it seems they preferred the term "Komunkul't," for it carried fewer negative connotations in society

[3] Semenko wrote, for example: "The Association of Komunkul'tists-Panfuturists was established in Kyiv in the fall of 1921....At the beginning of 1922...in the Association of

seeing through this transparent ruse, insisted, as did Vasyl' Ellan-Blakytnyi, that the Komunkul'tists were the same old unreformed Futurists they had always been. He was irked by their misleading alias and took to task officials in the Party for allowing them to use it (see Ellan-Blakytnyi 1930c, 166).

While the proletarian community looked on with skepticism, the Futurists embarked on a course that involved much more than minor cosmetic change. They began making an earnest effort to blend with their literary and political environment, so as to deprive their rivals of the argument that they shunned "dirty work" among the masses. The Futurists were determined to prove that they were not typical elitists alienated from peasants and proletarians (ibid., 165). To achieve this end, they had to overcome the glaring contrast between themselves (a group that appealed to a tiny minority) and organizations like Pluh and Hart, which had local branches in small towns and villages designed to cater to hundreds of individuals through workshops, public meetings, and literary discussions. It was this type of structure that Komunkul't set out to emulate. No longer would the Futurists be content with a few true believers in Kyiv. No longer would literature and art be their sole concern. Their ambition was to become a mass organization with All-Ukrainian, even All-Union status. Their function now would be to deal with culture in the widest sense, focusing in particular on the worker's *pobut,* that is, on all aspects of the workers' daily social existence. Futurists reasoned that they had to diversify beyond the narrow confines of art, if they were to effect the passage of society from bourgeois traditions and habits to new Communist values. To speed the process, AsKK set out to expand the Panfuturist system into a comprehensive theory of culture that would supplant what they considered to be the hopelessly inadequate muddle of Marxist and Leninist writings on this subject.[4]

One of AsKK's central theses was that even though Communist culture was only in its infancy, it was possible to predict that certain bourgeois cultural systems would not enter as components of the new culture. Religion was one of these, art another. Only science and technology had the potential to become the backbone of Communist culture. In giving direction to the new culture, it was necessary therefore to orient the masses toward science and technology, the emblems of rational thought, and away from art and religion. According to the Futurists, it was foolhardy

---

Komunkul'tists a plan for a new orientation —"Komunkul't"— was being devised..." (M.S. 1924, 278).

4 What follows is a schematic summary of the Panfuturist theory. For details see chapter six below.

to allow art to act as an organizing or structuring device of culture when this "emotional" (irrational) system was in its final stages of decline.

> [We must] stop trying to create cultural and educational organizations...around "artistic" formations or those related to them (e.g., literary societies)...[We must] orient, establish and organize all Soviet work on the third [i.e., cultural] front around scientific-technological organizations or those related to them ("Nashi ustanovki" 1924, 3).

AsKK's ambitions were anything but modest. The organization came to view itself as the "political center on the third front and the Gosplan [State Planning Commission] in the area of cultural production" (Semenko 1924f, 5). AsKK would establish chapters in every republic of the Soviet Union and have an All-Union, perhaps even an International, coordinating body.[5] Each republic would have a Research and Ideology Bureau [*Doslidcho-ideolohichne biuro*] directing the work of individual Komunkul't cells or clubs. AsKK members would work in villages, among urban proletariat, and in schools. In short, AsKK would be the guiding light in all types of cultural work and it would aim at producing a "harmoniously developed person" (Slisarenko 1924, 6).

AsKK planned to use two approaches in its work—one constructive, the other destructive. Destructive methods were to be employed against dying cultural systems, especially art and religion, so that their demise might be hastened and their influence on Soviet society neutralized. Constructive methods would be applied to two cultural "sectors," the scientific-technological and the social (*pobut*). As an antidote to art and religion, the masses would be directed toward biophysics, economics, politics, experimentalism, and ecology. In the science and technology sector Futurists also foresaw the pursuit of several "crafts"—short stories, rhetoric, posters, film, and photography (ibid.). In the social (*pobut*) sector Futurists were to promote physical culture, sports, personal hygiene, and recreation. The latter would be done according to the principles of "scientific management of labor" or, as it was literally known in the Soviet Union, "scientific organization of labor" (abbreviated NOP).[6] Not coincidentally, scientific management was at this time a prominent issue to which considerable attention was being devoted in the Soviet media. AsKK viewed any promoter of these principles as its natural ally;

[5] Slisarenko (1924, 6). See also (ibid., 17).

[6] NOP (*Naukova orhanizatsiia pratsi*) in Ukrainian and NOT (*Nauchnaia organizatsiia truda*) in Russian. The founder of scientific management was the American Frederick Winslow Taylor (1865–1915), often mentioned in the Soviet press.

it was particularly sympathetic to the All-Union "League of Time" [*Liga Vremia-NOT*], publisher of *Vremia* [Time] (1923–1925). AsKK considered the ideas of scientific management relevant not only in the social but also in the artistic realm. On several occasions Semenko brought up NOP in reference to art. A member of Berezil' even assessed NOP's meaning for the theater (Semenko 1924e, Bondarchuk 1924).

The core principles of the expanded Panfuturist theory were ready by January 1924. On 6 January Semenko gave a lecture to his fellow Futurists entitled "The Theory of Cults [Systems] as a Philosophical Foundation of Panfuturism."[7] Savchenko and Slisarenko were impressed by this report, saying that Semenko's views were of "great theoretical value for contemporary Marxist science," and urged that they be further elaborated ("Do poshyrennia" 1924). For precisely this purpose Aspanfut-Komunkul't met no less than six times during the month of January to discuss Panfuturism. The speakers at these meetings were Semenko ("The Foundations of Panfuturism"), Oleksa Slisarenko ("The Program and Perspectives for Panfuturist Prose"), Iakiv Savchenko ("The Relationship between Ideology and Facture"), Volodymyr Iaroshenko ("Ukrainian Literature and Meta-Art; Panfuturist Tactics"), Nik Bazhan ("The Mutual Relationship and Linkage Between Religion and Art"), and Geo Shkurupii ("An Examination of the Existing Views on Art in Marxist Literature and Their Differences; The Reform Panfuturism Introduces to This Question") (Kachaniuk 1930, 1–2: 186).

A final and comprehensive statement on the new Panfuturist system did not appear until late 1924 when Semenko published a thirty-two page article, "On Applying Leninism to the Third Front" (Semenko 1924b). Until then, Futurists relied mostly on their public appearances, open meetings, and press summaries to promote their views. On 16 March, for example, Geo Shkurupii gave a lecture at the Kyiv Medical Institute entitled "What is Panfuturism" (*Bil'shovyk* 61 [15 March 1924]: 4; and 63 [18 March 1924]: 6). Speaking before an audience made up of members of the Union of Workers of Art, Semenko raised the issue of "Art Today," expounding ideas that later were incorporated into "On Applying Leninism..." (*Bil'shovyk* 76 [4 April 1924]: 6). On 13 April, Geo Shkurupii was scheduled to speak before an AsKK meeting on the subject of "Destructive Work Today" (*Bil'shovyk* 81 [10 April 1924]: 6). Other announced topics in this series included "Art, Revolution, and Panfuturism" (Nik Sukhomlyn); "Expressionism and Its Place in the

7 See "Shyroke zasidannia" (1924, 6). This lecture was later published in *Chervonyi shliakh* 1924 (3) as "Mystetstvo iak kul't" (Semenko 1924d).

Panfuturist System" (Vira Cherednychenko); "Lef and Panfuturism" (Nik Bazhan); "Theater and Anti-Theater" (Geo Shkurupii) ("U Komunkul'tovtsiv" 1924). These topics were also brought up before audiences consisting of common laborers. Nik Bazhan, for example, spoke before a club of printers about "The Komunkul't System as a Factor in the Creation of a New Culture, New Society and [New] Living Conditions." According to a published summary, Bazhan agitated for the ideas of NOP, good hygiene, and the creation of a new person. Moreover, while promoting the utilitarian exploitation of art, he "hurled deadly slogans against classical art and against [all] degenerating phenomena that [continue to] exist to this day" (*Bil'shovyk* 85 [15 April 1924]: 4). A few days later, Bazhan spoke to a group of metal workers about building Communist culture and the problems of art in the age of transition ("Vystup Komunkul'tovtsiv" 1924). Speaking in the same vein, Savchenko appeared before an audience of students to advocate NOP, Marxism in art and the utilitarian exploitation of art for the creation of a new culture. He also reportedly rejected art as a "pure," personal category (*Bil'shovyk* 70 [28 March 1924]: 4).[8]

Appearances like these were characteristic of the methods Futurists used to court the masses. Such practices peaked between February and June 1924, tapering off thereafter. In the months of March and April alone AsKK reported having more than twenty appearances and lectures (*Bil'shovyk* 114 [21 May 1924]: 4; *Honh komunkul'ta* 1924, 13). Most often they took place at various institutes (pedagogical, technical, medical, metallurgical, polytechnical), schools (commerce and trade), factories, and workers' clubs. Futurists appeared less frequently in institutions like the Building of Culture and the M. Zan'kovets'ka Theater. Demand for the Futurists was apparently so high that AsKK was forced ultimately to limit these activities:

> Due to intensive internal organizational work in the Association, public appearances will not take place more than twice a week. Factories, clubs, institutions of higher learning and other organizations wishing to arrange the appearance of Aspanfut-Komunkul't at their location are requested to notify the Central Bureau [of AsKK] in advance so that

8 These and other lectures given by the Futurists were never published and, therefore, it is impossible to know what precisely was said in them. An exception is Slisarenko's lecture of this period ("Ukraïns'ka literatura i Panfuturyzm") which was published in Kachaniuk (1930, 1–2: 187–89). In March 1924 AsKK admitted that most of its theoretical material "awaits publication" due to "the absence of our own journal" (see *Bil'shovyk* 67 [23 March 1924]: 5).

the Association's calendar might be better regulated (*Bil'shovyk* 78 [6 April 1924]: 6).

These public forays had a relatively fixed format. A keynote speaker discussed an aspect of the Futurist program or theory. This was followed by "demonstrations of practical work," meaning that Futurists would read from their literary works. The floor was then opened for discussion and comments, including written questions from the audience. In a two-month period the Futurists received 813 inquiries. A majority of these referred to the lectures or readings but some were also "attacks, pranks, and rebukes" designed to discredit AsKK. It was said that the organization was assailed especially by advocates of "great, holy art." Some of AsKK's appearances turned into direct confrontations with the Neoclassicists (Sotnyk 1924, 13–14).[9]

If the reports that appeared in *Bil'shovyk* are to be believed, nearly everywhere the Futurists went they were given a warm reception. Typically, reports speak of "the auditorium's great satisfaction" or note that the "Komunkul'tists were received [by the audience] as active creators of a steel-like proletarian culture" ("Vystup Komunkul'tovtsiv" 1924; "Vystup Komunkul't-Aspanfut" 1924). In some instances resolutions were drafted by the spectators, commending AsKK's performance. For example, the following was adopted by students of the Higher Technical College of Trade and Economy [*Vyshchyi torhovel'nyi tekhnikum*]:

> The student body..., having heard the lecture about the work of Komunkul't and the basic principles of Panfuturism, stresses that it will always support revolutionary organizations in every manner possible and in particular Komunkul't, which stands at the forefront of the creation of a Communist culture (*Bil'shovyk* 55 [6 March 1924]: 4).[10]

Another resolution, passed by a club at the Kyiv Technical College of Commerce [*Kyïvs'kyi hospodars'kyi tekhnikum*], declared:

> In the name of the Taras Shevchenko Literary Club...we express sincere gratitude to [our] Panfuturist comrades for introducing us to contemporary literary movements and their work. Your appearance here...has broadened our knowledge [and] will give us the ability to develop our own work in the club in this direction (cited in Sotnyk 1924, 14).

The Futurists claimed that following their lectures Komunkul't cells were inevitably formed in the technical colleges, schools, or workers'

9 For more on the conflict between Futurists and Neoclassicists see Ia. Savchenko 1923a, 1924b; Demchuk 1924.

10 Reprinted in *Honh komunkul'ta* 1924, 14.

clubs where they had appeared (Sotnyk 1924, 15). For organizational and ideological reasons, these cells were highly prized by the Futurists. As the smallest units in their organizational structure, they were their most direct links to the "masses." These were agencies by which workers would give form and substance to the new society. A Komunkul't slogan declared: "Building a Communist culture Is a Task for the Hands and Brains of the Workers Themselves." Parenthetically, however, Futurists were wont to add: "...with the help of the intelligentsia" ("Klubni iacheiki 'Komunkul't'" 1924, 4; and Zatvornyts'kyi 1924b).

In general, there is little information about these cells, their numbers, and their activities. An exception is "The First of May Agitational Workshop of the Komunkul't," known as Agmas (Ahmas), a theatrical group founded and headed by Hlib Zatvornyts'kyi.[11] The purpose of Agmas was to rally workers around the ideas of AsKK and help them create a new social order on a "foundation of rationalism and NOP" (Zatvornyts'kyi 1924a, 8). Agmas activities seem to have been limited primarily to the Union of Kyiv Construction Workers [*Spilka budivel'nykh robitnykiv mista Kyieva*] where it engaged in anti-religious propaganda by performing agitational plays (*Bil'shovyk* 17 [20 January 1924]: 6).

Like Pluh and Hart, AsKK was determined to have its own theater and devoted considerable energy toward establishing one. The issue was first raised at an AsKK meeting in March, when members discussed the "organization of an Aspanfut theater" (*Bil'shovyk* 53 [4 March 1924]: 4). In June and July efforts were under way to create what was by then referred to as the Komunkul't Workers' Theater, with Zatvornyts'kyi as director (*Bil'shovyk* 162 [20 July 1924]: 6; *Chervonyi shliakh* 6 [1924]: 253). However, this plan apparently led nowhere because a few months later Zatvornyts'kyi was mentioned only in connection with Agmas (*Chervonyi shliakh* 6 [1924]: 320). Moreover, AsKK began speaking about a completely new entity, the Agit-Theater of the Komunkul't, which began work in the late summer of 1924. Directed by AsKK member O. Kapler, this theater staged several performances and reportedly "was already playing a perceptible role in Kyiv's theatrical life." AsKK prided itself on the fact that its initiative had "met with a positive and friendly reception from responsible party organs" (ibid.).

To realize its ambition of becoming a national organization, AsKK encouraged affiliate chapters wherever possible. Until 1924, Futurists had ignored such activity, even though there had been isolated cases of

[11] He was later assisted by Leonid Frenkel'. See "Ahmas im. 1-ho travnia," *Honh komunkul'ta* 1924, 13; *Chervonyi shliakh* 8–9 (1924): 320.

organizations sympathetic to their cause springing up in small towns as early as 1922. Now, however, AsKK pursued even the slightest sign of interest and sent associates to outlying areas to stimulate membership. Small AsKK affiliates were founded in places like Berezan', Viitovets', Pryluky, Rzhyshcheva, and Shepetivka. In Berezan', for example, students of the local AsKK chapter published two issues of a journal called *Dynamit* [Dynamite] "dedicated," as they said, "to Komunkul't's theory" (EM. Shch-k 1924, 15; *Bil'shovyk* 124 [1 June 1924]: 6). In April a chapter was established in the town of Fastiv. It prided itself on being formed from "the most conscious [and] active members of all the local organizations..." (*Chervonyi shliakh* 6 [1924]: 253). There is evidence that AsKK additionally tried to extend its influence into the Kuban' region (*Bil'shovyk* 149 [4 July 1924]: 6).[12]

AsKK's two most significant provincial organizations were located in Uman' and Odesa. The Uman' chapter was founded on 15 March 1924 following a lecture by Nik Bazhan. Headed by a certain Ia. Tytiunenko, this group was composed of students from the Lenin Agricultural Institute who, it was said, were "enthusiastically" engaged in work and requested further guidance and materials from the Kyiv center. This chapter anticipated publishing the journal *Panfut* on 30 March (Babiuk 1924).

The Odesa branch was the largest and most active of AsKK's organizations. Dubbed the Southern Regional Organization [*Pivdenna kraieva orhanizatsiia*], it had a sphere of influence that ostensibly included the districts of Odesa, Zaporizhzhia, Katerynoslav, Podillia, and Crimea (unfortunately, the nature and extent of its activities cannot be determined; *Chervonyi shliakh* 8–9 [1924]: 320). July reports stated that the Odesa chapter had established close ties with the Russian-language avant-garde journal *Iugo-Lef* and that they had initiated something called the Communist Coalition of the Arts [*Komunistychnyi blok mystetstv*]. These reports even indicated that *Iugo-Lef* merged with AsKK on 10 July (*Bil'shovyk* 163 [22 July 1924]: 4). The editor of *Iugo-Lef*, Leonid Nedolia (a Ukrainian who would later join Semenko in Kharkiv) explained that while "the program and practice of Komunkul't...is 99% congruent with the work of Lef..." and that while both groups "act everywhere in Odesa as a unified front," "the question of merging [the two organizations] was postponed" because of certain unstated "conditions in the South" (Nedolia 1924a). Iugo-Lef continued to function as an independent organization until February 1925, perhaps because Odesa-AsKK was opposed to a merger (Kachaniuk 1930, 1–2: 191). In the fall of 1924

[12] My copy of this issue is so defective that I cannot provide any details.

reference was made only to the good understanding and close contact between the two organizations (*Chervonyi shliakh* 8–9 [1924]: 320). It should be noted that *Iugo-Lef* published Nedolia's Ukrainian verse in addition to his Russian works, as well as his scathing criticism of Pluh leader Serhii Pylypenko (Nedolia 1924b and1924c).

It is impossible to calculate the exact number of people AsKK embraced through its organizations and cells. In Kyiv it claimed over sixty members and candidates (*Honh komunkul'ta* 1924, 12). The Odesa branch had a minimum of eighteen members (Kachaniuk 1930, 1–2: 191).[13] Uman' reported having seven members and eleven candidates when it was organized (*Bil'shovyk* 71 [29 March 1924]: 4). These figures, however, are incomplete and in most cases probably refer only to full-fledged members. This means that they do not reflect participants, students, and workers who frequented cells or took part in instructional workshops. Pluh offers an analogy. In February 1925 it claimed to have 800 individuals in its various branches throughout Ukraine, but called only 150 of them "real members" ("Meta 'Pluzhanyna'" 1925).[14]

When speaking about numbers one must bear in mind that many individuals collaborated with AsKK while belonging officially to other organizations. This was true of Berezil' members who had frequent dealings with AsKK. In March, twenty-five members of Berezil's Workshop No. 2 sent a letter to Aspanfut-Komunkul't expressing their "deep gratitude" to Semenko and Savchenko for lectures they had delivered, adding that they completely shared AsKK's ideological orientation and were hoping that Aspanfut would further expand its activities (*Bil'shovyk* 60 [14 March 1924]: 6). In May it was asserted that "in the last few months AsKK and Berezil' have been brought closer together" and that their "complete agreement" on the basic issues amounted to "a de facto organizational fusion between Berezil'" and AsKK (*Honh komunkul'ta* 1924, 13). This statement was given credence when AsKK published *Honh komunkul'ta* [Gong of the Komunkul't, 1924] in which Berezil' members Les' Kurbas, Hnat Ihnatovych, and Favst Lopatyns'kyi were listed as "co-workers." A month later, when AsKK announced it would begin publishing a series of literary collections under the title *Komunkul't* (unfortunately never realized), the editorial board, not surprisingly, was composed of, among others, Kurbas and Vadym Meller, Berezil's set and costume designer (*Bil'shovyk* 127 [5 June

13 This calculation is based on the number of persons who voted at a 1925 meeting. It is probably not an accurate gauge of membership.

14 In their almanac, *Pluh* (1924), they enumerated only 63 members.

1924]: 6). At a 31 August general meeting, Kurbas was accepted into AsKK as a "real member" ("U Kyïv AsKK" 1924).

In the fall of 1924 AsKK established a working relationship with Pluh. The latter was continually warring with Hart. As tensions between the two increased, Pluh began seeking closer alliances with other organizations, specifically VUAPP and AsKK (Lebid' 1925, 89).[15] Pluh then began allowing its own members to join AsKK (Ellan-Blakytnyi 1930c, 167). This brought several Pluh members under AsKK's influence (for example, Vira Cherednychenko and Hryts'ko Koliada). The two organizations even decided to collaborate on a joint publication, *Zhurnal dlia vsikh* [The Magazine for Everyone, 1925]. When it appeared several months later it featured a most unlikely editorial board: Semenko, Shkurupii, Mykhailo Ialovyi [Iu. Shpol], and the leader of Pluh, Serhii Pylypenko.

AsKK's ranks were also strengthened by defections from Hart's Kyiv branch. The first to abandon Kyiv-Hart was V. Voruns'kyi. He joined the Futurists in February, explaining that he did so because Aspanfut-Komunkul't was an organization where the "really revolutionary forces" were congregated (Zhorzh 1924). In March he was followed by N. Shcherbyna (N. Litak), who praised "the Panfuturists (Komunkul'tists) [for having] a Communist orientation," while denouncing Hart for being "ideologically superficial" in art and for pursuing an antiquated "aestheticism" (*Bil'shovyk* 58 [9 March 1924]; see Zhorzh 1924).

Hart ignored the first defection, but the second received an official reply. The two young men, it said, "would have [been] ejected [like] rubbish...sooner or later." Hart contended the desertions were staged by the Panfuturists (something they denied) and that the men were, at any rate, simply pawns in a dispute between organizations. Hart considered the incident not only an attack on itself but on the KP(b)U as well, because AsKK had insulted an organization founded on Marxism and Party resolutions (*Bil'shovyk* 61 [15 March 1924]: 4). Hart's letter ended by listing those Kyiv-Hart members who continued to be in good standing.

Ironically, soon after this reply was published, the Secretary of the Kyiv organization, Ievhen Kaplia-Iavors'kyi, and another member, a certain Skurativs'kyi, also broke ranks with Hart. In their joint letter to *Bil'shovyk*, they stated that Hart in general and Kyiv-Hart in particular lacked any consistent plan of action, had no artistic platform, and was merely spreading philistinism and anarchy. On the other hand, after

15 VUAPP stands for Vseukraïns'ka asotsiiatsiia proletars'kykh pys'mennykiv [The All-Ukrainian Association of Proletarian Writers].

"examining the work of Aspanfut (Komunkul't), one can see [several] positive features: sharply demarcated lines of work, production that is useful for the present, a practical program for differentiating the masses, a completely class-based definition of the role of art today...[and] activities...that are firmly allied to the work of the Communist Party and the Soviets....All this compels us to leave Hart and join Aspanfut (Komunkul't)" (Zhorzh 1924).

Although AsKK worked hard to establish its credentials as a social and cultural organization, it never abandoned its destructive and exstructive artistic interests. AsKK had a Literary Sector (paralleling the Science and Technology, and Social [*pobut*] Sectors) which consisted of a Production Bureau and a literary workshop. The Production Bureau met to discuss and criticize works written by senior members of AsKK and to set publishing goals. The literary workshop, which opened in February 1924, was called the Workshop for Word Montage [*Maisternia montazhu slova*]. Designed for young promising writers, it had sections devoted to the study of poetry, prose, drama, film scripts, journalism, and public speaking ("Maisternia Litsektora" 1924). The instructors were Iakiv Savchenko, Nik Bazhan, Mykhail' Semenko, Hlib Zatvornyts'kyi, Geo Shkurupii, Oleksa Slisarenko, and Volodymyr Iaroshenko ("Maisternia montazhu slova" 1924, 6; *Honh komunkul'ta* 1924, 13). Among the students who attended this workshop were Oleksa Vlyz'ko and Iurii Ianovs'kyi (ibid.).

AsKK had more literary plans than it was capable of bringing to fruition. *Honh komunkul'ta*, a theoretical and programmatic journal that appeared in May, was to have been supplemented in June by a "journal like *Lef*" (*Bil'shovyk* 114 [21 May 1924]: 4). Nothing of the kind appeared. Instead, AsKK announced in June that it had reached an agreement with the Kharkiv publishing house Red Path [*Chervonyi shliakh*] to publish a series of periodic collections entitled *Komunkul't*, the first of which was scheduled for the end of summer. An announcement read: "It is hoped that these collections will fill a great gap. Kyiv does not have the necessary journals where AsKK's long works, both theoretical and literary, can be published. This remains a roadblock to [our] normal and healthy development" ("Zbirnyky 'Komunkul't'" 1924). Simultaneously, AsKK revealed that two issues of *Honh komunkul'ta* would be published in Uman' and Odesa respectively, before becoming a regular bimonthly in Kyiv (*Chervonyi shliakh* 6 [1924]: 253).

Because of these publishing prospects, AsKK made a decision in September to move its headquarters from Kyiv to Kharkiv, where the organization hoped to publish not just *Komunkul't* but a bimonthly, mass-circulation magazine called *Radio-zhurnal* [Radio-Journal] (*Chervonyi shliakh* 8–9 [1924]: 321). Work had already begun there on AsKK's and Pluh's joint publication, *Zhurnal dlia vsikh*. In this way Kharkiv became the newest AsKK outpost. Delegated to manage it were Semenko, Slisarenko, Ialovyi, M. Shcherbak, Grigorii Petnikov (a Russian poet), Hryts'ko Koliada, and Mykola (Nik) Bazhan.

The move to Kharkiv was a turning point for AsKK. Between June and September, a perceptible shift of emphasis had occurred in the organization. Energy previously spent on expansion and establishing links with the masses was gradually being chanelled into literary and publishing pursuits. In September AsKK was sending out directives to its outlying organizations urging them to prepare materials for the collection *Komunkul't* and "other journals." Bazhan and Frenkel' were entrusted with preparing an artistic publishing plan (*Bil'shovyk* 210 [18 September 1924]: 4). Elsewhere AsKK announced that "in the upcoming year" the organization would be more "production" oriented with members taking "a most active part in all organs of the press and publishing houses" (*Chervonyi shliakh* 8–9 [1924]: 321).

What the announcement failed to say was that this programmatic about-face had been extracted at a high cost to the organization. In August, as the changes became more obvious and imminent, AsKK went through a serious crisis. The first sign was the expulsion of Volodymyr Iaroshenko and the suspension for two months of Iakiv Savchenko on account of his "unclear and ambivalent behavior" (*Chervonyi shliakh* 8–9 [1924]: 320; *Bil'shovyk* 198 [2 September 1924]: 4). A few weeks later Savchenko's membership was entirely revoked (*Bil'shovyk* 210 [18 September 1924]: 4). By then it was obvious what had happened. On 21 August a rift split the organization in two. Iaroshenko, Savchenko, and Mykola Tereshchenko seceded, taking with them a number of younger associates (Ianovs'kyi, Tadei Sliusarenko, Nik Sukhomlyn, Kaplia-Iavors'kyi, Oleksa Vlyz'ko, Borys [?] Kovalenko, and a certain Skurativs'kyi). This group formed a shadow organization with exactly the same name, AsKK.

An article written by Samiilo Shchupak immediately following this event gives a fairly good account of why the schism occurred. Entitled "The Struggle and Victory over Conservatism in Art," it was above all else a public endorsement of the secessionist group. Shchupak conceded that Ukrainian Futurists, by evolving from "pure Futurism" to Panfuturism, had played a "positive role in the development of their own organization and in the literary life of Ukraine." However, the time had come for everyone who was "sensitive to the needs of the revolution and the proletarian masses" to abandon "leftist formalism" and "theorizing" and engage in "real literary creativity." He saw a clear desire for this among the young writers of AsKK, who were being driven in this direction by "life itself." Unfortunately, said Shchupak, "the old generation of Futurists became an obstacle" when they insisted that Futurist principles must prevail "über alles." Despite their new name and practical activities, "the Panfuturist system remained the principal point in the work of the Komunkul'tists." The creators of Futurism refused to listen to the demands of the young and were dictatorially promoting their own line. These "maniacs of Futurism" were obstructing the growth of their organization, preventing it from making progress. In conclusion Shchupak said, "We are completely on the side of those who did not want to become stuck in the quagmire of impotent intellectual ruminations [*inteligenshchyna*] and who are advancing toward active creative work for the benefit of the proletarian revolution" (Shchupak 1924a).

The renegades themselves were at first less forthcoming about the reasons for their break. Even so, it is evident from a report of their first general meeting that they had been quite dissatisfied with AsKK's ideological position and especially with the lack of practical work among the masses. The meeting "sharply condemned all tactical or ideological mistakes that were made in the past year both by AsKK as a whole and by its individual members." It also declared that in the upcoming year it would put greater emphasis on visiting industry, workers' clubs, and cultural-educational institutions ("Zahal'ni zbory" 1924).

For the next five months the splinter group and the original organization continued their respective activities while becoming increasingly more alienated from one another. AsKK proper kept moving further and further away from the mass orientation, devoting itself to the literary publication *Hol'fshtrom* [Gulf Stream]. Eventually, the secessionists decided that it was time to renounce AsKK entirely. In February 1925 they formed a new body called Zhovten' [October]—an "organization of workers for a proletarian culture." In a declaration that appeared in *Proletars'ka pravda* [Proletarian Truth], a group of fourteen explained why a "schism" and then a "final organizational and ideological rupture" had taken place in AsKK.[16] The major problem, they contended, was that AsKK spouted revolutionary phrases but approached the building

[16] The fourteen were: Vasyl' Desniak, V. Dev'iatin, N. Denysenko, Ievhen Kaplia-Iavors'kyi, Ivan Le, S. Novin, Tadei Sliusarenko, Iakiv Savchenko, Mykola Tereshchenko, [?], Khrystyn, V. Shum, Feliks Iakubovs'kyi, Iurii Ianovs'kyi, and Volodymyr Iaroshenko.

of Communist culture with its entire Futurist heritage intact. The group felt AsKK had been wrong in rejecting the concept of a Proletarian culture and had failed to engage in adequate "mass civic activity." The signatories claimed they had tried to turn AsKK in the direction of genuine mass-oriented work, but had been barred by a leadership that suffered from the illness of Futurism and showed no sign of wishing to restore itself to health ("Lyst-Dekliaratsiia" 1930).

In step with these problems, AsKK's relationship with Pluh was deteriorating. The journal on which the two organizations had been collaborating, *Zhurnal dlia vsikh,* was suddenly aborted after the first issue appeared in February. That same month Serhii Pylypenko published a stinging attack against Semenko for his article, "On Applying Leninism to the Third Front." Writing in *Pluzhanyn* [The Plowman], Pylypenko rejected Semenko's notion that the Communist Party had an unclear position on art and accused him of "blasphemy" for invoking the great name of Lenin in connection with his own theories. The leader of Futurism, said Pylypenko, was a friend of "bourgeois art" (Pylypenko 1925).

It was Pluh, apparently, that began encouraging the secessionist camp in AsKK to form a separate organization, hoping in this way to establish a common front against Hart and AsKK. Not everyone in Pluh approved of this tactic. Shchupak, for example, was in favor of the disintegration of AsKK, but expressed misgivings about the prospect of two "revolutionary" organizations like Hart and Pluh fighting one another. He was vehemently against the creation of Zhovten', believing that it fostered divisiveness on the revolutionary front. He argued that the leadership of Pluh was correct in helping the splinter group in AsKK "to free itself from the chains of Panfuturism" but considered it reprehensible that Pluh should stimulate the birth of Zhovten' for the purpose of using it "as a weapon against Hart" (Shchupak 1925). Ironically, Pluh's maneuvering was not rewarded. When Zhovten' published its declaration, it disparaged not only AsKK, but Hart and Pluh, as well. In fact, Zhovten' said there were no literary-artistic organizations in Ukraine worthy of emulation and chose to model itself on the Russian group *Oktiabr'* [October].

In theory, the falling-away of Savchenko and his group opened the doors for AsKK to scale down its organization, consolidate its gains, and move forward with greater emphasis on literary matters. This did not occur. Rather than liberating the organization, the schism became a prelude to AsKK's total collapse.

The death-knell was sounded at the Kharkiv headquarters.[17] Sometime

[17] The following events are reconstructed on the basis of Ialovyi's article, "Do ob'iednannia AsKK (Komunkul't) iz Hartom" (Ialovyi 1930, 141–45).

at the end of March 1925, two members of the Central Bureau, the executive body of AsKK, began expressing a desire to join Hart. These two, presumably Slisarenko and Ialovyi (the source is not specific), were followed by a third (Shkurupii), who made it known that he too intended to quit AsKK. On 2 April 1925 Semenko, Slisarenko, Shkurupii, et al., met in Kharkiv to discuss the problem. The dissenting members were gracious. Shkurupii even rescinded his resignation as a gesture of good will to his colleagues, but remained adamant about withdrawing. Everyone wanted to separate amicably. To avoid the appearance of internal conflict and to ensure an orderly end, a resolution was drafted proposing a merger with a proletarian organization that did not contradict AsKK's tenets. Strangely, this turned out to be Hart. Voting in favor of this union were Slisarenko, Shkurupii and Ialovyi; voting against—Bazhan and Semenko. For the sake of harmony and "in order to carry out this resolution painlessly," the minority was asked to give its assent. Bazhan did after reflecting on the issue for a day. Semenko, however, refused. On 5 April *Visti VUTsVK* carried "An Agreement between the Organization Hart and AsKK (Komunkul't)" signed by all the above except Semenko. This marked the official end of AsKK and all its provincial organizations. Semenko made a last-ditch effort to side-track this merger by creating a new Central Bureau in Kharkiv and even a new regional bureau in Odesa headed by Dan Sotnyk, a photographer. But to no avail: on 17 April the Odesa branch met to discuss the events in Kharkiv; after hearing a report from Slisarenko, it passed a resolution by a vote of 14 to 4 in favor of accepting the 2 April decision. Moreover, the organization denounced Semenko and Sotnyk for their intrigues and stated that any organization that might emerge would be considered a fraud (Kachaniuk 1930, 1–2: 191). Such was the end of AsKK.

At first glance, the precipitous slide of this organization into extinction may seem baffling. Defections and attacks were obviously factors, but it is hard to accept them as the decisive blows that destroyed AsKK. The Futurists, after all, had experienced such things before and had always managed to survive. What is particularly curious about this sudden demise is that it occurred without denunciations or recriminations (leaving aside, of course, Semenko's desperate actions and the resolution of the Odesa branch). It appears that the members of the Central Bureau went out of their way to try to avoid a hostile confrontation. At the same time, they showed an unshakable determination to end the life of AsKK. Why?

AsKK died not because of any schism (although behind-the-scenes Party pressures probably played a role), but mainly from a lack of will to persevere. It seems that its members no longer cared to deal with the myriad of problems their institution was generating. Ialovyi spelled it out this way:

> It has become apparent that Komunkul't, having advocated pertinent contemporary slogans for the cultural and artistic front and, having been besieged by large numbers of "unpolished, gray" masses was confronted with [the problem of] insufficient cadres, both in terms of numbers and qualification, who would be capable, on the one hand, of elaborating and applying the fundamentals of Komunkul't to concrete daily situations and, on the other, to...prevent other organizations from exploiting them either for themselves or against AsKK... *The process of forming a mass Komunkul't organization is experiencing a deep developmental crisis...* (Ialovyi 1930, 142, 144; *emphasis added*).

The proposed solution was startling:

> The Association *must refuse at the moment to engage in extensive mass work,* it must narrow its organizational framework, take a brief respite and direct all its energy toward preparatory work, workshops and theory [in order] to create its own permanent and qualified cadres...(ibid., 142; *emphasis added*).

This, in effect, is what AsKK had set out to do in the fall of 1924 when it began de-emphasizing its civic activities and increasing its literary output. Organizational gamesmanship and public activism seem to have exhausted AsKK. Commitment to these pursuits waned radically after the schism. Judging by the organization's shift toward publishing, it is obvious that the idea of a civic, mass-oriented organization had lost its appeal to the leadership. It is equally clear that no one had the desire or strength to face down the criticism that such an admission would bring down on them. It was simply easier to do away with the organization. "Merging" with Hart proved to be an ideal solution, primarily because it was face-saving. Outright dissolution of AsKK would have been an embarrassing admission of defeat. A merger, on the other hand, obviated the need to cope with thankless internal reforms: they automatically became Hart's problem. Finally, this approach gave the appearance that Futurists were not rejecting the mass-orientation but were simply embracing it in another guise. Ialovyi said as much:

> Present adherents of Komunkul't have no other place to go except into the [cultural-artistic proletarian] organizations. [They] must be among the great masses of the proletariat.... In...Hart...every Komunkul'tist will find for himself a limitless field of opportunity for enhancing his theoretical work and for [engaging in] *extensive mass activities....* Komunkul'tists never brought up the rear, they never turned tail...and they will not now...All other organizations must follow in the footsteps

> of [the Odesa branch] in order that we might emerge from this crisis honorably, amicably, and well-organized and continue, in a new organizational form, along the path that leads to the creation of a Communist culture (ibid., 144–45; *emphasis added*).

By this time, Ialovyi was clearly paying only lip-service to an idea whose time had passed. The Futurists were not excited by the "mass activities" Hart offered; they were seeking a way to extricate their members from them so they might be able to pursue literary matters. Indicative of this was the appearance of *Hol'fshtrom* shortly after AsKK merged with Hart (*Hol'fshtrom* 1925).[18] Heralded as the first in a series, this miscellany was in fact the final act of the organization. As AsKK's only publication devoted exclusively to literature, it was a good indication of the direction the Futurists were heading before they abandoned ship.

The end of AsKK meant the end of a course along which the Futurists had traveled for almost four years. To be sure, that course was not peculiarly their own. It was characteristic of the general literary process that insisted on using literature as a tool of enlightenment and Marxist ideology. Like so many of their contemporaries, Futurists tried to give their own meaning to the empty terms "proletarian" and "communist." Under external pressure, they had acceded to the mass orientation, believing that in this way they could maintain and perhaps even expand the influence of the avant-garde.

It could be said, therefore, that the history of the Futurist movement up to 1925 ran parallel to the developments of Ukrainian literature as a whole. Conversely, the crisis of Futurism, its disillusionment with mass forms of organization, can be seen as a reflection in microcosm of a larger crisis in Ukrainian letters. The collapse of AsKK was just one in a series of signs that pointed to what Shchupak called "a reaction against the civic forms of literary organization." When he observed that "some young Ukrainian writers are tormented by the thought that perhaps all these literary organizations are superfluous and that perhaps it is better to exist independently as an individual writer," he was not speaking only about the Futurists (Shchupak 1925, 61). Disgruntlement with this form of literary life had spread to many writers and burst forth in the great Literary Discussion that began in April 1925.[19] This proved to be a

[18] The contributors here were: Geo Shkurupii, Oleksa Slisarenko, Mykola Bazhan, Hryts'ko Koliada, Leonid Frenkel', O. Kapler, Mykola Shcherbak, N. Shcherbyna, Grigorii Petnikov, and S. Levitina. Notably absent was Mykhail' Semenko.

[19] On the "Literary Discussion," see Luckyj 1956, Shkandrij 1992, Khvyl'ovyi 1986, and Khvyl'ovyi 1990a.

fundamental challenge to the principles that had governed Ukrainian literature until then. In a reversal that was both sudden and spectacular, a host of voices were heard criticizing the mass organizations as seats of ignorance and literary incompetence. The idea that sheer numbers could be a measure of an organization's success was dismissed as a bad joke, and the issue of literary quality was put forward for universal consideration. Perhaps the most revealing aspect of the change sweeping through the literary establishment was that the leader of this discussion was no other than Mykola Khvyl'ovyi, a former Proletkul'tist, member of Hart, and enemy of Formalists, Futurists, and Neoclassicists. Another sure sign of the times was that the Neoclassicist Mykola Zerov emerged as an informal ally and supporter of Khvyl'ovyi, and himself managed to gain a measure of respect and acceptance that he had not known since the revolution.[20]

As opinion turned against mass organizations, there arose a strong need for a truly professional literary association, composed of mature writers who would be free from civic and bureaucratic responsibilities. Such sentiments finally destroyed Hart at the end of 1925 and led to the creation of VAPLITE (*Vil'na akademiia proletarskoï literatury* [Free Academy of Proletarian Literature]), which marked a historic turning point in Ukrainian literature. Naturally, adherents of the mass orientation were not easily dissuaded, and they began a long campaign of attacks against VAPLITE for its elitism and formalism. There were some (for example, Samiilo Shchupak) who specifically faulted Futurists for the demise of Hart and the creation of VAPLITE, saying that they were, by their very nature, supporters of such causes, having "always [been] formalists and enemies of mass work" (Nevira 1925, 26). Such views were not necessarily fanciful. VAPLITE, after all, harbored many a former Futurist: Ialovyi (Shpol) was president; Slisarenko was Secretary, while Bazhan, Shkurupii, and Ianovs'kyi were members.

The consensus that gave birth to VAPLITE was not built around any particular literary school or movement (although Formalist ideas and romantic tendencies were popular). Rather it was founded on the general assumption that after years of organizational bustle, the writer deserved an opportunity to serve his craft. VAPLITE recognized that the masses needed guidance and education but felt it was not the duty of the professional writer to provide them. The writer had an equally urgent task to perform, namely, to defend high culture, to serve the young

[20] Consider Zerov's defense of Khvyl'ovyi and the access the Neoclassicists were given to *Chervonyi shliakh* and *Zhyttia i revoliutsiia*.

socialist Ukraine with literary works of outstanding caliber. Because the former Futurists were exhausted by their civic and organizational activity, they had no trouble identifying with these general goals and felt quite at home in VAPLITE.

Semenko, meanwhile, lived in "proud isolation" (Doroshkevych 1925, 127). Without supporters, he withdrew from active literary life and focused his attention on Ukrainian cinema, which was about to blossom under the direction of Oleksander [Alexander] Dovzhenko. His isolation, however, was only temporary. In just over a year he returned to Kharkiv and began mobilizing his former adherents around the cause of the avant-garde once again. His call to arms did not go unanswered. In 1927 Semenko finally realized a dream he had cherished for almost a decade. He became editor of a monthly journal whose life came to be measured not in days or weeks but in years. The journal and group he established was called The New Generation [*Nova generatsiia*].

Cover art from the journal *Nova generatsiia: top*, 1930, no.2; *bottom*, 1930, no. 3. *Reproduced with the kind permission of the Houghton Library, Harvard University.*

CHAPTER 5

The New Generation

Semenko's activities immediately after the fall of AsKK can be reconstructed only broadly.[1] For almost two years he withdrew from literary life to devote his energies to the youngest and, what Futurists considered, the most revolutionary of arts: film. He moved from Kharkiv to Odesa where he became an employee of VUFKU (*Vseukraïns'ke foto-kinoupravlinnia* [The All-Ukrainian Photo-Cinema Administration]), eventually serving as "chief editor of the Odesa film factory and chief editor of VUFKU's directorate" (Semenko 1929d, 6). The available information suggests he was close to the centers of power and wielded considerable influence, especially during the early period of his employment. "I worked conscientiously," he said. "I did whatever was possible at that time to integrate this industry into the Ukrainian cultural process. I think that I accomplished much" (ibid.).

It is not clear what role Semenko may have played in obtaining employment for his friends and allies, but VUFKU harbored several of them. Bazhan, who has described Semenko as "my careful patron and guardian," acknowledged that he and "another 'Panfuturist'...Iura [Iurii] Ianovs'kyi" were lured from Kyiv by Semenko. Ianovs'kyi eventually became "chief editor of the Odesa film studio" (Bazhan 1971, 181). A few years later Ianovs'kyi painted a kindly portrait of Semenko in his novel *Maister korablia* [The Shipmaster, 1928] which is set against the background of the film industry in Odesa:

> Mykhail' was my former mentor. More generally, he was the leader of the left poets in our country. He was a Futurist who was always lacking in some small detail, which prevented him from becoming a giant. I loved him, if anyone is interested in my attitude toward him. He came to the studio every day, invariably smoking a pipe, would go out to look at the sea and disappear, leaving behind the aroma of "Capstan" [tobacco] from his pipe.

[1] The account that follows is based on information culled from Hoholiev (1970 passim); Sulyma (1989, 299–301); and Sulyma (1987).

> One could always sense in him some kind of vibrancy, a flickering flame. He was a thorough romantic, but hid this behind grinning, somewhat cynical, teasing eyes. He would lay out bold and engaging projects rationally and seriously, as if scolding a wife for overcooking dinner. As I said, he was on the border of being a genius. But not quite. I felt his presence at the studio like some upbeat melody, animating and carefree. You felt that, standing next to you, whistling, was someone who was solving global problems. Meanwhile, following his example, you could continue working and working. A short while later he was given leave and then never again returned to the studio... (Ianovs'kyi 1954, 22).

Ianovs'kyi, Bazhan, and Shkurupii wrote film scripts for VUFKU, as did Semenko himself.[2] Les' Kurbas and Favst Lopatyns'kyi, both of Berezil', directed films; Vadym Meller served as art director. Interestingly, as a film director, Lopatyns'kyi espoused views about the cinema that were reminiscent of the Panfuturist theory. It is said that he sought the "destruction of psychologism" in film and "the substitution of interesting [cinematic] tricks for boring emotions" (Hoholiev 1970, 5).

Contact with his former supporters made it easier for Semenko to draw on their help when the opportunity arose to resume literary activities. During his sojourn in Odesa, Semenko also managed to broaden his circle by making the acquaintance of individuals in the film industry. Some of them (for example, the directors Oleksander Dovzhenko and O. Perehuda) subsequently were associated with his publishing projects. A young film theoretician by the name of Leonid Skrypnyk, whom Semenko probably met during this period, later became a regular contributor to *Nova generatsiia* [The New Generation] and one of the most original writers of the group.

When Semenko finally cut his ties to VUFKU in 1927 to resume his literary activities, he was confronted with a cultural and political situation radically different from the one in which he earlier had worked. Inasmuch as the change helps to explain the emergence of *Nova generatsiia*, a brief historical digression is in order.[3]

In 1923 the KP(b)U initiated the so-called Ukrainianization Policy to win over the disaffected intelligentsia and peasantry. The policy unleashed

2 Semenko is known to have worked on at least two film scripts, neither of which were produced. In 1926 he was writing *Chorna rada* [The Black Council] based on Panteleimon Kulish's romantic novel. Much later, in 1933, he was adapting Honoré de Balzac's *Le cousin Pons* to the screen. See Sulyma (1989, 301).

3 For details on the history and literary politics of this period see Mace 1983; M. Skrypnyk 1927; Shums'kyi 1927; Ievsieiev 1959; Shchupak 1927; Lapchyns'kyi 1927; Koshelivets' 1972; M. Skrypnyk 1974; Luckyj 1956; Shkandrij 1992.

powerful currents in Ukrainian society that were not easily contained within the narrow straits reserved for them by the Party. The support and encouragement Ukrainian cultural activities received from official circles, especially the introduction of Ukrainian into governmental, Party, and educational institutions, and the steady conversion of periodicals from the Russian to the Ukrainian language, rather than satisfying those whom they were designed to appease, made them bolder in putting forth greater demands. Under the relatively liberal conditions of the 1920s, the momentum of Ukrainian cultural expansion constantly threatened to outpace the Party's plans for it. Moreover, it stirred resentment among the Russian-speaking minority whose culture continued to dominate urban centers and whose influence in the KP(b)U remained disproportionately large. From the beginning of the decade, the KP(b)U fought repeated battles to restrain the Ukrainian movement. As indicated earlier, in 1920, it had refused to grant the Borot'bists the status of an independent political party; later, in 1924–25, it had to subdue a group of national communists, the so-called Ukapisty (Ukrainian Communist Party). Finally, in 1926–27, it once again came up against a powerful wave of discontent which was fed by the perception that de-Russification was proceeding too slowly and that the KP(b)U was not acting with sufficient vigor to stamp out Russian chauvinism.[4]

This latest challenge to the KP(b)U began innocuously in April 1925 as the "Literary Discussion," an attempt to deal with issues of quality in literature and the problems posed to it by mass literary organizations. However, it soon spilled over into more sensitive areas as Mykola Khvyl'ovyi, who set the tone and pace of the debates, linked Ukrainian cultural developments to Soviet political life. Khvyl'ovyi found surprisingly strong support among members of VAPLITE, the

[4] One instance of Russian superciliousness that shocked Ukrainian writers of all political hues was Maksim Gor'kii's letter of 1926 to a Ukrainian publishing house that had requested permission to translate his short novel *Mat'* [Mother] into Ukrainian. Gor'kii's response (dated 7 May 1926) came from Sorrento and read as follows: "It seems to me that a translation of [this] *povest'* into the Ukrainian dialect is...unnecessary. I am astounded by the fact that people who have one and the same goal not only affirm the dissimilarity of dialects—trying to make [the Ukrainian] dialect a 'language'—but even oppress those Great Russians who suddenly find themselves a minority in the domain of a given dialect. During the old regime I strongly protested against such phenomena. It seems to me that under the new regime it would be appropriate to strive toward the removal of everything that prevents people from helping one another. Otherwise, a curious thing happens: some people try to create a 'worldwide language,' while others do exactly the opposite." The letter was signed "A. Peshkov." Quoted from Khvylia (1929b, 11). This article, as well as Khvylia 1929a, gives other examples of Russian chauvinism.

Neoclassicists, certain circles of the pre-revolutionary intelligentsia, and even within the KP(b)U itself, most notably in the person of Oleksander Shums'kyi, the commissar for education. Khvyl'ovyi argued that Ukraine's dilemma stemmed from Russia's continued effort to maintain cultural hegemony on Ukrainian lands. The policy of the KP(b)U, he argued, should encourage the gradual retreat of Russian culture into its own ethnic boundaries and leave Ukraine free to pursue its own cultural development—within a European context. This idea was condensed in two pithy slogans, "Away from Moscow" and "Psychological Europe," which opponents interpreted to mean a rejection of a "proletarian" Russia in favor of a "bourgeois" Europe (Khvyl'ovyi 1925; Khvyl'ovyi 1926).[5] Khvyl'ovyi's position was bolstered by an economic argument formulated by Mykhailo Volobuiev, who suggested that even Ukraine's economic status in the USSR had not changed significantly from its colonial position in the Russian Empire (Mace 1983, 161–90). Thus, between 1926 and 1928 the Party had to face down three "nationalistic deviations," which received the names "Khvyl'ovism," "Shums'kism," and "Volobuievism."

Although echoes of these debates were to reverberate for more than three years, the Party moved decisively against Khvyl'ovyi and Shums'kyi, and by the middle of 1927 was fairly secure in the knowledge that it had vanquished both. Shums'kyi was forced to resign his post of commissar for education and quietly faded into oblivion somewhere in Leningrad. In the meantime, Khvyl'ovyi and his most vocal supporters in VAPLITE were compelled to recant their views by publishing apologies in the press.

What is paradoxical, especially in light of the brutal repression of Ukrainian cultural activities in the 1930s, is that—despite the Party's struggle with nationalism—Ukrainianization was not abandoned. Credit for this goes to Mykola Skrypnyk, a long-time Party member, who waged a merciless struggle against Shums'kyi and Khvyl'ovyi and succeeded the former to the post of commissar for education. While adhering closely to the Party line, Skrypnyk exploited every ideological argument to press forward with Ukrainianization. As he put it, this was to be proof positive that the Party was the true defender of Ukrainian interests and that it had the will to implement its own policies. In trying to wrest the nationality issue from the hands of the "deviationists," the KP(b)U rejected any culpability for the cultural problems in Ukraine, portraying itself as the morally superior party that was carefully negotiating the volatile path

5 His most controversial essay, "Ukraine or Little Russia" was never published during his lifetime. It first appeared in 1990. See Khvyl'ovyi 1990b. For translations of published essays see Khvyl'ovyi 1986.

between two chauvinistic extremes, one Russian, the other Ukrainian. KP(b)U resolutions of this period explicitly denounced Russian chauvinism but always in conjunction with attacks on Ukrainian nationalism. The fine balancing act is aptly illustrated by Andrii Khvylia, a member of the Central Committee and one of Khvyl'ovyi's fiercest opponents:

> *Old Russia is dead and will never be resurrected from the grave. The proletariat has sent her there, it has crushed and destroyed her.* In her place has emerged a union of nations: Ukrainian, Russian, Belarusian, Tatar, Georgian, and others. *He who dreams of resurrecting the corpse of Old Russia [and] of returning the creative, cultural work of the union of nations onto the old path is a criminal in view of the historical struggle of the proletariat against capitalism. Therefore, our first slogan is this: a stubborn and victorious struggle against all forms of Russian chauvinism.* Every Russian chauvinist, whoever he may be, is a specter of Old Russia stumbling between the feet of the victorious class, trying to reinstate the period of the Tsars. Death to this threat—this is our slogan. *At the same time, we must wage a decisive struggle against national Ukrainian chauvinism. It will not turn the task of cultural construction in Ukraine onto the path of enmity among the nations of the Union* (Khvylia 1926, 5; *emphasis in the original*).

The KP(b)U's affirmation of Ukrainianization was not a hollow promise. With Skrypnyk at the helm of the Commissariat for Education, the pace increased noticeably, especially in publishing. The years 1926, 1927, and 1928 saw an unusual burgeoning of literary organizations and journals. Associations such as Valeriian Polishchuk's Constructivist group Avanhard (Avant-Garde, 1926), Molodniak ("The Young Forest"—an organization of Komsomol writers, 1926), VUSPP (*Vseukraïns'ka spilka proletars'kykh pys'mennykiv* [The All-Ukrainian Union of Proletarian Writers] 1927), Zakhidna Ukraïna (Western Ukraine, 1927), and Tekhnomystets'ka hrupa A (Techno-artistic Group A, 1928) came into being. Virtually every group was granted the right to publish a journal. In 1927 *Hart*, *Literaturna hazeta*, *Molodniak*, and *Vaplite* appeared; in 1928, *Krytyka*, *Literaturnyi iarmarok*, *Universal'nyi zhurnal*, *Zakhidna Ukraïna* and *Biuleten' Avanhardu*.

It should be understood that the opening by the KP(b)U of the cultural floodgates was hardly an exercise in Ukrainian patriotism. By increasing the number of publications, the Party hoped to tip the scales against the so-called "nationalistic" groups, especially VAPLITE. It placed great stress on "proletarian" and "Marxist" ideology, indulging particularly the proletarian sector of the literary community. Groups espousing class rather than national or artistic values began to predominate. An organization like VUSPP had at its disposal several publications (for example, *Hart*, *Literaturna hazeta*). Ukrainianization, in short, also involved at this time a tightening of ideological controls.

While the KP(b)U condemned Khvyl'ovyi and his supporters for nationalistic deviations, it quietly acceded to their criticism that proletarian literature needed to be revamped. Notions of quality and literary professionalism quickly became a mainstay, and most organizations, including VUSPP and Pluh, at least paid lip service to them. The Party itself began to look askance at manifestations of "Onguardism" [*napostivstvo*] and Proletkul'tism (that is, vulgar sociological criticism). Such developments, naturally, did not absolve writers from promulgating a correct ideology in their work, but it did mean that critics and Party members—frequently the two were one and the same—were prone to underscore a writer's artistic duty as well. This was graphically illustrated during a literary forum in February 1928. Mykola Skrypnyk, who was the keynote speaker at this event, urged writers not to "limit themselves to a social-political approach" but to be "careful about style" (M. Skrypnyk 1928, 28).[6] Emphasizing quality and artistic form, Skrypnyk even argued (to the chagrin of many in the audience) that literary organizations should be formed on formal and artistic principles and not on quasi-political platforms.

> For the most part, our writers create organizations not on the basis of any artistic [or] purely literary principle or movement, but rather on semi-political platforms which unite various, sometimes even antagonistic artistic currents under a single roof.... To put it mildly, our literary organizations were and remain even now, largely, literary-political organizations and not organizations with artistic-literary characteristics.... (M. Skrypnyk 1928, 6–7).

Writers must have an artistic "self-definition," said Skrypnyk. "If they do not distinguish each other by style, it means they are not working on their style, they are not perfecting their style..." (ibid., 29). The Party, he maintained, had the right to give certain "pointers" about the content of a literary work, but "as far as form and style are concerned, there can be no pointers and there are none; in this respect there must be free competition among various currents" (ibid., 27). Skrypnyk singled out two avant-garde groups as examples of true literary organizations: Semenko's Nova generatsiia and Valeriian Polishchuk's Constructivist

6 Skrypnyk was echoing here views expressed earlier in a resolution of the Central Committee of KP(b)U. See "Polityka partiï v spravi ukraïns'koï khudozhn'oï literatury" 1927, especially pp. 354–55.

group, Avanhard. About the former he said:

> The journal *Nova generatsiia*, which has gathered around itself a small group of writers, [is a literary] movement that has established an organization on artistic principles.…I am not an admirer of the left front of art, but precisely because *Nova generatsiia* is founded on artistic, literary principles, *it has more significance than many others.* The existence of [this group] will force many other writers to define themselves in an artistic manner… (ibid., 8–9; *emphasis added*).

As is evident, the appearance of *Nova generatsiia* in 1927 was not a simple act of will on Semenko's part.[7] A host of political and cultural events conspired to make it feasible. The appearance of a new Futurist organization with its own journal was the result of far-reaching changes sweeping through Ukrainian society. After strenuous debates and arguments for nearly two and a half years, the cultural situation took on a dramatically different and, in some respects, more mature guise. The period when mass-oriented organizations were able to dictate the tone and direction of literature had come and gone. For the first time during the decade intrinsic artistic pursuits received a modicum of recognition. This was enough to make the next two years one of the most productive in Ukrainian letters, especially for the Futurists.

Bumeranh

The first issue of *Nova generatsiia* appeared in Kharkiv in October 1927. However, when Semenko left Odesa he had no assurance, nor even a hint that before the end of the year he would be editor of a major literary-artistic journal. In fact, his efforts during the first half of the year were directed elsewhere. At first he did not even venture to Kharkiv. Settling in Kyiv, the city that, in a manner of speaking, had nurtured Futurism, he set out to revitalize the avant-garde through a group called Bumeranh [Boomerang]. Although there is reason to believe Semenko had ambitions of turning Bumeranh into a full-fledged organization, it never amounted to more than a loose coalition between writers and members of the film industry. The history of this formation is brief, but memorable.

Bumeranh succeeded in producing two publications. The first was a miscellany, the cover for which was designed by Volodymyr [Vladimir] Tatlin,[8] *Zustrich na perekhresnii stantsiï* [Meeting at the Crossing

[7] Koshelivets' points out that Polishchuk's organization Avanhard was sanctioned by the People's Commissariat for Education. See Koshelivets´ (1972, 196). Logically, the same had to be true for Semenko's organization.

[8] Camila Gray refers to him as a "Ukrainian by nationality" (1970, 167).

Station],[9] subtitled *Rozmova tr'okh* [A Conversation among the Three]—a reference to Semenko, Shkurupii, and Bazhan. The other was *Bumeranh*, subtitled "a non-periodic journal of [polemical] pamphlets." Listed on its back cover as participants were Mykola Bazhan, Dmytro Buz'ko, Oleksander Dovzhenko, Hlib Zatvornyts'kyi, O. Kapler, S. Mel'nyk, O. Perehuda, B. Teneta, Mykhail' Semenko, Oleksa Slisarenko, Io. Stril'chuk, Leonid Frenkel', Geo Shkurupii, Mykola Shcherbak, Iurii Ianovs'kyi, and Volodymyr Iaroshenko. The catalogue of supporters was impressive, but only four actually contributed articles: Semenko (1927c), Bazhan (1927b), Shkurupii (1927c), and Perehuda (1927).

Zustrich was a smorgasbord of poetry and polemics, arranged into four sections, the first three of which were devoted, respectively, to the poems of Semenko, Shkurupii, and Bazhan. The fourth was an unsigned piece of prose, in all likelihood written by Semenko, bearing the same title as the publication. Semenko's poetry was overtly avant-gardist in a terse, dark, minimalist, and anti-aesthetic way.[10] Shkurupii's and Bazhan's, on the other hand, was more traditional in form and mood. The former offered a flawless cycle of romantic poems about the sea[11]; the latter indulged in references to the past and resorted to the sonnet.[12] A witness to this heterogeneity concluded: "while [one] can still speak about M. Semenko as a Futurist...[one] cannot say the same for G. Shkurupii and M. Bazhan; their poetry has as much in common with Futurism as does Nadson's" (Kovalenko 1927, 100).

If the verse only hinted at some kind of estrangement among the three, the final prose section seemed to confirm it openly. This third person narrative describes in an engaging manner the meeting and conversation of three "conquistadors" (Semenko, Bazhan, and Shkurupii) whose "tracks" had diverged for a time but who "finally came together again at this railroad station" (*Zustrich* 1927, 37). At first, the tone of this reunion is amicable. Soon, a discordant note enters the proceedings. Semenko reminds his friends about their treacherous role in the demise of AsKK, and Bazhan raises doubts about the wisdom of their former program:

> [Our] formulas—with the aid of which years ago we tried to lay down new tracks into the future—contained as much algebra and logarithms as the calculations of a building engineer. And what of it? The fiercest

9 Henceforth cited as *Zustrich*

10 "Zavod im. Myx. Semenka," "Krym," "Vona," "Pisnia trampa," "1 NP," "3 NP," "6 NP," "7 NP." *Zustrich* 1927, pp. 7–20.

11 "More." *Zustrich* 1927, pp. 23–27.

12 "Krov polonianok," "Zalizniakova nich." *Zustrich* 1927, pp. 31–33.

> and most diligent desire to prove that 2 x 2 = 5 is not always justified (ibid., 39).

To this Semenko responded with undisguised sarcasm: "You have become terribly clever.... Must be the stupid fences you climbed during our separation. This wisdom has been given to you by the provincialism that surrounds our [avant-garde] oasis and toward which you [Bazhan and Shkurupii] fled after your betrayal" (ibid.). Bazhan, however, was not deterred and pressed Semenko to come face to face with his theoretical and practical inconsistencies. Bazhan accused him of composing "sharp, guillotine-like formulas about the death of art" on one side of a page, while writing poems on the other (ibid., 40). Personally, Bazhan said, he could not do this and confessed that he had lost faith in their Futurist program:

> I admit: I have laid down my arms. I have stopped dreaming about new forms of art a thousand times more influential, stronger and more grand than the old. I have stopped believing that in place of a private, petty, domestic art (domestic cattle!), there will come tomorrow or the day after a new art of the masses, city squares, demonstrations and battles.... (ibid., 45).

It was obvious the three associates did not see eye to eye. The differences were especially palpable between Semenko and Bazhan; Shkurupii came across as less vocal in this narrative and sided with Semenko on most issues. Bazhan's artistic demands were now more immediate and simple. He asked for excellence and originality but did not revile tradition. In fact, when it came to posit an ideal, he turned to the elite culture of the Ukrainian Baroque and the Hetman State, a period Bazhan believed had been unfairly eclipsed by the peasant orientation of nineteenth-century culture (ibid., 44).

Semenko reacted to Bazhan's postulates by reiterating his faith in the New. Both he and Shkurupii expressed strong aversion to anything linked with tradition and the stifling past. A writer must be sensitive to the "pulse of the epoch." "One cannot habitually be nourished by canned food," claimed Semenko. "Even *Ukrnarkharch*[13] sometimes provides fresh hamburgers, so what about literature?" (ibid., 42).

Although the three agreed to disagree, in the final analysis they found enough common ground to affirm their association. First, everyone acknowledged they all had distinct creative personalities. As Semenko put it: "each one of us is individually responsible for his own literary snout [*pyka*]." But this was not a barrier to establishing "some kind of computational average" which could serve "as the backbone for our

[13] A government body responsible for food production.

group" (ibid., 45). Shkurupii pointed out they all had faith in the October Revolution. More importantly, they adhered to a formalist concept of art, they shared a common "method," and showed "a conscious awareness of what our material is and how to operate with it" (ibid.). Bazhan spoke for the group when he wrote in *Bumeranh*: "Our literature is not always a well made *thing*.... It is too moderate and serious. Let us have less dignity, more skill [*uminnia*] and ingenious carelessness.... A new thing, or, at least, a new way of seeing *things*—that is literature's forte," he insisted. "There are endless combinations of *things in literature* and of *literary things*" (Bazhan 1927b, 24–26; *emphasis added*).

Their aversions served as an equally strong bond. They all conveyed a distaste for backward bumpkins, folk art, embroidered shirts, apiaries, education with a mass appeal [*Prosvita*] (regardless of its "political hue"), the populist writer and activist Borys Hrinchenko (1863–1910), the Ukrainian National Republic, the Ukrainian Autocephalous Church, and, last but not least, "Marxist" critics. Shkurupii bracketed them with interrogators; Bazhan described any critic who "swears by the beard of Marx" as an old peasant "who burps loudly after dinner and says to his fat wife: 'this I like and this I don't like'" (*Zustrich* 1927, 40).

In the final analysis, this "conversation" proved heartening. The reunion concluded on a note of harmony, with Semenko enunciating the enormity of their mission, while reiterating themes from earlier manifestoes in a tone of mock seriousness:

> Who can tell what this reunion will bring? Perhaps there will be more of us.[14] But right now we must mobilize ourselves effectively for several years and set out in an *organized* manner; we cannot allow the creative combinations springing from our energetic, lively and incomparable heads to perish.... You know quite well that we are, after all, pioneers, and everyone who follows us is a pioneer. We must disembark here, on this hopelessly barren self-destructive shore. We must release our boomerangs, but the main thing is to work, to show others how to work. We will disembark and walk the Ukrainian prairies, bringing electricity to homesteads, defending the industrial treasures we brought into Ukrainian culture.... We must steer culture out of that worthless rut into which it has fallen.... We must follow the road of universal creative objectives and not stew in our own juice.... We must rid ourselves of provincialism.... Otherwise, we, the anti-provincials, will either suffocate or [be forced] to flee. [But since] there is nowhere to run, this means we must hit the beaches! We will ruffle the pot bellies of

[14] Elsewhere in the text, Semenko speculated that they might be joined by Iuliian Shpol (M. Ialovyi). This wishful thinking probably was based on the fact that Shpol, together with Khvyl'ovyi and Oles' Dosvitnii, had been expelled from VAPLITE on 28 January 1927.

> the self-satisfied literary kulaks. Let us light the flame of the self-sacrificing conquistadors who march toward the communist future not out of fear but out of conscience (ibid., 46, 48; *emphasis added*).

The appearance of *Bumeranh* and *Zustrich* created serious problems for Bazhan and Shkurupii who were at the time official members of VAPLITE. On 21 April 1927 this organization condemned *Bumeranh* as "a politically illiterate caper" and demanded the two writers quickly explain "their attitude toward VAPLITE" (Luckyj 1977, 99). A few days later the Secretary of the organization, Arkadii Liubchenko, wrote the culprits a letter stating that for "[our] organization your participation in *such* a journal is very surprising and strange" (ibid.; *emphasis in the original*).

VAPLITE's angst was well founded. It seemed obvious from the "Conversation of the Three" that Bazhan and Shkurupii were contemplating a separate association with Semenko and, what was worse, equating the "Free Academy" with parochialism. Semenko had told his two colleagues: "There are enough of us to begin a *movement*" and in the same breath made a truculent allusion to VAPLITE: "If someone needs to form a *group*, then let him do so on the principle of quality and his creative psyche [*psykhika*], not because he calls himself a 'Ukrainian writer.' Once again, it is necessary to embrace 'isms,' not one's 'home sweet home, where peace and quiet reign.'" To this Geo Shkurupii responded: "Where is this 'peace and quiet?' We need cooperation! In VAPLITE...." But Semenko interjected in ersatz French: "In VAPLITE? Oh, there *did t-e-la passe, baba l'on bié, sam pan sil très a ge ùo prive!* as the French say" (*Zustrich* 1927, 48; *emphasis added*). This "Gallic" expression (a parody of VAPLITE members' predilection for foreign words) was a phonetic rendering of the Ukrainian phrase: "The old man grazes a calf, the old woman beats flax, and the master himself grinds salt, while Geo sweats." The peasant and village imagery was clearly meant to offend the "Academy" which prided itself on defending high European cultural values.

But this was a minor irritant in comparison to Semenko's article in *Bumeranh*, "Reflections about Why Ukrainian Nationalism Is Bad for Ukrainian Culture, or, Why Internationalism Is Good for It" (Semenko 1927c). This was a smartly written apologia for an art that ought to have "significance...beyond the borders of [Ukrainian] national culture" (ibid., 5), and an aggressive attack on those who are "pleased by the parameters of Ukrainian culture" and use them as their point of departure in creativity (ibid., 4). Semenko scoffed at this "nationalistic" approach, condemning typical "Ukrainian" choirs, the cult of Shevchenko ("wrapped in embroidered ritual cloths"), Hart, Pluh, in short "every sort of cultural trivialization regardless of its political hue, including the red...and...proletarian" (ibid.). He belittled those who would build a proletarian culture on the basis of a "folk song," who would sit with their "bloated bellies" listening to a "tiresome, oft-heard 'European' opera"—in Ukrainian. Declared Semenko: "Every 'European' idea and novelty, when passed through such a parochial prism, hangs on the neck of Ukrainian culture like last year's [fashionable] 'wrap'; 'Europe' agrees with it about as much as *merci* and *pardon* do in the novels or feuilletons of Khvyl'ovyi and Arkadii Liubchenko..." (ibid., 3). Semenko urged that this retrograde "national" cultural reflex be replaced by a conscious avant-gardism, which he equated with "internationalism" and progress: "We must, intensely and seriously, encourage the *innate progressive processes* in our culture, because it is not through trafficking in old values but in the creation of *new values* that we will be able to attain not just a 'true Europe,' but a proletarian culture" (ibid., 8–9; *emphasis added*).

On May 18 Bazhan and Shkurupii answered Liubchenko by assuring him that "under no circumstances" did the appearance of *Bumeranh* "mean the creation of a new literary group or organization." In defending their participation, they made this additional point: "The Free Academy...is called Free because it does not try to cut each member's hair [according to the style] of a single school...." Bazhan explained the appearance of *Bumeranh* as the result of "specific Kyiv circumstances, [i.e.,] isolation from the Kharkiv literary community and the relationship amongst me, Shkurupii, and Semenko...." He pointed out that they had felt a "need to raise certain problems more sharply," but because this was impossible to do on the pages of the regular press, they resorted to *Bumeranh*. Both writers maintained that the "hounding of *Bumeranh* served no good purpose either for VAPLITE or for the literary community" as a whole. In any case, they stressed, their participation in the journal did not mean they were cutting themselves off from VAPLITE.

This answer was deemed unsatisfactory by VAPLITE and a few days later both Shkurupii and Bazhan were expelled. Nevertheless, they were quickly reinstated when some members (among them, apparently, Slisarenko) came to their defense. Bazhan published freely in VAPLITE's journal after this incident, but not Shkurupii.[15] When *Nova generatsiia* made its appearance in October and Shkurupii took a position on its editorial board, he was thrown out of VAPLITE permanently (Luckyj 1977, 100).

The pressure tactics used against Bazhan and Shkurupii were also employed against two other VAPLITE members, Oleksander Dovzhenko

[15] Shkurupii had a single story published in *Vaplite. Al'manakh* (1926).

and Iurii Ianovs'kyi. At virtually the same time as Bazhan and Shkurupii were busy defending themselves in Kyiv, Dovzhenko and Ianovs'kyi were penning a joint letter of explanation to VAPLITE from Odesa. Dated 24 May and written in a light and friendly tone, it, nonetheless, drove home a serious point, namely, that they had nothing in common with Semenko's goals and ambitions. The letter was published in *Vaplite* to make this fact clear to the community at large:

> In the first issue of Semenko's *Bumeranh* our names appear as members of the *group*, Bumeranh. In reference to this, we wish to provide an explanation. We love Mysha Semenko, author of *Kobzar No. 2*. We did, indeed, agree to have [our] articles on specific film topics published in *Bumeranh*. But, as we [now] see, the first page of the journal *Bumeranh* has *a highly convoluted platform*[16] about which Semenko did not notify us. Therefore, we ask that the inclusion of our names on the pages of *Bumeranh* be interpreted as Semenko's mistake (Dovzhenko and Ianovs'kyi 1927).

Semenko's first post-AsKK exercise at mobilizing the forces of the avant-garde into a coherent movement ended in failure. The animosity of VAPLITE (not to mention of other organizations like Molodniak and Pluh), and the vacillation of friends spelled its doom.[17] As Dovzhenko and Ianovs'kyi seem to imply, Semenko may have done himself a great deal of harm with his newest attack on "national art."

It is tempting to view Bumeranh as a prologue to *Nova generatsiia*. Chronologically, it certainly was, but in other respects it seems like an epilogue to Futurism's preceding history, an echo of such transient achievements as Flamingo, the Poet-Futurists' Shock Brigade, and to some extent Aspanfut and AsKK. Like these early embodiments of Futurism, Bumeranh was a private, self-funded, and self-supported organization that had limited resources and a poor publishing record. The fact that *Nova generatsiia* appeared regularly and without interruption for over three years is reason enough to distinguish it from preceding ventures. Of course, this was possible because for the first time Futurists received official governmental support. Unlike *Zustrich*, which was issued under the private Futurist imprint Bumeranh (reminiscent of Gulf Stream), *Nova generatsiia* was published by the State Publishing House [DVU]. This—and the fact that a change had occurred in the political and cultural climate—explains why the Futurist movement in a few short months succeeded in going from bust to boom.

16 The allusion is to Semenko's "Reflections about Why..." (1927c).

17 For contemporary opinions of *Bumeranh*, see Kovalenko 1927, Pylypenko 1927, and P.B. 1927.

Cadres

The fate of Bumeranh might have suggested that recruiting contributors to *Nova generatsiia* would be a problem for Semenko. Surprisingly, the opposite was true. On 1 October 1927 *Kul'tura i pobut* [Culture and Life, Kharkiv] ran a brief announcement under Semenko's initials informing the public that preparations were under way for the journal. Besides himself, the following individuals were identified as participants: Les' Kurbas, Geo Shkurupii, Vadym Meller, Oleksa Vlyz'ko, Anatolii Petryts'kyi, O. Perehuda, Leonid Skrypnyk, Dmytro Buz'ko, Geo Koliada, Oleksii Poltorats'kyi, Grigorii Petnikov, A. Buchma, Mykola Bazhan, S. Mel'nyk, R. Novosads'kyi-Lialin, and N. Shcherbyna (*Kul'tura i pobut* 37 [1 October 1927]: 7). This initial list proved to be both incomplete and too inclusive. When *Nova generatsiia* began appearing, it became clear that not every associate had been enumerated, while some, like Novosads'kyi-Lialin and Shcherbyna, were destined never to take part. Several months into its existence, the journal's back cover listed fifty-three participants (*Nova generatsiia* 1928 [1]). This increased to fifty-six in the next issue, dropping a little subsequently. During 1930 it was not unusual to see *Nova generatsiia* boasting more than eighty participants. These figures were somewhat inflated by pseudonyms (e.g., Levon Lain, M. Lans'kyi, Ole Vorm, Vil'm Iar, D. Holubenko). Moreover, not all "participants" were actual contributors. In some instances, they were little more than an honorary editorial board that added to the journal's prestige but did not affect its character. Still, there was a large and stable corps of supporters. The key players were Semenko, Shkurupii, and a newcomer, Oleksii Poltorats'kyi. Standing near this top leadership were Leonid Skrypnyk, Oleksa Vlyz'ko,[18] and the photographer, Dan Sotnyk. They were backed by steady contributions from Andrii Chuzhyi, Oleksander Mar'iamov, Dmytro Buz'ko, Ievhen Iavorovs'kyi, Leonid Frenkel', Leonid Chernov, Geo Koliada,[19] S. Voinilovych, O. Korzh, M. Skuba, Favst Lopatyns'kyi, Leonid Nedolia, Antin Pavliuk, Petro Mel'nyk, Ivan Malovichko, Mechyslav Hasko, Sava Holovanivs'kyi, Volodymyr Kovalevs'kyi, and others.

18 For his letter of resignation from VUSPP and Molodniak, see *Nova generatsiia* (1928 [10]: 274).

19 Koliada, who resided in Moscow, had vague connections to the Futurists in the early part of the decade. In 1927 he joined VAPLITE, which elicited a venomous response from *Nova generatsiia* (see Dans [Dan Sotnyk], 1927). After the dissolution of VAPLITE in January 1928, Koliada began to appear fairly regularly in *Nova generatsiia*. The Futurist publishing house Semafor u Maibutnie even released his novel *Arsenal syl* (Koliada 1929).

Nova generatsiia had a good many collaborators from arts other than literature. This was symptomatic of the journal's conscious "pan-artistic" philosophy which endeavored to embrace all avant-garde phenomena (Semenko 1928c, 360). Contributors came from film and theater (O. Perehuda, Marko Tereshchenko, Hlib Zatvornyts'kyi), from the easel arts (Anatol' [Anatolii] Petryts'kyi, Vasyl' Iermylov [Ermilov], Pavlo Kovzhun), photography (Dan Sotnyk), and especially architecture (I. Malozemov, O. Kas'ianov, L. Lopovok, M. Kholostenko, and others). In line with its Panfuturist philosophy—which defined art as a single universal process and rejected national introspection—the journal deliberately fostered an international climate. Titles and subtitles were frequently replicated in French, German, English or Esperanto (e.g., "Journal de nouvelle formation de l'art"; "Zeitschrift der linken Kunstformation," etc.) and foreign language summaries were provided for certain articles. More significant was the cosmopolitan editorial board. Among its foreign associates, the journal counted Herwarth Walden, the German impresario of the avant-garde; László Moholy-Nagy, the central figure of the Bauhaus movement; Enrico Prampolini,[20] Johannes Becher, and Rudolf Leonhard. There were also representatives from Russia (Osip Brik, Aleksei Gan, Sergei Eisenstein, Vladimir Maiakovskii, Aleksandr Rodchenko, Volodymyr [Vladimir] Tatlin, N. Chuzhak, Viktor Shklovskii, Dziga Vertov, Kazimir Malevych [Malevich]) and Georgia (Simon Chikovani, K. Kolidze, Levan Asatiani, L. Esakia, D. Shenhelaia, N. Shenhelaia, Beso Zhgenti). The actual participation of this foreign contingent was marginal. Few of them contributed original material to *Nova generatsiia*. The exceptions were Walden (1928)[21] and, especially, Malevich.[22] Most others, if they appeared, had their works reproduced from a foreign source.

[20] He sent the following letter to *Nova generatsiia* (Prampolini 1928): "J'ai appris du camarade Deslaw que votre journal est l'expression de la nouvelle activite spirituelle-artistique d'aujourd'hui en Ukraine. J'envoye mes souhaits et mes salutations amicables, je serais heureux si vous pouvez m'envoyer les copies du votre journal qui a publié des rensegnements sur mes creations artistiques, comme j'aimerais bien collaborer dans votre journal. A bien vous lire, Enrico Prampolini."

[21] His article, "Mystetstvo v Evropi" [Art in Europe], appeared in *Nova Generatsiia* 1928 [9]: 170. Several times *Nova generatsiia* advertised *Der Sturm* (see nos. 7 and 10 [1928]), the journal edited by Walden. During a visit to the Soviet Union in September 1929, Walden was also in Kyiv where he met the Futurists. He "promised to devote a separate issue of *Der Sturm* to left art in Ukraine [and] invited participation in this journal, promising also to publish a separate German edition of M. Semenko, Geo Shkurupii, and O. Vlyz'ko (see "Nimets'kyi pys'mennyk Hervart Val'den odvidav Kyiv," *Literaturna hazeta*, 20 [15 October 1929]: 7). In 1930 a special issue of *Der Sturm* appeared devoted to the Soviet Union, but contained only three sketches about Ukraine. See "Ukrainica," *Chervonyi shliakh* (1930 [7–8]: 197).

[22] Malevich, who was born in Kyiv, considered himself a Ukrainian. Speaking of his best

Probably the best expression of the journal's programmatic internationalism lay in the meticulous attention it paid to Western artistic developments. Reports on trends, personalities, and exhibits in the West were nearly a monthly feature. To give its readers the requisite pan-artistic and international perspective, the editors drew heavily on a host of foreign publications, especially German ones,[23] and in the process brought attention to a wide spectrum of artists.[24]

As is obvious, *Nova generatsiia* did not have a narrow sectarian profile. It freely accepted contributions from individuals outside its Futurist inner circle, trying to highlight the entire avant-garde as such. "Our journal is not a journal of a closed organization...The doors are open to all....Our demands are adherence to our platform...and to those attributes that are characteristic of the left formation of poets and publicists..." ("Lystuvannia z redaktsiieiu" 1928c, 237; Semenko 1928c, 360). A distinction was made between an unyielding nucleus of Futurists who embraced the so-called "program maximum" [*prohrama maksymum*] and avant-gardists or "leftists" in general. For example, Anatol' Petryts'kyi, who numbered among *Nova generatsiia*'s official "coworkers," was called a leftist but not a "Futurist" because he disagreed with their "program maximum" (L. Skrypnyk 1929c, 42). The relationship of Kurbas, Meller, and Bazhan to *Nova generatsiia* represented a special case.

---

friend Lev Krachevs'kyi, he wrote: "He and I were Ukrainians." See Malevich (1976, 115). On the subject of Malevich and Ukraine see Horbachov (1988, 11–14). Between 1928 and 1930 Malevich published a series of fourteen theoretical and historical articles on the new art in *Nova generatsiia* and one in the Kyiv Futurist organ, *Avanhard-Al'manakh proletars'kykh myttsiv Novoï generatsiï* (for details, see "References" below). A few have been translated. See Andersen 1971, vol. 2.

[23] The following is a partial list of the journals *Nova generatsiia* frequently cited (Russian journals are excluded): *Cahiers d'art* (Paris), *Der Sturm* (Berlin), *Filmliga* (Rotterdam), *Das Kunstblatt* (Berlin), *Das neue Frankfurt* (Frankfurt), *Praesens* (Warsaw), *Stavba* (Prague), *7 Arts* (Brussels), *Der Querschnitt* (Berlin), etc. The latter was acknowleged by Semenko to have been a model for *Nova generatsiia* (see 1928 [11]: 335). According to *Nova generatsiia* (1928 [6]: 54), *7 Arts* carried a positive response to the Ukrainian journal in an April 1928 issue. I was not able to verify this independently.

[24] The following is a sample of the Western names that appeared in *Nova generatsiia*. As is evident, they represent a variety of movements: Futurism, Cubism, Dada, De Stijl, Expressionism, the Bauhaus, Neue Sachlichkeit. Some were not, strictly speaking, "avant-gardist," but merely "leftist," in the political sense: Oleksander Arkhypenko [Alexander Archipenko], Hans Arp, Guillaume Apollinaire, Giacomo Balla, Marcel Breuer, Georges Braque, Willi Baumeister, Giorgio de Chirico, Otto Dix, Juan Gris, Walter Peterhans, Paul Klee, Le Corbusier, Fernand Leger, Walter Mehring, Jean Metzinger, Ludwig Mies van der Rohe, Pablo Picasso, Victor Servranckx, Oskar Schlemmer, Jan Tschichold. Others included W. Broniewski, Carl Sandburg, MacKnight Black, William Richard Titterton, J. S. Wallace, and so on.

Vadym Meller (1884–1962) was the artistic director of *Nova generatsiia* for the first seven issues. He severed ties with the journal in April 1928. His job went to Dan Sotnyk and then, at the beginning of 1930, to Anatol' Petryts'kyi. At exactly the same time as Meller departed, Kurbas also disappeared from the journal's monthly roster. This was a result of artistic tensions that had been simmering in the background for some time. In its first issue, *Nova generatsiia* still claimed Kurbas' Berezil' as an "ally" (*Nova generatsiia* 1927 [1]: 41), even though earlier, in *Bumeranh*, Semenko had expressed fears that Berezil' "was turning its face in the direction of the Philistine" (Semenko 1927c, 4). Semenko's notion that the theater should be both more political and more purely experimental (Semenko 1928c, 360) went counter to Kurbas' plans for Berezil'. His collaboration with the brilliant dramatist Mykola Kulish led him away from his earlier Constructivist and anti-psychological positions. This "betrayal" of the avant-garde spirit compelled Semenko to publicly disavow his friend in a later poem (Semenko 1928g).

As for Bazhan, his departure from the avant-garde camp came in February 1928. Considering the views he expressed in *Zustrich*, this probably was inevitable. Just prior to the final break, his work appeared twice in *Nova generatsiia*.[25] The February 1928 issue listed him as an official participant. Bazhan, however, wrote a brusque letter to *Chervonyi shliakh* (dated 20 February 1928) denying he had consented to work in *Nova generatsiia*. He stated that the manner in which he was extended an "invitation" could "hardly [be] to the benefit of the journal" (Bazhan 1928).

Semenko, it seems, was taken aback by this public rejection. In a response dated 5 March he offered a business-like explanation for why Bazhan had been described as a participant:

> Comrade Bazhan has warned me that he has sent you [the editors] his letter in which he registers surprise at seeing his name included among the coworkers of *Nova generatsiia*. I must state here [the following]: *Nova generatsiia*, No. 3, 1927 carried a poem by M. Bazhan under the title "Tsyrk" [Circus]; [it was published with] his consent and [after some] editing by him (the poem being an old one). He [Bazhan] requested that an appropriate comment be made about this poem by the editorial board and this, in fact, was done (cf. the editors' comments in *Nova generatsiia*, No. 3). Moreover, Comrade Bazhan received an honorarium for this poem. Therefore, we considered it completely natural to include his name among our journal's coworkers. At the moment this is all" (ibid.).

[25] The poem "Tsyrk" (written in 1924) was published in 1927 (3); "Elehiia atraktsioniv," in 1928 (1). The latter was actually a reprint from *Vaplite* 1927 (5): 118.

After this incident the two poets never again entered into any formal literary arrangements.

Platform and Program

In October, when the first issue of *Nova generatsiia* was published, the unusual happened: it received a positive review. Even more surprisingly, it appeared in *Pluzhanyn* [The Plowman], the official organ of Pluh. To be sure, the reviewer began tentatively by acknowledging that the "content" of *Nova generatsiia* would be alien to the "average village reader" and probably of little interest to the worker. But having said this, he went on: "for the city reader and especially for the Soviet *inteligent* everything [will be] of interest and full of significance." Apart from a few caveats, the reviewer's text was sprinkled with expressions of satisfaction and pleasure. He enjoyed the journal's "youthful enthusiasm," its tendency toward the exotic and the sarcastic; he characterized in glowing terms everything from the cover ("original and dazzling") to the final article. Semenko's verse was "unusually ardent, talented, sharp, decisive [and] original..."; Geo Shkurupii's contained "beautiful chords"; other works were "cultured in form and interesting in content." "The ideological section is no less interesting than the artistic section," continued the reviewer. Leonid Skrypnyk's article was "wonderful"; Oleksii Poltorats'kyi's was "scholarly," and Frenkel's "interesting." All in all, the platform of the new journal testified "to its genuine revolutionary character." "There can be no doubt about its communist ideology.... *Nova generatsiia* is undoubtedly a revolutionary, positive phenomenon which must be welcomed" (T.S. 1927).

Reactions from others came more slowly but were equally affirmative. VUSPP's organ, *Literaturna hazeta* [The Literary Gazette] stated the Futurists had produced "an interesting and, doubtlessly, a necessary journal for contemporary literature" ("Vid redaktsiï" 1928b). A few months earlier it ran the opinions of five commentators, all of whom had minor reservations (to the effect that there was too much formalism, too little stylistic consistency, too much ego, too many pseudonyms), but by and large gave *Nova generatsiia* high grades. For example, Iakiv Savchenko, the former Komunkul'tist, called the journal's slogans and orientation "unequivocally valuable and fruitful":

> I value most in *Nova generatsiia* its youth and enthusiasm, its incontestable love for Soviet culture and its pursuit of socially useful forms. The journal is a revolutionary factor in our culture. I want to stress particularly the valuable achievements of *Nova generatsiia*: a

> good, sometimes perfect reportage, a lively and energetic "notebook"[26] [section], a highly refined (considering our circumstances) technical appearance. Here you will find love, diligence, and an eye for detail. This is culture ("Nasha anketa" 1928).

The poet and critic Dmytro Zahul (a former Symbolist) was of the opinion that *Nova generatsiia* represented the avant-garde "rather well." Its design, he remarked, was better than that of the Russian *Lef* or *Na postu* [On Guard]. He saw good reason for its existence, since there was a need to educate the tastes of large segments of society, especially the "bourgeois tastes of the lagging majority." He too paid compliments to the "notebook" section, saying it was "biting, sharp, and lively" (ibid.). Antin Khutorian, a minor poet, who had more caveats than others, nonetheless avowed: "This journal is pleasant to look at, pleasant to hold; some things are even pleasant to read. Especially pleasant, in the old tradition of Futurism, are the attacks on the petty-bourgeoisie" (ibid.). Semenko's one-time ally and Symbolist poet, Mykola Tereshchenko declared: *Nova generatsiia* "must be considered a completely positive phenomenon." "It is a new progressive cultural factor, although, obviously, it also has a whole series of shortcomings" (ibid.). For prose writer Iakiv Kachura, the Futurist organ was "a fresh healing balsam," even if on occasion it did emit "an unpleasant smell" (ibid.). Vasyl' Atamaniuk, a poet and member of Zakhidna Ukraïna, observed that "among the majority of our publications, which are stale and bloodless, this is the only journal with a little spice and occasional bitters [*hirchytsi*]....[It] is needed. We require a little noise, even some pranks in our serious (at times, nearly boring) literary atmosphere" (ibid.).

Did this praise from the enemy camp mean the Futurists had modified in some way their theory and practice to suit their critics, or were their opponents mellowing in the face of Skrypnyk's insistence that writers organize along artistic (formal) lines? In reality, it was a little of both. Skrypnyk's speech of February 1928 obviously played a role; the ideologically-oriented organizations were forced to concede the legitimacy of *Nova generatsiia* and to acknowledge that they too would try to "foster writers with artistic attributes" ("Lysty do redaktsiï" 1929). VUSPP did not entirely accede at first to Skrypnyk's position and had to make belated efforts to fall in line. The organization became sensitive to criticism of its policies, at one point complaining that some individuals had interpreted Skrypnyk's speech as permission to "strike at VUSPP" (ibid.;

26 In Ukrainian: "Bloknot" or "Bl'oknot," a regular feature devoted to irreverent comments and observations about people, events, literature, and art.

"Lyst do redaktsiï" 1929a). This vulnerability may have prompted the organization to make a special effort of recognizing the Futurist journal.

Nova generatsiia certainly helped itself with declarations that were conciliatory both to the Party and the proletarian organizations. At a time when Khvyl'ovyi and VAPLITE were being severely criticized, the journal (following a general tendency) diligently toed the Party line with its own repudiation of Khvyl'ovyi and "Fascism," choosing to embrace as "allies" such politically correct groups as VUSPP and Molodniak. On the surface, at least, *Nova generatsiia* seemed to have come to terms with the long-held Party position that the masses must appropriate bourgeois culture; it tended to de-emphasize "destruction" in favor of "construction," and went as far as to affirm art a useful tool in the building of socialism ("Zhovten' i my" 1927, 29). Where there once was a radical theory about the liquidation of art, there now stood, to all appearances, a fairly uncontroversial series of slogans proclaiming what the Futurists were "for" and what they were "against." *Nova generatsiia*'s title page read:

> We are for communism; internationalism; industrialization; efficiency [*ratsionalizatsiia*]; inventiveness; quality; thriftiness [*ekonomnist'*]; social resolve; a universal orientation on communism in daily life, culture, science, technology; new [left] art. We are against national narrow-mindedness; unprincipled trivialization [of culture]; bourgeois fashions; amorphous artistic organizations; provincialism; rustic backwardness [*tr'okhpil'ne khutorianstvo*]; quasi-learning; eclecticism.[27]

While the careful observer may have noted that these slogans were permeated with Futurism's past, there was also no denying that now they had an uncharacteristically moderate appearance and tone. This was no accident. The Futurists prided themselves on their ability to adapt. Semenko said the Futurists were "Leninists" in their approach to art, not "utopian communists" (Semenko 1928c, 360). They were willing "to relinquish the purity of [their] leftist maxims for the sake of [dealing with] the concrete, local reality" (ibid.). In an age characterized by a "great confusion in tradition, customs, and tastes" ("Platforma i otochennia livykh" 1927, 41), it was occasionally necessary to tread lightly in order to exert influence on the course of events.

Subsequent developments would prove, however, that while the Futurists were willing to compromise, they were not willing to abandon their positions. Time and again, there would be a resurgence of their maximalist program. In later issues of *Nova generatsiia*, Panfuturism was

[27] These slogans were arranged in two columns and kept appearing from October 1927 to December 1928.

invoked unambiguously. From January 1929 to April 1930, in place of the noncommittal "for" and "against" slogans, the journal ran this declaration:

> Art as an emotional category of culture is dying. The gradual process of art's demise has been marked in the last decades by the destructive current. The rational demands placed upon art today are redirecting it into the constructive path of functional art. Functional art plays a socially useful role in the general process of socialist construction within the universal orientation toward communism. *Nova generatsiia* unites the destructive stage of art, which is drawing to a close, with the constructive, which is beginning, [and] considers both these stages as component parts of a single dialectical process in the development of the left [avant-garde] formation of art.

For those who may have thought that the Futurists had broken with their past, they made a point of tracing their genealogy from "naive Kvero-futurism," through Aspanfut, Komunkul't and Bumeranh ("Platforma i otochennia livykh" 1927, 39). For those who were frightened by the word "destruction," *Nova generatsiia* found a useful substitute—"experimentation." Poetry, painting, and theater were now prone to be affirmed in their avant-gardist (leftist) guise, rather than "destroyed" as institutions. These arts, it was said, would enter as elements into communist culture only after they were purged of their "bourgeois spirit" ("Zhovten' i my" 1927, 29), "after [undergoing] mandatory experimentation and [re-]invention" ("Platforma i otochennia livykh" 1927, 42).

The Futurists never confused their ideological and political alliances with artistic principles. In terms of politics, they subordinated themselves more or less to organizations like VUSPP and Molodniak but jealously guarded their independence on questions of art and culture, refusing to acknowledge others as authorities. From its first issue, *Nova generatsiia* declared itself in favor of "differentiation" in the artistic arena (ibid., 41; Semenko 1928f, 399). The journal argued that only through free competition among various movements would it become clear which artistic currents were in fact progressive and which reactionary ("Platforma i otochennia livykh" 1927, 41). There certainly was no doubt in the Futurists' mind to which category the proletarian corps of writers belonged:

> Within groupings that take a *proletarian* approach to the [artistic] process and are under the greatest [ideological] control, one very frequently encounters content that is counter-revolutionary in its ramifications.

> Here in the Ukrainian S.S.R., this occurs when "proletarian" critics begin to think of themselves as "spokesmen for proletarian social opinion...." In most cases, they predicate [their criticism] solely on their petty-bourgeois gut [*puzo*]. They begin analyzing and "criticizing" for "the greater glory of communism," but in fact do it a disservice. This happens when a "proletarian writer," supported by a "proletarian critic," tries to pass as "proletarian creativity" any "inspired" story or poem even if it is bereft of all structure.
>
> Therefore, we must expose unprincipled behavior and ignorance, in order that there be no whitewashing, no misunderstanding on the revolutionary front, in order that we might reject the "proletarian" which is counter-revolutionary, so that we might see the left [masquerading] under the right and the right under the left (ibid.).

Nova generatsiia thought of itself as a laboratory for the "qualified artist" and "scientific workers of art" who conducted "experiments" and implemented their "own methodology" (ibid., 43). It was expected that the rational and functional nature of their experiments would have a positive effect on the uncultured state and in the formation of a "new psyche, a new developing person, a new race" (ibid.). The Futurists considered themselves "just as essential as...builders and workers of the Dnipro hydroelectric plant or the liquidators of illiteracy" ("Zhovten' i my" 1927, 30). The journal treated readers as partners in this task of creating a new culture and a new man. Through their own efforts, readers would consolidate "the new tenets and principles" ("Platforma i otochennia livykh" 1927, 43). But the Futurists did not deem it important to appeal to the masses as such, stating that their focus was on the "prepared" and "cultured" reader (*Nova generatsiia* 1928 [5]: 391 and 1928 [11]: 357). When told that writing "to social order" meant not only satisfying "ideological" requirements but also "the specific literary tastes and demands of the reader" (Ruderman 1928, 105), the Futurists responded that their function was "to raise the masses" to a higher level (*Nova generatsiia* 1928 [4]: 301).

First Metamorphosis: VUARKK

During the first year of the journal's existence no special effort was made to flaunt Panfuturism or to pursue it in a militant fashion. As *Nova generatsiia* set out to "develop the entire front of new art in all its aspects and in its international dimension" (Semenko 1928c, 360), the theory was more frequently an implicit rather than an explicit presence. However, on the journal's first anniversary (October 1928) there was an attempt to do away with this amorphousness. It was announced that two organizations were being formed by associates of the journal, in order that each might specialize in a different aspect of the Panfuturist program. One was referred to as "The Constructivists-Functionalists" [*Konstruktory-funktsionalisty*]; the other, "The Futurists-Destructivists (meta-artists)" [*Futurysty-destruktory (meta–mysttsi)*]. The first group, which was headed by Shkurupii and included some of the newest recruits to the Futurist cause, that is, Iurii Paliichuk, Viktor Ver, and Oleksa Vlyz'ko, had intentions of establishing itself "in accordance with regulations [governing] artistic organizations" ("Konstruktory-funktsionalisty" 1928, 275). The participants of the second were not revealed, but there can be no doubt they were led by Semenko. Shkurupii's camp declared it would conduct its activities under the slogan "constructive functionalism in art" and would proceed to "specify its place within the system of the left formation of art." The Constructivists further declared they would publish an independent journal and a series of separate publications.

The Futurists-Destructivists defined themselves as a union of avant-garde literati, journalists, and poet-destructivists. Their aim was to "struggle with art as a separate category of culture," meaning that this "group would occupy the extreme left flank" in the artistic process. Like the Constructivists-Functionalists, they too were planning to publish a journal and even announced a title, *F* (for "Futurists"). Towards this end they established a cooperative publishing house, Semafor u Maibutnie. *F*, it was said, would be similar to the Russian *Novyi Lef*, but would pay particular attention to the "post-artistic significance of each type of art" ("Futurysty-destruktory" 1928, 276).

In the past, a split such as this would have signaled a crisis in the Futurist movement. In this instance, it was a premeditated step to develop and differentiate the program more fully. This view is supported by comments Semenko made a few months later. "We are *forced*," he said, "to express in a single organ [i.e., *Nova generatsiia*] two sides of our work: the destructive and the constructive. Among circles that have little knowledge of dialectics, this elicits the accusation that we [engage] in eclecticism. The best thing would be to publish a second journal, *but right now this is impossible*" (*Nova generatsiia* 4 [1929]: 73; *emphasis added*). Indeed, publishing something other than *Nova generatsiia* proved unworkable in April 1929 when this comment was made, as well as in October 1928 when the Constructivists and Destructivists expressed a desire to specialize. *F* was just one of a number of projected publications never realized, attesting to the fact that, without direct government subsidy and sanction, the Futurists remained powerless.[28]

[28] The Futurists planned and advertized the following publications, which never appeared: 1) *Al'manakh novoï generatsiï* [The Almanac of the New Generation], a series

Even though this attempt at "differentiating" their work failed and nothing more was heard about creating two distinct organizations, the episode did illustrate that the Futurists were intent on pursuing the Panfuturist program more vigorously. Because the publication of additional journals was impossible, this function fell to *Nova generatsiia* itself. At this time, it began showing signs of radicalization, frequently and overtly alluding to various aspects of Panfuturism. However, since the journal was compelled to serve two factions, the Constructive and the Destructive, it also betrayed evidence of genuine vacillation about which of the two directions to take. In the first few months of 1929 the destructivist current had a definite edge. Not only did a series of articles begin appearing written from a clearly "maximalist" position (Poltorats'kyi 1929a),[29] but in January 1929, as already stated, the journal jettisoned its innocent "pro" and "con" slogans in favor of statements proclaiming art a dying category. This was the unmistakable trademark of the Destructivists.

But just as this latter tendency appeared to be gaining ascendancy, Semenko suddenly moved to deny destruction altogether and to focus exclusively on "constructive work." As we shall see, the Futurists were indeed turning toward more radical positions in 1929, but they moved carefully and tried to emphasize, especially in their programmatic statements (less so in their practice), those elements of their theory that

---

of "thick" almanacs scheduled for release by the Kharkiv publisher Proletarii (see *Nova generatsiia* 1928 [5]: 384). 2) An untitled monograph series on Ukrainian and West European artists and special artistic problems and themes. Projected publisher: Proletarii (cf. ibid.). 3) A large collection, *P'iatnadtsiat' rokiv ukraïns'koho futuryzmu* [Fifteen Years of Ukrainian Futurism], scheduled for February 1929 from the publisher Semafor u Maibutnie to mark the fifteenth anniversary of Semenko's *Derzannia* (1914) (see *Nova generatsiia* 1928 [9]: 195; [11]: 358). This was to include Futurist works, a history of the movement and bibliography. 4) *Suchasna arkhitektura* [Contemporary Architecture] and *Al'manakh nevyznanykh* [The Almanac of the Unrecognized]. The latter, planned as a bi-monthly, was to accept only works that were rejected by at least three editors or publishing houses. Publisher: Semafor u Maibutnie (see *Nova generatsiia* 1929 [4]: 5, 81; 1929 [5]: 81). 5) *Front: Al'manakh proletars'kykh pys'mennykiv Novoï generatsiï* [Front: The Almanac of Proletarian Writers of the New Generation]. Publisher: Semafor u Maibutnie (see *Nova generatsiia* 1929 [10]: back cover). 6) The publisher Semafor u Maibutnie was to have released several works by individual Futurists, but only Koliada 1929 managed to appear.

29 Also, in April the journal began publishing the posthumous articles of Leonid Skrypnyk (L. Skrypnyk 1929h). Actually these were chapters from a book entitled *Art and Social Culture* (*Mystetstvo i sotsiial'na kul'tura*), which the editor admitted was written "from the point of view of the maximalist program of Panfuturism, on which the notion of the withering away of the arts is based..." (*Nova generatsiia* 1929 [4]: table of contents).

were prone to elicit the least amount of censure from the literary and political community at large.

Semenko's call for completely constructive work occurred at a 12 March 1929 meeting of *Nova generatsiia*'s Kharkiv associates ("Protokol zasidannia" 1929, 72).[30] It was then that he also warned his colleagues against allowing the group to develop into an "artistic sect" and urged that a link be established between "experimentalism and mass work [*masovist'*]" (ibid.). To achieve these objectives, Semenko proposed that the informal character of their association be transformed into an authentic organization, and he even advanced a name: "The Association of Workers of Communist Culture." Suddenly it appeared as if *Nova generatsiia* was on the threshold of retracing the history of Komunkul't.

Semenko's plan met with general approval. Everyone agreed on the need for a *bona fide* organization that would have a cultural instead of a purely artistic character. Not everyone, however, concurred at first with the proposed name. Two members (Malovichko and Ver) said that their group should carry the name "Futurists." Ver reasoned that the name had an honorable and spirited history and hence was not something they should repudiate. Nonetheless, when it came to a vote, a unanimous decision was taken in favor of Semenko's choice. ARKK [*Asotsiiatsiia robitnykiv komunistychnoï kul'tury*] (internally also called "Komunkul't") became the official name; a short while later it was modified to VUARKK—The All-Ukrainian Association of Workers of Communist Culture [*Vseukraïns'ka asotsiiatsiia robitnykiv komunistychnoï kul'tury*].

A few days following these developments, the Kyiv associates[31] of *Nova generatsiia* met to ratify the decisions taken in Kharkiv and established a branch of VUARKK in their own city. An executive "bureau" was elected consisting of Shkurupii, Parubochyi, Buz'ko, Frenkel', and Krychevs'kyi ("Protokol zboriv initsiatyvnoï hrupy" 1929, 77). In Kharkiv the leadership of the organization fell to Semenko, Sotnyk, and Poltorats'kyi. VUARKK also established three specialized "bureaus," each with its own head: "Research and Ideology" (Poltorats'kyi), "Production" (Ver), and "Propaganda" (Sotnyk).

The formation of VUARKK might suggest that, as in the past, the Futurists were trying to become civic activists instead of "workers" in art. While it is true that in some respects VUARKK resembled Komunkul't,

[30] Present were Mykhail' Semenko, Dan Sotnyk, V. Kashnyts'kyi, Hro Vakar, Ivan Malovichko, Oleksii Poltorats'kyi, V. Ver, and Oleksander Mar'iamov.

[31] Attending the meeting were: Shkurupii, Iu. Dritt, Dan Sotnyk, Oleksa Vlyz'ko, L. Frenkel', Hlib Zatvornyts'kyi, [?] Krychevs'kyi, [?] Kovalevs'kyi, [?] Kolomoitsev.

in practice it never came close to reproducing the history and activities of its predecessor. Members of *Nova generatsiia* did indeed venture out into the "masses," propagandizing their theories and showing off their "production." The organization even entered into several alliances with other groups and workers' clubs. In the final analysis, however, these activities were a minor aspect of VUARKK; they remained insignificant in comparison to efforts made on behalf of artistic issues and the journal.

When VUARKK was being established one member expressed the fear that, due to a lack of personnel, the new organization could find itself in the same unfortunate situation as Komunkul't had a few years earlier, when it tried to do too much with insufficient cadres. Significantly, Semenko countered by saying: "Of course, *Nova generatsiia* will not undergo great changes" ("Protokol zasidannia" 1929, 74). And, indeed, it did not. In retrospect, Semenko's call for linking experimentalism and work among the masses was not actually an invitation to his associates to involve themselves directly with the "people." The link, as he understood it, was to occur through "strengthening the constructive elements" in their program, meaning it would be achieved by means of their artistic production, specifically, via the development and practice of "functional arts." In a speech before the Research and Ideology Bureau, Semenko outlined how some of the traditional arts could be employed in a functional dimension. He urged his associates to work on a "functional" terminology (preferably one modeled on architecture), which would replace the artistic and aesthetic terminology peculiar to the old arts (Semenko 1929f). A few days later, Poltorats'kyi pursued this line of inquiry in a speech before the Production Bureau. After outlining several specific directions their work could take, Poltorats'kyi ended by saying that *Nova generatsiia* was "not a mass" periodical and that "the journal must be a laboratory....We must publish only progressive things; we must not repeat ourselves; we must print only new endeavors" (Poltorats'kyi 1929c). Although Poltorats'kyi's statement seemed to place the notion of "experimentalism" and "the masses" in opposition to each other, the two were apparently reconciled in the minds of the Futurists by virtue of the fact that experiments, although private and highly individualistic, were in the final analysis useful for the masses.[32]

If in March the Futurists tried to present themselves as constructive/functional workers, toiling for the benefit of the masses and communist

[32] In another context, the editors had noted: "The 'laboratory-experimental' work of chemists, while 'individualistic' to a great extent, is not (or should not be) cut off from the masses simply because the science of chemistry, as such, in its application to life, has to be, and is, a science for the masses." See "Shcho pyshut' chytachi" 1927.

culture, then in April, at a public debate held in Kyiv, they willingly embraced the opposite image. In what turned out to be a rather typical clash with the representatives of proletarian art and criticism (most notably members of VUSPP), the Futurists reaffirmed their commitment toward destruction and antagonized their audience by declaring art dead and useless for the proletariat.

The debate, entitled "Who Needs Art?" ("H." 1929), took place on 21 April, just a month and a half after the creation of VUARKK. The star attraction was Semenko who gave the keynote address; also present were Vlyz'ko, Shkurupii, Ver, Sotnyk, and others, all of whom read from their works. Before a large audience, Semenko gave what a reporter from *Literaturna hazeta* described as a "boring speech." The following remarks were attributed to Semenko: Art was dying as an emotional category; it will be subordinated to human reason; it must cease being an object of leisure and should perform a socially useful function; Futurists rejected beauty, for it was a bourgeois notion; they renounced all existing Marxisms, inasmuch as one Marxist contradicted another; Futurists made common cause only with the Party; they regarded themselves as builders of a proletarian culture and creators of completely new "left" forms; Volodymyr Sosiura's or Pavlo Tychyna's "soft-bodied" lyrics could not achieve this goal, for their work was nothing but "eternal little verses" covered "with proletarian sauce." The Futurists, he continued, promoted functional lyrics, destruction, a universal orientation on communist culture, feuilletons and reportage; they substituted the concepts of facture and ideology for the old "form and content" dyad (ibid.).

This performance elicited a hostile reaction from the floor. Everyone who was reported to have made a comment (among them Borys Kovalenko, Serhii Voskrekasenko, I. Dubkov, Iurii Perlin, and Ivan Vrona) condemned Semenko. Kovalenko, a leading figure in Molodniak and a close associate of VUSPP, set the tone when he described Semenko's theories as vulgarized Marxism and observed that the pursuit of "leftist" forms did not necessarily guarantee a revolutionary ideology. He considered Futurists' "constructive" work nothing but "leftist" formalism with a primitive ideology that reduced the complexity of art to a few pathetic forms. He viewed their individualism and endless desire to scandalize as a petty-bourgeois symptom.

Iurii Perlin at first almost refrained from speaking, saying that the cheap sensationalism and childish self-promotion to which he was witness virtually precluded serious discussion. He did, nevertheless, state that Semenko's positions were diametrically opposed to the tenets of classical Marxism and that the promotion of a rational art was a basic error.

Vrona, representing the painters' organization ARMU (*Asotsiiatsiia revoliutsiinoho mystetstva Ukraïny* [Association of Revolutionary Art of Ukraine]), said he was disappointed with Semenko's confused speech. In his view, it was not art but rather the Futurists who were self-destructing. Art, being an ideological factor, could not possibly be rejected, nor could it die as an emotional category.

Others expressed similar notions, pronouncing Futurist poetry incomprehensible to the masses and displeasing to the reader. The proletariat, it was said, needed beauty no less than the bourgeoisie. Some advised Semenko to stop playing with Marxism, for it was far too serious a discipline for games.

The most interesting moment of the debate occurred at the end, when Semenko rose to rebut his opponents. In a characteristically unperturbed fashion he called everyone who took the floor against him "natural [*stykhiini*] demagogues and chameleons" and declared VUSPP's slogans "senseless spontaneous [*stykhiine*] simplification[s]" that only retarded culture.

The virulent character of this public confrontation was not an isolated incident. The polite treatment the Futurists had received from the proletarians earlier had by now changed. The Futurists themselves were to blame for this, because they insisted on distinguishing between the positive ideological work of the proletarians and their negative, regressive art. *Nova generatsiia* regularly carried caustic observations about proletarian efforts in literature and literary criticism, paying particular attention to the activities of VUSPP. The critic H. Ovcharov, for example, overtly stated that "polemics against representatives of VUSPP hold first place" (Ovcharov 1930a) in *Nova generatsiia*. Journals like *Hart*, *Literaturna hazeta*, *Molodniak* and the critics who contributed to them (Samiilo Shchupak, Volodymyr Derzhavyn, Volodymyr Koriak, Ahapii Shamrai, Feliks Iakubovs'kyi, Mykhailo Dolengo) were frequent targets. Shchupak, who received more than his share of unwanted attention from the Futurists, was described by one of them as a person who "definitely disgusts us all" (Vlyz'ko 1928).[33] The feeling was mutual, and the proletarian groups did not hesitate to condemn the Futurists just as harshly, although in a vocabulary notably less figurative.[34]

33 See also the following: Poltorats'kyi 1928d; Holubenko 1928; Poltorats'kyi 1928e; "Bloknot 'Novoï generatsiï'" (1928, 335–38, 424); Poltorats'kyi 1929g

34 For a sampling see the following: Iakubovs'kyi (1928a, 93 and 107; and 1929e); Khvylia 1928; Ruderman (1928, 104); Shchupak 1928; Dolengo 1929a and 1929b; K—v 1929.

These frequently vicious polemics came to an abrupt end in May of 1929. The immediate cause was the second congress of VUSPP (26–31 May) which suddenly drove home certain political facts of life that until then the Futurists either had refused to acknowledge or failed to notice. The first Five Year Plan, introduced a year earlier, was having serious repercussions in the cultural realm. During VUSPP's congress it became evident that the organization the Futurists enjoyed baiting was going to play a central role in the period of "socialist reconstruction." Ivan Mykytenko, a leading member of VUSPP, spelled out the connection between the congress and the new sociopolitical situation:

> The second congress [of VUSPP] coincides with the entry of our country and the entire Union of Republics into a new period of reconstruction, [i.e.,] of rebuilding all of life [and] all of society on completely new foundations. In connection with the tasks of this period, *the third front, to which literature also belongs, ceases to exist separately.* A single socialist-reconstructive-class-front is being created into which proletarian literature must organically grow and be active (Mykytenko 1929, 24; *emphasis added*).

VUSPP was an organization exuding confidence. It had strong support from Pluh and Molodniak and embraced within its structures a broad spectrum of party-oriented critics and writers, among whom were Russians and Jews.[35] VUSPP had at its disposal *Literaturna hazeta* and *Hart*. In addition, the State Publishing House (DVU) issued under VUSPP's imprint various works of fiction and criticism. In 1928 VUSPP joined the Russian-sponsored VOAPP (Vsesoiuzne ob'iednannia asotsiatsii proletars'kykh pys'mennykiv [The All-Union Alliance of Associations of Proletarian Writers]), thus becoming the organization through which Ukrainian writers were eventually expected to enter into all-Union contacts and through which the unity of Soviet cultures would be achieved.

Mykola Skrypnyk, who was just one of many Party dignitaries to speak at the congress, paid VUSPP numerous compliments. At the same time he tried to restrain the ambitious organization. Referring to its hegemonic goals, Skrypnyk reminded the delegates that "VUSPP is not *all* of proletarian literature" and that it cannot have pretensions to being a "regulatory [*kerivna*] organization." He counseled tolerance and moderation toward fellow-travelers, even toward the avant-gardists, mentioning Semenko and Valeriian Polishchuk. He argued that those

[35] Russian and Jewish writers had their separate journals; the former published *Krasnoe slovo*, the latter, *Prolit*.

who err in the present should not be viewed as irrevocably lost to the proletariat. But for all these cautionary remarks, Skrypnyk did concede to VUSPP the right to pursue a policy that would unite all Ukrainian writers:

> We are faced with the task of consolidating all creative proletarian forces.... We, [i.e.,] all proletarian writers, stand before the task of...founding an All-Ukrainian Association of Organizations of Soviet Writers. This [task] must be done now when VUSPP has grown strong, when there are certain mobilized forces, when certain relationships have become manifest. The Union of Ukrainian Proletarian Writers [i.e., VUSPP] must be the organizer. Uniting the forces is an important task. You [VUSPP] members must take an active role in this.... (M. Skrypnyk 1929, 21–22).

In short, although the KP(b)U tried not to grant VUSPP complete monopolistic authority over literature, it did make clear this was a special organization. Ordered to practice restraint, VUSPP was given, nonetheless, an obvious mandate to integrate all Ukrainian cultural and literary organizations. For the Futurists it now became important to seek reconciliation with VUSPP, especially because they were mentioned at the congress as one of the wayward groups:

> The left-intellectualist [*livo-inteligents'ki*] writers are attempting to substitute naked functionalism for proletarian literature. They are faced with the danger of substituting reflexology [*sic*] for the dialectics of Marx and Lenin; [even] now they are attempting to prove with the help of [reflexology] that art as an emotional category is reactionary. If the Panfuturists do not renounce the production of 'artistic,' or should we say "functional" things, they can eventually arrive at a self-contradiction or at the falsification of art; [they are in danger of producing] artistic things far from the needs and demands of the working class. Proletarian literature...must influence these writers [and direct them] toward closer ties with proletarian creativity (Mykytenko 1929, 32).

It did not take long for the Futurists to assimilate these words. Before the congress came to a close, *Nova generatsiia* (VUARKK) submitted a proposal to VUSPP, urging it to join with the Futurists in a coalition "against the threat of the right." Surprisingly, VUSPP readily took up the offer. At the last session of the congress a declaration was issued by each organization which officially sealed the pact ("Bl'ok mizh VUARKK ta VUSPP-om" 1929).

VUSPP's willingness to deal with the Futurists stemmed from its obsessive desire to federate all writers under its own wing. The establishment of links with *Nova generatsiia* was viewed as another feather in VUSPP's cap, a sign of the same organizational prowess that had led to "close contacts" with Molodniak and Pluh ("Dekliaratsiia VUSPP" 1929). Coming as it did at the end of the congress, this announcement no doubt helped to heighten the organization's aura of success.

The coalition between *Nova generatsiia* (VUARKK) and VUSPP could not overlook, of course, their troubled past. Consequently, both organizations stressed in their respective declarations the need for renouncing further "sharp polemics." All "criticism and polemics should be conducted in a friendly tone..." stated the VUSPP declaration. It must be devoid of "unprincipled abuses" and refrain from becoming a "settlement of personal grudges" (ibid.). For its part, *Nova generatsiia* vowed to "stop the publication of material designed to compromise VUSPP in general or its representatives in particular" ("Dekliaratsiia VUARKK" 1929). Moreover, "*Nova generatsiia* considers that...the work of VUSPP reflects the needs of the working class....Our paths must meet....There can be no question of any antagonism between *Nova generatsiia* and VUSPP on questions of principle" (ibid.).

This did not mean, however, that polemics were to cease altogether. Both organizations conceded that theoretical disparities still existed between them and that further discussion was inevitable. "The theoretical platform of Panfuturism is presently far from being in complete agreement with the theoretical platform of VUSPP," stated *Nova generatsiia*. It identified several points of controversy, mentioning "the problem of form and content, the problem of the future of the artistic process, and the question of the role of the art object...and the individual arts" in society (ibid.). It was suggested further that both groups engage in "socialist competition" to test which of the two movements "pointed forward and which backward." This was, literally, the same suggestion made by *Nova generatsiia* in 1927. In short, the journal was again recognizing the ideological and political role of VUSPP but reserved the right to pursue its own artistic policy.

There was one phrase of *Nova generatsiia*'s declaration that could be construed as an attempt to accommodate itself to VUSPP's artistic position: "There can be no question about the liquidation of literature; the problem lies only in an appropriate directional transformation of [literature]"....(ibid.). Considering the importance the concept had in the Panfuturist system, this could be seen as a major concession to VUSPP. On closer examination, and especially in light of *Nova generatsiia*'s subsequent practice, it appears that this was more of a terminological refinement than a theoretical change of heart. By speaking about the "directional transformation" of literature, the Futurists were in fact implying its "death" but with more tact. According to their concepts, any transformation of a system in effect meant its demise and the emergence of something entirely new. It is hard, therefore, to see in this document and the coalition with VUSPP any serious break in the Futurists' position. Their declaration seems to have all the earmarks of a diplomatic ploy designed to ensure them a continued presence in the literary arena.

This conclusion is supported by a lengthy report on a meeting of the Research and Ideology Bureau which discussed developments in the Ukrainian theater. It was published in the same issue of *Nova generatsiia* that carried the declarations about the coalition. At this meeting, there was no sign of compromise as speakers pursued typically "maximalist" positions. Shkurupii, for example, argued that the theater must outgrow the limitations imposed on it by the stage and walls, and develop into "mass games"—a view similar to one espoused by Semenko back in the days of Aspanfut. The issues of *Nova generatsiia* that followed provide many examples which prove that despite a partial retreat and some obfuscation, the Futurists for the most part kept to their characteristic course.

Polemics with the Russians

When the last issue of the Russian avant-garde journal *Novyi Lef* appeared in December 1928, it carried a brief reference to *Nova generatsiia*:

> TO THE ATTENTION OF SUBSCRIBERS AND READERS OF "NOVYI LEF." During the absence of our own journal, we propose that our principal theoretical works, those which fail to find a place for themselves in the general press, be printed in the Ukrainian journal *Nova generatsiia*, published by the State Publishing House of Ukraine (*Novyi Lef* 1928 [12]: 45).

This announcement might suggest that there was a special rapport between the two journals. Indeed, in some respects there was. *Novyi Lef* had acknowledged a few months earlier that "friendly contacts and exchange of materials are in effect between the editorial boards of *Novyi Lef* and *Nova generatsiia*" ("Nam pishut o 'Novom Lefe' i 'Novoi Generatsii'" 1928). This impression was also conveyed by *Nova generatsiia*. As part of a strategy to strengthen its own position in the Ukrainian cultural and political sphere, *Nova generatsiia* adopted certain overt features that linked it to *Novyi Lef*. Like the Russian journal, *Nova generatsiia* subtitled itself the "Left Front of Arts"; when LEF became REF, *Nova generatsiia* too renamed itself the "Revolutionary Front of Arts." The Russian journal was said to be "required reading" (*Nova generatsiia* 1 [1927]: 79) for *Nova generatsiia*'s supporters. Russian Futurists and their journal were defended from attacks, as well as invoked for purposes of self-defense ("Lystuvannia druziv" 1928).

In late 1927 Ukrainian Futurists extended an invitation to the Russians to contribute to *Nova generatsiia*.[36] This led to the most conspicuous link between the two journals. The list of "participants" that *Nova generatsiia* began publishing on its covers in 1928 displayed names of several prominent "leftist" activists in Russia: Nikolai Aseev, Osip Brik, N. Chuzhak, Sergei Eisenstein, Aleksei Gan, Vladimir Maiakovskii, Kazimir Malevich, Viktor Pertsov, Grigorii Petnikov, Aleksandr Rodchenko, Viktor Shklovskii, Vladimir Tatlin, Sergei Tret'iakov and Dziga Vertov. The roster was impressive. But like other accoutrements of their "relationship," it proved to be mostly symbolic; the practical consequences for *Nova generatsiia* were negligible. Aside from a few minor pieces, the journal—and its sister publication in Kyiv, *Avanhard-Al'manakh proletars'kykh myttsiv Novoï generatsiï* [Avant-Garde—Almanac of Proletarian Artists of the New Generation]—published Dziga Vertov,[37] Aleksei Gan,[38] P. Neznamov (Neznamov 1928), and Sergei Tret'iakov (Tret'iakov 1930). Some Russian poetry in translation was published as well.

In short, despite expressions of fellowship, actual collaboration between Ukrainian Futurists and *Novyi Lef* were minimal. *Nova generatsiia* reported fairly regularly on *Novyi Lef* and publicized the contents of new issues. But it received no such systematic attention from the Moscow journal. In fact, there was only one article worthy of note in *Novyi Lef* about *Nova generatsiia*. Ironically, it only undermined the carefully wrought impression that the two movements were close associates. But before turning to this problem, it would be appropriate to point out certain broad analogies and areas of congruence between the Ukrainians and Russians.

First, it must be noted that by 1927 Ukrainian Futurism, as a movement, had attained certain organizational forms that made it roughly equivalent to the Russian movement. It now had the ability to maintain a journal, having won grudging tolerance from society. From 1927 Ukrainian Futurism had more in common with the Russian movement than at any previous time, largely because it had abandoned its earlier orientation on the masses. Both movements derived their identity from a periodical. Much like *Novyi Lef*, *Nova generatsiia* was primarily concerned with art and literature in a formalist and constructivist vein. To the degree that

[36] A letter to that effect, signed by Semenko and Dan Sotnyk, appeared in *Novyi Lef* (1927 [8–9]: 88)

[37] Vertov 1929. Dziga Vertov's film, "A Man with a Movie Camera," the subject of this article, was released in 1929 by VUFKU, the All-Ukrainian Photo-Cinema Administration.

[38] Han 1928. This was a translation and reprint from *S.A.* (*Sovremennaia arkhitektura*).

these were also the concerns of *Novyi Lef*, it can be said the two movements were roughly alike.

Thanks to such parallels and the editorial ties, *Nova generatsiia* found itself being accused both of imitating *Novyi Lef* and for deviating from its example. Readers wrote wishing to know what the differences were between the two publications. Did *Nova generatsiia* share *Novyi Lef*'s platform? If so, why did *Nova generatsiia* publish belles-lettres and reproductions of Picasso when *Novyi Lef* was against both? Did *Nova generatsiia* consider *Novyi Lef* a model for emulation or a vestige of the past? Why had *Novyi Lef* not responded to the appearance of *Nova generatsiia* if the two were such close associates? ("Lystuvannia z redaktsiieiu" 1928b).

In answering such queries, *Nova generatsiia* took pains to underscore its own independence and distinctiveness, while conceding that in certain spheres it shared a common platform with *Novyi Lef*. The Ukrainians argued that the avant-garde was greater than the sum of its individual parts. *Nova generatsiia*'s role was to inform readers about the avant-garde in the West and to pursue "destructive" and "constructive" work at home. "In this respect, as a dialectical conception of art, we consider our work to be more significant than Moscow's *Novyi Lef* because the latter stands only for practical [work] (leftist craftsmanship) [and does not] support its work with a specific philosophical system of Left art..." ("Vid redaktsiï" 1928a). The editors also pointed out that certain "differences" continued to exist between the two journals on the question of leftist prose, and argued that the "systematization" of the Left [that is, avant-garde] movements remained a matter for the future (ibid.).[39]

The divergence between the two journals came into sharper relief in those instances when *Nova generatsiia* was criticized for not following *Novyi Lef*'s lead. In July 1928, for example, the Ukrainian journal published a letter from I. Vertsman, a member of Moscow's VKhUTEMAS (Vysshie gosudarstvennye khudozhestvenno-tekhnicheskie masterskie [Higher State Artistic and Technical Workshops]), who declared the following:

> If you are LEF, then be consistent, the way your Russian colleagues are..., think about "things," not about art which has been rejected by them....The savoring of Picasso's charms can only be explained either by...[your] provincialism (one can't escape that, honored editors!), or by a theoretical eclecticism. Either you are LEF or you are not LEF (*Nova generatsiia* 1928 [7]: 62–63)!

Nova generatsiia responded:

> We do not like the tone of your letter ...Why do you take offense? Don't tell us that you, a person from Vkhutemas, are irritated by

[39] For similar sentiments, see Semenko 1928d.

> Picasso? Why shouldn't even you learn how Picasso is painting today? It can only be useful....You advise us to think about "things" rather than art with which you are finished. No. We don't want to end with art; there are various types of art. And about "provincialism," etc., you can go tell that to someone else. We have our own windbags like you. Why don't you forget about "the art of the capital." Study. Otherwise leftists will compare you to those "obliging friends" who are worse than the "enemy" (ibid.).

In late 1928 a long-awaited review of *Nova generatsiia* appeared in *Novyi Lef* (Trenin 1928).[40] Very reminiscent of Vertsman's unsolicited advice, it too urged its Ukrainian Futurists to adhere more closely to the principles of LEF. The review and the rebuttal it received revealed substantial differences between the two movements.

Novyi Lef's reviewer, Vladimir Trenin, began his critique by explaining to his Russian audience that *generatsiia* meant *pokolenie*. He complimented the journal on its slogans, singling out for praise those that pitted communism and internationalism against national restrictiveness, a vice "painfully visible in Ukraine lately." The rest of the review amounted to a refutation of what he described was a "widespread impression that *Nova generatsiia* personifies the Ukrainian LEF" and that it was a "detachment of the Left Front in Ukraine."

Trenin concluded that the "theoretical part of the [Ukrainian] journal stood in sharp opposition to the assertions of LEF." He accused *Nova generatsiia* of suffering from leftist "aestheticism and eclecticism" and compared it to *Veshch'* (Lissitzky and Ehrenburg 1922) and *Transition*,[41] saying that it resembled these journals right down to its "immaculate European outward appearance." Basically, he said, the journal embodied the principles of early Futurism.

A considerable part of the critique was devoted to *Nova generatsiia*'s prose practice. Trenin took sharp exception to the theoretical and practical attempts to synthesize genres, in particular the factual with the fictional—a favorite approach of Ukrainian Futurists. "It has been already constituted through experimentation," he said authoritatively, "that the novel cannot fixate facts, it cannot be a 'reflection of reality.'..." Trenin ended by demanding that *Nova generatsiia* "clearly explain whether the journal is a common international informational organ of leftist currents, of which there are many in the West, or a laboratory of workers of the Left Front of Arts in Ukraine. We hope that *Nova generatsiia* will really become the 'new generation' of LEF in Ukraine."

40 For an entirely different Russian perspective of *Nova generatsiia* see Timofeev 1929.

41 Published in Paris from April 1927, *Transition*, edited by Eugen Jolas and Elliot Paul, printed leading contemporary authors such as James Joyce.

Trenin's "warning" (*trevozhnyi signal*) was ill received in Ukraine. A veiled and strictly interim rebuttal appeared in the form of an editorial comment to an article on the literature of fact by P. Neznamov published by *Nova generatsiia* in October (Neznamov 1928). Ukrainian Futurists took this opportunity to emphasize that on certain "fundamental" issues their journal was "different from *Novyi Lef.*" They argued that the Russian journal treated "debatable questions" as "programmatic" and was forcing them on the entire avant-garde community. "We view *Novyi Lef*'s posture as a specific modification of futurist work, one which is not without its didactic benefits, but it remains only one of many possible variations." In contrast to LEF's so-called restrictive theories, Ukrainians pointed to their "concept, which is based on the dialectics of leftist movements in their historical evolution," and embraces both "maximalist and minimalist" positions (see the table of contents, *Nova generatsiia* 1928 [10]: 201–202).

A direct and much more temperamental response to Trenin was provided by Geo Shkurupii, who called the Russian article a "false alarm" founded on ignorance. He suggested that "before [anyone] begins attacking the leftist positions of [our] journal—which unquestionably reflects consistent principles of the new art and has a well argued dialectical orientation—he should carefully consider several issues and most certainly take into account the tone of the signal and advice" (Shkurupii 1928c, 332). With undisguised sarcasm, Shkurupii reassured *Novyi Lef* that *Nova generatsiia* was not hopelessly lost in the provinces. He observed that "internationalism" was a relevant principle not only in Ukraine but wherever national restrictiveness and chauvinism survived, and that included places like Russia.

Shkurupii was half bemused, half indignant at Trenin's insistence on comparing *Nova generatsiia* with other journals and his insinuation that Ukrainian poets were imitators of either Maiakovskii or Aseev. He wrote:

> *Nova generatsiia* cannot be the "personification" of a Ukrainian LEF, because there is no such thing as a "branch" of *Novyi Lef* in Ukraine.... We understand that there is no God except God, but we do feel that it is dangerous to judge unfamiliar depths on the experience of one's own river.... Our friends must understand once and for all that we are not *Novyi Lef*, we are not *Veshch'*, and we are not *Transition*. We are *Nova generatsiia*. Even if we were to have the same principles as *Novyi Lef*, we [still] have our own economic base and social conditions, a base which distinguishes our general work from the work of *Novyi Lef*.... Our friends must remember that Ukraine is not France and not Russia, and this means that the work of *Novyi Lef*, [even] if it were conducted in Ukraine, would have to undergo a suitable transformation (ibid., 328).

Shkurupii punctuated his remarks by daring *Novyi Lef* to work with its program in New York, implying that it would be as out of place in an American setting as it was in a Ukrainian one. "Can it really be that our friends from *Novyi Lef* are so immersed in their own group interests that they cannot conceive of the existence of a more original, and, let us suppose, a more correct conception [of art] than the one *Novyi Lef* has or *Veshch'* had?"

The Ukrainian Futurist system of art, explained Shkurupii, encompassed the constructive work of LEF, the experimentation of a poet like Il'ia Sel'vinskii, and the destructive practice of the Western avant-gardes. If there were any inconsistencies between theory and practice, then that was simply a consequence of unremitting experimentation. Absolute consistency, he maintained, could be found neither in *Nova generatsiia* nor in *Novyi Lef*. Moreover, only the ignorant demanded that things be written according to the "Laws of God" or the "ABCs of Communism."

The publication of Western avant-garde painters on the pages of *Nova generatsiia* was not a sign of aestheticism, explained Shkurupii. There was more aestheticism and less functionalism in Rodchenko's photographs, he claimed, than in the West European paintings *Nova generatsiia* reproduced. He reminded Trenin that Soviet painters continued to be reactionary in many respects, and insisted that European avant-garde paintings "performed a destructive role, helping to analyze and study the facture [*faktura*] of material." Because photography was a new and weak art, it could not as yet perform such a role.

> We are not at all confused by Cézanne, Picasso, or Rodchenko—as you suggest. When we publish George Grosz next to Chirico, this does not mean that we are hopeless aesthetes or eclectics. We have declared countless times that our universal communist orientation on the new art represents an entire dialectical process of leftist [i.e., avant-gardist] movements. We believe that the new art is a process which has many "isms" and one such "ism" is *Novyi Lef*.... *Novyi Lef* and the rest of [the Russian avant-garde] are not the alpha and omega of the new art. There are leftist artists who work under bourgeois conditions and there are those who work under the dictatorship of the proletariat, but *the artistic process is one* (ibid., 327).

Trenin's claim that "destruction" was a sign of aestheticism, eclecticism, and early Futurism was scoffed at by Shkurupii. The process of destruction "is taking place in art and..., of course, will continue for a long time." The work of a Khlebnikov, he maintained, was relevant for the contemporary—but essentially conservative—artistic process and Trenin's dismissal of it only demonstrated the narrowness of *Novyi Lef*'s program.

Novyi Lef's tendered solution to the problem of leftist prose also failed to satisfy Shkurupii. He countered Trenin's arguments by saying that there was a need to go beyond the reportage and the simple "fixation" of facts. If leftist prose was nothing more than what LEF defined it, then every contributor to a newspaper would have to be considered a member of LEF. "Left prose must not only fixate, but it must also organize facts," said Shkurupii. This meant that it had to discover an "architectonics" for fact.

Trenin had insisted that fictional and factual genres could not be synthesized without harming "fact"; he maintained that the novel, having become a purely aesthetic genre, had lost its ability to function as an agitational medium. Shkurupii disagreed on all counts. If properly constructed, the novel would not harm but rather strengthen factual material. He ended his rebuttal with these words:

> *Novyi Lef*, which is a specific element of the left process of art, should pay more careful attention to what is occurring in the leftist movement. We expect that the Moscow leftists will finally understand our conception [of art] and will avoid [writing] in [the chauvinistic] tone characteristic of old Russian literature. An exchange of ideas, materials, friendly advice, and close contacts between *Novyi Lef* and *Nova generatsiia* will only strengthen our influence and [our] common front against the VAPP-VUSPP vulgarities and the bureaucratic production of so-called "proletarian art." The only true workers of [proletarian art] are those who firmly stand on the international principles of the left front (ibid., 334).

Polemics with the "Right"

Following the coalition with VUSPP, the Futurists entered a period of relative tranquillity. Issues of *Nova generatsiia* appearing between June and December 1929 reflected a milder polemical tone and a lesser preoccupation with the art of confrontation. To be sure, VUSPP and other segments of the proletarian community did come under periodic scrutiny, with the Futurists making sardonic comments on writings in *Literaturna hazeta*, *Krytyka*, *Hart*, and *Molodyi bil'shovyk* [The Young Bolshevik]. These were not, however, the same militant attacks for which they were known in previous months. More or less, *Nova generatsiia* adhered to its promise of conducting "criticism and polemics...in a friendly tone."

The coalition with VUSPP had been formed under the pretext of combating the literary "right." It cannot be said, however, that the Futurists exhibited unusual fervor in this respect either. Their crusade amounted mostly to making cynical remarks in the "notebook" section of *Nova*

1. Portrait of Mykhail' Semenko, 1924. [Photo courtesy of Iryna Mykhailivna Semenko.]

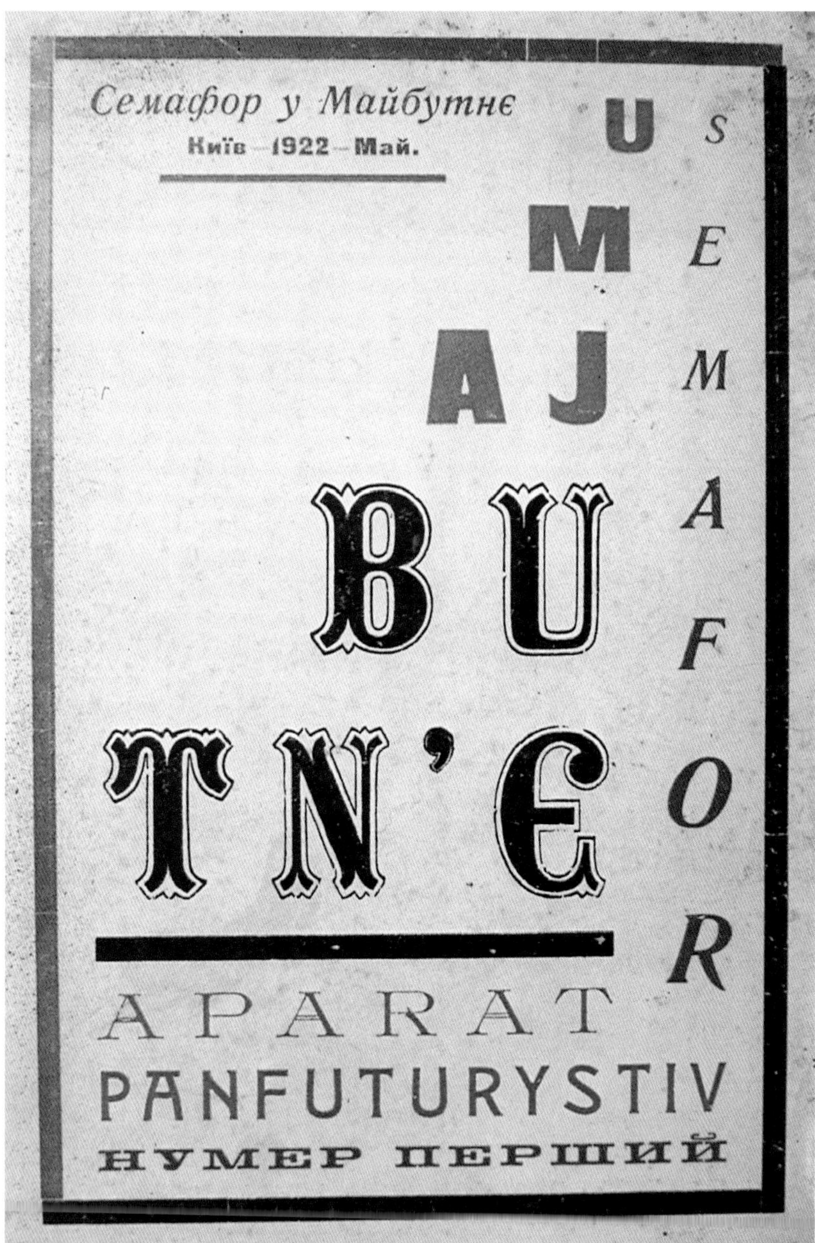

2. Cover art from *Semafor u Maibutnie. Aparat Panfuturystiv.* Kyiv: Hol'fshtrom, 1922, no. 1 (May).

3. *Top:* Caricature of *Nova generatsiia* (Semenko as Pierrot). From Mykola Sheremet, *Sharzhi ta parodiï.* Kyiv: Masa, 1931, p. 31; *Bottom:* “Nash literaturnyi Parnas.” Caricature of Mykhail' Semenko. From Mykola Sheremet, *Sharzhi ta parodiï.* Kyiv: Masa, 1931.

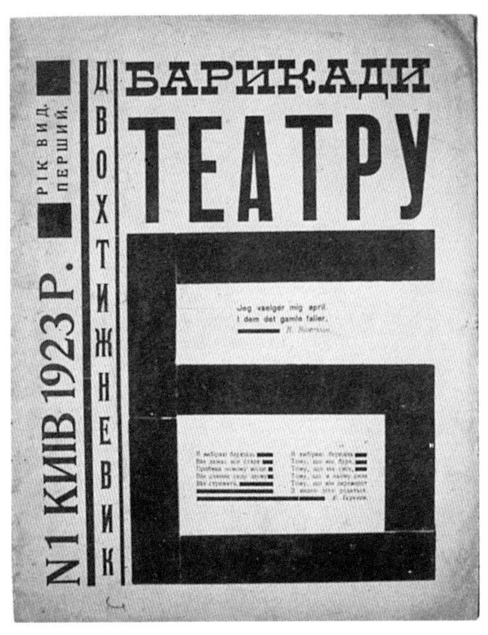

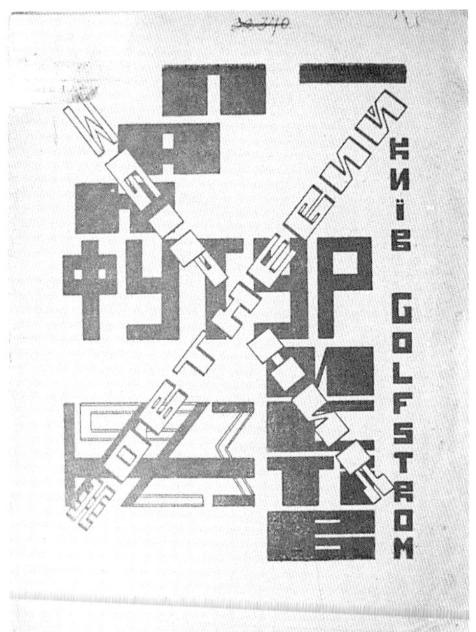

4. Cover artwork. *Top: Barykady teatru* 1923, no. 1; *Bottom: Zhovtnevyi zbirnyk panfuturystiv,* ed. Geo Shkurupii and Nik Bazhan. Kyiv: Gol'fstrom, 1923.

5. Cover artwork. *Top: Mystetstvo* 1920, no. 1; *Bottom:* Geo Shkurupii, *Baraban. Vitryna druha.* Kyiv: Panfuturysty, 1923.

6. Cover artwork for *Hol'fshtrom. Zbirnyk I. Litsektor AsKK.* Kharkiv: DVU, 1925.

7. Cover artwork. *Top:* Oleksa Slisarenko, *Neperemozhni syly. Vybrani opovidannia.* Odesa: DVU, 1929; *Bottom:* Mykhail' Semenko. "Poezomaliarstvo." *Semafor u Maibutnie. Aparat Panfuturystiv* no. 1 (May), p. 35.

8. Cover artwork for Mykhail' Semenko, *Evropa i my. Pamflety i virshi (1928–1929).* Kharkiv: Knyhospilka, 1930.

generatsiia about writers like Arkadii Liubchenko, Kost' Burevii, Pavlo Tychyna, Mykola Khvyl'ovyi, and Borys Antonenko-Davydovych, whom Shkurupii called "famous [only] for his hyphenated name" (Shkurupii 1928d, 40). Objections were also raised by the Futurists against "discredited" leftists like Valeriian Polishchuk, leader of the Constructivist organization Avanhard, and Les' Kurbas. Their sharpest attacks by far were reserved for a group of painters in ARMU (*Asotsiatsiia revoliutsiinoho mystetstva Ukraïny* [Association of Revolutionary Art of Ukraine]), the so-called Boichukists (followers of Mykhailo Boichuk), who drew much of their inspiration from Byzantine icons (Shkurupii 1929a). Provincialism and artistic backwardness were vices the Futurists lambasted most often. As was inevitable during this time, polemics did not remain purely cultural, but acquired a political hue as well. Relatively speaking, however, politics had a minor place in Futurist arguments, although there were notable exceptions. For example, one article in *Nova generatsiia* (to be sure, written by a critic from Molodniak) characterized Todos' (Teodosii) Os'machka as a "carrier of a hostile ideology" (Kovalenko 1929).

The major representative of the so-called "right" in 1929 was *Literaturnyi iarmarok* [The Literary Fair] of which twelve issues were published between December 1928 and February 1930. The journal served as a platform for a variety of writers—publishing at one point even the Futurist Oleksa Vlyz'ko (Vlyz'ko 1929)— but was recognized primarily as a successor to the controversial *Vaplite,* banned by the Party in late 1927 after only five issues. It also was considered by many a new haven for the "nationalist" Khvyl'ovyi and his associates, who were forced to dissolve VAPLITE in January 1928. VUSPP took a dim view of *Literaturnyi iarmarok* and was not at all timid about impugning it (Mykytenko 1930a).[42] In contrast, *Nova generatsiia* paid relatively scant attention to the journal, limiting itself mostly to mocking remarks; only toward the end of 1929 did polemics between the two turn into more insidious confrontations.

The first item of substance to appear in *Literaturnyi iarmarok* directed against the Futurists was an open letter signed by "a group of ARMU members," that is, the Boichukists. These artists had been close to VAPLITE and now associated with *Literaturnyi iarmarok.* The June issue (which actually appeared in late July) carried a letter dedicated to *Nova generatsiia* and its "chief," Semenko. Ripe with sarcasm, it listed the "dialectics" (i.e., inconsistencies) of Semenko's movement, implying

[42] See the section in the article entitled "Shliakhy 'Literaturnoho iarmarku.'" See also Novyts'kyi 1930.

that the war of words waged by the Futurists against Kurbas and the Boichukists in ARMU was a reflection of their mercenary mentality and political opportunism—their need to find a scapegoat ever since VUSPP was adopted by the powers that be. Concluding that Semenko's journal and movement were superfluous, the anonymous authors declared: "You must die. We say this in all seriousness. You [Semenko] and your boys must die not as a physical entity, but as a social factor.... Yes, Comrade Mike [*Mykhas'*], you must disappear" (Hrupa armistiv 1929, 279).

A month later *Literaturnyi iarmarok* taunted the Futurists once again by reviving an embarrassing incident involving the fictitious writer Edvard Strikha. Invented by Kost' Burevii, who by 1929 was an associate of *Literaturnyi iarmarok*, Strikha had appeared in December 1927 as a legitimate contributor to *Nova generatsiia*. So well did Strikha imitate the exuberant and boastful tone of Futurist poems that for a time his works were not taken as parodies. *Literaturnyi iarmarok* gleefully reminded its readers that Semenko was so thoroughly deceived by Strikha that he even attributed genius to his works (Burevii 1929, 2). When Semenko realized he had been duped, Strikha was gently divorced from the journal. At first, Semenko appropriated the pseudonym for himself, publishing several works under that name. Eventually he orchestrated Strikha's demise. *Nova generatsiia* revealed to its readers that Strikha had become the victim of a tragic accident. In a letter to the editor, Strikha's "wife" (created by the Futurists) gave public testimony to this sad fact. But in 1929 Burevii resurrected his alter ego in one of Valeriian Polishchuk's publications,[43] where he again poked fun at Semenko. It was to Strikha that the editorship of the eighth issue of *Literaturnyi iarmarok* was entrusted, giving him further opportunities to needle the Futurist. Strikha declared there: "You [Semenko] have thrown your journal into the mud" (Strikha 1929a, 323).[44]

In reacting to these taunts, the Futurists wisely ignored the Strikha incident, but took full advantage of the ARMU letter. In September *Nova generatsiia* carried a portfolio of records under the title, "The Case of the Corpse" (Semenko, Poltorats'kyi, and Petryts'kyi 1929). An editorial commentary noted that the VUSPP coalition had "stirred the circles of the right" and brought *Nova generatsiia* under attack from the "all-Ukrainian Philistine [*mishchanyn*]" who was seeking Semenko's death.

[43] Kost' Burevii and "E. Strikha" were first listed as participants in V. Polishchuk's *Mystets'ki materiialy Avanhardu* (1929, a continuation of *Biuleten' Avanhardu*). "Strikha's" work appeared in the next iteration of this changing periodical. See Strikha 1929b.

[44] For a history of the Strikha affair see Sherekh 1955.

In order to grant him this wish, the editors had requested that Semenko die—and he had graciously obliged. In memory of their fallen leader, they offered sympathetic readers a number of mock documents: a letter addressed to the local prosecutor asking for an investigation into Semenko's untimely passing; two letters found on Semenko's body; an obituary in the form of a ritual lament; and, lastly, a memoir about the late Futurist by Anatol' Petryts'kyi. One of the two letters, from Oleksii Poltorats'kyi, discussed ARMU's own "opportunistic" alliances; the second was Semenko's incomplete reply to Poltorats'kyi in which he characterized *Literaturnyi iarmarok* as a lowbrow journal: "This 'Fair' is an organ of uncle Taras from the Poltava region [and it has] the commensurate circle of Little Russian readers" (ibid., 28).

This harmless jousting took a pernicious turn toward the end of the year. In early January 1930 the long-overdue October issue of *Literaturnyi iarmarok* appeared, carrying a letter to the editor signed by Arkadii Liubchenko, Hryhorii Epik, Oleksander Kopylenko, and Iurii Vukhnal' (Liubchenko et al., 1929).[45] Except for Vukhnal' (a member of Molodniak), all signatories were coworkers of the journal. They were reacting to a letter that had appeared in both *Visti VUTsVK* [The News of the All-Ukrainian Central Executive Committee—one of two official dailies] and *Komsomolets' Ukraïny* [The Komsomolian of Ukraine] written by a coalition of five organizations—VUSPP, Pluh, Molodniak, VUARKK (*Nova generatsiia*) and Zakhidna Ukraïna. The coalition's letter was a rebuke to Hryhorii Epik for advocating the closure of *Nova generatsiia* and to *Literaturnyi iarmarok* for "associating" [*spilkuvannia*] with Valeriian Polishchuk's Avanhard.

The letter in *Literaturnyi iarmarok* flatly denied both allegations as groundless inventions. (As we shall presently see, this was untrue.) It also went on to suggest that the coalition's letter was a conspiracy to obscure the central question raised by Epik, namely, *Nova generatsiia*'s "pornography" and "political cynicism." The authors interpreted the coalition's letter as an attempt on the part of *Nova generatsiia* (which, they said, had been caught "red-handed") to evade "proletarian judgment" by hiding "behind the back of the other four organizations" who were not aware of all the facts.

Nova generatsiia was again cited for pornography (among other things) by Mykola Khvyl'ovyi in February 1930 when the twelfth issue for 1929 of *Literaturnyi iarmarok* appeared (Khvyl'ovyi 1929, 2). The Futurists answered Khvyl'ovyi lamely and briefly by citing the pornographic nature

[45] Although the issue of *Literaturnyi iarmorok* is numbered as no. 11 (1929), the actual date of publication (11 January 1930) is indicated opposite page 1.

of Oleksander Kopylenko's work in the previous issue of *Literaturnyi iarmarok* (*Nova generatsiia* 1930 [3]: 36–37). Their lackluster reply may have had something to do with the fact that by then they had significantly more serious accusations to contend with. On 27 January 1930 Khvyl'ovyi had published a diatribe in the newspaper *Komunist* [Communist]—an organ of the Central Committee of KP(b)U—in which the Futurists were branded nationalists, Mazepites, Iefremovites, and fascists (Khvyl'ovyi 1930e).[46] Counteracting these accusations would become their primary task.

The immediate stimulus to Khvyl'ovyi's article was the appearance in early January 1930 of the Futurist *Avanhard–Al'manakh proletars'kykh myttsiv Novoï generatsiï* [Avant-Garde–Almanac of Proletarian Artists of the New Generation].[47] Published in Kyiv and edited by Geo Shkurupii, it had among its contributors Oleksa Vlyz'ko, Oleksander Dovzhenko (represented by an excerpt from his film script *Zemlia* [Earth] which was about to be released), Petro Mel'nyk, Iurii Paliichuk, Ivan Malovichko, Mykola Bulatovych, Viktor Petrov, S. Vlasenko, and Mykola Kholostenko. Although subtitled "an almanac of proletarian artists" (an obvious obeisance to the spirit of the day and a reflection of the fact that *Nova generatsiia* too had changed in January 1930 from a journal of "left" art to one of "revolutionary" art), the publication still managed to assert on the first page and in bold letters that art was dying as an "irrational category." Even though slightly more conservatively designed than *Nova generatsiia*, the almanac was in other respects the perfect offspring of the parent journal. Like *Nova generatsiia*, it contained within the table of contents editorial comments about all contributions; like the journal, it was consciously international and pan-artistic (the title appeared in Ukrainian and German). The almanac featured an article by De Stijl leader Theo van Doesburg, ran a report on *Der Sturm* and on the avant-garde in Czechoslovakia. There were also items on architecture, city planning, and film. None of this, however, attracted Khvyl'ovyi's attention. He saw only evidence of the most heinous nationalism in *Avanhard–Al'manakh*.

Khvyl'ovyi chose Vlyz'ko as his primary target, zeroing in on his humorous "Istoriia zakordonnoho pashportu" ["History of the Travel Passport"] (Vlyz'ko 1930a), which was a chapter from Vlyz'ko's book,

46 This article was reprinted in *Prolitfront* 1930 [1]: 247–53. My references will be to the latter source. It is significant that Khvyl'ovyi also published other articles in *Komunist* during the early part of 1930. See his "Z bl'oknotu korespondenta" of which several installments appeared in *Komunist* (46 [16 February 1930]: 2); (49 [19 February 1930]: 3); and (69 [11 March 1930]: 3).

47 Henceforth cited as *Avanhard–Al'manakh*.

Poïzdy idut' na Berlin [The Trains Are Leaving for Berlin]. Vlyz'ko's ironic reportage—called an editorial by Khvyl'ovyi—was written from the point of view of a naive, rambling, and ever-digressing traveler. Khvyl'ovyi, however, discovered in it "an undisguised apologia for [that] Mazepism [*mazepynstvo*] of which Ukrainian fascists are so proud" (Khvyl'ovyi 1930a, 247). He marshaled his evidence against Vlyz'ko with a quotation (taken out of context) that had the narrator remarking, ironically and in passing, that he cannot forgive Tsar Peter I for defeating Ivan Mazepa "because this was our best Hetman." On the basis of this and other passages, Khvyl'ovyi argued that Vlyz'ko's work "reeks with malice toward Peter I" while "sing[ing] panegyrics to Mazepa." Khvyl'ovyi stated that Vlyz'ko grieved for a "militant Ukrainian nationalism," especially the "imperialistic" variety. Generalizing from this example, Khvyl'ovyi went on to declare that "these apologists of Mazepism are none other than the well-known, relentless opponents of Khvyl'ovism, the Panfuturists-Komunkul'tists from *Nova generatsiia*."

Khvyl'ovyi's second target was Geo Shkurupii's "The New Art in the Process of Development of Ukrainian Culture" (Shkurupii 1930e), an essay that examined the avant-garde's role in helping Ukrainian culture overcome its "traditions," "atavism," and "narrow domestic interests" in favor of a broad "international" orientation on "world proletarian culture" (ibid., 37). Shkurupii depicted this as an on-going struggle against those who would "shut the development of culture in a frame of provincial interests and national restrictiveness," a weakness he identified primarily with those individuals who associated with *Literaturnyi iarmarok*, ARMU, and Berezil'. Arguing that "the new art in the entire world has lost its national flavor—there is no new German, English, French, Ukrainian art—it is international, but with very clear and sharp class characteristics" (ibid., 41), Shkurupii pointed to modern "functional" architecture (Frank Lloyd Wright, Le Corbusier, Gropius) as the clearest embodiment of this tendency. He concluded: "the new art...pushes our culture forward toward socialism" (ibid., 42). While this was a faithful rendering of Futurism's long-standing positions, Shkurupii offered several phraseological and ideological concessions to the proletarian community to mitigate the overall impact. At one point he wrote that, inasmuch as "nationalism has not yet been outgrown," "art in a national form" (i.e., "regressive" art) has "a complete right to exist," as long as it adheres to class principles (ibid., 40). It was on these latter passages that Khvyl'ovyi chose to converge, taking them as proof that Shkurupii was a "consistent Khvyl'ovist" and a representative of "one hundred percent [pure] National-Bolshevism" (Khvyl'ovyi 1930a, 250).

The last person to be singled out by Khvyl'ovyi was Viktor Petrov, a scholar who also wrote fiction under the pseudonym V. Domontovych.[48] Petrov's contribution to *Avanhard-Al'manakh* fell under the heading "literature of fact," being a chapter from a biographical novel about the Romantic novelist and poet, Panteleimon Kulish. It was Petrov's chapter heading ("Movchuche bozhestvo"—The Silent Deity) that Khvyl'ovyi parodied when he named his assault on the Futurists "Krychushche bozhestvo" [The Screaming Deity]. He described Petrov's chapter as a "programmatic article" that, in the age of reconstruction, offered readers only "bourgeois nonsense." By publishing him, the Futurists were guilty of giving refuge to a "Neoclassicist." Khvyl'ovyi ended by recalling that the Futurists still suffered from the illness of pornography and were responsible for the publication of "toilet works."

Khvyl'ovyi's *Komunist* article received several replies from the Futurists. The first appeared at very short notice and, therefore, was no more than a paragraph long. Dashed off by Semenko for the January issue of *Nova generatsiia*, it was a caustic observation about Khvyl'ovyi's newfangled conversion to the age of reconstruction. More importantly, however, it was also a diplomatic but obvious rebuke to the editors of *Komunist* for publishing an article like Khvyl'ovyi's without any editorial qualification (Semenko 1930c). A much longer response appeared in the February issue, written by V. Antoniuk. This was a virtual reprint of Khvyl'ovyi's article, with a running commentary on its distortions (Antoniuk 1930a).[49] The final reply was Geo Shkurupii's, which appeared in April, that is, in the second and, as it turned out, the last issue of *Avanhard-Al'manakh* (Shkurupii 1930b).[50] Ironically, Shkurupii's answer was published the same month that Khvyl'ovyi's article was reprinted in *Prolitfront*, a journal that succeeded *Literaturnyi iarmarok*. Aside from demonstrating once again how Khvyl'ovyi misrepresented the texts he cited, Shkurupii argued that Khvyl'ovyi's "lies," "falsehoods," and "slander" were motivated by inter-group rivalries. He registered surprise at his defense of Emperor Peter I and accused Khvyl'ovyi of becoming an inadvertent spokesman for Russian great-power chauvinism, a role that automatically discredited him as a true communist (ibid., 64–65).

[48] See his novel, *Doctor Serafikus*, dating from 1928–29 (Petrov 1947), which contains references to Futurism. It was recently republished in Domontovych (1988, 1: 359–509).
[49] Antoniuk was also the author of two other articles that appeared in the Kharkiv daily press. See Antoniuk 1930b. The other article, which appeared in *Vechirnia robitnycha hazeta* , was not available to me.
[50] The third issue of the almanac, "No. c," was advertized but never appeared.

The dust had not settled from "The Screaming Deity" when Khvyl'ovyi appeared in the press with still more ominous and far-fetched accusations against the Futurists. On 16 March 1930 the newspaper *Kharkivs'kyi proletar* [Kharkiv Proletarian][51] carried "And Who Else Sits among the Indicted?" (Khvyl'ovyi 1930f),[52] an article inspired by the trial of the so-called Union for the Liberation of Ukraine that had begun in Kharkiv a few days earlier.[53] In this piece Khvyl'ovyi set out to "ideologically disarm" the "counter-revolutionary Iefremovites" [*kontr-revoliutsiina iefremovshchyna*] and to unmask "Khvyl'ovism" (that other "nationalistic deviation") which continued to "hide either behind exceptionally '*r*revolutionary' [*sic*][54] phrases or even behind genuine party membership cards" (Khvyl'ovyi 1930f, 2). At first through insinuation and then quite explicitly, Khvyl'ovyi paints the Futurists as a politically reactionary and dangerous force. The brunt of the attack is directed at Geo Shkurupii—pointedly identified as a "member of *Nova generatsiia*"—whom he describes as a "disseminator of Iefremovite lies" [*pidbrekhach Iefremovshchyny*] (ibid., 3). The only proof Khvyl'ovyi offers are several quotes culled from a poem of 1921–23, "Likarepopyniada," more recently republished in Shkurupii's collection, *Dlia druziv poetiv suchasnykiv vichnosty* [For My Poet Friends, the Contemporaries of Eternity, 1929].[55]

51 Note well the paper's subtitle: "Orhan Okruzhkomu KP(b)U, Okrvykonkomu, Okrprofrady i Mis'krady" [Organ of the Okruh Committee of the Communist Party (Bolsheviks) of Ukraine, the Okruh Executive Committee, Okruh Professional Council, and the City Council]. Anything published here would have the Party's sanction.

52 Two days later, in a letter to the editor, Khvyl'ovyi introduced a few minor corrections to the above text. See Khvyl'ovyi 1930h.

53 SVU (*Spilka vyzvolennia Ukraïny* [The Union for the Liberation of Ukraine]) was alleged to have been an anti-Soviet organization created by intellectuals of the older generation, former supporters of the UNR (Ukrainian National Republic) and Symon Petliura. Forty-five individuals were tried between 9 March and 19 April 1930, among them members of the Ukrainian Academy of Sciences and the noted critic and literary historian Serhii Iefremov. The accussed were found guilty and sent to Soviet concentration camps where most died. It was alleged by Soviet security organs that SVU had links to another underground nationalist organization, SUM (*Spilka ukraïns'koï molodi* [Union of Ukrainian Youth]) and the Ukrainian Autocephalous Orthodox Church. For an example of the orchestrated condemnation of SVU and the role literary organizations played in this see "Zukhvalyi zamakh" 1929. Even during the final days of the Soviet Union, it was freely acknowledged that the Union for the Liberation of Ukraine was a fabrication of the NKVD.

54 The double "r" was a transparent allusion to the Futurists whom Edvard Strikha had parodied in the poem "*Rr*revolutsiia." See Strikha 1955, 21.

55 Sections of "Likarepopyniada" initially appeared in *Semafor u Maibutnie* (1922). Its first full publication came in Shkurupii 1923e.

The motifs in this poem, argued Khvyl'ovyi, were "inspired [*naviiani*] by Iefremov's preparation for an armed uprising" against Soviet rule.

So incredible was Khvyl'ovyi's faultfinding that *Nova generatsiia* immediately set out to parody it. In "Mistyfikatsiia (?)" [Hoax (?)] (Holubenko 1930b), which appeared in the polemical "notebook" section of the journal, Khvyl'ovyi is pictured incriminating Semenko as a disseminator of "global bourgeois lies" as well as those perpetrated by bourgeois "intelligence services." This Khvyl'ovyi, much like the real one, asks rhetorically "do you want proof?" and then explicates Semenko's poem of 1913 ("Osin'" [Autumn]) as an "editorial" imbued with "kulak ideology" that calls on the masses "to organize sabotage and mischief in the cultural field." "Proof" is offered (*à la* Khvyl'ovyi) in the form of a harmless phrase *u sertse* [into the heart], whose letters "u," "s," and "r," are deciphered as an abbreviation for the "counter-revolutionary" *U*krainian *SR* (Socialist Revolutionary) Party. In another case of typical Khvyl'ovist exegesis, the parodist makes *sum* (sadness) stand for the nationalist organization SUM (*S*pilka *u*kraïns'koï *m*olodi). This lampoon of Khvyl'ovyi's polemical style ends with the assertion that Semenko had been passing secret messages to the enemy on the "other side of the barricades."

A more serious response to Khvyl'ovyi's wild accusations came from Geo Shkurupii himself a few pages later in the same issue. This took the form of an open letter (dated 20 March 1930), addressed to the Federation of Organizations of Revolutionary Writers of Ukraine (FORPU—Federatsiia orhanizatsii revoliutsiinykh pys'mennykiv Ukraïny).[56] In defending his good name from Khvyl'ovyi's "despicable" articles, Shkurupii asserted that the former member of VAPLITE was trying to atone for his former ideological errors by slandering innocent opponents with his own sins. Shkurupii argued that he had been struggling against "nationalist deviations" long before Khvyl'ovyi. His letter ended with an appeal to "authorities" (i.e., FORPU) to defend "revolutionary writers" from the "dirt" spread by people like Khvyl'ovyi.

Khvyl'ovyi's articles of January and March marked the beginning of a vicious and ignoble struggle between the Futurists and the Khvyl'ovist camp. By 1930 *Literaturnyi iarmarok* had reorganized itself into PROLITFRONT—The Proletarian Literary Front—and began publishing a journal of the same name. Now *Nova generatsiia* and *Prolitfront* accused

[56] Shkurupii 1930c. Shkurupii erroneously refers to FORPU as the "Federation of Soviet Writers," an understandable lapse, given that the organization was barely three months old. For details see below.

each other of the worst conceivable political transgressions. Traditionally, it has been argued that the Futurists were the aggressors in this war and that Khvyl'ovyi and PROLITFRONT responded in kind only after losing patience with a group that, ostensibly, subjected them to endless torments. This position has been enunciated forcefully by Hryhorii Kostiuk:

> During the period of PROLITFRONT Khvyl'ovyi did not publish a single new story.... All his creative energy, all his polemical passion was focused on literary polemics directed mainly against *Nova generatsiia*. He dedicated to the organization of Ukrainian Futurists and, especially, to its member, the critic O. Poltorats'kyi, three long, sharp, exposé articles.[57] Moreover, *Prolitfront* published articles by I. Momot (under the pseudonym O. Mak),[58] I. Senchenko,[59] and Varvara Zhukova (Kost' Burevii)[60] [all of which were] directed against *Nova generatsiia*. How can we explain why *Prolitfront* [showered] *Nova generatsiia* with such "attention?" This was not some kind of whim on the part of *Prolitfront*; [it was] especially not [a whim on the part of] Khvyl'ovyi. This sharp attitude was triggered by two factors: 1) the very negative attitude of *Nova generatsiia* toward PROLITFRONT as an organization; and [the journal's] continuous, issue after issue, defamation of [PROLIT-FRONT]; 2) the provocative article by O. Poltorats'kyi against Ostap Vyshnia's works which played a fatal role in the subsequent destiny of Ostap Vyshnia. These are the basic reasons for the all-out war Khvyl'ovyi [waged] against *Nova generatsiia* (Kostiuk 1978, 82–83).

Kostiuk elaborates by saying that from 1927 to 1930 *Nova generatsiia*

> stubbornly, issue after issue, published various derisive, malicious inventions, pamphlets, annoying provocations, and even common political denunciations [*donosy*] against M. Khvyl'ovyi and his followers. The most active author of such "literature" was the young critic O. Poltorats'kyi. His long political denunciation [*donos*] of Ostap Vyshnia (it spanned several issues) incensed not only numerous readers of Ostap Vyshnia but the entire literary community that was close to PROLITFRONT.... Such spiritually filthy, amoral types [like Poltorats'kyi] set the tone in *Nova generatsiia* for the attacks against PROLITFRONT. Finally, they destroyed M. Khvyl'ovyi's equilibrium and became one of the fundamental causes for M. Khvyl'ovyi's and PROLITFRONT's total counter-attack against *Nova generatsiia*. These conflict-laden situations should not be forgotten by any investigator (ibid.).[61]

57 Khvyl'ovyi 1930a, 1930b, 1930c [Kostiuk's notes]. Kostiuk makes no mention of Khvyl'ovyi 1930f.

58 "Z bl'oknotu chytacha," *Prolitfront* 1930 (nos. 1, 3, 4) [Kostiuk's note].

59 *Prolitfront* 1930 (2): 177–210 [Kostiuk's note].

60 *Prolitfront* 1930 (3): 205–228 [Kostiuk's note].

61 Kostiuk's view of Poltorats'kyi is echoed in Osadchyi 1987.

The two opposing camps could hardly have been described in more contrasting terms. The above leaves little doubt as to who were the heroes and who were the villains in this confrontation. The Futurists are depicted as merciless predators while Khvyl'ovyi's group is the distraught victim engaged in self-defense. Khvyl'ovyi's—and more generally, PROLITFRONT's—attack on the Futurists is justified not just by immediate actions taken by *Nova generatsiia* (the purported attacks on *Prolitfront* and Poltorats'kyi's article) but also by its behavior from as early as 1927. Khvyl'ovyi's actions are to be understood as the pent-up response to endless provocations and "political denunciations." A closer examination of the facts reveals a far different situation.

As we have seen earlier, the Futurists and Khvyl'ovyi had been at odds since the beginning of the decade (recall the publications *Zhovten'*, *Arena*, and the organization Hart). While politics were not irrelevant to their early debates, the conflicts had essentially a cultural and artistic character. This changed with the creation of VAPLITE in November 1925, when strictly political divisions around the question of nationalism exacerbated their tense relationship. However, inasmuch as the Futurists did not constitute a formal organization during the zenith of the "Literary Discussion," that is, when VAPLITE was under fire from the Party and proletarian circles, these divisions did not assume any concrete forms until the appearance of *Bumeranh*. The attacks here on Khvyl'ovyi and VAPLITE were indeed biting but continued to be cultural rather than political in nature. It is clear that Semenko used the term "nationalism" to mean "provincialism," and held to his long-standing conviction that the "national" period in Ukrainian culture was over. It was only when *Nova generatsiia* appeared that the Futurists, toeing the Party line, resorted to strong political language, saying they were "against Khvyl'ovism...in such an organization as VAPLITE" because it might lead "to fascism" ("Platforma i otochennia livykh" 1927, 40–41).

It is worth noting, nonetheless, that *Nova generatsiia*'s position on VAPLITE was hardly original. By October 1927, when the latter statement was made, such views amounted to little more than a ritual and were almost irrelevant. Early in the course of the Party's criticism of Khvyl'ovyi, even VAPLITE distanced itself from the controversial writer by expelling him from the organization (January 1927). A year later (February 1928), Khvyl'ovyi himself renounced his own views, becoming a passionate foe of "Khvyl'ovism" by 1930. For the Futurists, just as for VAPLITE, being against "Khvyl'ovism" was a necessary act of political conformity. It was the price everyone paid to preserve a foothold in the artistic community. Moreover as the events of 1930 were about to prove, when the Party and the proletarian camp were given a choice, they were more willing to accept a reformed "nationalist" like Khvyl'ovyi than a perennial "internationalist" and avant-gardist like Semenko.

While there can be no dispute that *Nova generatsiia* baited the Khvyl'ovists, it is a gross exaggeration to imply that they besieged them in every issue of the journal from 1927 to 1930. There simply is no evidence for such sweeping assertions. The Futurists did not take cognizance of the "right" as zealously or as consistently as Kostiuk suggests. There is even less truth to the imputation that during these same years the Futurists were engaged in political denunciation. While they certainly were not known for their tact, it is incorrect to suggest that they always debated in the style peculiar to 1930, a year of growing restrictions and intolerance on the cultural front. Prior to this, there is nothing in *Nova generatsiia*, either in manner or tone, that corresponds to Khvyl'ovyi's articles in *Komunist* and *Kharkivs'kyi proletar*. Although Futurist polemics and literary works did attack Ukrainian nationalists and, on occasion, lumped Khvyl'ovyi and his associates into the so-called "counter-revolutionary" camp, in most cases this was done in the spirit of opposing a cultural stance they considered provincial or parochial. This explains, for example, why the "fellow-traveler" Antonenko-Davydovych was accused of "Little Russian nationalism" (Shkurupii 1928d, 41). For the Futurists, VAPLITE and, especially, *Literaturnyi iarmarok*—with its *intermedii* and Gogolian banter—were living proof that these writers were "nurturing" a "museum-like," "provincial" culture. From the Futurists' perspective, the Khvyl'ovists were regressive even when they invoked European culture, since their view of Europe was "antiquated by at least 50 years" (Shkurupii 1930e, 37). Semenko urged the government to support only avant-garde theaters because, in his words, "it is not in the interest of the Soviet state and its leadership to make the Ukrainian Soviet Socialist Republic an eternal province" (Semenko 1929e, 76). This was Futurism's primary line of argument. It had little in common with "political denunciations" and certainly had no relationship to Khvyl'ovyi's attack in 1930.

Oleksii Poltorats'kyi's article about the humorist Ostap Vyshnia is the other and, perhaps, the more central explanation put forth for PROLITFRONT's and Khvyl'ovyi's onslaught against *Nova generatsiia*. It is alleged that this essay not only provoked Khvyl'ovyi but was responsible for Vyshnia's tragic ten-year experience in the Gulag. It is also taken as typical of the "moral filth" with which the Khvyl'ovists were forced to contend. A careful review will show that this interpretation, too, is not sustained by the facts.

Poltorats'kyi's article can be eliminated as the *casus belli* of the 1930 polemics on chronological grounds alone: its serialization began only in February, that is, after the Futurists were charged with pornography and political cynicism in *Literaturnyi iarmarok* and after Khvyl'ovyi's "The Screaming Deity" appeared in *Komunist.* If anything, Poltorats'kyi's essay is easier to construe as a possible rejoinder than a provocation. Its tenor and content are also at odds with the monstrous role assigned to it.

Poltorats'kyi's "Shcho take Ostap Vyshnia?" [Just What Is Ostap Vyshnia?] ran in three installments in *Nova generatsiia.* The professed stimulus to its writing was the publication of a two volume edition of Vyshnia's works (Vyshnia 1929–1930), although other motivations cannot be ruled out. Poltorats'kyi resolved to investigate why Vyshnia had become "king of the Ukrainian *tyrazh* [print run]," why he was being promoted by publishing houses, and why he was considered useful in the task of "Ukrainianization." Poltorats'kyi wished to refute the notion that Vyshnia played a positive role in Ukrainian society. In the first installment, he made these principal points: Vyshnia was a representative of the uncultured peasant masses; his linguistic style was characteristic of this (quoting Marx) "idiotic" stratum of society and therefore reactionary, conservative, and reminiscent of nineteenth-century populists' ideals. Consequently, Vyshnia was bad for Ukrainianization and demoralizing in the struggle to lift the masses to a higher cultural level. In the face of Vyshnia's low-brow appeal, Poltorats'kyi made a plea for greater sophistication.

> Whereas several years ago Vyshnia's "popular language" [*prosta mova*] could have been greeted as the best language for the masses, now, when the masses have matured extraordinarily in the cultural sense, such a language as Vyshnia's can only be detrimental to the process of cultivating the language of the Ukrainian masses.... Ostap Vyshnia's linguistic practice can only have a negative influence on workers... who are being Ukrainianized.... In our opinion the proletarian circles of Ukrainian society should condemn the reactionary linguistic practice of Ostap Vyshnia (Poltorats'kyi 1930a, 2: 32).

A corresponding criticism was directed at Vyshnia's "comic technique," which purportedly vulgarized everything by focusing on anal, genital, and bathroom humor. In Poltorats'kyi's view, Vyshnia's human beings were no better than animals.

Whereas the first installment managed for the most part to retain a descriptive and analytical thrust, the second and third betrayed strong political indignation at what was seen to be Vyshnia's negative and cynical view of Soviet socialist reality. Pointing to Vyshnia's attitudes about the village, city, and machine, Poltorats'kyi argued that he had eyes only for the primitive and retrograde but remained blind to the achievements of the revolution. The "literary mask" that was Ostap Vyshnia (the author's real name was Pavlo Hubenko), argued Poltorats'kyi, was not the intrepid propagandizer of Party tenets as generally believed; in truth, this was an unprincipled, uneducated bourgeois with a dubious political past. Vyshnia "as a literary figure," insisted Poltorats'kyi, was a prime example of the conservatism that plagued the Ukrainian village in the recent past (ibid., 3: 19). "Independently of the personal sympathies of the author," Vyshnia had emerged as "a reactionary figure, a brake on the train of the cultural revolution in Ukraine" (ibid., 3: 20). In view of Vyshnia's "militantly anti-cultural character," his "cheap and primitive" artistic devices, Poltorats'kyi was forced to conclude:

> We must openly state that the creativity of Ostap Vyshnia is not [our] wealth; it is not an achievement of Ukrainian culture. Ostap Vyshnia is our poverty because in his works we have the fullest expression of the self-centered backwardness [khutorianstvo], lack of culture and provincialism, from the clutches of which Ukrainian Soviet literature is liberating itself with much effort (ibid., 4: 28; *emphasis in the original*).

Above and beyond these manifestly literary and cultural issues, Poltorats'kyi's article contained several political innuendoes. The names of Petliura, Vrangel, the White Army, and the Cadet Party sprung up in the course of his analysis and comparisons. He described Vyshnia as a bourgeois with kulak sympathies. He deliberately chose to apply humorless, puritanical, and literal criteria to a writer for whom such standards were inappropriate. It must also be added that on balance Poltorats'kyi's article was far less obnoxious than those of Khvyl'ovyi and his *Prolitfront* associates. The latter were nothing less than out-and-out accusations of treason. Poltorats'kyi at least made an effort to distinguish between the writer (Hubenko) and his literary persona (Vyshnia). Ultimately he condemned the mask, not the creator.

Vyshnia received a defense of sorts from Khvyl'ovyi in the form of a fifty-six page article (Khvyl'ovyi 1930c). For all its length, Khvyl'ovyi's argument was simple and crude: Regardless of what the elitist and formalist Poltorats'kyi might think, Vyshnia was a good writer because he was loved by the peasant and working masses, and had been recognized as such by leading orthodox proletarian critics. The only detractors of Vyshnia were nationalists, fascists, and untrustworthy Soviet writers. As examples of the latter, Khvyl'ovyi pointed to Dmytro Dontsov, the West Ukrainian journalist and nationalist theorist, and to an anonymous Ukrainian author writing in a nationalist publication in Prague; strangely, he also placed Antonenko-Davydovych in the same company.

Poltorats'kyi's characterization of Vyshnia, argued Khvyl'ovyi, was completely consonant with that of "counter-revolutionaries" (ibid., 307):

> As we see, the views on Ostap Vyshnia divide along class lines: fascists—and those who sing to their tune on this issue—look at Vyshnia...as if [he were a] member of the Cheka [*chrezvychaika*]. Communists declare that Vyshnia is "necessary," they place him next to academician Tychyna and call him "one of the most noted, most influential contemporary Soviet writers." It cannot be otherwise: there is no apolitical literature; there is only class literature. And inasmuch as classes war among one another, a Soviet writer will never find a place in the heart of a bourgeois critic (ibid., 306–309).

In light of the content, can one reasonably maintain that Poltorats'kyi's article had some bearing on Vyshnia's tragic fate? Could an article written in 1930 have been instrumental in the arrest of a man in December 1933? This question can be answered by posing another. Are Khvyl'ovyi's articles (and those of his friends) responsible for the execution of Vlyz'ko in 1934, or the shooting of Semenko and Shkurupii in 1937? Certainly not. The same holds true for Poltorats'kyi. The causes of these tragedies must be sought in the immediate temporal context in which they occurred—for example, the fall of Mykola Skrypnyk, the rise to power of Pavel Postyshev, and the growing terror in general. They can hardly be attributed to a specific article or individual. There can be no true causality between Poltorats'kyi's writings and Vyshnia's fate if only because the time span between the two was so great. In an environment as politically volatile as Ukraine's at the start of the thirties, where a few months and even weeks brought radical transformations in the political situation, seeking such causality between distant events cannot be convincing.

The alleged evil nature of the Futurists clearly does not explain why Khvyl'ovyi waged such a virulent struggle against them. Chronology as well as the tone and content of Poltorats'kyi's article argue against the proposition that the Futurists instigated the harsh polemics of 1930. The facts indicate that responsibility for the qualitative deterioration in the Futurist-Khvyl'ovist debate rests squarely with the Khvyl'ovist camp. It started in *Literaturnyi iarmarok*, gained momentum through Khvyl'ovyi's January and March articles and by April, when the journal *Prolitfront* began appearing, was canonized, more or less, as the style of the period. It is hard, indeed, to accept the argument that PROLITFRONT was merely responding to the attacks of *Nova generatsiia* when it is clear that Khvyl'ovyi initiated the attacks before PROLITFRONT was founded. *Nova generatsiia* could not have originated the attacks against *Prolitfront* because the very first issue of *Prolitfront* already contained virulent anti-Futurist statements in the form of Khvyl'ovyi's reprinted article from *Komunist* and an editorial ("Do chytacha" 1930). In short, the image of an innocent group of writers defending themselves against vicious Futurists is hardly plausible. If anything, the opposite was true. When *Nova generatsiia*'s articles about PROLITFRONT and Khvyl'ovyi (see Muzychenko 1930a and 1930b; Malovichko 1930a) are examined for content and timing, it becomes clear that they were primarily written in response to attacks that first appeared in *Prolitfront*.

The Khvyl'ovists began their anti-Futurist campaign for a simple reason: to gain admittance into the proletarian circle from which they were being excluded. It was a device to repudiate their past and reinstate themselves into the good graces of the Party. This will become clear once we examine the literary-political situation during this period.

It was pointed out above that *Literaturnyi iarmarok* had been severely censured by VUSPP. As this journal was being ostracized, exactly the opposite was happening to the Futurists. Their coalition with VUSPP had made them nominal members of the proletarian community and sheltered them from active persecution. Symbolic of the legitimacy *Nova generatsiia* enjoyed was the presence of its members at a meeting on 21 October 1929 in Kyiv which weighed the question of creating a "revolutionary coalition" ("Do utvorennia" 1929). VUSPP, Molodniak, Pluh, and Zakhidna Ukraïna were also party to these proceedings. This was the same group of five that would shortly take Epik and *Literaturnyi iarmarok* to task for advocating the liquidation of *Nova generatsiia* and for associating with Valeriian Polishchuk.

This meeting in Kyiv focused largely on *Literaturnyi iarmarok*. It was discussed not just as the most important opponent of the "revolutionary" orientation, but also as the organization around which other members of the "right" tended to coalesce. It is interesting to observe that whereas the critic Borys Kovalenko from Molodniak spoke about the "recidivism" of nationalism in *Literaturnyi iarmarok*, Geo Shkurupii, who represented *Nova generatsiia* at the meeting—typically for the Futurists—linked the "right's" "national tastes in literature and film" to their provincialism, in other words, he avoided blatantly political accusations. Moreover, Shkurupii bluntly reiterated that differences of a formal (artistic) nature continued to exist between VUSPP and *Nova generatsiia*, but insisted that they should not be a cause for enmity between the two organizations (ibid., 8).

In November 1929 *Nova generatsiia* again improved its position when the coalition to which it was party expanded to include the All-Ukrainian

Association of Revolutionary Cinematographers, or VUARK (*Vseukraïns'ka asotsiiatsiia revoliutsiinykh kinematohrafiv*) for short. Previously known as UARDIS (*Ukraïns'ka asotsiiatsiia rezhyseriv, dramaturhiv i stsenarystiv* [The Ukrainian Association of Directors, Dramatists, and Scenarists]), it recognized Semenko as one of its founders. Now he was "deputy head" [*zastupnyk holovy pravlinnia*] of the renamed organization (Semenko 1929d). To avoid confusion with the cinematographers' organization, *Nova generatsiia* altered its formal name VUARKK to VUSKK, becoming a "union" [*spilka*] rather than an "association" of workers of communist culture (Luckyj 1956, 148).

This obsession with coalitions was part of a mushrooming tendency to form a single unifying body for all "revolutionary" organizations. VUSPP had received a mandate for exactly this at its May 1929 congress and by the end of the year it was on the verge of launching what eventually came to be known as FORPU (*Federatsiia orhanizatsii revoliutsiinykh pys'mennykiv Ukraïny* [Federation of Organizations of Revolutionary Writers of Ukraine]). As the moment of federation approached, *Literaturnyi iarmarok* came under tremendous pressure to justify its continued estrangement from the proletarian camp. Although the journal resisted these pressures, the breaking point came in November 1929 when every major forum lacerated Valeriian Polishchuk for his *Avanhard 3* (no relationship to the Futurist *Avanhard-Al'manakh*).[62] Accused of pornography and a host of other offenses, Polishchuk was coerced into confessing his errors and disbanded his organization (Kulyk 1929; "Polishchukiiada" 1929; Ovcharov 1932a). When this occurred, *Literaturnyi iarmarok* was also forced to throw in the towel. Polishchuk had been a close associate of the journal and the condemnation he received at the hands of the proletarians threatened to spill over to *Literaturnyi iarmarok*. To forestall the inevitable, the journal decided to join the chorus of denunciations. When the tenth issue appeared, it contained a strongly worded attack on Polishchuk ("Odvertyi lyst do redaktsiï" 1929).[63] The events that followed are by now familiar. Before *Literaturnyi iarmarok*'s repudiation of Polishchuk had a chance to be noticed (the issue in which it appeared was published very late), the aforementioned coalition of five organizations, among them *Nova*

[62] *Avanhard 3* (1929). The forerunners of this publication were *Mystets'ki materiialy Avanhardu* (1929 [2]) and *Biuleten' Avanhardu* (1928 [1]).

[63] The letter accused Polishchuk of "counter-revolutionary stunts" and "gross pornography." Its signers were Mykola Kulish, Iurii Ianovs'kyi, V. Vrazhlyvyi, Mykhailo Ialovyi, Mykola Khvyl'ovyi, Arkadii Liubchenko, Oles' Dosvitnii and Hryhorii Epik. It was dated 10 November 1929.

generatsiia, released a letter chastising the journal for its "association" with Polishchuk. *Literaturnyi iarmarok* angrily rejected this accusation, calling it an "invention of a sick mind." It then proceeded to build a case against the Futurists.

When *Literaturnyi iarmarok* wrote that it had not associated with Polishchuk it was deliberately lying. Polishchuk as well as other members of his entourage (for example, Leonid Chernov) had made appearances on the pages of *Literaturnyi iarmarok*, while writers like Kost' Burevii (Edvard Strikha) and Ivan Senchenko appeared in Polishchuk's publications. Contemporaries went so far as to speak about a coalition between the two groups. The "coworkers of *Literaturnyi iarmarok* had a coalition [*bl'okuvalys'*] with [Polishchuk's] Avanhard," said Mykola Skrypnyk in May 1930 (M. Skrypnyk 1930, 25; Sukhyno-Khomenko 1930a, 34). There was confirmation of this even in one of Polishchuk's publications which carried the following notice: "A new literary organization has been formed [by the name of] Proliten [a preliminary name for PROLITFRONT] (Khvyl'ovyi, Senchenko, Kulish, Epik and many others). Proliten will live with Avanhard in a relationship of good neighborliness" (cited in Tovarets' 1930, 95).

The abandonment of Polishchuk and the creation of PROLITFRONT in late November or early December were symptomatic of the serious change taking place in *Literaturnyi iarmarok*. With issue Number 10 (formally designated as the September issue but actually published in mid-November), the journal unofficially entered the PROLITFRONT era. The tone of the last two issues of *Literaturnyi iarmarok* already prefigured the journal *Prolitfront*. Observers at the time were quite aware of this. In January 1930 one of them said:

> Two months ago there was reason to fear that this group of writers [*Literaturnyi iarmarok*] had an organic, "pessimistic" illness; today we can say with assurance that this illness is not organic and that the majority of [these] "pessimists" will become our own troubadours. *They have begun to speak a different language....* If you take Number 10 of *Literaturnyi iarmarok* you will see that it already signals the end of the age of *Literaturnyi iarmarok*...[and signals] a transition to...an organization [that is part] of the proletarian literary front. *It was exactly in November and December* that the long process of drawing nearer to the creative obligations of proletarian and revolutionary literature came to an end for members of *Literaturnyi iarmarok* (Sukhyno-Khomenko 1930a, 31, 34; *emphasis added*).

All this points to the fact that, in the face of the complete rout of one of its allies (Polishchuk) and the imminent creation of FORPU, *Literaturnyi iarmarok* made a resolute decision to gain entry into the proletarian camp regardless of cost. The implications of not belonging to a nationwide federation were too grievous to contemplate. But since it was obvious that *Literaturnyi iarmarok* as such was not going to be accepted into FORPU, Khvyl'ovyi's group quickly formed a new organization, PROLITFRONT. This was nothing but a maneuver to gain entry into FORPU. PROLITFRONT, incidentally, embraced and advocated the concept of "work among the masses," the very same concept against which VAPLITE had been formed five years earlier. On 31 December 1929, PROLITFRONT, a completely unknown organization, with no organ of its own, became one of seven signatories of the document that created FORPU ("Dekliaratsiia Vseukraïns'koï federatsiï revoliutsiinykh" 1930).[64] Not until April 1930, when the first issue of *Prolitfront* appeared, would the public know what PROLITFRONT actually was. Meanwhile, it was to gain an accurate foretaste from the final two issues of *Literaturnyi iarmarok* and especially from Khvyl'ovyi's articles.

In fighting the Futurists, PROLITFRONT had no need to look for real arguments, for there were several ready-made issues at hand. Polishchuk's downfall showed that an accusation of "pornography" was lethal; the trial of the Union for the Liberation of Ukraine (*Spilka vyzvolennia Ukraïny*—SVU) suggested nationalism as the second potent weapon. The Futurists, moreover, were a relatively easy target because of all the members of FORPU, they were the group with the least support. It was no secret that except for VUSPP, the organization with which PROLITFRONT now set out to compete, no other association really desired closer contacts with the Futurists. Pluh openly voiced opposition to VUSPP's alliance with *Nova generatsiia*, calling it an "incorrect tactic." Significantly, Pluh's attitude toward PROLITFRONT was much more forthcoming. It went out of its way to "greet the psychological breach that occurred among members of PROLITFRONT in favor of...proletarian literature" (Shymans'kyi 1930).

The ease with which PROLITFRONT entered FORPU and the affable way it was hailed by Pluh suggests that it had strong support from official circles. Permission to form this organization as well as funding for the journal doubtlessly came from the Party and probably involved some kind of *quid pro quo*. Consider what Hryhorii Kostiuk says about the formation of PROLITFRONT: "Khvyl'ovyi informed [us] that he had

64 The other co-signers included VUSPP, *Nova generatsiia* (VUSKK), Pluh, Molodniak, Zahkhidna Ukraïna, Hrupa A. This declaration was widely published in other journals and newspapers.

[agreement] from 'higher spheres' for the creation of a new organization and a promise to insure the financing of a monthly" (Kostiuk 1978, 80). Clearly, the KP(b)U, having destroyed one avant-garde group in the person of Polishchuk, apparently decided to use PROLITFRONT to orchestrate the demise of the second. This was not, after all, 1927 when Skrypnyk personally gave the avant-gardists a new lease on life. Artistic and organizational pluralism had come to an end. Now the catch-words were "federation" and "consolidation." With the capitulation of *Literaturnyi iarmarok*, the Futurists remained the last significant organization with an autonomous program. To set this anomaly straight, the Party unleashed Khvyl'ovyi against them. The facts clearly point to a collusion between the Khvyl'ovists and the KP(b)U on this issue.

The Futurists seemed to have been genuinely unaware that they were being singled out for liquidation by the Party. Khvyl'ovyi's articles were interpreted as private initiatives, just another instance of inter-organizational rivalries. Semenko had registered surprise that Khvyl'ovyi's article appeared in *Komunist* without any editorial comment; he seemed to have believed that the absence of a disclaimer was an oversight. S. Antoniuk, too, assumed that he was responding merely to a personal vendetta. So certain was he of this that he ended his rebuttal with the following smug apostrophe to Khvyl'ovyi: "Your stand [*vystup*] has not been supported by Party and public [*partiino-hromads'ka*] opinion" (Antoniuk 1930a, 28). Soon, it became obvious that the Futurists had miscalculated. A number of official commentaries in the press condemned the Futurists for their attempt to exonerate themselves, asserting in no uncertain terms that Khvyl'ovyi had been correct in exposing the Futurist threat.

The first to shatter *Nova generatsiia*'s illusions was Andrii Khvylia, member of the KP(b)U and a leading spokesman on literary matters. Khvylia had been one of Khvyl'ovyi's foremost critics during the VAPLITE era, but when Antoniuk and Shkurupii censured the *Komunist* article, Khvylia came to the defense of his former ideological foe. Not only did he see fit to reiterate the basic accusations against the Futurists (pornography, nationalism), but he went out of his way to acknowledge that Khvyl'ovyi's article was proper and demanded that the Futurists acknowledge as much:

> Articles have already appeared in our press critical of Shkurupii's work. There was the article by M. Khvyl'ovyi which *quite justly* noted that Shkurupii's book, *Dlia druziv poetiv suchasnykiv vichnosty* [To My Poet-Friends, the Contemporaries of Eternity], contained a passage that can be called nationalistic. Comrade Khvyl'ovyi *justly exposed* this sick phenomenon in Geo Shkurupii's work. Let us assume that Geo

> Shkurupii wrote these things in 1921–1922....But why, then, when Comrade Khvyl'ovyi reacted against [these] elements of Geo Shkurupii's work and exhorted our proletarian community to take note of this phenomenon..., why, [then], did Comrade Shkurupii in his letter to the press[65] and Comrade Antoniuk in his articles...react with such indignation, such outcries against "the new capers," "the new tricks" of Khvyl'ovyi? Is there any evidence of Khvyl'ovism in Khvyl'ovyi's article? Nothing of the kind. The attempt to call this Khvyl'ovism has nothing in common with [literary] criticism. This is an unwarranted attempt to persecute [*ts'kuvannia*] *a proletarian writer, a member of the Party, Comrade Khvyl'ovyi.* This is an attempt to cover up one's own ideological vacillations, one's own mistakes, an attempt to distort the general line of proletarian literature....We note again that all three of Comrade Antoniuk's articles contained attacks [*ts'kuvannia*] against Comrade Khvyl'ovyi (Khvylia 1930a, 35–36; *emphasis added*).

Antoniuk was also severely chastised in *Kharkivs'kyi Proletar* by its editor V. Furer, who expressed amazement that Antoniuk would dare to "polemicize" with an article like Khvyl'ovyi's which appeared "in the central organ of the KP(b)U" and do it, moreover, in *Nova generatsiia*, "a non-party journal" [*pozapartiinyi zhurnal*]. Accusing Antoniuk of covering up "manifestations of Ukrainian nationalism," Furer rhetorically asks: "Who and for what reason authorized Comrade Antoniuk to criticize Comrade Khvyl'ovyi?" (Furer 1930a).

A month later Mykola Skrypnyk made this observation: "M. Khvyl'ovyi's *great service* lies in the fact that he raised his voice as early as January of this year to expose the fallacious elements manifesting themselves in *Nova generatsiia*'s *Al'manakh*, No. 'a'" (M. Skrypnyk 1930, 26; *emphasis added*).

The Futurists were not alone in failing to realize immediately that they were the object of a Party-orchestrated attack. Two months after Khvyl'ovyi's "The Screaming Deity" appeared in *Komunist*, it received a negative appraisal in the VUSPP journal, *Hart*. The author, V. Sukhyno-Khomenko, accused Khvyl'ovyi of seeking "revenge" and of discovering "Khvyl'ovism in places where it is completely superfluous" (Sukhyno-Khomenko 1930b). This earned him a long, trenchant rebuke from Furer (Furer 1930b), and a much longer and harsher rebuttal from Khvyl'ovyi himself in an article entitled, "With What Has *Nova generatsiia* Enchanted Comrade Sukhyno-Khomenko?" (Khvyl'ovyi 1930b). Between bouts of self-flagellation, Khvyl'ovyi not only subjected the VUSPP critic to his sharpest sarcasm, but set out to prove once again that the Futurists

65 The reference is to Shkurupii 1930c.

(especially Shkurupii) were indeed permeated with "nationalism," "counter-revolutionary theories," and "Khvyl'ovism"; that they were, in effect, no better than Petliurites, Iefremovites, and Dontsovites. Bristling at the suggestion made by Sukhyno-Khomenko that he, Khvyl'ovyi, was out of step with the Party's views, Khvyl'ovyi directed this blunt remark at his detractor:

> If [my article] was anti-Party...Comrade Sukhyno-Khomenko, then, first of all, it would not have been printed in *Komunist* and, moreover, without any commentary; in the second place, I bring to your attention that you were not being addressed from the pages of the central organ of the Party by a Khvyl'ovist who [mistakenly] got mixed up with members of PROLITFRONT while [continuing to] dream about counter-revolutionary "revenge." [No. You were addressed] by a member of the Communist Bolshevik Party of Ukraine (ibid., 233).

To emphasize that his articles were not quixotic outbursts, Khvyl'ovyi linked his own efforts with those of prominent Party members:

> *Avanhard* [No. a]...has been condemned. It has been condemned by responsible workers of the Party. It has been condemned by Comrade A. A. Khvylia...; it has been condemned by the People's Commissar for Education, Comrade M. O. Skrypnyk....Moreover, Party opinion has condemned not only the almanac in question, but *the entire orientation* of the *Nova generatsiia* poets (ibid., 229; *emphasis added*).

As late as September 1930, in the course of an overview of contemporary literary criticism, the critic H. Ovcharov, known as "Skrypnyk's right hand and his closest aid in the NKO" [People Commissariat for Education], once again returned to the errors committed by the Futurists and the positive role that Khvyl'ovyi played in exposing them. At this stage, Ovcharov did concede that Khvyl'ovyi's article in *Komunist* contained "significant mistakes in several instances" (Ovcharov 1930b, 85), among which were his description of *Avanhard–Al'manakh*'s defects, an incorrect assessment of the dangers on the literary front,[66] "untruthful quotations" and "distortions" (ibid., 106). Nonetheless, Ovcharov concluded that Khvyl'ovyi's article was "necessary and beneficial" and that it had an "objectively positive meaning" (ibid., 85, 106). Sukhyno-Khomenko, Shkurupii, and Antoniuk were criticized for not recognizing this fact. In addition, the latter two were singled out for not exhibiting any self-criticism. Instead of confessing their errors, these Futurists

[66] Khvyl'ovyi had stated that his former opponents were trying to monopolize proletarian ideology for themselves, a remark that upset certain members of VUSPP. See "Za hehemoniiu proletars'koï" 1930.

engaged in "tantrums" [*vykhvatky*] whose sole purpose was to "compromise" Khvyl'ovyi (ibid., 97, 100).

It is clear that once Khvyl'ovyi capitulated to the Party and members of *Literaturnyi iarmarok* gained access to the proletarian fold, he became a prized and protected instrument of its policy. His function was to rein in an independent-minded literary organization and lend credence to the Party's fabricated trial against the intelligentsia. It should be noted that Khvyl'ovyi's attack on the Futurists went hand in hand with his fulminations against the Union for the Liberation of Ukraine (SVU). A better part of "And Who Else Sits among the Indicted?" was devoted to the trial. That very same month he wrote an abusive two-part diatribe against one of the chief defendants, Serhii Iefremov, based, apparently, on the man's private diary. Khvyl'ovyi defended the ethics of using a living person's papers by referring to Iefremov as a political corpse. The personal journal itself was characterized thus: "No, this is not a diary, this is a reeking toilet that never had a fan. This is the most shameful document of our time."[67]

The events recounted here set the stage for the last act in the history of Ukrainian Futurism. With the onset of Khvyl'ovyi's offensive, the Futurists entered into a period of irreversible and rapid decline. The conditional acceptance they had enjoyed in the proletarian community was about to disappear thanks mainly to the "revelations" made by Khvyl'ovyi. Within weeks of his articles, the Futurists were once again isolated on the literary front. Out of favor with the Party, out of favor with VUSPP, *Nova generatsiia* was about to go through the final desperate months of its existence.

OPPU: Final Metamorphosis and the End of a Movement

The show trial of the Union for Liberation of Ukraine was a watershed for intellectuals and artists in Ukraine. Since at least 1928, when the Soviet Union embarked on the first Five Year Plan and Stalin consolidated his power, there had been a steady tightening of ideological and cultural controls. The trial signaled a vicious turn for the worst, betraying an imminent turn against Ukrainian culture itself—certainly against Ukrainianization—and an all-out war on artistic and intellectual diversity.

In January 1930 Semenko observed that the new phase of socialist construction on which the Soviet Union was embarking demanded from writers and readers alike "emphasis on a new creative psychology." He

[67] In Ukrainian: "Ні, це не щоденник—це вонючий кльозет, що ніколи не мав вентилятора. Це найганебніший документ наших днів." See Khvyl'ovyi (1930g, 65: 2).

expressed concern that the reader's psychology was outpacing the writer's and urged that literature remain in the "vanguard rather than at the rear" of this important transformation. "We need not fear a certain schematism" in our work, he said. "We must fear extraneous psychologism which retards our tempo." "Writers who produce class-conscious works yet remain primitives with respect to their productive and creative qualifications [and] identify the study of the classics with proletarian literature might even now be failing to satisfy their readers...." Semenko was particularly pessimistic about the role peasant writers' organizations were playing:

> Independent peasant literary organizations like Pluh may have a temporary, intermediate significance, [but] in my opinion they have outlived their usefulness....They may inadvertently turn into *conservative* mechanisms that retard or impede the reconstruction of the new "village." Former peasant work must be developed by regular proletarian literary organizations...like VUSPP and VUSKK [*Nova generatsiia*] (Semenko 1930f).

The point of these ruminations came down to this:

> There is a need to take into account the experience gained from the so-called leftist work conducted in the Union Republics....In my view it would be a mistake...to require the new [leftist] formations to merge with VUSPP-[type organizations]. The Party leadership should give them [i.e., the avant-garde] the chance [and] the help to take an independent road, creating the conditions [whereby] such leftist...organizations [can establish] close coalitions with the [other] VUSPPs in the Union Republics (ibid.).

Under the circumstances, these were bold suggestions. Not only did Semenko raise a pet concern of the Futurist program (anti-psychologism) and belittle Pluh, but he also managed to challenge VUSPP's ambition to absorb other literary groups into its own structure, arguing that it was preferable to maintain coalitions rather than create a single large organization. It should be kept in mind that these views were expressed the same month Khvyl'ovyi began vilifying the Futurists in *Komunist*. In fact, the issue of *Nova generatsiia* that carried this particular article also contained one of the Futurist rebuttals to Khvyl'ovyi (i.e., Semenko 1930c).

Semenko's claim to both organizational and artistic independence is all the more striking because only two months later he was obliged to reverse his stand completely. On 20 March 1930 *Literaturna hazeta* carried a notice from Semenko requesting that VUSPP rule quickly on the question of *Nova generatsiia*'s "merger" [*zlyttia*] with VUSPP. The reason: he considered the existence of parallel proletarian organizations

(VUSPP and *Nova generatsiia*) superfluous.[68] Significantly, such requests for a merger were not coming from *Nova generatsiia* alone. In late February and early March other segments of the literary community were expressing similar interests. For example, a number of critics, members of the Ukrainian Institute of Marxism-Leninism (V. Sukhyno-Khomenko, Mykhailo Novyts'kyi, Ievhen Hirchak, H. Ovcharov and others), voiced their desire to see a "consolidated" and "unified" literary front and asked to be made members of VUSPP. On 8 April 1930 Semenko followed up his petition to VUSPP with this statement:

> There can be no separate (Futurist), independent artistic system other than the Marxist-Leninist. There is also no need for any walls and barriers between movements that consider themselves genuinely proletarian; these can only introduce confusion.... Very frequently terminology (futurism, leftism, constructivism, etc.) pollutes the ideational side of the cause [and] attracts into its orbit people who are psycho-ideologically alien; [it can also attract] entire movements that have a formalistic or other character.... Through its creative work, through the crystallization of its ideological positions and through the application of its own methodological, artistic-formal quest, *Nova generatsiia* has been unceasingly moving toward proletarian literary ranks. To be sure, it has been doing so through the obstacle of its formalistic conceptions.... It should be noted that there were negative instances in our work and that [this] could have... prevented us from successfully overcoming Futurism. As a petty-bourgeois concept, it had played a positive role in Soviet art, but it hindered [us] in drawing closer to other proletarian literary groups, with whom, essentially, *Nova generatsiia* shared a single ideological and political foundation... (Semenko 1930i).[69]

Khvyl'ovyi's denunciations were achieving their purpose. The Futurists petitioned for entry into VUSPP to find shelter from PROLITFRONT. As required, they were ready to plead guilty to all charges. Semenko conscientiously noted that *Nova generatsiia* had now "liberated itself" not only from its "maximalist view of art," but was also free of "nationalism," specifically "Khvyl'ovism and other manifestations" (Semenko 1930b).

The Futurists' application to VUSPP was greeted "very warmly." Obviously, their coalition partners had not yet adopted the negative attitude that prevailed toward them in PROLITFRONT. But this was to change soon. Already at the end of March, Ivan Kulyk had written an

68 For the full text see Semenko 1930a. This document is dated 1 March 1930.

69 See also Semenko 1930j. Although this particular document also called for union with VUSPP, it was far less apologetic about the Futurist program than the above.

article for the Party organ *Komunist* in which he urged VUSPP to re-examine its relationship with the Futurists. It appeared in the middle of April and a month later was reprinted in *Hart* (Kulyk 1930). If the Futurists thought their long-standing coalition would entitle them to swift and uncontested passage into VUSPP's ranks, Kulyk's article must have deeply disappointed them.

Kulyk observed, first of all, that *Nova generatsiia*'s (VUSKK) desire to join VUSPP was a brilliant victory for the Party's literary policy. He acknowledged the Futurists had been useful in the past but saw no role for them either now or hereafter. A movement that was concerned only with destruction and scandal could hardly be the basis on which to unite the masses, he argued. Moreover, the majority in VUSPP, contended Kulyk, was not ready to admit every single Futurist into the organization. Membership could be granted to individuals but not to the entire organization. He worried especially about the "political-artistic position of the leadership" in VUSKK and the "policies" [*liniia*] of their journal. The real question, as far as he was concerned, was whether the Futurists had indeed evolved sufficiently in the direction of proletarian literature to warrant VUSPP's embrace. Kulyk felt they had not. The benign attitude displayed by the Futurists toward VUSPP was fine, but he tended to believe this was merely a "warfare tactic." The problem was that the principles of *Nova generatsiia* were not in line with VUSPP's; the journal was far from overcoming its past and present ideological mistakes and it showed no sign of self-criticism. In his view "only the class enemy can derive pleasure and service" from the Futurists' theories on nationalism and national cultures. "We have not only confusion here, we have something worse, something politically harmful." He pointed to a few instances of this in the journal, but was particularly incensed by Semenko's reaction (i.e., Semenko 1930c) to Khvyl'ovyi's censure of *Avanhard–Al'manakh*:

> There is no denying that M. Khvyl'ovyi's condemnation of Shkurupii's uncommunist...article ["The New Art in the Process of Development of Ukrainian Culture" in *Avanhard–Al'manakh*] was entirely just. Will M. Semenko dare to suggest that Shkurupii's evaluation of our policies on national-cultural construction was correct and Leninist in manner? It is hardly conceivable that a person who stands solidly on the positions of proletarian literature would dare to assert this. And if that is the case, then M. Semenko should have acknowledged and condemned [these errors] regardless of who exposed [them]. *Nova generatsiia* did not do this, therefore, it was quite natural to fear that G. Shkurupii's mistakes on the nationality question were not accidental and personal, but that they were shared by all of VUSKK (Kulyk 1930, 190–91).

Kulyk ended on this note:

> We cannot evaluate VUSKK's...desire to enter VUSPP in any other way except as an incontestably positive fact, a fact of significant literary-political importance. But we want to know exactly what the Comrades from VUSKK are prepared to bring into our organization. And above all we want to be sure that they are capable of liberating themselves from that confusion and harmful nihilism that characterized their position on the nationality question in the past. Only under such conditions will we be able (and have the right as a proletarian organization) to seriously consider and raise in a practical manner the question of allowing a portion of VUSKK's membership entry into our organization. Such, at least, is my view (ibid., 191).

For a month the issue of whether the Futurists would be allowed into VUSPP lay dormant. It was not raised again until VUSPP's Plenum (20–24 May), at which time it became the most controversial item of discussion, turning this celebration of VUSPP's pre-eminence on the literary front into a major scandal.

From the start of the Plenum it became obvious that VUSPP had adopted Kulyk's recommendations. The Futurists would be acceptable to VUSPP only if they capitulated completely. Ivan Mykytenko, a leading figure in the organization, stated as much: "A genuine consolidation of forces...can take place only...if *Nova generatsiia* decisively condemns the ideological defects in its previous work and completely recognizes the ideological and *creative platform* of VUSPP as obligatory for itself. Without this we cannot even imagine *Nova generatsiia*'s entry into our organization" (Mykytenko 1962, 100; *emphasis added*). Specifically, the Plenum asked the Futurists to condemn their "nihilism" on the nationality question, confess that they "failed to understand the Leninist [nationality] policy," and renounce "formalism" as an approach to art ("Postanova Plenumu rady VUSPP" 1930, 192). In putting forth these demands, VUSPP was aware that the Futurists were in no position to refuse; with the Party behind it, VUSPP was simply too powerful to be denied. Moreover, it was obvious from Semenko's March statement that the Futurists were in a mood to compromise. To the Plenum's shock and amazement, however, something entirely different happened. Instead of throwing themselves at the mercy of VUSPP, the Futurists came to the Plenum to negotiate as equals.

Nova generatsiia's delegation consisted of Semenko, Ivan Malovichko, Oleksii Poltorats'kyi, Leonid Nedolia (former editor of *Iugo-Lef*), and Mykola Skuba. During the opening ceremonies, Nedolia greeted the delegates by saying the Futurists never had any intentions of abandoning their platform. He characterized Kulyk's article as "harmful...for proletarian literature" and suggested that he be "put in his place."[70] This so unnerved the Plenum that it nearly eliminated the Futurists from its agenda then and there. Quick intervention by other representatives, however, saved the day. VUSPP's resolution noted that "only a correction of Comrade Nedolia's statement...made it possible to approach this question [again] in a realistic manner" ("Postanova Plenumu rady VUSPP" 1930, 192).

With this incident contained, the Futurists were granted permission to make an appearance before a commission examining their petition; Semenko was also given the opportunity to address the entire Plenum. In granting these privileges, VUSPP expected the Futurists to be contrite, confess their errors, and engage in public self-criticism. Instead, the unexpected came to pass: the Futurists tried to convince the Plenum that their avant-garde positions were correct. While insisting that they wanted to become members of VUSPP, they refused to make any major concessions. The persistence with which the Futurists pursued their goals finally forced the Plenum to abandon negotiations. It "is impossible to discuss at present the question of *Nova generatsiia*'s entry into VUSPP," declared the Plenum and tabled the entire motion (ibid., 193). As a result of this action, the coalition between the two groups was officially terminated (M. Skrypnyk 1930, 25).

Rather than savoring an unconditional surrender, the Plenum thus became witness to a major scandal. The behavior of the Futurists (especially of Semenko) so shocked VUSPP that a special resolution was adopted censuring them. Nearly half of it was devoted to a criticism of Semenko's "futuro-anarchistic" and "recidivistic" address, which was "categorically condemned" for being "anti-proletarian," an "attack on the basic positions of proletarian literature and its Party leadership," an "unworthy attempt at revising the Leninist Party policy on the nationality question," and a revision of the "developed and set view in Marxist literary scholarship [on the question] of the origins of October proletarian literature" ("Postanova Plenumu rady VUSPP" 1930, 193). The last point was an insinuation that Semenko was trying to include himself among the "first bold ones" [*pershi khorobri*], who were officially recognized as founders of proletarian literature.[71]

[70] This incident is reported in Mykytenko 1930b.

[71] The expression the "first bold ones" comes from Vasyl' Ellan-Blakytnyi's poem "Udary molota i sertsia" [The Beat of Hammer and Heart, 1920]. It was adopted in the twenties as a reference to the writers (most of them Borot'bists) who first sided with the October revolution and were associated with the journal *Mystetstvo* [Art], which, as we recall, was edited by Semenko. In addition to Blakytnyi, the phrase was normally associated with

Weeks and even months later, commentators continued to recall Semenko's speech, expressing amazement and indignation at its brazenness. Mykytenko observed that the Futurist leader "felt as relaxed on the podium of the Plenum...as he does on a boulevard" (Mykytenko 1930b, 4). Khvyl'ovyi raised it when he impeached Futurism: "Did the Panfuturists repent? Did they begin correcting their mistakes? Nothing of the kind. At the VUSPP Plenum the chieftain of *Nova generatsiia*, M. Semenko, read such a speech (I would say, such an 'ideologically steadfast' speech) that even his coalition partners [VUSPP] had to reject it" (Khvyl'ovyi 1930b, 229). In late September, H. Ovcharov felt compelled to remind readers of how rashly Semenko attacked Andrii Khvylia at the Plenum and how he was "categorically and decisively" denounced for it (Ovcharov 1930b, 86–87).

The resolution and summary of the Plenum proceedings only hint at the animosity and tensions that prevailed there (Mykytenko 1930a). A more palpable recreation of the atmosphere comes from two articles that appeared soon after the event: Mykytenko's "'Live' shakhraistvo" ["Leftist" Fraud] (Mykytenko 1930b) and Semenko's temperamental retort, "Nu i repliky" [Wow, Some Answer!] (Semenko 1930d).

Semenko's article was one of the most impassioned, angry, and desperate he had ever written. Although Mykytenko was his primary target, Semenko was in fact responding to the entire literary front that stood against him. He presented the Futurists' side of what happened at the VUSPP Plenum, defended the principles and history of his organization, and insisted that it had a right to an autonomous existence: "Do you [Comrade Mykytenko] think that two [proletarian organizations]—VUSPP and PROLITFRONT—are enough? We, however, are NOT satisfied with this. Indeed, there can be three proletarian organizations; why necessarily two? We will see later what will come of them" (ibid., 31). Remarkably, in October 1930 Semenko was still defending the notion of artistic competition and pluralism, demanding that *Nova generatsiia* be accepted as an equal.

What is most astonishing about this sometimes eloquent performance is both the boldness and force with which Semenko attacked the lofty figure of Ivan Mykytenko.[72] Accusing him of lies, misrepresentations,

---

Vasyl' Chumak, Hnat Mykhailychenko, and Andrii Zalyvchyi. Interestingly, it was never applied to Semenko, even though it probably should have. An early example of the phrase appears in Ialovyi 1923.

72 The Plenum elected Mykytenko to VUSPP's Council [*Rada*] as well as to the Secretariat; it chose him as one of VUSPP's representatives to the Russian VOAPP [The All-Union Alliance of Associations of Proletarian Writers] and he served on the editorial board of *Hart* and *Zaboi*. See Mykytenko 1930a, 209.

and conscious distortion of history, Semenko freely made use of *ad hominems*. He ridiculed the "great dexterity" of Mykytenko's "loose tongue"; he accused him of "envy," "brazen lies and ignorance"; he called him a "naked ignoramus," "naive," and referred to him sarcastically as "smart." At one point Semenko exploded: "Come to your senses [Comrade Mykytenko]! I am not such a careerist as you" (Semenko 1930d, 33).

Semenko rejected Mykytenko's contention that for the last eight to nine years the Futurists were engaged in nothing but "burying art." He emphasized that they practiced destruction and construction simultaneously, that in destroying bourgeois art they were also creating proletarian art. On the subject of whether or not he was promoting a revisionist view of the origins of Soviet Ukrainian literature, which was by then being canonized, Semenko had this to say:

> Comrade Mykytenko! Once and for all try to remember this: A. Zalyvchyi, H. Mykhailychenko, V. Chumak [and] V. Ellan-Blakytnyi are the first bold ones [*pershi khorobri*], the organizers of Soviet and proletarian literature. But in addition there is also Comrade Semenko, M., who was engaged in this same task together with them; Ukrainian Futurism was a Soviet movement on a par with others; it did not appear later as some would have it. If you have a head..., repeat this [fact] about forty times; it will do you good....What [after all] is the crime here? Was [it a crime] that we really worked and worked together with the first bold ones? This is not a flaw. One can be proud of this. Yes or no, Comrade Mykytenko? (ibid.).

Semenko also denied that he had attacked the Party leadership, namely, Khvylia and Kulyk. He asserted that he respected Khvylia as a "serious worker" in literature, but, nevertheless, he considered himself completely within his rights "to criticize, even sharply, when Comrade Khvylia, on a par with us, treats those problems of applied criticism that are debatable and do not have the character of a directive" (ibid.). (The argument was about Geo Shkurupii who had been criticized both by Khvylia and Kulyk.) But if Semenko showed at least a modicum of deference for Khvylia, he had absolutely none for Kulyk: "I leave aside Comrade Kulyk's ideas about G. Shkurupii's 1922 period because Comrade Kulyk is no better a theoretician than I. Mykytenko, nor [is he] a worse obfuscator than many of our [other] organizational literary scholars."

A large part of Semenko's article dealt directly with the negotiations at the Plenum. He maintained that when *Nova generatsiia* petitioned for entry into VUSPP, the Secretariat had not asked the Futurists to meet any preconditions. They had not been asked to re-examine their principles, they had not been accused of misunderstanding the nationality policy, they had not been cited for formalism and most of all they had not been asked to accept VUSPP's ideological and creative platform. Referring to Nedolia's speech at the Plenum, Semenko said: "Nedolia did the correct thing. In *Nova generatsiia*'s previous course, just as in Comrade Mykytenko's, there were lapses, mistakes, and even common stupidities, but, basically, the course was revolutionary and had a positive effect on proletarian literature, especially if it is compared with other proletarian organizations. Why then should [this course] be denied...? Why, especially when the older members of *Nova generatsiia* stood on communist principles longer than Comrade Mykytenko and have done more for proletarian literature than he?" (ibid., 32).

According to Semenko, the merger between VUSPP and *Nova generatsiia* failed not because of any "fraud," "hooliganism," or "deception" on the part of the Futurists (as Mykytenko contended), but because there were "artistic-creative" differences between them and because they had differing attitudes toward "certain unproletarian literary organizations (PROLITFRONT)."

> In his naiveté (?) Mykytenko does not understand the true essence of our differences.... *We believe the creative method of proletarian literature is an open question at the present moment.* [This is] contrary to VUSPP's assertion that its own creative method...is the only method [for proletarian literature]. This means our method of work [proletarian functionalism] must enjoy the same rights and privileges [as VUSPP's]. The wholesale rejection of Futurism, the confusion between (1) Maiakovskii's Futurism and (2) Marinetti's Futurism...is harmful and we, naturally, have no reason to reject anything. Therefore, the position of *Nova generatsiia*'s delegation at the VUSPP Plenum was entirely correct (ibid., 34).[73]

The Futurist "position" as outlined by Semenko consisted of these major points:

1. *Nova generatsiia* would not reject its platform because it was correct; nor would it condemn its past, believing as it did that the works it produced corresponded to the needs of the period in which they were written.

2. The organization had no political-ideological differences with VUSPP.

3. Individual Futurists had made mistakes just as individuals in other groups (for example, VUSPP), but there was no reason to assign blame to the entire organization.

4. Attacks (like Kulyk's) were nothing but "tomfoolery" and

[73] Emphasis added. The question mark in the first sentence appears in the original.

"irresponsibility" inasmuch as *Nova generatsiia* had already condemned its own errors.

5. The Futurists felt their formal development had contributed toward the strengthening of proletarian literature. Although they were willing to work within VUSPP, they advocated "socialist competition" among all the separate formal currents in that organization.

6. *Nova generatsiia* would merge with VUSPP but only if VUSPP recognized that the Futurists had played an essentially positive role in the past. Furthermore, VUSPP had to accept the entire Futurist organization, not separate individuals.

7. The maximalist articles in their journal were acknowledged as "debatable," but so were the minimalist articles that appeared in VUSPP's organs.

8. The union between *Nova generatsiia* and VUSPP would not mean the end of work pursued by the Futurists; it would imply its expansion and continuation within the confines of VUSPP.

9. All these conditions were considered "completely normal" and "feasible" inasmuch as VUSPP was not a literary movement, only an organization (ibid., 34–35).

Semenko's account demonstrates that the Futurists refused to capitulate before VUSPP. They had come to the Plenum determined to concede as little as possible. VUSPP, naturally, expected the opposite. If the Party had made the decision to liquidate the Futurists, as it seems it did, VUSPP obviously could not settle for anything less. The Futurists probably sensed what was in store for them, because there was an element of desperation in Semenko's quixotic struggle for the recognition of their current rights and their past contributions. It is as if he foresaw that more was at stake than just his organization's immediate survival; Futurism's very place in history was being threatened.

When the Futurists failed to gain entry into VUSPP they became a marked organization, a group beyond the pale of the proletarian community. For a few weeks they maintained a low profile, "organizationally deactivating" themselves. But just as it seemed they might be quietly fading into oblivion, they emerged again. Exactly a month after the Plenum, a small announcement appeared in the press, revealing that *Nova generatsiia* (VUSKK) had formed a new organization called The Union of Proletarian Writers of Ukraine or OPPU [*Ob'iednannia Proletars'kykh Pys'mennykiv Ukraïny*] ("'Nova generatsiia' na novomu etapi" 1930). According to this notice, OPPU was "not a new organization" but represented *Nova generatsiia* "at a new stage of its work." OPPU declared it would not publish any "ideational [or] political platform...because it shared VUSPP's...." OPPU would "struggle for the consolidation of proletarian literary forces around this platform, but with [the understanding] that...free competition among various creative methods...would be guaranteed."

The formation of OPPU triggered Mykytenko's savage article, "'Leftist' fraud." OPPU literally sent the proletarian camp into a frenzy and the reasons are obvious. First, the Futurists had dared to appropriate for themselves the venerable title "proletarian." This was an affront to VUSPP, which considered itself *the* proletarian organization. Second, OPPU was clearly an obstacle on the path toward "consolidation," frustrating VUSPP's ambition to absorb other groups. Third, the Futurists were demonstratively challenging VUSPP's choice of literary method (realism). And perhaps worst of all, they were continuing to parade their disregard for the Party, VUSPP, and PROLITFRONT by harboring in OPPU such "anti-proletarian" elements as Shkurupii. Earlier, when *Nova generatsiia* sued for membership in VUSPP, it made a gesture of good will by dismissing from its organization four individuals who had resisted the merger (Viktor Ver, Volodymyr Kovalevs'kyi, A. Sanovych, and Hro Vakar [ibid., 86; Semenko 1930i, 64]), but when OPPU was created no such gesture was made: Shkurupii was retained as a member, allowed to published in *Nova generatsiia* (of all things, on the subject of Taras Shevchenko; see Shkurupii 1930f), and was even elected to a position of leadership.[74]

The course on which the Futurists embarked was daring but hopeless. Following the creation of OPPU, they came under virtual siege: VUSPP was against them, PROLITFRONT was against them, and, most importantly, the Party was against them. It was probably no accident that Mykytenko called OPPU as dangerous as Valeriian Polishchuk's late Avanhard (Mykytenko 1930b, 4).

Under these circumstances *Nova generatsiia* turned virtually into a journal of polemics, self-defense, and even self-criticism. The journal did succeed in publishing a few interesting items that reflected the Futurist platform, but often the affirmation of a Futurist principle in one issue would lead to its denial in another.[75] Nothing demonstrates better how

[74] The other official members of OPPU were Semenko, Leonid Nedolia, S. Antoniuk, M. Skuba, Ivan Malovichko, Oleksii Poltorats'kyi, Oleksa Vlyz'ko, O. Korzh, L. Zymnyi, Iu. Poliichuk, Petro Mel'nyk, Mykola Panchenko, and O. Perehuda. Candidates for full membership included: S. Voinilovych, A. Mykhailiuk, Mykola Ivanov, Ol. Ian, M. Bulatovych. See "'Nova generatsiia' na novomu etapi" (1930, 86).

[75] See, for example, Kovalevs'kyi 1930. This article was criticized by O. Poltorats'kyi (Poltorats'kyi 1930b).

quickly the Futurists were losing ground in their war against the proletarians than the fact that by October OPPU had to announce that it was expelling Shkurupii, Vlyz'ko, and Antoniuk—the three men who had drawn the sharpest fire from the opposition. A short statement from the "OPPU Bureau" stated that Antoniuk was expelled for "intellectualist [*inteligents'ki*] vacillations," the others for their "unwillingness and inability" to follow the proletarian model of creativity (*Nova generatsiia* 1930 [10]: 64). Ironically, the issue that carried this notice also contained Semenko's response to Mykytenko with its defense of Shkurupii. This contradiction was corrected the following month when Ivan Malovichko published a short but vile article about Shkurupii (Malovichko 1930b, 65–66).

Despite such difficulties, *Nova generatsiia* announced that subscriptions were being accepted for the year 1931. This optimism, however, went unrewarded. The last and final issue of the journal appeared for the months of November and December 1930, the third time in 1930 that a double issue was published (the previous were Nos. 6–7 and 8–9). There were no other signs of an imminent demise. Nevertheless, in January 1931, both OPPU and *Nova generatsiia* officially expired.

It would be simplistic to reduce the death of Ukrainian Futurism to a single cause. The movement was undermined by a multitude of political and cultural factors, most of them completely beyond its control. But if one were to identify the proverbial straw that broke OPPU's back, then it would have to be a play by Leonid Nedolia or, to be more precise, the review it received from Khvylia, who at that time was head of the Cultural Propaganda Section of the Central Committee of the KP(b)U.

The play in question was "Khoroba: Pobutova khronika 1929 r." [Illness: An Everyday Chronicle of 1929] (Nedolia 1930). The theme was Ukrainianization. Its protagonist was Ivan Liubota, a decent, highly respected Ukrainian Bolshevik whose goal is to introduce the Ukrainian language into a Russified workers' union. His efforts to implement the Party's policy is met with strong resistance from a group of Russian chauvinists and Ukrainophobes. In order to deprive Liubota of his leadership position in the union, the chauvinistic clique launches a slander campaign, accusing him of anti-Semitism, Ukrainian nationalism, and anti-social behavior. Although completely innocent, Liubota falls victim to these charges; he is severely reprimanded by a supervisory committee [*kontrol'nyi komitet*] and dismissed from his position of responsibility.

In November, Khvylia published an analysis of the play entitled, "Khto zakhvoriv?" [Who is Ill?] (Khvylia 1930b). He expressed concern not about Russian chauvinism but about Nedolia's ideological health. He took issue with his portrayal of Ukrainianization, namely, his suggestion that the policy was instituted only because the Party feared Ukrainian nationalism. The notion put forth by the play—namely, that the Party allowed Ukrainians to speak their language and pursue their culture simply to prevent them from joining the underground or becoming Petliurites—was considered reprehensible. But even worse was Nedolia's implication that official Soviet institutions were nothing but agents of Russian nationalism, bent on sabotaging the Party's nationality policy:

> As we can see, the author...stresses that not only is the Union *aparat*...against Ukrainianization [but so is] the regional supervisory committee. [According to Nedolia], our Union and Party *aparat* is against Ukrainianization [and] any member of the Party who attempts to actively implement the Party's principles on the nationality question will be confronted with the invincible force of the Union and Party *aparat*—and this force will destroy him....In an "artistic" form, Nedolia shows that the regional supervisory committee is a tool in the hands of Great Russian power nationalists....In this play the Party and union *aparat* is [shown to be] in opposition to the workers and the decisions of the Party (ibid., 57–59).

Khvylia admitted that there were opponents to the Party's policy, but maintained that they were a minority and the exception. Nedolia's mistake was that he only saw Russian chauvinism in Ukraine and overlooked Ukrainian nationalism, which was the greater evil. Nedolia should have stressed in his play that Ukrainian nationalism "is a great force" and that it was "putting pressure on separate links of our *aparat*." He should have emphasized "that struggling against Ukrainian nationalism and its manifestations in the Party and the unions is an unusually important matter. Why did Nedolia forget about this? He has forgotten this because he is following the path of Ukrainian nationalistic slander against the Party; he sees in Ukraine and in the Union and Party *aparat* only Russian nationalism." Khvylia concluded that Nedolia had written a nationalistic and Trotskyite play (ibid., 60, 61). Just over a month later, *Nova generatsiia* ceased publication.

On 20 January 1931 *Literaturna hazeta* published a "Resolution on the Dissolution of the Union of Proletarian Writers of Ukraine—OPPU (*Nova generatsiia*)," signed by Semenko, Nedolia, and Mykola Panchenko. The resolution had been passed "unanimously" on 11 January 1931 at a general meeting of OPPU ("Postanova pro rozpusk Ob'iednannia proletars'kykh pys'mennykiv Ukrainy—OPPU [Nova generatsiia]" 1931). It read as follows:

> During its entire existence, right up to VUSPP's Plenum in 1930, VUSKK-*Nova generatsiia*, doubtlessly, conducted useful work for the

> proletariat [while] overcoming its own mistakes.... VUSKK...exposed the anti-proletarian essence of [various] phenomena. At the same time VUSKK supported positive phenomena in literature and art.... In all its work, VUSKK always followed the lead of the Party and...VUSPP..., struggling decisively and openly for a proletarian ideology in art. VUSKK worked at crystallizing its own creative method and at educating new cadres of writers only in this direction. Such was the case up to the VUSPP Plenum. It is affirmed that the conduct of VUSKK's representatives at the...Plenum, both on the issue of consolidating the forces of proletarian literature and on the question of who directed the literary process, was completely wrong. Instead of confessing thoroughly and decisively to these errors, [instead of] correcting them and merging immediately with VUSPP, VUSKK took the completely erroneous step of transforming this organization into...OPPU. The very fact that this organization came into existence [meant] that it was opposing itself to VUSPP, the organization that stood closest to the Communist Party and the only one that should have gathered about itself all the forces of proletarian literature....Due to such opposition to VUSPP, [OPPU] became a vehicle for anti-proletarian elements....The continued existence of OPPU is considered objectively harmful and, therefore, it is resolved that the organization be dissolved. In addition, members of OPPU take upon themselves the obligation of [demonstrating] proletarian self-criticism [and] of acknowledging in the Soviet and Party press the mistakes of the organization [and] its...members. All members of OPPU consider VUSPP the sole organization of proletarian literature. Within its bounds it will be possible to develop all methods of creativity that are beneficial for proletarian literature, including the creative method of the former *Nova generatsiia*-VUSKK-OPPU.

Although contrite, this resolution failed to satisfy VUSPP. Quite obviously the Futurists were not prostrating themselves sufficiently and were too adamant about seeing positive features in their past. Moreover, they failed to repudiate their artistic method, inexplicably insisting that they would be able to employ it as members of VUSPP. An editorial comment in *Literaturna hazeta* observed:

> We consider this "document" clearly deficient....The authors evaluate the entire ideological course of *Nova generatsiia* positively [and have] no reservations [about it]. Their organizational independence is seen as their only mistake..., as if the existence of [OPPU] had been their only form of opposition to [VUSPP]. In this way the authors...have blotted out their class, "leftist," petty-bourgeois essence which [served as] the foundation of their opposition. The "resolution" does not say a word about the anti-proletarian manifestations in *Nova generatsiia*, especially [those] contained in the last issues. These were unscrupulous attacks on the policies of proletarian literature and the Party leadership

> that guides it. [This] made *Nova generatsiia* a vehicle for petty-bourgeois rebellion against the policies of the Communist Party in literary matters (*Literaturna hazeta* 4 [20 January 1931]: 2).

To appreciate just how reluctantly the Futurists succumbed to VUSPP, one must only compare their statement of dissolution with that of PROLITFRONT's, which disbanded a week after OPPU. The declaration of Khvyl'ovyi's organization was longer, went into greater details about its errors, and diligently enumerated the virtues of VUSPP. Among the achievements for which PROLITFRONT gave itself credit was the role it played, "together with VUSPP," in exposing the "petty-bourgeois essence" of the "Futurist organization *Nova generatsiia*, which under a 'leftist' guise concealed [its] rightist essence" ("Rezoliutsiia zahal'nykh zboriv 'Prolitfrontu'" 1931).

VUSPP was very pleased with PROLITFRONT's resolution. A headline in *Literaturna hazeta* blared: "The Policy of VUSPP Has Proven to Be Correct. PROLITFRONT Admits to Its Mistakes and Has Liquidated Itself. The Basic Cadres of PROLITFRONT are Entering VUSPP" (*Literaturna hazeta* 5 [30 January 1931]: 3). The organization's Secretariat elaborated, saying that it

> welcomes the resolution of... PROLITFRONT; it attests to the fact that, basically, these Comrades have realized their mistakes, that [they] have condemned them and have found their bearings on the road [leading] toward the development of Ukrainian proletarian literature. The Secretariat of VUSPP views this as a great and undeniable victory for the Communist Party... ("Vid Sekretariatu VUSPP" 1931).

The Secretariat also stated that it would admit PROLITFRONT's members into VUSPP as soon as possible and would "not close its doors" to anyone in that organization who had repudiated his past. On 11 February 1931 the Secretariat announced the names of eighteen former PROLITFRONT members who were made members of VUSPP; among them were Mykola Khvyl'ovyi, Oles' Dosvitnyi, Petro Panch, Arkadii Liubchenko, Pavlo Tychyna, Ivan Dniprovs'kyi, and Hryhorii Epik (*Pluh* 1931 [3]: 130). At the end of January, Khvyl'ovyi began appearing as a member of *Literaturna hazeta*'s editorial board, sharing responsibilities for the newspaper with such Party stalwarts as Ivan Mykytenko, Serhii Pylypenko, Andrii Richyts'kyi, and Pavlo Usenko. When the Kharkiv chapter of VUSPP convened its general meeting on 24 February 1931, Khvyl'ovyi was there to read one of the longest speeches. He praised VUSPP, denounced PROLITFRONT's past and urged the Futurists to provide a more "extensive and sincere criticism of the petty-bourgeois essence of [their] principles" (Khvyl'ovyi 1931). Facts such as these leave little room for doubt as to which of the two organizations were more politically conformist as the final curtain descended on the 1920s.

It is apparent that after their decision to disband, the Futurists came under further pressure to make a better act of contrition (Kulyk 1931). It is worth observing that when VUSPP accepted PROLITFRONT's members, it also admitted several from *Nova generatsiia*, but only those who began publishing in the journal quite late (for example, L. Zymnyi, M. Bulatovych, A. Mykhailiuk) or those who were complete unknowns in the organizations (B. Stepanova, [?] Pyn'kova). The only exception to this rule was Nedolia; he entered VUSPP thanks to a solid confession (Nedolia 1931). The major figures of the movement, however, were not admitted. It was, therefore, only a question of time before they, too, would be forced to repudiate their past in a manner pleasing to VUSPP.

A few weeks after OPPU's resolution was published, Poltorats'kyi, Shkurupii, Vlyz'ko and Petro Mel'nyk began making appearances in the press with their own personal recantations, faithfully and tediously cataloguing the errors that VUSPP wanted to hear. Poltorats'kyi, Shkurupii, and Mel'nyk were the most diligent and systematic in their self-criticism (Poltorats'kyi 1931a; Shkurupii 1931b; P. Mel'nyk 1931). In scrambling to clear their own names, there were instances when they even implicated one another; this led to further counter-accusations or denials (Vlyz'ko 1931; Poltorats'kyi 1931b).

Semenko made peace with VUSPP by publishing a long confessional poem (Semenko 1931d). "Objectively, impartially, sincerely—I condemn my erroneous steps," he wrote. These he identified as "bohemian self-delusion," "formalism" and "futuro-formalism," "nihilism," "dandyism," the promotion of a "mechanistic" "bourgeois" "intellectualist" literary "method," and unfair criticism of PROLITFRONT, Mykytenko, Khvyl'ovyi, and Kulyk. The poem stressed that Semenko would no longer remain an outsider because he was entering the common ranks. Perhaps the saddest and most revealing statement in the poem was this one: "I am now Semenko, *Mykhailo;* hitherto I was Semenko, *Mykhail'*." Finally, the system had coerced him into conformity.

The movement was finished. During the early 1930s some of the former Futurists would appear in print sporadically. Official criticism would even note with satisfaction that they were adequately rehabilitating themselves.[76] But for the most part, the Futurists played no role in the literary process after their dissolution; literary histories and criticism made a conscious effort to overlook them. Many of the younger writers

[76] For comments on Semenko, see Kovalenko 1934.

who had sought guidance from the Futurists early in their career seem to have abandoned literature altogether; their names, at least, never again appeared in any literary context.

The 1930s, of course, were not just a disaster for the Futurists. They were a tragedy for many writers and for all of Ukrainian culture. Whereas in the 1920s the Party struggled primarily against political deviation and ideological error, in the 1930s it launched a campaign against Ukrainian culture itself. The Ukrainian intelligentsia (both communist and non-communist) was decimated; Ukrainianization was abandoned and supplanted by *de facto* Russification; the peasantry, still the overwhelming majority of the Ukrainian population—in whose name, essentially, Ukrainianization had been carried out—was ravaged by an artificial famine (1932–1933; see Conquest 1986). When writers, like Mykola Bazhan, turned to writing odes to Stalin during this terrible period, they were no longer engaged in literature but in the art of survival. Unfortunately, there were many who never perfected this demanding craft and, hence, perished. In 1933 Khvyl'ovyi and Mykola Skrypnyk committed suicide; in 1934 Vlyz'ko was executed; and, in 1937 both Semenko and Shkurupii, the "king of the Futurist prairies," died before firing squads. Ironically, among Shkurupii's last published words were these: "Our creativity is prospering like exuberant flowers, for it is guided by the hand of our Party" (Shkurupii 1933a).

II

The Theory of a Movement

CHAPTER 6

Panfuturism: Blueprint for the Avant-Garde

No literary group of the 1920s devoted more attention, nor attached greater significance, to theoretical pursuits than the Futurists. This tenacious determination to articulate a systematic vision of art and culture sometimes gives the impression that theorizing about art was almost as important to the Futurists as creating it. The pages of *Katafalk iskusstva*, *Semafor u Maibutnie*, and *Honh komunkul'ta* were, in fact, overwhelmingly devoted to programmatic musings. *Nova generatsiia* was not as one-sided in this respect but likewise addressed a host of conceptual questions on a regular basis. Several members of the movement (most notably Mykhail' Semenko, Oleksii Poltorats'kyi, and Leonid Skrypnyk) donned the mantles of theoretician or critic, or both, producing a significant body of writings in these genres. At one stage of his career (1923–24), Semenko seemed almost on the verge of abandoning poetry in favor of theory. As we noted in previous chapters, the Futurists recurrently held private and public meetings to discuss the philosophical aspects of art.

Theory served several functions in the movement. On the one hand, it was a form of propaganda, a vehicle by which the Futurists fashioned their public image. The loud, consciously "revolutionary" proclamations on art were meant to delineate their positions in a bewildering cultural environment and, it was hoped, bring new members into their fold. On the other hand, theory was a form of justification, a "scientific" explanation of their motives, designed to pacify their detractors and puzzled audience. These writings were a reflection of their grand ambition to affect the course of Ukrainian cultural development. In this respect, it was a competing ideology and aesthetic to the ones offered by proletarian organizations and *Kulturträgers* like Khvyl'ovyi and the Neoclassicists. The Futurists expected, naively in retrospect, that a rationally articulated theory would convince politicians to elevate avant-garde principles to the level of official policy. Futurist theorizing, in short, had a messianic element.

The Futurists worked on the assumption that Ukraine and, by extension, the entire Soviet Union was a cultural backwater. Early in the decade, Geo Shkurupii expressed dismay that he and his comrades were "surrounded by a dark night," believing that only they "gave out passes into the Future to the bold" (Irchan and Shkurupii 1922). Oleksa Slisarenko likened his country to a banana republic in which writers vied for power but produced only "slobbering little poems" (Slisarenko 1923a, 7). All in all, the Futurists held that both their literary competitors and the Party were confounded by cultural matters and lacked any cogent plan of action. They obstinately maintained that "proletarian" and "Marxist" views of art were confused and meaningless. As a result, innovative artistic practices were being retarded. Semenko observed, "Today there are all sorts of Marxists...Marxism [is being] interpreted in every which way" (Semenko 1924d, 226). Referring to organizations like Pluh and Hart, Slisarenko professed that there was "no serious work of any kind being done to lay a philosophical foundation" for art. Moreover, in both Russia and Ukraine, the influence of the Academy outweighed that of the proletariat (Slisarenko 1930b, 188). Semenko went as far as to say that Marxism, in its current form, was powerless to solve the cultural dilemma facing the young revolutionary state.

> Revolutionary Marxism's lack of a solid philosophical foundation in the area of culture and, particularly, [in the area] of art is the root cause of the present horrendous divergence of ideas [in these fields]. [For this same reason] there is no communist policy for art; this leads to serious negative consequences. Our artistic reality is being inundated by the turbid stream of bourgeois, petty-bourgeois, and anarchic deviations. [These assume] a proletarian guise and, by exploiting the uncertainty of [our] situation, [succeed] in penetrating and poisoning the young proletarian body (Semenko 1924d, 222).

Under the circumstances, Semenko contended: "[Only] THEORY WILL SAVE US!" (ibid.; *emphasis in the original*). More specifically, he meant "Panfuturism," touted as the application of Leninism to the cultural front.

Art as a Process

"Panfuturism," said Slisarenko, was not a term coined by accident. For individuals grouped around Semenko, it symbolized an acceptance of "the revolutionary achievements of Futurism" and its traditions (Slisarenko 1930b, 190). Its implications, however, were broader. Panfuturism was "*at once* Futurism, Cubism, Expressionism, and Dadaism" but was not simply a "synthesis of these useful things" ("What Futurism Wants" 1930; *emphasis added*). Panfuturism was "not a literary school" (Slisarenko 1930b, 189) but a general theory or "system" of art (Semenko 1930m, 120). As such its goal was to explain the avant-garde as a historically unprecedented phenomenon, and to draw practical conclusions about what it meant for the further development of art. "The Panfuturist system embraces all 'isms,' considering them discrete elements of a single organism"(ibid.).[1] Unlike other European movements that pursued "private" problems of art, Panfuturism approached art as a "poly-problematic organism" ("What Futurism Wants" 1930, 126).

Central to this view was the notion of art as a process. Semenko had spoken in this vein as early as 1914 in *Kvero-futuryzm* ("Art is striving. Therefore, it is always a process...[A]rt is always change..."), but a full elaboration of the idea came only in 1922. From then, it remained Panfuturism's central article of faith. In defining art in this way, the Futurists were in effect debunking a host of traditional views of art that enjoyed popularity among broad segments of the literary community, especially the proletarians. They rejected art as an innate emotional human reflex and did not believe that it needed to have an expressly aesthetic function. Art as a reflection of reality, as an imitation or representation of life in images was an alien concept to them as well. They pointed to the multiplicity of definitions of art as proof that it remained fundamentally a complex and protean process. To settle for one traditional view and to canonize it, as most literary groups did, was to act against the very essence of art. Poltorats'kyi reminded his readers that "to say that art always plays one and the same role is in principle false. As is well known, there is no permanent or lasting phenomenon on earth that throughout its existence has only a single function" (Poltorats'kyi 1929a, 2: 43).

The theoretical attitude of Ukrainian Futurists toward their European and Russian brethren was ambivalent. On the one hand, their work was considered historically inevitable and intrinsically valuable. On the other, it harbored a potentially fatal flaw. The narrow and narcissistic nature of these avant-gardes made them insensitive to the artistic process as a whole. Without an overview and a sense of their own place in history, there was a danger that the practice of these vanguards could degenerate into mere self-centered aggrandizement and jeopardize the entire revolutionary process. In fact, they strongly suspected that some movements and artists were already unproductive from this point of view.[2] To avoid the danger of a "private" orientation, Panfuturism took

1 One contemporary underscored this fact, although he failed to note Panfuturism's international orientation: "With significant enthusiasm this group has thrown itself into work and uses every available means to unite all Ukrainian 'ists' (Futurists, Imaginists, Dynamists, etc.) into a single artistic 'Panfuturist' group" (Donets' 1922, 33).

2 Recall Semenko's and Shkurupii's attitude toward Russian Futurists during the Aspanfut period (above, p. 60). The Ukrainians represented Panfuturism as an alternative to such "sickly or accidental examples and phenomena" as Dadaism (Semenko 1922f).

what can be called a "pan-avant-gardist" approach, treating all revolutionary movements as a single phenomenon and a special stage in the overall artistic process.

According to Panfuturism, one of the key characteristics of the artistic process was that it respected neither political nor national boundaries. "There are leftist artists who work under bourgeois conditions and there are those who work under the dictatorship of the proletariat, but *the artistic process is one*" (Shkurupii 1928c, 327; *emphasis added*). In practice, the process could be (and usually was) more advanced in some countries than others, but the moment it attained a new level in one place, it became universally relevant, serving as a universal benchmark for all further artistic development. It was essential, therefore, for avant-gardists to have an international orientation. Their duty was to respond to the process, to meet its challenge at each new evolutionary stage. The process—perceived as an impersonal and external force—placed demands on the artist and not the other way around. Poltorats'kyi phrased it this way:

> When we [Futurists] have occasion to hear words such as "Proletarian literature, like every other decent literature, must depict a living person, a new hero, etc.," we can only laugh because we know that art develops not by taking a path which returns it to the past but [by taking one] which leads toward differentiation. We know that artists, the cultural activists of each epoch, are not destined to rediscover some previously established slots in "decent literature"; rather, they must think about the differentiating obligations that the art process places on them. [Furthermore, they must ask themselves] whether this process, generally speaking, places any obligations on them at the present and [whether it will] in the future (Poltorats'kyi 1929a, 1: 42–43).

Towards the Liquidation of Art

In their frequent attempts to enlighten opponents about the obligations the artistic process placed on them, the Futurists ultimately arrived at a coherent, if not an altogether detailed, account of its history and current status. The one aspect that concerned them most was its perilous condition. The avant-garde itself was proof of this: on the one hand, it was an organic and logical development of the old art but, on the other, it signaled its degeneration and imminent demise. As a new and unique occurrence in the history of art, the vanguard was understood to be the tail-end of a long development that had now entered a period of self-contradiction and self-destruction (B—n 1925).[3]

[3] See also *Semafor u Maibutnie*, passim.

The Futurists traced the origin of the artistic crisis to France, dating it to approximately the middle of the nineteenth century (Trirog [Semenko]1922, 2). From there it spread to other countries. Sculpture and painting betrayed the degenerative symptoms first, with Impressionism recognized as the earliest of the crisis movements. Walt Whitman, Paul Cézanne, and the French Symbolist Gustave Kahn were counted among typical representatives (Semenko 1930m, 121). The developments that occurred "on the corpses of Impressionist and Neo-impressionist painting and Parnassian and Symbolist poetry" heightened the critical situation further, leading ultimately to its most extreme manifestation—Futurism (Semenko 1930o, 113).

Semenko referred to the period before the crisis as the age of Great Art (or "bourgeois art") (Semenko 1923b, 50). The long history of Great Art was a single organic process (B—n 1925, 55). A style typically defined an entire age, affecting all the arts. Throughout its evolution, the process of Great Art had been relatively stable. Mutations had always been integral or systemic. Crises were resolved dialectically, always resulting in a new synthesis. However, by the middle of the nineteenth century something entirely new transpired. Great Art suddenly became incapable of further organic evolution. The single, unified process began splintering into lesser processes (movements), many of which were mutually antagonistic and not prone to any new synthesis. Great Art as such began to unravel.

Of all the movements that the splintering artistic process produced, Marinetti's was the most significant. Futurism was a watershed—it represented the most radical and categorical denial of the ancient process. It challenged timeworn assumptions about art, shattering its organic unity and traditional divisions. The individual formal elements of art ceased being subordinate components in a greater whole; they themselves became objects of investigation and experimentation, the "private" tasks of a host of movements (Semenko 1930o, 114pt3). As each formal element became a subject rather than a means (device), the organism known as Great Art stopped evolving. The various arts with their clear divisions and formal identities began crumbling. Painting and sculpture began to merge; poetry and prose lost their distinctive features; music and noise become more difficult to differentiate (Semenko 1922c, 34; Shkurupii 1922c).

Ukrainian Futurists were careful to draw a distinction between the ideological deficiencies of the Italian movement—its imperialism, militarism, chauvinism (political as well as sexual), characteristics which they described as "accidental and non-immediate" ("What Panfuturism Wants" 1930, 127)—and the significant formal and historical role it played in the artistic process. Addressing all "enemies of Futurism who are weak in the head," Slisarenko drove the point home: "The first Futurists, like the first socialists, had many faults; but it should not follow from this that Futurism and Socialism were destined to die" (Slisarenko 1922, 39). The real significance of Marinetti's movement lay in the fact that it broke "the continuous line of the artistic process" (Semenko 1930o, 114pt3). Marinetti's ideological "excrescences" were attributed to the social and political evils of capitalism and were considered immaterial to the artistic process ("What Panfuturism Wants" 1930, 127).

The incessant metamorphosis of art was neither automatic nor spontaneous. Art had a natural tendency toward inertia, that is, toward canonization and stagnation. The driving force behind all innovations was the creative revolutionary who consciously placed himself in opposition to conservative forces. Declared Slisarenko: "The petite bourgeoisie of art—the one that trembles in fear of its reputation and is afraid of ruining its relationship with the dull *Privatdozent* (lest it should succumb to the wild, creative process)—only retards the progress of forms" (Slisarenko 1930a, 315). Because of this, change normally took place in a violent manner. When "the waters of evolution," continued Slisarenko, "have gathered into a large mass, they suddenly destroy the dam in order to continue the eternal process. These are moments of revolution and from them emerge the new forms that become more perfect in the process of evolution" (ibid.).

It was understood that forms could not advance and metamorphose endlessly—no social or biological phenomenon did (Semenko 1924b, 171). There had to be a stage in the growth of all things when further evolution became impossible and a degenerative process ensued, leading "to the negation of the beautifully constructed form that had been sustained by the revolutionary process."

> Form dies, degenerates the way nations die that have reached a high level of culture and civilization. There comes a time when there is a need for a fresh infusion of blood so that the exhausted organism of form might be revived. Such an infusion of blood, such a change of artistic forms typifies the entire course of human art. The last such infusion was the futurization of art which for a short period energized the rotten body of the Muse (Slisarenko 1930a, 315).

Futurism, however, did not revitalize the artistic process because Futurism was no longer just "art" (Semenko 1930o, 114). Far from attempting to "perfect" form, it actually spearheaded the attack on the process that had given birth to it. With Futurism, the cycles of an earlier epoch came to an end. Futurism, and the vanguards that succeeded it, represented the final destructive phase of the old artistic process. Knowing this, all artists had a clear duty: they were obliged to bring the ancient process to its logical culmination by dedicating themselves to the liquidation of Great Art. To do otherwise was to engage in useless restorationist activity (Semenko 1930o, 122; B—n 1925, 56).

> Destruction for us is the last stage of the development of art [i.e., Great Art], not merely one of its bifurcations or deformations. That which is called art is for us an object [destined] for liquidation. Art is a remnant of the past. A specter roams Europe—the specter of Futurism. The futurization of art is the liquidation of art. Death to art! Long live Panfuturism! (*Semafor u Maibutnie* 1922, 1–2).

This apocalyptic scenario also held out the promise that an entirely new organic process would eventually emerge from the pulverized ruins of Great Art. In the meantime, however, the Futurists proclaimed: "The liquidation of art is our art" (ibid., 1).

The Theory of Cults

In its early redactions, Panfuturism addressed itself almost exclusively to issues of art. The theory took little note of social factors, although it did allude to the orthodox Marxist idea that art was a function of the economic base. Toward the end of 1923 Panfuturism underwent an important revision both in detail and in scope. By then it was promoted as a theory not just of art but also of culture:

> Panfuturism is a system that seeks the solution to the greatest contemporary problem: the problem of culture in a communist society. Panfuturism is a corollary of Marxism. Panfuturism is the introduction of Marxism into culture...(Slisarenko 1930b, 189).

As was pointed out earlier, the Futurists' concern with issues other than art was at least partly stimulated by their opponents' charge that they were elitists who were unconcerned with the broad cultural welfare of the Soviet people. The response to this criticism, on the organizational level, led to the formation of "Komunkul't" (AsKK). On the theoretical level, it involved expansion of the Panfuturist system. If the first step ultimately ended in disaster, the second gave the entire theory a deeper resonance.

Semenko expanded Panfuturism by means of what he called the "Theory of Cults" [*Teoriia kul'tiv*]. Although it sounded exotic, Semenko used "cult" to mean "system" and, in fact, frequently employed the two words interchangeably (Semenko 1924b, 189). Accordingly, "culture" was defined as a "system of systems" (Semenko 1924d, 224), or, in other words, a system of multiple cults (e.g., art, politics, law, religion, philosophy, science, technology). The systems that made up culture were further composed of subsystems. Thus, for example, art was a system of culture, but sculpture, painting, theater, etc., were subsystems of art (Semenko 1924b, 190).

All systems in a culture were dynamic, but their processes were not identical. Each system, after all, had its own unique formal properties and hence its own laws and rates of change. There was, however, constant interaction among systems, and stronger systems were capable of affecting weaker ones. In fact, Semenko argued that a culture always had a dominant system that influenced other systems. As an example he pointed to religion, a system that dominated the human race for three-quarters of its existence, impacting the development (or underdevelopment) of such systems as philosophy, science, and art (ibid., 179ff.).

In proposing this model Semenko stressed that culture was not a permanent or fixed aggregate of systems. As an ever-changing system of systems there could be no guarantee that the component systems of one age would necessarily be equivalent to those of another or that they would always exist in the same relative relationship to one another. While the systems in a culture never simply disappeared (such things were impossible), they were susceptible to such radical transformations as to lose their former identity and function. Because systems were not absolutes, and their existence was not guaranteed for all time, it was possible to assert that under certain circumstances some systems would become obsolete and die (ibid., 174; also Semenko 1930o, 118n2).

The above held true because culture, and its component parts, was subject to a dialectical law—namely, the law of birth and atrophy, the law of flowering and decay or, as it was most frequently expressed, the law of "construction and destruction." This was a universal axiom applicable to all phenomena (Semenko 1924b, 169–73). The law of construction and destruction worked in the following way:

> Every wave of construction pushes into the past those forces and things that have performed their constructive task in an earlier segment of history [and then] at a given moment decay [and] self-destruct. Every wave of construction goes into a decline, [that is] it self-destructs in relationship to a new wave that begins to expand. The concentration of constructive elements occurs under destructive conditions (Semenko 1924d, 224).

In short, construction and destruction were the dynamic principles inherent in all systems. But because they constructed and destructed at different rates, that is, according to their own internal "formal" laws, at any particular moment of history some systems of culture might be constructing while others were destructing.

A constructing system underwent cycles of construction and destruction. These short-term phases were organic, systemic transformations that had no detrimental effect on the system; they represented the life-history or stages in that system's evolutionary process.

> This entire process of growth—[namely, the] periodic decline and renascence [which leads] to a higher, more brilliant and fuller development [of the system]—represents a step-like, gradual constructive line within the confines of the entire cult. Following which, there begins a descending, destructive wave that ends the existence of the entire cult (Semenko 1924b, 178).

Using religion as an example, Semenko stated that "the system of religion, as a cult, contains sub-systems, sub-cults that are elements or forms of equal value and importance [because] they constitute within the process [of the system's evolution] separate phases of historical development" (ibid., 180). Thus in the history of religion, the discrete phases of construction and destruction are equivalent to specific stages of its development (for example, fetishism, polytheism, monotheism). Each new phase in the history of the cult constituted a brief period of construction in relationship to some earlier phase that had undergone destruction.

A system as a whole enters the destructive phase of its existence when the short-term stages fail to end in a dialectical synthesis and instead lead to endless differentiation, meaning that dependent or subordinate elements of a system break off and begin developing as if they were entire systems unto themselves. According to Semenko, differentiation was the clearest evidence of a system's imminent demise (ibid., 182; Semenko 1924d, 225). In practice this expressed itself as a wide branching out of the system into independent streams. At such a point there could be no further unity in the system since elements that once functioned cooperatively now functioned autonomously. The differentiation process, unlike short-term phases of destruction and construction, never ended in a new integration.

Semenko made a point of distinguishing "division" from "differentiation" (Semenko 1924b, 182). The former was a positive feature of all systems. Science, for example, was divided into various disciplines; art was divided into specific types. Such divisions never worked to the detriment of a system. However, when a system such as religion splintered into sects, then this became a symptom of decay. The same was true for the various independent avant-garde movements: these "isms" were no longer "art" (i.e., Great Art); they pursued only separate elements of the artistic process (sound, perspective, color) yet tried to function as the old "complete" system did.

The destruction of a system took a long time; therefore, it could exist in a destructing or a constructing phase for ages or find itself somewhere in between. Polytheism and monotheism, for example, coexisted for some time, meaning that the destructing phase (polytheism) overlapped with the formative moments of the constructive phase (monotheism). Although boundaries between the two phases were frequently vague and fluid, sensitive cultural observers and, especially, revolutionaries would be able to discern which system was actually constructing and which was destructing. Knowing this, they would be in a position to choose the historically promising path.

The final destruction of a system, as noted above, was not construed as its sudden liquidation or disappearance. Destruction was primarily an unraveling of old structural relationships and functions. The elements that constituted the old system did not vanish, they instead became building blocks for a new constructing system of relationships and functions based on some new organizing or structuring principle (ibid., 178). Panfuturism foresaw that after the final destruction of Great Art, its elements, restructured on some new "non-artistic" principle, would become the foundation of a fresh, constructing cult.

Ideology and Facture

Besides "construction" and "destruction," Panfuturism operated with two other terms, "ideology" and "facture" [*faktura*].[4] At first these concepts were applied only to art but with the theory's expansion they were judged relevant for the description of any system. However, to be useful, they had to be seen as complements of the first pair. Thus "construction" and "destruction" described the dynamics of a cult; "ideology" and "facture" referred to its structure.

Ideology and facture entered the Panfuturist idiom against the background of the so-called form and content debate of the early 1920s.[5] Both terms constituted an explicit argument against those in the Marxist and non-Marxist camp who exhibited a dependence on this traditional

4 The term "facture" was actually used by the Futurists in the English version of their manifesto, "What Panfuturism Wants" (1930, 127).

5 The following are some of the more interesting contributions to this debate: Koriak 1922, Koriak 1923c, Koriak 1923a, Mezhenko 1923a, Kovalivs'kyi 1923, Hadzins'kyi 1923, and Iakubs'kyi 1923. Also consult Navrots'kyi 1925.

description of art. To some extent they were also a polemical rejoinder to Russian Formalism, whose lessons Ukrainian Futurists digested rather thoroughly.

Semenko rejected the "form and content" dichotomy on the grounds that it was an impediment to the creation of a scientific theory of art. In this respect, he clearly shared the Formalists' view. "Content," said Semenko, "is not something permanent; therefore, it cannot be relied upon. Form, too, is not a static phenomenon that might serve as a foundation for a theoretical formulation" (Semenko 1930o, 116). "The system of form and content is closed, limited, and unenlightening in its essence" (Semenko 1924d, 223). Poltorats'kyi, who in the late 1920s reviewed the context in which Semenko's two terms came into being and briefly sketched the background to the "form and content" debate among earlier literary scholars, gave credit to Georgii Plekhanov for stressing that form and content were one and the same in a literary work. Nonetheless, Poltorats'kyi concluded that Plekhanov's "terminology is absolutely outdated" (Poltorats'kyi 1929a, 4: 52) and that ultimately he failed "to give a correct solution to the problem" (ibid.). Therefore, he discouraged contemporary critics and writers from blindly following Plekhanov's dictums. As for the Formalists, they were embraced but not unconditionally:

> The Formalists...tried to define the artistic work as a complex of devices that operates with verbal material. This terminology was much more skillful and useful than the terms "form" and "content." Nonetheless, it had one great drawback: this terminology was too one-sided; it correctly...established the techniques of an artistic work, its dialectical essence, but it did not allow for any further generalizations. In particular, it was inimical to the Marxist theory of base and superstructure. This terminology was most suited for Shklovskii's idealistic declarations about literary evolution as the substitution of one form for another (ibid.).

The feeling that Formalism, for all its achievements, was somehow inadequate had also been voiced by Semenko in 1924, when he called the Formalist approach "scholastic" (Semenko 1924d, 222).

In promulgating the terms "ideology" and "facture," Semenko stressed that his concepts were not simply a change of labels but a "new generalization that significantly clears the air" (ibid.). On the surface, however, there were rather obvious similarities between his formulation and the old one. The art object continued to be defined in binary terms: it still consisted of external (facture) and internal (ideology) features. The innovations became apparent only in the definition of the terms.

"Ideology" in Semenko's understanding of the word was a much less restrictive term than "content." It was construed to be "identical to the philosophy of the age," a "given element" in art (Semenko 1930o, 116, 117). Poltorats'kyi characterized ideology as the "tonality of the [art] object, a force that lies outside the work but guides it in one direction or another." For him, too, ideology was equivalent to the "general aspirations of an age" and hence was "reflected in every work of that age" (Poltorats'kyi 1929a, 4: 53, 55). Semenko considered "ideology" to be dependent on the "bio-social" base of human society, the sum of a myriad of factors: economic, social, even natural (such as geography); (Semenko 1924b, 175). In short, ideology was never individual; normally, it was expressed through the ruling class (Semenko 1930o, 117). Semenko wrote that it was not "content" but "ideology [that] guides every poet, painter, director. A consummate class consciousness...guides not only the politician and the economist but also the belletrist, actor, and musician. Ideology is the basic impulse of all social action" (Semenko 1924d, 223). Poltorats'kyi phrased it this way:

> ...Ideology can be called, in part, a class apperception of a work. An artist who has a need to express his observations receives them from the outside in correspondence with the ideological apperception of the class to which he belongs....The selection of phenomena [in an artistic work] is dictated by the ideology of the age and class (Poltorats'kyi 1929a, 4: 53).

During periods of transition from one age to another, from the supremacy of an old class to a new, there was usually conflict between a dying ideology and the one ascending the stage of history (Semenko 1924b, 175).

If "ideology" was a force outside art, then "facture" was "the materialization of ideology in objects"; it was "the arsenal of instruments and devices that go into the production of an object; [it was] the physical characteristic of a cult" (Semenko 1924d, 223; also 1930o, 117; 1924b, 177). Facture was the distinguishing feature of a system, making each one unique, setting apart systems from subsystems, permitting discrimination between, say, poetry and painting. Furthermore, facture was considered a composite term, subsuming and implying unity of at least three elements: "material," "form," and "content." Facture was considered a superior concept because it treated as a unit those elements that traditionally where conceptualized as discrete and in opposition to one another.

The constituents of facture (material, form, content) were to be perceived as "relative" elements; the synthetic concept, facture, was the "absolute." The reason for this relativity lay in the fact that each system was composed in its own unique way and, therefore, the components that went into forming its facture had to be specific to that system (for example, poetry's "material" was "words"; in painting it was "paint"). Semenko put it this way:

> Facture is made of material, form, and content. You may apply any meaning to these three synthesized concepts of facture. They may be broadened, made more complex, subdivided, and generalized. But these three constituent elements are the most frequently used and known (1924d, 223).

In 1929, while reassessing facture, Poltorats'kyi took Semenko at his word and proposed a more detailed analysis. Applying it specifically to literature, he argued that facture should be considered the sum of the following: verbal material, theme, composition, stylistics, and genre [*zhanrystyka*] (Poltorats'kyi 1929a, 4: 55). But regardless of how facture was ultimately broken down, Semenko viewed it, together with "ideology," as the basic key to understanding a system. These two concepts formed the "ultimate model" of all systems (Semenko 1924d, 223; also 1924b, 175).

Defining "Communist" Culture

A great deal of importance was attributed in the Panfuturist theory to the economic base, understood to be the foundation of culture. The base supported "ideology" ("ideology exists in a functional dependence on the base") as well as all the systems of culture (Semenko 1924d, 223). The systems, obviously, were not ontological or permanent phenomena; they were dependent and "utilitarian" manifestations of the base and susceptible to change as the base changed. While the base was capable of supporting any number of systems (depending on the needs of the culture), there was, normally, only a single, common ideology for all systems. Ideology, thus, served as a unifying or binding force in culture (Semenko 1924b, 176). Exceptions to this rule occurred during periods of transition, that is, periods when the economic base itself was undergoing transformation. At times like these, an old ideology (the one generated by an earlier economic order) and a fledgling ideology (the one emerging from a new economic order) would, of course, conflict as the systems came under the influence of contradictory forces. Under such circumstances, a culture would not exhibit any organic unity, and individual systems—for example, art—would not be capable of manifesting a single coherent style. The Futurists believed that they lived precisely in an age such as this. Their "Age of Transition" did not yet have a full-fledged ideology (the economic transformation was incomplete) and, therefore, talk of a "proletarian" culture was, at best, premature. Applied specifically to art, this argument developed as follows:

> ...New socio-economic formations always lay the foundation for new forms of art. But as long as the new changes [in the means] of production and exchange have not constructed and formed a new culture, there can be no new art and, moreover, there cannot be even talk of creating a specific, new [and] general style or form. During times of transition, only tendencies exist, only forerunners of a future [style] appear. If we now consider our present conditions and examine the various manifestations of our art in all its forms, we come up with this question: Have the Revolution and contemporary developments led to the construction and formation of a new art, new forms, a new style? Frequently we speak, for example, about proletarian culture, about proletarian art and sometimes even about socialist art. In fact, we even have individual artistic groups (associations) that are trying to create a communist culture. But there are all sorts of indications proving that, despite their firm convictions in this matter, they are not creating [a new culture]...No matter how hard we look for examples in the development of contemporary art, we will not be able to prove that our art is already formed, that it has succeeded in creating from all its constituent parts (literature, theater, music, painting, sculpture, architecture, etc.) a single organic whole and that we are now facing a *fait accompli* of the new culture...It is true that the old culture is coming to an end, that the old art is receding into history, that contemporary revolutionary tendencies in art (destruction and construction) point in the direction of a new culture of the future; but we cannot say that we already have a new art, a new culture. They do not exist yet....Regardless of the tempo of development of these new tendencies in art, we do not have now, strictly speaking, a new art. It is being born, it is sprouting its first shoots on the virgin soil of socialism which [itself] is only now coming into being...But we do not have a new life; we do not have socialism. Therefore, art cannot show us the face of this new existence. Our world of feelings and thoughts, even that of a communist, is still [fixed] in the past; this is not the world of feelings and thoughts of a person living in a communist society. Consequently, we cannot yet speak, in the strict sense of the word, of a new art....We still face the need to destroy the old culture and the old art. This destruction has already shown itself to be the antithesis to the old art. The synthesis, the construction, and the formation of a new communist art is still a task of the future (B—n 1925, 55–56).[6]

[6] For now it remains an open question who "B—n" actually was (perhaps Mykola Bazhan). There is, however, no doubt that the author must have been a Futurist.

The Futurists deemed it important that the present generation develop a clear theoretical notion of what constituted a communist culture. Otherwise, the appropriate measures that might ensure the emergence of a new culture would not be taken, and the cause for which the Revolution was fought would be further retarded.

A major priority in this respect was shifting the "present 'Marxist' discussion" away from concepts like "bourgeois" and "proletarian"—which were judged to be abstract, metaphysical and based largely on personal taste and habit (Semenko 1924b, 183)—to more precise and scientific formulations:

> The division of culture into bourgeois and proletarian is possible, but [these terms must be viewed as] relative and not [suitable for a] working [hypothesis]. [They are] not useful for any kind of political action on the cultural front. At best, [they are suited] for non-binding, demagogic polemics. This division in practice...carries the seeds of great misunderstandings, precisely because it is inexact and unscientific. This division contains an imprecise, unobjective, [and] unscientific formulation of the concept of culture and its content (ibid.).

Because culture, as a complex of systems, was neither monolithic nor an absolute constant value, it was not enough to define it simply in ideological or class terms. It was primitive to suppose that "bourgeois" culture could become "proletarian" simply through an infusion of "proletarian" content. Semenko contended that it did not suffice to "clean" the systems of culture of their "bourgeoisness" or "to find for them 'proletarian' forms" (ibid., 189). The new culture could not be the old, bourgeois culture dressed in new proletarian clothes; communist culture, to be truly new, had to possess significantly altered structural features. The aggregate of systems known as "bourgeois" culture could not be identical to the aggregate that would eventually represent "communist" culture. The new economic base, after all, would eliminate the *raison d'être* for systems that had been supported by the capitalist order. (In fact, certain systems were destructing even at the present moment.) Moreover, one could not conceive of the constituent elements of the new culture drawing on decaying systems. "It is important to understand," emphasized Semenko, "that only constructing cults will enter communist culture" (Semenko 1924d, 224). These constructing cults could be designated "proletarian," but according to Semenko this would be superfluous (ibid., 225).

To drive home the need for a structural or systemic definition of the future culture (instead of an ideological or class one) Semenko again turned to religion as an example. A term like "bourgeois religion" or "proletarian religion," he noted, was so manifestly absurd that it was hardly worth discussing. No one would seriously argue that religion had a place in a communist or proletarian culture. This meant religion was only possible under conditions of the old economic order. As a system, it could not be made proletarian because it was a destructing cult, undermined by the relatively new cults of science and learning. Religion was no longer a living, active system; it showed no further tendency toward development. Its survival among the masses was not a sign of vitality but a testament to social inertia (Semenko 1924b, 192). Thus, if religion was destined to disappear from the complex of systems to be known as "communist culture," then this suggested that other systems might suffer the same fate. The future culture would therefore indeed be a new structural entity.

It was easy to condemn religion to oblivion, but when the Futurists also argued that "the communist revolution...removed the economic preconditions for the existence of the cult of art" (Semenko 1924d, 226), they came up against stiff resistance, especially when declaring the following:

> Bourgeois art [and] proletarian art, just as bourgeois culture [and] proletarian culture, are completely relative definitions; they can be used for general purposes, but they have no scientific significance (Semenko 1924b, 186).

For Semenko, dividing art into class categories was a preposterous proposition. "Throughout history, there was never a cult or a culture that was divided from the onset into a culture of the ruling class and a culture of the downtrodden" (Semenko 1924d, 225). Systems were not class categories; there could not be separate artistic processes for the bourgeoisie and for the proletariat ("the artistic process was one"). Each class merely "exploits" a system at whatever particular historical phase it happens to find that system (ibid.). The bourgeoisie used art when it was in a constructing phase; the proletariat inherited this system when it was destructing and, therefore, useless as a cultural category. Conventionally, therefore, all art was "bourgeois." "Proletarian" art was a contradiction in terms, since the system bearing that name was disappearing. "Proletarian art," said Semenko, "...will not exist at all and does not exist now" (Semenko 1924b, 187). What did exist was the final, destructive stage of the artistic process. If, at this moment of truth, the proletariat wished to have some relationship to this process, then it had to involve itself in destruction. Should the proletariat do otherwise, should it engage in creating "proletarian art" by modeling itself on the artistic process as it had once existed in the "bourgeois" past, then it was engaging in an activity as futile as trying to create a "proletarian religion." Such action could only retard the inevitable triumph of the new culture.

Beyond "Great Art"

The Futurists were firmly convinced that "present-day artistic principles, as well as the practice of contemporary masters, demonstrated that art is already ceasing to be art, that it is an entirely different cult or [at least] the introduction, the beginning of another cult" (Semenko 1924d, 225). Here, as on other occasions, they insisted that the death of Great Art, as a coherent and traditional system, would lay the foundation for an entirely new system.[7] This allowed them to maintain that their cry for the liquidation of art was not nihilism, as critics contended, but a positive step on the road toward the realization of something novel and inevitable.

> We are participants in a worldwide process of the destruction of art and we stand on the edge of a gigantic integration that is destined to erect the second arch of the history of art for thousands of years to come (Semenko 1930m, 120).[8]

Panfuturism, in short, was not just a theory that "embraced the process of destruction." It was also "a means for [laying] the first foundations of construction," an effort to create another organic and holistic system or, as the Futurists put it, "to rediscover the lost watershed of the artistic process" so that its diverse streams and currents might be funneled back into a single mighty movement (Semenko 1930o, 115; cf. ibid., 114pt3).

Two important preconditions had to be met before the new constructing cult could begin its formation. First, a communist social order [*pobut*] had to emerge. Second, the old artistic system had to become extinct. To date neither had occurred. The revolution continued to be a local rather than a universal achievement. Within the Soviet Union itself there were vacillations in policy that tended to favor the resurgence of old ways in both society and art (ibid., 114). While "the fate and future of every art has been decided" (ibid.) in theory, the actual practice of art did not reflect this. Destruction was not yet fully realized in all the arts (that is, "in a pan-artistic context" (Semenko 1922g, 15), and without a complete liquidation of the old system nothing new could be erected.

7 The new system, for the sake of convention, was often referred to as "art." As will be evident below, however, the tendency was to use "art" in quotation marks in order to distinguish it from the old system.

8 See also Semenko (1930o, 115pt7).

Destruction was to take place in specific subsystems (such as painting or poetry) by reducing them to their "atoms," that is, their basic elements (Semenko 1930o, 115pt6). Moreover, activities were to be directed toward liquidating the boundaries that set subsystems apart. "The task of destruction is to decompose 'the arts' to the point where the boundaries [among them] will be absolutely erased" (ibid.). These two operations would lead to "the liquidation of bourgeois art..., of 'art' in general" (ibid.). Naturally, such destructive operations had to focus on the facture of each art, namely, on that which gave the arts their separate identity. "The breaking up of the facture of art is the present destructive process" (ibid., 117). Once the "physiognomy" (Semenko 1922g, 15) of each of the traditional arts was transformed beyond recognition and the "characteristic and specific facture" of each art was atomized, the individual atoms of one facture would begin to recombine with those of another and a new system would be born. In short, the "construction" of new systems (or "new arts") was the reorganization, the recombination of the old "atomized" elements. "The sum of the original elements" of facture were to serve as "building blocks" for a new synthesis. Said Semenko: "I consider it possible to have an integration and chemical fusion of the sum of [all] the arts..." (ibid., 17). This integration, of course, would no longer be Great Art but something entirely different.

The originality of the new system would rest on more than a novel recombination of old elements. Any reintegration implied a complete change in the rules that made the new cohesion possible. Systems, after all, had to be integrated or structured on some principle if they were to be something other than just a random and chaotic assemblage of parts. Great Art, for example, had been governed by "irrational," "emotional," and "aesthetic" principles; it was an "emotional" cult, an idealistic form of human creativity ruled by an individual's feelings. Inspiration (often assumed to be "divine") had been the backbone of this system. Consequently, Great Art tended to breed professionals called "poets" who posed as prophets or high priests [*zhrets'*] (Semenko 1924d, 227; Semenko 1924b, 193; Poltorats'kyi 1929a, 2: 13, 14). The new system was to be a wholesale rejection of such attitudes and principles. "The time had come to liquidate the rich, luscious farm on which a variety of muses have been cultivated" (Semenko 1922c, 32). Instead of relying on intuition and related faculties, the new system would be based on the laws of reason. Scientific principles would hold sway; beauty would be replaced by functionalism. The new system would be served not by prophets and high priests but by engineers (Semenko 1924e, 3).

> The great vocation of the poet, [his] torments of creation...have lost all sense...The poet is superfluous; only from habit [do people] continue

> to expect something from him; the word "poet" sounds as unnatural [today] as does "archimandrite"...When a poet fogs up a clear head with iambs and other secrets, then this must be considered nothing but filth; this is speculation at the expense of immature minds who wait to hear what Comrade Poet will say. Poetry is dying and her high priests, the poets, vegetate through sheer inertia; through contortions they make themselves into some kind of prophets, even though no one has paid any attention to them for a long time (Tryroh 1922a).

To understand why the new system would be integrated expressly on rational premises and not any other, one had to apprehend that communism was going to be an age of science and technology (Semenko 1924d, 227). This was easily inferable from the fact that these two systems were on the threshold of a new limitless development. They were the preeminent "constructing cults." Actually, Semenko viewed them as aspects of a single system that he called "techno-science" [*naukotekhnika*] (Semenko 1924b, 184). As religion had once done in the past, so now "techno-science" would permeate all facets of culture, stamping its principles even on unrelated systems. "Techno-science," said Semenko, "represents that hegemonic cult that will imbue the entire complex of [communist] culture with the requisite tonality...; [it will become] that axis of the cultural front that will penetrate the entire frame of social existence" (ibid., 185). Once all the systems of culture became structured on the rational principles of "techno-science," human "creativity" would also abandon its emotional, irrational, and aesthetic foundation. At that point Great Art would be dead. Reason, rationalism, and functionalism were destined to become the hallmarks of the new system. Semenko observed: That which "people wish to call proletarian art [that is, the new system] will resemble art the way religion resembles communism" (Semenko 1924d, 225).

The new rational and scientific system that would put an end to Great Art was given the name "Great Technology" [*Velyka Tekhnika*] (ibid., 227; Semenko 1924e). The period of transition leading up to that age was to be characterized by "meta-art," "the craftsmanship [*kustarnyts'kyi*] period" of Great Technology. "After passing through a period of *craftsmanship* the producers of so-called 'aesthetic' values [and] objects will be replaced by the machine, the apparatus, the engineer, the technician, [and] the fitter," predicted Semenko (1924d, 225; *emphasis in the original*). The new system, obviously, would not cultivate "beauty" for its own sake. Beauty would no longer be conceived as an ontological quality but as a function of usefulness or purposefulness. "The 'beautiful' is not beautiful in and of itself; the beautiful is a thing that in its totality results in a purposeful [*dotsil'nyi*] product" (Tryroh 1922a, 13). To imply this quality in the new system, the Futurists resorted to several words connoting "ability," "dexterity," "skill" [*umilist', shtuka*]. Meta-art was even defined as "a synthesis of deformed art with sport" (ibid.). Like "craft," the word "sport" here implied "doing," "making."[9]

Meta-art approached the edges of the new system, characterizing the work of the avant-garde, the entire left front of art (Semenko 1924e). This activity was no longer "art," although it still wore "'artistic' clothes" (ibid., 2). For the moment, the avant-garde gave the impression of being a great achievement, but one day when meta-art came to be compared with Great Technology, it would appear as an "awkward product of craftsmanship or, at best, a dilettantish engineering model for present or future machine production" (Semenko 1924b, 191). As meta-art progressed and the old system crumbled, Semenko foresaw that so-called "'artists' will abandon their art one by one; at first they will call themselves tradesmen, fitters, builders, and engineers; finally, they will engage in 'normal' human work" (ibid., 193).

The last remark points to a theme that, in an understated fashion, occupied an important place in the Panfuturist theory. Put succinctly it was this: The destruction of Great Art was to lead to the formation of a system that, in contrast to the former, would be completely integrated into the common and general life of humanity. Creativity would no longer be the unusual, esoteric matter that it was at present; it would cease to be the domain of a select group standing aloof from society. Instead, this new system would be an intrinsic part of life. Great Art, it was pointed out, had become alienated and separated from the daily concerns of man. It was an activity that had turned inward on itself, pursuing its own "aesthetic" goals ("art for art's sake"), ignoring life and, in fact, falling far behind the general tempo of social development (Shkurupii 1922b, 8–9; B—n 1925, 55–56; Semenko 1924d, 227; Tryroh 1922a). Poltorats'kyi noted that at one time humanity had no use for such a separate, self-oriented system. In the primordial communist society, life and art had not been discrete; the aesthetic and the utilitarian had not been differentiated; they constituted a continuum. Poltorats'kyi rejected the notion advanced by some that games and songs, for example, were a form of art or aesthetic pleasure for primitive man. He sided with those who interpreted them as practical activities, as avenues by which the

9 The Futurists' notion of art evokes associations with Plato's word for art, *techne*, which embraced virtually everything made and done by man. "Great Technology," "meta-art," and "art as process" suggested something similar.

individual acquired valuable skills. Songs and games "were certainly not an object of aesthetic pleasure," insisted Poltorats'kyi (Poltorats'kyi 1929a, 1: 44). They were training [sport!] and preparation for the eventualities of life. Far from being passive and contemplative, the way Great Art was, these activities were highly active and purposeful.[10] Only later did society develop a fetish for the "aesthetic." When this happened, an activity that was socially mobilizing and constructive turned into one that was exactly the opposite.

In the new "classless socialist society" of the future, when Great Art will have disappeared as a "separate category of culture" (ibid., 49), human creativity would assume the characteristics it had in its earliest stage but on a much more sophisticated level. Imbued, as it must be, with the principles of science and technology, this new form of creativity would stand among society's rational systems. Unlike Great Art, which influenced the "reactionary" "emotional centers" (ibid., 44) of man, Great Technology would appeal to logic. The triumph of Great Technology would simultaneously be the triumph of Reason. It would signal that humanity had at last outgrown its "childhood" and had finally attained the maturity that its entire intellectual history had foreshadowed (Semenko 1930o, 118).

Exstruction: A Compromise with the Age of Transition

Most literary and cultural organizations as well as the Party leadership worked on the assumption that art was useful in education and propaganda, never dreaming of denying it a place in society. The Futurists, as we saw, clearly thought otherwise. But if they quarreled with the majority view concerning the ultimate fate and role of art in a communist society, they accepted the utilitarian principles behind it, agreeing that there was a need for a system that would be in harmony with the revolution and new culture. Unlike their opponents, however, they did not believe that this system would or could be art in the traditional sense. In their opinion, the "organizational"[11] role that the proletarians tried to ascribe to art was incongruous because art in "its essence" was unfit to perform it

[10] These issues were in the air at this time. They were even discussed in Hrushevs'kyi (1959, 26–29). Poltorats'kyi and Hrushevs'kyi also make reference to the same German author, Karl Bucher, when presenting their arguments.

[11] In Ukrainian: *orhanizatsiinyi*. The word was used to denote a rational method of activity that had practical social consequences. The term came from the NOP movement (*Naukova orhanizatsiia pratsi* [Scientific organization of labor]). See above, chapter 4, pp. 85–86.

(Tryroh [Semenko] 1922a). If society wanted a system that was useful, one which would mobilize ("organize") human energy for the creation of communism, then it should not look toward an emotional and irrational system. For the Futurists it was obvious that once the utilitarian and rational factors were introduced into Great Art, it ceased being Great Art. "There cannot be an organizing art. One contradicts the other. A consistently carried out organizational analysis [of Great Art] does not give a new 'art'; it only gives a dead schema of art" (Semenko 1930o, 118). The proletarians could not have it both ways. They could not have Great Art (or Proletarian Art) and have a utilitarian, rational system. Great Art "had only its own goals" and it "stopped being art when it became a utilitarian tool..." (B—n 1925, 56). Any rational principle introduced into art destroyed art, just as their theory predicted.

The above, in the words of the Futurists, was their "maximalist" position—a posture, as we saw, they had difficulty sustaining in the face of proletarian criticism. Consequently, they made room in their theory for a less extreme stance, based on the premise that although "there will be no art" in the future, "there is art" now (Semenko 1924d, 227). Drawing an analogy to a familiar sphere, they argued that the predicament of art was akin to the peasantry as a class. The peasantry existed in the present but according to Marxist theory was destined to disappear in the future. The Party had adjusted to reality by adopting appropriate measures directed specifically at the peasants. The Futurists saw themselves as capable of doing the same in relation to art. They too would adjust to the fact that art continued, for the time being, to play a role in society, that it had no small effect on the masses who were "accustomed" to it, and continued thinking "in artistic terms" (ibid.). Given this situation, the Futurists proposed that art's remaining "strength" be utilized for the promotion of the future culture (Semenko 1924b, 194). While "the cultivation of art as some kind of self-serving category is inappropriate and dangerous," it was acceptable to "exploit" the familiar devices of this system to agitate for and propagandize the ideals of the working class (Semenko 1924d, 227). This type of practice was dubbed "*ex*struction" (as opposed to *de*struction) and implied "practical" or "positive" artistic work with an educational function (Voinilovych 1929a, 7: 22–32).[12] Exstruction, of course, was "not really art"; it was merely the exploitation of "external artistic form" for the promotion of a desired ideology (B—n 1925, 56). Semenko viewed exstruction as "approximately that which is necessary in the age of transition" and included proletarian literature in

[12] See also the editorial comments to this article on the contents page.

this category (Voinilovych 1929b, 63).[13]

The Futurists embraced exstruction unenthusiastically. It never figured in their theory as prominently as did "construction," "destruction," "ideology," and "facture." Semenko bluntly stated that "the significance of exstruction is limited" (Semenko 1924b, 194). Unlike destruction and construction, exstruction "did not have a tendency toward development." Its relationship to the artistic process was marginal at best, since it was really a category of activity belonging to the "political-practical front" and hence was explicitly alien to "art as a cult." Exstruction had only the immediate, temporary function of promoting social and political goals. Once these were attained, "exstructive art...falls away like a useless, inactive thing" (ibid.).

The Futurists were acutely aware that the short-term benefits of exstruction did not completely compensate for its harmful effects. Their official attitude toward this practice therefore remained skeptical. Exstruction was "dangerous" because, when it exploited Great Art, it also inadvertently "cultivated," "galvanized," and "dragged out" the existence of a system slated for destruction (ibid., 195). "Exstruction is an enemy of construction," pointed out Semenko, because it was a detour in the destructive process, stalling the eventual triumph of the new constructing cult. He concluded: "Under our present conditions the entire exstructive policy can be put to question...Personally, I am negatively disposed toward exstruction" (ibid., 195 n. 2). The Futurists made a distinction between "practical" art like exstruction and their own "constructive" work. The former affirmed Great Art as a system, made use of it in its most traditional and conservative guise, while construction fashioned a new system and, hence, was inimical to Great Art. Again Semenko: "Exstruction is the exploitation of art..., construction...rejects [*vidkydaie*] art" (Voinilovych 1929b, 63).

Functionalism

The rejection of exstruction by the Futurists did not, naturally, mean that they were in favor of an art detached from the cares of this world. Their theory clearly expressed scorn for the notion that either the artist or his work could stand aloof from society. If artistic or meta-artistic activity was to have merit, it had to perform a useful function in society. The demise of Great Art, after all, was directly attributable to the fact that it

[13] Semenko's observations, cited here and below, were made during the discussion period following Voinilovych's lecture.

evolved into a dead-end of formalistic and introspective experimentation. Because the Panfuturist system viewed art as a direct participant in the transformation of society (rather than as a method for "discovering," "contemplating," or "adorning" life through images), any asocial art was rejected out of hand (Semenko 1930j, 58; Poltorats'kyi 1929a, 1: 47 and 1929a, 2: 42–50). Of all the Futurists, Leonid Skrypnyk pursued this line of argument most vehemently.[14] According to him, a majority of the traditional arts were hopelessly dysfunctional and, therefore, had to be liquidated.[15] Some, however, could be reformed through innovation and experimentation. Those that were susceptible to this would gradually be transformed into meta-art, becoming keystones of a new "constructing" system. It was in this intellectual context that the expression "functionalism" came into being. "The Panfuturist theory uses this term to mean the social effectiveness [of art] in the context of construction" ("Bl'oknot 'Novoï generatsiï'" 1929, 32). Put another way, "functional literary production" was considered to have an "objectively social significance" but only as long as it was made in accordance with "leftist practice."[16]

Inasmuch as "functionalism" was linked to the constructing phase of a new system, it clearly implied the rejection of Great Art. Functionalism, like rationalism, when introduced into Great Art, led to its destruction. Thus the Futurists were able to speak of the "disappearance of art in an atmosphere of rationalistic, functional demands."[17] In place of Great Art's "aestheticism," the new constructing system embraced the principle of efficacy and practicability (Poltorats'kyi 1929c, 76–77). The Futurists also referred to functionalism as "agitation and propaganda" but with the proviso that these words be understood in the "broad, not the simplistic" sense (Semenko 1930j, 58).[18]

14 See the following articles by Skrypnyk: L. Skrypnyk 1929h, 1929d, 1929g, 1929a, and 1929e.

15 Speaking ironically, Skrypnyk declared: "One must stage as quickly as possible operas on themes like 'The Industrialization of the Country,' 'Highways,' 'Agricultural Cooperation,' and 'The Rational Manuring of Land.' When we finally hear The First Lovers' aria on the subject of the comparative value of horse manure and superphosphate, when we admire for the last time the dance or the 'airy ballet' of locksmiths [...] we will then be able to close down the opera. On the other hand, we can do that even sooner." See L. Skrypnyk (1929h, 47).

16 See the editorial comment in the table of contents to Geo Shkurupii's poem, "Armiia armii," *Nova generatsiia* 1928 (2).

17 See the editorial comment in the table of contents to L. Skrypnyk 1929h.

18 See also Poltorats'kyi: "What do the odious words 'ideological steadfastness' [*ideolohichna vytrymanist'*] mean? We will not defend the vulgar point of view that calls a

Thus, despite certain similarities to exstruction, "functionalism" clearly implied concern for the facture of a work, i.e., for experimentation, something the former did not. As an element of "construction," functionalism obviously left Great Art behind and represented a union of novelty with utility. The functional work was understood as a crafted, "produced" object. Its mode of existence was compared to architecture, namely, to structures dependent on the service they rendered. These were to be judged by their performance, not by some abstract measure of beauty. Functionalism, thus, guarded against the danger of avant-garde "aestheticism" (Poltorats'kyi 1929c, 78). The Futurists made a point of differentiating between "functional 'craftsmanship'" and "refined aestheticism" ("Nash dysput pro teatr" 1929, 61).

Functionalism gained wide currency after the creation of VUARKK. It was, without question, designed to mitigate the destructive or experimental character of the Panfuturist theory by giving it more of an art-affirming appearance. Even so, Panfuturism's maximalist proclamation about the inevitable demise of art continued to be affirmed indirectly. It is interesting to note that as late as March 1930, in a summary of Futurist goals, Semenko openly acknowledged that

> the first stage [of our program]—destruction—...led later to the theory and practice of functional art. Panfuturism agitated simultaneously for construction, implementing its maximalist program of denying art; [this] in reality [meant] transforming [art] into [one of the] production arts which [we] understood as the introduction of engineering [techniques] into artistic devices. Practically speaking, [this] was, in effect, a denial of art in the old understanding [of the word] as a category separate from science and technology (Semenko 1930j, 57).

Functionalism allowed the Futurists to remain faithful to the principle of novelty that they so cherished and, at the same time, allowed them to argue that their work had practical and ideological value for the revolution. It must be admitted, however, that the term was somewhat of a chameleon. On the one hand, it was used to denote an experimental work, a type which in the past, probably, would have been simply called "destructive." On the other hand, it was also used to denote a work that was especially transparent and top-heavy with a political message. The meaning of functionalism was easily affected by political circumstances and expediency, consequently a certain ambiguity surrounds it. One example

---

work ideologically steadfast when the positive types are communists and the negative are the bourgeoisie, and where everything necessarily ends with the singing of the Internationale" (Poltorats'kyi 1929a, 2: 48).

will suffice. A few months before *Nova generatsiia* was dissolved, Petro Mel'nyk, in an article on the functional poem, clearly spoke about the necessity of muting the experimental and formalistic aspect of a work and urged more emphasis on ideology (Mel'nyk 1930a; also 1930b). In such an interpretation functionalism began to tip dangerously close toward exstruction.

CHAPTER 7

Aesthetics and Poetics

The diverse and seemingly contradictory literary legacy of Ukrainian Futurism derives its coherence and unity from one dominant premise: experimentation, that is, an unstinting commitment to novelty. Although compelled time and again by cultural and political circumstances to demote or even camouflage this principle, the movement was motivated by it, literally, to the very end. Even in 1930, Mykhail' Semenko kept insisting that "we must be concerned not only about the present day in art, but also about tomorrow. This calls for certain testing and experiments. In effect [this calls for] successful and unsuccessful experiments..., for achievements as well as failures" (Semenko 1930j, 58). Leonid Frenkel' pointed out that "without experiments there are no inventions" (Frenkel' 1928a, 372). And *Nova generatsiia* told its readers and contributors: "Without [experimentation] further development...is impossible" (*Nova generatsiia* 1927 [3]).[1] Oleksii Poltorats'kyi warned: "One must not learn to do as the masters did in earlier periods; one must learn *not* to do [as they did; one must] do things in a new way" (Poltorats'kyi 1930d, 34). Leonid Skrypnyk defined the avant-gardist as "an artist who has gone at least one step further than other artists"; anyone who "stops and waits to be reached or overtaken ceases to be a leftist" (Lans'kyi [Skrypnyk] 1927, 38). "When we write stories or novels," echoed Geo Shkurupii, "we pay attention to the originality of their architectonics.... [Given] a lot of room for inventiveness, we shall create new things, more useful than [those] that are being re-made and restored" (Shkurupii 1927a, 34). In one of his short stories, he elaborated: "To show [people] things the way they are accustomed to seeing them is to betray one's own graphomania [*hrafomanstvo*]" (Shkurupii 1929b, 19). The stress on originality was such that potential contributors to *Nova generatsiia* were cautioned not to imitate other Futurists, especially not Semenko. One budding author was given this sober advice:

[1] This statement was made on the table of contents page in connection with the publication of M. Bazhan's poem "Tsyrk."

> Your...[poem] is an empty play on foreign words. When you saw them in Semenko, they were not as numerous (you have two to a line). Moreover, there was a time when it was necessary to protest against the hackneyed Ukrainian poetic language and this was done successfully. [But now] there is no need to repeat an earlier stage; there are new tasks....Under no circumstance should [you] separate yourself from the [requirements of] the present....("Vidpovidi chytacham" 1928).

Even acknowledged innovators were encouraged by the Futurists to keep up with "progress" in the arts. About Les' Kurbas Semenko said: "We appreciate [his] past [achievements]....But there is need for further work" (Semenko 1929e, 76).[2]

Nova generatsiia willingly published unorthodox works even on those occasions when they came into conflict with the journal's program. When serialization of Andrii Chuzhyi's novel *Vedmid' poliuie za sontsem* [The Bear Hunts the Sun] was begun, a disclaimer announced that "the editors do not agree with such experiments but, nonetheless, offer it to the attention of readers" (*Nova generatsiia* 1928 [7]: [table of contents]). Yet, when the work attracted negative criticism, these same editors immediately came to its defense: "Although A. Chuzhyi's work is permeated with the scent of early Futurism, it is not without positive significance *in the context of our literary practice* and at any rate, the positive sides [of the novel] outweigh the negative" (*Nova generatsiia* 1928 [10]: [table of contents]; *emphasis added*). As the last statement suggests, novelty was, at least in part, a relative concept. Within a culture still ensnared by "old rotten methods" (Poltorats'kyi 1928c, 432), even belated practices could retain their relevance. In the face of the "restorationist" poetics of Modernism, Symbolism, Neoclassicism, Impressionism, Romanticism, and Realism that prevailed around them, the Futurists justified not only early vanguardistic practices but even certain traditional modes of literary inquiry (popular fiction, for example) as potentially revolutionary.

The New was frequently promoted in the language of Formalism. Poltorats'kyi maintained that "proletarian art must experience several revolutions in its development. The fundamental revolution that must occur within proletarian art is a revolution of its artistic devices....The object of experimental work lies precisely in the constant struggle with bourgeois artistic devices, in their destruction, in experimenting [with them], in creating and trying new ones" (Poltorats'kyi 1930d, 32). An art

[2] See also "Protokol zasidannia VUSKK (Novoï generatsiï) v spravi kino 10.XII.1929," 1930. In the latter document the actor Buchma and other members of the Futurists organization VUSKK attacked conservatism in Ukrainian cinema.

work was defined as "a complex of devices" which organized "the material of life [into] a 'teleological' whole, a construction that [acted] in a certain direction, influence[d] a reader in one [particular] way instead of another" (Poltorats'kyi 1928a, 50). Literature was thought of as something fabricated (made) rather than inspired. Writers were craftsmen rather than seers or messiahs. Accordingly, one Futurist maintained that in place of inspiration, "the architectonics [of a novel] demand typical 'engineering'...and 'administrative'...skills" (Lans'kyi [Skrypnyk] 1927, 36).

Poltorats'kyi's writings demonstrate better than most the extent to which Formalist thinking permeated Ukrainian Futurist poetics and aesthetics. A useful guide in this respect is his book *Literaturni zasoby* [Literary Devices], and in particular the chapter "Praktychna i poetychna mova" [Practical and Poetic Language] (Poltorats'kyi 1929e). A brief overview of its major tenets will shed light on how Futurists conceptualized literature.

Like the Formalists, Poltorats'kyi found the work of Oleksander Potebnia a useful foil for his own ideas. One of his major arguments began with a citation from Potebnia's *Mysl' i iazyk* [Thought and Language, 1862]:

> Symbolism of language, obviously, can be called its *poeticalness* [*poetychnist'*]; on the contrary, the absence of an internal form appears as a word's *prosaicness* [*prozaichnist'*]....The question of the transformation of the word's internal form is, apparently, equivalent to the question of the relationship of poetry to prose, that is, to literary form in general (Poltorats'kyi 1929e, 30; *emphasis in the original*).

This was interpreted by Poltorats'kyi to mean that, for Potebnia, "there are two ways of perceiving phenomena of the external world: an emotional-poetic and a practical (scientific). Figurativeness...[according to Potebnia] is a sign of poetic language" (ibid.). Poltorats'kyi rejected this conclusion. More to his liking was the position of the Formalists who, in his opinion, convincingly demonstrated that figurativeness was not a necessary characteristic of artistic language. But in accepting their view, he also criticized them for adhering to a dichotomous conception of literature, in particular, for trying in their own way to distinguish poetic language from the practical.[3] Poltorats'kyi argued that such attempts must end in failure because poetic language did not exist as an

[3] On the subject of Potebnia, and the concepts of "poetic" and "practical" language, see Erlich (1955, 23–26); Pomorska (1968, 23–24); and Fizer 1982. Further details on this subject are found in Fizer (1986, *passim*).

absolute or independent category. "Elements of artistic [poetic] and practical language are so tightly connected that they cannot in any way be separated. All attempts to discover static, absolute differences [between them will] prove nothing" (ibid., 39). He considered the idea of a special language, that is, one which alone elicited aesthetic emotions, as basically false. "In principle, there is no difference between prose and poetic language…" he insisted (ibid., 43). According to him there was only one way to define "poetic" language, namely, as a *convention* [*umovnist'*], a tacit agreement between reader and writer. Poetic language had no absolute or permanent characteristics because it changed with time and circumstance (ibid., 37–39).

The merits or flaws of Poltorats'kyi's position need not concern us here, but his "relativism" in these matters is noteworthy, for it is symptomatic of how Futurists conceived not just "poetic" language but all of literature (writing). One and the other were regarded as historically and culturally determined forms, normative stereotypes to which writers adhered only through inertia. Futurist practice leaves no doubt that they approached the institution called "Literature" (and, by extension, "Art") as an impermanent phenomenon, as a changing "convention" to which they owned no particular allegiance. Consequently, they disavowed any literary practice that led to a rigid separation of "poetic" language (style) from other forms of discourse, and at the same time rejected all sharp divisions between "Literature" and other forms of writing. A linguistic or stylistic practice that self-consciously aspired toward some preconceived idea of "Literature" was frowned upon. Strictly speaking, Futurists saw themselves not as "writers" or "artists," but as "workers in language." As such, their activities were circumscribed neither by a specific "artistic" discourse nor by established "literary" modes (genres). Their true vocation was not the practice of "Literature" but the testing of its boundaries. The limited universe from which "Literature" derived its themes and forms had to be rejected. In their view, "Literature" (i.e., the institution served by "artists"), together with the dichotomy between "poetic" and "practical" language, would yield ultimately to a "verbal meta-art of the future" (ibid., 43). In practical terms, this meant that Futurists had to strive for two major goals: a) they must escape from the slavery of conventional "poetic" subject matter and language; b) they must render "artistic" (literary) rules obsolete by obliterating distinctions not only among separate genres but even among the individual sovereign arts.

Futurism's approach to language entailed above all else a repudiation of the aristocratic, precious lexicon and diction inherited by Ukrainian letters from Modernism, Symbolism, and Neoclassicism. As an antidote to these traditions, the movement espoused a discourse based either on journalism, science, and technology or on informal speech unencumbered by rules of decorum—meaning, it permitted locutions both colloquial and profane. Linguistic purism or prescriptivism had no place in the Futurists' theory and practice. Moreover, their discourse was conditioned to a large extent by a desire to divorce art from emotions, by a refusal to arouse in readers conventional, totally arbitrary, "feelings." Thus, where the language of the heart had once reigned, coarseness appeared; where only lyricism inhered, rhetoric surfaced. This programmatic anti-sentimentalism was registered most of all through wit, skepticism, and irreverence. Irony, satire, and parody became fundamental features of their aesthetic, almost as if the Futurists had a congenital need for frivolity. Their polemics, their pseudonyms (Sandi Good, Ars Librysto, Ole Vorm), and, naturally, their poems and prose were laced with mockery, sarcasm, flippancy, caricature, and humor. They deliberately promoted the anecdote and farce as genres.[4] At times, the Futurists found it necessary to caution even themselves against turning these tendencies into a "canon" (P. Mel'nyk 1930a, 42). Nevertheless, the theoretical justification for such modalities was that they "neutralized" old devices, methods, and themes, destroyed traditional attitudes by making "rational" (conscious) those things that otherwise swayed "emotionally":

> Through the present practice of Panfuturism, it is possible to discern how a theme becomes a device for shifting the perception of art from emotions to reason.... One of the [ways of doing this] is destructive, [i.e.,] by taking an ironic approach to a theme. A particular Futurist work may retain an old theme, but it is not approached in the normal way; that would be stereotypical and [act] as an emotional stimulus. [In the Panfuturist approach] the theme is parodied and hence its power to influence aesthetically is destroyed (Poltorats'kyi 1929a, 2: 47).

In view of the above, it is obvious that literature was hardly a solemn enterprise for Futurists. Their formalism easily translated into play. Lofty sentiments, profundity of thought were sneered at. Even their political engagement—pompous and bombastic as it was at times—nearly always carried overtones of irony, rarely betraying the wooden earnestness of their proletarian comrades.

One is able to compile a virtual handbook of Futurist likes and dislikes from an article written by Poltorats'kyi about Arkadii Liubchenko

4 See Frenkel' 1927 and Frenkel' 1928b. Opponents tended to interpret such attitudes as contempt for socialist reality, but judging by remarks that appeared in *Nova generatsiia*, readers found it refreshing. "Generally speaking," wrote one, "[your] journal has a very original character; it is light and humorous. It lacks our standard 'khokhol'-like boredom, tears and sentiments, [all of which] have become simply loathsome to us all..." See "Lystuvannia z redaktsiieiu" 1928a.

(Poltorats'kyi 1930c). This prominent member of VAPLITE was taken to task for writing works "designed for 'eternity'" and for orienting himself on "unchanging aesthetic values" (ibid., 5: 40). His aestheticism and conscious preoccupation with Beauty were found unacceptable. Liubchenko was mockingly called "Arkadii Chrysostom" and "Arkadii the Eloquent" [*Arkadii krasnomovets'*] for using archaic words, for speaking "beautifully in the noble, lyrical landscape style" of Fet, Turgenev, Kotsiubyns'kyi, and Ukraïnka. Poltorats'kyi disparaged his lyricism, melodrama, his *mystère profane*, his philosophical, funereal tone, and his "perfumed drivel" [*parfumerni slynozlyvy*]. "If we focus on such details as epithets and images..., we see that they fit into the general idealistic framework of our author," says Poltorats'kyi. "They are consistently of an 'ornamental' kind, belonging mostly to the category of 'luxury items' (emerald chords, azure plafonds, etc.). Sometimes [they have] a religious-mystical origin..." (Poltorats'kyi 1930c 8–9: 24). Ultimately, the criticism boiled down to Liubchenko's so-called archaic and provincial manner:

> All the ornamental tendencies that are evident in A. Liubchenko's style appear very naive at the present moment. The point is that in the course of bourgeois art's development, these ornamental tendencies had begun to self-destruct back in the [period] of early Futurism. Having been parodied, they lost all their artistic force. Only the *provincialism* of A. Liubchenko's artistic qualifications and artistic tastes can account for such completely sincere exploitation of this already parodied theatrical appurtenance [*butafors'ka perukarshchyna*] (ibid., 8–9: 28).

Preoccupation with genre became a logical extension of the Futurists' rejection of "poetic" language. Just as they were not prepared to exclude a particular discourse from their work, so too they were not ready to disqualify untraditional "writings" from "Literature." Practice shows they did not limit themselves to any predetermined class of genres. Their works ranged from the "artistic" to "non-artistic," from the "factual" to the "fictional," and avoided at all times making a fetish of any one kind.

The "literature of fact," although not as popular as among Russian Futurists, had a conspicuous place in the Ukrainian movement as well.[5] Characteristically, this implied the *reportazh* (what Poltorats'kyi preferred to call *faktazh*; Poltorats'kyi 1930d, 35), a designation that included travelogues and journalistic reports. "Documents," "diaries," "letters," "memoirs," "biographies," and simple "materials" were among the other

[5] Ukrainians followed the Russian trend closely; the works and ideas of Sergei Tret'iakov and N. Chuzhak were especially popular.

purportedly "factual" genres in their repertoire. Ukrainian Futurists, however, never exaggerated the documentary value of this prose. As with their other writings, "fact" was a legitimate object of mystification and play. Thus, on the one hand, *Nova generatsiia* was apt to request from its readers "language documents, reportages, and jottings [*zapysy*]" instead of "poems and stories on 'serious' themes..."[6] (the latter, it declared, "inevitably end up in the [editor's] trash bin") but, on the other, it would also print outrageous parodies of "fact" (e.g., Myrhorods'kyi and Malovichko 1929; Meter 1929). As a result, titular "novellas" (like those of Viktor Petrov [1930b] and Geo Shkurupii [1930f, 1930g]) were frequently closer to "reality" than so-called "letters" and "diaries."

By resorting to popular canonical genres, namely, fiction in which action and plot predominate, the Futurists found yet another way to undermine the high seriousness of "Literature." *Nova generatsiia* offered stories of adventure, mystery, science fiction, and horror-suspense, even stylizations on the American Western. Such works were justified by the novelty they introduced into Ukrainian letters.[7] It was said that they brought "our literature closer to the literature of Europe" (Poltorats'kyi 1928a, 52) and America. They were an escape from nineteenth-century Realism or what was derisively labeled as the "Hrinchenko" tradition, that is, "stories of tragic love and fate" (ibid., 50, 59). Shkurupii viewed this fiction as an antidote to the dearth of good Ukrainian reading material:

> There exists a great literature with many famous names, but there is nothing to read. There is much bread but nothing to eat. There is much water but nothing to drink. The reader is like a brave sailor sailing the seas without fresh water. Naturally, there are things to read, just as there is water in the sea, but reading old Ukrainian prose is boring and drinking sea water is salty (Shkurupii 1927c, 13).

"Left" prose, as this fiction was dubbed, had one other very important goal: it was meant to cure "the illness of disorganized material"—to do away with effusive, lyrical, and ornamental prose. Such writings became an excellent pretext for manipulating the structures of literature and playing games with its self-imposed rules, all of which dovetailed with the movement's formalist preoccupations, its deep-seated hostility toward psychologism and subjectivism. The Futurist publication exemplifying this penchant best was *Hol'fshtrom* (1925), a collection that placed heavy

6 These comments appear in the table of contents of *Nova Generatsiia* 1929 (2).

7 Publication of Vil'm Iar's [Ievhen Kaplia-Iavors'kyi] science-fiction story "Plan mistera Roka" [The Plan of Mr. Rock] was accompanied by this editorial comment on the contents page: "[This] is a common fantastic [story], but it is not widely disseminated in Ukrainian literature." See *Nova generatsiia* 1927 (3): 48.

emphasis on plot-centered literature (both in prose and poetry). Its appearance was immediately scored as an unwelcome "American" trend. One reviewer, who entitled his critique "Under the banner of Ukrainian 'Americanism'," drew attention to the "back-breaking [literary] tricks" employed by the authors, and noted their fascination with all things American. Indeed, *Hol'fshtrom*'s cover bore a photograph of a black man, while some texts compared Ukraine to Mexico and California; mention was even made of James Fenimore Cooper. Thanks to the poem "Povist' pro mistera Iuza i trampa Dzheka" [A Tale about Mr. Hughes and Jack the Tramp], Bazhan was accused by the reviewer of "a desperate 'Americanism,' a desire, at all cost, to be more American than the Americans" (Iakubovs'kyi 1925).

While popular fiction and documentary genres in their "pure" guise were deemed acceptable to the movement because they were an exotic addition to the traditional Ukrainian canon, theoretical and practical preference was given to those works that actually transgressed against an established artistic category or class and led to some new "synthesis." This was the principle of relativism at its most extreme, for synthesis respected neither the identity of genres nor the individuality of the arts. It involved melding unrelated literary forms (such as the novella and the narrative poem), mixing "artistic" and "non-artistic" genres (for example, a novel and a reportage), or blending "literary" arts with the "visual." Futurists had numerous suggestions about how to proceed on this path. Poltorats'kyi counseled writers of the "left" story to draw on the "lapidary style" of the film scenario (Poltorats'kyi 1928a, 57). Leonid Skrypnyk strove to bring the novel closer to film and the screenplay through the use of "montage" techniques and other cinematic devices. Frenkel' declared that "the novel, [when] constructed thematically according to the design of a memoir, opens up new formal possibilities...The plotting of fact must begin from memoirs; in our day and age, this constitutes a part of the problem of the left novel" (Frenkel' 1928a, 371). By combining the traditional plotted story with fact (the reportage), Futurists were purportedly bringing "art closer to life" (Poltorats'kyi 1928a, 59). But the real reason synthesis remained one of their principal preoccupations was that it was simultaneously "destructive" and "constructive," that is, it undermined old genres and arts while creating new ones.

By fusing "factual" literature with "artistic," Futurists produced various hybrid, ad hoc genres like the *faktopoema* [narrative fact-poem] or *fakto-opovidannia* [fact-story]. The pages of *Nova generatsiia* saw "letter-poems," "pamphlet-poems," "editorial-poems," "charade-poems," "radio-poems," and even "speech-poems." Geo Shkurupii worked on a novel in verse (Shkurupii 1925d). Favst Lopatyns'kyi (a director of film and theater) contributed a film scenario in free verse (Lopatyns'kyi 1928c). Geo Koliada used verse and prose simultaneously in his single "novel" (Koliada 1928 and 1929). Semenko wrote *poezofil'my* (poetry-films) and advocated the synthesis of literary and non-literary works, specifically, painting and poetry (*poezomaliarstvo;* Semenko 1922c, 32).

Ukrainian Futurism was ill disposed toward all regulative and prescriptive notions of literature. It combined animosity toward art (Panfuturism, after all, promoted its destruction and death) with a paradoxical affirmation of its autonomy through a formalist orientation and an emphasis on innovation. But the Futurists' concept of autonomy was a far cry from the quasi-modernist notions of art for art's sake that still dominated the artistic thinking of the literary elite. The Futurists did not subscribe to the idea that literature's function was simply to exist and be alluring. They were not committed to any metaphysical concept of art, nor did they encourage disinterested contemplation of it. The aesthetic life as such was not idealized, and qualities like harmony and proportion, decorum and good taste, were alien to them.

The Futurists put faith in a new art or "system" that would end the current isolation and alienation of the artist from society. In their own practice, they tried not to draw an absolute distinction between artistic and other types of written forms. But even as they knocked literature from its august pedestal and brought it closer to the ordinary experience of life through the literature of fact, through urban and political themes, they were careful not to restore to it (in the manner of proletarians) its old social and national functions. As long as Great Art remained a living impediment to the future system, the emphasis had to be placed on destroying the old, in revealing its conventions and illusions to those who would still believe in its efficacy.

III

The Literary Legacy

A Survey of the Major Practitioners

Cover artwork by Anatol' Petryts'kyi for M. Semenko, *P'iero mertvopetliuie. Futuryzy. 1914–1918. Poezii. Knyzhka 3-a.* Kyiv: Flamingo, 1919.

CHAPTER 8

The Poetry

> Поет молодий. Енергія його велика. Читав чимало. Читане тямить. Отже додавши до цього очевидний поетичний хист, можемо сподіватися, що з цього дива буде пиво.
> *The poet is young. His energy is great. He has read much. He understands what he has read. Thus, if we add to this his obvious poetic talent, we can expect this strange seed to bear fruit.*
>
> Andrii Nikovs'kyi, *Vita Nova* (1919, 98)

> Я хочу кожний день все слів нових
> *I want ever new words each day.*
>
> M. Semenko (1914)

> Мій девіз—несталість і несподіваність.
> *My motto is: change and surprise.*
>
> M. Semenko (1918)

Mykhail' Semenko (1892–1937)

During Semenko's lifetime there was only one notable instance when a critic tried to assess—and reassess—his poetic work in a relatively calm and non-partisan manner. This was done in 1925 by the scholar Borys Iakubs'kyi, following the publication of Semenko's *Kobzar*, that is, his collected works from 1910 to 1922 (Iakubs'kyi 1925). Unlike preceding critics, Iakubs'kyi saw in Semenko a "first-rate revolutionary poet," a "real artist," an "honest lyric poet" (ibid., 257). He said that Ukrainian literary criticism had failed to do justice both to him and his movement. In trying to "understand and explain" Semenko, Iakubs'kyi stressed the unique historical role his verse played in Ukrainian literature and emphasized its preoccupation with formal tasks.

One reason scholarship has had less than total success in "understanding" and "explaining" Semenko is that, unlike his straightforward public image, the work he produced did not lend itself to easy categorization or definition. When viewed in its entirety, the poetry refuses to coalesce into an orderly whole or accept a simple label. It is replete with loose ends, takes unexpected turns, and offers strains that seem at first glance uncharacteristic for a self-professed leader of the avant-garde. Pigeonholing this body of work is made all the more difficult because of its sheer size: between 1913 and 1936 Semenko issued some thirty separate books (the *Kobzar* alone totaled 646 pages). While a few were reprints, many more were new and original. If judged by standards of continuity and logical evolution, these books and cycles immediately evoke puzzlement, even frustration, on account of their dissimilarity. Quite palpable is the continuous experimentation with various aspects of verse: sound and rhyme, stanzaic form, rhythm and meter, punctuation and syntax. Genre in Semenko's oeuvre tends to be a particularly shifting category and, frequently, an object of outright invention. His first poems, for example, were conventional "lyrics," followed by *poezy* and *poezopisni* [poetry-songs]. Later, he turned to the *poema* [narrative poem], as well as "intimate poetry," and wrote two verse dramas. On the heels of these came *poezofil'my* [poetry-films], *revfutpoems* [*rev*olutionary *fut*urist poems], sound (trans-sense) and visual poetry, to name just a few.

Thematically, this work is also eclectic. The urban landscape with its automobiles, trains, airplanes, electricity, fumes, cafes, and prostitutes coexists with idyllic scenes of nature. Paeans to speed do not preclude "Hymns to St. Theresa" [*Himny Sv. Terezi*], a cycle from 1918 (Semenko 1920). The exoticism of large cities (New York, Paris, Melbourne, Chicago) and distant places (America, Greenland, Africa, the Amazon, Patagonia, and even Mars) proves as attractive as life's banalities, which can elicit from the poet phrases like these: "I'd like to be Jack/ To forget all art and wisdom.../ I'd like to grab splendid Jill's breasts / and wear a hat all year round.."[1] The venting of his *mania grandiosa* (to borrow Iakubs'kyi's phrase) alternates with lines of meekness and self-abasement. All these aspects are materialized, of course, through an exuberant lexicon and diction. Sometimes, Semenko's voice is that of an urban *inteligent*, at other times, a tramp or a clown. His texts exploit barbarisms, Russianisms as well as the terminology of the social and natural sciences and technology. Neologisms and "nature" vocabulary also hold an important place in his poetry.

1 Хотів би я Іваном буть, / Мистецтво й мудрість все забуть... / Хватать за перса пишну Гапку, / І круглий рік носити шапку... ("Ivan"; Semenko [1925a, 116–17], written in 1914).

Faced with this disparity, critics have nonetheless sought to establish for Semenko a single true identity. Their approach has been to simplify, primarily by dismissing certain works as worthless scribbling. Late Soviet criticism, when not ostracizing Semenko outright, was prone to present him in a sanitized version, preferring to put as little emphasis as possible on his "destructive" work.[2] Even Mykola Bazhan, who knew better, wrote that the experimental and outrageous "...did not and does not represent the essence of the poet's creativity..." (Bazhan 1985, 6). Distanced thus from the purported ills of the avant-garde, the "real Semenko" would become in the eyes of one critic "a romantic and subtle lyricist" (Chernysh 1989a, 85) and in the eyes of another the cofounder of Socialist Realism (Hariaïv 1987).

In striving to bring order and harmony to this unruly oeuvre, critics remained blind to the fact that Semenko never intended to project a coherent or monolithic image. On the contrary, through his many collections and, especially, the compilations of his "complete works," (Semenko 1924c, 1925a, 1929–31) he took great pains to impress upon the reader the protean character of his poetic personality. It bears remembering that Semenko had absolute control over of all his editions and could have molded, through judicious selection, a polished and homogenous picture of his craft and a complimentary and integral image of himself as "the poet." As it turns out he did the opposite: he consciously swelled editions like the *Kobzar* with poems that previously had not found their way into print, diligently registering his obscure periods and haphazard efforts. In 1927 this determined thoroughness betrayed itself in the belated publication of a highly conservative and atypical work from 1921, the lyrical verse drama *Marusia Bohuslavka*. In fact, Semenko knowingly included his amateurish writings alongside the polished. That he was well aware of his own weaknesses is revealed in his review of an anthology edited by Mykola Zerov. Writing under the pseudonym M. Tryroh, Semenko took Zerov to task for an anthology, especially his "perfectly bad taste" in selecting contemporary verse—including, ironically, Semenko's. Four of the five poems in the anthology, claimed Tryroh, were completely uncharacteristic of Semenko and worthless (Tryroh [Semenko] 1922b). The tendency to publish without undue discrimination led one reviewer to make this observation:

> [Semenko]...is like a self-taught man who sits down at an instrument, letting his fingers strike anywhere in an attempt to play chords. Once in a while he strikes a pleasant note, but generally it is simply noise. He

2 See my review of Mykhail' Semenko, *Poezii* (Semenko 1985) in Ilnytzkyj 1985.

> should write less and be more selective. After all, the Lord did not deny him talent (Volok 1920, 92).

Of course, talent was not the issue. Semenko purposely cultivated this air of randomness in defiance of the principles that governed Great Art (i.e., consistency, selectivity, and artistic perfection). A hint as to what he was trying to accomplish comes as early as 1914 in *Kvero-futuryzm*:

> Art is striving. Therefore, it is always a process. The soul of man lives in time. Therefore, art—as an expression of the soul—is movement. The soul is change. Therefore, art is always change....In art anything that has been discovered and experienced is of no interest to the person who has discovered and experienced it, therefore everything that has been accomplished is not art, [because it has] lost the dynamism of the quest....*Art is the process of searching and experiencing without fulfillment* [*zdiisnennia*]....Kvero-futurism in art declares the beauty of the search, of dynamic flight. *The goal and fulfillment in art is the search itself.* It rejects the possibility of perfection [*zakinchenist'*] and ceases being art at the point where canons and the cult of self-satisfaction and reverence begins (Semenko 1914b, 1; *emphasis added*).

The *Kobzar* and later the *Povna zbirka tvoriv* [The Complete Collected Works, 1929–31] were not designed to canonize Futurism or to elevate his own "poetic" reputation. Clearly, Semenko's compendia of verse were records of his "quest" and creative process; they were monuments to his "dynamic flight." Their comprehensive and nearly always chronological and retrospective structure was a device to convey to the reader a sense of movement, progress, and change. To achieve his goal, Semenko elevated the principle of "completeness" above "selectivity,"that is, he treated raw or uncharacteristic work in the same way as he did the *tours de force*, because both constituted a stage in the creative process. Semenko endeavored to leave a record of his search, regardless of whether it diminished or enhanced his literary stature. As the *Kobzar's* epigraph suggested—"The finished product is no longer yours" (the words of Russian poet Elena Guro)—texts took precedence over poetic reputation. In keeping with the theory of Panfuturism, the poet's individuality is subordinated to the literary process. This notion finds expression again in a poem introducing the third volume of the *Povna zbirka tvoriv*:

> Комусь попаде і ця книжка.
> Історії літератури—не обійти,—
> якби я не заплющував очі і не спускав їх низько.
> Не обдуриш історії, читачу, й ти.

Знайдуться моськи, що будуть плювати,
доводячи свою
«революційність теж:"
«і яке, мовляв, хутористичне нахабство,
і яке не сучасне, і чуже без меж."

Що їм література, історія, дати.
Їм би хоч жменьку письменницьких благ...
("Do vykhodu tomiv moieї 'Povnoї zbirky tvoriv'"; Semenko 1931a).

Even this book will fall into someone's hands.
There is no way to escape the history of literature,
even if I were to lower my eyes and feign modesty.
Nor will you, dear reader, fool history.

There will be drooling wise men
proving
"they too were revolutionary":
"what futuristically backward boorishness,
how uncontemporary and infinitely alien."

What is literature, history, time to them
When all they want is a handful of writing awards.

There is no question that the vast heterogeneous material of Semenko's corpus speaks poorly of him as a consistent, full-blown Futurist, or even as a "great" artist. In that respect—by publishing and republishing works which were manifestly immature or unpolished—he did himself a disservice. But therein lies his avant-gardism and the key to his baffling oeuvre: it is not constructed solely as a showcase for the individual aesthetic object (arrayed for the passive delectation of the reader); these are texts arranged to highlight the various phases of the creative process itself, warts and all.[3] Recall his previously cited words: "We must be concerned not only about the present day in art, but also about tomorrow. This calls for certain testing and experiments. In effect [this calls for] *successful and unsuccessful experiments..., for achievements as well as failures"* (Semenko 1930j, 58; *emphasis added*). It could be said therefore

3 In the second volume of *Povna zbirka tvoriv*, Semenko admonishes his critics to pay attention to his development: "You better take note where my selfpropeller has propelled me and where my spearhead is pointing" ("Подивіться краще, куди мій самопер / попер / тепер / і куди моє вістря), adding that, for their sake, he was and will be "shameless and agitated" ("для вас і був / і буду— / безсоромний і схвильований") (Semenko 1929–31, 2: 5).

that in 1914 Semenko did not so much *become* an instantaneous Futurist, as he embarked on an avant-garde journey. For him the trip mattered more than the arrival. The oeuvre is a summary of his travels, detours, and discoveries.

The *Kobzar* (first printing, 1924) proved that Semenko's initial three books of poetry—*Prélude* (Semenko 1913), *Derzannia* (Semenko 1914a), and *Kvero-futuryzm* (Semenko 1914b)—were just tips of the iceberg, revealing only a small facet of the actual process by which he came to repudiate the conventions of his day. *Derzannia*, after all, consisted of no more than seven poems, *Kvero-futuryzm* of twenty-five. This was a marked contrast to the *Kobzar*: here *Derzannia* and *Kvero-futuryzm* were integrated with the previously unpublished cycles "Erotezy" [Erotheses] and "Poezofiry" [Poetry-offerings], yielding a total of one hundred poems. But the *Kobzar* painted not only a more complete picture, but a more complex one. It blurred the boundaries between *Prélude* and the two Futurist publications by portioning out a number of poems from each of these into a new cycle called "Naive Little Poems" [*Naïvni poeziiky*], suggesting a reinterpretation on Semenko's part of his early avant-garde undertakings.

Naive or not, *Derzannia* decidedly abandoned *Prélude*'s melodious, syllabic-accentual verse, its lexicon derived from romances and songs and, most of all, its rhapsodic intonations in the minor key. If *Prélude* had given the impression of wholeheartedly embracing Modernist clichés, *Derzannia* gave evidence of a conscious groping toward originality at any price. Semenko's cadence, for one, became entirely different here. Accentual verse, tending sometimes toward *vers libre*, eclipses the sing-song meters of *Prélude*. Neologisms assert themselves, as do more original rhymes. Most importantly, *Derzannia* manifested the first signs of what would emerge after several fitful starts as one of Semenko's major stylistic marks: a prosaic, colloquial inflection, the antidote to *Prélude*'s breathless, exalted emotionalism. In concert with the latter, a note of levity enters the love poetry, taking the edge off Semenko's serious impassioned ardor. This in turn gives birth to an entirely different persona: in place of one that is woeful and delicate, an assertive and extravagant figure emerges. At least one poem indicates that the habitat of this new individual is no longer *Prélude*'s protective nature, but the city.

These tendencies were advanced further in *Kvero-futuryzm*, which became a kind of laboratory where Semenko freely moved from experiment to experiment. Here he seemed to be sampling a variety of modes rather than perfecting a single manner. Many poems deliberately deviated from traditional poetic and linguistic practices. Some amounted to little more than snippets of prose: "about white nights, about pink twilights. about lulling..." [про білі ночі, про рожевий сутінок. про колихання...]) (Semenko 1914b, 24); others violated punctuation rules, obliterated word boundaries ("silentlyebbs thisriver of the soul" [тихоплеще сярічка душі]), or abandoned meaning for pure sound ("ste kliu vliu pliu" [сте клю влю плю]). There was a noticeable gravitation toward an exotic lexicon (e.g., Anitra, cancan; ibid.). For the first time Semenko resorted to declarative, programmatic, and polemical verse—either to affirm his new movement or to ridicule his literary opponents. Parody and humor made their first appearance here as well in the form of primitive rhymes, rhythms, and alliterations. What once Semenko himself practiced in earnest and utmost seriousness now becomes the butt of mannered jokes:

Білі білі як коралі
білі зуби зуби Галі
тіло біле все у неї
тіло білої лілеї...
("Zuby Hali"; Semenko 1914c).

White white as coral
white teeth teeth of Halia
hers is an entirely white body
the body of a white lily...

Perhaps the most interesting aspect of *Kvero-futuryzm* was its experimentation with diction. During this time, Semenko was still trying to subdue his mournful mellifluousness, the high-serious tone of *Prélude*—an air that would bedevil him for quite a long while. As a step toward overthrowing it, he elaborates a manner (tried also in *Derzannia*) based on the natural rhythms and syntax of ordinary, day-to-day speech. *Kvero-futuryzm* gives reign not only to a loud and definitely unsubtle voice, but demonstrates that his prosaic and colloquial utterance is capable of psychological nuances that previously eluded him:

І я, і Ви—почули голос мая
Щось затремтіло—там, біля серця.
Мчимо в хвилях мототрамвая.
Почнемо інтермеццо.

Ми в Дарниці. Так гарно. Мило.
Пахучососни. Гуляємо. Десь плеще.

Груди затопило...
...Ви: —«Що се ще?”

Ми поверталися. Ні слова. Кепсько.
Безмовно йшли. Прощались біля ліфта.
І зникли Ви. І зник кудись Семенко.
...Дома я взявся за Свіфта
(“I ia i vy—pochuly holos maia”; Semenko 1914d).

Both you and I heard the voice of May
Something quivered there, near the heart.
We fly on waves of the motortram.
We'll start an intermezzo.

We're in Darnytsia. So nice. Sweet.
Scentlypine. We stroll. Somewhere a splashing.
Flooding my heart...
...You: "And what's this?"

We were returning. Not a word. Dicey.
Silently we walked. Parted near the lift.
You disappeared. And somewhere Semenko disappeared.
...At home I picked up Swift.

Я....і футурист і антиквар.
I am...both a futurist and an antiquarian.

M. Semenko (1916)

After four years of prolific writing in Vladivostok, Semenko emerged in 1918 to face a society that had neither evidence nor knowledge of his labors. This was a situation he was determined to change. Almost immediately, Semenko set about establishing a literary history for himself by publishing a huge backlog of poems that previously had not seen the light of day. At the same time, he began issuing more current works meant to delineate a new creative course which, in effect, rejected the Vladivostok period, one marked by a certain psychological ambivalence and a retreat from his radical positions of 1914. These contradictory imperatives led to the appearance during the years 1918–1919 of a host of collections and cycles, many of which seemed mutually exclusive. In some Semenko was seen rehearsing the past, in others he openly wrestled with it, while still in others he demonstratively broke with it. Not without reason does he admit in 1918: "Dissonant am I" [Дисонантний я].

Semenko's post-Vladivostok period opened in September 1918 with *P'iero zadaiet'sia* [Pierrot Brags]—verses from 1915–1917—designated, curiously, as "Book One" (Semenko 1918e).[4] Two more Pierrot collections followed—*P'iero kokhaie* [Pierrot Loves, 1918d] and *P'iero mertvopetliuie* [Pierrot Does the Death Spiral, 1919e]—resulting in a fairly comprehensive reconstruction of his creative efforts from 1914 to 1918. As the titles suggest, these assorted collections were held together by an extended series of lyrics devoted to love as well as the less noble but attendant emotions, like jealousy. *P'iero kokhaie,* the chronological start of this cycle, introduced a lyric hero with exceptionally mercurial moods, few of which were endearing. His frankness in questions of love bordered on shamelessness. Cynical, spiteful, nonchalant, Semenko's Pierrot treats love as a farce and a game. At one point he declares: "Love hates candor / Love likes games" [Кохання не любить щирости / Кохання любить гру] (Semenko 1925d). Behind this brave facade, however, lurked another personality: ingenuous, vulnerable, and idealistic. Pierrot, in short, spoke from both sides of his mouth. At times, he was parodic and mocking, his verse a caricature of all that is sincere and sentimental. On other occasions, he was capable of refined psychological vignettes devoid of bluster and posturing. These emotional vacillations were expressed in a technique that ranged from thumping rhythms and grammatical rhymes to prose-like simplicity. For the most part, Semenko continued to organize his verse into quatrains, but essayed invariably toward the natural rhythmical movement of colloquial speech. If he was often thwarted in achieving success here, it was because of the shortness of his periods and the tightly end-stopped lines with their perfect or near-perfect rhymes, as in this instance:

> Цікаво знати хто був мій предок?
> Сухорлявий і смілий козак
> Підлесливий маленький неборак
> І вмів дівчат збирати в оберемок...
> ("Мої predky"; Semenko 1925e).

4 By 1921 Semenko had eight consecutively numbered collections. Book six ("Naïvni poeziiky," a cycle from 1913) and book seven ("Osinnia rana," a cycle from 1916) never appeared, although they were, apparently, sent to the printer. In *Prominnia pohroz. Vos'ma knyha poezii, 1919-1920* (Semenko 1921b) these two books were said to be "in press."

I'm curious, who was my ancestor?
A lean and daring Cossack
A flattering, slight drifter
Who knew how to collect the girls by the armload...

There were occasions, however, when he overcame these lumbering rhythms by resorting to longer periods:

Я з Вами розстанусь і буду десь в Чікаго чи Мельбурні
І там капризна доля може звести нас.
Я буду вагоновод на трамваї, улиці будуть димні і
хмурні—
І раптом я зобачу між пасажирів Вас.
Ви скинете очима і я спостережу, як здригнуться кутики Ваших
губ.
Ви пригадаєте Владивосток і зробите рух щось вимовить, ніби в
вагоні для нас немає нікого.
Я змагаюсь, щоб не заплющити очі.... Але у нас не виникне
розмови про колись омріяний шлюб,
Бо вагоноводові розмовляти забороняється строго
("Vahonovod"; Semenko 1929g).[5]

You and I will part ways and I will end up somewhere in Chicago or
Melbourne
Capricious fate may bring us together even there.
I will be a motorman on the streetcar, the streets will be hazy and
gloomy—
And suddenly I will see you among the passengers.
You'll cast a glance and I'll note how the corners of your mouth twitch.
You'll recall Vladivostok and try to say something, as if there was
no one but us in the coach.
I struggle to keep my eyes open... But we will not bring up the wedding
we once dreamed of,
Because a motorman is strictly forbidden to talk.

In the second phase of the cycle, *P'iero zadaiet'sia* [Pierrot Brags] Semenko's emotional range narrows considerably: the tone becomes confessional, contemplative, and melancholy. Powerless and tormented, Pierrot speaks primarily in the lexicon of the heart and soul. He suffers pain, sadness, boredom, and spouts sentiments like these: "The worm of doubt gnaws and strangles me" (Черв'як зневір'я гризе і душить; "Do pobachennia"; Semenko 1925f); "My heart bears immeasurable wounds"

5 In an earlier version, Semenko used the title "Vahonovozhatyi." See Semenko (1925a, 208–209).

(В моїм серці безліч ран; "Reministsentsiia"; Semenko 1925g); "I have lost my strength entirely" (Я цілком розгубив свої сили; "Emanatsiia"; Semenko 1925h). Sometimes he manages brief fanfares of bravado, saying, "I am sick of inspired poets" (Мені набридли поети натхненні; "Zaklyk"; Semenko 1925i), and yearns "to slap the face" (дати...по морді; "Nu"; Semenko 1925j) of every sentimentalist, thereby betraying as much frustration with himself as with the Symbolists and Modernists to whom these words were ostensibly addressed.

This was the Pierrot of 1916–17. He underwent a dramatic metamorphosis in the last installment of the cycle, "Mertvopetliuiu" [I Do the Death Spiral], written in Kyiv during 1918 and published in *P'iero mertvopetliuie* a year later (Semenko 1919e).[6] Gone suddenly was the mask of the timorous, tender lover Semenko created in Vladivostok; this Pierrot was "liberated" (Я звільнивсь) and arrogant ("I cast about me a disdainful glance"—Я кинув довкола зневажливий зір). Laughter replaced moans and, to all intents and purposes, the poet's spiritual afflictions vanished ("I do not feel my wounds"—Я не чую ран). Pierrot is now actually capable of stepping back and examining his own split personality:

Я—жертва погасаючого світу.
Я—поранений звір [...]
Дух мій в захопленні можливостей футурних
І в крові—безліч архаїчних атавіз...
("Zhertva. Ego-Ego futuryza"; Semenko 1919m).

I am a victim of a dying world
I am a wounded animal...
My spirit is in the throes of future possibilities
But my blood is full of countless archaic atavisms.

While admitting that he is an adolescent chasing girls ("I am a boy and my dream is a debutante"—Я ще хлопчик, і моя мрія—панна), Pierrot nevertheless predicts that he will become Harlequin ("Wait, tomorrow I will rise as Harlequin"—Чекайте, завтра я арлекіном встану; Semenko 1919g; see also 1925a, 343). In essence, Pierrot strives to free himself from the world of feeling and sentiment to which he is hostage. He expresses a loathing for "idiotic sniveling" (Я ненавидю...ідіотські похлипування) (Semenko 1925a, 348), he seeks skies "devoid of metaphysics" and yearns for a poetry that does not "agitate the soul with memories" (ibid., 342 and Semenko 1919e, 13). In the poem, "Pierrot is Able," subtitled, "An

[6] This book was subdivided into three sections: "Mertvopetliuiu," poetry of 1918; "Poezofiry," poetry of 1914, and "Erotezy," poetry of 1914–1916.

Inimitable Poeza," Pierrot suggests that he is no longer vulnerable to the romantic and symbolist world view, declaring that whatever inadvertent links there may have existed are now severed:

Я готовий приймати отруєні стріли!
Я готовий до зустрічі символістів і крамарів!
Всі нитки між нами перегоріли!
Але я не згорів!
("P'iero mozhe. Poeza bezzrazkovosty"; Semenko 1919f).

I am ready to accept poisoned arrows!
I am ready to meet symbolists and shopkeepers!
All threads between us have gone up in flames!
But I am not burned out!

In tandem with this psychological transformation, the last act of Pierrot's melodrama inaugurates obvious innovations in theme and form. Semenko's alter ego embraces the city: steel, concrete, rocks, and smokestacks become the new emblems of his poetry, marking a sharp departure from the natural environment (for example, the sea) that had nourished his spirit to this point. Most important, however, is the way Semenko consciously tries to deviate stylistically from his previous work. The lyrical properties retreat in the face of a decidedly rhetorical manner. A stichic organization of the verse begins supplanting what was to this point a predominantly strophic structure. There is an attempt to eschew rhymes, use enjambment, and endow the line with more consonantal timbres. In some poems even the voice of the protagonist disappears, together with punctuation. The last few poems of the cycle become fragmented, elliptical, and cryptic. Semenko had not written anything like the following since 1914:

фффф
дмухкало пирхкало
шшшш
шипіло шумно за машиною [...]
("Misto"; Semenko 1919d).

ffff
it puffed it huffed
shshshsh
it swished shrilly behind the machine

The same is true for "Memoir," which begins:

Трикнуло, зойкнуло—
                                        безпідставно—
—розгублено.
Схопилися.
Хе, всміхнулись!
Хрустнуло в животі.
    Звір! [...]
("Spohad"; Semenko 1919h).

A crack, a howl—
                                        without reason—
—confused.
They leaped up.
Ha! They smiled!
A crunching in the stomach.
    Animal! [...]

Months before the Pierrot complex played itself out in public, Semenko had already published *Dev'iat' poem* [Nine Narrative Poems]. This was the second collection of 1918, and one of the earliest expressions of a desire to break free from his psychological and formal impasse. The first poem of *Dev'iat' poem* actually prefigured the struggle that would only later emerge full-blown in *P'iero mertvopetliuie*:

Зір мій опереджує електричний ток
моя безсонність переборює в мені звіря
моє натхнення увільняє мене від аморфности
моя геніяльність зруйновує спокій обставин
я почуваю себе без меж
я почуваю себе над-расовим
і над-культурним
я змагаюсь з безсиллям погасаючих атавіз,
я становлюся майбутнім і сильним...
("La futurition. Poème philosophique"; Semenko 1918c)

My gaze anticipates the electric current
my sleeplessness vanquishes the animal in me
my inspiration frees me from amorphousness
my genius destroys the calm of the status quo
I feel myself without limits
I feel myself above races
and above cultures
I struggle with the weakness of receding atavisms
I am emerge future-like and strong...

For the first time in *Dev'iat' Poem* Semenko abandoned his favorite genre, the lyric, for the narrative poem—albeit, for now, a very short one. The poems were not only longer than anything he had written before, but more importantly were less obviously subjective and egotistic than his previous work. Semenko successfully effaced himself, curbed the first-person approach in favor of a detached, almost impersonal portrayal of city life. Each poem, save one, had a French subtitle denoting its "type" (Poème philosophique, Poème éléctrique, Poème objectif, Poème social, etc.). Semenko's entirely novel manner of exposition here—couched in long, rambling periods of prose-like verse—focused on urban commonplaces, in particular the seamy and aberrant:

> Перед фонтаном, в заснувшому скверику, самотньо ворушив
> заломленими губами маніяк.
> Публіка з садів і електричних театрів розходилась по каварнях.
> Садист на темнім розі, перестрінувши солодку мрію, притулив
> енергійно до жіночої спини свій стек.
> Маленький цуцик зупинивсь отриножено біля загороженого
> корня.
>
> Верлен сидів очезпідбровено за мармуровим столиком,
> Спостерігаючи силуетні рухотіни за вікном отемреним.
> В телефонній будочці панна інтимно-випадково розмовляла
> з Семенком.
> Електрика освітлювала дзеркальну залю обезпаморочено...
> ("Intérieur. Poème objectif"; Semenko 1918b).
>
> *Near a fountain, in a sleepy square, a maniac was desolately moving his*
> *broken lips.*
> *Crowds emerging from gardens and electric theaters disappeared into*
> *cafes.*
> *A sadist on a dark corner apprehended his sweet dream and energetically*
> *pressed his horsewhip into the woman's spine.*
> *A small puppy froze like a tripod near a fenced stump.*
>
> *Verlaine sat with downcast eyes behind a marble table,*
> *Watching the silhouettes of moving shadows behind a darkened window.*
> *In a telephone booth a debutante spoke intimately and casually with*
> *Semenko.*
> *Electric lights soberly lit up a mirrored hall...*

Even though his rhymes and quatrains called to mind earlier practice, there can be no doubt that in *Dev'iat' Poem* Semenko made important strides in turning his back on the past.

Much the same can be said for the eighty lyrics of *Bloc-Notes* [Writing Pad] composed during 1918 but published only in the winter of 1919. In this instance Semenko held on to the lyric form but stripped it of its intimate character, again avoiding, for the most part, references to his own persona. These were not records of feelings or emotions but rather representations, frequently wry and cynical, of urban life. The typical work here was laced with cloying neologisms (most frequently based on the prefix *o*-, as in "окінематографований," "оковдрадиться," "оалеєний," etc.) and dealt with erotic motifs, which, significantly, were neither romantic nor sentimental. This environment was preeminently carnal, populated with amorous couples, provocative prostitutes, and sensuous young ladies (*panny*).

З насмішкуватою посмішкою похитувавсь розпалено
Ілюмінований по японському електричний монастир.
Ще лише 10 годин вечору—вона прямує впевнено
У чорний сквер.

Була відважна елеґантка і мила
Виріз колін на сукні випадково зменшений
Приставала розводила руками і говорила:
Це ж свинство. Невже ніхто не хоче женщини!
("Vona"; Semenko 1919l).

Smiling sardonically, the electric monastery,
Illuminated à la Japanese, swayed ablaze.
It's only 10 P.M. but she heads confidently
Into the black square.

She was a brave fashion plate and precious
The casually short skirt showed her knees
She would approach, spread her arms and say:
"This stinks. Doesn't anyone want a woman!"

In *Bloc-Notes,* as in *Dev'iat' poem,* Semenko was moving further and further away from the literary repertoire that cherished nobility, beauty, and idealism. He develops an eye for the "Maniac with a Gothic soul" [Маніяк з душею ґотичною] and for "Mounds of blue female bodies" [Купи блакитних жіночих тіл]. Even his turn of phrase suggests Semenko would sooner speak as a bureaucrat than as a "poet":

Приймаючи до уваги, що місто сьогодні ілюміноване,
А також те, що панни йдуть у сад у білих строях,—

Я скину почування поміркуване
І спущусь на улицю в гороховім настрої…
("Sv. Sil'vestru"; Semenko 1919i).

Taking into account that the city today is illuminated,
And moreover that the ladies are entering the orchard in white outfits,—
I will cast off my sensible feelings
And go down into the street in a really bad mood.

As we have seen already, Semenko's attempt to regenerate his poetic self hardly proceeded in an unbroken line. In 1918, along with the above, he wrote several cycles that easily were more retrospective than prospective. Not all of them were published immediately (some appeared as late as 1920), as a result of which Semenko's literary persona remained in continuous flux. Take "Vinok tremtiachyi" [Trembling Wreath] which made its debut in December of 1918 (Semenko 1918f). On the surface it resembled a crown of sonnets, except that it violated nearly every rule of the form. Its impersonal, almost epic invocation of a metropolis is reminiscent of *Dev'iat' poem,* but here everything is couched in a magisterial, sonorous lexicon and atmosphere—гірлянди [garlands], смерть [death], сон [dream], чорний жах [black fear], дракони [dragons]—which can only be described as symbolist: "The park whispered: Christ's strength is with us" [І парк шептав: Христова сила з нами].

Another cycle from 1918—*V sadakh bezroznykh* [In the Roseless Gardens], subtitled "Saturnalia" [*Saturnalii*]—shows Semenko in an equivocating, transitional mood, greeting young aviators in one breath (Я вітаю вас молоді авіятори) and confessing to the agonies of his quest in the next [Мені—моїх шукань агонії] (Semenko 1919k). In the twenty-six lyrics of "Himny sv. Terezi" (Hymns to St. Theresa, 1918; Semenko 1920; 1925a, 287–97),[7] the voice of the paladin is monolithically weak and lovelorn. In tones at once prayerful and erotic, he addresses his beloved without either shame or cynicism.

Semenko reached a clear watershed in his poetic career in 1919, the year that saw the publication of three long narrative works—"Tov. Sontse" [Comrade Sun], "Vesna" [Spring], and "Step" [Steppe] (Semenko

7 The year of composition is indicated in *Kobzar* (Semenko 1925a). For a recent reprint and discussion, see Semenko 1992 and Sulyma 1992, respectively.

1919-20a, 1919-20b, and 1919-20c, respectively). Devoted as they were to the theme of revolution, these poems marked the beginning, so to speak, of Semenko's "Soviet" period. After all, to this point his work had almost completely eschewed overtly social and political topics. The appearance in 1919 of the last of his love cycles (*P'iero mertvopetliuie* and *V sadakh bezroznykh*) was thus symbolic: they culminated a long preoccupation with intimate themes that had started with *Prélude*. While the subject of women and love would certainly recur in his later writings, Semenko would never again devote an entire collection to such private matters, and certainly would not approach them with the same direct ingenuous passion. In 1919 the question of Semenko's own dualism, i.e., his disparate and contradictory personality, would be raised several more times and then conclusively and effectively buried.

The imminent demise of his "Pierrot complex" was signaled most unambiguously in the short verse drama, *Lilit* (*Scènes pathétiques*) [Lilith], a parody of Symbolist writings (Semenko 1919c).[8] The work incorporates the tradition of the *commedia dell'arte,* but in place of Pierrot, Harlequin, and Columbine, the cast consists of Lilith and two antipodal male characters, identified simply as The First [*Pershyi*] and The Second [*Druhyi*]. The First is a poet with a typically modernist-symbolist sensibility, preoccupied with divine and utopian dreams. At one point he declares: "I am a romantic. My songs are sad and naive" (Semenko 1925a, 429). Lilith is the embodiment of his ideals. In contrast, The Second is a self-proclaimed "villain" [*kham*], a "victor and tramp" with "no room for sadness," having been "redeemed by the automobile." Lilith associates The First with "inspiration"; The Second evokes in her "dissonance." In the struggle for Lilith's heart, The First offers her "eternal" dreams and beauty; The Second promises only "temporary" carnal pleasure, to which Lilith succumbs. Eventually, The First dies:

Ліліт:
Як прекрасно він умирає—
Від туги смертної, від блідих думок! [...]
Другий:
І як це льогічно—наш романтик сконав! [...]
І з ним умирають усі похилі....
(*Lilit;* Semenko 1925a, 450).

Lilith:
How beautifully he dies—
A consequence of deathly yearning and pale thoughts!...

8 Published earlier also in *Mystetstvo* 1920 (1): 17–33 and reprinted in *Kobzar'* (1925a).

> The Second:
> *And how logical this is—our romantic has croaked!...*
> *And with him die all the forlorn...*

The Second predicts that Lilith will forget the late romantic during a "morning of metal hours." As the curtain drops, Lilith sings farewell to her dead "dreams."

Dualism is rejected again, this time in a less absurd manner, in *Prozopisni* (*spirali*) [Prose-songs (Spirals), 1919], a cycle of nineteen prose poems narrated by Semenko's romantic, sensitive, and lyrical persona (Tryroh [Semenko] 1919). The mode is entirely abstract, symbolist, and subjective. The axis around which these "Spirals" turn is the self. As in previous works, there is tension between the old and the new ("Everything old follows me. My heart pursues the new"), even as the narrator anticipates an immanent transformation: "I weep before the new resurrection." The cycle is bereft of any irony or sarcasm until nearly the very end. At that point, the object of ridicule becomes Semenko himself. In a charming instance of self-parody, he, playing the role of a bumpkin, enters the city...and is immediately run over by an automobile:

> Одверто виставив душу—розхрістаний і неохайний. Стою на порозі—слухаю й розмикаю рота.
> Чи не з лісу я?—
> Мене витягли з—під автомобіля. Він полетів далі, застерігаючо сурмлячи в тумані
> ("Prozopisni. (Spirali)"; Tryroh 1919, 18).

> *Candidly I exposed my soul—unbuttoned and slovenly. I stand on the corner—listening, gaping.*
> *Am I perhaps a native of the forest?—*
> *They dragged me from under the automobile. It flew on, the horn sounding a warning in the fog.*

Unfazed, the poet moves on, declaring:

> Брати мої близькі, я за вас ліг на шляху міськім і пізнаю вагу машин і колес....витягайте мене знову, в останній раз...
> (ibid., 19).

> *My dear brothers, I have fallen in the city streets for your sake and I am discovering the weightiness of cars and wheels....Pull me out again, one last time...*

As these works attest, there is no question that by 1919 the private, vulnerable, and lyrical persona—the wounded animal in him, to use Semenko's phrase—was swiftly losing ground to a voice at once public, assertive, and ironic. This was also a time when Semenko's formal vicissitudes became less frequent and sharp, although they did not disappear entirely. His neologisms—which in some cycles tended to be employed to the point of distraction—were tamed and found a more functional and natural place in the poetry. His spoken, informal vocabulary and syntax began to show a broader range, ultimately encompassing everything from low slang and intentionally substandard utterances to a neutral accentual verse that attained a certain rhetorical eloquence. Some of these qualities are already manifest in the long revolutionary poems of 1919.

The *revfutpoema* (i.e., revolutionary futurists narrative poem) "Tov. Sontse" [Comrade Sun] (Semenko 1919–20a), and the *poezofil'my* (i.e., poetry-films) "Vesna" [Spring] (1919–20b) and "Step" [Steppe] (1919–20c) introduced more than just a sociopolitical dimension into Semenko's poetry: they introduced a new genre. These three lyrico-epic narrative poems were the longest works Semenko ever wrote. Critics were sharply divided about them. Andrii Nikovs'kyi was convinced they were "worthless," even though he thought the title, "Tov. Sontse" was brilliant, expressing "almost everything about those who have been swept up by the wave of revolution." The colloquial style of the works, however, struck him as uncontrollable chatter; the dynamic compositional technique was compared to an abandoned movie camera recording events haphazardly, and only on occasion "fixating individual phenomena rather accurately and interestingly." On the whole he was quite appalled by these "colossal vermicelli" (Nikovs'kyi 1919, 113–14). Iakubs'kyi was of a different mind. For him these poems signaled a new beginning. He too complained about "Vesna's" length (the longest of the three works), but ranked them all among Semenko's best achievements (Iakubs'kyi 1925, 252–54).

"Tov. Sontse" is a dynamic and enthusiastic work. Its structure combines revolution with Semenko's favorite themes: the city, art, and self-aggrandizement. The opening lines are—again—an exorcism of the "Pierrot complex," an address to the "pale and tender" followers of Saturn, which, naturally, included himself, the author of various "saturnalia." Semenko embraces the revolution here in the voice of the "victor and tramp." The tone ranges from grandiloquence to coarseness ("We'll make hamburgers of the bourgeoisie"—З буржуя ми зробимо котлету), even to blasphemy ("And God leaned over the curbstone and died"—І Бог схилився на тумбу і вмер). Epic scenes of revolution alternate with down-to-earth episodes, banalities ("I have thick boots, and lice in my mouth"—У мене чоботи грубі, І є воші в губі), references to friends (Kurbas, Marko Tereshchenko), politicians (Volodymyr Zatons'kyi) and, of course, himself:

> Роздягнусь біля Хмельницького,
> Покажу всім
> Що в мене красиве тіло…
> ("Tov. Sontse"; Semenko 1919–20a)
>
> *I will undress near Khmel'nyts'kyi's monument,*
> *and show everyone*
> *that I have a beautiful body.*

The theme of social and, to some extent, personal renewal permeating "Tov. Sontse" animates "Vesna" as well. This is a hopeful and optimistic poem that begins on a melancholy note, almost as stream of consciousness:

> Весна.
> Злетіло з нервових уст.
> Потер рукою лоб.
> Але хто повірить?
> Від палтьо відірвався ґудзик,
> Відтягує руку футляр.
> Хе, музикант!
> Ти покажи скрипку
> І настрой гучно.
> Тоді я повірю, що ти уже був на Володимирській горці.
> Сіпни за рукав бльондинку
> І відмовся від сонетів.
> Хе, музикант!
> Весна
> ("Vesna"; Semenko 1919–20b; 1925a, 469).
>
> *Spring.*
> *It flew off nervous lips.*
> *He rubbed his forehead.*
> *But who will believe it?*
> *A button was missing on the coat.*
> *A violin case tugged at the hand.*
> *Huh, a musician!*
> *Show me the fiddle*
> *And tune it well.*
> *Then I'll believe that you've been on Volodymyr Hill.*[9]
> *Tug a blonde by the sleeve*
> *And reject all sonnets.*
> *Huh, a musician!*
> *Spring.*

9 A park in Kyiv above the Dnipro River.

The first section of the poem stands out from the other four rather starkly. It is a series of disjointed, cryptic thoughts, phrases and observations, very reminiscent of Semenko's "divided" self: one moment mischievous ("I will shave my head as last year"—Я поголю голову, як торік), the other morose ("I weep"—Я плачу). But after acknowledging his duality ("O sun! Let's start a spring riot and share a splintered heart"—Сонце! Здіймемо весняну бучу і поділимось серцем розколотим!), the poet shifts from subjective, ego-centered concerns to external, social themes. The poem unfolds as a kaleidoscope of revolutionary events and impressions, alternately visionary and exhortative. The change in tone and orientation implies that personal doubt and divisiveness can find resolution in social action. Typically, the revolution is seen as an occasion for psychological renewal.

Ще не всі однакові
Перед відновленням,
Нецікаво заплакані,
Затурбовані виконанням
Ще не в усіх наперед очі
І на устах прийдешнє,
Один ще ласий до борщу,
Другий агітує за яєшню. [...]
Ні, ще не всі ми варті
І не всі розплутані [...]
Не ми вторимо ясність
І прийдешність нового слова
Ми підбиті й зламані
Зойкаєм під галас промов,
Але в очах немає сліз,
І ми, безхвості, веселі [...]
(ibid., 482)

As yet, not everyone is equal
Before the renewal,
Some are insipidly weepy
Worried about performance
Not all eyes gaze straight ahead
nor lips speak the future
Some have an appetite for borscht
Others agitate for scrambled eggs [...]
No, not all of us are worthy
And not all are untangled [...]
It is not for us to create clarity
And the future of the new word

We are trampled and broken
We moan to the sound of speeches,
But there are no tears in our eyes,
And we are tailless and happy. [...]

Semenko's personal fate assumes tragic dimensions in this poem: he sees himself as the "last corpse," destined for death precisely because of his dualism ("I'm condemned, condemned to die / Because one can't live divided"—Засуджено, засуджено вмерти, / Бо не можна жити надвоє).

"Step," with its allusions to class struggle and communes, is the most "social" of the three works. Revolution implies the city, the machine ("The steppe will be filled with the aroma of gasoline"—запахне бензиною серед степів), and the retreat of the past:

Умерло степу дідівське й звичне
діди старі доживають кутках
("Step"; Semenko 1919–20c; 1925a, 506).

The ancestral and familiar died [in] the steppe
old men end their days [in] corners.

The omission of prepositions in the preceding lines is indicative of a characteristic practice during this period.[10] The asyndeton, for example, is regularly employed in the cycle *Preriia zor* [Prairie of Stars], completed in early 1920.[11] Subtitled "a poem-novel," it chronicles a love affair in halting accentual verse set in quatrains. The frequent ellipses of prepositions as well as other words make the meaning ambiguous in places and the syntax problematic.

February 1921 saw the release of *Prominnia pohroz* [Rays of Menace], a small collection of poems from the years 1919–1920 (Semenko 1921b).[12] In tone and style, this was one Semenko's most polished and harmonious books, although not necessarily his most optimistic. The short lyrics—intimate, but not subjective or sentimental—had neither neologisms nor flashy rhymes. Although purposely understated, they possessed vivid details and sharply delineated psychological moods, the most dominant of which was expressed in these lines:

10 The Soviet Ukrainian edition of his works consistently reinstates the prepositions. See Semenko 1985.

11 This cycle was scheduled for publication in 1921 but appeared only in *Kobzar* (Semenko 1924c).

12 There were 34 poems in this publication. When Semenko republished these works in *Kobzar* he expanded the cycle by an additional nine poems.

Я не хочу думати, я не хочу думання,
Думка стомлена
("Zhertva vechirnia"; Semenko 1921d).

I do not want to think, I do not want thinking,
Thought is exhausted.

Elsewhere Semenko says, "and sad, sad am I" (і сумно, сумно мені). His dark disposition can be traced to revolution and war, here divested of the romantic enthusiasm that characterized the "poetry-films." The theme is no longer change and renewal, but death:

Після пожарів
місто в кістяках чорних...
(ibid., 28).

After the fires
the city is full of black skeletons.

Such images recur:

Їх лежало 23 роздітих—
без голів і обідраних—
вони теж були материні діти
і волосся тремтіло на вітрі.

Без шкури й напівзасипані
вони поєднують живих і мертвих
це ж трупи, кров'ю зліплені,
і я не боюся вмерти
(ibid., 25).

Twenty-three lay naked—
missing heads and in shreds—
these too were mothers' children
and the wind rustled their hair.

Skinless and half-buried
they unite the living and the dead
they are corpses, joined in blood,
and I am not afraid of death.

Elegiac tones also prevail in two poems dedicated to the slain Hnat Mykhailychenko and Vasyl' Chumak. But *Prominnia pohroz* does not aspire toward tragedy; it is sooner a testament to emotional exhaustion and numbness. About the only surviving feelings are pity and empathy, as in this unusual poem:

Вузенькою стежкою на передмісті,
Спираючись на стек
Прислухалися вуха до завірюхи
І рот ловив сніжинки.

Упала одна за комір—
Бідна сніжинка—
І розтала.
Бідна сніжинка впала.
Бідна сніжинка.

Запалив люльку
Руку міцніше стис.
Довга, вузенька—
Стежка—
В снізі на передмісті.

Куталось серце в хутро,
Щулилось в муфті—
Бідна маленька ручка
Змерзла.
Крутились сніжинки
("Snizhynky"; Semenko 1921c).

Along a narrow path on the outskirts,
Leaning on a stick.
Ears were listening to the winter storm
And the mouth was catching snowflakes.

One fell behind my collar—
Poor snowflake—
And melted.
A poor snowflake fell.
Poor snowflake.

I lit my pipe
Firmly squeezed my hand.
A long, narrow—
Path—
On the outskirts, covered in snow.

My heart snuggles in the fur,
Sheltering in the muff—
Poor tiny hand
Frozen.
Snowflakes swirling.

In *Prominnia pohroz* Semenko proved, again, rather convincingly that his discursive, idiomatic voice was a complex instrument, capable of subtlety, not just ostentation.

Semenko's most uncharacteristic and unexpected composition of this period must be *Marusia Bohuslavka* (Semenko 1927b). Penned in 1921, this verse drama was based entirely on folklore motifs. It is a traditional tale about the liberation of Cossacks from Turkish captivity. In manner, language, and style it could pass for one of Lesia Ukraïnka's works, especially in view of its elevated style, nobly expressed passions, and psychological, deftly drawn characters. Except for the erotic theme—focus is on the tragic love between Marusia and the sultan—the play embodied everything Semenko on other occasions consciously avoided. Its presence in his oeuvre can be explained only by the fact that it was written as a libretto to an opera being composed by Mykhailo Verykivs'kyi (1896-1962).[13] Conventional though it was, *Marusia Bohuslavka* did serve Semenko as an occasion for mystifying his critics. When it was published for the first time in 1927, reviewers were chagrined by the unexpected absence of all "destructive" elements in the Futurist leader's work.[14]

During the years 1921–1922, Semenko completed a series of "visual" poems,[15] a cycle of lyrical verse with the mysterious title "Zok" (1921), a long, rhetorical "Poema povstannia" ["Poem of Rebellion," 1920] and a short but humorous "Promova" ["Speech," 1922], which commemorated an imaginary "festive public meeting of the jubilee committee marking Mykhail' Semenko's ten years of literary activity." This group of works ranged from satire, parody, and exhortation, to egotism, obnoxiousness, and eroticism. Formally and ideologically, they were some of Semenko's most radical works to date. Especially noteworthy was "Poema povstannia," which prefigured in style and tone his own later poetry and the works of others in *Nova generatsiia*. Whitmanesque and Maiakovskian, it employed rather effective, free-flowing rhetoric. It recalled a few of Semenko's other poems, dating back as far as 1913, in which he foretold his transformation and entry into the modern age. "Poema povstannia" was at once programmatic, confessional, scandalous, humble, and egotistical:

13 This is made plain in *Arena* 1 (1922) March: 18.

14 See Iu. Savchenko 1927.

15 "Kablepoema za okean" [Cablepoem Across the Sea, 1920-21]; "Moia mozaika" [My mosaic, 1922]. For details see below chapter 10, "Visual Experiments in Poetry and Prose."

Я перегорів за вас всіх
Я перестраждав за сучасність […]

Поети, на нас дивиться всесвіт!
Забудьте про минуле
І свої грішки […]

Поете
Зроби
Злочин!
Щоб батько вважав за жулика
Щоб відцуралась рідня! […]

Я щедрий і безсоромний
Я сиджу з вами за одним столиком
І б'ю вас по фізіонімії
А ви всміхаєтесь. […]

Я ні над чим не задумуюсь
І повторюю чужі слова
І кажу що це мої
Що це з душі. […]

Я гасло сучасности,
Центральна фігура доби. […]

Я
Наївний і великий […]
("Poema povstannia [Spetsial'noho pryznachennia]"; Semenko 1925l)

I have burned out for the sake of you all
I have suffered in the name of the present […]

Poets, the universe looks upon us!
Forget the past
And your peccadilloes […]

Oh, Poet
Commit
A crime!
So that your father might consider you a rogue
While your dear ones renounce you! […]

I am generous and shameless
I sit with you at one table
And slap your face
But you smile. […]

I don't belabor anything
I repeat the words of others
And claim them as my own
As products of my soul. […]

> *I am the slogan of the present,*
> *The central figure of this age* [...]
> *I am*
> *Naive and great.* [...]

The final poem in Semenko's *Kobzar* was dated December 1922. Emblematic of just how far Semenko had traveled since 1910 was the fact that his last lines were a Dadaesque "ready-made" poem, consisting of nothing more than the seven days of the week arranged in a column ("Ponedilok" [Monday]; 1925m). Its first publication (in Russian translation!) had been a joke in itself.[16] Viktor Petrov (V. Domontovych) would later capture the spirit that animated poems like this by writing: "Why must we consider the poetry of Lesia Ukraïnka or Ryl's'kyi more interesting than numbers enumerated to a hundred or a thousand?" (Domontovych 1947, 29).

Semenko composed no poetry in 1923 and 1924. The extant published record indicates that he resumed writing only in 1925. Prior to this, his only original works were full-page revolutionary slogans *(hasla)*, published in *Zhovtnevyi zbirnyk panfuturystiv* (1923). Reprints made up the bulk of his literary output. The year 1925 saw the appearance of a second edition of *Kobzar* (Semenko 1925a); a collection of previously published poetry dating from 1919–1920 entitled *V revoliutsiiu* [Into the Revolution] (Semenko 1925c),[17] and a revised edition of "Steppe" (Semenko 1925b). A half dozen new poems were published during 1925–26 in the periodic press. But the first substantial concentration of works (eight to be exact) was printed only in *Zustrich na perekhresnii stantsiï* (1927). A year later *Malyi kobzar i novi virshi* [The Small Kobzar and New Poems] was issued, containing forty-four works from 1918–20, and eleven for the period 1925–26 (Semenko 1928j). Obviously, as Semenko turned his energies elsewhere (i.e., toward organizational matters, the editorship of Futurist publications and theoretical writings), his poetic productivity dropped off precipitously.

The poetry of 1925–26 is at once similar and different from what came before.[18] Semenko's basic themes remain intact. He writes personal,

16 It appeared originally as "Stikhotvorenie" in *Katafalk iskusstva* 1922 (1): 1. See Semenko (1925a, 627).
17 This cycle of poems appears in *Kobzar* under the title, "Prominnia pohroz II."
18 I refer to works published in *Zustrich na perekhresnii stantsiï. Rozmova tr'okh* (Kyiv, 1927) and *Malyi kobzar i novi virshi* (Semenko 1928j).

intimate verse about himself, exposing his vulnerability and pain; the erotic motifs (love, sex, women) remain strong; the city continues to occupy a prominent place, as do literary-artistic themes. On the whole, however, the poems acquire distinctly severe and dark colors; this is especially true of his love lyrics which speak of prostitutes and abortions.

The group of poems published in *Zustrich na perekhresnii stantsiï* begins, appropriately enough, with what could be construed as an overture to his second debut. "Zavod im. Mykh. Semenka" [The Mykhail' Semenko Factory] signals the start-up of Semenko's poetic "production" after an acknowledged lull. It is a sturdy, concise poem rendered in accentual verse of one and two stresses per line, exploiting a "proletarian" language that fluctuates between Russianisms and the standard norm:

...знову прийшло
времня
моє—
запрацювала моя машина:
Хто сказав—що
без труб?
Хто ето
сказав—що
без
диму?
("Zavod im. Mykh. Semenka"; Semenko 1927h).

...again
my time
has come—
my engine starts:
Who said—
no smokestacks?
Who is it
that said—
no
smoke?

Another poem on the subject of art and creativity from this period bears the title "Vseukraïns'ke puzo" [The All-Ukrainian Gut], a satirical invective against bourgeois tastes in art. Foul-mouthed, employing a Ukrainian-Russian lingo, the poem is in the tradition of the anti-aesthetic poetry found in *Nova generatsiia*[19] and prefigures a tendency especially prominent in several works by Mykola Bazhan (for example, "Rozmova

[19] See, for example, Ievhen Iavorovs'kyi, "Reabilitatsiia T. H. Shevchenka" (Iavorovs'kyi 1928).

serdets'" [A Conversation of Hearts]). Semenko's poem opens with these lines:

Лізе—лізе на нас—
стид і срам—
(з очима виряченими)
не ананас а
поетичний
бізнесман,—
....
«Ідеї твої—...
дайош нам!"
    А слина в роті,
    а ноги точаться,
    а рило свиняче [...]
Вишкірило пельку
беззубу
всеукраїнське пузо....
("Vseukraïns'ke puzo"; Semenko 1928l).

It's coming—it's coming at us
shame and disgrace—
(eyes bulging)
not a moron
but a poet-
businessman,—
....
"Give us [...]
your ideas!"
    Mouth foaming
    legs wobbling
    and the snout of a pig [...]
The all-Ukrainian gut
displayed
its toothless gullet...

A markedly different tone takes over in the urban poetry, which ranges from solemn praise of the new communist city (for example, "Remont" and three poems entitled "Leningrad"; Semenko 1928j, 91, 93–103) to more personal lyrics, defining the meaning of the city in his own life and work. The following lines are from the poem "Misto" [City]:

Так зрадив я предків,
і дітей, і жінку,
і зробивсь для степів

чужинцем,
і серце моє отверділо
для минулих ран,—
що мені за діло
до чумацьких караванів,
до свиток і плахт—
коли я не Робінзон Крузо
й улицями міста
сновигають брати мої
в синіх
блузах?

Я довірився місту,
що стукотить і реве...
("Misto"; Semenko 1928m).

Thus I betrayed my forefathers,
and children and wife,
and became a foreigner
in the steppe,
and my heart grew numb
to past wounds,—
what are wagon caravans
to me
peasant jackets and skirts
when I'm not Robinson Crusoe
and my brothers scurry
on city streets
dressed in blue
shirts?

I've put my faith in the city
that rattles and roars.

Although Semenko claimed here that his "heart was growing numb," other verses revealed a far more thin-skinned individual. The poem "Krym (samotnist')" [Crimea (Solitude)] (Semenko 1927e) and "Pisnia trampa (Moïi dochtsi)" [Song of a Tramp (To My Daughter)] (Semenko 1926) are excellent evocations of loneliness and ostracism. They are rendered with utmost emotional restraint and couched in a depressing calmness. As in his earlier poetry, love proves to be the most debilitating of forces. In the following lines it is conveyed ironically.

Коханням
зараз поранений я
і вийшов—на час—з лав.

Я почуваю себе йолопом зрання—
вас не дивує, що я такий став?
("3 NP"; Semenko 1927a).[20]

By love
I am wounded
I leave—for now—its ranks.
I feel myself an idiot, early in the morning—
are you not surprised at what I've become?

But this theme has a darker side as well, and the lyrics in *Zustrich* are some of Semenko's most painful. They are primarily about prostitutes. "Vona" [She] (Semenko 1927f) portrays the varying personalities of several women and their relationship to the narrator; "Pisnia trampa (Ти—горе—горе моє)" [Song of a Tramp, (Oh, Misery, My Misery)] (Semenko 1927g) expresses the revulsion and pain involved in loving a streetwalker. The most unusual of the poems is the enigmatically titled "6 NP," a mournful apostrophe to a fetus which is about to be aborted. It is simultaneously brutal and tender, written in Semenko's typical prosaic style. The fetus is addressed both as a human being and as bodily waste that is about to be dropped in a bucket and flushed as sewage into the sea. This poem is a far cry from Semenko's Pierrot cycle. Whereas before he expressed himself with excitable pathos, here his feelings are tightly curbed and brought under rational control.

Тобі—дитино моя—що завтра на аборт підеш—
Тобі—що тільки місяць йому—
Тобі—що місяць як зародилося, а живеш мільони віків у
животі цієї жінки що я люблю—
Місяць уже тобі, а завтра ти—ніщо, викинуть твій кавалочок у
відро з помиями—
І попливеш ти каналізаційною трубою аж у Чорне море, де й
зародилось од мене—
Тобі—
Тобі—
Тобі це
("6NP"; Semenko 1927i).

For you—my child—who will be aborted tomorrow—
For you—who is only one month old—

[20] The meaning of "NP" in the title and in other poems of this cylce remains unclear (perhaps, *nova poeziia* [new poetry]). M. Khvyl'ovyi suggested (spitefully, of course) that it stood for "horse power." See "Vstupna novela" (1927) in Khvyl'ovyi (1989, 16).

For you—who was born last month but lived a million years in
the belly of this woman I love—
You are a month old; tomorrow you'll be—nothing. They will throw your
little scrap in a bucket with slop—
And you will float down the sewers into the Black Sea, where you were
conceived by me.

For you—
For you—
This is for you....

Except for the three long narrative poems of 1919 and a few others written at various times, it can hardly be said that Semenko's verse belongs to the category of *littérature engagée*. However, there is no difficulty in applying this designation to works that appeared in *Nova generatsiia* and in the collection *Evropa i my* [Europe and We, 1930] (Semenko 1930l). In fact, the period from 1927 to 1930 saw his work become increasingly more topical, civic-minded, and political, reflecting the growing politicization of literature and society. While some poems narrowly responded to the sociopolitical orders of the day (singing the praises of communism, the five-year plan, or combating alcoholism; Semenko 1927d, 1928k, 1930k), others succeeded in fusing situational requirements with such typically Futurist concerns as urbanization, electrification, and mechanization (Semenko 1928b; 1929b). In terms of form Semenko's poetry shows no retreat, but the eccentric and scandalous elements steadily wane. Satire and irony remain a potent weapon in his artistic arsenal, but they are less frequently used against targets of his own choosing. More often than not, the butt of his criticism also suffers official political censure.

The "social" character of Semenko's verse is conveyed in part by the genre designations it receives (for example, "pamphlets" and "open letters"). Moreover, his highly individualistic, somewhat perverse, and fickle alter egos yield to a more "responsible," public voice, given to oratory. Significantly, this period contains very few lyrical, subjective, or personal works, the only possible exception being two poems that bear the identical title, "My Raid into the Future," but even these are not without sociopolitical connotations.[21] Semenko's primary focus now

[21] The first poem appeared in the Latin transliteration used in *Semafor u Maibutnie* (1922): "Mii reid u vichnist' [Мій рейд у вічність]" (Semenko 1928e). The second was printed traditionally: "Mij Rejd U Viqnist'" (Semenko 1929c). However, the comments to this poem (in the table of contents) were transliterated in Latin letters.

turns to literary and cultural politics, and related issues like the nationality question, attitudes toward the political emigration, and the global confrontation between capitalism and socialism (Semenko 1928i). However, for the time being, even these august issues are not entirely safe from his humor:

Соціялізм—
це не прекрасні
очі,
що про них ми
мрісмо
глупої
ночі
("Sotsializm i alkohol'"; Semenko 1931f).

Socialism
is not "beautiful
eyes,"
which we dream
about
on sottish
nights.

Semenko's literary-cultural polemics are exemplified by two "open letters," one addressed to the Marxist critic Volodymyr Koriak, the other to the director Les' Kurbas (Semenko 1928h and 1928g, respectively). The epistle to Koriak was derisive and sarcastic, touching on the literary battles that had taken place between him and Mykola Khvyl'ovyi. In 1927 Koriak had taken Khvyl'ovyi to task for advocating the separation of Ukrainian culture from Russian influence and other ideological deviations (Koriak 1927). Shortly afterwards, in the journal *Vaplite*, Khvyl'ovyi attacked Koriak for identical "political errors" that were committed eight years earlier in the journal *Mystetstvo* (Khvyl'ovyi 1927).[22] Semenko's letter-in-verse gleefully alludes to these events and takes a well-aimed shot at both opponents by revealing that it was he, as former editor of *Mystetstvo*, who had brought Koriak's article to Khvyl'ovyi's attention. Khvyl'ovyi, without expressing gratitude for this "bibliographical" reference, says Semenko, used it to attack Koriak. Semenko's "letter" serves as a mock apology to the critic:

Я перед Вами завинив—
своїми власними руками
ах!

[22] See also Koriak's article "Chystylyshche" (Koriak 1919).

о ах !
о жах !
Хвильовому очі розкрив—
щоб потім він Вас
У Вапліте вбив.
("Odvertyi lyst do tovarysha Volodymyra Koriaka"; Semenko 1928h)

I stand guilty before you—
with my own hands
ah!
oh, ah!
oh, horror!
I opened Khvyl'ovyi's eyes—
and let him destroy you
in Vaplite.

The letter to Kurbas is realized in a different tone, reflecting the close relationship the two had earlier. The poem is at once intimate and cold:

Говорять всі і
знають всі, що
ми з Вами—давні особисті
друзі.
Кинемо старі краватки й
коридорні плітки
й поговоримо
про нашу теперішню
в наших відносинах
смугу.

Почнемо з того, що не всім
відомо:
що ми перестали буть друзями.
("Odvertyi lyst do tov. L. Kurbasa"; Semenko 1928g)

Everyone says and
Everyone knows that
You and I are ancient personal
friends.
Let's drop all pretense and
corridor gossip
and talk
about the present phase
of our mutual
relationship.

Let's begin with what
many do not know:
namely, that we are friends no more.

Semenko attributes the rift between himself and Kurbas to the latter's insincerity, as well as his abandonment of the avant-garde in favor of "restorationist" art and the playwright Mykola Kulish. Although there is evidence in the poem that the parting of ways was painful, it also suggests that both men ultimately valued their respective artistic principles more than the friendship:

Я наговорив «прикростей» і «нетактовностей»,
зворушений образою.
Але я не хочу, щоб в нашу культуру
дмухнуло боягузною
заразою!
(ibid.).

I've said much that is "unpleasant" and "untactful,"
having been moved by indignation.
But I can't allow into our culture
gutless winds of
debilitation.

The artistic differences between Semenko and the group around Kurbas was the subject of another poem several months later. In "Pro epokhy i s'ohodnishnikh blikh" [About Epochs and Contemporary Fleas] he satirized Kurbas, Khvyl'ovyi, and Kulish as "epochal people" who think of "eternity" but fail to perceive the present (Semenko 1930g).

Semenko's major poetic contribution to *Nova generatsiia* was a lengthy five-part work under the title "Povema [*sic*] pro te iak povstav svit i zahynuv Mykhail' Semenko"[23] [A Novem[24] About How the World Was Created and Mykhail' Semenko Died], a parody on nationalism, provincialism, and narrow-mindedness. In effect, the poem summarizes Semenko's long-standing antipathy for those who did not take a broad international and contemporary approach to Ukrainian culture. The

[23] See Semenko 1927–29. Two excerpts, under the title "Povema pro te, iak povstav svit," appeared in *Suchasni virshi* (Semenko 1931e) and in *Poezii* (Semenko 1932c, 146–53).

[24] "Povema" is Semenko's neologism which is derived from a fusion of the words *povist'* and *poema* (novella and poem). Hence, my English translation.

work is innovative, clever, and amusing—no doubt one of Semenko's wittiest satires. It also remains unfinished.

The "Povema"—deliberately published in a random chronology—recounts, mostly in the form of inane dialogues, the adventures of six members of an imaginary "All-Ukrainian Chapter of the International Club of Inventors, Eccentrics, and Interplanetary Communication," who set out to explore past eras in a time-machine operated by Semenko. He is joined by Kh. Vyl'ovyi (a footnote tells the reader not to confuse this character with M. Khvyl'ovyi), D. Dontsov, V. Vynnychenko, a Bishop of the Ukrainian Autocephalous Church, and an Old Man (a co-op activist). The travels of these eccentrics include an encounter with the First Man, which elicits from each character a highly typical response:

> *Єпіскоп* [*sic*]:
> Адам! Адам!
> *Всі:*
> Де?
> *Єпіскоп:*
> Та он із-за скелі дивіться яка чортяка суне.
> *Винниченко:*
> Людина!..
> *Єпіскоп:*
> Свят! Свят! Свят!
> *Дід:*
> Ох ти ж боже ж мій!..
> *Донцов:*
> Стійте! [...]
> Хто сказав—печерна людина? [...]
> Та це ж свій чоловік! [...]
> Це—українська печерна людина!
> і повстала вона
> таки з нашої української
> малпи. [...]
> Ви подивіться на тип писку—
> український предок наш
> ("Povema pro te iak povstav svit i zahynuv Mykhail' Semenko"; Semenko 1927–29, 1: 4–5).
>
> Bishop:
> *Adam! Adam!*
> All:
> *Where?*
> Bishop:
> *There, behind the cliff. Look at that fiend approaching.*

Vynnychenko:
It's Man!
Bishop:
Holy! Holy! Holy!
Old Man:
Oh, dear Lord!
Dontsov:
Hold on! [...]
Who said it's a cave man?
Why, he's one of ours! [...]
This is a Ukrainian cave man!
and he evolved
most certainly from our own Ukrainian
ape. [...]
Just look at that archetypal kisser—
Our Ukrainian ancestor.

The work is full of playful literary allusions, like the following to Pavlo Tychyna's lyric poem "Arfamy, Arfamy..." [Like Harps, Like Harps...]:

Дід:
Невже весна?
красна?
закосичена?..
(ibid., 1: 3).

Old Man:
Is it spring already?
beautiful?
braided?

The "Povema" employs unusual devices, including backward syntax and truncated words. Compare the following dialogue which takes places immediately after the creation of the world:

Х. Вильовий:
Готова!
Куля!
Земна!
Дід:
То можна й сходити вже?
Семенко:
Ні!
Зачекати краще,
доки проведуть
меридіяни й
паралé.

Під'їхати
ближче
можна,
але…
Винниченко:
Я прошу
сло!..
Семенко:
Хто про?
Нема.
Але говоріть коротко,
швидко
зима
бо.
Винниченко:
Шановні товариші!
Перед на…
куля земна.
Дід:
Й ні
душі.
Винниченко:
Як і всі,
я дуже ра…
Семенко:
Це вам не в Центральній
Зра…
Донцов:
Гальо! Я побачив
Укр !
Гальо! Гальо! […]
(ibid., 2: 105–106).

Kh. Vyl'ovyi:
Ready!
Planet!
Earth!
Old Man:
Can we disembark now?
Semenko:
No!
Better wait,
until they
lay down meridians and
latitu[des].

> *Approaching*
> *closer*
> *is possible*
> *but...*
> Vynnychenko:
> *I request*
> *the flo!*
> Semenko:
> *Who says na*[y]*?*
> *No one.*
> *But speak briefly,*
> *soon*
> *winter*
> *because.*
> Vynnychenko:
> *Dear Comrades!*
> *In front of u[s]...*
> *the planet earth.*
> Old Man:
> *And not*
> *a soul.*
> Vynnychenko:
> *As is everyone*
> *I am very hap...*
> Semenko:
> *You're not speaking in Betrayal*
> *Central.*
> Dontsov:
> *Hello! I saw*
> *Ukra!*
> *Hello! Hello!*

Semantic meaning is sometimes reinforced through graphic emphasis, as here:

> *Семенко:*
> Ми спускаємось
> знов на якусь землю.
> Землю
> емлю
> млю
> ю
> (ibid., 2: 23).

Semenko:
We are descending
again onto some planet.
Planet
anet
net
t.

At other times punctuation marks (e.g., "?", "!") replace words entirely to imply surprise, inquiry, or mute silence. The tongue-in-cheek atmosphere, the puppet-like characters, and the strange language create the impression of a modern-day *interludium.*

Of the poetry Semenko published in journals other than *Nova generatsiia*, his poems about Berlin (written in January of 1929 when he was a visitor in that city) are especially noteworthy. In these works the poet recreates a majestic, bourgeois, decadent, and capitalistic city, suspended perilously between fascism and proletarian revolution. Poems like "Chornyi Berlin" [Black Berlin] (Semenko 1930p) and "Alt-Berlin" [Old Berlin] (Semenko 1929a) are written in long lines of heavy eloquent accentuated prose that strictly adhere to the standard literary language. These poems are a far cry from the minimalist, sparse, colloquial, and jocular "Povema," even though the chronological distance separating the two is insignificant (the last installment of the "Povema," for example, appeared in February 1929). Compare:

Чорний Берлін зустрів мене гуркотом важких машин,
чорний Берлін зустрів мене в грудні димом своїх відтулин,
чорний Берлін осліпив мене гулом своїх вогнів,
чорний Берлін зустрів мене, чужоземця, ґранітом генеральських
чобіт, вдавлених монументами в землю
("Chornyi Berlin"; Semenko 1930p).

Black Berlin welcomed me with the rumble of heavy machines,
black Berlin welcomed me in December with the smoke of its chimneys,
black Berlin blinded me with the noise of its fires,
black Berlin welcomed me, a stranger, with the granite of generals' boots,
buried by monuments into the soil.

Between 1930 (the year of *Nova generatsiia*'s demise) and 1933 Semenko managed to publish eight books of poetry, including the last two volumes of *Povna zbirka tvoriv*.[25] In 1936, approximately one year before his execution, he published *Vybrani tvory* [Selected Works] (Semenko 1936b). This last collection contained the long narrative poem "Nimechchyna" [Germany] which Semenko had been writing since 1933. Its opening stanza grotesquely paraphrased Whitman while paying obeisance to Stalin:

> Я ще раз співаю радянське життя!
> Я захвату повний знову,
> і знову вдихаю бадьорий цвіт—
> епохи Сталіна мову
> ("Nimechchyna"; Semenko 1936a, 93).
>
> *I sing once more the Soviet life!*
> *I'm full of zeal again,*
> *and again inhale the cheerful bloom—*
> *the language of Stalin's epoch.*

These lines illustrate how inexorably the political situation of the late 1920s and early 1930s chipped away at Semenko's poetic personality. For all its polemics and partisanship, the collection *Evropa i my*—which contained works from 1928 and 1929—still bore traces of Semenko's trademark, namely, a predilection for experimentation, urban themes, and parody. But the liberty of filtering social and political events through one's own eccentric self was swiftly being eliminated with every new poem and publication. In the late 1920s Semenko's temperament still came through in lines like these:

> Subway, Metro, Untergrund, підземка—
> які чудесні потвори—плюс ще 1000-тонний кран!
> Це ж не урбанізм тільки, а якась індустріялізована істерика
> для наших радянських хуторян!
> ("Pidzemka"; Semenko 1930e).
>
> *Subway, Metro, Untergrund, Underground—*
> *what wondrous monsters—plus a thousand-ton crane!*
> *This is not just urbanism, but some kind of industrial hysterics*
> *meant for our Soviet yokels.*

[25] *Evropa i my. Pamflety i virshi (1928–1929)* (Semenko 1930l); *Povna zbirka tvoriv* (Semenko 1929–31, II and III); *Suchasni virshi* (Semenko 1931g); *Kytai v ohni. Poezii* (Semenko 1932b); *Poezii* (Semenko 1932c); *Z radians'koho shchodennyka. Poezii, 1930–1931* (Semenko 1932d); *Mizhnarodni dila. Publitsystychni virshi 1932–33* (Semenko 1933).

and in parodies (this one on Shevchenko but in reference to Germany):

Село.…І серце відпочине…
З вікна ваґону, над шосе—
висока кірха, маґазини,
циґар реклями і касет
("Selo"; Semenko 1930h).

A hamlet…And the heart breathes easy…
Through the train's window, above the highway—
a church stands tall, department stores,
ads for cigars and cassettes.

Even when Semenko turned toward partisan politics, he managed to maintain his own peculiar voice, lexicon, and point of view, as in this work from January 1929, which bore the improbable title, "Konkretna propozytsiia do vsikh literatury, mystetstva i nauky robitnykiv, shcho ïkh NKO chy inshi vidpovidni ustanovy maiut' vidriadzhaty u zakordonnu poïzdku" [A Concrete Proposal to All Workers in Literature, Art, and Science Who Are Being Sent by the NKO {The People's Commissariat of Education} or Other Comparable Ministries on a Foreign Trip] (Semenko 1931c). The poem begins by stressing the importance of Europe:

Товариші!
Говорю серйозно: без европ нам—
як попам
без душі:
обійтись ніяк не можна —[…]
("Konkretna propozytsiia…"; Semenko 1931c, 46)

Comrades!
In all seriousness: without Europe we
are like priests
without souls:
it's difficult to manage […]

The contradiction between the need to travel and the Soviet Union's hard currency shortage is solved in this way:

…Отже, коли Респулбіка каже, що валюти
чорт–ма,
і щоб не було між нами зайвих спорів,—
давайте урегулюємо командировочну ділему,
щоб не було тут страшної
проблеми.
Я пропоную виробити спеціяльний список,

щоб зобов'язував би кожний командирований
писок...

Тоді
за невеличку валюти горку
ми їздили б
за кордон
усі
щороку
(ibid., 46–47).

...Thus, when our Republic tells us it has a goose egg's worth
of hard currency,
and to avoid needless arguments among us,
let's regulate our foreign trips,
to avoid some terrible
problem.
I propose we make a special list
that would oblige each traveling stiff. [...]

Then
for a small hill of money
we'd all travel
to a
foreign
country yearly.

By 1930 these sort of light-hearted and irreverent verses were increasingly more difficult to justify. Irony, sarcasm, a sense of distance (even alienation) from one's own milieu—traits so characteristic of Semenko's work—became politically untenable. Semenko compensated to some extent for this loss of individualism by republishing earlier works. Sixty percent of the poems included in *Suchasni virshi* [Contemporary Poems, 1931] (Semenko 1931g) had been composed before 1930, among them one against Russian imperialism, dated 1925 ("Imperiia i my" [The Empire and We]). A section of the poem contained this ditty:

Гей,
Москва, Москва,—
ти кров пускала
і кров ссала
не раз, не два...
("Imperiia i my"; Semenko 1931b).[26]

[26] By 1936 the reference to Moscow was deleted and replaced by the word "tsars." See Semenko (1936b, 16).

Hey,
Moscow, Moscow,—
you spilled blood
and you sucked blood
not once, nor twice [...]

Poezii [Poetry, 1932] (Semenko 1932c), too, provided a broad overview of work from 1914 to 1931. However, the scales tipped in the other direction with *Z radians'koho shchodennyka* [From a Soviet Diary, 1932] (Semenko 1932d), poems from the years 1930–31. The sentiments and themes here were totally predictable, synchronized with the political currents of the day. Semenko donned a sober voice, and in tones of humorless communal pathos, patriotism, and xenophobia, sang exhortative, boastful, and didactic songs about interventionists, party cadres, hard-working miners, counter-revolutionaries, and the leading role of the Communist Party.

The book *Mizhnarodni dila* [International Affairs, 1933] (Semenko 1933) continued in the same vein, but with a slight increase in technical ingenuity. The effect this had on the two narrative cycles contained therein ("German Affairs" and "American Stories") was dubious. They gave the impression of being a cross between political invective and nonsense verse.

If Semenko's three decades of writing proves anything, it is that he was a restless poet. He dared to take Ukrainian poetry into new territory and use the Ukrainian language in unthinkable ways. Through methods both subtle and forthright, he challenged his readers to think of poetry, literature, and the writer in completely new ways.

Geo Shkurupii (1903-1937)

Shkurupii published his first collection of poetry at age nineteen. Its cryptic title *Psykhetozy* [Psychetosis, 1922] (Shkurupii 1922e) bore an equally puzzling subtitle: "Display Window Three" [*vitryna tretia*]. Soon afterwards *Baraban* [Drum, 1923] appeared as "Display Window Two" (Shkurupii 1923e). A major literary periodical of the day greeted Shkurupii's debut with the headline "Fools" (Rolenko 1922). The reviewer's verdict: anachronistic, derivative, and without any promise of an artistic future. *Psykhetozy*'s thirty-two pages, it was said, manifested the influence of no fewer than twelve writers.[27] Shkurupii, averred the

[27] Mentioned were Igor' Severianin, Vladimir Maiakovskii, Filippo Tomasso Marinetti, Fedor Sologub, Aleksei Apukhtin, Leonid Andreev, Mykhail' Semenko, Iakiv Mamontov, Oleksander Oles', Charles Baudelaire, Velemir Khlebnikov, and Valeriian Polishchuk.

critic, had no identity. "There is no Shkurupii. None at all. Emptiness prevails." And on a more ominous note: "There will [never] be a proletarian poet Shkurupii. There will [only] be a café clown, a little gentleman, a scribbler" (ibid., 62).

A year passed and Shkurupii's talent was appraised again. This time, Maik Iohansen, a theoretician and innovative writer in his own right, discerned only the imprint of Aleksei Kruchenykh's and Vladimir Maiakovskii's "ingenious" sound experiments which, he said, dwarfed Shkurupii's own efforts. "With all due respect to...*Psykhetozy*, there is nothing in it that can be singled out. It is simple *épatement* that is ten years too late" (Iohansen 1923a). *Baraban*'s so-called "healthy elements," however, evoked a more sanguine comment. Iohansen argued that as soon as "Shkurupii removes from his head the theatrical headgear of the 'King of the Futurist Prairies' [a sobriquet that appeared on the collection's cover], and renounces the honorific rank of 'Sidewalk Poet,' then he will become, if not a poet of the revolution, than a prominent poet of the revolutionary period" (ibid.). Several years hence, on the occasion of Shkurupii's collection *Dlia druziv poetiv suchasnykiv vichnosty* [For My Poet-Friends, the Contemporaries of Eternity, 1929] (Shkurupii 1929f)—a volume summarizing nearly a decade of verse—one reviewer came to this overdue conclusion: "The relationship between poet and critic, especially in cases where the poet belongs to a leftist [i.e., avant-garde] movement, remains, as always, fairly complex: the conservative doctrinairism of a conscientious but shortsighted criticism elicits haughty contempt from the 'free genius.' [C]riticism...does not know how to tackle, how to approach these insulting 'enfants terribles' of our poetry..." (Starynkevych 1929a).

Notwithstanding Shkurupii's rough treatment at the hands of critics, there is every reason to regard him, in Iohansen's phrase, as a "prominent poet of the revolutionary period" and to treat his poetic work as a "significant achievement" (Iohansen 1923a, 189).[28] In the Futurist repertoire, his poetic oeuvre is one of the best and largest.[29] Thanks to a penchant for innovation, an antipathy to lyricism, a deliberate engagement in political and literary polemics—Shkurupii's legacy stands as an apt and an ample example of the movement's poetic practice.

[28] Quite unexplicably, Shkurupii's poetry is missing from a recently published six volume anthology of Ukrainian poetry. See *Antolohiia Ukraïns'koï poeziï v shesty tomakh*, 1984–1986. An analogous publication in the 1950s—*Antolohiia ukraïns'koï poeziï v 4-kh tomakh*, 1958—contained three of his poems.

[29] Besides the collections mentioned above, Shkurupii also published *Zharyny sliv. Vybrani poeziï* (Shkurupii 1925c).

A survey of Shkurupii's poetry must necessarily begin with a closer examination of that first offending publication, *Psykhetozy*. While it contained much that could have exasperated conservative literary tastes (eroticism, narcissism), the collection, contrary to what Iohansen would have his readers believe, was not concerned simply with bashing the bourgeoisie. A consciously "constructed" book, it was a sophisticated fusion of poetry with graphic design—a typical manifestation of the Futurist movement. From the visually arresting cover and intermittent use of Latin script, to the layout of its twenty-three poems (printed without capitalization or punctuation, with titles running vertically in large block letters beside the text) *Psykhetozy* made an immediate claim to being more than an ordinary reading experience. This was driven home by four accompanying illustrations (in effect, posters) depicting various machines. Each carried a slogan that oscillated between earnestness and humor. "Science, Technology, Sport and Art of All Countries, Unite!" declared one in Ukrainian and German. Beneath an image of a turbine, the message continued with a Dadaesque twist: "Build New Machines and Factories, New Instruments and Sound Orchestras! Let Us Perfect the Music of Noise." Another picture of a locomotive proclaimed: "By Means of Engines, by Means of Engines of the Intellect, We Will Destroy the Prejudices of the Heart." On a more personal and clearly comic note, Shkurupii advertised his personal "word products." One bilingual Ukrainian-French placard ("Fabrication mécanique et non chimique") provides mostly bogus publication sites[30] for Shkurupii's books and cautions buyers: "Beware of Imitations." The subtitle, "Display Window Three," was obviously an allusion to the visual and commercial motifs permeating the volume. Certain poems make direct reference to this: "I will smelt wonderful words / and exhibit them in display windows" [переплавлю слова чудесні / і виставлю у вітринах] (Shkurupii 1922a). In other verse, he purportedly employs words for the manufacture of industrial goods. Thus, in "Vyrobnytstvo" [Production], "porcelain and steel words" turn out, among other things, tanks and women's clothes.

However, the primary "products" of this collection were not material but psychological. This may explain the neologism *Psykhetozy*. But even the titles of the poems attest to an overwhelming focus on internal (that is, mental) realities: "Ochikuvannia" [Expectations], "Radisno" [Joyfully], "Hniv" [Anger], "Bozhevillia" [Frenzy], "Sum" [Sadness], "Zazdrist'" [Envy], "Odchai" [Despair]. Significantly, none of the works becomes an occasion for sentimentality or lyrical introspection. Shkurupii may have

30 Three Ukrainian cities are listed as well as Vienna, Prague, and Winnipeg.

enjoyed flaunting his ego, but he betrayed emotions reluctantly. For the most part, therefore, passions are depersonalized. "Odchai" [Despair], for example, renders its psychological mood rather grotesquely, by being at once sad and ludicrous. Characteristically, it almost completely effaces the persona experiencing this condition:

Собакою диким вовком
вити на місяць
душить пече
синій камінь
душить пече
рогом незґрабним корова нещастя
саданула в груди
ой ой ой
кишки
з живота падають не зупинить
уп'ялась аж у місяць
незґрабна рогами
уукає корова нещастя
а ай а ай
("Odchai"; Shkurupii 1922f).

Dog-like wolf-like
to howl at the moon
chokes burns
the blue stone
chokes burns
with its clumsy horn the cow of misery
thrusts into my breast
ouch ouch ouch
guts
come tumbling from the belly no way to stop
horns sunk into the moon
the awkward
mooing cow of misery
oh my oh my

"Odchai" reveals much not only about *Psykhetozy's* anti-lyrical posture, but also about the collection's formal features, in particular, its free verse, the liberties it takes with syntax, and the way it exploits abstract sounds. Here Shkurupii's syntax is highly elliptic; the sense units are mostly disjointed words or phrases. The poem "Vokhko [*sic*]" [Humid], for example, contains a line made up only of an interjection and two pronouns: "ох ми я" [oh we I]. But few works are as atomized. The majority tend toward a more traditional word order, using short colloquial phrases or incomplete sentences.

Although Shkurupii's sound experiments were disparaged by Iohansen, they deserve attention. Some were inspired by the contemporaneous Dada movement (one poem is actually titled "Dada").[31] Others drew on a wide spectrum of avant-garde traditions, Italian as well as Russian. "Avtoportret," for example, represents both a visual exercise and a play with etymology and morphology. Shkurupii's first name, Geo, is employed in a narcissistic game of free association (*geo*grapher, ego, *geo*logist). The following, rendered in the original Latin script, is the text of the full poem:

geo O ge
ego
geo Wkurupij
geometr i
ja
geograf i
ja geo
log i ja ego
evrop A f r i k
si
merik A vstrali A
geo O ge ego
Geo Wkurupij
A V T O P O R T R E T
("Avtoportret"; Shkurupii 1922g)[32]

This poem is clearly analogous to Semenko's self-portrait of 1914, which, however, used the Cyrillic alphabet and gave less emphasis to graphic elements:

Хайль семе нкоми
Ихайль кохайль альсе комих
Ихай месен михсе охай
Мх йль кмс мнк мих мих
Семенко енко нко михайль
Семенко мих михайльсе менко
О семенко михайль!
О михайль семенко!
("Avtoportret"; Semenko 1925k, 112).

In both instances an apparently Cubist principle is at work: the authors fragment the self, take an analytical approach to their own person,

[31] In *Zharyny sliv* (Shkurupii 1925c) the title was changed to "Kolyskova" [Lullaby] but was later restored again to "Dada" in Shkurupii (1929f, 47).
[32] The transliteration system is identical to one used in *Semafor u Maibutnie* 1922 (1).

examining it from several perspectives. Shkurupii tries on a number of identities (geographer, geologist, egotist, etc.). For both poets, but especially for Semenko, the exercise, leads to an epiphany, a sudden discovery about one's self.

Shkurupii's other poems took pleasure in pure sound, striving apparently to liberate language from meaning. Such was "Lialia" [La-La], which contained a single comprehensible word, "boomerang," suggesting perhaps an invocation of Australian aborigines. The relevant section reads:

бумеранґ бумеранц
пфуїті твіті лю
лю
банґ банґ
ре мікі мікі мікі
шанґ танґ
("Lialia"; Shkurupii 1922i).

boomerang boomerants
pfuiti tviti liu
liu
bang bang
re miki miki miki
shang tang

A more frequently employed sound technique involved using interjections, abstract and onomatopoeic sounds to evoke or reinforce subconscious, primordial emotions. The intention was most frequently parodic and subversive. "Dada," for example, creates a false sense of warmth and nurture through soothing nonsense sounds and diminutives (Уо / Маленький хлочику / Уо, аа) [ooh oh/ O Little boy / ooh oh, ah ah], but shatters the mood brutally with an unanticipated crude ending: "Your big-breasted mommy / is all embraces, / all love" [Твоя цицата пенька / вся обійми, / вся любов]. "Sum" [Sadness] intensifies a melancholic mood by resorting to pathetic, meaningless sounds: "Like a fly struggling / confused feelings / buzz stubbornly: ah mem yamy mem!" [...б'ються мухою / зплутані почуття, / дзичать настирливо: а мем ями мем!]. The poet's disdainful attitude toward this frame of mind is revealed at the conclusion by a sudden vulgarism: "Unnoticed tears flow / along the silken snout of pensiveness..." [Непомітні сльози котяться / по єдвабній морді задумливости...]. In another poem ("Misiashno" [*sic;* Moonlit]), Shkurupii recreates sounds of dogs and humans howling at the moon: "uu vav av uu av." Such devices, clearly, had nothing in common with etymological experiments à la Kruchenykh. Shkurupii's sounds appealed to the irrational and subconscious, and was more in the spirit of Dada.

Another prominent characteristic of the collection was its mannered exoticism, embodied in references to the Eiffel Tower, mustangs, alligators, remote continents and lands (Klondike, Yukon, Alaska). While much of what Shkurupii did in *Psykhetozy* was not destined to be repeated in later works, this fondness for the strange and distant would survive well into the decade.

Psykhetozy can give the impression that Shkurupii entered poetry as a full-fledged disciple of the avant-garde. A glance backward and sideways at his career paints a more complex picture. Like Semenko, but to a much lesser degree, he deliberately worked at purging himself of lyricism and emotionalism. Shkurupii went through a period in which his effete and timid voice—an undesirable remnant of Modernism and Symbolism—was gradually restrained. This process is evident in "Neniufary" [Water-Lilies, 1921] (Shkurupii 1921), a poem of feeling, personal transformation, and avowed vulnerability. Here, the poet still vacillates between life and death, coldness and passion, the old world and the new. His psychological and philosophical dualism is expressed through formal equivocations: on the one hand, free verse and neologisms bring to mind Semenko (for example, *optashylys', omoleni*); on the other, his sense of cosmic consciousness evokes memories of Pavlo Tychyna. The lexicon of love, soul and heart, church and prayer combines awkwardly with expressions like "factory smoke stacks," "human masses," and "red terror." Shkurupii manages to suggest in "Neniufary" a new adamant spirit but does so only tenuously and haltingly.

Some aspects of this psychological discord survive in "Tykhshe, misto" [Be Still, City] (Shkurupii 1925e), one of his many urban poems. In this instance, the city is anarchic, depraved, exotic. The opening lines are rendered in a futuristically eccentric syntax, but words like "*molytvy*" [prayers], "*sviatyi iezuit*" [holy Jesuit], "*sviata*" [holidays], "*panna v chornomu*" [maiden in black] continue to be reminders of Symbolism (and most obviously Aleksandr Blok). Within this context, rather unexpectedly, one also encounters words like "bushmen," "Mexico" and "prairies," which makes "Tykhshe, misto" a strange and stilted linguistic brew.

Doubt and diffidence are banished more resolutely in "Semafory"[33] [Semaphores, 1922]. Moreover, as a counterpoint to his prevailing

[33] First published in *Semafor u Maibutnie* (1922 [1]); republished in *Shliakhy mystetstva* 1922 (1): 8–9.

egocentrism and narcissism, certain signs appear implying that the poet is beginning to identify with the collective. Even though an occasional religious image still intrudes—"The semaphores stretched their hands / to the sky / in despair…" [І семафори руки простягнули / до неба / з одчаю…"]—and "all people still suffer from epilepsy" [всі люди хворіють на чорну неміч], the poem's dominant mood is conveyed by the phrase, "the beauty of Ruin" [краса руїн].

An even more cardinal transformation in tone takes place in "Zalizna brama" [The Iron Gate] (Shkurupii 1922h). It contains the lines "Brothers and sisters / We will feel how sorrow perishes" [Брати і сестри! / Ми відчуємо, як гине печаль] and the refrain: "Woe, woe to the powerless!" [Горе, горе безсилим!]. A loud, expansive poem that has nothing in common with the sotto voce utterances of "Neniufary," "The Iron Gate" advances its exhortative message against a background of brutal images: war, violence, rape, and prostitution. Some of its rhetorical flourishes are rather effective:

Коли заломлять руки,
в отчаї заплачуть над трупом,
коли уб'ють мого батька,
заріжуть матір,
зґвалтують сестру,
я буду мовчать
і келих печалі не дам другому вихилити.
Коли ж запитають, чому мовчу,
я відповім:
—Горе, горе безсилим! […]
("Zalizna brahma"; 1922h)

When they wring their hands,
weep in despair for the corpse
when they murder my father,
butcher my mother,
rape my sister
I will remain mute,
and I will deny others the cup of sorrow.
When they ask, why are you silent,
I will respond:
"Woe, woe to the powerless!" […]

"Semafory" and "Zalizna brama" were included, rather appropriately, in *Baraban* where there were relatively few traces of Modernism or Symbolism, and where a marked tendency toward an aesthetics of ugliness and coarseness made an appearance. "Kapeliukhy na tumbakh" [Hats on Posts], for example, purposely debases its content which, on the surface, is high and noble. The lyric voice of this poem belongs to a self-professed "savage and poet" who sings of "tramps" and "waifs" [*patsany*]. This thoroughly urban, déclassé mentality exploits religious terms (for example, icon, prayer, church, incense, Mother of God) for the sake of parody and shock:

А навколо люде і коні,
ватаги пацанів і трампів,
вітрин блискучі ікони
з хлібом і наїдками.

Мій товариш
до шкла приплюсне носа,
і фанатично молиться
гладкій ковбасі,
цій богородиці нашого храму,
де ладаном курить автомобіль
("Kapeliukhy na tumbakh"; Shkurupii 1923h, 7).

All around—humans and horses,
droves of waifs and tramps,
and the shiny icons of storefronts
brimming with bread and foodstuffs.

My friend
glues his nose to the glass,
and utters fanatical prayers
to the fat sausage,
this madonna of our temple
in which the incense of automobiles burns.

An aesthetic credo of sorts is espoused by Shkurupii toward the end of this poem. It calls for the embrace of things urban and uncommon, and advocates a rhetorical strategy that is destructive, aggressive, and hectoring:

Вітаю танець будинків,
розклад і смерть всього звиклого!
І коли критики
Облізлими мордами
Щирять на мене
Зуби лисих коняк,
Я люблю їх,
Як алігатор любить пташину,
Що колупається
в його зубах [...]
(ibid., 9).

I welcome the dance of buildings,
the decay and death of the ordinary!
And when critics
With their shedding snouts,
Flash at me
The teeth of balding nags
I love them,
The way an alligator loves a birdie,
that picks
at the dirt of his teeth. [...]

As the above shows, invective and vituperation (modes popular with the Futurists) readily went hand in hand with locutions designed to offend polite society. Shkurupii, in particular, was inclined to vulgarities (e.g., *svoloch*, *stervo*), and coarse, almost clinical, description.

Ціла армія
одвислих цицьок
і задниць
приймає військовий смотр. [...]
("Vy"; Shkurupii 1923d, 10).

Коли місяць,
гнилим носом сифілітика,
понюхає цегли міста,
ваше пузо
псом скиглить [...]
(ibid., 11).

A whole army
of dangling tits
and butts
line up for an army inspection. [...]

When the moon,
sniffs the bricks of the city
with the nose of a syphilitic,
your gut
whines like a dog [...]

This style is used in the inscrutably titled "Likarepopyniada," a political jeremiad which occupied seventeen of *Baraban*'s sixty-two pages. This quasi-epic sings the "disgrace" [*han'ba*] of a host of weak-kneed enemies of Ukraine. History and politics are couched in a language that is, at best, indelicate:

На нашу Вкраїну,
на вашу неньку,
на цей шматок падла
без ніг
і без голови,
історія висипала пригод опеньки,
—всю бутафорію
революцій і війн [...]
Зосталась
величезна задниця,
з хліба, сала
і цукру [...]

Голову загубив Хмельницький,
а ноги Мазепа,
залишилась одвисла цицька
і приголомшений степ [...]

Ох! в задницю в'їлися раки:
праворуч Москва,
ліворуч поляки,
а прямо шибениця!
О, загубилась,
заблукалась
між трьома цими соснами
українська душа!
("Likarepopyniada"; Shkurupii 1923a).

On our dear Ukraine,
on your motherland,
on this piece of carrion
without legs
and no head,
history has spilled mushrooms of mishaps—
all the baggage
of revolutions and wars [...]
What's left is a
huge rump
made of bread, lard,
and sugar [...]

Khmel'nyts'kyi lost her [Ukraine's—OI] *head,*
Mazepa—her feet
All that's left is a drooping tit
and a comatose steppe [...]

Oh, crabs nip at her rump:
on the right—Moscow,
on the left—the Poles,
and ahead—the gallows!
Among these three pines
Ah, is lost,
gone astray—
the Ukrainian soul.

Less frequently, and with more irony, this anti-aestheticism finds application in renderings of one's self. In "Liryka futurysta" [Lyric of a Futurist], Shkurupii paints this unflattering self-portrait:

У мене розпухла морда
і болить зуб
У мене стала пика гордою
од одвислих губ [...]

і тепер я подібен
до бога готентотів [...]
Собі мій гімн я складаю з охотою [...]
("Liryka futurysta"; Shkurupii 1923b).

I have a bloated snout
and a tooth that hurts
My mug looks proud
thanks to a sagging mouth [...]

and now I resemble
the Hottentot god [...]
I gladly compose a hymn to myself [...]

Not all poems of *Baraban* adopt this base approach, however. "Holod" [Famine] (Shkurupii 1925i) is realized as a first-person, rhetorically elevated supplication. "Feed me, comfort me" [Нагодуйте мене, зогрійте!] are the opening lines spoken by a personified Famine. In place of a low lexicon, Shkurupii resorts here to the grotesque. Famine is portrayed as a pathetic hybrid, a cross between a patrician and a mongrel:

Я загорнувся в подерту ковдру,
мов римський патрицій у тогу,
і мені страшенно зимно в ноги.

О сонце!
Я хочу потертися спиною
об твоє гаряче обличчя [...]
("Holod"; 1925i).

I am wrapped in a tattered quilt
like a Roman patrician in his toga,
and my feet are frozen stiff.

Oh, sun!
I'd like to rub my back
against your smoldering visage [...]

If in some early poems, Shkurupii worked hard to rid himself of the past, "Aerokoran" (Shkurupii 1923i)[34] shows him unwaveringly embracing the future. This is a prophetic vision of speed, machines, and global urbanization, inspired by the rhythms of an airplane's propeller. In elevated, exalted tones, the poet surveys past and future, and finds solace among the human masses: "I see enraged mobs of people, / I comprehend their frenzy, / inside these mobs I feel myself" [Я бачу роздратовані юрби людей, / я розумію їх сказ, / в цих юрбах я відчуваю себе]. In this context, too, backward Ukrainians are infused with a new boundless, inquisitive spirit:

Ех, коли б хоч раз:
- На Марс!
- На Марс!
Чухає потилицю кожний дядько
("Aerokran"; Shkurupii 1923i).

Oh, if only once:
—To Mars!
—To Mars!
Says every old man, scratching his nape.

After *Baraban*, Shkurupii's repertoire continued to include modishly destructive works. Among the more interesting is "Mashyna" [Machine] (Shkurupii 1925j). Ostensibly a sound poem, it is, however, less abstract than other works of this category. Because of its rudimentary syntax, recognizable vocabulary, it is susceptible to a coherent, if not entirely precise, understanding. The obstacle toward full comprehension lies in "Mashyna's" barrage of recurring sounds and staccato rhythms, which constantly work to subvert its semantics and threaten to strip it of its embryonic meaning:

Мент дум
не жде,
грому глум
дінеш де?

[34] Appeared originally in *Semafor u Maibutnie* (1922 [1]).

Блиск спис,
мент зойк
болю тиск [...]
Ах!
Кров [...]
("Mashyna"; Shkurupii 1925j).

The instant of thoughts
doesn't wait,
thunder's scorn
do what with?
Glint of spears
moment shriek
throbbing of pain [...]
Ah!
Blood [...]

In contrast to Semenko who was obsessed with intimate and erotic themes, Shkurupii seems almost intentionally evasive on this score. The only strictly intimate cycle to emanate from his pen bore the name "Romansy banali" [Romances of the Banal],[35] a title which speaks volumes about his approach to matters of the heart. In general, there is greater indirection and restraint in Shkurupii's treatment of these themes; his persona is less emotional, less softhearted than Semenko's. Therefore, one cannot describe as entirely characteristic poems like "Mantry" [Mantras, 1921] and "Barabany pechali" [Drums of Sorrow, 1922], which treat love (either as an emotion or as a physical act) sincerely, without passing the experience through some intellectually distorting prism. In most cases, however, his erotic verse is infected by irony or facetiousness, as in "Ieva" [Eve, 1921]:

Моя Єва навчилась носити
великі капелюхи,
курить папіроси
і цілувать зів'ялі айстри
("Ieva"; Shkurupii 1929l).

My Eve is good at wearing
giant hats,
at smoking cigarettes
and kissing wilted asters.

[35] This title was applied to three poems that appeared initially in *Chervonyi shliakh*: "Vohkist' vust" (Shkurupii 1923c), "Zhdan'" (Shkurupii 1924b) and "Predsontszoria" (Shkurupii 1924c). In *Dlia druziv poetiv suchasnykiv vichnosty* (Shkurupii 1929f) fourteen poems fell under this heading.

Shkurupii's "Zhdan'" [Expectation, 1924] (Shkurupii 1924b) may well exemplify the proper way a Futurist should handle love, especially one who, on principle, rejects writings about paramours and abjures going public with "petty emotions" and the grieving soul (Shkurupii 1924a, 11). "Zhdan'," paradoxically, does all these things but in an aggressively de-idealized manner, as if begrudging these emotions their power. Thus, the poem begins with exaltations [о, як пізно приходиш ти!—"Oh how late is your arrival!"], but ends on a note of pure animal lust:

> Мої руки твої перса пестили,
> і всі женщини мене дратують стегнами тепер [...]
> У мене в грудях од цього пес виє
> і я те й те зжер би [...]
> ("Zhdan'"; Shkurupii 1924b).

> *My hands caressed your breasts,*
> *and now all women tease me with their thighs* [...]
> *This sets off a dog howling in my chest*
> *and I could devour both this and that* [...]

"Predsontszoria" [Beforesundawn, 1924], with its neologism for a title, is considerably less coarse and even has moments of genuine tenderness. Nevertheless, the lyrical hero treats himself wryly:

> Моя голова, як великий дзвін,
> дзвонить одчайно в присмерк,
> а серце потрапило в каламутний плин,
> де нема ні сигналів ні іскор
> ("Predsontszoria"; Shkurupii 1924c).

> *My head is like a huge bell,*
> *ringing despondently in the dusk,*
> *and my heart floats into a turbid liquid,*
> *where there are no beacons or sparks.*

The poet, however, cannot muster the same flippant attitude toward the object of his affection. Concern for the woman's emotional welfare comes across sincerely:

> [...] мене турбує твій одчайний захват,
> солона роса твоїх повік
> (ibid.).

> [ ] *I am concerned by your desperate rapture*
> *the salty dew of your eyelids.*

If there is any cycle in which Shkurupii betrays genuine enthusiasm and frankness, then it is in the five short poems of "More" [Sea] (Shkurupii

1927b). Love may be banal, but the sea is truly full of romance. Unlike his intimate works, these poems are completely bereft of irony, sarcasm, or belligerent crudity. All are unfeigned in their sincerity and delight; they extol adventure, danger, and exoticism: "I am bored with events of yesterday" [Набридло те, що було вчора] and "There, into the gulf of watery marvels / I also go" [Туди, в затоки водограйних див / і я йду]. The poet has no wish to de-aesthetisize this particular reality, perhaps because it serves as a metaphor of the Futurist ethos—namely, its sense of heroism and quest. A case could be made for a similar reading of another "sea" poem, "Pisnia zarizanoho kapitana" [Song of the Murdered Captain], which begins with these words:

Відвага пригод
нас у море жене.
відвага пригод
нас турбує, пече...
("Pisnia zarizanoho kapitana"; Shkurupii 1928f).

Fearless adventures
drive us to the sea.
Fearless adventures
agitate and set us ablaze...

In 1924 Shkurupii expressed the view that a Futurist should use "the word as an agitational device." This was proposed as an antidote to various "poetic schools that spoil young writers, [by] transforming them into common poets, high priests, and dreamers— individuals useless in contemporary life." Shkurupii envisioned a "worker in words" who would be politically aware and committed to society. In place of "petty emotions," his work would focus on slogans, exhortations, the life of the proletariat, revolutionary romanticism, and the experience of the collective. But equally important in this undertaking would be the development of one's literary prowess and rejection of classical devices. As Shkurupii put it, in the final analysis all Futurists were to "exploit technique, make inventions" (Shkurupii 1924a).

These twin imperatives—ideology and novelty—plainly converge in Shkurupii's own work. Many a poem has a blatantly expedient quality, affirming, even mythologizing the new life. But although Shkurupii's civic and communal sentiments may frequently be pedestrian, his verse, at its best, has a verbal, oratorical appeal. To be sure, there are instances when message overwhelms form, and invention is sacrificed to tradition.

In works of the mid-1920s this happens only rarely, but by the early 1930s it becomes virtually the rule.[36]

Shkurupii's political poems, with minor exceptions, assume a narrative form. Among them are ballads: "Sherk sertsia" [Sound of the Heart] (Shkurupii 1923f) and "Zhovtnevyi roman" [October Love Affair] (Shkurupii 1923g). Both works are condensed and telescoped stories that couple erotic and revolutionary themes. In each instance, the dramatic prevails over the sentimental. "Zhovtnevyi roman" has the characteristics of an improvisation, flaunting ready-made, essentially folklore formulas ["Ось гайдамака, як лютий вовк," "Гей, дівчино, частуй…Чим багата…," "дівчина…важкою кулею, гайдамацьку душу з тілом розлучила" (ibid.)].

"Chudesnyi patychok" [The Magic Wand] (Shkurupii 1925f) is a long narrative poem, or more precisely, a versified political fable. The pathos-laden plot speaks of a poor village orphan girl who finds refuge in the city. Written in quatrains, for a young audience, this tendentious work manages somehow to avoid becoming a complete failure through its disarming charm. In "Doktor Stvard" [Doctor Stvard] (Shkurupii 1925d), Shkurupii spins a parodic tale laden with clichés. Promoted as "an excerpt from a novel" and executed in parodic sing-song iambs, it relates the dastardly deeds of a class enemy through the voice of an artless proletarian journalist.

While both preceding works were conspicuous for their lack of technical virtuosity, "Zakhyshchai Kytai" [Defend China] (Shkurupii 1924d, 1925g) is one of Shkurupii's better examples of how experimentation and politics can be combined successfully. Alternating between exhortation ("Rip the imperial flag, / Wave the red banner!"—Прапор імперії рви, / стягом червоним май!) and narration, the poem recounts a coolie's struggle against British imperialism. For all its plainness of theme, the poem is rhythmically resourceful, contains original rhymes [e.g., Скоро, скоро не буде / Буди], and employs an uncommon oriental terminology.

Shkurupii's political and polemical verse always displayed strong rhetorical tendencies. This was already apparent in the works of the early 1920s, but became especially pronounced in poetry written for *Nova generatsiia*. "Desiatyi" [Tenth] (Shkurupii 1927d) was identified as a narrative poem (*poema*) but might be described more accurately as a

[36] This is especially true for the following: *Bozhestvenna komedia. Pamflety* (Shkurupii 1931d) and *Zyma 1930 roku. Frahmentarni maliunky, vykonani virshamy ta prozoiu* (Shkurupii 1933b). Excerpts from these two collections appeared earlier in the press. See Shkurupii 1930a, 1931a, 1931c.

political ode commemorating the tenth anniversary of the revolution. Ceremonial in function, eloquent and exalted in tone, global in perspective, it made good use of the lexicon of revolution and industrialization. Obviously intended for declamation, "Desiatyi" was composed in step-ladder verse and was full of dynamic, hortatory cadences. It created its special effects primarily through repetitions, parallelisms, recurrent morphological and syntactic structures and catalogues.

"Iuvileina Promova" [A Jubilee Oration] (Shkurupii 1927e), also written on the occasion of the tenth anniversary, belongs to the same ceremonial genre. The tone, however, is significantly more subjective in that the orator's voice and persona play a central role in the poem. The range of rhetorical flourishes, moreover, is much wider. At one moment satirical, at another indignant and pompous, this "speech" becomes a broadside against elitism in literature, Ukrainian nationalism and, in particular, Russian chauvinism (Gorkii and Maiakovskii are mentioned as examples). The editors of *Nova generatsiia* maintained that the poem "conformed completely"[37] to all their requirements:

Сьогодні
обурений я
Сурмлю в сурми.
Слухайте, голосномовці, авдиторії!
На десятому році революції
скиньте тягар з коліс істроії.
Геть—
шовінізму скрип [...]
("Iuvileina Promova"; Shkurupii 1927e).

Today
incensed I
trumpet trumpets.
Listen, loudspeakers, audiences!
On the tenth year of the revolution
throw off the dead weight from history's wheels.
Away with—
chauvinism's squeak [...]

Rhetoric assumes a different dimension in "Moia oratoria" [My Oratorio] (Shkurupii 1928g), "a poetic pamphlet" that appeared as part of *Nova generatsiia*'s series "The Rehabilitation of T. H. Shevchenko" (see Ilnytzkyj 1989). This is a diatribe against philistines who would appropriate the memory of a genius for retrograde ritualistic purposes. It

[37] See the table of contents in *Nova generatsiia* 1927 (1).

satirizes the bucolic, populist, folkloric, and sentimental reading of Shevchenko, while promoting an image of him as a European, a ladies' man, an iconoclast, and a "witty bohemian" [*dotepnyi bohemets'*]. True to its polemical purpose, the "Oratorio" is frequently crude and rude: "buckweat cereal oozes from philistine heads, lard dangling from their ribs…" [пре / каша гречана / з міщанських голів / з одвислими салом ребрами…] (Shkurupii 1928g).

One of the last strictly futuristic poems Shkurupii published was entitled "Mirkuvannia Geo Shkurupiia pro Kryms'ki hory i vichnist'" [A Meditation by Geo Shkurupii on the Crimean Mountains and Eternity]. It can be taken as a paraphrase of the movement's major attitudes and literary stratagems. Written in rhetorical free verse and a colloquial tone (dedicated, quite appropriately, to Mykhail' Semenko), the poem waxes philosophical while avoiding the cerebral or highbrow. Bravado combines with just a hint of nostalgia as Shkurupii reflects on the Futurist movement and its fate. He defines himself and his cohorts (naming Vlyz'ko, Bazhan, and Semenko) as "knights of speed and machines" [Ми, лицарі швидкости і машин], and expresses confidence that, literary critics notwithstanding, Futurism will be vindicated by history:

> Друзі!
> Не бійтесь!
> Вічність витягне нас
> з-під руїн
> за волосся,
> її не обдурять в статтях
> Дорошкевич, Коряк,
> або
> Фелікс Якубовський
> ("Mirkuvannia Geo Shkurupiia pro Kryms'ki hory i vichnist'"; Shkurupii 1929j).

> *Friends!*
> *Fear not!*
> *Eternity will yank us from*
> *beneath the ruins*
> *by the hair,*
> *she will not be deceived by the articles*
> *of Doroshkevych, Koriak,*
> *or*
> *Feliks Iakubovs'kyi.*

Echoes of Shkurupii's early struggle with his emotions are contained in this pithy statement:

А далі,
забувши образу
та біль,
в'їдеш в історію
сівши в автомобіль
(ibid.).

And then,
forgetting insult and bile,
you'll enter history
riding an automobile.

Elsewhere the poem consciously de-aestheticizes and de-romanticizes nature ["Forgive me, Honored Comrades Mountains, but your appearance is so repugnant"—Вибачте, шановні Товариші Гори, але ваш вигляд такий огидний], parodies pastoral scenes ["Living shishkebabs graze in herds"—пасеться отарами живий шашлик] and plays havoc with good taste ["There: toward the sea...we carry our mistress and soft belly"—Туди: до моря...веземо коханку і гладкий живіт] (ibid.).

As a poet, Shkurupii was more holistic and complete than Semenko. If he had emotional wounds, he obviously preferred not to show them or make them the stuff of his writings. He explored the idea of the avant-garde broadly, happily juxtaposing himself to the tastes of his reading public. His anti-aestheticism no doubt influenced and had much in common, formally and even philosophically, with Mykola Bazhan's later, analogous tendencies. Perhaps the best compliment one can give Shkurupii, using his own words, is that he had "an objective, conscious knowledge of what constitutes [his] material" and knew "how to manipulate it, so that it would yield exactly what a master wants" (*Zustrich* 1927, 45).

Oleksa Slisarenko (1891-1937)

For a decade, Slisarenko's poetic reputation rested on two collections: a Symbolist volume, *Na berezi Kastal's'komu* [On the Castalian Shore] (Slisarenko 1919c), and *Poemy* [Narrative Poems] (Slisarenko 1923b), a book of Futurist verse that appeared in Kyiv under the imprint "Panfuturists," with a cover designed by Mykola (Nik) Bazhan. Only in 1928 did he publish *Baida*, a comprehensive edition of "selected lyrics" dating from 1911 to 1927 (Slisarenko 1928j).[38] In a foreword he explained:

[38] A second edition appeared a few years later (Slisarenko 1931). For a recent short survey of Slisarenko's life and work, see Aheieva 1990 and Musiienko 1992.

"I have mercilessly discarded everything that in my opinion was accidental or uncharacteristic, putting into this book only that which exemplifies an artistic and ideological stage of my poetic work" (Slisarenko 1931, 3).

Baida consisted of five sections arranged in reverse chronological order. Besides "Na berezi Kastal's'komu" (poems of 1919–1923), and "Poemy" (poems of 1911–1918), it presented three previously unknown cycles: "Zemnymy dorohamy" [Along Earthly Paths, poems of 1919–1922], "Baida" (poems of 1924–27), and an untitled group of verse from 1926. The dimension of each cycle varied significantly: Symbolist works occupied 46 pages, Futurist—41, "Zemnymy dorohamy"—32, "Baida"—18, and poems of 1926—only 5. These numbers make clear that throughout the decade poetry declined steadily as a factor in Slisarenko's creative work. *Baida* also proves that whatever Slisarenko's reason for abandoning Futurism for VAPLITE, the poetry he wrote under the auspices of the avant-garde was not something he was prepared to relegate to the "accidental or uncharacteristic." Significantly, the cycle *Poemy* was included both in the first (1928) and second edition (1931) of *Baida*, and was even enlarged by five additional poems that were not previously seen in the original publication of 1923.

Slisarenko declared himself a Futurist in 1919 with the poem "Tsarivna ostann'oho (Prohnozy)" [Princess of the Ultimate (Prognoses)], published in Semenko's *Mystetstvo* (Slisarenko 1919b). Shortly afterwards, he participated with Semenko and M. Liubchenko in *Al'manakh tr'okh* (Slisarenko 1920). This Futurist debut, however, was overshadowed by his own Symbolist book which was just then being recognized and reviewed,[39] and by the appearance of the much delayed *Muzahet* in which he was represented by three Symbolist poems (Slisarenko 1919a).[40] While in this situation the embrace of Futurism may have seemed sudden and unexpected to some, there was ample evidence—especially in the cycle "Zemnymy dorohamy"—to suggest that the meditative and frequently elegiac tenor of Slisarenko's poems was being challenged by another orientation.

In the *Muzahet* poems Slisarenko's sensibility is still typically Modernist and Symbolist. "Chernychka" [Nun] (ibid., 30) recounts how a young woman fends off the temptations of spring; "Rabynia"[41] [Slave Girl] (ibid., 32) is about love for a nobleman. When these were subsequently

[39] There were at least four reviews of *Na berezi Kastal's'komu*. See Zerov 1919; Fylypovych 1919a; Iavirs'kyi 1919; and Iakubs'kyi 1919a.

[40] See "Chernychka," "Poshliu svoiu dushu v iurbu," "Rabynia."

[41] In *Baida* the title of this poem is "Rozhnivavsia sukhyi viter..." See Slisarenko (1931, 97).

incorporated into the cycle "Zemnymy dorohamy," they merged seamlessly with other melancholy, contemplative lyrics containing religious and sacramental images (*sviate prychastia* [Holy Communion], *Isus* [Jesus]). Still, there was some foreshadowing of new realities and attitudes even in this context. One of the *Muzahet* poems ["I Shall Send My Soul into the Throng"—Пошлю свою душу в юрбу] (ibid., 31), for example, offered a rather unexpected variation on the Symbolist theme of solitude and social estrangement, positing a previously impossible accord between the poet and the mob. It was even more unusual to see Slisarenko in other works of this cycle trading in his unfeigned sincerity and emotionalism for an ironic, somewhat self-deprecating intellectualism:

У кав'ярні за нудною кавою
Висмоктую мозок віршем,
А панночка усмішкою лукавою
Нагадала про інше.

Розгубив рими і ритми—
У серці-вулику інші рої!
Відчуваємо світ ми
Через призми настроїв!
("U kav'iarni"; Slisarenko 1928i).

In a café, drinking insipid coffee
A poem sucks at my brain,
While a debutante's crafty smile
Reminds me about something else.

Rhymes and rhythms scatter—
Something else is abuzz in this hive of a brain
We encounter the world
Through the prism of moods!

While the above posture was rare for Slisarenko in 1919, it was nonetheless an obvious hint that the poet's persona was open to new possibilities. He was retreating from the Castalian fount and the Parnassian locale to a setting significantly less "literary" and idyllic:

Ріки з асфальтовими берегами,
З прибережними кручами кам'яниць
Заглушили мої пшеничні гами
Звуками бетонів і криць.

І я не той, що був серед пшениць і гречки
Серед оксамитного коливання нив—

Розгубилися мої овечки,
Налякані голосами гудків.

І хоч інколи сумую за степом,
Та вже знаю—не заберу отар [...]
Став шофером фірми Шульц і Леппе
Степовий вівчар
("Riky z asfal'tovymy berehamy"; Slisarenko 1928g).

Rivers lined with asphalt shores,
With cliffs of stone buildings,
Drown out the wheat fields of my music
With the sound of concrete and steel.

I am not the man who once stood in stretches of buckwheat
Amidst the silken swaying of fields—
Scattered are my little lambs,
Frightened by the sounds of sirens.

And sometimes though I yearn for praries,
I know now that my flock is gone [...]
The shepherd of the steppe
Is now a driver for Shultz and Leppe.

Slisarenko was obviously shifting gears into a more cerebral and self-critical mode, embracing (somewhat reluctantly) an urban culture.

With "Tsarivna ostann'oho (Prohnozy)" Slisarenko completely reinvented himself as a poet and illustrated the self-conscious resourcefulness to which Futurism obliged its members. The ubiquitous quatrains and inevitable exact rhymes of his short lyrics gave way to a relatively long narrative in accentual meter. Sonority and melodiousness retreated in favor of a prose-like diction. Most dramatic of all was his departure from Modernist/Symbolist discourse; now scientific (especially chemical) and technical terminology took over his verse (e.g., *fibry* [fibers], *protoplazmy* [protoplasms], *klityny* [cells], *elektrony* [electrons], *instynkt* [instinct], *narkoz* [narcosis], *amputovanyj* [amputated], *retorty* [retorts], *milihramy* [milligrams], *kryshtaliuiets'sia* [crystallizes]). The poem sets out to demythologize and debunk the established cultural order, elevating reason as the key to progress and human happiness. "Tsarivna ostann'oho (Prohnozy)" opens with these lines:

Крицею думки
крешеться кремінь
Майбутнього.

1.
У лабораторіях
вібрують звиви мозку.
У лабораторіях
над таємницею матерій
еластично силкується Розум
("Tsarivna ostann'oho (Prohnozy)"; Slisarenko 1923c).

With the steel of thought
is forged the flint
of the Future.

1.
In laboratories
vibrate the coils of the brain.
In laboratories
working on the mysteries of matter
the mind struggles resiliently.

Slisarenko's other Futurist verse was published in *Mystetstvo* (1919–20), *Al'manakh tr'okh* (1920),[42] *Semafor u Maibutnie* (1922), and *Zhovtnevyi zbirnyk panfuturystiv* (1923). Similar in form to "Tsarivna ostann'oho," these works were punctuated by the themes of reason, science, and progress. They evoked an awakening urban mechanistic age, but one which continued to be arrayed in a natural context and viewed from a panoramic, cosmic perspective. As the titles suggest ["To the Wheat Fields"—*Poliam pshenyshnym*; "Cyclones"—*Tsyklony*; "Spring Sound"—*Vesnohuk*], nature and the new era of global electronic communication ["Communication"—*Komunikatsiia*] were not necessarily in conflict.

As was stated above, Slisarenko's publications in the periodic press generated relatively little awareness of his Futurist work. It took *Poemy* to elicit a discernible critical response. And, as always, opinion was divided. Naturally, Nik Bazhan praised Slisarenko's "virile poems with [their] clearly delineated sexual characteristics" (N.B. 1923), while also taking a swipe at the listless spirit of his first (Symbolist) collection. Maik Iohansen, on the other hand, reproached Slisarenko for his hyperbole and, especially, for his language which he considered inappropriate for verse: "He endeavors to extol scientific declarations in a scientific language and, of course, nothing comes of this" (Kramar 1923).

Although poles apart in their evaluation and understanding, the reviewers did capture some of the cardinal features of Slisarenko's new

42 Two short cycles appeared here ("Prahnennia" [Desire; pp. 9–12] and "Zakokhannia" [Love; pp. 13–18]) and were later reprinted in *Poemy* (Slisarenko 1923b).

work. As Bazhan pointed out, *Poemy* signaled a radical change in tone and timbre. Sanguine and boastful, this poetry served as a vehicle for a brazen ego (see "Poema znevahy" [A Poem of Disdain]; Slisarenko 1928d), as a platform for denouncing folk ways ["Let's move away from teamster wagons that are as boring as ethnography"—Од чумацьких маж, нудних, як етнографія] (Slisarenko 1928c) and a stuffy intelligentsia ["The day is gray, / like the soul of an intellectual"—Сьогодні сіро, / як на душі інтеліґента...] (Slisarenko 1928a). They exuded a genuine vitality, an enthusiasm for life. In one poem Slisarenko declares: "Glory to life pregnant! [Слава життю вагітному!] (Slisarenko 1928b); and in another: "I impregnate language with the sperm of bold images [Я заплоднюю мову / Спермами сміливих образів] (Slisarenko 1928d).

Such avowals offended Iohansen's notion of literary decorum. He advised Slisarenko that lines like "over thick-skinned backbones" [по товстошкірих хребтах] were best reserved for agricultural studies. Of course, the point of such expressions was to defy traditional notions of beauty and propriety. A good share of Slisarenko's Futurist work, like that of his colleagues, was permeated with anti-aesthetic imagery and vocabulary. Take these examples:

З смердючої стайні
на соковиті паші
гонимо тупих биків
("Tsyklony"; Slisarenko 1928h).

From a fetid stable
to a succulent grazing field
we drive the witless bulls.

...трупами
абортованих днів
майбутній час
угною!
("Poliam pshenychnym"; Slisarenko 1928e).

...with the corpses
of aborted days
we will fertilize
the future!

Лиже минуле
спину мою
язиками холодними згадок
("Prahnennia"; Slisarenko 1928f).

The past licks
my spine
with the cold tongues of memories.

Slisarenko's Futurist corpus was small, his stylistic and thematic range relatively narrow, but there is no question that his work represents one of the most concentrated and clear expressions of the movement's literary ethos.

Iuliian Shpol (1895-1937)

His real name was Mykhailo Ialovyi. In 1926 he became the first president of VAPLITE— The Free Academy of Proletarian Writers. But prior to assuming the mantle of an "academician," Shpol served briefly in the ranks of the Futurists. He made his debut as a poet in the almanac *Zhovten'* (1921) and the journal *Shliakhy mystetstva* (1921). His official association with the Futurists was through *Semafor u Maibutnie* (1922), where he published seven poems. These early works laid the foundation for his only book of poetry, *Vèrkhy* [Astride, 1923], published by the Futurist house "Gol'fshtrem" (Shpol 1923a).[43] In the mid-1920s Shpol broke with the movement, embraced prose and achieved short but unwelcome notoriety for a formalistic novel, *Zoloti lyseniata* [Little Gold Foxes, 1929] (Shpol 1929).[44]

Vèrkhy is composed primarily of short poems, all untitled and undated. Much of the volume deals with the theme of change. As was the case with other Futurists, Shpol forswears the old world and exhorts the weak and afflicted to regenerate themselves in the name of a brave new tomorrow. The impetus toward this spiritual transformation (the word "soul" comes up repeatedly) is provided by the revolution which permeates the poetry as an implicit force. Most of the collection is imbued by a timeless and cosmic perspective— typical for the early years of the new order.

Vèrkhy's forty-eight pages contain two numbered cycles and a single relatively long poem. One cycle of five brief poems tenders stylistic echoes of Pavlo Tychyna, whose influence is felt elsewhere too. It is a montage of elusive images, sometimes grotesque and violent, which fuse religion, revolution, nature, and industry. There are also occasional deviations into the diction of folk songs. The longest of the poems begins as an extended apostrophe to the city:

43 See Pylypenko's review in *Chervonyi shliakh* (Pylypenko 1923).

44 See the review by Iurii Savchenko in *Krytyka* (Savchenko 1929) and by Feliks Iakubovs'kyi in *Zhyttia i revoliutsiia* (Iakubovs'kyi 1929c). The first chapter of this novel was published in *Vaplite* 1927 (4).

Місто
Кремезне!
Загартцьоване,
Засмоктане,
Запльоване.
Тобі в пащу
Я кладу
Свою
Розкуйовджену голову
("Misto"; Shpol 1923b, 42).

City, you are
Robust!
Hardened,
Exhausted,
Covered in spit.
Into your jaws
I place
My
Disheveled head.

While Shpol's work clearly gravitates toward the avant-garde, strong Modernist and Symbolist traces survive, either in the form of morbidity ("Corpses everywhere. / Among the corpses, I"—Скрізь трупи. / Між трупів я; Shpol 1923a, 18) or as a tendency to worship at the cult of feeling. Some poems—with their morphological rhymes, excessive use of consonance, alliteration, and synonyms—recall the simplistic formal and euphonic devices of Oleksander Oles' and Hryts'ko Chuprynka (e.g., Дзвінкими дзвіночками / Дзінькає снотне повітря; ibid., 20). Still, there is no doubt that Futurism affected Shpol's world view and literary technique. One manifest sign of this was the "Ante scriptum" that graced the title page of *Vèrkhy:*

> The author has had the misfortune of living like everyone else: all the way from the cradle to age twenty-something. He wallowed in emotions. He impaled them on a rhymed lance. These impaled items, re-arranged, he now publishes.

These deprecating lines distance the author from his past and help rationalize the retrograde elements current in the collection. But the struggle with "emotions" is not just a programmatic position; it is manifested also in the poetry:

В залізні пута
Загнуздався розум.
Скривавлене чуття

У розпачі забилося в куток [...]
("V zalizni puta"; Shpol 1923c).

Into iron fetters
the mind is bridled.
Bloodied feeling
Desperately huddles in a corner.

Shpol resorts to other typically Futurist stratagems: he de-poeticizes and de-aestheticizes; he marshals coarseness, shock, and vanity ("I'm a genius"—Я геній); he relies on prosaisms, scientific terminology, colloquialisms, neologisms, and accentual verse. The following is one of the more successful amalgamations of all these diverse elements into a single whole:

Фістульно тонкою ниткою
Ми зв'язані з тобою,
Адаме.
На біса танок первісний
Витанцьовують у душах наших
Бігом часу
Скалічені дами.
На право!—
Вигавкує мохнатий примат.
До стінки! À gauche.
Туди—твою—мать!—
Гремить
Залізом і кров'ю вкритий
Новий Адам [...]
Годі дзвонить на подзвіння.
Зігніть, прокляті, коліна.
Бо в зуби фістульні
Дам!
("Fistul'no tonkoiu nytkoiu"; Shpol 1923d).

With a fistulously thin thread
We are bound to you,
Adam.
Why the hell
Do dames maimed by time
Perform primordial dances
In our souls.
To the right!—
Shouts the shaggy primate.
Up against the wall! À gauche.
Move it—your—mother!—

The New Adam
Thunders
Covered in iron and blood [...]
Enough tolling for the dead.
On your damned knees.
Or else I'll break your fistulous
teeth!

As a writer, Shpol occupies a modest place in the literature of the 1920s. His achievements as a Futurist are equally unexceptional. The collection *Vèrkhy* did not move Ukrainian Futurist poetry into uncharted waters, but it serves as a useful example of the commonplaces preferred by the movement.

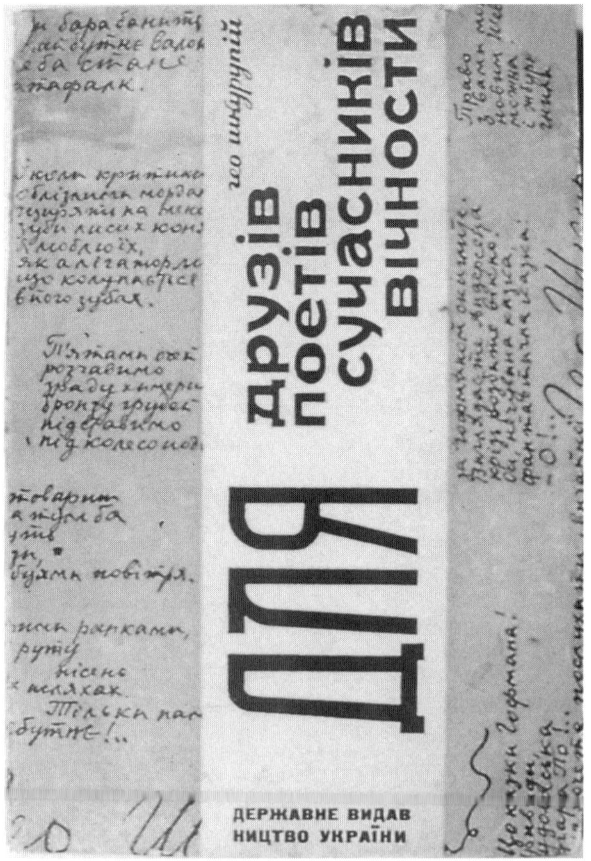

Cover artwork for G. Shkurupii, *Dlia druziv poetiv suchasnykiv vichnosty.* Kyiv: DVU, 1929.

CHAPTER 9

The Prose

Introduction

> Не можна, звичайно, вважати, що «лівий роман" є стала форма. Найбільш «сталий" елемент лівого роману (як і всього лівого мистецтва)—перманентний рух вперед.
> *Naturally, one cannot consider the "left novel" a stable form. The most "stable" element of the left novel (as of all left art) is the permanent movement forward.*
>
> M. Lans'kyi, "Livyi roman" (Lans'kyi 1927, 36).

> Термін «ліве оповідання" ми вважаємо за термін умовний.... [Його] не можна було б визначати якимись абсолютними постійними ознаками.
> *We consider the term "left story" a relative term... [It] cannot be defined by some absolute, permanent characteristics.*
>
> O. Poltorats'kyi, "Praktyka livoho opovidannia" (Poltorats'kyi 1928a, 50).

Prose was a relative latecomer to the Futurist repertoire. Most members of the movement began their literary careers as poets, while those that branched out into prose did so only gradually, either before or after the mid-1920s. Such was the case with Geo Shkurupii, Oleksa Slisarenko, Andrii Chuzhyi, and Oleksa Vlyz'ko. The "born" prose writers—Dmytro Buz'ko, Oleksii Poltorats'kyi, Leonid Skrypnyk, to name a few—did not appear on the literary scene until the second half of the decade. Early publications like *Semafor u Maibutnie* (1922), *Katafalk iskusstva* (1922), and *Zhovtnevyi zbirnyk panfuturystiv* (1924) did not contain any prose fiction. Not until *Hol'fshtrom* (1925) was this genre identified as a Futurist interest, although works and collections by individuals were known earlier.[1] Both in *Nova generatsiia* and *Avanhard–Al'manakh* prose had a major presence.

The movement's drift toward prose must be seen in the larger context of Soviet Ukrainian literature. By 1923 it was increasingly apparent that poetry was no longer the dominant force it had been in the period before and immediately after the revolution.[2] But not only was prose resurgent (thanks to the improving economic conditions and the rise of periodic publications), but it also began undergoing a marked stylistic transformation. The "poetic," "lyrical," and, mostly, short works of writers like Khvyl'ovyi, Kosynka, or Kopylenko, with their impressionistic and ornamental features, started giving way (in the words of Ia. Savchenko) to prose "in the strict sense of the word" (Leites and Iashek 1930, 1: 447). The "poetic" gave way to the "prosaic" and the "lyrical" to the "fabular."

Critics of the day were quick to note that Futurists played an important role in this transformation. In 1924 Mykhailo Dolengo complained that Ukrainian writers suffered from an "anarchic absence of architectonics," "lack of discipline," and "pan-lyricism." "But," he added, "here one must differentiate a few authors...whose work reflects a West European tradition of developing interesting plots. All the latest belletristic experiments of the Panfuturists (or Komunkul'tists) are maintained in the spirit of western adventures, a fact that testifies to their sense of timing." Among those cited for their ability to tell a good story and handle plot was Geo Shkurupii (Dolengo 1924, 173). Futurists were also singled out by Oleksander Bilets'kyi, one of the most distinguished critics of the twenties:

> Both G. Shkurupii and Iu. Ianovs'kyi were connected to the Futurist group of writers—the former, of course, still being a member of this school. [Futurism] helped [these writers] to liberate themselves from tradition, it "Europeanized" them. O. Slisarenko...also belonged to this same group (Bilets'kyi 1926, 156).

An early example of the new prose was provided, surprisingly, by Semenko. His "Mirza Abbas-Khan" (dated 11 February 1922) was a mystery-adventure tale with subtle political overtones (Semenko 1923e, 1). Terse, journalistic, narrated in the first person, and with loose

1 The prose contributions in *Hol'fshtrom* were by O. Kapler ("Shchaslyvyi vypadok"), Slisarenko ("Shpon'chyne zhyttia ta smert'", "Sotni tysiach syl"), Shkurupii ("Shtab smerti"; "Patetychna nich"), and Mykhailo Shcherbak ("Prokliata nich").

2 Dmytro Zahul wrote the following in 1924: "Yes, the lyric was strong and countless during the revolutionary years. Next to it (strange to say!) there were almost no signs of any epic creativity, virtually not a single decent novelist [or] storyteller. And that's the way it was until last year" (Tyverets' 1924).

references to autobiographical fact, the story takes place in the fall of 1921 on a crowded train heading from Moscow to Berlin. Among the narrator's traveling companions is an Afghan diplomatic mission headed by Mirza Abbas-Khan. Exoticism gives way to mystery as the narrator discovers that the Afghan speaks perfect Russian, has nothing but scorn for his entourage and praise for the Soviet regime. The anecdotal nature of the story is revealed when Mirza Abbas-Khan's paeans begin to wane in direct proportion to the distance the train recedes from Moscow. The swiftly unraveling plot contains appropriate literary allusions (for example, the narrator is reading Jules Verne) and humor. As the narrator (by now clearly identified as Semenko) parts company with Mirza Abbas-Khan, he gives him a copy of Shevchenko's *Kobzar*, declaring: "Taras Shevchenko is my literary pseudonym." In 1927 Shkurupii hailed this story for its plot, narrative technique, and ability to depict a psychological "type" without "boring psychology" (Shkurupii 1927c, 19). Astute as Semenko was in anticipating the new trend, he did not emerge as one of its representatives—after this single experiment, he published no other fiction.[3]

Geo Shkurupii

Among Futurists the man who best epitomized "plot-oriented" literature was Geo Shkurupii. Bilets'kyi spoke of him as "this *Wunderkind* of our contemporary literature":

> Shkurupii, understandably, is oriented toward Europe. His youth... makes [his] collections[4] overly literary: almost every story calls forth bookish associations...but, let us agree that, on the whole, Shkurupii's collection is an interesting phenomenon in our young prose.... (Bilets'kyi 1926, 154).

Similar sentiments were held by other critics. Feliks Iakubovs'kyi praised Shkurupii for breaking with Ukrainian tradition and for "stubbornly seeking out compositional devices" (Iakubovs'kyi 1927, 58). He described him as one of "the most outstanding representatives of the plot school..." (Iakubovs'kyi 1928b, 22). In 1929 Poltorats'kyi called his twenty-five-year-old colleague "almost an accomplished master" (Poltarats'kyi 1929d). Opinion became increasingly more polarized, however, toward the late 1920s as critics became alarmed at his "formalism."

3 Recently, a few other fragments of his unpublished prose have appeared. See Chernysh 1989a.

4 The reference here is to *Peremozhets' drakona* (Shkurupii 1925a) and *Pryhody mashynista Khorna* (Shkurupii 1925b).

Although Shkurupii was identified with "plot," his work as a whole confounds such simple definition. Plot and intrigue are better understood as just one aspect of his extreme literary self-consciousness, which assumed several guises. Shkurupii could play with language as much as with composition. He was just as likely to exploit a device as to reveal it. He could satisfy a reader's desire for convention or he could thwart it. Sometimes, Shkurupii willingly subordinated himself to the dictates of genre, and at other times he consciously challenged them.

Between 1925 and 1930 Shkurupii published several collections of short prose and two novels.[5] One of his earliest efforts, "Tysiacha proidysvitiv" [A Thousand Vagabonds, 1923], was an exercise in mystification and defamiliarization [*ostranenie*]. Here he was concerned more with manner than message, less with plot than with language. The story's opening lines intentionally lead the reader astray: "A fierce northeast wind blew toward the bow of my ship, which heaved and tossed in the squalls of a strong storm. Resolutely I gathered all the sails and wrapped them around the single mast of my ship." The abrupt beginning and sense of impending danger point to an adventure at sea. But although the tale is told virtually throughout in a mariner's language and is filled with the requisite paraphernalia of storms and ports, it is not what it seems. As Oleksander Bilets'kyi wrote, "the 'defamiliarization' is done so simply and effortlessly that even the most experienced reader will fall into the author's trap..." (Bilets'kyi 1926, 154). Only after several paragraphs, does it become apparent that this is a story about an alcoholic, bound for home in a rainstorm, drunkenly weaving his way through dark city streets and, unexpectedly, encountering the militia, who are construed here as pirates. On rereading, the "bow of the ship" turns out to be the vagabond's nose, cutting a swath through the rain. What promised to be an adventure becomes instead a lesson in literary subterfuge. Rather appropriately, Bilets'kyi noted that the collection containing "Tysiacha proidysvitiv" was "not so much for the ordinary reader, as for those people who in one way or another have a vested interest in literature. This would include our young prose writers who, like it or not, have been educated on 'populist' literature" (ibid.).

Shkurupii took a diametrically opposite approach in "Provokator" [The Provocateur, 1927] (Shkurupii 1929d) in which he diligently exploited canons of the detective story. It was done so well that soon after

5 *Peremozhets' drakona* (1925a), *Pryhody mashynista Khorna* (1925b), *Shtab smerti* (1926), *Sichneve povstannia* (1928e), *Dveri v den'* (1929g and 1931e), *Patetychna nich, Narkom* (1929h), *Strashna myt'* (1929i), *Zhanna batal'ionerka* (1930h), *Zruinovanyi polon* (1930i).

publication the tale was analyzed as a model of its type (Maifet 1928). Indeed, although it has lapses in logic and detail, and strikes today's reader as naive, it was an interesting adaption of the genre to Soviet reality (the detective is a Komsomol member; the murderer is motivated by anti-Soviet designs). The action takes place on a fittingly eerie night, in a post office cut off from the world by a storm that traps detective, victim, and murder suspects. The problem for comrade detective Pavliuk is to discover who in this motley group is the actual miscreant.

As close as he adheres to the detective genre, Shkurupii cannot, in the final analysis, restrain himself from shattering the illusion he has created. The spell is broken, the artifice is revealed when the investigator turns to literature for his solution: Pavliuk "grew pensive, as if solving a difficult task. Anxiously he recalled the crime novels he read, he remembered Sherlock's detective work, but could not understand how and why the telegraph operator was killed" (Shkurupii 1929d, 24). Later, Arthur Conan Doyle and Holmes are mentioned again. Shkurupii's fictional characters tend to imitate art on other occasions as well. A heroine from "Patetychna nich" [Piteous Night, 1925] returns home through streets that appear "to her like jungles from any one of Fenimore Cooper's novels" (Shkurupii 1929c, 26). The extent to which both author and characters are trapped in literature's web can be gleaned from this same story when a confused narrator tries to explain certain things to the reader:

> Як бачимо, обидва потяги вже вийшли зі своїх протилежних пунктів, —значить… Але це нічого не значить, бо тут є ще третя особа, —значить… Значить, треба ввесь час пам'ятати, що в цьому оповіданні тільки дві особи беруть участь, всі останні—це просто бутафорія (Shkurupii 1929c, 12–13).
>
> *As we see, both trains have already left their respective stations. This means… Actually, this does not mean anything, because there is a third person here, which means… It means one must always remember that in this story only two characters are involved, all the rest are just simple accessories.*

Despite such cravings to divulge the scaffolding of his trade, Shkurupii proved on numerous occasions that he could spin a tale without undue authorial asides or self-conscious references to the literary act. Take, for example, "Shtab smerty" [Death Headquarters, 1925] (Shkurupii 1925h), a tale done in the lyrico-epic vein, whose protagonist, a bandit leader named Chuchupak, rains terror on the armies of the UNR (Ukrainian National Republic). The historical context is virtually immaterial here—for the story is not about politics but Chuchupak's exploits, which account for one episode after another and lead to a surprise ending. While not a psychological study, this work draws its strength as much from character as it does from plot.[6] The protagonist's name and activities invite comparison to Panas Myrnyi's Chipka.[7] Shkurupii underscores his vengeful nature by explicitly likening him to the Haidamak leaders Gonta and Zalizniak. By being both sinister and pathetic, Chuchupak emerges as something more than a one-dimensional character. The murder of his sister, the reader learns, has changed him into a mentally disturbed killing machine. He is a man "without heart and without blood" in whom death inspires erotic feelings, while love serves as an occasion for carnage.

"Strashna myt'" [A Terrible Moment, 1926] (Shkurupii 1929e) evokes memories of Nikolai Gogol' ("Vii," "A Terrible Vengeance") and E. T. A. Hoffmann. Mykola Bazhan thought it was written in the "expressionistic manner" (Bazhan 1927b, 24). Dark and foreboding, permeated with a surrealistic sense of time, the work combines elements of a mystery and an adventure story. The ambiguous opening might even suggest a ghost tale: "Amidst sodden cigarette smoke phantoms glimmered: the once executed Oleksa Krevych, the half-dead [*nedobytyi*] Samuïl Mazur, and the half-raped [*nedogvaltovana*] Jewish girl, Mirel'. They are all alive, but their faces are dead, their gazes frozen... They are visitors in the Present" (Shkurupii 1929e, 36). A well-written chase sequence in which Oleksa and Samuïl escape from White Army officers sets in motion political motifs. One episode includes grotesque scenes of death: "At the train station, women and children, emaciated old men dressed in lice-infested rags were dying amidst filth and garbage. Among the corpses hungry dogs roamed, fighting like wolves over some poor fellow's chewed-off leg..." (ibid., 40). The general setting is that of a decadent city, alive with cafés, music, lights, cabarets and trolley cars. The plot is purposely obscure. Time and reality are deformed (at one point clocks begin moving backward). Only the last few lines betray that the events portrayed are the momentary hallucinations of a man in the grips of a heart attack.

When *Zhanna batal'ionerka* [Joan of the Women's Battalion, 1929][8] made its appearance, a reviewer noted with surprise that Shkurupii "did not set for himself any destructive tasks" in this novel (Pidhainyi 1930,

[6] In the early 1930s Shkurupii divided his prose into three categories: "Reportorial tales" (*Noveli reportazhni*), "Tales of Mystery" (*Noveli taiemnyts'*) and "Psychological tales" (*Psykholohichni noveli*). Among the latter was "Shtab smerty," which was renamed "Chuchupak." See Geo Shkurupii, *Noveli nashoho chasu. Proza.* (Shkurupii 1931f).

[7] The main protagonist of *Khiba revut' voly, iak iasla povni* (1880).

[8] This novel was first serialized in *Zhyttia i revoliutsiia* (Shkurupii 1929k) and later published separately: Geo Shkurupii, *Zhanna batal'ionerka* (Shkurupii 1930h). Since then it was not republished in the Soviet Ukraine; it did, however, appear in the West in *Suchasnist'* (Shkurupii 1982).

150). Nonetheless, it did possess an element of playfulness: one chapter employed a type of cinematic "fade-in" and "fade-out" technique (chapter 8: "Poema pro klaptyk paperu"[A Narrative Poem about a Piece of Paper]), another turned out to be a false ending (chapter 13: "Nemozhlyvyi kinets'" [An Implausible Ending]). At the conclusion, an unexpected twist occurs in what has been shaping up as a predictable love plot. The first chapter is realized as an adventure (the chase here is reminiscent of one in "Strashna myt'"); the second (portraying a Theosophical séance) recalls an outtake from a Russian realistic novel. On the whole, however, the text is fairly consistent in tone and style; it makes no conspicuous appeal to its manner or devices.

Zhanna batal'ionerka is set during the Kerenskii period. The protagonist is a student, Stefan Boiko, member of a socialist group, who refuses to serve in the army, resents the regime's chauvinistic policies and wants to ameliorate Ukraine's "colonial" status in the Russian Empire (the "national" theme is quite prominent in the novel). Boiko falls in love with a politically incompatible young woman, Zhanna, a Russian patriot with romantic notions of defending the imperial fatherland. This fervor leads her to join the "Women's Legion." Weaving together romance, ideology, and adventure, Shkurupii creates a highly readable, fast-paced work. The narrative, shifting between events in Boiko's life and Zhanna's, is handled deftly. Dialogues are crisp and, when appropriate, coarse. A few mild erotic moments disturbed critics. Zhanna's "intimate sexual feelings are described too carefully," noted one reviewer (Pidhainyi 1930, 150).

Among Shkurupii's more typically formalist endeavors was "Misiats' z rushnytseiu" ["A Month With a Rifle," 1928]. When these "pictures of Red Army life" first appeared, they were described in *Nova generatsiia* as a "story that borders on the leftist reportorial sketch" (Shkurupii 1928a).[9] Indeed, even though later it was published in a collection with "Provokator" and "Strashna myt'," this "story" had little in common with traditional "fiction."[10] As a narrative that ostensibly is about civilians undergoing a month of military training, it is best relegated to the "literature of fact."

Ranging in tone from the serious to the humorous, this distinctly unmilitary reportage divides its eighteen pages of content into seven brief chapters. Each begins with a philosophical meditation on some universal topic (e.g., friendship, love, fear); this is followed by a concrete episode, anecdote, or character-sketch that bears a descriptive title (for

[9] The comments appear on the contents page.

[10] Compare the contents in *Strashna myt'* (Shkurupii 1929i).

example, "In the Camp," "The Three Musketeers," "A Chemical Alarm," "We Peel Potatoes"). This highly structured narrative contains several references to the conventions of literature and art. Some statements are ironic and clearly polemical.

> Страх—це єдина релігія всіх безвірників. І як у релігії є відступники, так серед безвірників є ті, що не бояться страху, таких людей звуть героями.
>
> Люди майбутнього всі будуть героями, бо вони нічого не боятимуться. А тепер ще страшно навіть прочитати книжку, яку не так написано, як до цього звикли (Shkurupii 1929b, 16–17).
>
> *Fear is the only religion of unbelievers. And just as religion has it heretics, so among unbelievers there are those who are not afraid of fear. Such people are called heroes.*
>
> *All people in the future will be heroes, for they will fear nothing. But in the meantime even a book written in an uncommon manner inspires fear.*

"Misiats' z rushnytseiu" concludes with this "Epilogue:"

> За вимогами знавців і теоретиків літератури, кожний роман, кожне оповідання мусить кінчатись певним виплутуванням героїв з інтриґ, подій і положень. Живу людину виплутує з роману життя смерть....
>
> Місяць кінчився, як театральна вистава. Ми розходимось по домах. Чотири сотні смертей логічно мусили б розв'язати наше оповідання про чотириста людських романів. Але ми не будемо такі безжалісні, як теорія літератури, і відпустимо наших героїв на всі чотири сторони гуркотливого й бундючного життя. Хай ще трошки поживуть (ibid., 19–20).
>
> *According to experts and theoreticians of literature, every novel, every story must end with the heroes being extricated from their intrigues, adventures and predicaments. But human beings are extricated from the novel of life only by death....*
>
> *Like a theatrical performance, the month has come to an end. We all go our separate ways. Four hundred deaths would logically end our story about four hundred human dramas. But we will not be as merciless as literary theory and will disperse our heroes—noisy and flamboyant—in all four directions of a life. Let them live a short while longer.*

Another interesting fusion of "fact" with the narrative techniques of fiction occurs in the unfinished "Povist' pro hirke kokhannia poeta Tarasa Shevchenka" [A Novella about the Poet Taras Shevchenko's Bitter Love

Experience"].[11] The extent chapters employ recognizable biographical and historical facts from Shevchenko's life, including short quotes from his diary. The focal point is the poet's St. Petersburg period following his return from exile. But the actual chronological boundaries are widened considerably through flashbacks and other devices. Episodes include Mykola Kostomarov and Shevchenko in a restaurant; Shevchenko at a high society ball; Engel'hardt in bed; a historical digression on Tsar Nicholas I; and conversations with Turgenev. The erotic motifs promised by the title are prominent throughout but especially in a chapter that carries the long title, "First Love of Childhood. Oksana. Dunia Hashkovs'ka. A Nice Little German Girl Named Maria. Princess Varvara Repnina. At the Crossroads. Kateryna Piunova. Kharytia. Late Desire" (Shkurupii 1930g, 22).

For all its reliance on biography and history, this is hardly a scholarly account of the poet's life. It is instead fictionalized, partisan, and personal—a continuation of the Futurists' attempt to "rehabilitate" Taras Shevchenko, to show, in Semenko's words, that he too "had a pot belly and brains" and was "not a sacred relic, dry and greased with oil."[12] The "Novella" takes a stab at the political and national cult of Shevchenko by substituting an urban and bohemian image for the populist one. In this way the demiurge is humanized and demystified. In some respects he is even made to resemble a "futurist," for Shkurupii highlights Shevchenko's "pranks" and makes an issue of his admiration for the steam engine. A scene—lifted directly from a nineteenth-century memoir—in which Shkurupii depicts Shevchenko being initiated into the "Society of Boozers" [*mochymordy*], reads like a Dada sound poem.

> шевченко ще досі пам'ятає веселий хор голосів, що ним починався ритуал пиятства.
> бас гудів
> — ром, пунш, ром, пунш...
> тенори підхоплювали:
> — півпиво, півпиво, ґлінтвейн, ґлінтвейн...

[11] Parts of the "Novella" were published in *Nova generatsiia* (Shkurupii 1930f) and *Zhyttia i revoliutsiia* (Shkurupii 1930g). An editorial note in *Nova generatsiia* states that the complete work was scheduled to be published "soon" by the State Publishing House (DVU), but apparently it was not. It thus remains incomplete.

[12] These words were from one of two epigraphs that accompanied the "Novella." They came from Semenko's poem "Bez ikon i bez trupiv" (Semenko 1928a). The other epigraph cited Semenko's infamous words from *Derzannia* (Semenko 1914a): "Today, Shevchenko is under my feet." The latter, incidentally, was not included in the chapters printed in *Zhyttia and revoliutsiia*. For more detail on this subject see Ilnytzkyj 1989.

а дисканти вигукували:
— солодка, біла, червона, горілка.... (*punctuation in the original;* Shkurupii 1930f, 12).[13]

shevchenko could still remember the merry chorus with which the drinking ritual began.
the basses buzzed
"rum, punch, rum, punch..."
the tenors chimed in:
"beer, beer, Glühwein, Glühwein..."
And the sopranos shouted in descant:
"sweet, white, red, vodka...."

What makes this narrative baffling is its mindful inconsistency of discourse, its purposeful avoidance of settling into a recognizable style or genre. The chapters that appeared in *Nova generatsiia* can easily be construed as sections of a novel. Aside from quotations from Shevchenko's diary, they are a traditional third-person narrative, for the most part neutral and objective in tone, skillfully blending Shevchenko's recollections of the past with present events. The chapters in *Zhyttia i revoliutsiia* are much more heterogeneous. The first, describing the slothful life of the landowner Engel'hardt , opens in a novelistic vein, but as the topic shifts to the brutal reign of Tsar Nicholas I, the text acquires characteristics of a "history" but without its "objective" stance. Engel'hardt and Nicholas I are treated subjectively and sarcastically. The narrator is far from being a neutral observer: his attitude is critical, evaluative, even polemical. He writes from "national" and "class" positions. But this is not sustained for long; abruptly, the subject and tone changes to this:

Боротьба з оточенням і урядами—це доля геніїв, що дають людськості нові ідеї....Трагічний кінець лише краще підреслює їхню прекрасну біографію. Геніям нудно вмирати в ліжкові своєю смертю. Куля пістоля, вдар шаблі, віриьовка й нещасний випадок—неодмінні аксесуари кінця. Навіть звичайним людям нудно, коли геній вмирає так само, як вони.

Од Франсуа Війона до мого друга Олекси Влизька лише один маленький крок, хоч він і нараховує кілька століть. Можливо, я навіть і не помилюся, коли скажу, що його повісять.[14] Можливо, що такої ж думки про своїх друзів і Олекса Влизько (Shkurupii 1930g, 11).

13 This particular section was taken virtually verbatim by Shkurupii from the memoir of Oleksander S. Afanas'iev-Chuzhbyns'kyi, "Vospominaniia o T. G. Shevchenko."

14 Oleksa Vlyz'ko was actually executed by firing squad in 1934 on trumped-up charges that he belonged to SVU [The Union for the Liberation of Ukraine].

> *The fate of geniuses, those who give humanity its new ideas, is to struggle against society and government... Their tragic death only helps to underscore their wonderful biography. Geniuses consider dying in bed boring. A bullet from a gun, a blow from a sword, a noose or an unfortunate accident—these are the inevitable accessories of their death. Even common people are bored if geniuses die in a manner similar to their own.*
>
> *Although several centuries separate them, the distance between François Villon and my friend Oleksa Vlyz'ko is just one little step. I am probably not mistaken when I say that he will be hanged. Oleksa Vlyz'ko is probably of the same opinion about his friends.*

The chapter portraying Shevchenko and Turgenev at a Petersburg "salon" is mostly dialogue and, again, resembles a novel. Objective for the most part, it does, however, contain some editorializing. When the conversation turns toward the topic of Ukrainian language and literature, and Turgenev betrays his reactionary views, the narrator offers this observation:

> Нам тепер дивно читати такі суперечки великих людей, коли Україна стала радянською республікою. Але тоді такі розмови про мову були часті серед великих людей, як тепер серед недоукраїнізованих урядовців (ibid., 15).

> *Today, when Ukraine has become a Soviet republic, we find it strange to read about such conflicts between great men. But at that time such conversations about language were as frequent among great men as they are now among insufficiently Ukrainianized bureaucrats.*

The last chapter (the one with the long title cited above), is essentially an "article," a popular, somewhat sentimental, synoptic and synthetic piece of "scholarship" about Shevchenko's love life. Unlike the other chapters it is totally undramatic: Shevchenko is no longer portrayed as a character, but is the subject of a study.

As is evident from this summary, Shkurupii appears to have been purposely tampering with the generic unity of traditional narratives. It may be unsound to draw definitive conclusions about an incomplete novella, but it seems obvious that he was constructing this work from diverse textual modes. Reading the "Novella" is like confronting several different genres simultaneously, all dedicated to one subject. Shevchenko's biography may bind these stylistically autonomous texts, but the polyphony of modes unquestionably undermines the subject and raises in the reader's mind anxious questions of a formal, compositional, and narrative nature.

The protocols that governed the "Novella" become less puzzling in light of Shkurupii's novel *Dveri v den'* [Gateway into Day, 1929] (Shkurupii 1929g, 1931e). Here is how one contemporary critic described it:

> [In *Dveri v den'*] the author has created a mechanical mixture of literary and quasi-literary forms: scenario, reportage, stenographic notes, lectures, journalism. In the work itself all these represented forms do not merge into one another to become a single unified stylistic whole; they are mechanically joined together and pasted into what is basically a realistic novella...(Iakubovs'kyi 1929a).

And another stated: "All the mentioned inserts of various genres not only fail to help the basic novella in delineating character [and] developing action, etc., but do quite the opposite: [they] contradict it...The style of the novel does not form a single whole..." (Smilians'kyj 1929).

One can better understand what the critics meant by charting an outline of *Dveri v den'*. The first chapter introduces the reader to the main character, Teodor Hai, sitting in a bar late at night, surrounded by the noise of a jazz band and prostitutes. The descriptions of the environment are done in a Bazhanian manner. In fact, both Bazhan and Semenko make cameo appearances in this chapter. The allegorical nature of the novel's title emerges as it becomes obvious that Hai yearns to escape "into daylight" from this squalid environment. The second chapter, unexpectedly designated as the "Peredmova" [Preface], spells out in no uncertain terms the author's concern with the "material" of his art, the importance he places on experiencing the very "process" of creativity. The next chapter ("Rich" [Thing]) is a two-page description of a painting depicting a prehistoric landscape. The chapters that follow are written in a mystery and horror style: a man waits on a street corner for an accident to occur. When it does, he steals the victim's body from the morgue. From this point, the work turns into a prehistoric novel in which Hai figures as the major character. One critic said this section gives the impression of being "a report about another author's novel on the same subject" (Smilians'kyi 1929). This confusion is resolved in the following way: the prehistoric novel turns out to be Hai's dream; the stolen corpse becomes a device for Hai to stage his own death and start a new life. *Dveri v den'* ends anti-climatically with a professorial lecture about the Dnipro dam where Hai sets out to work. Another chapter, describing Hai's trip down the Dnipro, was a case of self-plagiarism (Shkurupii 1929g, 199–220): this section appeared in *Nova generatsiia* two years earlier under the combined authorship of Dmytro Buz'ko and Geo Shkurupii. At the time the editors described it as "a type of leftist reportage that uses journalistic structural devices" (Shkurupii and Buz'ko 1927). Shkurupii incorporated this piece into *Dveri v den'* with only minor changes, additions, and elisions.

Toward the end of the 1920s critics became increasingly frustrated with Shkurupii's work. On the one hand, they could not deny his obvious talent, but on the other, they were taken aback by his literary trials, by what one critic called his "unprincipled eclectic search," which prevented him from establishing an "organic relationship with the stylistic orientation of our present day" (Pidhainyi 1930, 152). Shkurupii's work was found wanting on the grounds that it was "unrealistic" and ideologically useless. Critics demanded a logical plot and development, consistency of character, a stable tone, and a meaningful message (see Iakubovs'kyi 1929b).[15] The following comment was characteristic:

> More than any other Ukrainian writer, Geo Shkurupii's literary development is complex and convoluted. His entire corpus is a single experiment of a formal nature. It is no wonder, therefore, that after almost ten years of being involved in literature Shkurupii has been unable to produce a completely finished work, about which it could be said that it is a harmonious synthesis of his creative search.... Of course, one cannot be against experimentation as long as it does not become a goal unto itself. But in Shkurupii's case, unfortunately [experimentation] has, it seems, become the goal. Everything is subordinated to it, including style, plot, and ideological clarity..." (Khutorian 1929).

While this is not the most balanced summary of Shkurupii's career, it does capture an essential truth about his work. He may not have subordinated everything to experimentation, but it certainly occupied a preeminent place in his writings. What proletarian critics viewed as a sin, Shkurupii pursued as a virtue.

Oleksa Slisarenko

During the 1920s, critics and readers alike associated Geo Shkurupii's name with Futurist prose. Such was not the case with Oleksa Slisarenko. While it was customary to distinguish a Futurist period in his poetry, the prose never attained that same clear-cut recognition. Iakiv Savchenko, for example, interpreted Slisarenko's first prose collection as an entirely new stage in his career, distinct from Symbolism and Futurism. He wrote:

[15] This article appeared originally as "Pered 'Dveryma v den''" (Iakubovs'kyi 1929a).

> Slisarenko—the Symbolist poet; Slisarenko—the Futurist-Panfuturist: these are generally recognized stages in his career.... And suddenly we have a *new* Slisarenko, who has *absolutely nothing in common* with his earlier writing tradition, with that world view and sensibility that we knew from his poetry collections *Na berezi Kastal's'komu* and *Poemy* (Ia. Savchenko 1925, 141; *emphasis added*).

It is easy to understand why such a view took hold and survives to this day.[16] Slisarenko embarked on a career in fiction just as his association with the avant-garde was winding down (namely, on the eve of the demise of AsKK). Prose was just emerging as a recognized activity among the Futurists and, of course, they did not hold a monopoly on promoting "plot." Since Slisarenko kept to this course for the rest of the decade (when he was already outside the movement), the context from which his fiction originated became gradually blurred. Yet there can be no doubt that the roots of his prose are indeed traceable to Futurism. His first stories were written in 1924, a period when he actively participated in Aspanfut-AsKK. One story made its debut in the Futurist-inspired magazine *Hlobus*, where Semenko's, Shkurupii's, and Ianovs'kyi's works also appeared. Two others were published in the almanac *Hol'fshtrom*. Thus, it seems appropriate to consider at least his first collection of prose as relevant to our study of the movement.[17]

When *Sotni tysiach syl* [Hundreds of Thousands of Horsepower] was released, Savchenko and Mykola Zerov were among its early reviewers (Ia. Savchenko 1925; Zerov 1925). Both critics took a comparative approach, examining the collection in concert with one just published by Oleksander Kopylenko (an associate of Pluh, later of VAPLITE) and concluded that Slisarenko was the more mature and original writer. Savchenko expressed unreserved praise and admiration for Slisarenko, saying that his stories demonstrated an "irreproachable mastery." Zerov tendered a few polite remarks but was not overly impressed. Both critics, however, were drawn to the collection's formal properties. *Sotni tysiach syl* "must be recognized as a positive phenomenon in our prose first of all because it constitutes a new formal manner, uncharacteristic of our

[16] In the introduction to the most recent edition of Slisarenko's works, Mykhailo K. Naienko states that Futurism relates "purely to the poetic period of Slisarenko's creativity," although further on, Naienko is less categorical. See Slisarenko (1990, 6). More recently, another author is slightly more forthright in admitting a Futurist influence on the prose. See Aheieva (1990, 33 and 40).

[17] *Sotni tysiach syl. Opovidannia* (Slisarenko 1925b) appeared in April or early May. His second collection was published later that same year, when AsKK no longer existed. See *Plantatsiï. Opovidannia* (Slisarenko 1925a).

revolutionary belles-lettres," said Savchenko (Ia. Savchenko 1925, 141). The Neoclassicist tried to explain Slisarenko's form-consciousness by pointing to Futurism as one of several possible influences:

> O. Slisarenko's book makes a completely different impression [than Kopylenko's]. Whereas Kopylenko writes his books without considering questions of form (why search for one's own style when one can borrow Khvyl'ovyi's!), Slisarenko is drawn toward prose primarily by theoretical considerations. At least such is my first impression. [It is hard to say] whether these considerations are the general convictions of an "Aspanfutist" [who believes] that poetry has had its day and that a forward-looking Panfuturist should try his hand at literature only in the prose medium—and only by writing adventure stories—or whether this is Slisarenko's own idea inspired by some critical voice. Perhaps it is simply that Ehrenburg—the author of the famous [*Adventures of*] *Julio Jerenito* [1922]—having deprived him of sleep and peace, forced him at last to turn toward chronicling adventures. But [whatever the reason, one thing is obvious]: the intentionality, deliberateness [*nadumanist'*] of Slisarenko's literary approach is manifest from the very beginning of his book. At the same time, there is no evidence that this author writes from the "gut," on account of some internal necessity, or that prose, to use an ancient expression, is his "vocation." The situation is quite simple: there is a type of prose called "adventures" (O. Henry, for example), a genre which has not been tried in Ukrainian literature. Why then should not Slisarenko lay a foundation for it?
>
> The truth is that Slisarenko's stories are somewhat unusual for Ukrainian literature: they neither have descriptions of everyday life [*pobut*], nor psychology. The author is only interested in endless events, adventures, [and] episodes... (Zerov 1925, 36).

Slisarenko's language and tone was another aspect that weighed on the two critics. Savchenko was receptive to what he encountered:

> His vocabulary is everyday, common. You will not find a poetic image, a simile or an epithet embellishing something.... There is not an ounce of lyricism or psychologism here. The word is used very efficiently, it is used purely in a compositional sense, completely subordinated to the task [it performs] in the plot. Beyond this the word has no independent meaning. But it is so well placed within the contours of the story that when you throw out even a few words, the story immediately falls apart (Ia. Savchenko 1925, 141).

Zerov saw things differently. In his opinion, the author "has not found an appropriate tone for his new experiments. The language of his stories is insuperably and needlessly coarse. Moreover this coarseness cannot be justified, as it can in Kopylenko's case, by literary immaturity." Zerov was offended in particular by the immodest humor, by the exaggerations and sarcasm. Such attributes evoked in him memories of Slisarenko's "destructive" Futurist poetry. "Our literature has such a poor verbal culture," went on Zerov, "that even an experienced *litterateur* [like Slisarenko] repeatedly falls into artlessness [*sproshchennia*] and vulgarity..." (Zerov 1925, 36–38).

Zerov raised objections to Slisarenko's prose practice also at another forum—during the famed literary discussion held at the Ukrainian Academy of Sciences on 24 May 1925. Amidst debates about literary quality, provincialism, and the role of Europe, Slisarenko's name was brought up as an example of what ailed Ukrainian letters. Speaking of European literary achievements, Zerov chose him as an illustration of Ukrainian mediocrity, calling him a second-rate Pierre Benoit.[18] Iurii Mezhenko (no doubt inspired by Zerov's review) described him as a "vulgarized O. Henry" who littered every page with "indecent words" (*Shliakhy rozvytku* 1925, 13, 15, 29). Approximately a year later Bilets'kyi tried to place this controversy in perspective:

> I must admit that I personally was not able to confirm the accuracy of [Mezhenko's] criticism. At the first reading, I did not find those incriminating words and now, having again perused the volume, was not able to track them down. The critic clearly exaggerated this trait.... It is also obvious that Pierre Benoit was brought up only for the sake of polemics. Slisarenko is neither better nor worse than Benoit: he simply has nothing in common with him. After the debate, Benoit was never again mentioned. Instead another author was chosen, one who quite accidentally has become fashionable among us through Russian translations even though he is not a contemporary author. [I have in mind] the American, O. Henry. His name has been firmly affixed to characterizations of Slisarenko's stories even though no one has done any comparative analysis, [the majority of] observations being limited to superficial comments about plot. Slisarenko's reputation as the "most plot-oriented" among our prose writers has grown stronger and, from this perspective, defenders of "plot" are ready to acknowledge him as one of the foremost powers in our literature (Bilets'kyi 1926, 156–57).

Slisarenko's prose as represented in the first collection can be divided roughly into three categories: satires ("Shpon'chyne zhyttia ta smert'," "Sotni tysiach syl," "Prezydent kyslokapustians'koï respubliky"), adventures ("Vypadkova smilyvist'," "Kriuchkovar"), and works of an

[18] Prolific French author (1886–1962) of exotic adventure novels, notably *Koenigsmark* (1918), *L'Atlantide* (1919), and *Pour Don Carlos* (1920).

anecdotal nature ("Pryhoda Sydora Petrovycha," "Dva pistony kukharchuka").[19] The satires have a certain predilection for low street language, slang, and obscenities, but it would be wrong to exaggerate these characteristics. These narratives tend to betray a more overt literary self-consciousness, through techniques like addressing the reader, revealing a device, or parody. The so-called adventure stories are, in contrast, far less self-reflecting. Carefully crafted, they place emphasis on pure storytelling without conspicuously attracting the reader's attention to their stratagems; these in particular make good use of surprise endings. Finally, the stories that resemble extended anecdotes share many of the same characteristics of Slisarenko's other works, but they are, as a rule, limited in scope and complexity.

Slisarenko's stories normally take place during the early revolutionary period, when the new order was in flux and the old had not entirely given up its positions. The settings are provincial, out-of-the-way places where "bandits" put up resistance to Soviet rule. "Shpon'chyne zhyttia ta smert'" [The Life and Death of Shpon'ka] is that rare instance of a story that takes place in a city. It tells of the proletarization and ultimate death of an aristocratic dog named Zizi who, after the revolution, becomes known by the pedestrian name Shpon'ka. It is a parodic fable with a political lesson, in which the new reality is made exotic and foreign by being depicted through the eyes of a dog. A self-conscious narrator makes literary asides, like this allusion to Modernism/Symbolism: "The author... is a coarse prose writer and does not like to digress from contemporary events into the beautiful, semi-mystical past." In the "epilogue," he addresses the reader: "Don't think, dear reader, that I wanted to present a moral here. It is true that Shpon'ka died while reacting to the call of the old life, but she could have lived, were it not for the passing trolley car. On the other hand, if you wish, you can take it as a moral lesson.... This will simply be another excuse to praise the author" (Slisarenko 1965, 374).

"Prezydent kyslokapustians'koï respubliky" [President of the Sauerkraut Republic] is a political satire. Subtitled "historical materials collected by an objective person," this anti-story is a collage of speeches, letters, and rumors loosely tied together by an incompetent chronicler who wants to serve "truth." It recounts how the village of Kapustianka [Cabbageville], proclaims itself the Ukrainian National Republic (UNR)

19 *Sotni tysiach syl* contained ten stories (see "Slisarenko, Oleksa Andriiovych," in Leites and Iashek (1930, 1: 448). The original collection was not accessible to me. I base my analysis on later editions of his prose: Slisarenko 1929 and 1965. Three of the original ten stories ("Zapalivs'ka istoriia," "Shtany," "V bolotakh") have not been reprinted. They remain outside my investigation.

and conducts an unsuccessful war against a neighboring Bolshevik settlement. The ending is partly an apology for the story's compositional chaos, and partly a Futurist rejection of Great Literature in the name of scholarship and fact:

> Моє писання про Кислокапустянську республіку та її президента має багато неґативних рис, але автор у тому не винен. Моє бажання було подати матеріяли, а не писати оповідання, коли ж матеріялів не вистачало, я не хотів вигадками заповнювати пробіли. От чому, хоча критики мене й вилають, зате Академія Наук похвалить. Автор у цьому твердо переконаний (Slisarenko 1929, 160).
>
> *My writings about the Sauerkraut Republic and its president have many negative aspects, but the author should not be faulted. My goal was to convey certain materials; it was not to write a story. When the materials proved insufficient, I did not want to fill the gaps with my personal inventions. Although critics will scold me, the Academy of Sciences will praise me. The author is absolutely certain of this.*

Of all Slisarenko's tales, this one especially is full of stylistic and compositional absurdities. It also accounts for much of the offending vocabulary[20] that so disturbed Zerov's literary sensibility and led him to argue that nothing—neither language, nor ideas, nor interesting events—could justify its publication (Zerov 1925, 38). These objections notwithstanding, the story, in fact, works quite well. Its style is dictated by the provincial nitwits who constitute the cast of characters. It manages to be politically scathing without becoming cloyingly tendentious. In general, Slisarenko had a remarkable ability to maintain an ironic distance from his subjects. This quality endows his prose with a certain air of impartiality even when he is being blatantly partisan.

"Sotni tysiach syl" was described by one critic in 1928 as an "unusually apt caricature… that pointed out unhealthy phenomena without becoming anti-Soviet" (Stepniak 1928).[21] The plot of this Gogolian story centers around "Professor" Shakhryns'kyi [Cheater], a bold confidence man with a nationalist political past. On the strength of bluster ("I invite you to California, to the Ukrainian California, where we will… have thousands of horsepower, utilizing just milligrams of effort!" [Slisarenko

[20] These included expressions such as "sukyn syn" [son of a bitch], "hivno" [shit], "morda, pyka," [snout, mug], "zasranyi" [shitty], "chort patlatyi" [hairy devil].

[21] This story was not republished in *Bunt* (Slisarenko 1965), but has now appeared in Slisarenko 1990.

1929, 161]) and the blessing of Soviet authorities, he sets in motion a scam to create a Polytechnic Institute in an out-of-the-way village, using Red Army deserters for students. The first-person narrator and co-conspirator is a lowly teacher who is made dean of this Institute.

Among the works written in a "serious" adventure vein, "Vypadkova smilyvist'" [Accidental Courage] is doubtlessly the best. It is a lean narrative, efficiently and effectively rendered in an understated manner. It builds suspense and mystery gradually and resolves them, literally, in the last sentence. Like most of the tales, this one is told in the first person by a character who relates his experience as a communist informer in a village resisting Soviet order. The banter between narrator and listener introduces a countervailing levity to what is otherwise a tense account. Slisarenko uses many of his typical devices here. The work begins abruptly *in media res*. The setting is sketched out in minimalist fashion, long description is eschewed. The language is simple, colloquial, and transparent, virtually without tropes or epithets. "Accidental Courage" is remarkable also for the way it depicts political realities. Slisarenko shows that not only was there deep suspicion of the Bolsheviks, but that they themselves were distrustful even of those who sided with them. This candor proved too much for censors: the ending—the very heart of the story—was excised in a recent Soviet edition, effectively destroying the work.[22]

Bilets'kyi had at one time drawn a comparison between Slisarenko and Shkurupii, and was struck by the "plainness" of Slisarenko's stories (Bilets'kyi 1926, 157). Indeed, Shkurupii's prose is almost ornamental and lush in comparison to Slisarenko's. Where the former is grandiose, the latter is understated. Where Shkurupii is heroic, Slisarenko is ironic; where Shkurupii's characters are in some way extraordinary, Slisarenko's are common. Shkurupii is unquestionably much more complex in the projection of his literary self-consciousness. Slisarenko has a highly developed sense of composition, form, and genre, but his goal (with some important exceptions) is neither their destruction nor their reification. Bilets'kyi had a point when he said that "the smell of life in [Slisarenko's] stories is stronger than the smell of literature" (ibid., 160). Indeed, unlike Shkurupii who compelled his reader to confront the nuts and bolts of "literature," Slisarenko's work has a tendency to linger in the reader's mind as a vicarious thrill.

[22] Compare the ending in *Bunt* (Slisarenko 1965, 352) with the one in *Neperemozhni syly* (Slisarenko 1929, 146). The ending was not restored in the most recent edition of Slisarenko's work (see Slisarenko 1990).

Dmytro Buz'ko (1890–1937)

While Oleksa Slisarenko gradually disassociated himself from Futurism, others were attracted into its ranks as much by the logic of their own creative work as by the movement's program. This was the case with Dmytro Buz'ko, who joined the movement in 1927.[23] If we put aside his earliest endeavors—those of 1918–1921, written (to quote him) when he was "an earnest nationalist" and "consciously" craved to "harm" the Soviet order (Buz'ko 1930d)—the beginning of Buz'ko's literary career can be dated with the publication of the short novel [*povist'*], *Lisovyi zvir* [The Forest Animal] (Buz'ko 1923; Buz'ko 1924a). A popular work, it immediately appeared in Russian translation (Buz'ko 1925) and was made into a film for which Buz'ko wrote the scenario.[24] This marked the start of his employment as a scriptwriter in VUFKU's Odesa studios, where he came into contact with Semenko.[25] In 1925 he established a literary relationship with the Futurists when his story "L'olia" [Lola] was published in *Zhurnal dlia vsikh*, where Semenko, Shkurupii, and Ialovyi (Shpol) served on the editorial board. Later, when *Nova generatsiia* was launched Buz'ko became a prominent participant, contributing to the journal well into the middle of 1930. The very first issue contained a short story and polemical article by him. As already noted, he also shared billing there with Shkurupii as co-author of a reportage that was subsequently integrated into the latter's *Dveri v den'*. In ensuing years, Buz'ko contributed to *Nova generatsiia* several more stories as well as one piece of "factual" writing—a two-part memoir of his experiences as a political prisoner in tsarist Russia (Buz'ko 1930a). Among the works he wrote as a tenured Futurist were an acclaimed study of the Ukrainian film industry (Buz'ko 1928a)[26] and two novels, one of which became a classic of Futurist "destructive" prose.

23 For an overivew of Buz'ko's biography and career, see Boiko 1991. Boiko offers here a much improved reading of Buz'ko over one he published twenty years ago (see Boiko [1971]). Among other things, he provides a new year for Buz'ko's birth (1890 vs. 1891) and a more definite date for his death, which, it turns out, was by firing squad on 14 November 1937. Previously, it was asserted that he had died from illness in 1943. See also Musiienko 1991.

24 The film was directed by A. Lundin in VUFKU's Odesa studios. Completed in 1924, it premiered in Kyiv on 17 June 1925 and a week later in Moscow.

25 Buz'ko wrote filmscripts for several other productions: "MacDonald" (1924, directed by Les' Kurbas); "Son Tovstopuzenka" (directed by Les' Kurbas), "Dymivka" (1926, directed by P. Sazonov), "Zhyttia Tarasa Shevchenka," co-authored with M. Panchenko (1926, directed by P. Chardynin). See Korniienko (1970, 189–190).

26 See the review of this work by M. Bush [Nik Bazhan] (Bush 1929).

One can better grasp Dmytro Buz'ko's writings by dwelling briefly on his article "A Problematical 'Problematicalness'" (Buz'ko 1927b), subtitled "A Reader's Protest"—an outcry not only against "philosophy" and "deep human problems" in literature but also a rejection of the writer-as-mentor. "I hated L. Tolstoy for assuming the role of mankind's teacher," he begins.

> I, a diligent student of philosophy, was struck by the difference that existed between the humble language of genuine specialists who tackled complex problems and the tone of this Russian count who dressed in a peasant shirt. From that time I harbored, so to speak, a sacred hostility for every writer who continued to uphold this tradition in his literary creativity, tried to teach the reader something, to educate him in some fashion, in short, to present, as is often said, a profound issue.... (ibid., 58).

"It is my conviction," proceeded Buz'ko, "that the pseudo-philosophical epidemic, this classic consequence of prerevolutionary ideology, effectively continues to control our literature," with the difference that at present it has a "sociological" accent.

> I recall that Western European [and] American literature comfortably distinguishes itself from our own in that the author hardly ever assumes the pose of a philosopher, a teacher, but remains a pure belletrist, dedicated to perfecting... his craft. His ideology, his world view are expressed in his work effortlessly, naturally, without force or sweat....
>
> The tendency toward profound problems in belles-lettres is, without doubt, a consequence of our low level of material culture, the weak development of our technology, [and a result of the fact that] the principle of division of labor (differentiation) has not penetrated the consciousness of society.... [Consequently] there is ample room for dilettantish omniscience, for bold attacks on the reader by villains who disguise themselves as wise men and philosophers.... (ibid., 59).

Buz'ko believed writers should foster their craft and leave the solution of philosophical and sociological problems to experts. "The writer's progenitor," he argued, was not "the philosopher but the comedian-storyteller...." In his view, contemporary philosophical writers were not only cheats but disgraceful traitors to their profession (ibid.).

Sentiments such as these were to animate much of the writing of Buz'ko himself, who happily "engaged in [the] honorable business" of the "storyteller." Utilizing devices of popular fiction, he sought to express—"effortlessly, naturally, without force or sweat"—the ideology of his new society. Characteristically, his works combined "relevant" contemporary themes with compositional techniques designed to capture the reader's interest.

This orientation was already apparent in *Lisovyi zvir*—a first-person narrative, purportedly autobiographical (Buz'ko 1930d, 68), that recounts how a writer with a dubious political past makes amends before the Soviet regime by voluntarily going underground as a Cheka operative. His assignment is to bring to justice a nationalist rebel leader whose band terrorizes the countryside and attacks Red Army units. This "noble" theme surrenders largely to plot as the narrator, imagining himself to be Sherlock Holmes, describes his infiltration of the opposition and his adventures in their midst. Scenes, episodes, and locales change feverishly. Suspense is created by the constant threat of discovery that hangs over the narrator. In 1930, when the Party became more stringent in matters of theme, Buz'ko felt obliged to confess that the characters in this novel were "silhouettes—not living people" and that the causes behind the "banditry" as well as the class relationships were poorly described (ibid.). Of course, his original intention had been to avoid such things at all cost. In *Lisovyi zvir*, Buz'ko was obviously slipping from under the influence of prerevolutionary aesthetics, although as he conceded, the novel did retain certain "impressionistic" traits (ibid.). In places it was quite opaque and lapsed into lyricism: "The day appeared to be calm. The sun sat atop tall birches and covered the forest with a golden web. The forest enjoyed this: 'More, more,' it begged and fell silent in ringing expectation" (Buz'ko 1924a, 73). This was a manner Buz'ko would eventually abandon, but not before succumbing to it completely in "Po shchyrosti" [In All Sincerity] (Buz'ko 1924b), a tale that shared certain thematic lines with the novel *Lisovyi zvir* (e.g., banditry and ideological vacillation on the part of the hero). Here, however, Buz'ko placed emphasis on mood rather than external conflict, imbuing his short story with a dream-like quality by showing events through the disfiguring prism of the narrator's fragile consciousness.

The three short stories in *Nova generatsiia* were fairly typical of Buz'ko's output in the second half of the decade.[27] In one form or another they were all satires on some aspect of bourgeois society and manners. Executed through clever and dynamic compositional techniques, they placed a premium on the unexpected denouement. "Asta Nil'son" [Asta Nielsen] (Buz'ko 1927a), for example, is set in Copenhagen during World War I where Buz'ko had lived briefly as a political émigré. A story of love, jealousy and assassination, it is imbued with a sardonic tone toward Danish mercantile values and maintains an overtly capricious attitude toward the narrative process itself. Self-referential and self-conscious, it is replete with digressions ("I must interrupt this story...") and authorial

[27] For his other works see Buz'ko 1930c and Buz'ko 1930e.

asides ("Don't think that my Asta Nielsen is the famous movie star..."). Because of the theme and composition, Buz'ko considered "Asta Nielsen" his best work (Buz'ko 1930d, 70).

Not all of the author's prose was as "effortless" as he would have liked it to be. In fact, some proved quite stilted precisely because of his insistence on compositional surprise. Works like "Tsinoiu krovy"[28] [At the Price of Blood] (Buz'ko 1928c), about a medical student making ends meet by donating blood to an anemic "bourgeois" hag, and "Opovidannia pro Sofochku i Dzhyma" [A Story about Little Sophie and Jim] (Buz'ko 1929b), in which marriage and prostitution are made synonymous, succeed in garnering interest but ultimately fail because the endings are contrived and incongruous. They retain, however, a modicum of seductive power owing to their "shocking" treatment of the extravagant and unwholesome aspects of life. This is particularly true of the jaundiced and vituperative "Tsinoiu krovy" which is contemptuously anti-aesthetic in its use of a low, physiological lexicon ("Natalka says that her 'friend' is a decent guy. True, a bit old. Doubtlessly he has hemorrhoids. So what? His profession—accounting—is also hemorrhoidal...").

Nothing Buz'ko wrote was as controversial as his anti-novel *Holiandiia* [Nudia, 1930] (Buz'ko 1930b),[29] which he openly admitted was wrought "under the influence" of *Nova generatsiia*'s theories (Buz'ko 1930d, 74). The Futurists spoke of it as "a montage of the reportage, polemical writings [*publitsystyka*], and parodic fragments of the 'pure' novel" (*Nova generatsiia* 1930 [2]: 64). They called it an "experimental novel" in which "the author destroys old novels [and] literary forms" in order to link them with the "factuality of the reportage" (Buz'ko 1929a).[30] Buz'ko himself explained that "the basis for this 'novel' is the author's sincere acknowledgment that he is incapable of treating the commune and collectivization themes through the devices of a common novel" (ibid.). Elsewhere, the emphasis was placed not so much on the abilities of the author as on the shortcomings of literature itself: "The formal theme is to prove that the [above-mentioned] subjects cannot be treated through the devices of 'artistic literature'" (*Nova generatsiia* 1930 [2]: 64).

[28] Buz'ko called this a "very bad story." See Buz'ko (1930d, 71).

[29] An excerpt from the novel first appeared in *Nova generatsiia* (Buz'ko 1929a). The Ukrainian title derives from the word "naked" [*holyi*], hence my English translation. Until very recenty, most works of criticism and bibliographies assumed, incorrectly, that the novel refers to Holland and cite it as *Hollandiia*. See, for example, Boiko (1971, 6, 8) and Koval' and Pavlovs'ka (1988, 93).

[30] This description appears on the contents page.

Holiandiia can be thought of as a critical and analytical discourse on the stratagems, artifice, and subterfuge of the literary craft. Its primary preoccupation is literature and narration. In the course of a reluctant attempt to write a relevant novel about collectivization, Buz'ko lays bare the conventions of genre, character, plot, and motivation. He approaches his venture with skepticism, futility and not without some antagonism toward the reader whose retrograde expectations tie the narrator's hands. Literature is viewed as a lie and the novelist as nothing less than a swindler who substitutes "literary" thinking for regular, logical "human" thought.

It is the first-person narrator who gives this centrifugal work its unity. He is both creator and critic of the novel. But even he is recognized as little more than a convention and his authority is intentionally undermined. "I must observe," says a voice, "that I am not I. I am the wind. Changing and uncertain.... Let this novel be written by this other, invented I. While I will continue to search for the factual, documentary truth..." (Buz'ko 1930b, 4). This evasive and protean mouthpiece of the author (who also figures as a separate entity) frequently engages the reader in conversations about the ever-evolving novel:

> ...Бо ж читач із обуренням скаже:
>
> — Якого ж біса ви тоді вивели Гафійку й Петра на сцену? Щоб вони ото посварилися й розійшлися? Поганий ви романіст.
>
> Знаю я це, читачу, через те й стараюся. В мене ж бо дві фабульні нитки. Одна—колективізація села Сокільчого. Друга—романтичний трикутник: Петро, Гафійка, Тамара. За літтеорією дві фабульні нитки обов'язково повинні сплестися в одну. Інакше й не треба, щоб їх було дві. А як же мені не мати їх дві, коли про саму колективізацію вийшло б нудно...
>
> — Як? Що?—обурюється читач.—Нудно про колективізацію писати? Таке складне, таке цікаве явище й нудно? (ibid., 125–26).
>
> *The reader will say indignantly: "Why the hell did you [the narrator] introduce Hafiika and Petro [two central characters] into the scene? Just so they can have an argument and then go their separate ways? [If so,] you are a bad novelist."*
>
> *Dear reader, I am aware of this, and for that reason I am trying the best I can. I have, after all, two plot lines. One is the collectivization of the village of Sokil'che. The second is a romantic triangle: Petro, Hafiika, and Tamara. According to literary theory these two plot lines must, most definitely, merge into one. Otherwise there is no need for two. But how can I not have two plots, when writing about collectivization itself would be boring?*
>
> *"How's that? What did you say?" the reader says indignantly. "You say it's boring to write about collectivization? Such a complex, such an*

interesting phenomenon and you say it's boring?"

Formal and compositional issues (almost always spoofed) are the central concern of *Holiandiia*. To avoid exposition and description, Buz'ko sometimes uses names of well-known authors as ready-made formulas and short-cuts to evoke requisite literary situations, characters, or emotions ("Here, dear reader, I am imitating Kuprin, Vynnychenko, etc. All of them wrote about such prostitutes..."). Instead of delving into the psychology of his character's sexual urges, the narrator simply sends the reader to learn about these facts from "our solid writer [V.] Pidmohyl'nyi [who] elaborated these feelings carefully in his novel *Misto* [The City, 1928]" (ibid., 201).

Among the more whimsical devices used in the novel to undermine the mimetic and realistic expectations of the reader is a character named Iankovs'kyi "who crawls out" from *Lisovyi zvir*. He is assigned a pivotal but purposely anticlimactic role: in one episode Iankovs'kyi nearly assassinates Buz'ko, his creator. Real individuals also figure in *Holiandiia*. The author hails his poet-friends from *Nova generatsiia* (ibid., 175) and pokes fun at Geo Shkurupii's manner of writing ("...inspiration comes to him when [his three-year old son] Hoha spills ink on the manuscript and punches his father's nose with his fists..."; ibid., 40).

Within the parameters of the two plots (a love triangle and collectivization), Buz'ko pursues several themes that are typical not only of his other works but of the Futurist movement as a whole. The most prominent of these are the sexual motifs and the opposition between city and village. Considering the time and circumstances of writing, the erotic moments in the novel are handled with surprising candor and in an openly anti-romantic, anti-sentimental manner. The antagonism between village and city betrays a characteristically Futurist disdain for the rural way of life as something primitive and insipid.

It goes without saying that on publication *Holiandiia* received a cold reception. One reviewer held that it was "in general an interesting novel, written in the experimental vein" but that, unfortunately, the issues dealt with by the work were "handled in such a difficult and absolutely unintelligible form" that they would create "in the uninitiated reader" "contradictory impressions" (S. 1930). At a time when Soviet critics wanted to see "life of the Ukrainian village during the reconstruction period," Buz'ko's exploitation of this theme for purely formal play was deemed irresponsible and downright hostile. His depiction of communal life was called a parody of the real thing and a warning was issued: "Buz'ko... must take into account the consequences that flow from his contemporary literary activities. He must remember that works such as

Holiandiia will be properly evaluated not only by literary criticism but also by the mass readership..." (H.H. 1930). Being no fool, Buz'ko immediately resigned from *Nova generatsiia*.

Leonid Skrypnyk (1893–1929)

> Талант є талант і він, сукин син, завжди проб'ється і посяде те місце на яке заслуговує.
>
> *A genius is a genius and the son-of-a-bitch will always come through and assume his rightful place.*
>
> L. Skrypnyk (1928b, 295).

A theoretician and prose writer, Skrypnyk was one of the most accomplished and interesting Futurists. Today he is also the most obscure. On 23 February 1929, at age 36, he died of tuberculosis.[31] Due, largely, to the unpopularity among official circles of his radically "destructive" views on art and formalist writings, memory of this talented individual disappeared almost completely after his passing.

Skrypnyk was an engineer by training. Initially he was interested in aerodynamics and before World War I engaged in early flight attempts ("Leonid Skrypnyk" 1929b). Later, as was noted above, he would write that writers needed "administrative" and "engineering" skills to maintain control over their literary material and devices. In the early 1920s he abandoned his profession and turned toward film, working in the Odesa studios. This led to the writing of one book on photography and another on film theory (L. Skrypnyk 1927; L. Skrypnyk 1929f).[32] Like Buz'ko, he became a regular contributor to *Nova generatsiia* when it began publication.

Skrypnyk's prose legacy includes one novel, *Intelihent*[33] [The Intellectual] (L. Skrypnyk 1929b), one short story, "Materiialy do biohrafiï pys'mennyka Loputs'ky" [Materials Toward a Biography of the Writer Loputs'ka] (Skrypnyk 1928b), and two chapters from an incomplete novel, *Epizody z zhyttia chudnoï liudyny* [Episodes from the Life of a

[31] This date is given in his obituary. See "Leonid Skrypnyk" 1929a. *Krytyka* lists 26 February as the day of death. See "Leonid Skrypnyk" 1929b.

[32] The latter work was positively reviewed by D. Buz'ko (Buz'ko 1928b) and Ol. Ozerov (Ozerov 1928).

[33] *Intelihent* was first serialized in *Nova generatsiia* under the pseudonym Levon Lain. See Lain 1927–28.

Strange Person] (L. Skrypnyk 1928a and 1928c). Although each of these works is peculiarly distinctive, all draw in one form or another on the "biographical" mode. Every narrative amounts to a "life" of a male character, told with a maximum sense of literary self-awareness, analytical acumen, and stylistic economy.

In "Materiialy do biohrafiï pys'mennyka Loputs'ky" these traits manifest themselves as flagrant satire and parody. The writer in the story is a hack and, hence, the darling of the literary establishment which bestows on him wealth and free trips abroad. In Germany, Loputs'ka is awed by clean toilets and machines dispensing condoms. The story ridicules proletarian art, Marxist criticism (it has transparent allusions to such organizations as VAPP, MAPP, and VUSPP),[34] provincialism, and such popular literary clichés as "unity with the masses" and "orientation on Europe." All this is achieved in a demonstratively formalist manner that includes pseudo-scholarly footnotes and pedantic explanations. The heading of one section, for example, reads: "Episode eight (not necessarily a continuation of [episode] seven, for it can exist independently)." "Materiialy..." is actually composed of fifteen such "episodes" as well as several "non-episodes," all haphazardly assembled into a narrative that is the very antithesis of what "proletarian classicism" required—namely, a work that would be "understandable, clear, precise, forged and hardened by the proletarian cultural revolution..." (Skrypnyk 1928b, 294).

The two extant chapters of *Epizody z zhyttia chudnoï liudyny* take fewer liberties with narrative convention, although they too telegraph their literary self-consciousness through short digressions and asides that debunk "poets and prose writers," especially their approach to the subject of love. Skrypnyk, who prefers the role of "historian" to that of "writer," chronicles the erotic experiences of a certain Ivan Petrovych. He does this in a coldly dispassionate "scientific" style ("From this moment on, Ivan Petrovych's love entered a third stage...") (Skrypnyk 1928a, 21), carefully anatomizing the behavioral and psychological manifestations of love in a young man during two periods of his life: at age thirteen and seventeen. The protagonist's emotions are virtually dissected. They are portrayed as a primordial, dark force irrevocably in conflict with the intellect, inflicting agony on him and death on the object of his desires. While there are moments of irony and sarcasm (for example, in scenes describing the lasciviousness of Old Russia's aristocracy), the

34 The acronyms stand, respectively, for: the All-Union Association of Proletarian Writers; its Moscow branch; and, the All-Ukrainian Association of Proletarian Writers.

narrative for the most part evolves in cold efficient steps to a tragic conclusion. There is a hint of this at the end of the chapter entitled "The First Love of Ivan Petrovych":

> Поети й белетристи-прозаїки, коли дорівнюють зародження любови до прекрасного ранку, —брешуть...Любовний порив—це порив у майбутнє, а майбутнє, —це не ми. Людина обмежена в часі, і життя її—в її сучасному. Майбутнього в неї нема. В майбутньому в неї смерть. Любов—це міст у майбутнє, але пройти цим мостом не судилося нікому... (Skrypnyk 1928c, 47).
>
> *Those poets and prose writers who have compared the birth of love to a beautiful morning are liars....The love impulse is an impulse—toward the future, but we are not the future. A human being is circumscribed by time, and his life is in the present. A human being has no future. For him the future holds only death. Love is a bridge into the future but no one has yet managed to cross it.*

Eros is not a romantic concept for Skrypnyk. In the excerpt "Ivan Petrovych and Felis" an innocent, sensitive, and idealistic young man finds his love being reciprocated by a young woman who, he imagines, descended from a Pre-Raphaelite painting. The narrator emphasizes that this couple is destined "to repeat the experience of millions and billions of lovers" (Skrypnyk 1928a, 21). Their "fairy tale," however, is short-lived. To Ivan Petrovych's horror, Felis (the girl he loves) is not the vision of purity he fancied, but a sexually experienced woman, wantonly abused as a child and presently the unwilling mistress of several old men. Coolly, Skrypnyk shows how the young man responds to "canons and principles born of emotions," which "humanity has preserved within itself for hundreds of thousands of years...." Against the better judgment of his "intellect," Ivan Petrovych gives in to a primitive axiom: "The woman I love must not have belonged to anyone else in the past" (ibid., 23). Skrypnyk continues:

> [Іван Петрович] закликав на допомогу свою людську гордість, гордість самоосвідомленого розуму, —але вона розбивалась об ображену й розпечену вогнем помсти гордість чоловіка. Іван Петрович в одчаї проклинав богохульственно страшні кайдани законів почуття...Стародавні закони почуття впали на нього всією тисячолітньою вагою, розчавили й знищили його... (ibid., 24).
>
> *[Ivan Petrovych] sought help in his human pride, the pride of a self-conscious intellect, but it was decimated by his insulted and incendiary masculine ego. In despair, Ivan Petrovych cursed blasphemously at the*

terrible chains [thrust upon him] by the laws of feeling, but he was powerless against their weight.... Ancient emotional laws fell on him with all their thousand-year-old weight, crushing and destroying him....

While Ivan Petrovych dies a thousand spiritual deaths, the desperate and despondent Felis, who discovers in him her first true love, ends her life under a tramcar. For the narrator this is symbolic of the relationship between the sexes. As Ivan Petrovych stands besides Felis' corpse, he must contend with the silent rebuke of a nurse:

> В тоні сестри була така ненависть, що Іван Петрович відвів голову й подивився їй в очі. В цих безбарвних очах палала злість. Півтора мільйони років жіночого рабства зникли в присутності трупа жінки, вбитої лише за те, що любила. Літня сіра дівчина повстала проти мужчини, володаря життя, чиє право давати життя і вбивати.
>
> Як колись сам Іван Петрович зробив з старим небесним богом так зараз ця дівчина, нащадок тисяч поколінь рабинь, жорстоко осудила його—мужчину, і мужчина—володар, мужчина—вбивець, не витримав тягаря вироку і схилив голову... (ibid., 31).

> *The hatred in the nurse's voice was such that Ivan Petrovych raised his head and looked into her eyes. Inside those colorless eyes there was blistering anger: a million and a half years of female oppression disappeared in the presence of this woman's body, killed only because she loved. An average, aging Woman stood up against Man-the-Ruler-of-Existence whose right it was to give life and take it away.*
>
> *As Ivan Petrovych had done a long time ago with the old heavenly God, so now this woman—a descendant of thousands of generations of slaves—sternly condemned him, a Man. And Man-the-Ruler, Man-the-Murderer could not bear the weight of her verdict, and he bowed his head....*

The notion of love and sex as an atavism that contravenes reason and intellect survives in Skrypnyk's *Intelihent*, his longest and most polished work, although here the theme evolves in conjunction with other concerns—the question of art.[35] But *Intelihent*'s first and most arresting feature is not necessarily its subject; it is the form. Called a "screened novel" [*ekranizovanyi roman*], it is written as a film scenario that includes running commentaries by the author, as well as his conversations with

[35] The novel was reviewed—not very well—by L. Starynkevych in *Krytyka* (Starynkevych 1929b). For a spirited defense of *Intelihent* see Oskar Reding [Volodymyr Hadzins'kyi] 1929.

the reader. These two narrative modes are made visually and stylistically discrete. The scenario is a matter-of-fact, third-person description of events taking place on a silent movie screen that is being "viewed" simultaneously by reader and author. Typography establishes the scenario as the primary text: the author's remarks are indented and set in small type. Moreover, they are conducted in the first-person and contain frequent apostrophes to the reader. The commentator introduces himself thus:

> Я, автор і ваш друг, ввесь час поруч вас. Я буду для вас тим тлумачем, що завжди присутній в кожнім японськім кіно. З увагою слухайте й мене, хоч я й говоритиму тільки пошепки, на вухо, дрібним шрифтом (Skrypnyk 1929b, 8).
>
> *I, the author and your friend, will at all times be near you. I will be that interpreter who is always present in every Japanese film. Be sure to listen to me carefully even though I will only whisper into your ear in small print.*

This author allows himself great liberties. He judges the action taking place on the "screen" and evaluates the director's skill in setting up his "shots." He interprets the actors' gestures, pointing out their hidden meanings. He is alternately sarcastic, ironic, naive and philosophical. In this interplay between an astute author and the "objective" screen-events, thirty-five years of a man's life unfolds. He has no name, just the epithet "Intellectual." This is Skrypnyk's Everyman, very much related to his equally common Ivan Petrovych. "My dear hero is a thousand years old. He has changed his name often, very often....He is extremely resilient and has carried his fundamental biological features from the darkness of millennia to our day" (ibid., 145). "My hero lives among you and is, frequently, within you" (ibid., 7). The author admits that there was a time when he loved his hero, "considered him a higher order of being. I took great pains to become like him.... I sincerely believed that any person that wore a pince-nez and collar was... a superman" (ibid, 8).

The novel begins in the 1890s with the birth of the Intellectual; it dwells on his adolescence, the first stirrings of his libido, his early sexual experiences. It shows him as a successful member of Russian society, a patriot of Mother Russia during the time of the provisional government. After the Bolshevik revolution, he flees to Ukraine, but here, too, the communist regime overtakes him. Nevertheless, thanks to his oratorical skills he becomes a prominent functionary. Only overzealous adherence to regulations leads to his downfall.

This plot allows Skrypnyk to satirize hypocrisy, political opportunism, and bureaucracy. But he is at his best when casting a jaundiced eye at the sexes, at the psycho-social complex and protocols that define their relationship and roles. Sexuality, which "respectable" society tries to sweep under the rug, is shown to be life's prime motive force. Biology and emotion are at the root of all actions, even as man pretends that he is guided by intellect.

> Ми ставимось до нашого мислення з величезною офіційною повагою. Ми часто буваємо щиро переконані, що наш хазяїн—мозок. Це тільки тому, що в нас його ще мало. Так мало, що дуже багатьом удається впевнити себе, що його багато. Не вірте навіть собі в цьому. Це небезпечна помилка. Більшість людей процес відчуття називають здебільшого „думанням". Чи звернули ви увагу на те, як надзвичайно часто ми чуємо навколо себе слова: „Я думаю". Можна подумати, що ми живемо вже в справжньому світі розуму.—Не вірте. Дев'ятсот дев'яносто дев'ять чоловіка з тисячі думають дуже рідко. Але вся тисяча постійно, безперервно щось та відчуває... (ibid., 129).
>
> *We take our thinking with great official seriousness. We are often sincerely convinced that intellect is our master. That's because there is so little of it. There is so little of it that many manage to convince themselves that there is a lot of it. Don't even trust yourself on this score. This is a dangerous mistake. Most people call the process of feeling—"thinking." Have you noticed how often we hear the words: "I'm thinking." One would imagine that we live in a genuine world of reason. Don't believe it. Nine hundred, ninety-nine out of a thousand people think only very rarely. But every single one of them feels something, constantly and without end....*

Of all the Futurists, Skrypnyk was probably most successful in embodying the movement's twin philosophical pillars: formalism and rationalism. His works achieve this end so naturally and organically that they lend some credence to the Futurist slogan that "art was dying as an emotional category."

Top: Cover art for Geo Shkurupii, *Noveli nashoho chasu. Proza.* vol. 1. Kharkiv-Kyiv: LiM, 1931. *Bottom:* Cover art for Leonid Skrypnyk, *Intelihent. Ekranizovanyi roman na shist' chastyn z prolohom ta epilohom.* Kyiv: Proletarii, 1929.

CHAPTER 10

Visual Experiments in Poetry and Prose

Ut pictura poesis.

Horace, *Ars Poetica.*

Futurist literature was produced in a distinctly polyartistic atmosphere. It will be recalled that two of the three co-founders of Futurism were painters (Vasyl' Semenko and Pavlo Kovzhun). Later, the movement found allies in the theater (Marko Tereshchenko, Les' Kurbas) and cinema (Oleksander Dovzhenko). Many a Futurist (Mykola Bazhan, Dmytro Buz'ko, Mykhail' Semenko, Leonid Skrypnyk, Oleksii Poltorats'kyi, Geo Shkurupii) was intimately connected with the film industry either as a scriptwriter, editor, or theoretician. Futurist publications were nearly always close collaborative ventures involving artists: V. Tatlin designed the cover of *Zustrich na perekhresnii stantsiï*; *Nova generatsiia*'s layout was fashioned by prominent figures in set design (Vadym Meller), photography (Dan Sotnyk), and painting (Anatol' Petryts'kyi). Not without reason has *Semafor u Maibutnie* been called a masterpiece of publishing (Poltorats'kyi 1966).

Given this context and the Futurists' penchant for "synthesis," it is not unexpected that writing itself was shaped by the influence of other media. We have previously mentioned Semenko's "poetry-films" [*poezofil'my*], Skrypnyk's "screened novel" [*ekranizovanyi roman*] *Intelihent*, and Shkurupii's "Shop Windows" [*vitryny*], that is, the collection *Baraban*. These were not anomalies, but manifestations of a broad and diverse effort to interrelate the visual element with the literary. Thus writers and photographers collaborated to investigate whether photographs could be used "not as an illustration to the text, but as an inseparable part" of it (Poltorats'kyi and Sotnyk 1929).[1] In *Zhovtnevyi zbirnyk panfuturystiv* (1923) a symbiosis was established between posters and poetry. Two texts here were actually classified as "posters" (Iaroshenko 1923;

[1] The comment appears on p. 2 of *Nova generatsiia*'s table of contents.

Savchenko 1923c). But even so-called "poems" succumbed to the dictates of this promotional graphic genre: flamboyant and highly politicized in content, they were done in a striking layout and with an imaginative use of typography. The entire publication employed "montage" as the principle for organizing its diverse material of "words," "posters," and "slogans" into a single whole.[2]

Experiments such as these were meant to shift literature away from an exclusively semantic plane. Text was not treated as a mere sign. It acquired the properties of a material object, giving Futurist works a new ontology. The unit of meaning was no longer simply the individual word: the page and line took on relevance and signification, as did size and placement of text. A concerted effort was made to draw attention to the technology of writing and printing itself. Hence, typography became an integral part of many works. On the most elementary level, this was manifested as an increased awareness of the verse line and its arrangement on the page. At another, it involved bringing the alphabet into relief, thereby endowing language with an unexpected tangible quality. As mentioned earlier, the Futurists repeatedly turned their backs on Cyrillic in favor of Latin script. On some occasions they even banned upper-case letters from their publications (see *Nova generatsiia* 1930). Such actions served as a form of visual "interference," meant to contravene habitual responses to the printed word by drawing readers away from the denoting text to its physical form.

In 1922 Mykhail' Semenko had argued that the final "death throes" of traditional poetry demanded "energetic experimentation" with "the material of poetry" (that is, "the word") so that "new ways of writing poetry" might be found. Words were to be "dissolved" into their "primary" ("visual" and "aural") elements. In fusing them into a new art—one that would be "completely unlike [any] previous" art—the writer was to govern himself by principles derived either from painting or music (Semenko 1922c, 32). Relying on the former, Semenko began work a year earlier on a genre he called "poetry-painting" [*poezomaliarstvo*], a type of intermediary art between "poetry" and "posters."

Semenko published two cycles in this vein: "Kablepoema za okean" ["Cablepoem Across the Sea," begun in 1920, completed in 1921], and "Moia mozaïka" ["My Mosaic," 1922]. Both are composed of a series of separate "cards" ("Kablepoema za okean" has eight, "Moia mozaïka," ten), sporting elaborately arranged text and, in one instance, mathematical

2 The "montage" is attributed to Geo Shkurupii and Nik Bazhan.

symbols. Each "card" of the "Kablepoema..." is printed on an off-white cardboard page in black and red ink.[3] "Moia mozaïka," likely, was executed in the same manner, but there are no known color reproductions of this work.[4] Cyrillic (in various styles, shapes and sizes) predominates; however, text in Latin transliteration appears in both works as well. Virtually all these texts—or, more precisely, verbal constructions—are enclosed in a frame-like border. The works, therefore, take place not directly on the "page" but within a secondary and independent environment defined by Semenko. One can actually speak of a "canvas"—a notion reinforced by the fact that all "cards" bear the author's (painter's?) name, are titled, and (in the case of "Moia mozaïka") are even dated just beneath the "frame."

For all their similarities, "Kablepoema za okean" and "Moia mozaïka" are wholly different works.[5] The title of "Kablepoema..." suggests it to be a synthesis of at least two types of "written" media: the telegram and the narrative poem. This is reflected in the style which is not only terse, laconic, and elliptical but also distinctly narrational. A consecutive numeration of the cards largely predetermines just how this visual work will be "read" and "looked at." The continuity and unity of the "Kablepoema" is further underscored by a consistent graphic format and single theme. Two vertical panels (rectangles), one of which is additionally segmented into horizontal boxes, alternate from left to right on each consecutive card. The theme, developed in a provocatively Futurist manner, is a celebration of the new cultural and industrial world order.

Within this graphic framework, the unsegmented panel always contains a syntactically coherent text, in other words, a poem in free verse complete with title.[6] In contrast, the horizontal boxes of the segmented panel contain individual words or brief phrases realized in large, bold and, occasionally, oddly shaped type.

[3] "Kablepoema za okean" appeared first in *Shliakhy mystetstva* (Semenko 1921a) as a straightforward text in two columns. Semenko claimed it was published here without his permission (see Semenko 1922b). Its only full color publication as "poetry-painting" occurred in *Semafor u Maibutnie* (Semenko 1922a). Half of the text (minus formatting and layout) is also extant in a Russian translation by Iu. Nikitin (see Semenko 1922d). It was reprinted in a reduced format and without color in Semenko 1924c and again in Semenko (1925a, 575–82). The work also appeared in Semenko 1925c.

[4] "Moia mozaïka" first appeared in Semenko 1924c; reprinted in Semenko (1925a, 607–16). Reprinted again in Semenko (1929–31, vol. 2). There are minor differences between the 1925 and 1930 editions of this work (see below).

[5] For more on these two works, see Mudrak 1986. I have expressed my views on this publication in Ilnytzkyj 1987.

[6] The first poem, on "Card No. 2," is called "Introduction." "Card No. 1" has no poem since it is designated as the "Cover."

If arranging words into a graphic pattern is Semenko's way of fusing the literary and visual arts, his heterogeneous verbal material indicates a desire to exploit and combine a variety of language styles. The "Kablepoema" uses discourse reminiscent of telegrams, political slogans ("Proletarians Unite!"), even graffiti ("Semenko=idiot"). All this linguistic material is mounted on the cards for the amusement of the reader. However, one cannot possibly approach it in a uniform manner. Some texts (the free verse, for example) must be read for content in the normal manner. The large single words—and the card as whole—make more sense when "viewed" or "surveyed." Still other words (e.g., the slogans) encourage vocalization.

Unlike the preceding work, the individual cards of "Moia mozaïka" do not combine to produce a thematic, narrative, or visual whole. Each card in this instance is a separate entity. More light-hearted and less political than the "Kablepoema," "Moia mozaïka" has two conspicuous motifs running through the cards: one tends toward the personal, the other toward literary and artistic themes. Both are handled in a Futuristic and Dadaesque manner: the humor is irreverent and absurd, while the polemics are strident and bombastic.

As visual poems, the works of "Moia mozaïka" fall into two general categories. At the core of one group, there is normally a text with a linguistically coherent sequence of words. One could argue that these are little more than graphically embellished poems. Another group consists of works whose text is deliberately disconnected, nonsequential, arranged without recourse to syntax. They give the impression of being random arrangements of separate words and sounds, and are, therefore, more ambiguous since the reader has no common, ready-made system to fall back on when deciphering their meaning. In such cases the message, if it exists at all, must be laboriously extracted using the implicit, largely spatial "syntax" of the works themselves.

Works of the first category, that is, those with normal sentences and syntax, tend to use visual and typographic elements primarily as aids for oral or semantic interpretation. Large or bold text, for example, helps establish the proper intonation of an utterance, its relative volume in relation to other words. In lines of pure phonetic text such stylistic features may indicate correct pronunciational stress (e.g., "a-KA, a-KA, a-KA"). Some typographical devices serve as visual tautologies, reiterating semantic meaning through graphic means. Take for example the card entitled "Panfuturysty" [Panfuturists]. The word "down" [*vnyz*] is rendered thus:

в
н
и
з

while the phrase "at the bottom" [*na dni*] appears as the lowest element in a block of words:

червоїди
В МУЛІ
НА ДНІ

w o r m s
I N M U D
AT THE BOTTOM

Of the works in which syntax plays no role, "Suprepoeziia" [Suprepoem] and "Systema" [System] are especially worth a closer examination. "Suprepoeziia" is constructed as four identical and adjoining rectangles, each of which is filled with discrete words (arranged either horizontally or vertically) in stern typefaces of different sizes and styles. In addition, one rectangle contains numerals marking pivotal years in Semenko's life: 1892 (birth); 1914 (publication of his first collection); 1917 (his return to Ukraine from Vladivostok); 1922 (inauguration of activities of The Association of Panfuturists). These dates as well as other words—for example, "Kybyntsi" (Semenko's birthplace)—give this enigmatic work a certain autobiographical patina. Some words (*rozbyshaka, khvorist'* [scoundrel, illness]) allude to the literary scandals in his life; still others, by their proximity and juxtaposition, seem to be designed to do little more than provoke the ire of literary traditionalists (*liryka kurka* [lyric chicken]). But what the poem lacks in semantic clarity, it more than makes up by its direct homage to Kazimir Malevych [Malevich]. The very title, the simplicity and pureness of its geometrical arrangement, and its studied flatness make this an unambivalent adoption of Malevych's artistic ideas (that is, suprematism) to literature.

"Systema" is entirely different. In place of rectilinear order, this poem gives us "words in freedom." It is composed almost entirely of place names, personal names, and literary titles that float at odd angles and arcs. A variety of typographic styles and sizes create a dynamic, circus-like mood—quite appropriate for a work whose theme is modernism and the avant-garde.

There are, so to speak, two basic semantic groupings in this poem. One is "western," consisting of the following words: Picasso, Marinetti, New York, London, Paris, Cézanne, van Gogh, [Umberto] Boccioni,

Gérard de Nerval, Walt Whitman, Gauguin. The other set is "Ukrainian" and evokes Futurist personalities and publications from 1914 to 1922. It is salient that the "western" and "Ukrainian" sets are clustered separately. Western names occupy the upper third of the page. They are segregated from the rest (the "Ukrainian" part) by the word "revolution" which is repeated four times across the page and lodged between two black horizontal bars. Below the lower bar stands the word "Moscow"—significantly, the only Russian reference in the entire poem.

Despite an absence of syntax, this work is manifestly meaningful. Not only is the lexicon here less subjective and private than it was in "Suprepoeziia," but the spatial positioning acts as a form of substitute "syntax," a relational code that allows the reader to engage in interpretation and evaluation. Thus, although at first glance "Systema" seems disjointed, closer inspection reveals that this jumble of words has a logical organization and functions sensibly. It not only has a "message" but actually succeeds in being polemical, humorous, and self-deprecating.

"Systema" is arranged to be "read" from the bottom up.[7] One infers the merit, quality, and stature of the various items by noting their relative distance from the bottom of the page: the higher the position of a name, the more importance it carries. Naturally, the value system of this work is avant-gardist. Consequently, Taras Shevchenko and his *Kobzar* occupy the lowermost position. In contrast, Semenko's own *Kobzar* is centrally located. Just above Shevchenko stand the Modernists (Oleksander Oles', Mykola Voronyi, and Hryts'ko Chuprynka) and next to them, in a gesture of objective self-evaluation, Semenko places his first collection, *Prélude*. As the eye travels further up the page, it re-traces a rough chronological history of Futurism, its various theoretical and organizational stages (Kvero-futuryzm, Aspanfut), its major publications and personalities. The schema also includes foes of the Futurists (Dmytro Zahul, Pavlo Tychyna). Semenko even has fun at the expense of a fickle member of his movement, Iakiv Savchenko: by adding the first initial of the latter's name (*Ia*kiv) to Zahul's surname, Semenko creates the phrase "Zahul*ia* Savchenko" (i.e., "Savchenko will go on a spree").[8] Finally,

7 In a later edition a set of arrows, pointing upward, were added to emphasize this (see Semenko 1929–31: 2).

8 This critique of Savchenko appeared only in the 1930 edition of "Moia mozaïka" (see above). In the 1924–25 editions, Savchenko ranks low (together with Zahul and Tychyna) but is not yet ridiculed. Semenko's harsher treatment is a reflection of the animosity he felt toward Savchenko, who briefly associated with the Futurists (1923), but then turned his back on the group (see chapter 3 above, pp. 73ff).

towering above all this is the word "Panfuturism," the theoretical "system" to which the title alludes.

The visual language of this work (specifically, the two black horizontal bars) invites the interpretation that art in Ukraine has been severed from that of the West by the October Revolution. Nonetheless, what prevails is the Panfuturist notion that there can be only a single universal artistic process for East and West. "Systema" implies as much by harboring both within the body of a single work.

The placement and size of "Moscow" speaks volumes about Semenko's cultural politics. The word has a lofty position in the work, but it is small and easily dwarfed by "New York" and "London." By placing it adjacent to the word "revolution," Semenko seems to be assigning Russia a political role but denying it a role in Ukraine's culture. It is rather striking that not a single Russian avant-garde artist or writer is incorporated into this composition.

The visual experiments we have examined thus far involved poetry. A noteworthy exception to this rule is the novel *Vedmid' poliuie za sontsem* [The Bear Hunts the Sun] by the largely forgotten writer Andrii Chuzhyi (1897–?).[9] Serialized in *Nova generatsiia* during 1927 and 1928, this unfinished novel numbers about forty pages.[10] It consists of twelve brief chapters, all with obscure titles that foreshadow a strange, somewhat surrealistic prose (e.g., "Tvorchist' od 13 do 17 misiatsiv, vid beky do olivtsia" [Creativity from the age of 13 to 17 months, from poo-poo to pencils]; "Bat'ko vdruhe vchyt'sia khodyty nakarachky" [Father learns to walk on all fours again]; "Ia ovolodiv tr'oma pal'tsiamy livoï ruky Moskvy" [I took control of three fingers of Moscow's left hand]. A highly atomized narrative, it does not so much have "characters" as effusive, almost disembodied "voices." Plot and setting are reduced to a minimum, while an elevated, life-affirming tone prevails.

A large part of *Vedmid' poliuie za sontsem* is given over to a description of the narrator's childhood, especially the loving relationship with his mother. Scenes include descriptions of the narrator's own birth, his prenatal consciousness, his erudite conversations with the mother (for example, when he is one week old and again when he is 396 days old). Other episodes focus on his alcoholic father as well as on anti-revolutionary "bandits." Within this context we encounter observations on class differences, freedom, and liberation. This is rendered in a diffuse,

9 For information on Chuzhyi see Poltorats'kyi 1968.

10 *Vedmid' poliuie za sontsem* appeared in the following issues: 1927 (3); 1928 (3–4), (7), (10–11). See Chuzhyi 1927–28.

opaque, rhythmic prose that frequently resorts to onomatopoeia. Dialogues sometimes acquire the ritual quality of incantations.

As this description suggests, *Vedmid' poliuie za sontsem* is an anti-mimetic, anti-realistic, consciously "difficult" piece of avant-gardistic prose. Yet this is just one side of its complexity. What sets the novel apart, and what gives it a unique status both in the Futurist movement and in Ukrainian literature of the twenties is the liberties Chuzhyi takes with the layout of the text. His is not the average linear prose with its straight horizontal lines and aligned margins. Most of the novel unfolds visually more like poetry than prose: sentences are indented in midstream, short phrases are centered on the line or aligned to the right margin, groups of words are arranged in step-ladder formation. Nor does it end here; in some sections, text is employed to create large outline figures on the page (for example, animals, arrows).[11] In a word, where one expects a rectangular block of text, one finds instead undulating or jagged shapes. Thus, Chuzhyi not only compels his reader to navigate a conceptually difficult prose, but compounds the problem by presenting it in a physical form that undermines semantic meaning and comprehension. Inasmuch as sentences and words are subordinated to the images they are forming, they stop functioning as efficient signifiers. Frequently, understanding of a passage is temporarily suspended as the eye roams through blank space searching either for the next line, the logical end of a sentence, or tries to piece together a word that has been left unnaturally truncated at the outer edge of an image. A novel like this turns reading into a new and disquieting experience: the knowledgeable consumer of literature becomes virtually a stumbling illiterate.

Some of the images Chuzhyi creates with text extend beyond the boundaries of a single page. Their continuity is vertical, that is, the bottom of an image on one page is logically continued at the top of the next page. The convention of the "bound" page, however, disrupts this continuity. To be truly appreciated, these pages need to be removed from the environment of the journal in which they appeared and joined together to form a seamless scroll. When read or viewed in this form, the pages of the novel would properly be "unrolled" rather than flipped or turned, thereby revealing the textual image in its entirety. In short, Chuzhyi's visual novel forces a re-examination of some of the most basic conventions of reading, writing, and printing.

The scenario was another genre that reached for the expressive powers of typography and page-layout techniques. In 1928 *Nova generatsiia*

[11] See especially Chuzhyi (1927–28, 7: 22–27).

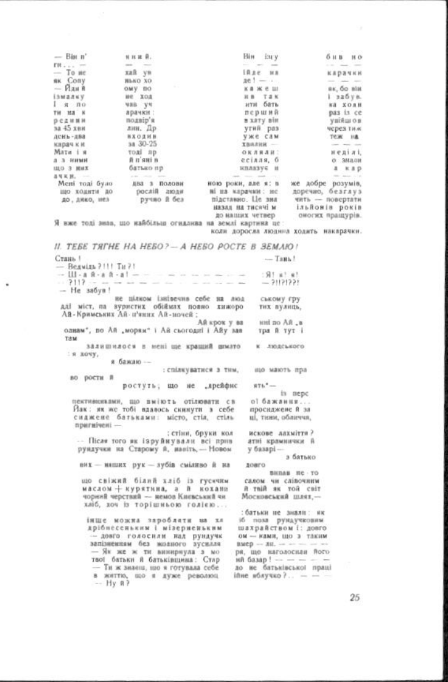

Four pages from Andrii Chuzhyi, *Vedmid' poliuie za sontsem. Nova generatsiia* 1928, 7: 23, 24, 25, 27. [Reproduced with the kind permission of the Houghton Library, Harvard University.]

published "Dynamo," an eleven-page film script inspired by H. G. Wells' short story, "The Lord of the Dynamos" (Lopatyns'kyi 1928c). The author, Favst Lopatyns'kyi, was a professional director of theater and film who had become frustrated by the "boring" and "useless" scripts that encroached on his artistic prerogatives with pointless and uninspiring camera directions. To set an example for young screenwriters, Lopatyns'kyi proposed an entirely "new structure for the scenario," one that would convey "the screenwriter's emotions immediately to the...director." This was to be achieved by endowing the scenario with various typographical devices, musical notations (to suggest the rhythm of a scene), layout techniques, and highlighted words (Lopatyns'kyi 1928b, 8).[12]

Lopatyns'kyi was explicit in stating that "Dynamo" was not a traditional literary work and that he was not interested in the "subtlety of words." Yet, visually this scenario does give the impression of being free verse. Only closer inspection reveals that the layout is much more complex than in the average poem. Above and beyond the expected pattern of unpredictable line lengths, "Dynamo" exploits an array of symbols and punctuation marks in an unorthodox manner. The text contains equal signs, slurs, braces, arrows, lines, parentheses, and endless em-dashes. The size and style of print vary frequently; words occur at forty-five-degree angles and some are boxed to suggest placards. Although "Dynamo" could conceivably be read as a poem, the graphic organization of the text discourages it: oral interpretation of some signs is nearly impossible and a purely aural apprehension of the work would be quite problematic, for much of the semantically relevant visual information would be lost. To be wholly appreciated "Dynamo" must actually be seen.

Lopatyns'kyi employs typography, text, and layout as a kind of graphical notation system that tries to create on the page analogs to the language of cinema. His dynamic narrative is entirely biased toward visual action. Text is arranged to suggest the rhythms of a motion picture and to invoke its devices. Words function as equivalents to the shot or scene, describing actions and mimicking them. By modifying the physical appearance of a word and its placement on the page, Lopatyns'kyi can suggest certain cinematic attributes, for example, the illusion of a changing (zooming) perspective, of action approaching or receding into the distance. "They went [illegible]" is rendered thus:

[12] See also Favst Lopatyns'kyi, "Lyst do moioho pryiatelia-stsenarysta" (Lopatyns'kyi 1928a).

Пішли...

Пішли...

Пішли...

Пішли...

Other typographical and graphic devices simulate slow motion and simultaneous (parallel) action.

Visual experiments in the Futurist movement were designed to tear down art and genre barriers. Literature (and writing in general) was targeted for amalgamation and infusion with properties inherent in other arts. Essentially, this meant returning to the word its materiality, overcoming its predominantly semiotic, symbolic function, transforming "reading" (i.e., scanning for abstract information) into "viewing."

It is apparent that Ukrainian Futurists rarely pursued visual experimentation for its own sake. For the most part, they marshalled it for such goals as the destruction of traditional genres or for synthesis. Moreover, there is no indication that they wanted to endow their visual works with pure iconic properties or to distill from language only the graphic element and elevate it to a position of complete autonomy. Virtually all visual works remain highly charged semantically and make a strong appeal to an idea. Semenko clearly assigned an ideological function to poetry-painting ("It is necessary to embody great liberated thoughts in an appropriate form"; Semenko 1922c). This explains why so many "visual" works are at the same time "narratives." Ideally, Ukrainian Futurists aspired toward a verbal art that would simultaneously communicate on several levels: as sign, as image, and as sound. Chuzhyi, for example, referred to his poems of 1921 as "drawings for the eyes and ears" (Chuzhyi 1980, 9). Characteristically, there is no sharp boundary between an acoustic and a visual poem in the movement: both will be found in a "pure" form, but most works indicate that the Futurists preferred to see these elements fused into a greater whole.

Сауг
(Дзя . . .)
Сауг
(Впа =) = в Сауг
Ніч . . .
Лондон . . .
(*Ритмострічка*)
(вулиця, шинок). Виходить Джемс.
Джемс — шинок
закрутився, зник
скривився, захитавсь, побрів
Джемс . . .
Джемс . . .

як собака під тином
лежить Сауг.
Сауг . . .
на його ноги; зачепились } Сауг
мацають, що це лежить }
Думає Джемс (п'яний) згадав:
= розлите масло
= брудні частини
= в динамо — відділі
оце ж помічник!
підняв за чуприну зомлілого Сауга.
Сауг
— будеш служити?: = витирати масло?
= чистить частини?
= в динамо — відділі?
чи будеш?
— О так! о так! о так!
Жбурнув позад себе Сауга Джемс:
— Іти - меш слідком!
— О так! о так! о так!
Пішли . . .
Пішли . . .
Пішли . . .
Пішли . . .
Лоооннн . . .
дооонннн . . .
(*Ритмострічка*)
ГІМН ДИНАМО
(тридцять кадрів)

12

Сауг . . .
Сауг! . .
Саaауг!!
Джемс (грубо штовхнувши),
Джемс:
— Динамо!
Джемс до Сауга:
(Сауг)
— Бачив?! Динамо!!
Ди — и — и — и — намо!
Сауг.
Джемс
рвонув маленького „Дзяо", що висів
у Сауга на шиї,
Дзяо — бог,
Сауг: — віддай!!
Джемс відштовхнув —
— к'бісу таких „богів"!
кинув фігурку у лязг динамо
Са — у — у — у — г
Бог — в порошок
Сауг
Дииииииин . . .
Сауг
. . . наммммм . . .
Сауг
о
о о
О О
О О
. . . О О!
Джемс.
Джемс — непевно до розподіл - дошки.
Впевнено перемикає.
Рубильники кажуть:
(Ритм)
Сауг:
„Не чіпай! ти зробиш їй боляче!"
Джемс
(повернувся, засміявся, нахмуривсь, глянув у бік)
де грубий мідяний дріт
Джемс 'го підняв
Джемс (рука — мідяний дріт)
Сауг
Джемс глянув в куток

13

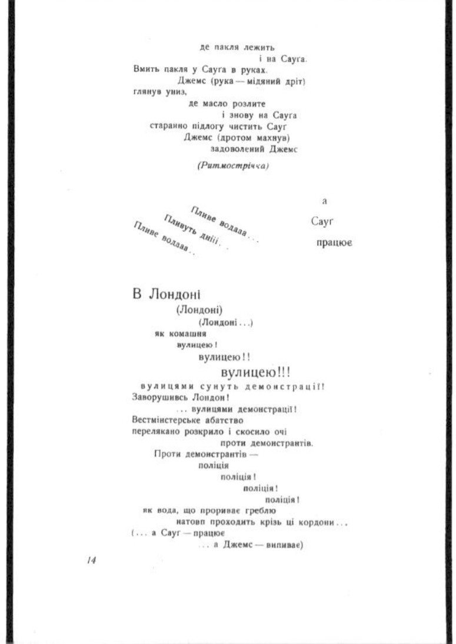

де пакля лежить
і на Сауга.
Вмить пакля у Сауга в руках.
Джемс (рука — мідяний дріт)
глянув униз,
де масло розлите
і знову на Сауга
старанно підлогу чистить Сауг
Джемс (дротом махнув)
задоволений Джемс
(*Ритмострічка*)

Пливе водааа . . .
Пливуть дніiі . .
Пливе водааа . .

а
Сауг
працює

В Лондоні
(Лондоні)
(Лондоні . . .)
як комашня
вулицею!
вулицею!!
вулицею!!!
вулицями сунуть демонстрації!
Заворушивсь Лондон!
. . . вулицями демонстрації!
Вестмінстерське абатство
перелякано розкрило і скосило очі
проти демонстрантів.
Проти демонстрантів —
поліція
поліція!
поліція!
поліція!
як вода, що проривае греблю
натовп проходить крізь ці кордони . . .
(. . . а Сауг — працює
. . . а Джемс — випиває)

14

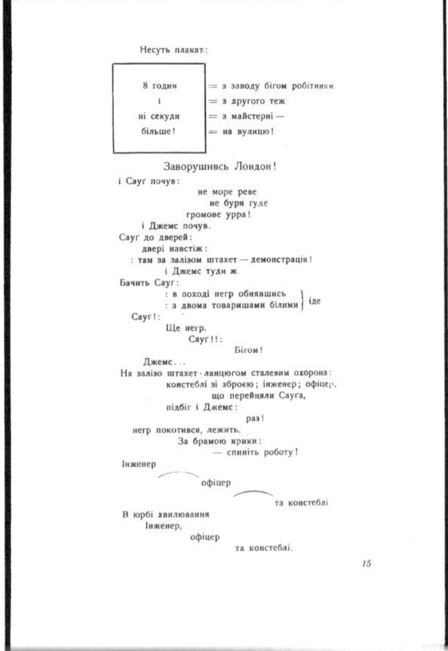

Несуть плакат:

8 годин
і
ні секуди
більше!

= з заводу бігом робітники
= з другого теж
= з майстерні —
= на вулицю!

Заворушивсь Лондон!
і Сауг почув:
не море реве
не буря гуде
громове урра!
і Джемс почув.
Сауг до дверей:
двері навстіж:
: там за залізом штахет — демонстрація!
і Джемс туди ж.
Бачить Сауг:
: в поході негр обнявшись } іде
: з двома товаришами білими }
Сауг!:
Ще негр.
Сауг!!:
Бігом!
Джемс . . .
На залізо штахет - ланцюгом сталевим охорона:
констеблі зі зброєю; інженер; офіцер,
що перейняли Сауга,
підбіг і Джемс:
раз!
негр покотився, лежить.
За брамою крики:
— спиніть роботу!
Інженер
офіцер
та констеблі
В юрбі хвилювання
Інженер,
офіцер
та констеблі.

15

Four pages from Favst Lopatyns'kyi, "Dynamo. (Asotsiiatsiia vid Vel'sovoho 'Boh dynamo.') Kino-stsenarii." *Nova generatsiia* 1928 (7): 12–15. [Reproduced with the kind permission of the Houghton Library, Harvard University.]

Conclusions

More often than not, Ukrainian Futurism has been *compared* rather than *studied*. Invariably, comparisons found it deficient, a faint echo of some purportedly more original, more perfect proto-movement. Blinded by the name, critics saw in it little else than what they had already witnessed in a foreign "source."[1]

This work has purposely avoided comparative excurses on the premise that one first needs to know a subject before it can be productively juxtaposed to others. Consequently, the primary task here has been to allow Ukrainian Futurism to define itself by elucidating its history, theory, and writings. These concluding remarks take a tentative step further, endeavoring to locate Ukrainian Futurism in the context of the European and Russian avant-gardes, and record, albeit superficially, some of the more salient ideological and artistic features that it shared with its contemporaries and immediate predecessors.

In trying to conceptualize Ukrainian Futurism, it is apparent that the name by which the movement went, in and of itself, tells us little. Both theoretically and practically the Ukrainian phenomenon is not accommodated by reference to some "classical" notion of Futurism, be it Italian or Russian. The tenacious adherence to the name by Ukrainians had an honorific and theoretical function: it was a recognition, first of all, of Marinetti's movement as *the* watershed in art history. "Futurism," in some sense, served Ukrainians as a synonym for all of the avant-garde, a fact also reflected in their pan-avant-gardistic philosophy, which eschewed taking a narrow or restricted perspective on art. As we have seen, Ukrainian Futurists were disarmingly frank in referring to other

[1] A classic, although by no means isolated, case of this syndrome is Mykhailo Levchenko's "Maiakovs'kyi ta ukraïns'kyi futuryzm" (Levchenko 1971). Ukrainian Futurism is characterized here as "belated" and "unoriginal." It is redeemed and made the pretext for an article primarily because the author can link it to Maiakovskii and Russian literature. Even in the 1920s Semenko reacted to this approach with indignation: "The provincials and populist Europeans…, being devoid of the most elementary culture [and] full of national indolence, cannot consider and concentrate on that which is taking place before their eyes. [They can only] reject, cover up seditiously the significance of all leftist work and achievements, and they do this in approximately the following manner: Semenko? Maiakovskii wrote it yesterday, Semenko copied it today. Kurbas? Meyerhold staged it yesterday, Kurbas reproduced it today. And it means nothing [to them] that they did not read Maiakovskii and never saw Meyerhold.…" See Semenko (1927c, 6–7). On this subject, see also Ilnytzkyj 1992b.

movements. In fact, so diverse is the material on record in this respect that it is difficult to ascertain at first glance which of the many "influences" were central and which peripheral.

It might be argued, for example, that one should begin seeking parallels between Ukrainian Futurism and artists like Igor' Severianin, Konstantin Bal'mont, Andrei Belyi, and Mikolajus Čiurlionis—all of whom Semenko recognized (somewhat reluctantly) as his predecessors. Presumably, Cubism, Futurism, Expressionism, and Dadaism must also be considered prime candidates for comparative deliberation, inasmuch as Panfuturism claimed to represent all of them "at once" ("What Futurism Wants" 1922).[2] On the other hand, an investigator could not be considered overzealous if he were to cast his net even wider given that Panfuturism was a dialectical process of *all* avant-garde movements. "The Panfuturist system," to quote Semenko again, "embraces all 'isms,' considering them partial elements of a single organism" (*Semafor u Maibutnie* 1922 [1]: 10), a claim well substantiated in practice by *Nova generatsiia*. Indeed, one of the primary and unique attributes of Ukrainian Futurism was its cognizant embrace of the entire spectrum of the avant-garde—not in the sense of individual movements, but as one coherent and self-contained stage of art history. This was not eclecticism but an axiom.

Despite the great variety within the avant-garde, it is fair to say that most movements of the early twentieth century share certain common ideas and features. As a rule they have an international character, a formalistic attitude toward art, and are vehemently anti-traditional. Most betray an element of messianism and utopianism. These qualities are found in the Ukrainian movement as well. But if these features might be called universal, there are also any number of traits that distinguish and individualize these movements. Take the issue of politics. Cubism and Italian Futurism would have to be judged poles apart in this respect, whereas Ukrainian and Russian Futurism, not to mention the Dada movement, would exhibit many commonalities. Similarly, not every avant-garde movement rejected the intuitive, emotional, and subjective world (certainly not Expressionism) the way Ukrainian Futurism did. The latter shares, for example, with Surrealism a penchant for Marxism but has nothing in common with its subjective and Freudian premises. In short, regardless of the confluences, it is proper to bear in mind that Ukrainian Futurism clung rather consistently to a specific and coherent set of ideas, and these will allow us to place the movement in a rather specific location on the avant-garde spectrum.

2 Quoted from Leites and Iashek 1930: 2, 126. The original is in English.

❧ ❧
❧

If we take away Italian Futurism's nationalistic and fascist ideology, its glorification of war, its disdain for women and take into account Marinetti's financial fortune and Semenko's lack of one, there emerges a fairly accurate picture of Ukrainian Futurism in at least one of its major aspects. Although there are obvious parallels between the movements (devotion to speed, dynamism, urban life, and technology) it is primarily in the struggle they waged against traditional values and tastes that the two are most alike.[3] While Italy and Ukraine were, obviously, worlds apart, both futurisms labored against their own peculiar variant of cultural stagnation; both were determined to drag their respective nations into the nucleus of the European artistic revolution. (Russian Futurism, on the other hand, was more of a reaction to the Silver Age.) Ukrainian Futurism seems to have assimilated fully the Italian movement's posture and belligerence. Its polyartistic tendencies find analogs in the Italian situation which saw Futurism extend its influence to many other arts. Italian Futurism's rejection of art with a capital A, its anti-psychologism, its disdain for the cultured intellectual, academic art and learning are all features peculiar to Ukrainian Futurism. The social and public character of their art and activities also bind them.

It is noteworthy that in the early 1920s, the Italian movement and Dada were featured on the pages of Ukrainian publications side by side (*Semafor u Maibutnie* 1922 [1]). This is hardly surprising, since the two were in many respects similar. As the Dadaist Hans Richter put it, "we had swallowed Futurism—bones, feathers and all" (Richter 1978, 33). From the point of view of Ukrainians, Dada may very well have seemed not only as an extension and complement to Futurism, but also, in view of the claim that "Dada is German Bolshevism" (Motherwell 1981, 44), a distinct improvement. In preserving Futurism's most outrageous positions, Dada betrayed none of the latter's chauvinistic and nationalistic attributes, something which must have appealed to the Ukrainians. Like its predecessor, Dada made an art of the manifesto and the provocative statement. It was consciously heterogeneous and international, and, most importantly, it was outspokenly anti-art. Dada's tone in this respect was remarkably like that of Ukrainian Futurism.

> Dadaism for the first time has ceased to take an aesthetic attitude toward life.... Dadaism leads to amazing new possibilities and forms of

[3] On Italian Futurism see Tisdall and Bozzolla 1978, Apollonio 1973, and Flint 1972.

> expression in all the arts....The word Dada in itself indicates the internationalism of the movement which is bound to no frontiers, religions, or professions. Dada is the international expression of our times, the great rebellion of artistic movements....Under certain circumstances to be a Dadaist may mean to be more a businessman, more a political partisan than an artist—to be an artist only by accident—to be a Dadaist means to let oneself be thrown by things, to oppose all sedimentation; to sit in a chair for a single moment is to risk one's life....Blast the aesthetic-ethical attitude (Huelsenbeck 1981, 242–46).

There were two sides to Dada. One was rationalistic and technological; it called for turning "decisively away from the speculative," from "metaphysics" in order to reveal Dada's "understanding of itself as an expression of this age which is primarily characterized by machinery and the growth of civilization" (Motherwell 1981, 42). Another trend embraced the concept of chance and was concerned with the unconscious (Richter 1978, 51, 59, 60). This path ultimately led to Surrealism. It must be stressed, therefore, that for all the similarities between Ukrainian Futurism and Dada, this second bias had little influence on Ukrainians who rarely strayed from their faith in the machine, rationalism, and science.

The ideas of Marcel Duchamp offer an interesting parallel between Ukrainian Futurism and Dada. Richter has observed that in Duchamp's ready-mades "art has been 'thought through to a conclusion'; in other words, eliminated. Nothing, *nihil*, is all that is left. An illusion has been dispelled by the use of logic" (ibid., 91). Richter continues, saying that the ready-mades "are not works of art but of non-art, the result of discursive rather than sensory insight." He calls Duchamp "the nihilist of art, who gave expression and concrete form to his hope—the hope of achieving wonder not through chance but through exact knowledge, the interplay of scientific forces" (ibid., 92, 93). Such sentiments can easily be attributed to Ukrainian Futurism, although it is hard to say at present how well Ukrainians knew Duchamp's works and writings. His name appears in one Futurist publication (*Semafor u Maibutnie* 1922, 51). Moreover, one cannot help but be struck by the similarity between his works and Semenko's own famous ready-made poem of 1922 "Ponedilok": "Monday / Tuesday / Wednesday / Thursday / Friday / Saturday / Sunday" (Semenko 1925m).

Ukrainian Futurists' most obvious West European orientation was on Germany. The Dada movement seems to have been known to them primarily in its Berlin form. Another current that had a strong impact on them was Expressionism, assimilated primarily through Herwarth

Walden's *Der Sturm*. It will be recalled that during the early 1920s Ukrainians not only made frequent references to, but also translated Georg Kaiser, Georg Trakl, Ernst Toller, Karl Sternheim, and Rudolf Leonard. Later in the decade, *Nova generatsiia* carefully tracked the developments in *Der Sturm*, reproducing works of many a German Expressionist painter. Nevertheless, it would be wrong to think that Expressionism swayed Ukrainians as a method for articulating subjective states. It attracted them for another reason. In Germany, Expressionism was understood as the "discovery of all modern art," as a reaction against impressionism and naturalism (Richard 1978, 12).[4] It was identified with a heterogeneous group of movements, including Cubism, Futurism, The Fauves, Die Brücke, and Der Blaue Reiter. What is significant for us is that this was how Herwarth Walden understood the term and how it was reflected in the editorial policy of *Der Sturm*. It is reasonable to assume, therefore, that thanks to their own all-embracing and universal approach to the avant-garde, Ukrainian Futurists found a natural ally in Walden whose views probably reinforced their own.

Between 1920 and 1923, that is, at exactly the time Ukrainian Futurism was re-establishing itself, the Soviet Union and the West saw a rapid flowering of the international Constructivist movement. Described by one critic as a delayed reaction against Romanticism and spontaneity (Bann 1974a, xxviii, xxx), it was this current that gave ultimate expression to the ideas of rationalism, technology, functionalism, and utilitarianism.

The overt signs of Constructivism in early Ukrainian Futurist publications are few. In December 1922 *Katafalk iskusstva* made some disparaging comments about El Lissitzky's and Ilya Ehrenburg's *Veshch' / Gegenstand / Object* (Berlin) which had appeared in March of that year.[5] An unrealized issue of *Katafalk iskusstva* had been scheduled to delineate the differences between Panfuturism and Constructivism. However, van Doesburg's *De Stijl* and the Bauhaus movement would not be invoked until the period of *Nova generatsiia*. And Tatlin's brush with Ukrainian Futurism dates to 1927. Thus, while the Constructivist strain seems, perhaps, not as conspicuous as the Futurist and Dadaist, there can be no doubt that it did constitute a strong ideological undercurrent.

Several Constructivist manifestoes offer striking parallels to the Ukrainian movement. Naum Gabo's and Antoine Pevsner's "The Realistic Manifesto" (1920) contains a number of concepts found in Panfuturism.

4 On the problems of defining Expressionism see Weisstein 1973a and 1973b.

5 It is interesting to recall that, like *Veshch'*, future issues of *Katafalk iskusstva* were to have been tri-lingual.

Among them is the certainty that art has reached an "impasse" (not an uncommon belief for the period) and the desire to create a "system of art" that would be based on "the real laws of Life." When Gabo and Pevsner declare that "life does not know beauty as an aesthetic measure...efficacious existence is the highest beauty" or compare artists to engineers, complaining that "art is still nourished by impression, external appearance, and wanders helplessly back and forth from Naturalism to Symbolism, from Romanticism to Mysticism," it becomes obvious that there is a basic consonance of views between them and Semenko (Bann 1974b, 5, 7, 8, 9).

Taken together, the various Constructivist manifestoes defended the following essential principles. They consistently linked art, technology and science; rationalism was opposed to subjectivism, mysticism, and "lyrical arbitrariness" (ibid., 68).[6] Synthesis was a strong leitmotif (for example, in the work of Rodchenko), while utilitarianism and functionalism were often explicitly joined to Communist ideology. The de-aesthetization of art was likewise a major tenet.

Two Constructivist declarations in particular have much in common with Ukrainian Futurism. The first is the "Program of the Productivist Group" (1920) which strove to build a Communist culture through "practical activity." The Productivist Group declared "ruthless war against art in general," contending that an "evolutionary transition of the past's art-culture into the Communistic forms of constructive building is impossible" (Bann 1974b, 20). The "Program" ended with six "Slogans" which among other things avowed: "Down with art, Long live technic; Religion is a lie, Art is a lie; Kill human thinking's last remains tying it to art; Down with guarding the traditions of art; the collective art of the present is constructive life" (ibid.).

The second document whose tone and ideas parallel those of Ukrainian Futurism even closer is Aleksei Gan's *Konstruktivizm*, characterized by one critic as "a declaration of the industrial constructivists" (Bowlt 1976, 215). Gan called for a "struggle with the supporters of traditional art" and an "uncompromising war on art" (Bann 1974b, 33). He decried the fact that art was "permeated with the most reactionary idealism" and complained that individualism "shoves it in the direction of...refining subjective beauty" (ibid., 35). For Gan, as for Semenko, art was "indissolubly linked: with theology, metaphysics, and mysticism." He proclaimed "Death to Art," arguing that it "arose naturally, developed

[6] The quote came from the "Statement by the International Faction of Constructivists," which was originally published in *De Stijl* (1922).

naturally and disappeared naturally" (ibid., 36). The objective of Constructivism was "to find the Communist expression of material construction, i.e., to establish a scientific base for the approach to constructing buildings and services that would fulfill the demands of Communist culture in its transient state, in its fluidity, in a word, in all the formations of its historical movement beginning with the period of destruction..." (ibid., 39).

Such statements might tempt one to treat Gan's book as an important source for Ukrainian Futurist theory. Perhaps it was. Circumstantial evidence, however, raises a few doubts. *Semafor u Maibutnie* and *Katafalk iskusstva*, the two publications that most thoroughly mirror *Konstruktivizm*, appeared, respectively, in May and December of 1922. Gan's book was published in Tver' either in May or October of the same year (Bowlt 1976, 215). To have influenced Ukrainians, it would have had to reach Kyiv with lightning speed—not likely at the time. Moreover, as was pointed out earlier, Ukrainian Futurist publications had serious difficulty finding their way into print and, therefore, there is every reason to believe that articles for *Semafor u Maibutnie* and *Katafalk iskusstva* were probably written long before they were actually published. Finally, it has to be said that Gan's ideas were not in themselves unusual for 1922. Sentiments such as his filled the air and, hence, it would probably be unwise to attribute to them an exclusive power of influence.[7]

The "destructive" and "anti-art" trend to which Ukrainian Futurism obviously belongs was not the most typical manifestation of Constructivism. A publication like *Veshch'/Gegenstand/Object* explicitly rejected this attitude. It declared "the days of destruction, laying siege, and undermining lie behind us....The negative tactics of the 'dadaists'...like [those of] the first futurists...appear anachronistic to us...It is as laughable as it is naive to talk nowadays about 'wanting to throw Pushkin overboard'..." (Bann 1974b, 55). Such a position may well account for the dim view *Katafalk iskusstva* took of *Veshch'*. Clearly, the Futurist and Dadaist heritage served as the primary influence on Ukrainians; elements that accrued from other movements were adopted and subordinated to this dominant strain.

The relationship between Ukrainian and Russian Futurism deserves separate comment. As was pointed out at the onset of this study, the origins of Ukrainian Futurism were intimately tied to Ukrainian Modernism. However, there is also no doubt that it was nourished by the broader imperial cultural context. The founding of the movement in

7 Gan figured as a "participant" much later in *Nova generatsiia* (see 1928 [12]).

Kyiv in February 1914 came on the heels of the Cubo-Futurist tour through Ukraine (the Russians were in Kyiv on 28 January 1914) as well as Marinetti's famous visit to Russia. Futurism was then an object of intense curiosity. It is reasonable to assume, therefore, that the charged atmosphere had no small effect on the founders of Ukrainian Futurism. Semenko, moreover, studied in St. Petersburg from 1911. There is even some evidence that he had connections to the Moscow *Literaturno-khudozhestvennyi al'manakh* [The Literary-Art Almanac] published by Valerii Briusov (Kriger 1979, 25). The first overt signs of a Russian influence on his poetry begin in 1913–14. While we cannot at this time go into the specifics of this "influence," one thing is certain: Semenko's and, by extension, the movement's approach toward art was not dictated by strictly Ukrainian factors.

The Ukrainian movement's modest pre-revolutionary history does not allow for any serious comparisons to Russian Futurism until the early 1920s. At that time Ukrainian Futurists behaved in a demonstratively independent manner *vis-à-vis* their Russian colleagues, either ignoring or addressing them in belligerent tones. This contrasted vividly with their admiring references to Western movements. However, by 1923 Ukrainians underwent a change of heart mainly because of the attacks they were sustaining from the Party and mainstream cultural organizations. Under these circumstances they were compelled to find an officially agreeable form of artistic activity or face ruin. The emergence of the journal *Lef* in March of 1923 seemed to offer a solution. Ukrainian Futurists reasoned that by adopting a profile similar to LEF's, they might win the same acceptance from local authorities that their Russian competitors enjoyed in the north. They put great stock in being able to create their own avant-garde periodical, a cherished goal that kept evading them for most of this period. Thus, in 1923 they suddenly stopped treating Russian Futurism as a bankrupt movement. In a dramatic reversal, the Ukrainians claimed to be abandoning Futurism and Dadaism (the destructive "bourgeois" movements of the West, as they put it) for LEF's Constructivism, which Semenko defined as "the latest phase of Futurism in its healthy Eastern offshoot" (Semenko 1923b, 51–52).

> To become construction engineers, masters of artistic creativity for the purpose of building the "city of the future"—here is the contemporary problem of proletarian art, here is proletarian art itself. This is what Constructivists say.... Speaking practically, the Constructivist declaration sounds naive, but in principle, this is a normal, healthy way for artists to escape from a dead end. Here, essentially, a cross has been raised over art as such (ibid.).

As the last sentence indicates, Semenko was not about to retract his view that art was dying. He was, however, rephrasing the issue less provocatively.

The practical effects of this new orientation meant that during the years 1923–25 the Ukrainian movement (much like the Russian) ended up espousing a form of "Bogdanovism" (Utechin 1958; Crouch, Jr. 1979). The ideas of Aleksandr Bogdanov had widespread influence on the Proletkul'ts and also had an impact in the socioeconomic realm. Two former members of Proletkul't, Aleksei Gastev and Platon Kerzhentsev, devoted a great deal of attention to the problem of "scientific organization of labor" or NOT (Ukrainian, NOP). Some of these concepts were injected by Semenko into his own writings of 1924 where he invokes Gastev, NOT, TsIT [Tsentral'nyi institut truda—The Central Institute of Labor, founded by Gastev], and the All-Union League "Vremia-NOT." This trend attracted Semenko because it emphasized "rationalizing" work and "organizing" the workplace. By applying this same reasoning to artistic creation, Semenko argued that Great Art would be transformed completely and eventually die (Semenko 1924b, 199). In this way he again managed to reiterate in a more orthodox manner his "destructive" tenets.

Some of these Bogdanovite and Proletkul'tist tendencies were equally characteristic of LEF's theories. As Halina Stephan makes clear, the Russian Futurists turned to Bogdanov because they needed an acceptable ideological foundation on which to build a constructive and positive program (Stephan 1981, 59–64). Ukrainian Futurists turned to him much for the same reason. Consequently, the Ukrainian and Russian movements came to resemble one another in some important respects. Both were a mixture of Bogdanovite, Constructivist, and Formalist ideas (although not in the same proportions). Their ideological and artistic profile shared certain general features: they had faith in technology and science; both viewed art as a craft and were prepared to produce "useful," "agitational" objects that would "organize" the psyche of the worker and help create the New Man; their art was frequently and aggressively anti-psychological; and both movements showed a proclivity for strongly plotted, popular fiction.

Despite such confluences, LEF and Ukrainian Futurism were not identical. Ukrainian Futurism, to its own detriment, was clearly the more radical in its Bogdanovism during this period. It centered its attention not on art and literature but on social and cultural questions, devoting most of its energies to the creation of a "mass" organization and agitational work. Symptomatic of this is that throughout these years, try as they might, the Futurists were unable to publish a "journal like *Lef*" (*Bil'shovyk*

21 May 1924 [114]: 4). On the basis of such evidence it might be argued that LEF, in its struggle against the "belief in the permanence of artistic standards" (Stephan 1981, 61), was devoted, in theory and in practice, to the production of "useful" art objects, while Ukrainian Futurists, with their industrial models and social activism were, in effect, questioning the very usefulness of the artistic "system." In the final analysis, the two movements did share at least one unfortunate trait: they both collapsed in 1925 and, curiously, reemerged almost simultaneously in 1927. The first issue of *Novyi lef* appeared in March while *Nova generatsiia* began publishing in October.

From what has already been said about the relationship between these two journals in chapter 5, it should be clear that the two movements had mutual interests but ultimately differed on specifics as well as on broad theoretical issues. The problem of prose, as we saw, was one. Although the Ukrainians embraced the "literature of fact" and were acquainted with *Novyi lef*'s theoretical positions, this prose cannot be described as *Nova generatsiia*'s "theoretical and practical core" (Barooshian 1974, 135), a phrase used to characterize the Russian journal. For the Ukrainians "fact" was just one of several choices open to the avant-gardist, and was not considered a privileged category: like most things in their relative theory of literature, "fact" was fair game for parody or "destruction." In general, their practical and theoretical approach was less restrictive than *Novyi lef*'s. The Ukrainians preferred experimenting with genres and narrative modes, simultaneously "destroying" literature and creating hitherto unknown forms. The "literature of fact" was pursued less for its own sake than as an opportunity to fuse devices of journalism with those of art. *Nova generatsiia*'s basic goal was the reification of form and structure. For the Russians the notion of a "left" novel was irrelevant ("Nam pishut o 'Novom lefe' i 'Novoi generatsii'" 1928, 46); the Ukrainians, on the other hand, enthusiastically embraced the idea as a practical means to undermine tradition.

Another significant area of disagreement between the two movements involved their respective conceptualization of the avant-garde. Panfuturism espoused a synchronic view; *Novyi lef*'s was diachronic. Trenin, for example, betrayed a hierarchical notion of the avant-garde, relegating certain activities and movements to the past. He spoke of "early futurism" and of inappropriate activities such as "destruction," suggesting that Ukrainian Futurists were regurgitating the past.[8] This

[8] *Novyi lef* expressed this view of *Nova generatsiia*'s artistic practice: "We feel that the futurist devices surviving not only in the Ukrainian LEF, but in the Georgian (and

was fundamentally unlike the Ukrainian position which conceived the tactics, devices and strategies of *all* the avant-gardes as a single system standing in opposition to the system of Great Art. The practices of previous and present movements were deemed necessary during the current period of "transition" when art was being reanimated by ignoramuses. What men like Vertsman and Trenin disparaged as "eclecticism" and "impeccable Europeanism" was an endeavor to apprehend the avant-garde globally. Not surprising, LEF appeared to Ukrainians as exceedingly cliquish, self-centered, and lacking in historical vision. Shkurupii put it this way:

> We were never some kind of artistic "ism," a literary school or a narrow group that cultivates favorite little forms to the point of metaphysical self-love. Our theory and practice always stood in the mainstream of art's entire development or else was a continuation of it; it never stopped at some "ism." Because of this our friends from LEF called us eclectics; having fallen in love with a concrete task or "ism," they cultivated it to the point of self-contradiction (Shkurupii 1930d).

Ukrainian Futurism was a broadly-based, heterogeneous avant-garde movement. It was not, strictly speaking, a style or a mannerism. It was an attitude toward art. Its "aesthetics" were novelty and surprise. Seen in a broad context, it was part of the great twentieth-century reaction against naturalism, realism, and representational art. It was formalist, highly self-conscious of its own artifice and technique. In place of the metaphysics of modernism, it subscribed to rationalism. It believed it could reintegrate art and life.

The Panfuturist theory aptly reflected the character of the movement. Although in its particulars it was consonant with many other movements, as a finished "system," it occupies its own unique place among avant-garde theories. It was an original attempt to understand and cure the "crisis" of art. Panfuturism's particular virtue may lie in its proto-structuralist features. The notion of a "system," the historicism which is fundamental to it, the attempt to link art to other cultural phenomena—

---

according to rumor, in Belarus) exist only due to inertia, not because they serve a useful purpose." The defense of *zaum* by Ukrainians was characterized as "a kind of constant lagging behind [*kakoi-to neprestannyi khvostizm*]." See "Nam pishut o 'Novom lefe' i 'Novoi generatsii'" (1928, 45–46).

all this was quite innovative at the time. We can note, for example, that the Formalists' attempts to "relate imaginative literature to other domains of culture" (Erlich 1965, 111) did not appear until 1928, whereas Semenko's theory was basically complete by 1924. Some of his central ideas seem less far-fetched today than originally thought. Peter Bürger's recent work on the theory of the avant-garde, for example, offers many remarkable parallels to Panfuturism and should garner Semenko belated respect as a theorist of modern art (Bürger 1984).

Ukrainian Futurism was a movement in almost constant evolution. In part, this can be attributed to its philosophy, but in large measure it was a consequence of political and cultural pressures. In this respect the movement was not entirely self-made. It was shaped by politics and owes it some of its features. Occasionally, it was forced to compromise, be false to itself. Nonetheless, on close examination, behind the smoke screen of theories and organizational facades, the true core and aims of the movement stand out sharply.

Ukrainian Futurism was a movement with a mission. It set out to alter the course of Ukrainian culture, to bring it into the twentieth century, if necessary, against its will. This explains its propaedeutic streak, its short-lived "mass" orientation, the constant polemics with tradition, and its obsession with maintaining an "influence" in the cultural arena. This is also reflected in the informational character of *Nova generatsiia*, a journal that was determined to introduce an aspect of Europe that neither VAPLITE nor the Neoclassicists cared for.

René Wellek and Austin Warren have written that "to spend time and attention on a poet or a poem is already a judgment of value" (Wellek and Warren 1956, 250). No doubt this applies to a movement as well. Indeed, in describing Ukrainian Futurism, I have implicitly argued throughout this study that it is worthy of study and represents a value both for Ukrainian and European literature. Certainly, it was loud, brash, pretentious, intolerant and (according to the "cultured intelligentsia") in bad taste, but these traits (common to virtually the entire avant-garde; Poggioli 1968) were just the tip of the iceberg. Beneath this exterior "idiocy" there was complexity and sophistication.

The importance of Ukrainian Futurism can be summarized in this way: First, it was a major historical event that continues to have repercussions for interpreting and understanding an entire period of

Ukrainian cultural history. Second, it was an original literary phenomenon that left behind works of intrinsic value and appeal. This study has tried to show that Ukrainian Futurism was neither insignificant, nor small (especially not by avant-garde standards), nor "unpatriotic." It was one of the most important movements of its day and any history that overlooks its ideology and aesthetic positions gives an incomplete and distorted picture of the literary process.

The movement was vibrant, tenacious, and possessed an indomitable spirit. It faced down opponents from almost every quarter of Ukrainian society and demonstrated repeatedly its independence. It acted as a major force against cultural stagnation. In 1914 Semenko anticipated many issues of the great Literary Discussion, particularly the concern with intrinsic artistic problems and the provincial ("sincere") character of Ukrainian literature. For this, he deserves as much recognition as has been given to members of VAPLITE. Like the latter, Semenko's organizations helped contain and combat the influence of vulgar literary groups like Pluh and VUSPP. As a vanguard, Futurism obviously faced natural limits on the size of its audience, but its influence in the cultural field was far greater than most critics give it credit. The Futurists had reasonable success in recruiting followers and writers to their cause, and their impact certainly extended beyond their membership. Precisely because of its radicalism, Futurism helped pave the road for other innovative writers and contributed significantly to the spirit of discovery that characterized Ukrainian culture during this period. There can be no doubt that it affected the general ambiance and helped the flowering of free verse and experimental prose. Writers like Iurii Smolych, Maik Iohansen, and Iurii Ianovs'kyi cannot be discussed without taking into consideration the ideas of "leftist" prose. In verse, even a poet like Tychyna (e.g., in *Chernihiv*) cannot be fully appreciated without Futurism. The interest in reportorial genres and travelogues also cannot be separated from similar developments in Semenko's movement.

There is no need to admire all Futurist works or every Futurist writer to realize the movement made important contributions. Mediocrity will certainly be found within this group as in any, but that is not a reason for discounting the phenomenon as a whole. It had successes and it had failures. One cannot define Ukrainian Futurism by a single author or a single work. It had a wide stylistic, thematic, and tonal range. The *agitka* is no more typical of the entire movement than some of Semenko's personal and somber poems. At times it was simplistic; on other occasions highly complex. It purposely tried not to be pinned down. Not only was it highly critical of Ukrainian reality but it projected in its writings a deep alienation from its own society—an unusual occurrence in Ukrainian cultural history. It was truly one of the "strangest" movements of the 1920s and for this reason earned the reputation of being "inorganic" in Ukrainian culture.

If we borrow, as well as distort, a phrase from elsewhere, it can be said that Futurism did not produce works from "tractable material (euphony, pleasing visual images, 'poetic subjects')"; its works were "wrested from materials which, as materials, are recalcitrant: the painful, the ugly, the didactic, the practical" (Wellek and Warren 1956, 243–44). In the context of the avant-garde, such works were not unusual. In the context of Ukrainian literary traditions this was shocking, disturbing, and, most importantly, easily misunderstood. It bears repeating that the movement was misconstrued not only by the unsophisticated but also by the well-read. One can only conclude that Ukrainian scholarship and criticism did not live up to the challenge of the avant-garde. The temperament, ideology, and aesthetics of Futurism remained alien to both. The fact is that critics and scholars were generally conservative and inclined toward populist or modernist sentiments. For them Futurism represented an impenetrable barrier. Clearly, there was no mediation between the Ukrainian avant-garde and the public. Critics, who should have played such a role (as Formalists did in Russia), failed to do so and actually took the side of the uninformed audience. Ukrainian Futurists compensated as best they could by trying to perform the task themselves. In short, the sad fate of Futurism in Ukrainian literary history cannot be considered the just deserts of a worthless movement: it was actually a consequence of the shortcomings of scholarship. Its failures and omissions are what this study has hoped to redress.

Abbreviations

ARMU	*Ukr.* Asotsiiatsiia revoliutsiinoho mystetstva Ukraïny [Association of Revolutionary Art of Ukraine]
AsKK	*Ukr.* Aspanfut-Komunkul't
Aspanfut	*Ukr.* Asotsiiatsiia Panfuturystiv [The Association of Panfuturists]
DVU	*Ukr.* Derzhavne vydavnytstvo Ukraïny [State Publishing House of Ukraine]
FORPU	*Ukr.* Federatsiia orhanizatsii revoliutsiinykh pys'mennykiv Ukraïny [Federation of Organizations of Revolutionary Writers of Ukraine]
Gosplan	*Rus.* Gosudarstvennaia planirovannaia kommisiia [State Planning Commission]
HART	*Ukr.* Hart Amatoriv Robitnychoho Teatru [The HART of Supporters of Workers' Theater]
Komunkul't	*Ukr.* Asotsiiatsiia komunistychnoï kul'tury [The Association of Communist Culture]
KP(b)U	*Ukr.* Komunistychna partiia (bil'shovykiv) Ukraïny [The Communist Party (Bolsheviks) of Ukraine]
LEF	*Rus.* Levyi front iskusstv(a) [The Left Front of the Arts]
MAPP	*Rus.* Moskovskaia assotsiiatsiia proletarskikh pisatelei [The Moscow Association of Proletarian Writers]
NKO	*Ukr.* Narodnyi komisariiat osvity [The People's Commissariat of Education]
NOP	*Ukr.* Naukova orhanizatsiia pratsi [Scientific organization of labor]
NOT	*Rus.* Nauchnaia organizatsiia truda [Scientific organization of labor]
OPPU	*Ukr.* Ob'iednannia Proletars'kykh Pys'mennykiv Ukraïny [The Union of Proletarian Writers of Ukraine] *prev.* VUSSK
Proletkul't	*Ukr.* Proletars'ka kul'tura [Proletarian culture]
PROLITFRONT	*Ukr.* Proletars'kyi literaturnyi front [The Proletarian Literary Front]
REF	*Rus.* Revoliutsionnyi front iskusstv(a) [The Revolutionary Front of the Arts] *prev.* LEF
RSDRP	*Rus.* Rossiiskaia sotsial-demokraticheskaia rabochaia partiia [Russian Social-Democratic Revolutionary Party]
SUM	*Ukr.* Spilka ukraïns'koï molodi [Union of Ukrainian Youth]

SVU	*Ukr.* Spilka vyzvolennia Ukraïny [Union for the Liberation of Ukraine]
TsIT	*Rus.* Tsentral'nyi institut truda [Central Institute of Labor]
UARDIS	*Ukr.* Ukraïns'ka asotsiiatsiia rezhyseriv, dramaturhiv i stsenarystiv [The Ukrainian Association of Directors, Dramatists, and Scenarists]
UNR	*Ukr.* Ukraïns'ka narodnia respublika [Ukrainian National Republic]
VAPLITE	*Ukr.* Vilna akademiia proletars'koï literatury [The Free Academy of Proletarian Literature]
VAPP	*Rus.* Vsesoiuznaia assotsiiatsiia proletarskikh pisatelei [The All-Union Association of Proletarian Writers]
VKhUTEMAS	*Rus.* Vysshie gosudarstvennye khudozhestvenno-tekhnicheskie masterskie [Higher State Artistic and Technical Workshops]
VOAPP	*Rus.* Vsesoiuznoe ob"edinenie assotsiiatsii proletarskikh pisatelei [The All-Union Alliance of Associations of Proletarian Writers]
VUAN	*Ukr.* Vseukraïns'ka akademiia nauk [The All-Ukrainian Academy of Sciences]
VUAPP	*Ukr.* Vseukraïns'ka asotsiiatsiia proletars'kykh pys'mennykiv [The All-Ukrainian Association of Proletarian Writers]
VUARK	*Ukr.* Vseukraïns'ka asotsiiatsiia revoliutsiinykh kinematohrafiv [The All-Ukrainian Association of Revolutionary Cinematographers] *prev.* UARDIS
VUARKK	*Ukr.* Vseukraïns'ka asotsiiatsiia robitnykiv komunistychnoï kul'tury [The All-Ukrainian Association of Workers of Communist Culture] *later* VUSKK
VUFKU	*Ukr.* Vseukraïns'ke foto-kinoupravlinnia [The All-Ukrainian Photo-Cinema Administration]
VUSKK	*Ukr.* Vseukraïns'ka spilka komunistychnoï kul'tury [The All-Ukrainian Union of Communist Culture] *prev.* VUARKK, *later* OPPU
VUSSP	*Ukr.* Vseukraïns'ka spilka proletars'kykh pys'mennykiv [The All-Ukrainian Union of Proletarian Writers]
VUTsVK	*Ukr.* Vseukraïns'kyi Tsentral'nyi vykonavchyi komitet [The All-Ukrainian Central Executive Committee]

References

Several challenges arise from the presentation of the materials used in the preparation of this volume. A large number of the authors used pseudonyms—either singlets or multiple names. Within the bibliography I have given primary listing to the name under which a piece was written, but have cross-listed it with the author's primary *nom de plume* (in most cases his or her actual name, but sometimes a pseudonym), so that all the cited works of an individual are listed together. Many of the pre-WWII imprints are rarities. For this reason, publishers are listed for these works. Spelling of titles and names reflects the orthography in the original. As noted, the period under consideration was a time of great orthographic flux for the Ukrainian language, thus there may appear to be inconsistencies from title to title (e.g., *Avanhard* and *Avangard*). Relevant variants are indicated within brackets. Finally, to avoid cumbersome repetition, periodicals, almanacs, and miscellanies are listed by short title when referenced within other bibliographic entries.

Futurist Periodicals, Almanacs, and Miscellanies

2. Kyiv, 1922.

Al'manakh tr'okh. O. Slisarenko, M. Liubchenko, M. Semenko. Kyiv: Vyd. T–va Ukraïns'kykh Pys'mennykiv, 1920.

Avanhard–Al'manakh proletars'kykh myttsiv Novoï generatsiï. Kyiv, 1930, no. a (January)–no. b (April).

Bumeranh. Neperiodychnyi zhurnal pamfletiv. Kyiv, 1927, no. 1.

Hol'fshtrom. Zbirnyk I. Litsektor AsKK. Kharkiv: DVU, 1925.

Honh komunkul'ta. Kyiv-Kharkiv, 1924, no. 1 (May).

Katafalk iskusstva. Ezhednevnyi zhurnal pan-futuristov-destruktorov. Kyiv, 1922, no. 1 (13 December).

Neo-lif. Literaturno-vyrobnychyi zhurnal livoho frontu. Ed. Hryts'ko Koliada. Moscow: SiM, 1925, no. 1.

Nova generatsiia [*heneratsiia*]. *Shchomisiachnyi zhurnal livoï* [*revoliutsiinoï*] *formatsiï mystetsv*. Kharkiv, 1927–1930.

Semafor u Maibutnie. Aparat Panfuturystiv. Kyiv: Hol'fshtrom, 1922, no. 1 (May).

Zhovtnevyi zbirnyk panfuturystiv. Ed. Geo Shkurupii and Nik Bazhan. Kyiv: Gol'fstrom, 1923.

Zustrich na perekhresnii stantsiï. Rozmova tr'okh. M. Semenko, G. Shkurupii, M. Bazhan. Kyiv: Bumeranh, 1927.

Contemporary Periodicals, Almanacs, and Miscellanies

Arena. Orhan Vseukraïns'koï federatsiï proletars'kykh pysmennykiv i myttsiv. Kharkiv, 1922 .

Avanhard 3. Kharkiv, 1929.

Barykady teatru. Kyiv, 1923–1924.

Bil'shovyk Ukraïny. Kharkiv, 1924–1933.

Bil'shovyk. Orhan Kyïvs'koho Hubkomu Komunistychnoï partiï bil'shovykiv Ukraïny i Kyïvs'koho Hubvykonkomu. Kyiv, 1919–1925.

Biuleten' Avanhardu. Kharkiv, 1928.

Chervonyi shliakh. Hromads'ko-politychnyi i literaturno-naukovyi misiachnyk. Kharkiv, 1923–1932.

Grono [*Hrono*]. *Literaturno-mystets'kyi zbirnyk.* 1920. Ed. Valeriian Polishchuk. Kyiv.

*Hart. Literaturno-khudozhnii ta krytychnyi zhurnal Vseukraïns'koï spilky proletars'kykh pys'mennykiv. Hart. Literarische und kritische Monatsschrift des Allukrainischen Verbandes Proletarischer Schriftsteller [*sic*] "WUSPP."* Kharkiv, 1927–1932.

Hlobus. Dvotyzhnevyi iliustrovanyi universal'nyi zhurnal. Kyiv, 1923–1935.

Iugo-lef. Zhurnal levogo fronta iskusstv Iuga S.S.S.R. Odesa, 1924–1925.

Kharkivs'kyi proletar. Orhan Okruzhkomu KP(b)U, Okrvykonkomu, Okrprofrady i Mis'krady. Kharkiv.

Knyhar. Kyiv, 1917–1919.

Komunist. Orhan Tsentral'noho komitetu i Kharkivs'koho Mis'kkomu Komunistychnoï partiï (bil'shovykiv) Ukraïny. Kharkiv, 1919–1943.

Krytyka. Zhurnal-misiachnyk marksysts'koï krytyky ta bibliohrafiï. Kharkiv, 1928–1932.

Kul'tura. Zhurnal kul'turnoho, suspil'noho i politychnoho zhyttia. Lviv, 1928–1931.

Kul'tura i pobut. Dodatok do Vistei VUTsVK. Kharkiv, 1925–1928.

Literatura, Nauka, Mystetstvo. Kharkiv, 1923–1924.

Literaturna hazeta. Dvotyzhnevyi Orhan Vseukraïns'koï Spilky proletars'kykh pys'mennykiv. Kyiv, 1927–1930.

Literaturnyi iarmarok. Al'manakh–misiachnyk. Kharkiv, 1928–1930.

Literaturno-krytychnyi al'manakh. Knyha persha. Kyiv, 1918.

Literaturno-naukovyi visnyk. Lviv, 1898–1906; Kyiv, 1907–1914, 1917–1919; Lviv, 1922–1939.

Molodniak. Literaturno-mystets'kyi ta hromads'ko-politychnyi iliustrovanyi zhurnal-misiachnyk orhan TsK LKSMU. Kharkiv, 1927–1934.

Muzahet. Misiachnyk literatury i mystetstva. Kyiv, 1919, January-February-March, Nos. 1–3.

Mystets'ki materiialy Avanhardu. Kharkiv, 1929.

Mystetstvo. Kyiv, 1919–1920.

Mytusa. Literatura i mystetstvo. Lviv, 1922.

Na literaturnom postu. Desiatidnevnyi [Dvukhnedel'nyi] zhurnal marksistskoi kritiki. Moscow, 1923-1932.

Na zustrich. Dvotyzhnevyk. Literatura. Mystetstvo. Nauka. Hromads'ke zhyttia. Lviv, 1934.

Nova kul'tura. Lviv, 1923–1926.

Nova Ukraïna. Neue Ukraine. Misiachnyk pys'menstva, mystetstva, nauky i hromads'koho zhyttia. Prague, 1922–1928.

Novyi lef. Zhurnal levogo fronta iskusstv. Moscow, 1927–1928.

Pluzhanyn. Orhan Tsentral'noho komitetu Spilky selians'kykh pys'mennykiv "Pluh." Kharkiv, 1925–1927.

Prolitfront. Kharkiv, 1930.

Shkval. Odesa, 1924–1933.

Shliakh. Visnyk literatury, mystetstva ta hromads'koho zhyttia. Kyiv, 1917–1919.

Shliakhy mystetstva. Kharkiv, 1921–1923.

Shtabel.' Kharkiv: Vseuklitkom, 1921.

Sterni. Misiachnyk literatury, mystetstva, nauky ta students'koho zhyttia. Prague, No. 1, July, 1922.

Ukraïns'ka khata. Shchomisiachnyi literaturno-naukovyi zhurnal. Kyiv, 1909–1914.

Universal'nyi zhurnal. Kharkiv, 1928.

Vaplite. Literaturno-khudozhnii zhurnal. Kharkiv, 1927.

Visti VUTsVK [Vseukraïns'koho Tsentral'noho vykonavchoho komitetu Rad robitnychykh, selians'kykh i chervono-armiis'kykh deputativ ta Hubvykonkomu Kharkivshchyny]. Kharkiv, 1918–1933; Kyiv, 1934–1941.

Vyr revoliutsii. Katerynoslav, 1921.

Za marksolenins'ku krytyku. Kharkiv, 1932–1934.

Zakhidna Ukraïna. Kyiv, 1927–1930; Kharkiv, 1930–1933.

Zhovten'. Zbirnyk prysviachenyi rokovynam Velykoï proletars'koï revoliutsiï. Kharkiv: Vseukraïns'kyi literaturnyi komitet, 1921.

Zhyttia i revoliutsia. Misiachnyk. Kyiv, 1925–1934.

Zshytky borot'by. Kyiv: Borot'ba, 1920.

General References

Adel'heim, Ie. H. 1987. "Mykhail' Semenko: dolia, tvorchist', poetyka (Z istoriï ukraïns'koho poetychnoho avanhardyzmu)." In his *Kriz' roky. Vybrani pratsi,* pp. 47–135. Kyiv.

Aheieva, V. P. 1990. *Oleksa Slisarenko. Do 100-richchia vid dnia narodzhennia.* Kyiv. [=Seriia 6 "Dukhovnyi svit liudyny," no. 8.]

Andersen, Troels, ed. 1971. *K. S. Malevich: Essays on Art, 1915-1933,* vol. 2. Copenhagen.

Antolohiia ukraïns'koï poeziï. 1957. 3 vols. Kyiv.

Antolohiia ukraïns'koï poeziï v 4-kh tomakh. 1958. 4 vols. Ed. Maksym Tadeiovych Ryl's'kyi and Mykola L'vovych Nahnybida. Vol. 3. Ed. Mykola L. Nahnybida, intro. Leonid Mykolaiovych Novychenko. 2nd ed. Kyiv.

Antolohiia ukraïns'koï poeziï v shesty tomakh. 1984–1986. 6 vols. Ed. Mykola Platonovych Bazhan et al. Kyiv: Dnipro.

Antoniuk, S. 1930a. "'Bozhestvo' serdyt'sia, abo novi podvyhy konkvistadora Khvyl'ovoho." *Nova generatsiia* 2: 23–28.

———. 1930b. "Proty Khvyl'ovyzmu." *Literatura i mystetstvo* 8: 1–2.

Apollonio, Umbro, ed. 1973. *Futurist Manifestos.* New York.

Art et poésie russes, 1900–1930. Textes choisis. 1979. Comp. Troels Andersen and Ksenia Grigorieva, ed. Olga Makhroff and Stanislas Zadora. Paris.

"Asotsiiatsiia komunkul'tovtsiv (panfuturystiv)." 1924. *Chervonyi shliakh* 4–5: 278.

"Asotsiiatsiia panfuturystiv." 1923. *Chervonyi shliakh* 6–7: 224.

B—n, Mykh. 1925. "Od staroho do novoho mystetstva." *Zhyttia i revoliutsia* 5: 53–56.

Babiuk, O. 1924. "Komunkul'tovtsi v Umani." *Bil'shovyk* 71 (March 29): 4.

Ball, Hugo. 1974. *Flight Out of Time: A Dada Diary.* Ed. John Elderfield. New York.

Bann, Stephen. 1974a. "Constructivism and the New Man." In Bann 1974b. pp. xix–xxiii.

———comp. and ed. 1974b. *The Tradition of Constructivism.* New York.

Barooshian, Vahan D. 1974. *Russian Cubo-Futurism, 1910–1930: A Study in Avant-Gardism.* The Hague.

Bazhan, Mykola Platonovych [N. B.]. 1923a. Review of "Oleksa Slisarenko. Poemy. Kyiv: Panfuturysty, 1923." *Barykady teatru* 1 (20 November): 12. [Originally printed in *Bil'shovyk* 170 (31 July 1923): 4.]

——— [Panfuturyst-ekstruktor]. 1923b. "Les' Kurbas i Vsevolod Meiierkhol'd." *Bil'shovyk* 138 (June 23): 2.

——— [Nik Bazhan]. 1927a. "Krov polonianok." *Zustrich na perekhresnii stantsiï*, p. 31.

———. 1927b."Odiahnit' okuliary!" *Bumeranh. Neperiodychnyi zhurnal pamfletiv* no. 1, pp. 21–26.

———. 1927c. "Zalizniakova nich." *Zustrich na perekhresnii stantsiï*, pp. 32–33.

———. 1928. "Lysty do redaktsiï." *Chervonyi shliakh* 3: 160.

———. 1971. "Mytets' shukaie puti." *Vitchyzna. Literaturno-khudozhnii zhurnal Spilky radians'kykh pys'mennykiv Ukraïny* 1: 173–82.

———ed. 1973. *Slovnyk khudozhnykiv Ukraïny.* Kyiv .

———. 1985. "Vstupne slovo." In Semenko 1985, pp. 3–14.

———et. al., eds. 1984–1986. *Antolohiia ukraïns'koï poeziï v shesty tomakh.* Kyiv.

"Berezil'." 1923. *Barykady teatru* 1: 1.

"Berezil'." 1924. *Iugo-lef* 2 (September): 14.

Bilets'kyi, Oleksander Ivanovych. 1926. "Pro prozu vzahali ta pro nashu prozu 1925 roku." *Chervonyi shliakh* 3: 133–63.

———. 1929. "Mykola Voronyi. Krytychno-biohrafichnyi narys." In Voronyi 1929, pp. 15–52.

——— [Aleksandr Ivanovich Beletskii] et al, eds. 1954. *Ocherk ukrainskoi sovetskoi literatury.* Moscow.

———. 1965–66. *Zibrannia prats' u p'iaty tomakh.* Kyiv.

———et al. 1960–1965. *Ukraïns'ki pys'mennyky. Bio-bibliohrafichnyi slovnyk.* 5 vols. Kyiv.

Blakytnyi, Vasyl', et al. 1930. See Ellan-Blakytyni 1930d.

"Bl'ok mizh VUARKK ta VUSPP-om." 1929. *Nova generatsiia* 6: 56.

"Bloknot 'Novoï generatsiï.'" 1928. *Nova generatsiia* 11: 335–40, 12: 421–26.

"Bl'oknot [*sic*] 'Novoï generatsiï.'" 1929. *Nova generatsiia* 7: 32–37.

Bohats'kyi, Pavlo. 1923. *S'ohochasni literaturni priamuvannia.* Prague-Berlin: Nova Ukraïna.

———, Mykyta Shapoval, and Arkadii Zhyvotko. 1955. *Ukraïns'ka khata (Kyïv, 1909–1914).* New York.

Boiko, Leonid Serhiiovych. 1971. "Dmytro Buz'ko i ioho tvorchist'." In Buz'ko 1971, pp. 3–15.

———. 1991. "Shliakhom borot'by i shukan'." In Buz'ko 1991, pp. 5–25.

Bondarchuk, Stepan. 1923. "Teatral'nyi Hart." *Barykady teatru* 2–3: 11–12.

———. 1924. "Teatr i NOP." *Barykady teatru* 4–5: 4–5.

Bowlt, John E., ed. 1976. *Russian Art of the Avant-Garde: Theory and Criticism, 1902–1934.* New York.

Breton, André. 1978. *What is Surrealism? Selected Writings.* Ed. and intro. Franklin Rosemont. New York.

Budivnytstvo Radians'koï Ukraïny. Zbirnyk. Protsesy ideino-tvorchoï konsolidatsiï pys'mennyts'kykh syl Radians'koï Ukraïny (1917-1932). N.d. Ed. Volodymyr Zatons'kyi et al., pt. 1: "Za Lenins'ku natsional'nu polityku." Kharkiv: DVU.

"Bumeranh." [Unsigned review article.] 1927. *Pluzhanyn* 8: 29.

Burchak, L. 1919. Review of "M. Semenko. P'iero kokhaie. Misteriï (1916–1917). Intymni poezii. Knyha druha. V-vo 'Siaivo.' Kyiv, 1918. 93 st. Tsina 15 hryven'." *Knyhar* 18: 1149.

Burevii, Kost'. 1929. "Biohrafiia Edvarda Strikhy, avtora intermedii 138 knyhy, 'Liternaturnoho Iarmarku.'" *Literaturnyi iarmarok* 8: 1–3.

——— [Edvard Strikha]. 1929a. "Odvertyi lyst do 'Novoï generatsiï,' M. Semenka i inshykh khutorystiv [*sic*]." *Literaturnyi iarmorok* 8: 321–23.

——— [Edvard Strikha]. 1929b. "ZozendrOpiia [*sic*]." *Avanhard* 3: 126–33.

——— [Varvara Zhukova]. 1930. "Fashyzm i futuryzm." *Prolitfront* 3: 205–228.

——— [Edvard Strikha]. 1955. *Parodezy. Zozendropiia. Avtoekzekutsiia.* Ed. Iurii Sherekh. New York.

Bürger, Peter. 1984. *Theory of the Avant-Garde.* Trans. Michael Shaw. Minneapolis.

Bush, Mykola [Mykola Bazhan]. 1929. Review of "Buz'ko, D. Kino i kinofabryka. Kharkiv: DVU, 1928." *Zhyttia i revoliutsiia* 4: 189–91.

Buz'ko, Dmytro. 1923. "Lisovyi zvir." *Chervonyi shliakh* 9: 43–110.

———. 1924a. *Lisovyi zvir.* Kharkiv: DVU.

———. 1924b. "Po shchyrosti." *Kvartaly. Al'manakh pershyi.* Kharkiv: 55–72.

———. 1925. *Lesnoi zver'.* Kharkiv: GIU.

———. 1927a. "Asta Nil'son." *Nova generatsiia* 3: 36–46.

———. 1927b. "Problematychna 'problemnist'.' Protest chytacha." *Nova generatsiia* 1: 58–59.

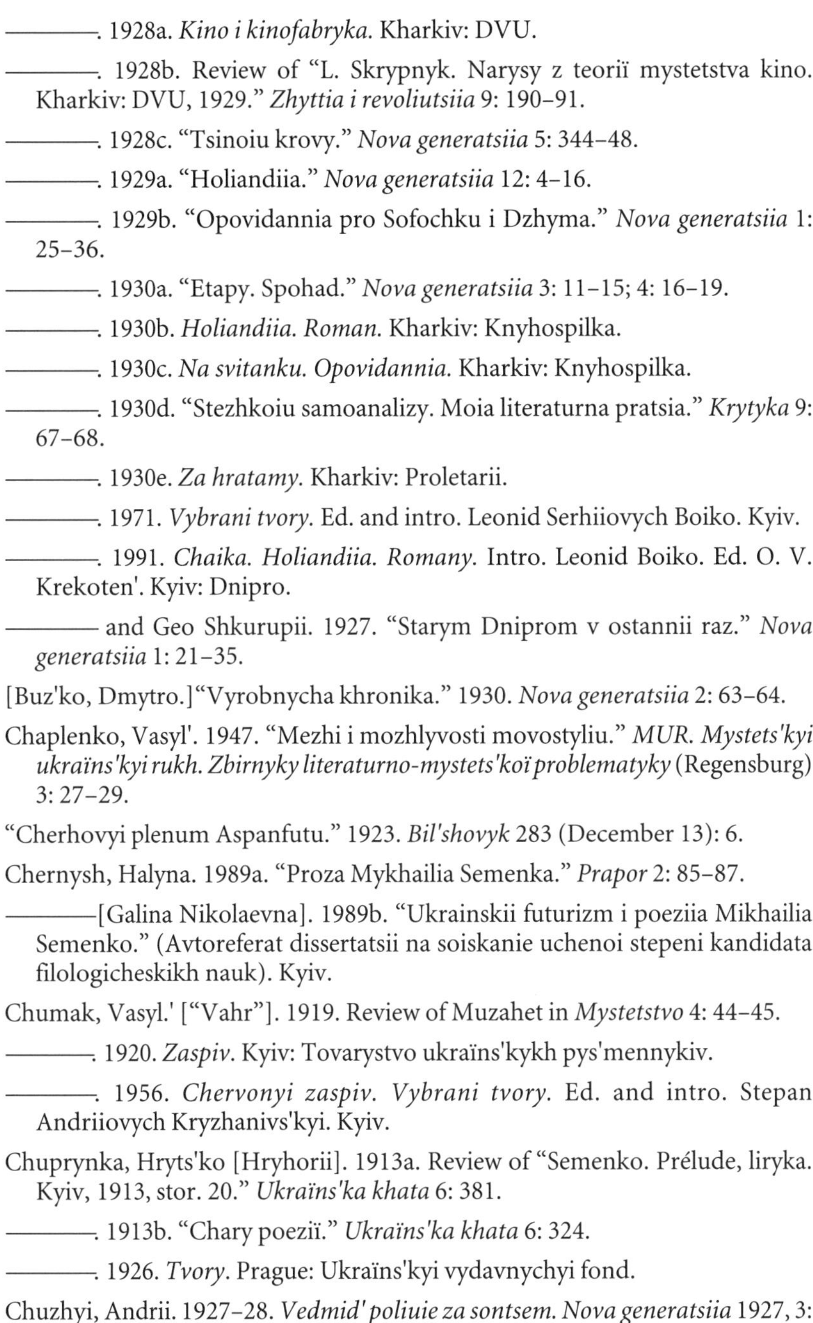

———. 1928a. *Kino i kinofabryka*. Kharkiv: DVU.

———. 1928b. Review of "L. Skrypnyk. Narysy z teoriï mystetstva kino. Kharkiv: DVU, 1929." *Zhyttia i revoliutsiia* 9: 190–91.

———. 1928c. "Tsinoiu krovy." *Nova generatsiia* 5: 344–48.

———. 1929a. "Holiandiia." *Nova generatsiia* 12: 4–16.

———. 1929b. "Opovidannia pro Sofochku i Dzhyma." *Nova generatsiia* 1: 25–36.

———. 1930a. "Etapy. Spohad." *Nova generatsiia* 3: 11–15; 4: 16–19.

———. 1930b. *Holiandiia. Roman*. Kharkiv: Knyhospilka.

———. 1930c. *Na svitanku. Opovidannia*. Kharkiv: Knyhospilka.

———. 1930d. "Stezhkoiu samoanalizy. Moia literaturna pratsia." *Krytyka* 9: 67–68.

———. 1930e. *Za hratamy*. Kharkiv: Proletarii.

———. 1971. *Vybrani tvory*. Ed. and intro. Leonid Serhiiovych Boiko. Kyiv.

———. 1991. *Chaika. Holiandiia. Romany*. Intro. Leonid Boiko. Ed. O. V. Krekoten'. Kyiv: Dnipro.

——— and Geo Shkurupii. 1927. "Starym Dniprom v ostannii raz." *Nova generatsiia* 1: 21–35.

[Buz'ko, Dmytro.]"Vyrobnycha khronika." 1930. *Nova generatsiia* 2: 63–64.

Chaplenko, Vasyl'. 1947. "Mezhi i mozhlyvosti movostyliu." *MUR. Mystets'kyi ukraïns'kyi rukh. Zbirnyky literaturno-mystets'koï problematyky* (Regensburg) 3: 27–29.

"Cherhovyi plenum Aspanfutu." 1923. *Bil'shovyk* 283 (December 13): 6.

Chernysh, Halyna. 1989a. "Proza Mykhailia Semenka." *Prapor* 2: 85–87.

———[Galina Nikolaevna]. 1989b. "Ukrainskii futurizm i poeziia Mikhailia Semenko." (Avtoreferat dissertatsii na soiskanie uchenoi stepeni kandidata filologicheskikh nauk). Kyiv.

Chumak, Vasyl.' ["Vahr"]. 1919. Review of Muzahet in *Mystetstvo* 4: 44–45.

———. 1920. *Zaspiv*. Kyiv: Tovarystvo ukraïns'kykh pys'mennykiv.

———. 1956. *Chervonyi zaspiv. Vybrani tvory*. Ed. and intro. Stepan Andriiovych Kryzhanivs'kyi. Kyiv.

Chuprynka, Hryts'ko [Hryhorii]. 1913a. Review of "Semenko. Prélude, liryka. Kyiv, 1913, stor. 20." *Ukraïns'ka khata* 6: 381.

———. 1913b. "Chary poeziï." *Ukraïns'ka khata* 6: 324.

———. 1926. *Tvory*. Prague: Ukraïns'kyi vydavnychyi fond.

Chuzhyi, Andrii. 1927–28. *Vedmid' poliuie za sontsem*. *Nova generatsiia* 1927, 3: 17–23; 1928, 3: 186–94; 4: 279–85; 7: 22–27; 10: 230–35; 11: 304–309.

———. 1980. *Poezii. Virshi ta poemy.* Kyiv.

Conquest, Robert. 1986. *The Harvest of Sorrow: Soviet Collectivization and the Terror-Famine.* New York.

Crouch, Garland E., Jr. 1979. "Bogdanov, Aleksandr Aleksandrovich." *The Modern Encyclopedia of Russian and Soviet Literature.* Vol. 3, ed. Harry B. Weber, pp. 74–81. Gulf Breeze, Florida.

Dada Almanach. Im Auftrag des Zentralamts des deutschen Dada-Bewegung herausgegeben von Richard Huelsenbeck. Mit Bildern. 1920. Berlin: Erich Reiss Verlag.

Dei, Oleksii Ivanovych. 1969. *Slovnyk ukraïns'kykh psevdonimiv ta kryptonimiv, XVI–XX st.* Kyiv.

"Dekliaratsiia Vseukraïns'koï federatsiï proletars'kykh pys'mennykiv i myttsiv." 1922. *Arena* 1 (March): 3–4.

"Dekliaratsiia Vseukraïns'koï federatsiï revoliutsiinykh radians'kykh pys'-mennykiv." 1930. *Molodniak* 1: 124–27.

"Dekliaratsiia VUARKK." 1929. *Nova generatsiia* 6: 57.

"Dekliaratsiia VUSPP." 1929. *Nova generatsiia* 6: 57.

Demchuk, Ostap. 1924. "Deiaki lektsiï po istoriï suchasnoï ukraïns'koï literatury abo neokliasychni hastroli Zerova v Zhytomyri." *Bil'shovyk* 149 (July 3): 6.

Desniak, Vasyl' [Vasyl' Vasylenko]. 1922a. "Hartsiuiut' na mistsi (Lyst z Moskvy)." *Semafor u Maibutnie. Aparat Panfuturystiv* no. 1 (May), p. 45.

———. 1922b. "Iak kyslooki poety lovliat' na hachok durniv." *Semafor u Maibutnie. Aparat Panfuturystiv* no. 1 (May), pp. 47–49.

"Do chytacha." 1930. *Prolitfront* 1: 8–10.

"Do poshyrennia plenumu idbiuro komunkul'tovtsiv." 1924. *Bil'shovyk* 6 (8 January): 4.

"Do utvorennia revoliutsiinoho bl'oku v literaturi." 1929. *Literaturna hazeta* 21 (1 November): 8.

Dolengo, Mykhailo [Mykhailo Klokov]. 1924. "Impresionistychnyi liryzm u suchasnii ukraïns'kii prozi." *Chervonyi shliakh* 1-2: 167–73.

———. 1929a. "Poeziia po nashykh zhurnalakh." *Krytyka* 6: 118–142.

———. 1929b. "Ohliad poeziï po zhurnalakh." *Krytyka* 10: 75–93.

Domontovych, Viktor [Viktor Petrov]. 1947. *Doktor Serafikus.* Munich: Ukraïns'ka trybuna.

———. 1988. *Proza.* 3 vols. Ed. Iurii Shevelov. Munich.

Donets', Roman. 1922. "Suchasne mystetstvo Ukraïny." *Nova Ukraïna* 10–11 (September): 30–33.

Doroshenko, Dmytro. 1969. *Moï spomyny pro nedavnie mynule, 1914–1920.* Munich.

Doroshkevych, Oleksander. 1924a. "Do pytannia pro utvorennia radians'koho mystets'koho bloku. Pro literaturu, krytyku i shche pro deshcho." *Bil'shovyk* 1 (1 January): 6; 2 (3 January): 6; and 3 (4 January): 4.

———. 1924b. "Konsolidatsiia revoliutsiino-mystets'kykh syl Ukraïny." *Bil'shovyk* 276 (4 November): 6.

———. 1925. Review of "Hol'fshtrom. Zbirnyk I. Litsektor AsKK. Kharkiv: DVU, 1925." *Zhyttia i revolutsiia* 6–7: 127–128.

Dovzhenko, Oleksander and Iurii Ianovs'kyi. 1927. "Lyst do redaktsiï." *Vaplite* 3: 210.

Drahomanov, Mykhailo. 1906. *Shevchenko, ukraïnofily i sotsiializm.* Intro. Ivan Franko. 2nd ed. Lviv: Ukraïns'ko-rus'ka vyd. spilka.

———. 1914. *Shevchenko, ukraïnofily i sotsiializm.* 3rd ed. Kyiv: Krynytsia.

———. 1970. "Shevchenko, ukraïnofily i sotsiializm." In his *Literaturno-publitsystychni pratsi u dvokh tomakh.* Ed. Oleksii Ie. Zasenko et al. Vol. 2, pp. 7–133. Kyiv.

Dykyi, V. 1919. Comments on introductions to "Universal Library" by Les' Horenko [M. Semenko]. *Knyhar* 18 (February): 1141–42.

Ellan-Blakytnyi, Vasyl' [Vasyl' Ellans'kyi]. 1920. *Udarom molota i sertsia.* Kyiv: Vseukrderzhvydav.

———. 1930a. "Deiaki uvahy do propozytsiï Aspanfut." In Leites and Iashek 1930, 2: 103–107.

———. 1930b. "'Hart,' 'Pluh,' i inshi ob'iednannia." In Leites and Iashek 1930, 2: 106–112.

———. 1930c. "Pered orhanizatsiinoiu kryzoiu v ukraïns'kii revoliutsiinii literaturi." In Leites and Iashek 1930, 2: 165–67.

———. 1930d. "Vidozva v den' pershoho travnia." In Leites and Iashek 1930, 2: 72–74.

———. 1958. *Tvory v dvokh tomakh.* Ed. and comp. L. Ie. Vovchyk and M. Vovchyk-Blakytna, intro. Andrii Volodymyrovych Nedzvids'kyi. 2 vols. Kyiv.

———, Mykola Khvyl'ovyi, and Ivan Dniprovs'kyi. 1923. "Lyst do redaktsiï." *Bil'shovyk* 207 (14 September): 5.

EM. Shch-k. 1924. "Komunkul'tovtsi na peryferiï." *Honh komunkul'ta* no. 1 (May), p. 15.

Erlich, Victor. 1955. *Russian Formalism: History and Doctrine.* The Hague.

Ermolaev, Herman. 1963. *Soviet Literary Theories, 1917–1934: The Genesis of Socialist Realism.* Berkeley and Los Angeles.

F—l' [Leonid' Frenkel']. 1924. “Etapy roboty Komunkul'tovtsiv.” *Honh komunkul'ta* no. 1 (May), pp. 12–13.

Fediuk, Mykola. 1924. *Pavlo Kovzhun. Grafiky. Persha zbirka*. Kyiv-Lviv: Treti pivni.

Fizer, John. 1982. “Potebnia’s Views of the Structure of Poetic Art: A Critical Retrospection.” *Harvard Ukrainian Studies* 6 (1) March: 5–24.

———. 1986. *Alexander A. Potebnja's Psycholinguistic Theory of Literature. A Metacritical Inquiry*. Cambridge, Massachusetts.

Flint, Richard Warren, ed. 1972. *Marinetti: Selected Writings*. New York.

Franko, Ivan. 1906. “Perednie slovo.” In Drahomanov 1906, pp. iii–xi.

———. 1950–56. *Tvory v dvadtsiaty tomakh*. Ed. Oleksandr Ievdokymovych Korniichuk et al. Kyiv.

Frenkel', Leonid [F—l']. 1924. “Etapy roboty Komunkul'tovtsiv.” *Honh komunkul'ta* no. 1 (May), pp. 12–13.

———. 1927. “Anekdot.” *Nova generatsiia* 1: 56–57.

———. 1928a. “Memuary. Kompozytsiia faktiv.” *Nova generatsiia* 5: 369–72.

———. 1928b. “Rekonstruktsiia farsu.” *Nova generatsiia* 9: 173–76.

Furer, V. 1930a. “Nationalistychni vybryky ta ïkhni zamazuvachi.” *Kharkivs'kyi proletar* 70 (27 March): 2.

———. 1930b. “Iak t. Sukhyno-Khomenko shukav ‘Vykhid iz zapomorochenoho stanu’ i shcho vin znaishov.” *Kharkivs'kyi proletar* 88 (17 April): 2; 89 (18 April): 2.

“Futurysty-destruktory (metamystsi).” 1928. *Nova generatsiia* 10: 276.

Fylypovych, Pavlo. 1918. Review of “M. Semenko. P’iero zadaiet'sia. Fragmenty. Intymni poezii. Knyha persha. Kyiv. 1918. 96 st. tsina 5 karb. V-tvo Grunt.” *Knyhar* 14: 858–60.

———. 1919a. Review of “O. Slisarenko, Na berezi Kastal's'komu. Poeziï. Kharkiv: Siaivo, 1919.” *Muzahet* 1–3: 148–51.

———. 1919b. Review of “M. Semenko. Dev’iat' poem. 1918. V-vo Siaivo. Kyiv, 32 st. Tsina 10 hryven'.” *Knyhar* 18: 1147–49.

———. 1919c. “‘Literaturno-naukovyi vistnyk [*sic*]’ u 1918 rotsi.” *Knyhar* 20: 1361–62.

Gray, Camilla. 1970. *The Russian Experiment in Art*. New York.

Guillén, Claudio. 1971. *Literature as System*. Princeton.

H. 1929. “Komu potribne mystetstvo.” *Literaturna hazeta* 5 (1 May). 6.

H.H. 1930. Review of “Holiandiia. Roman. Knyhospilka, 1930.” *Chervonyi shliakh* 10: 190–92.

Hadzins'kyi, Volodymyr. 1923. “Shche kil'ka sliv pro pytannia ‘formy i zmistu.’” *Chervonyi shliakh* 4–5: 174–79.

———. 1928. "Hnat Mykhailychenko." *Zhyttia i revoliutsiia* 6: 131–43.

——— [Gadzins'kyi]. 1929a. "Hnat Mykhailychenko (Zhyttia i tvorchist')." In Mykhailychenko 1929, vol. 1, pp. 19–84.

——— [Oskar Reding]. 1929b. "Lyst do chytachiv L. Skrypnykovoho 'Inteligenta.'" *Nova generatsiia* 10: 48–53.

Han, Oleksii [Aleksei Gan]. 1928. "Spravka pro Kazymyra Malevycha." *Nova generatsiia* 2: 124–27.

Hariaïv, Volodymyr. 1987. "Mif pro Mykhaila Semenka. Do analizu dyversiï suchasnoï radianolohiï." *Prapor* 10: 166–74; 11: 147–56.

Herwarth Walden and DER STURM: Artists and Publications. February 27 through May 1981. 1981. Intro. Monica Strauss. New York.

Hirniak, Iosyp. 1982. *Spomyny.* New York.

Hoholev, L. D. ed. 1970. *Kriz' kinoob'iektyv chasu. Spohady veteraniv ukraïns'koho kino.* Kyiv.

Holubenko, D. 1928. "Istoryk literatury Shamrai." *Nova generatsiia* 10: 238–49.

———. 1930a. "Antonenko-Davydovych á la russe." *Nova generatsiia* 2: 60.

———. 1930b. "Mistyfikatsiia (?)." *Nova generatsiia* 4: 57–58.

Horbachov, Dmytro Oleksiiovych. 1988. "Vsesvit Malevycha z tsentrom u Kyievi." *Ukraïna* 29: 11–14.

Hordyns'kyi, Iaroslav. 1939. *Literaturna krytyka pidsoviets'koï Ukraïny.* Lviv and Kyiv: Ukraïns'ka mohylians'ko-mazepyns'ka akademiia nauk.

———. 1943. *Pavlo Kovzhun (1896–1939).* Cracow-Lviv: Ukraïns'ke vydavnytstvo.

Hrupa armistiv. 1929. "Lyst do iarmarkomu. 'Dialektyka.'" *Literaturnyi iarmarok* 7: 277–80.

Hrushevs'kyi, Mykhailo. 1959. *Istoriia ukraïns'koï literatury.* Vol. 1. New York.

Hrushevs'kyi, Oleksander. 1918. Review of "P'iero zadaiet'sia. Fragmenty. Intymni poeziï. Knyha persha." In *Literaturno-naukovyi visnyk* 2: 136.

Huelsenbeck, Richard. 1974. *Memoirs of a Dada Drummer.* Ed. Hans J. Kleinschmidt. New York.

———. 1981. "Collective Dada Manifesto." In Motherwell 1981, pp. 242–46.

Hundorova, Tamara. 1992. "Suspil'no-literaturnyi rukh 'Molodoï Ukraïny' i problema modernoï natsiï." *Suchasnist'* 3: 108–13.

Iakubovs'kyi, Feliks. 1925. "Pid praporom ukraïns'koho 'amerykanizmu.'" *Bil'shovyk* 115 (23 May): 4.

———. 1927. "Ukraïns'ka khudozhnia proza v Kyievi." *Hlobus* 4: 58.

———. 1928a. "Po ukraïns'kykh zhurnalakh." *Krytyka* 3: 106–20, 11: 93–106

———. 1928b. *Syluety suchasnykh ukraïns'kykh pys'mennykiv.* Kyiv: Kul'tura.

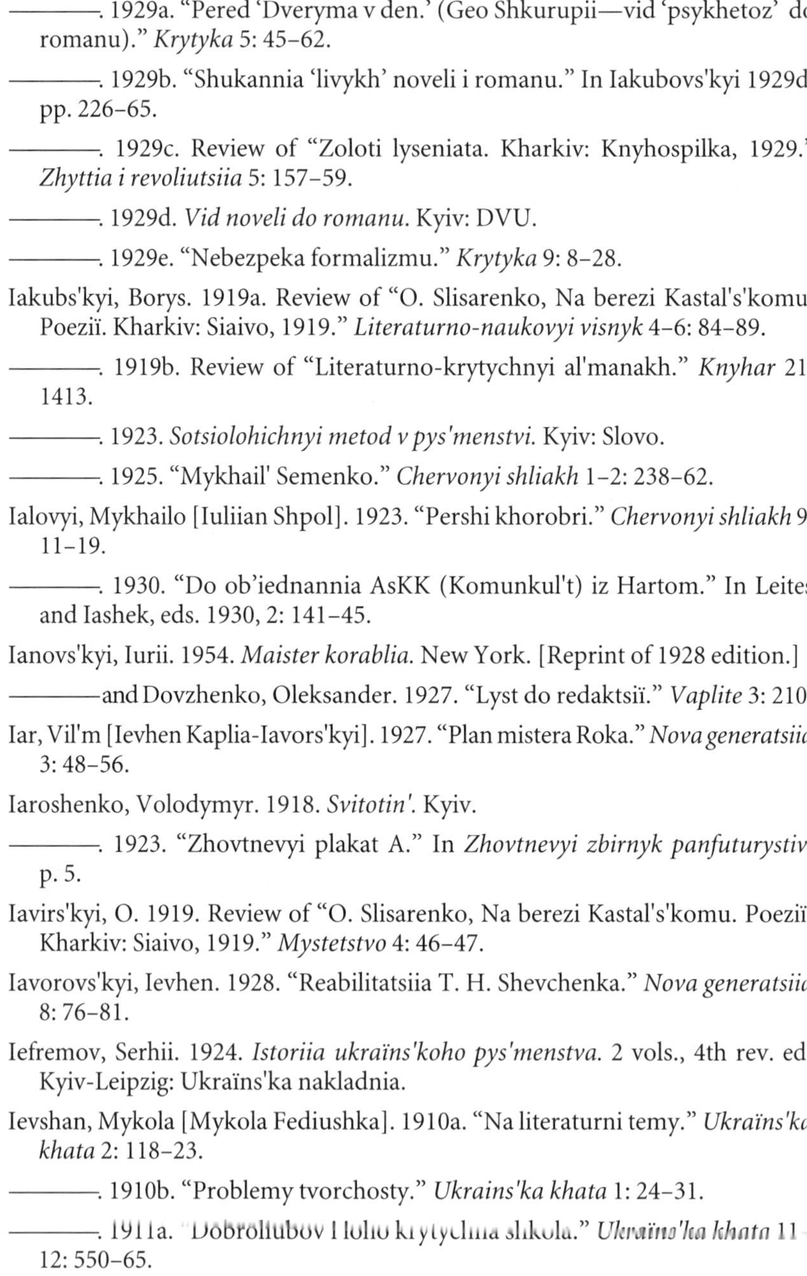

———. 1929a. "Pered 'Dveryma v den.' (Geo Shkurupii—vid 'psykhetoz' do romanu)." *Krytyka* 5: 45–62.

———. 1929b. "Shukannia 'livykh' noveli i romanu." In Iakubovs'kyi 1929d, pp. 226–65.

———. 1929c. Review of "Zoloti lyseniata. Kharkiv: Knyhospilka, 1929." *Zhyttia i revoliutsiia* 5: 157–59.

———. 1929d. *Vid noveli do romanu*. Kyiv: DVU.

———. 1929e. "Nebezpeka formalizmu." *Krytyka* 9: 8–28.

Iakubs'kyi, Borys. 1919a. Review of "O. Slisarenko, Na berezi Kastal's'komu. Poeziï. Kharkiv: Siaivo, 1919." *Literaturno-naukovyi visnyk* 4–6: 84–89.

———. 1919b. Review of "Literaturno-krytychnyi al'manakh." *Knyhar* 21: 1413.

———. 1923. *Sotsiolohichnyi metod v pys'menstvi*. Kyiv: Slovo.

———. 1925. "Mykhail' Semenko." *Chervonyi shliakh* 1–2: 238–62.

Ialovyi, Mykhailo [Iuliian Shpol]. 1923. "Pershi khorobri." *Chervonyi shliakh* 9: 11–19.

———. 1930. "Do ob'iednannia AsKK (Komunkul't) iz Hartom." In Leites and Iashek, eds. 1930, 2: 141–45.

Ianovs'kyi, Iurii. 1954. *Maister korablia*. New York. [Reprint of 1928 edition.]

———and Dovzhenko, Oleksander. 1927. "Lyst do redaktsiï." *Vaplite* 3: 210.

Iar, Vil'm [Ievhen Kaplia-Iavors'kyi]. 1927. "Plan mistera Roka." *Nova generatsiia* 3: 48–56.

Iaroshenko, Volodymyr. 1918. *Svitotin'*. Kyiv.

———. 1923. "Zhovtnevyi plakat A." In *Zhovtnevyi zbirnyk panfuturystiv*, p. 5.

Iavirs'kyi, O. 1919. Review of "O. Slisarenko, Na berezi Kastal's'komu. Poeziï. Kharkiv: Siaivo, 1919." *Mystetstvo* 4: 46–47.

Iavorovs'kyi, Ievhen. 1928. "Reabilitatsiia T. H. Shevchenka." *Nova generatsiia* 8: 76–81.

Iefremov, Serhii. 1924. *Istoriia ukraïns'koho pys'menstva*. 2 vols., 4th rev. ed. Kyiv-Leipzig: Ukraïns'ka nakladnia.

Ievshan, Mykola [Mykola Fediushka]. 1910a. "Na literaturni temy." *Ukraïns'ka khata* 2: 118–23.

———. 1910b. "Problemy tvorchosty." *Ukrains'ka khata* 1: 24–31.

———. 1911a. "Dobroliubov i ioho krytychna shkola." *Ukraïns'ka khata* 11–12: 550–65.

———. 1911b. *Taras Shevchenko*. Kyiv.

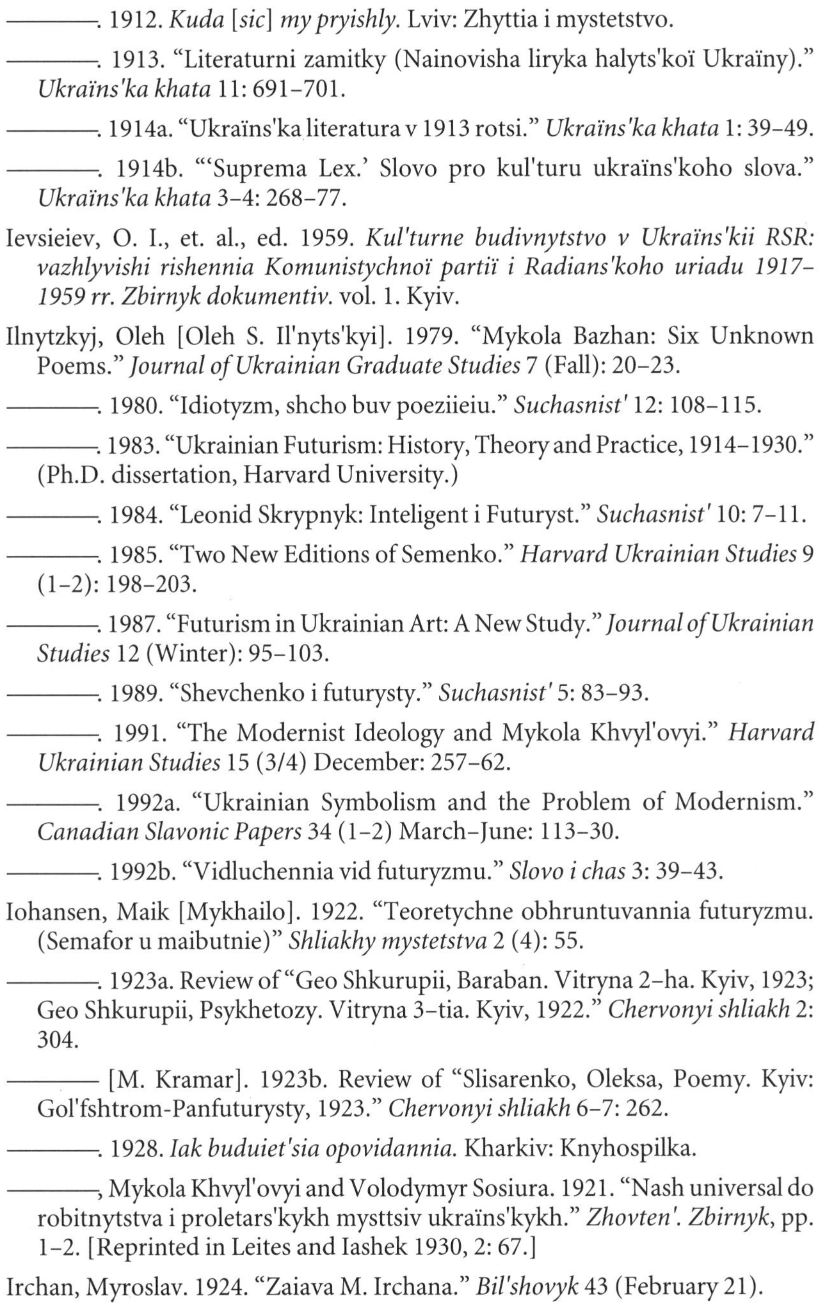

———. 1912. *Kuda* [*sic*] *my pryishly*. Lviv: Zhyttia i mystetstvo.

———. 1913. "Literaturni zamitky (Nainovisha liryka halyts'koï Ukraïny)." *Ukraïns'ka khata* 11: 691–701.

———. 1914a. "Ukraïns'ka literatura v 1913 rotsi." *Ukraïns'ka khata* 1: 39–49.

———. 1914b. "'Suprema Lex.' Slovo pro kul'turu ukraïns'koho slova." *Ukraïns'ka khata* 3–4: 268–77.

Ievsieiev, O. I., et. al., ed. 1959. *Kul'turne budivnytstvo v Ukraïns'kii RSR: vazhlyvishi rishennia Komunistychnoï partiï i Radians'koho uriadu 1917–1959 rr. Zbirnyk dokumentiv*. vol. 1. Kyiv.

Ilnytzkyj, Oleh [Oleh S. Il'nyts'kyi]. 1979. "Mykola Bazhan: Six Unknown Poems." *Journal of Ukrainian Graduate Studies* 7 (Fall): 20–23.

———. 1980. "Idiotyzm, shcho buv poeziieiu." *Suchasnist'* 12: 108–115.

———. 1983. "Ukrainian Futurism: History, Theory and Practice, 1914–1930." (Ph.D. dissertation, Harvard University.)

———. 1984. "Leonid Skrypnyk: Inteligent i Futuryst." *Suchasnist'* 10: 7–11.

———. 1985. "Two New Editions of Semenko." *Harvard Ukrainian Studies* 9 (1–2): 198–203.

———. 1987. "Futurism in Ukrainian Art: A New Study." *Journal of Ukrainian Studies* 12 (Winter): 95–103.

———. 1989. "Shevchenko i futurysty." *Suchasnist'* 5: 83–93.

———. 1991. "The Modernist Ideology and Mykola Khvyl'ovyi." *Harvard Ukrainian Studies* 15 (3/4) December: 257–62.

———. 1992a. "Ukrainian Symbolism and the Problem of Modernism." *Canadian Slavonic Papers* 34 (1–2) March–June: 113–30.

———. 1992b. "Vidluchennia vid futuryzmu." *Slovo i chas* 3: 39–43.

Iohansen, Maik [Mykhailo]. 1922. "Teoretychne obhruntuvannia futuryzmu. (Semafor u maibutnie)" *Shliakhy mystetstva* 2 (4): 55.

———. 1923a. Review of "Geo Shkurupii, Baraban. Vitryna 2-ha. Kyiv, 1923; Geo Shkurupii, Psykhetozy. Vitryna 3-tia. Kyiv, 1922." *Chervonyi shliakh* 2: 304.

——— [M. Kramar]. 1923b. Review of "Slisarenko, Oleksa, Poemy. Kyiv: Gol'fshtrom-Panfuturysty, 1923." *Chervonyi shliakh* 6–7: 262.

———. 1928. *Iak buduiet'sia opovidannia*. Kharkiv: Knyhospilka.

———, Mykola Khvyl'ovyi and Volodymyr Sosiura. 1921. "Nash universal do robitnytstva i proletars'kykh mysttsiv ukraïns'kykh." *Zhovten'. Zbirnyk*, pp. 1–2. [Reprinted in Leites and Iashek 1930, 2: 67.]

Irchan, Myroslav. 1924. "Zaiava M. Irchana." *Bil'shovyk* 43 (February 21).

——— [Andrii Babiuk] and Geo Shkurupii. 1922. "Lystuvannia z EM [*sic*] Irchanom." *Katafalk iskusstva* no. 1 (13 December), p. 2.

Ishchuk, Arsen Oleksiiovych. 1966. "Tvorchist' Mykoly Tereshchenka." In Tereshchenko 1966.

Istoriia ukraïns'koï literatury. 1954–57. Ed. Oleksandr Ivanovych Bilets'kyi. 2 vols. Kyiv.

Istoriia ukraïns'koï literatury u vos'my tomakh. 1967–71. Ed. Borys Spyrydonovych Buriak. 8 vols. Vol. 5 (1968); vol. 6 (1970). Kyiv.

Istoriia ukraïns'koï radians'koï literatury. 1964. Ed. Stepan Andriiovych Kryzhanivs'kyi et al. Kyiv.

Iu.S. [Dmytro Zahul?]. 1923. "Mystetstvo v Kyievi." *Chervonyi shliakh* 4–5: 255.

Ivanenko, I. 1925. "Do nashykh literaturnykh sprav (vydavnytstvo-pys'mennyk)." *Hlobus* 22 (November): 515.

Ivaniv-Mezhenko, Iurii [Iurii Mezhenko]. 1919. "Tvorchist' indyviduuma i kolektyv." *Muzahet* (January, February, March): 65–78.

K—v., R. 1929. "Pro panfuturyzm Ol. Poltorats'koho." *Hart* 4.

Kachaniuk, M. 1930. "Materiialy do istoriï futuryzmu na Radians'kii Ukraïni." In *Literaturnyi arkhiv*, Books 1–2: 186–92; 3–4: 312–18.

"Kalendar AsPF [Aspanfut]." 1924. *Bil'shovyk* 60 (14 March): 6.

"'Karnaval.' Kompozytsiia 'Mykhailychenkivtsiv.'" 1923. *Chervonyi shliakh* 6–7: 222.

"Khronika. Kyievs'ki [*sic*] futurysty." 1922. *Mytusa* (Lviv) 2 (February): 63.

Khutorian, Antin S. 1929. "U poloni eksperymentiv." *Literaturna hazeta* 23 (1 December): 4.

Khvylia, Andrii Ananiiovych. 1926. *Pro nashi literaturni spravy.* Kharkiv: Proletarii.

———. 1928. "Notatky pro literaturu." *Krytyka* 11: 3–30.

———. 1929a. "Pid znakom internatsional'noï proletars'koï iednosty." *Krytyka* 6: 3-15.

———. 1929b. "Zustrich." *Krytyka* 5: 3–24.

———. 1930a. "Notatky pro literaturu." *Krytyka* 4: 6–40.

———. 1930b. "Khto zakhvoriv? (pro p'iesu L. Nedoli 'Khvoroba')." *Krytyka* 11: 47–61.

Khvyl'ovyi, Mykola [Mykola Hryhorovych Fitil'ov]. 1925. *Kamo hriadeshy. Pamflety.* Kharkiv: Knyhospilka.

———. 1926. *Dumky proty techiï. Pamflety.* Kharkiv: DVU.

———. 1927. "Odvertyi lyst do Volodymyra Koriaka." *Vaplite* 5: 158–73.

———. 1929d. "Proloh do knyhy sto sorok druhoï." *Literaturnyi iarmarok* 12: 1–4.

———. 1930a. "Krychushche bozhestvo." *Prolitfront* 1: 247–52. [Originally appeared in Khvyl'ovyi 1930e.]

———. 1930b. "Chym prycharuvala '*Nova generatsiia*' tov. Sukhyno-Khomenka?" *Prolitfront* 3: 229–69.

———. 1930c. "Ostap Vyshnia v svitli 'livoï' balalaiky." *Prolitfront* 4: 254–310.

———. 1930e. "Krychushche bozhestvo (z pryvodu odniieï nebezpeky)." *Komunist. Orhan Tsentral'noho komitetu i Kharkivs'koho Mis'kkomu Komunistychnoï partiï (bil'shovykiv) Ukraïny* (Kharkiv) 26 (27 January): 4.

———. 1930f. "A khto shche sydyt' na lavi pidsudnykh? (Do protsesu 'Spilky vyzvolennia Ukraïny')." *Kharkivs'kyi proletar* 62 (1782) 16 March: 2–3.

———. 1930g. "Za shchodennykom S. O. Iefremova—vozhdia, akademika, 'sovisty zemli ukraïns'koï,' shcho palakhkotyt' 'Velykym Polum'iam.'" *Kharkivs'kyi proletar* 65 (1785) 21 March: 2; 68 (1788) 25 March: 2.

———. 1930h. "Do statti M. Khvyl'ovoho—'A kto shche sydyt' na lavi pidsudnykh?'" *Kharkivs'kyi proletar* 63 (1782) 18 March: 5.

———. 1931. "Konsolidatsiia ukraïns'koï proletars'koï literatury. Skorochenyi stenohrafichnyi zvit zahal'nykh zboriv Kharkivs'koï orhanizatsiï VUSPP, 24–II–1931. Promova tov. Khvyl'ovoho." *Literaturna hazeta* 10 (30 March): 1–2.

———. 1978–86. *Tvory u p'iat'okh tomakh*. Ed. and intro. Hryhorii Kostiuk. 5 vols. New York.

———. 1986. *The Cultural Renaissance in Ukraine. Polemical Pamphlets, 1925–1926*. Trans. Myroslav Shkandrij. Edmonton.

———. 1989. *Syni etiudy. Novely, opovidannia, etiudy*. Kyiv.

———. 1990a. "Lysty Mykoly Khvyl'ovoho do Mykoly Zerova." *Radians'ke literaturoznavstvo* 7: 3–15; 8: 11–25.

———. 1990b. "Ukraïna chy Malorossiia." Ed. and intro. Viktor Pohrebniak. *Vitchyzna. Literaturno-khudozhnii zhurnal Spilky radians'kykh pys'mennykiv Ukraïny* (Kyiv) 1: 181–88; 2:168–78. [Also *Slovo i chas* 1: 7–31.]

———, Volodymyr Sosiura, and Maik Iohansen. 1921. "Nash universal do robitnytstva i proletars'kykh mysttsiv ukraïns'kykh." *Zhovten'. Zbirnyk*, pp. 1–2. [Reprinted in Leites and Iashek 1930, 2: 67.]

"Klubni iacheiky 'Komunkul't.'" 1924. *Bil'shovyk* 16 (19 January): 4.

Kolasky, John, comp., ed., and trans. 1990. *Prophets and Proletarians. Documents on the History of the Rise and Decline of Ukrainian Communism in Canada*. Edmonton.

Koliada, Geo [Heo; Hryts'ko]. 1928. "Arsenal syl. Roman novoï konstruktsiï." *Nova generatsiia* 12: 376–406.

———. 1929. *Arsenal syl. Roman novoï konstruktsiï*. Kyiv: "Semafor u Maibutnie."

"Konsolidatsiia proletars'kykh literaturnykh syl. Zaiavy do Vseukraïns'koï Spilky proletars'kykh pys'mennykiv." 1930. *Literaturna hazeta* 5 (20 March): 2.

"Konstruktory-funktsionalisty." 1928. *Nova generatsiia* 10: 275.

Koriak, Volodymyr. 1919. "Chystylyshche." *Mystetstvo* 3: 20–21.

———. 1921. "Futuryzm ukraïns'kyi i pol's'kyi." In *Zhovten'. Zbirnyk*, pp. 106–128.

———. 1922. "Forma i zmist." *Shliakhy mystetstva* 2: 40–46.

———. 1923a. "Ukraïns'ka literatura pered VII Zhovtnem." *Chervonyi shliakh* 8: 180–205.

———. 1923b. "Vid shyrokoï koalitsiï do marksivs'koho bloku." *Literatura, Nauka, Mystetstvo* 6 (11 November).

———. 1923c. "Naukova krytyka." *Shliakhy mystetstva* 5: 45–52.

———. 1927. "Khvyl'ovystyi sotsiolohichnyi ekvivalent." *Hart* 1: 74–103.

Korniienko, Ivan. 1970. *Pivstolittia ukraïns'koho radians'koho kino.* Kyiv.

Korsuns'ka, Berta L'vivna. 1967. *Poeziia novoho svitu.* Kyiv.

———. 1968. "Mykhail' Semenko." *Radians'ke literaturoznavstvo* 6: 19–33.

Koshelivets', Ivan. 1964. *Suchasna literatura v URSR.* New York: Proloh.

———. 1972. *Mykola Skrypnyk.* New York.

Kostenko, Anatolii Illich. 1959. Editorial introduction to *Iz poeziï 20-kh rokiv. Zbirnyk.* Kyiv.

Kostenko, Natalia Vasylivna. 1971. *Poetyka Mykoly Bazhana (1923–1940).* Kyiv.

Kostiuk, Hryhorii. 1978. "Mykola Khvyl'ovyi—zhyttia, doba, tvorchist'." In Khvyl'ovyi 1978–86, vol. 1, pp. 15–106.

Koval', Vitalii Kyrylovych and Vira Petrivna Pavlovs'ka, eds. 1988. *Pys'mennyky radians'koï Ukraïny, 1917–1987. Biobibliohrafichnyi dovidnyk.* Kyiv.

Kovalenko, Borys. 1927. "Literaturna klounada." *Molodniak* 5: 100.

———. 1929. "Pokryvdzhena zemlia." *Nova generatsiia* 11: 53–58.

———. 1934. "Pid znakom perebudovy." *Za marksolenins'ku krytyku* 7: 57–58.

Kovalevs'kyi, B. 1930. "Rytmovi shukannia v suchasnii ukraïns'kii poezii." *Nova generatsiia* 1: 26–31.

Kovalivs'kyi, Andrii. 1923. "Pro sotsiial'no-ekonomichnyi metod v istoriï literatury." *Chervonyi shliakh* 3: 195–215.

Kovzhun, Pavlo. 1934. "Muzaget." *Na zustrich. Dvotyzhnevyk. Literatura. Mystetstvo. Nauka. Hromads'ke zhyttia* (Lviv) 3 (1 February): 3.

Kramar, M. [Maik Iohansen]. 1923. Review of "Slisarenko, Oleksa, Poemy. Kyiv: Gol'fshtrom-Panfuturysty, 1923." *Chervonyi shliakh* 6–7: 262.

Kravtsiv, Bohdan [Krawciw]. 1955. *Obirvani struny*. New York.

———. 1973. "Semenko, Mykhailo." *Entsyklopediia Ukraïnoznavstva: Slovnykova chastyna*, vol. 7, pp. 2748–49. Paris and New York.

Kriger, Leo [Iryna Mykhailivna Semenko]. 1979. "Mikhail Semenko (1892–1937)—osnovopolozhnik ukrainskogo futurizma." In Semenko 1979–1982, vol. 1, pp. 15–118.

Kriz' kinoob'iektyv chasu. Spohady veteraniv ukraïns'koho kino. 1970. Kyiv.

Kryzhanivs'kyi, Stepan Andriiovych. 1956. "Vasyl' Chumak." In Chumak 1956, p. 9.

———. 1989. ed. *Pys'mennyky Radians'koï Ukraïny 20-30 roky. Narysy tvorchosti*. Kyiv.

Kulyk, Ivan. 1921. "Realizm, futuryzm, impresionizm." *Shliakhy mystetstva* 1: 35–39.

———. 1922a. "Na shliakhu do proletars'koho mystetsva." *Shliakhy mystetstva* 2[4]: 32. [Reprinted in Leites and Iashek (1930, 2: 44).]

——— [Vasyl' Rolenko]. 1922b. "Iolopy (pro knyhu Psykhetozy H. Shkurupiia)." *Shliakhy mystetstva* 2: 62.

———. 1929. "Nakhabstvo, shcho ne viz'me horoda." *Hart* 12: 126–31.

———. 1930. "Konechna umova." *Hart* 5: 185–91. [Reprinted in *Komunist. Orhan Tsentral'noho komitetu i Kharkivs'koho Mis'kkomu Komunistychnoï partiï (bil'shovykiv) Ukraïny* (Kharkiv) 103 (14 April).]

———. 1931. "Lyst do t.t. VUSPPivtsiv." *Literaturna hazeta* 8 (28 February): 2.

———. 1934. "Dopovid' na pershomu vseukraïns'komu z'ïzdi radians'kykh pys'mennykiv." *Radians'ka literatura* 7–8: 183–230.

Kurbas, Les'. 1923a. "Psykholohizm na stseni." *Barykady teatru* 2–3: 5.

———. 1923b. "Estetstvo." *Barykady teatru* 2–3: 2–3; 4–5: 2.

———. 1923c. "Krakh akademichnykh teatriv." *Bil'shovyk* 205 (12 September): 6.

"Kyïv. Kul'turne zhyttia (dopys)." 1923. *Chervonyi shliakh* 6–7: 218.

Lain, Levon [Leonid Skrypnyk]. 1927–28. "Intelihent. Ekranizovanyi roman na shist' chastyn z prolohom ta epilohom." *Nova generatsiia* 1–3 (1927); 1–8 (1928). [Reprinted in *Suchasnist'* 10 (1984) and subsequent issues.]

Lans'kyi, M. [Leonid Skrypnyk]. 1927. "Livyi roman." *Nova generatsiia* 2: 34–38.

Lapchyns'kyi, Heorh. 1927. "Natsional'na polityka za desiat' rokiv sotsial'noï revoliutsiï." *Zhyttia i revoliutsiia* 5: 243–49.

Lavrynenko, Iurii. 1955. "Kost' Stepanovych Burevii." *Ukraïns'ka literaturna hazeta* (Munich) 3 (March).

——— [Jurij Lawrynenko]. 1959. *Rozstriliane vidrodzhennia. Antolohiia 1917-1933. Poeziia - Proza - Drama - Esei.* Paris. [=Biblioteka "Kultury," vol. 37.]

Lebid', A. 1925. "Do revoliutsiinoï kryzy v ukraïns'kii revoliutsiinii literaturi." *Zhyttia i revoliutsiia* 3: 88–89.

"Lektsiï pro panfuturyzm v Cherkasakh." 1923. *Bil'shovyk* 291 (22 December): 4.

Leites, Aleksandr Mikhailovich and Mykola Fedorovych Iashek, eds. 1928. *Desiat' rokiv ukraïns'koï literatury (1917-1927).* 1st ed.; 2 vols. Kharkiv: DVU. [Reprinted 1986, Munich: Verlag Otto Sagner.]

———, eds. 1930. *Desiat' rokiv ukraïns'koï literatury (1917–1927).* 2nd revised and expanded ed.; 3 vols. Kharkiv: DVU.

"Leonid Skrypnyk." 1929a. *Nova generatsiia* 3: 5.

"Leonid Skrypnyk." 1929b. *Krytyka* 3: 125.

Levchenko, Mykhailo. 1971. "Maiakovs'kyi ta ukraïns'kyi futuryzm." *Radians'ke literaturoznavstvo* 6: 19–29.

Liber, George L. 1992. *Soviet Nationality Policy, Urban Growth, and Identity Change in the Ukrainian SSR 1923–1934.* Cambridge. [=Soviet and East European Studies, 84.]

Lissitzky, El, and Ilya [Elie] Ehrenburg. 1922. *Vesch'. Mezhdunarodnoe obozrenie iskusstva. Gegenstand. Internationale Rundschau der Kunst der Gegenwart. Objet. Revue Internationale de l'Art Moderne.* Berlin.

"Literaturne zhyttia." 1924. *Nova Ukraïna* 1–3: 210.

Liubchenko, Arkadii et al. 1929. "Lyst do redaktsiï." *Literaturnyi iarmarok* 11: 313–15.

Liubchenko, Mykola. 1920. [Poems]. In *Al'manakh tr'okh*, pp. 21–32.

Lodder, Christina. 1983. *Russian Constructivism.* New Haven and London.

Lopatyns'kyi, Favst. 1928a. "Lyst do moioho pryiatelia—stsenarysta." *Nova generatsiia* 5: 361–63.

———. 1928b. "Druhyi lyst do moioho pryiatelia—stsenarysta." *Nova generatsiia* 7: 8–9.

———. 1928c. "Dynamo. (Asotsiiatsiia vid Vel'sovoho 'Boh dynamo'.) Kino-stsenarii." *Nova generatsiia* 7: 9–21.

Luckyj, George, S. N. 1956. *Literary Politics in the Soviet Ukraine, 1917–1934.* New York: Columbia University Press. [Revised and updated edition, Durham and London, 1990.]

——— [Iurii Luts'kyi]. 1977. *Vaplitians'kyi zbirnyk.* Oakville, Ontario

"Lyst-Dekliaratsiia Ob'iednannia robitnykiv proletars'koï kul'tury." 1930. In Leites and Iashek 1930, 2: 146–49.

"Lyst do iarmarkomu. Dialektyka." 1929. *Literaturnyi iarmarok* 7: 279.

"Lyst do redaktsii." 1929. *Literaturna hazeta* (Kyiv) 21 (1 November): 8.

"Lystuvannia druziv." 1928. *Nova generatsiia* 5: 389.

"Lystuvannia z redaktsiieiu." 1928a. *Nova generatsiia* 4: 317.

"Lystuvannia z redaktsiieiu." 1928b. *Nova generatsiia* 7: 60.

"Lystuvannia z redaktsiieiu." 1928c. *Nova generatsiia* 3: 234–38.

"Lysty do redaktsiï. Vid sekretariatu VUSPP." 1929. *Hart* 1: 150.

M.K. 1923. "Zhovtnevyi Blok Mystetstv." *Bil'shovyk* 254 (9 November 1923): 5.

M.S. [M. Semenko]. 1924. "Asotsiiatsiia Komunkul'tovtsiv (Panfuturystiv)." *Chervonyi shliakh* 4–5: 278–79.

M.T. [Mykola Tereshchenko?]. 1923. Review of Sulyma 1923. *Bil'shovyk* 1 (1 January): 3.

Mace, James E. 1983. *Communism and the Dilemmas of National Liberation: National Communism in Soviet Ukraine, 1918–1933.* Cambridge, Massachusetts.

Maifet, Hryhorii. 1928. "Analiza dedektyvnoï noveli." *Zhyttia i revoliutsiia* 1: 66–72.

"Maisternia litsektora Aspanfut (Komunkul'tovtsiv)." 1924. *Bil'shovyk* 48 (27 February): 4.

"Maisternia montazhu slova." 1924. *Bil'shovyk* 52 (2 March): 6.

Majstrenko, Iwan. 1954. *Borot'bism: A Chapter in the History of Ukrainian Communism.* New York.

Mak, O. [Ivan Momot] 1930. "Z bl'oknotu chytacha." *Prolitfront* 1, 3, 4.

Malevych, Kazimir S. [Malevich]. 1928a. "Maliarstvo v problemi arkhitektury." *Nova generatsiia* 2: 116–24.

———. 1928b. "Analiza novoho ta obrazotvorchoho mystetstva, Pol' Sezann." *Nova generatsiia* 6: 438–46.

———. 1928c. "Nove mystetstvo i mystetstvo obrazotvorche." *Nova generatsiia* 9: 177–85.

———. 1928d. "Nove mystetstvo i mystetstvo obrazotvorche." *Nova generatsiia* 12: 411–17.

———. 1929a. "Prostorovyi kubizm." *Nova generatsiia* 4: 63–67.

———. 1929b. "Lezhe, Gri, Herbin, Mettsinger." *Nova generatsiia* 5: 57–67.

———. 1929c. "Konstruktyvne maliarstvo rosiis'kykh maliariv i konstruktyvizm." *Nova generatsiia* 8: 47–54.

———. 1929d. "Konstruktyvizm i rosiis'ki konstruktyvisty." *Nova generatsiia* 9: 53–61.

———. 1929e. "Kubo-futuryzm." *Nova generatsiia* 10: 58–67.

———. 1929f. "Futuryzm dynamichnyi i kinetychnyi." *Nova generatsiia* 11: 71–80.

———. 1929g. "Estetyka." *Nova generatsiia* 12: 56–58.

———. 1930a. "Arkhitektura, stankove maliarstvo ta skul'ptura." *Avanhard-Al'manakh* no. b (April), pp. 91–94.

———. 1930b. "Sproba vyznachennia zalezhnosty mizh kol'orom ta formoiu v maliarstvi." *Nova generatsiia* 6–7: 64–69.

———. 1930c. "Sproba vyznachennia zalezhnosty mizh kol'orom ta formoiu v maliarstvi." *Nova generatsiia* 8–9: 55–59.

———. 1976. "Detstvo i iunost' Kazimira Malevicha. (Glavy iz avtobiografii khudozhnika)." Ed. and intro. Nikolai Khardzhiev [Nikolaj Chardiev]. In *K istorii russkogo avangarda. Nikolai Khardzhiev: Poeziia i zhivopis'. Kazimir Malevich: Avtobiografiia. Mikhail Matushkin: Russkie kubo-futuristy.* Ed. Jan Benedikt et al., with a postscript by Roman Jakobson, pp. 85–127. Stockholm.

"Maliars'ka maisternia prof. V. Melera [*sic*]." 1923. *Chervonyi shliakh* 6–7: 221–22.

Malovichko, Ivan. 1930a. "Iak zasypavsia M. Khvyl'ovyi na zakhysti Ostapa Vyshni." *Nova generatsiia* 11–12: 26–36.

———. 1930b. "Henii po-shkurupiïvs'komu." *Nova generatsiia* 11–12: 65–66.

———and Pavlo Myrhorods'kyi. 1929. "Dva shchodennyky." *Nova generatsiia* 2: 29–40.

Marcadé, Valentine. 1980. "Vasilii Ermilov [Yermilov] and certain aspects of Ukrainian Art of the early Twentieth Century." In *The Avant-Garde in Russia, 1910–1930: New Perspectives*, p. 46–50. Los Angeles (Los Angeles County Museum of Art).

Markov, Vladimir. 1968. *Russian Futurism: A History.* Berkeley-Los Angeles.

Maslov, Serhii Ivanovych, and Ievhen Prokhorovych Kyryliuk, eds. 1945. *Narys istoriï ukraïns'koï literatury.* N.p.: Akademiia Nauk URSR.

Mel'nyk, Petro. 1930a. "Funktsional'nyi virsh." *Nova generatsiia* 8–9: 36–49.

———. 1930b. "Try roky." *Nova generatsiia* 11–12: 17–25.

———. 1931. "Shche pro 'Novu generatsiiu.'" *Literaturna hazeta* 12 (April 20): 3.

Mel'nyk, Volodymyr Kononovych. 1987. "U vidblyskakh revoliutsiinoï zahravy." *Vitchyzna. Literaturno-khudozhnii zhurnal Spilky radians'kykh pys'mennykiv Ukraïny* (Kyiv) 1: 154–57.

"Meta 'Pluzhanyna.'" 1925. *Pluzhanyn* 1: 1.

Meter, Es. 1929. "Roman, shcho ioho nazvano romanom." *Nova generatsiia* 3: 16–38.

Mezhenko, Iurii. 1919a. "Mozhlyvosti i obov'iazky ukraïns'koï poeziï." *Shliakh* 1: 62.

———[Ivaniv-Mezhenko, Iurii]. 1919b. "Tvorchist' indyviduuma i kolektyv." *Muzahet* (January, February, March): 65–78.

———. 1923a. "Na shliakhakh do novoï teoriï." *Chervonyi shliakh* 2: 199–210.

———. 1923b. "Literaturnyi Kyïv 1923 r." *Chervonyi shliakh* 2: 263–65.

Motherwell, Robert, ed. 1981. *The Dada Painters and Poets: An Anthology*. Boston. [=The Documents of Twentieth Century Art.]

Mudrak, Myroslava M. 1986. *The New Generation and Artistic Modernism in the Ukraine*. Ann Arbor, Michigan.

Musiienko, Oleksa, ed. 1991. "Dmytro Buz'ko. Pys'mennyky Ukraïny—zhertvy stalins'kykh represii." *Literaturna Ukraïna* 23 (6 June): 8.

———. 1992. "Oleksa Slisarenko. Pys'mennyky Ukraïny—zhertvy stalins'kykh represii." *Literaturna Ukraïna* 2 (16 January): 8.

Muzychenko, Iu. 1930a. "Zapysky z 'prolitfrontu.'" *Nova generatsiia* 10: 36–44.

———. 1930b. "Pidruchnyk peresmykuvannia (polemichnyi reportazh)." *Nova generatsiia* 11–12: 36–46.

Mykhailychenko, Hnat. 1919. "Proletars'ke mystetsvo." *Mystetstvo* 1: 27–29.

———. 1929. *Tvory*, I. Odesa: DVU.

Mykytenko Ivan Kindratovych. 1929. "Proletars'ka literatura v dobu rekonstruktsiï (shliakhy ta perspektyvy VUSPP)." *Krytyka* 6: 24–33.

———. 1930a."Za hehemoniiu proletars'koï literatury." *Hart* 5: 206–209. [Reprinted in Mykytenko 1962, 84–122.]

———. 1930b. "'Live' shakhraistvo." *Komunist. Orhan Tsentral'noho komitetu i Kharkivs'koho Mis'kkomu Komunistychnoï partiï (bil'shovykiv) Ukraïny* (Kharkiv) 172 (26 June): 4. [Reprinted in *Hart* 6 (1930).]

———. 1962. *Na fronti literatury 1927–1937. Statti, dopovidi, promovy*. Eds. Iurii Svyrydovych Kobylets'kyi et al. Kyiv.

Myrhorods'kyi, Pavlo and Ivan Malovichko. 1929. "Dva shchodennyky." *Nova generatsiia* 2: 29–40.

N.B. [Nik Bazhan]. 1923. Review of "Oleksa Slisarenko. Poemy. Kyiv: Panfuturysty, 1923." *Barykady teatru* 1 (20 November): 12. [Originally printed in *Bil'shovyk* 170 (31 July 1923): 4.]

"Nam pishut o 'Novom lefe' i 'Novoi generatsii.'" 1928. *Novyi lef* 9: 47.

"Nash dysput pro teatr. Protokol zasidannia Doslidcho-ideolohichnoho biura ARKK vid 5-ho chervnia." 1929. *Nova generatsiia* 6: 59–64.

"Nasha anketa pro 'Novu generatsiiu.'" 1928. *Literaturna hazeta* 25 March (6): 2.

"Nashi ustanovki." 1924. *Honh komunkul'ta* no. 1 (May), pp. 1–3.

Navrots'kyi, B. 1925. *Mova ta poeziia*. Kyiv: Knyhospilka.

Nedolia, Leonid [Luk'ian Honcharenko]. 1924a. "Iugolef na literaturnykh pozitsiiakh." *Iugo-lef* 2 (September): 12.

———. 1924b. "Bude!" *Iugo-lef* 3 (October): 5.

———. 1924c. "Zapozdalym Pilipen'kalam." *Iugo-lef* 3 (October): 9–11.

———. 1930. "Khoroba [*sic*]. (Pobutova khronika 1929 r.)." *Nova generatsiia* 6–7: 11–45.

———. 1931. "Konsolidatsiia ukraïns'koï proletars'koï literatury. Skorochenyi stenohrafichnyi zvit zahal'nykh zboriv Kharkivs'koï orhanizatsiï VUSPP, 24–II–1931. Promova t. Nedoli." *Literaturna hazeta* 10 (30 March): 2.

Nevira, Kharyton. 1925. "Po storinkakh hazet ta zhurnaliv." *Pluzhanyn* 5: 24–27.

Nevrli, Mykola [Kol'a Nevrlý]. 1966. "Mykhail' Semenko, ukraïns'kyi futuryzm i slovats'ki davisty." *Duklia* 3: 23–28.

Neznamov, P. [Pavel Lezhakin.] 1928. "Na fronti faktu." *Nova generatsiia* 10: 254–57.

Nikovs'kyi, Andrii. 1919. *Vita Nova. Krytychni narysy: P. Tychyna, M. Semenko, Ia. Savchenko, M. Ryl's'kyi.* Kyiv: Drukar.

"'Nova generatsiia' na novomu etapi–OPPU." 1930. *Nova generatsiia* 6–7: 85–86. [Originally in *Visti VUTsVK* 22 June.]

Novyts'kyi, Mykola. 1930. *Na iarmarku*. Kharkiv: Hart.

O.B. 1923. "Mykhail' Semenko—panfuturyst." *Barykady teatru* 1 (20 November): 5.

Ocherk ukrainskoi sovetskoi literatury. 1954. Ed. Aleksandr Ivanovich Beletskii, et al. Moscow.

"Odvertyi lyst do redaktsiï 'Literaturnoho iarmarku' (M. Kulish, Iu. Ianovs'kyi, V. Vrazhlyvyi, M. Ialovyi, M. Khvyl'ovyi, Ark. Liubchenko, Ol. Dosvitnyi, Hr. Epik)." 1929. *Literaturnyi iarmarok* 10: 303–304.

Obiurten, Viktor. 1918. *Mystetstvo vmyraie.* Trans. Les' Kurbas. Kyiv: Grunt. [=Mystetst'ka biblioteka, pt. 1.]

Osadchyi, Mykhailo Hryhoryvych. 1987. "Ostap Vyshnia—svidok naikrashchoho tvoru Mykoly Khvyl'ovoho." *Ukrains'kyi visnyk* (Kyiv-Lviv) 7 (August): 33–34. (New York: Suchasnist', 1988.)

"Oseredok komunkul'tovtsiv na Kubanshchyni." 1924. *Bil'shovyk* 149 (July 4): 6.

Ostashko, T. S. 1987. "Pochatok formuvannia radians'koï systemy kerivnytstva khudozhnim zhyttiam u respublitsi (1919 r.)." *Ukraïns'kyi istorychnyi zhurnal* 5: 56–66.

Ovcharov, Hryhorii. 1930a. "Pro zhurnal'nu krytyku 1929 roku." *Krytyka* 3: 106–118.

———. 1930b. "Ohliad zhurnal'noï krytyky." *Krytyka* 9: 77–106.

———. 1932a. "Proty mishchans'kykh vykhvatok u literaturi (z pryvodu 'Avangardu')." In Ovcharov 1932b, 136–53. [Originally published in *Krytyka* 1: 9–29.]

———. 1932b. *Narysy suchasnoï ukraïns'koï literatury*. Vypusk pershyi. 2nd ed. Kharkiv: LiM.

Ozerians'kyi, V. 1923. "Produktsiia ukraïns'koï knyzhky v Kyivi." *Chervonyi shliakh* 3: 273.

Ozerov, Oleksii. 1928. Review of "L. Skrypnyk. Narysy z teoriï mystetstva kino. Kharkiv: DVU, 1929." *Krytyka* 3: 145–46.

P.B. 1927. Review of "*Bumeranh* no. 1." *Pluzhanyn* 8: 29.

Panfuturyst-ekstruktor [Mykola Bazhan]. 1923. "Les' Kurbas i Vsevolod Meiierkhol'd." *Bil'shovyk* 138 (June 23): 2.

"Panfuturysty pratsiuiut'." 1922. *Bil'shovyk* 56 (December 7): 3.

Pavliuk, Antin. 1922. "Nova ukraïns'ka poeziia." *Sterni. Misiachnyk literatury, mystetstva, nauky ta students'koho zhyttia* (Prague) 1 (July): 113–14.

Perehuda, O. 1927. "Okhmadyte, ty spysh!" *Bumeranh. Neperiodychnyi zhurnal pamfletiv* no. 1.

———. 1970. "Kinematohraf i Les' Kurbas." In Hoholiev (ed.) 1970, 39–51.

Petrov, Viktor. 1930a. *Romany Kulisha*. Kyiv: Rukh.

———. 1930b. "Movchushche bozhestvo." *Avanhard-Al'manakh* no. a (January), pp. 25–36.

———. 1947. [Viktor Domontovych.] *Doktor Serafikus*. Munich.

———. 1988. [Viktor Domontovych.] *Proza. Try tomy*. Ed. Iurii Shevelov. Munich.

Petryts'kyi, Anatol'. 1929. "Chy potribna komu opera?" *Nova generatsiia* 10: 34–39.

Pidhainyi, L. 1930. Review of "Geo Shkurupii, Zhanna batal'ionerka." *Krytyka* 6: 148–52.

Pipes, Richard. 1954. *The Formation of the Soviet Union: Communism and Nationalism, 1917–1923*. Cambridge, Massachusetts.

Pivtoradni, Vasyl' Ivanovych. 1968. *Ukraïns'ka literatura pershykh rokiv revoliutsiï 1917–1923*. Kyiv.

"Platforma i otochennia livykh." 1927. *Nova generatsiia* 1: 39–43.

Plevako, Mykola. 1923–1926. *Khrestomatiia novoï ukraïns'koï literatury*. 4 vols. Kyiv: Rukh.

Poeziia russkogo i ukrainskogo avangarda: istoriia, ètika, traditsii (1910–1990 gg.). 1990. *Tezisy Vsesoiuznoi nauchnoi konferentsii*. Kherson.

Poggioli, Renato. 1968. *The Theory of the Avant-Garde*. Cambridge, Massachusetts.

Polishchuk, Klym. 1923. *Z vyru revoliutii*. Kyiv-Lviv: Mamai.

Polishchuk, Valeriian [Mykyta Volok]. 1920. Review of "O. Slisarenko, M. Liubchenko, M. Semenko, Al'manakh tr'okh. Kyiv: Vyd. T—va Ukr. Pys'mennykiv, 1920." *Grono*, pp. 91–93.

——— [Valer'ian]. 1921. "Credo." *Grono*, p. 4.

———. 1922. "Shliakhy ta perspektyvy v suchasnii ukraïns'kii literaturi." *Shliakhy mystetstva* 2(4): 35–36.

——— [Vasyl' Sontsvit]. 1922b. "Halyts'ke molode mishchants-tvo." *Shliakhy mystetstvo* 2 (4): 56–57.

"Polishchukiiada." 1929. *Hart* 12: 174–77.

"Polityka partiï v spravi ukraïns'koï khudozhnoï literatury." 1959. In Ievsieiev 1959, pp. 351–56.

Poltorats'kyi, Oleksii Ivanovych. 1928a. "Praktyka livoho opovidannia." *Nova generatsiia* 1: 50–60.

———. 1928b. "Iak vyrobliaty roman." *Nova generatsiia* 5: 364–69.

———. 1928c. "Na zakhyst marksysts'koï teoriï mystetstva." *Nova generatsiia* 6: 429–38.

———. 1928d. "S. Shchupak khoche buty marksystom, abo problema ukraïns'koho Polons'koho... ." *Nova generatsiia* 10: 249–53.

———. 1928e. "Dyvna knyzhka Koriaka." *Nova generatsiia* 11: 322–26.

———. 1929a. "Panfuturyzm." *Nova generatsiia* 1:40–50; 2: 42–50; 4: 50–55.

———. 1929b. "Cherez holovy krytykiv." *Nova generatsiia* 2: 9–21.

———. 1929c. "Protokol pershoho zasidannia Vyrobnychoho biura ARKK, 21-ho bereznia 1929, r.; Dopovid' O. Poltorats'koho: 'Ustanovka prohramy literaturnoï roboty ARKK.'" *Nova generatsiia* 5: 76–80.

———. 1929d. "Heo Shkurupii." In Shkurupii 1929h, p. 3–6.

———. 1929e. "Praktychna i poetychna mova." In Poltorats'kyi 1929f, pp. 27–43.

———. 1929f. *Literaturni zasoby. Sproba sotsiolohichnoï analizy*. Kharkiv: DVU.

———. 1929g. "Tovarys'ki porady z komentariiamy nashomu krytykovi R. K—mu." *Nova generatsiia* 6: 42–47.

. 1930a. "Shcho take Ostap Vyshnia?" *Nova generatsiia* 2: 28–31; 3: 15–25; 4: 21–28.

———. 1930b. "Proty nedobytkiv formalizmu." *Nova generatsiia* 5: 49–52.

———. 1930c. "Arkadii Zlatovust." *Nova generatsiia* 5: 40–44; 6–7: 59; 8–9: 19–28.

———. 1930d. "Pro faktychnu literaturu." *Nova generatsiia* 8–9: 32–36.

———. 1931a. "Pro teoretychni khyby 'Novoï generatsiï.'" *Literaturna hazeta* 5 (30 January): 3.

———. 1931b. "Lyst do redaktsiï." *Literaturna hazeta* 11 (10 April): 4.

———. 1966. "Mykhail' Semenko ta 'Nova generatsiia.'" *Vitchyzna. Literaturno-khudozhnii zhurnal Spilky radians'kykh pys'mennykiv Ukraïny* (Kyiv) 11: 193–200.

———. 1968. "Znaiomtesia zanovo...Stattia—tsytata. [A. Chuzhyi]." *Vitchyzna. Literaturno-khudozhnii zhurnal Spilky radians'kykh pys'mennykiv Ukraïny* (Kyiv) 12: 172–81.

——— and D. Sotnyk. 1929. "Donbas na pivdorozi." *Nova generatsiia* 6: 7–21.

Pomorska, Krystyna. 1968. *Russian Formalist Theory and its Poetic Ambiance.* The Hague-Paris.

"Postanova nadzvychainykh zboriv aktyvu odes'koï kraievoï orhanizatsiï AsKK (Komunkul't) vid 17 kvitnia 1925 r." In Kachaniuk 1930, vol. 2, p. 191.

"Postanova plenumu rady VUSPP u spravi 'Novoï generatsiï.'" 1930. *Hart* 5: 192–93.

"Postanova pro rozpusk Ob'iednannia proletars'kykh pys'mennykiv Ukraïny-OPPU (Nova generatsiia)." 1931. *Literaturna hazeta* 4 (20 January): 2. [Also reprinted in *Chervonyi shliakh* 1–2 (1931): 157–58.]

Prampolini, Enrico. 1928. Letter to *Nova generatsiia* 2: 158.

"Pro proletkul'ty. Lyst TsK RKP. 1 hrudnia 1920 r." 1959. In Ievsieiev et al. 1959, pp. 78–80.

"Pro teatr. Protokol zasidannia... rady pry N.K.O. Promovy t.t. Shramenka, Semenka, Sotnyka, Savchenka, Kulyka, Poltorats'koho." 1929. *Nova generatsiia* 10: 74–80.

"Protokol zasidannia Kharkivs'koï hrupy spivrobitnykiv zhurnalu 'Nova generatsiia.'" 1929. *Nova generatsiia* 4.

"Protokol zasidannia VUSKK (Novoï generatsiï) v spravi kino 10.XII.1929." 1930. *Nova generatsiia* 1: 57–64.

"Protokol zboriv initsiatyvnoï hrupy v spravi orhanizatsiï kyivs'koï filiï Komunkul'tu, shcho vidbulysia 19-ho bereznia 1929 r." 1929. *Nova generatsiia* 4: 77–78.

Pryhodii, Mykhailo. 1972. *Vsesoiuzna konsolidatsiia literatur.* Kyiv.

Pylypenko, Serhii. 1923. Review of "Iul'ian [*sic*] Shpol *Vèrkhy.* Vydavnytstvo Hol'fshtrem [*sic*]. Kyïv-Moskva-Berlin. 1923. st. 48." *Chervonyi shliakh* 4–5: 280–82.

———. 1924. "Tykho plavaiut' v tumani." *Literatura, Nauka, Mystetstvo* 7 (17 February): 2–3.

———. 1925. "Prohrama kompartiï pro mystetstvo i 'likvidatory.'" *Pluzhanyn* 1: 7.

———. 1927. "Semaformaibutnyky bumeranhuiut'." *Pluzhanyn* 6: 24–25.

Radziejowski, Janusz. 1983. *The Communist Party of Western Ukraine, 1919–1929.* Edmonton, Alberta.

Radzykevych, Volodymyr. 1952. *Ukraïns'ka literatura XX stolittia.* Philadelphia.

———. 1955–1956. *Istoriia ukraïns'koï literatury.* 3 vols. Detroit.

Reding, Oskar [Volodymyr Hadzins'kyi]. 1929. "Lyst do chytachiv L. Skrypnykovoho 'Inteligenta.'" *Nova generatsiia* 10: 48–53.

"Rezoliutsiia zahal'nykh zboriv 'Prolitfrontu' v spravi konsolidatsiï syl proletars'koï literatury vid 19-I-1931 r." 1931. *Chervonyi shliakh* 1–2: 155.

Richard, Lionel. 1978. *Phaidon Encyclopedia of Expressionism.* New York.

Richter, Hans. 1978. *Dada, Art and Anti-Art.* New York-Toronto.

Rod'ko, Mykola D. 1970. "Vid futuryz pro tr'okh P'iero do temy revoliutsiï." *Ukraïns'ke literaturoznavstvo* 8: 111–18.

———. 1971. *Ukraïns'ka poeziia pershykh pozhovtnevykh rokiv.* Kyiv.

Rolenko, Vasyl' [Ivan Kulyk]. 1922. "Iolopy (pro knyhu Psykhetozy H. Shkurupiia)." *Shliakhy mystetstva* 2: 62.

Rubchak, Bohdan. 1968. "Probnyi let. Tlo dlia knyhy." In *Ostap Luts'kyi—molodomuzets'.* Ed. Iurii Luts'kyi, pp. 9–43. New York.

Ruderman, M. 1928. "Pro 'Novu heneratsiiu.'" *Molodniak* 3: 104–112.

Ryl's'kyi, Maksym Tadeiovych. 1918. *Pid osinnimy zoriamy (liryka, knyzhka 2. 1910–1918).* Kyiv: Grunt.

———. 1956. "Iasna zbroia (Iz dumok pro ukraïns'ku movu)." In his *Tvory v tr'okh tomakh* 3: 63–80. Kyiv.

———. 1966. "Mykola Zerov—poet i perekladach." In *Mykola Zerov. Vybrane.* Ed. Maksym Ryl's'kyi. Kyiv. [Originally published in *Zhovten'* 1 (1965): 78–86.]

——— and Mykola L'vovych Nahnybida, eds. 1958. *Antolohiia ukraïns'koï poeziï v 4-kh tomakh.* 2nd ed. 4 vols. Kyiv.

S. 1930. "Buz'ka 'Holiandiia.' Zauvazhennia redaktsii. . . ." *Chytach-retsenzent. Shchomisiachnyi dodatok do "Kul'trobitnyka"* 5: 13.

"Samolikvidatsiia 'Novoï generatsiï' ta 'Prolitfrontu.'" 1931. *Pluh* 3: 130.

Sarab'ianov, A. D. 1992. *Neizvestnyi russkii avangard v muzieiakh i chastnykh sobraniiakh.* Moscow.

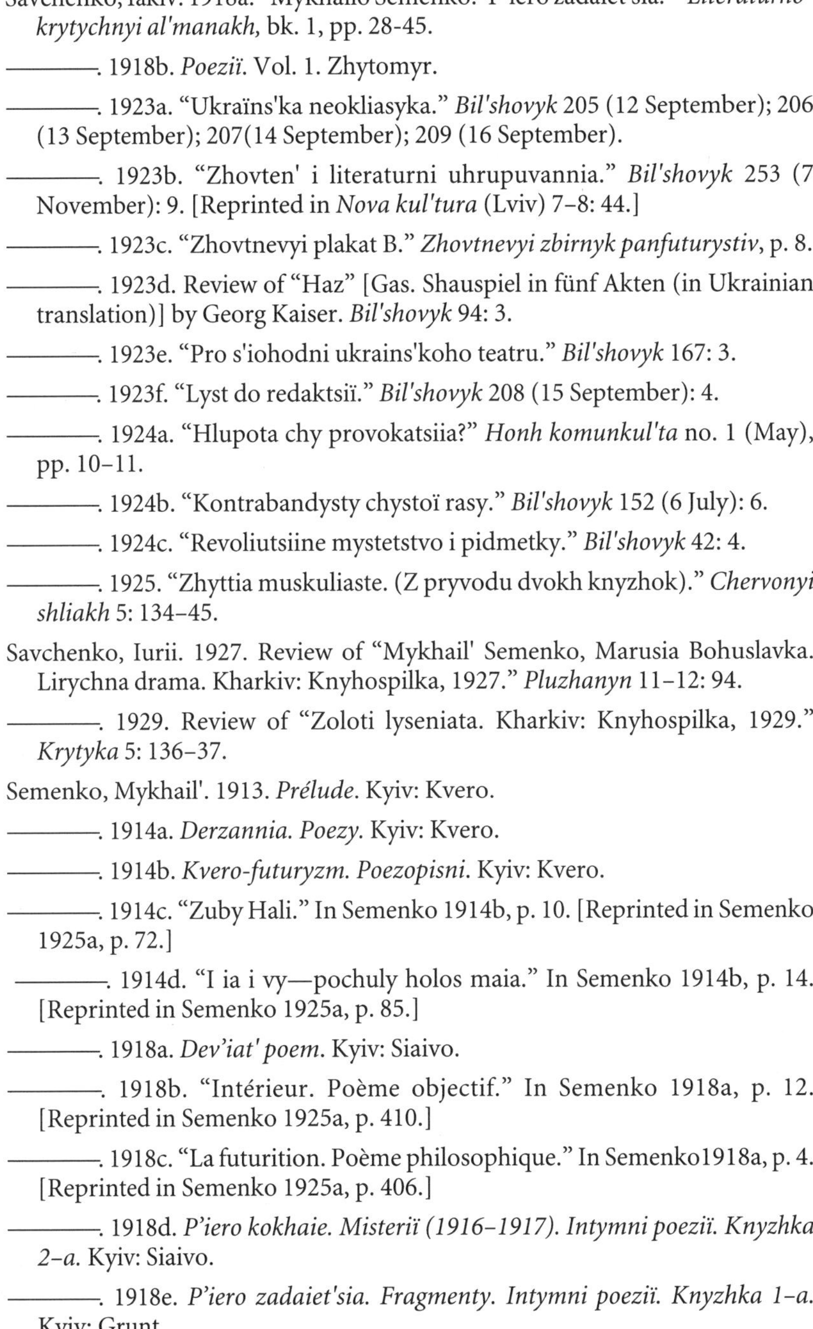

Savchenko, Iakiv. 1918a. "Mykhailo Semenko. 'P'iero zadaiet'sia.'" *Literaturno-krytychnyi al'manakh,* bk. 1, pp. 28-45.

———. 1918b. *Poezii.* Vol. 1. Zhytomyr.

———. 1923a. "Ukraïns'ka neokliasyka." *Bil'shovyk* 205 (12 September); 206 (13 September); 207(14 September); 209 (16 September).

———. 1923b. "Zhovten' i literaturni uhrupuvannia." *Bil'shovyk* 253 (7 November): 9. [Reprinted in *Nova kul'tura* (Lviv) 7–8: 44.]

———. 1923c. "Zhovtnevyi plakat B." *Zhovtnevyi zbirnyk panfuturystiv,* p. 8.

———. 1923d. Review of "Haz" [Gas. Shauspiel in fünf Akten (in Ukrainian translation)] by Georg Kaiser. *Bil'shovyk* 94: 3.

———. 1923e. "Pro s'iohodni ukrains'koho teatru." *Bil'shovyk* 167: 3.

———. 1923f. "Lyst do redaktsii." *Bil'shovyk* 208 (15 September): 4.

———. 1924a. "Hlupota chy provokatsiia?" *Honh komunkul'ta* no. 1 (May), pp. 10–11.

———. 1924b. "Kontrabandysty chystoï rasy." *Bil'shovyk* 152 (6 July): 6.

———. 1924c. "Revoliutsiine mystetstvo i pidmetky." *Bil'shovyk* 42: 4.

———. 1925. "Zhyttia muskuliaste. (Z pryvodu dvokh knyzhok)." *Chervonyi shliakh* 5: 134–45.

Savchenko, Iurii. 1927. Review of "Mykhail' Semenko, Marusia Bohuslavka. Lirychna drama. Kharkiv: Knyhospilka, 1927." *Pluzhanyn* 11–12: 94.

———. 1929. Review of "Zoloti lyseniata. Kharkiv: Knyhospilka, 1929." *Krytyka* 5: 136–37.

Semenko, Mykhail'. 1913. *Prélude.* Kyiv: Kvero.

———. 1914a. *Derzannia. Poezy.* Kyiv: Kvero.

———. 1914b. *Kvero-futuryzm. Poezopisni.* Kyiv: Kvero.

———. 1914c. "Zuby Hali." In Semenko 1914b, p. 10. [Reprinted in Semenko 1925a, p. 72.]

———. 1914d. "I ia i vy—pochuly holos maia." In Semenko 1914b, p. 14. [Reprinted in Semenko 1925a, p. 85.]

———. 1918a. *Dev'iat' poem.* Kyiv: Siaivo.

———. 1918b. "Intérieur. Poème objectif." In Semenko 1918a, p. 12. [Reprinted in Semenko 1925a, p. 410.]

———. 1918c. "La futurition. Poème philosophique." In Semenko1918a, p. 4. [Reprinted in Semenko 1925a, p. 406.]

———. 1918d. *P'iero kokhaie. Misterii (1916–1917). Intymni poezii. Knyzhka 2-a.* Kyiv: Siaivo.

———. 1918e. *P'iero zadaiet'sia. Fragmenty. Intymni poezii. Knyzhka 1-a.* Kyiv: Grunt.

———. 1918f. "Vinok tremtiachyi." *Literaturno-krytychnyi al'manakh*, bk. 1, pp. 17–19. [Reprinted in Semenko 1925a, pp. 403–405.]

———. 1919a. *Bloc-Notes. Poeziï 1919 roku. Knyzhka 4–a.* Kyiv: Flamingo.

———. 1919b. *Dvi poezofil'my.* Kyiv: Vseukrlitkom.

———. 1919c. *Lilit. Scènes pathétiques.* Kyiv: Siaivo. [Reprinted in Semenko 1925a, pp. 429–52.]

———. 1919d. "Misto." In Semenko 1919e, p. 38.

———. 1919e. *P'iero mertvopetliuie. Futuryzy. 1914-1918. Poeziï. Knyzhka 3-a.* Kyiv: Flamingo.

———. 1919f. "P'iero mozhe. Poeza bezzrazkovosty." In Semenko 1919e, p. 9.

———. 1919g. "Poeza moieï dushi." In Semenko 1919e, p. 14.

———. 1919h. "Spohad." In Semenko 1919e, p. 40.

———. 1919i. "Sv. Sil'vestru." In Semenko 1919a, p. 25. [Reprinted in Semenko 1925a, p. 365.]

———. 1919j. *Tov. Sontse. Revfutpoema.* Kyiv: Vseukrlitkom.

———. 1919k. *V sadakh bezroznykh. Saturnaliï. Poeziï. Knyzhka 5–a.* Kyiv: Flamingo. [Reprinted in Semenko 1925a, pp. 310–24.]

———. 1919l. "Vona." In Semenko 1919a, p. 55. [Reprinted in Semenko 1925a, p. 382.]

———. 1919m. "Zhertva. Ego-Ego futuryza." In Semenko 1919e, p. 12.

——— [M. Tryroh]. 1919n. "Prozopisni. (Spirali)." *Mystetstvo* 4: 15–19.

———. 1919–20a. "Tov. Sontse. (revfutpoema)." *Mystetstvo* 1: 6–11.

———. 1919–20b. "Vesna." *Mystetstvo* 2: 6–13. [Reprinted in Semenko 1925a, pp. 469–82.]

———. 1919/20c. "Step." *Mystetstvo* 3: 7–12. [Reprinted in Semenko 1925a, p. 000.]

———. 1920. "Himny sv. Terezi." *Al'manakh tr'okh*, pp. 37–62. [Reprinted in Semenko 1925a, pp. 287–97.]

———. 1921a. "Kablepoema za okean." *Shliakhy mystetstva* 2: 11–14.

———. 1921b. *Prominnia pohroz. 8–ma kn. poezii. 1919–1920.* Kharkiv: Vseukraïns'ke derzhavne vydavnytstvo.

———. 1921c. "Snizhynky." In Semenko 1921b, p. 12. [Reprinted in Semenko 1925a, pp. 511–12.]

———. 1921d. "Zhertva vechirnia." In Semenko 1921b, p. 14. [Reprinted in Semenko 1985, p. 247.]

———. 1922a. "Kablepoema za okean." *Semafor u Maibutnie. Aparat Panfuturystiv* no. 1 (May).

———. 1922b. "Lantukh i estrada." *Semafor u Maibutnie. Aparat Panfuturystiv* vol. 1(May), p. 46.

———[Myqail' {*sic*}]. 1922c. "Poezomaliarstvo." *Semafor u Maibutnie. Aparat Panfuturystiv* no. 1 (May), pp. 32–36. [Reprinted in Semenko 1979–1982, vol. 2, pp. 161–65.]

———. 1922d. "Tekst iz Kablepoemy za okean (1920). Perevod z ukrainskogo Iu. Nikitina." *Katafalk iskusstva* no. 1 (13 December), p. 3.

———. 1922e. "Telegramma Lit. A. Moskva, Vladimiru Maiakovskomu, futuristu." *Semafor u Maibutnie. Aparat Panfuturystiv* no. 1 (May), p. 18. [Reprinted in Semenko 1979–1982, vol. 2, p. 176.]

———. 1922f. "Postanovka pytannia v teoriï mystetstva perekhodovoï doby." *Semafor u Maibutnie. Aparat Panfuturystiv* no. 1 (May), pp. 3–7. [Reprinted; see Semenko 1930o.]

———[Miqail' {*sic*} Semenko]. 1922g. "Deiaki naslidky destruktsiï." *Semafor u Maibutnie. Aparat Panfuturystiv* no. 1 (May), pp. 15–17.

———[M. Trirog]. 1922h. "Chto takoie destruktsiia." *Katafalk iskusstva* no. 1 (13 December), p. 2.

——— [M. Tryroh]. 1922i. "Orhanizatsiinyi pryntsyp i mystetstvo slova." *Semafor u Maibutnie. Aparat Panfuturystiv* no. 1 (May), p. 13. [Reprinted in Semenko 1979–1982, vol. 2, pp. 138–45.]

———[M. Tryroh]. 1922j. Review of "Deklamator slovo. Kyiv: Slovo, 1923." *Bil'shovyk* 65 (28 December): 3.

———[Anatol' Tsebro]. 1922k. "Futuryzm v ukraïns'kii poeziï (1914–1922)." *Semafor u Maibutnie. Aparat Panfuturystiv* no. 1 (May), pp. 40–43. [Reprinted in Semenko 1979–1982, vol. 2, pp. 166–75.]

———. 1923a. "Do spravy pro radians'ke kino (v poriadku obhovorennia)." *Bil'shovyk* 294 (28 December): 4.

———. 1923b. "Suchasnyi stan svitovoho mystetstva." *Nova kul'tura* (Lviv) 7–8: 50–53. [Originally printed in *Bil'shovyk* 205 (12 September): 6.]

———. 1923c. "Umovy stvorennia, zavdannia i naslidky zhovtnevoho bloku (propozytsiia predstavnyka Aspanfutiv)." *Literatura, Nauka, Mystetstvo* 11 (16 December).

———. 1923d. "Do dyskusiï pro Zhovtnevyi blok." *Literatura, Nauka, Mystetstvo* 12 (23 December).

———. 1923e. "Mirza Abbas-Khan (Opovidannia)." *Hlobus* (Kyiv) 1 (1 November): 1–8.

———. 1924a. "Bez kerma i bez vitryl." *Literatura, Nauka, Mystetstvo* 7 (17 February).

———. 1924b. "Do postanovky pytannia pro zastosuvannia leninizmu na 3-mu fronti." *Chervonyi shliakh* 11–12: 169–201.

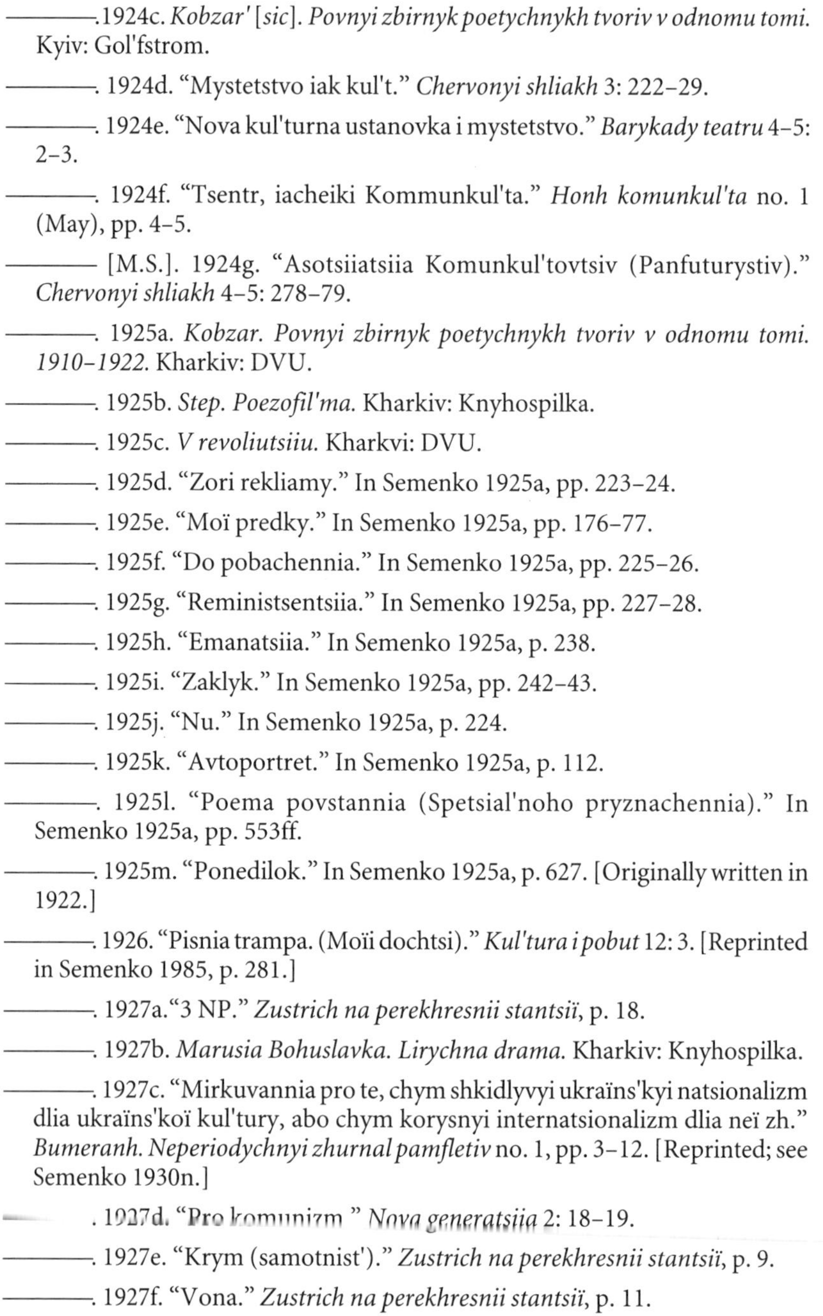

———. 1924c. *Kobzar'* [*sic*]. *Povnyi zbirnyk poetychnykh tvoriv v odnomu tomi.* Kyiv: Gol'fstrom.

———. 1924d. "Mystetstvo iak kul't." *Chervonyi shliakh* 3: 222–29.

———. 1924e. "Nova kul'turna ustanovka i mystetstvo." *Barykady teatru* 4–5: 2–3.

———. 1924f. "Tsentr, iacheiki Kommunkul'ta." *Honh komunkul'ta* no. 1 (May), pp. 4–5.

——— [M.S.]. 1924g. "Asotsiiatsiia Komunkul'tovtsiv (Panfuturystiv)." *Chervonyi shliakh* 4–5: 278–79.

———. 1925a. *Kobzar. Povnyi zbirnyk poetychnykh tvoriv v odnomu tomi. 1910–1922.* Kharkiv: DVU.

———. 1925b. *Step. Poezofil'ma.* Kharkiv: Knyhospilka.

———. 1925c. *V revoliutsiiu.* Kharkvi: DVU.

———. 1925d. "Zori rekliamy." In Semenko 1925a, pp. 223–24.

———. 1925e. "Moï predky." In Semenko 1925a, pp. 176–77.

———. 1925f. "Do pobachennia." In Semenko 1925a, pp. 225–26.

———. 1925g. "Reministsentsiia." In Semenko 1925a, pp. 227–28.

———. 1925h. "Emanatsiia." In Semenko 1925a, p. 238.

———. 1925i. "Zaklyk." In Semenko 1925a, pp. 242–43.

———. 1925j. "Nu." In Semenko 1925a, p. 224.

———. 1925k. "Avtoportret." In Semenko 1925a, p. 112.

———. 1925l. "Poema povstannia (Spetsial'noho pryznachennia)." In Semenko 1925a, pp. 553ff.

———. 1925m. "Ponedilok." In Semenko 1925a, p. 627. [Originally written in 1922.]

———. 1926. "Pisnia trampa. (Moïi dochtsi)." *Kul'tura i pobut* 12: 3. [Reprinted in Semenko 1985, p. 281.]

———. 1927a. "3 NP." *Zustrich na perekhresnii stantsiï*, p. 18.

———. 1927b. *Marusia Bohuslavka. Lirychna drama.* Kharkiv: Knyhospilka.

———. 1927c. "Mirkuvannia pro te, chym shkidlyvyi ukraïns'kyi natsionalizm dlia ukraïns'koï kul'tury, abo chym korysnyi internatsionalizm dlia neï zh." *Bumeranh. Neperiodychnyi zhurnal pamfletiv* no. 1, pp. 3–12. [Reprinted; see Semenko 1930n.]

———. 1927d. "Pro komunizm." *Nova generatsiia* 2: 18–19.

———. 1927e. "Krym (samotnist')." *Zustrich na perekhresnii stantsiï*, p. 9.

———. 1927f. "Vona." *Zustrich na perekhresnii stantsiï*, p. 11.

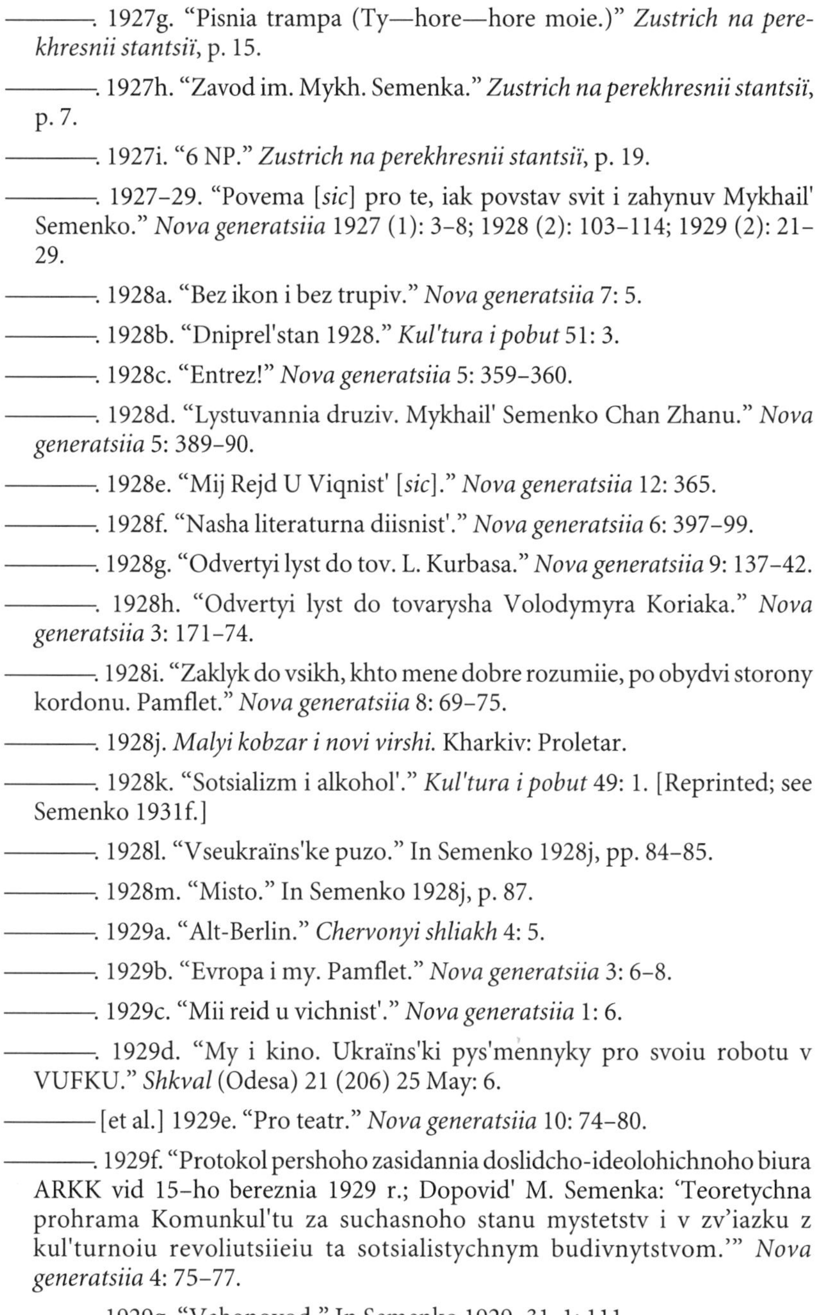

———. 1927g. "Pisnia trampa (Ty—hore—hore moie.)" *Zustrich na perekhresnii stantsiï*, p. 15.

———. 1927h. "Zavod im. Mykh. Semenka." *Zustrich na perekhresnii stantsiï*, p. 7.

———. 1927i. "6 NP." *Zustrich na perekhresnii stantsiï*, p. 19.

———. 1927–29. "Povema [*sic*] pro te, iak povstav svit i zahynuv Mykhail' Semenko." *Nova generatsiia* 1927 (1): 3–8; 1928 (2): 103–114; 1929 (2): 21–29.

———. 1928a. "Bez ikon i bez trupiv." *Nova generatsiia* 7: 5.

———. 1928b. "Dniprel'stan 1928." *Kul'tura i pobut* 51: 3.

———. 1928c. "Entrez!" *Nova generatsiia* 5: 359–360.

———. 1928d. "Lystuvannia druziv. Mykhail' Semenko Chan Zhanu." *Nova generatsiia* 5: 389–90.

———. 1928e. "Mij Rejd U Viqnist' [*sic*]." *Nova generatsiia* 12: 365.

———. 1928f. "Nasha literaturna diisnist'." *Nova generatsiia* 6: 397–99.

———. 1928g. "Odvertyi lyst do tov. L. Kurbasa." *Nova generatsiia* 9: 137–42.

———. 1928h. "Odvertyi lyst do tovarysha Volodymyra Koriaka." *Nova generatsiia* 3: 171–74.

———. 1928i. "Zaklyk do vsikh, khto mene dobre rozumiie, po obydvi storony kordonu. Pamflet." *Nova generatsiia* 8: 69–75.

———. 1928j. *Malyi kobzar i novi virshi*. Kharkiv: Proletar.

———. 1928k. "Sotsializm i alkohol'." *Kul'tura i pobut* 49: 1. [Reprinted; see Semenko 1931f.]

———. 1928l. "Vseukraïns'ke puzo." In Semenko 1928j, pp. 84–85.

———. 1928m. "Misto." In Semenko 1928j, p. 87.

———. 1929a. "Alt-Berlin." *Chervonyi shliakh* 4: 5.

———. 1929b. "Evropa i my. Pamflet." *Nova generatsiia* 3: 6–8.

———. 1929c. "Mii reid u vichnist'." *Nova generatsiia* 1: 6.

———. 1929d. "My i kino. Ukraïns'ki pys'mennyky pro svoiu robotu v VUFKU." *Shkval* (Odesa) 21 (206) 25 May: 6.

——— [et al.] 1929e. "Pro teatr." *Nova generatsiia* 10: 74–80.

———. 1929f. "Protokol pershoho zasidannia doslidcho-ideolohichnoho biura ARKK vid 15-ho bereznia 1929 r.; Dopovid' M. Semenka: 'Teoretychna prohrama Komunkul'tu za suchasnoho stanu mystetstv i v zv'iazku z kul'turnoiu revoliutsiieiu ta sotsialistychnym budivnytstvom.'" *Nova generatsiia* 4: 75–77.

———. 1929g. "Vahonovod." In Semenko 1929–31, 1: 111.

———. 1929–31. *Povna zbirka tvoriv*, Vol. 1. Kharkiv: DVU, 1929; Vol 2. Kharkiv: LiM, 1930; Vol 3. Kharkiv: LiM, 1931.

———. 1930a. "Do Vseukraïns'koï spilky proletars'kykh pys'mennykiv." *Nova generatsiia* 3: 59–60.

———. 1930b. "Konsolidatsiia proletars'kykh literaturnykh syl. Zaiavy do Vseukraïns'koï spilky proletars'kykh pys'mennykiv." *Literaturna hazeta* 5 (March 20): 2.

———. 1930c. "Krychushcha nikchemnist' (z pryvodu odniieï nebezpeky)." *Nova generatsiia* 1: 57.

———. 1930d. "Nu i repliky." *Nova generatsiia* 10: 30–35.

———. 1930e. "Pidzemka." In Semenko 1930l, p. 18.

———. 1930f. "Potribna rekonstruktsiia proletars'koho frontu literatury." *Nova generatsiia* 1: 32

———. 1930g. "Pro epokhy i s'ohodnishnikh blikh." *Nova generatsiia* 5: 4.

———. 1930h. "Selo." In Semenko 1930l, p. 18.

———. 1930i. "Vid kerivnoï kolehiï 'Novoï generatsiï.'" *Nova generatsiia* 4: 63–64.

———. 1930j. "Za konsolidatsiiu proletars'kykh syl v ukraïns'kii literaturi." *Nova generatsiia* 3: 57–58.

———. 1930k. "Zhovtnia udar." *Nova generatsiia* 11–12: 3.

———. 1930l. *Evropa i my. Pamflety i virshi (1928–1929)*. Kharkiv: Knyhospilka.

———. 1930m. "Panfuturizm. (Iskusstvo perekhodnogo perioda)." In Leites and Iashek 1930, vol. 2, pp. 120–22. [Originally published in *Semafor u Maibutnie* no. 1 (May), pp. 10–12.]

———. 1930n. "Mirkuvannia pro te, chym shkidlyvyi ukraïns'kyi natsionalizm dlia ukraïns'koï kul'tury, abo chym korysnyi internatsionalizm dlia neï zh." In Leites and Iashek 1930, vol. 2, pp. 375–80. [Reprint of Semenko 1927c]

———. 1930o. "Postanovka pytannia v teoriï mystetstva perekhodovoï doby." In Leites and Iashek 1930, vol. 2, pp. 113–19.

———. 1930p. "Chornyi Berlin." In Semenko 1930l, pp. 5–6.

———. 1931a. "Do vykhodu tomiv moiei 'Povnoï zbirky tvoriv.'" In Semenko 1929–31, vol. 3, p. 5. [Reprinted in Semenko 1931g, p. 93.]

———. 1931b. "Imperiia i my." In Semenko 1931g, p. 5.

———. 1931c. "Konkretna propozytsiia do vsikh literatury, mystetstva i nauky robitnykiv, shcho ïkh NKO chy inshi vidpovidni ustanovy maiut' vidriadzhaty u zakordonnu poïzdku." In Semenko 1931g, p. 46–47.

———. 1931d. "Pochynaiu riadovym." *Literaturna hazeta* 10 (March 30): 2.

———. 1931e. "Povema [*sic*] pro te, iak povstav svit." In Semenko 1931g, pp. 57–80.

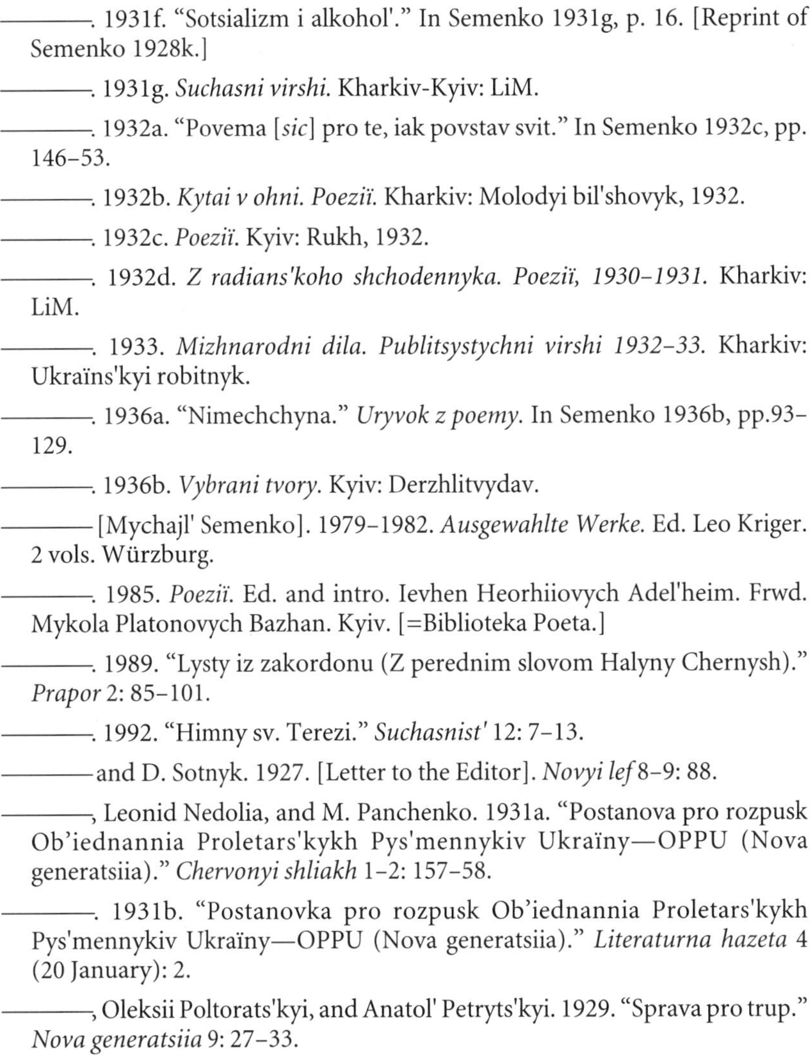

———. 1931f. "Sotsializm i alkohol'." In Semenko 1931g, p. 16. [Reprint of Semenko 1928k.]

———. 1931g. *Suchasni virshi.* Kharkiv-Kyiv: LiM.

———. 1932a. "Povema [*sic*] pro te, iak povstav svit." In Semenko 1932c, pp. 146–53.

———. 1932b. *Kytai v ohni. Poezii̇.* Kharkiv: Molodyi bil'shovyk, 1932.

———. 1932c. *Poezii̇.* Kyiv: Rukh, 1932.

———. 1932d. *Z radians'koho shchodennyka. Poezii̇, 1930–1931.* Kharkiv: LiM.

———. 1933. *Mizhnarodni dila. Publitsystychni virshi 1932–33.* Kharkiv: Ukraïns'kyi robitnyk.

———. 1936a. "Nimechchyna." *Uryvok z poemy.* In Semenko 1936b, pp.93–129.

———. 1936b. *Vybrani tvory.* Kyiv: Derzhlitvydav.

——— [Mychajl' Semenko]. 1979–1982. *Ausgewahlte Werke.* Ed. Leo Kriger. 2 vols. Würzburg.

———. 1985. *Poezii̇.* Ed. and intro. Ievhen Heorhiiovych Adel'heim. Frwd. Mykola Platonovych Bazhan. Kyiv. [=Biblioteka Poeta.]

———. 1989. "Lysty iz zakordonu (Z perednim slovom Halyny Chernysh)." *Prapor* 2: 85–101.

———. 1992. "Himny sv. Terezi." *Suchasnist'* 12: 7–13.

——— and D. Sotnyk. 1927. [Letter to the Editor]. *Novyi lef* 8–9: 88.

———, Leonid Nedolia, and M. Panchenko. 1931a. "Postanova pro rozpusk Ob'iednannia Proletars'kykh Pys'mennykiv Ukraïny—OPPU (Nova generatsiia)." *Chervonyi shliakh* 1–2: 157–58.

———. 1931b. "Postanovka pro rozpusk Ob'iednannia Proletars'kykh Pys'mennykiv Ukraïny—OPPU (Nova generatsiia)." *Literaturna hazeta* 4 (20 January): 2.

———, Oleksii Poltorats'kyi, and Anatol' Petryts'kyi. 1929. "Sprava pro trup." *Nova generatsiia* 9: 27–33.

"Shcho pyshut' chytachi." 1927. *Nova generatsiia* 1: 61.

Shchupak, Samiilo. 1924a. "Borot'ba i peremoha nad konservatyzmom v mystetstvi (do toho shcho stalos' v asotsiatsiï Komunkul'tovtsiv)." *Bil'shovyk* 198 (2 September): 4.

———. 1924b. "Odvertyi lyst chlenam literaturnoho ob'iednannia 'Aspanfut.'" *Bil'shovyk* 27 (2 February): 4.

———. 1925. "Zauvazhennia shcho do teperishn'oï sytuatsiï v literaturno-hromads'komu rukhovi na Ukraïni." *Zhyttia i revoliutsiia* 6–7: 61.

———. 1927. "Problema natsional'noï kul'tury." *Zhyttia i revoliutsiia* 6: 398–402.

———. 1928. "Komunkul'tivs'kymy manivtsiamy." *Hart* 2: 90–98.

Sherekh, Iurii [George Shevelov]. 1955. "Istoriia odniieï literaturnoï mistyfikatsiï." In Strikha 1955, pp. 249–64.

Shevchenko, Ivan I. 1923. "Chy mozhlyvyi Zhovtnevyi blok mystetstv?" *Literatura, Nauka, Mystetstvo* 6 (11 November).

Shevelov, George [Hryhorii Shevchuk]. 1947. "Istoriia Edvarda Strikhy." *Arka* (Munich) 6: 10–14.

——— [Iurii Sherekh]. 1955. "Istoriia odniieï literaturnoï mistyfikatsiï." In Strikha 1955, pp. 249–64.

Shkandrij, Myroslav. 1992. *Modernists, Marxists and the Nation: The Ukrainian Literary Discussion of the 1920s.* Edmonton.

Shklovskii, Viktor Borisovich. 1970. *A Sentimental Journey: Memoirs, 1917–1922.* Trans. Richard Sheldon. Ithaca, New York.

Shkurupii, Geo. 1921. "Neniufary" (Poema). *Zhovten'. Zbirnyk* (Kharkiv), pp. 20–22.

———. 1922a. "Ia." In Shkurupii 1922e, n. p.

———. 1922b. "Manifest Marinetti i panfuturyzm." *Semafor u Maibutnie. Aparat Panfuturystiv* no. 1 (May), pp. 8–10.

———. 1922c. "Muzyka shumiv (Musique bruitiste)." *Semafor u Maibutnie. Aparat Panfuturystiv* no. 1 (May), p. 23.

———. 1922d. "!Nevidannyi poiedinok!" *Semafor u Maibutnie. Aparat Panfuturystiv* no. 1 (May), p. 46.

——— [Korol' Futuroprerii]. 1922e. *Psykhetozy. Vitryna tretia.* Kyiv: Panfuturysty.

———. 1922f. "Odchai." In Shkurupii 1922e, n. p.

———. 1922g. "Avtoportret." In Shkurupii 1922e, n. p.

———. 1922h. "Zalizna brama." *Shliakhy mystetstva* 1: 9.

———. 1922i. "Lialia." In Shkurupii 1922e, n.p.

———. 1923a. "Likarepopyniada." In Shkurupii 1923e, p. 54.

———. 1923b. "Liryka futurysta." In Shkurupii 1923e, p. 22.

———. 1923c. "Vohkist' vust." *Chervonyi shliakh* 9: 20–21.

———. 1923d. "Vy." In Shkurupii 1923e, pp. 10–11.

———. 1923e. *Baraban. Vitryna druha.* Kyiv: Panfuturysty.

———. 1923f. "Sherk sertsia." *Zhovtnevyi zbirnyk panfuturystiv,* p. 25. [Reprinted in Shkurupii 1925c, p. 3.]

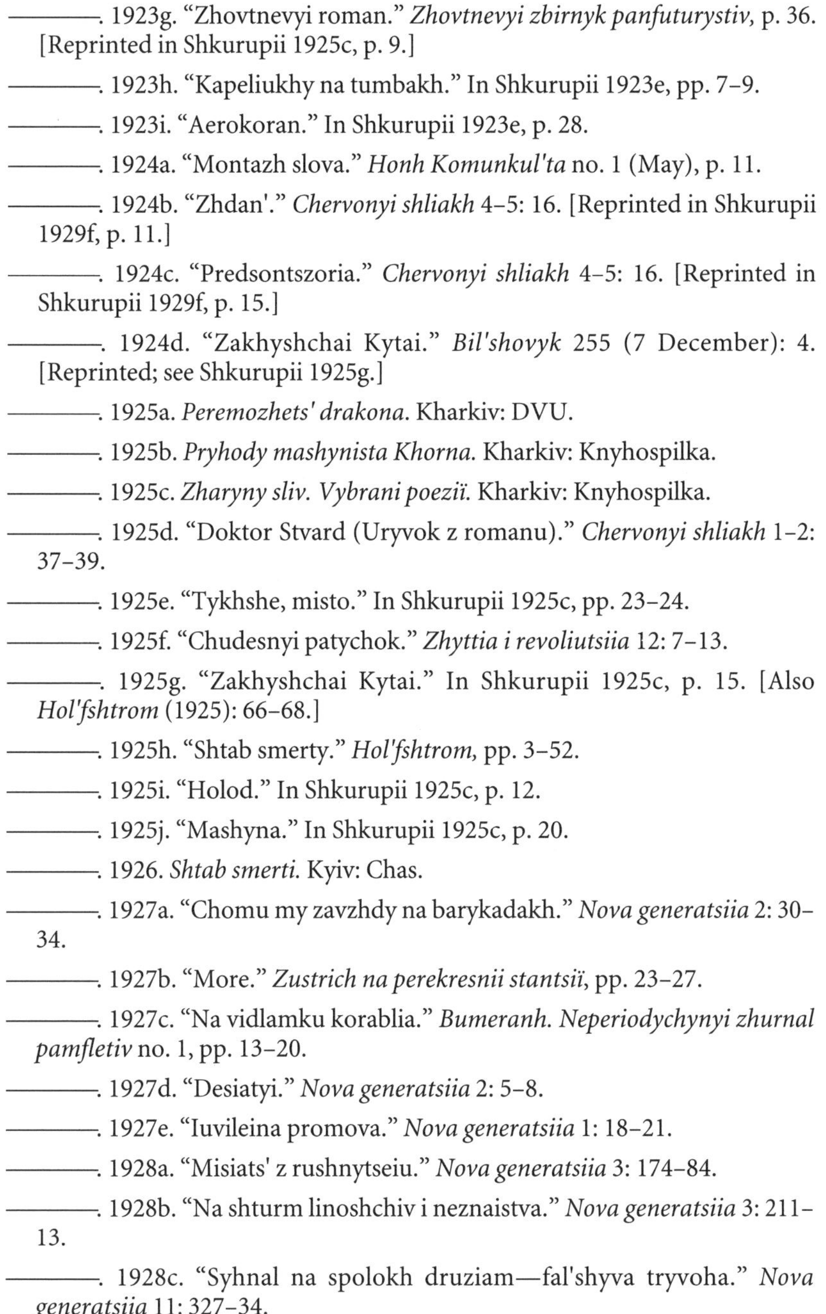

———. 1923g. "Zhovtnevyi roman." *Zhovtnevyi zbirnyk panfuturystiv*, p. 36. [Reprinted in Shkurupii 1925c, p. 9.]

———. 1923h. "Kapeliukhy na tumbakh." In Shkurupii 1923e, pp. 7–9.

———. 1923i. "Aerokoran." In Shkurupii 1923e, p. 28.

———. 1924a. "Montazh slova." *Honh Komunkul'ta* no. 1 (May), p. 11.

———. 1924b. "Zhdan'." *Chervonyi shliakh* 4–5: 16. [Reprinted in Shkurupii 1929f, p. 11.]

———. 1924c. "Predsontszoria." *Chervonyi shliakh* 4–5: 16. [Reprinted in Shkurupii 1929f, p. 15.]

———. 1924d. "Zakhyshchai Kytai." *Bil'shovyk* 255 (7 December): 4. [Reprinted; see Shkurupii 1925g.]

———. 1925a. *Peremozhets' drakona*. Kharkiv: DVU.

———. 1925b. *Pryhody mashynista Khorna*. Kharkiv: Knyhospilka.

———. 1925c. *Zharyny sliv. Vybrani poeziï*. Kharkiv: Knyhospilka.

———. 1925d. "Doktor Stvard (Uryvok z romanu)." *Chervonyi shliakh* 1-2: 37–39.

———. 1925e. "Tykhshe, misto." In Shkurupii 1925c, pp. 23–24.

———. 1925f. "Chudesnyi patychok." *Zhyttia i revoliutsiia* 12: 7–13.

———. 1925g. "Zakhyshchai Kytai." In Shkurupii 1925c, p. 15. [Also *Hol'fshtrom* (1925): 66–68.]

———. 1925h. "Shtab smerty." *Hol'fshtrom*, pp. 3–52.

———. 1925i. "Holod." In Shkurupii 1925c, p. 12.

———. 1925j. "Mashyna." In Shkurupii 1925c, p. 20.

———. 1926. *Shtab smerti*. Kyiv: Chas.

———. 1927a. "Chomu my zavzhdy na barykadakh." *Nova generatsiia* 2: 30–34.

———. 1927b. "More." *Zustrich na perekresnii stantsiï*, pp. 23–27.

———. 1927c. "Na vidlamku korablia." *Bumeranh. Neperiodychynyi zhurnal pamfletiv* no. 1, pp. 13–20.

———. 1927d. "Desiatyi." *Nova generatsiia* 2: 5–8.

———. 1927e. "Iuvileina promova." *Nova generatsiia* 1: 18–21.

———. 1928a. "Misiats' z rushnytseiu." *Nova generatsiia* 3: 174–84.

———. 1928b. "Na shturm linoshchiv i neznaistva." *Nova generatsiia* 3: 211–13.

———. 1928c. "Syhnal na spolokh druziam—fal'shyva tryvoha." *Nova generatsiia* 11: 327–34.

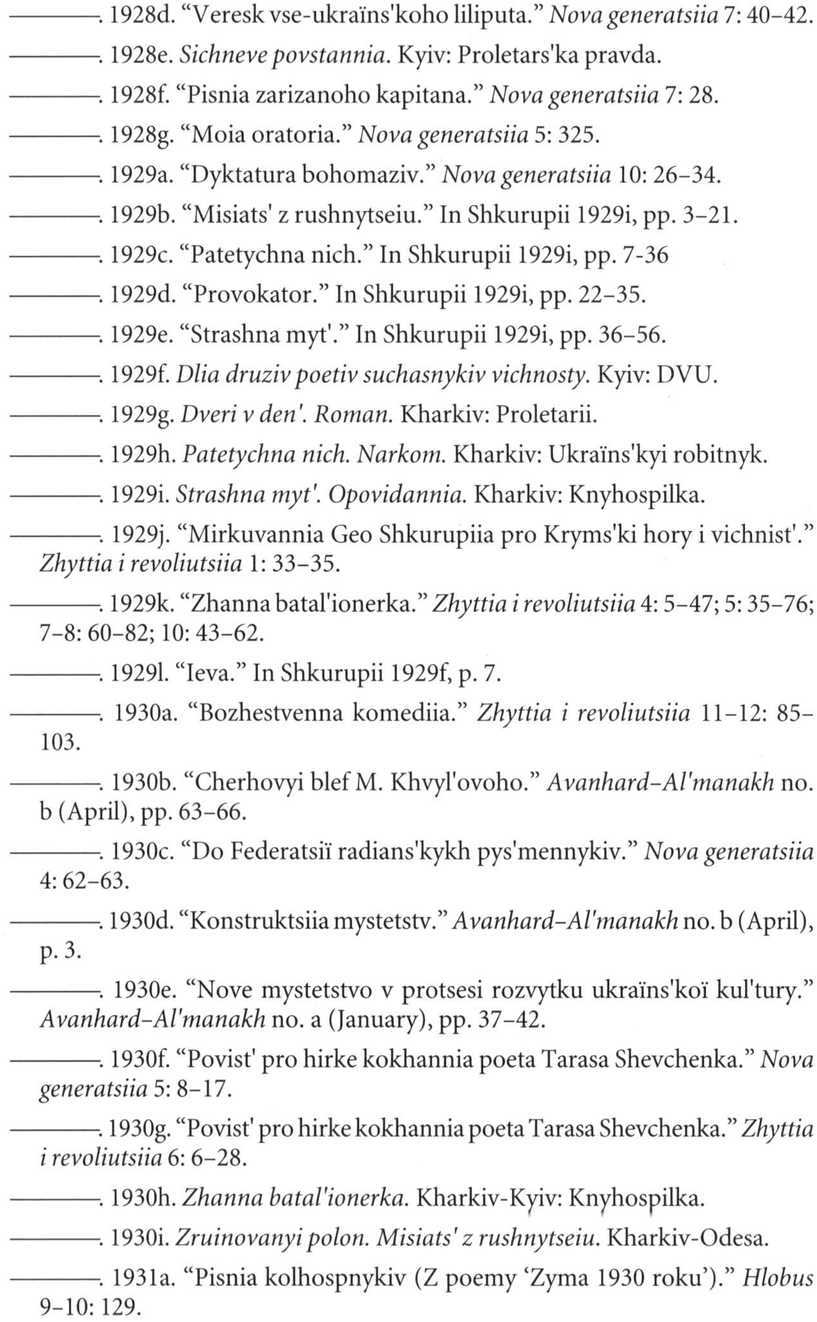

———. 1928d. "Veresk vse-ukraïns'koho liliputa." *Nova generatsiia* 7: 40–42.

———. 1928e. *Sichneve povstannia*. Kyiv: Proletars'ka pravda.

———. 1928f. "Pisnia zarizanoho kapitana." *Nova generatsiia* 7: 28.

———. 1928g. "Moia oratoria." *Nova generatsiia* 5: 325.

———. 1929a. "Dyktatura bohomaziv." *Nova generatsiia* 10: 26–34.

———. 1929b. "Misiats' z rushnytseiu." In Shkurupii 1929i, pp. 3–21.

———. 1929c. "Patetychna nich." In Shkurupii 1929i, pp. 7-36

———. 1929d. "Provokator." In Shkurupii 1929i, pp. 22–35.

———. 1929e. "Strashna myt'." In Shkurupii 1929i, pp. 36–56.

———. 1929f. *Dlia druziv poetiv suchasnykiv vichnosty*. Kyiv: DVU.

———. 1929g. *Dveri v den'. Roman*. Kharkiv: Proletarii.

———. 1929h. *Patetychna nich. Narkom*. Kharkiv: Ukraïns'kyi robitnyk.

———. 1929i. *Strashna myt'. Opovidannia*. Kharkiv: Knyhospilka.

———. 1929j. "Mirkuvannia Geo Shkurupiia pro Kryms'ki hory i vichnist'." *Zhyttia i revoliutsiia* 1: 33–35.

———. 1929k. "Zhanna batal'ionerka." *Zhyttia i revoliutsiia* 4: 5–47; 5: 35–76; 7-8: 60–82; 10: 43–62.

———. 1929l. "Ieva." In Shkurupii 1929f, p. 7.

———. 1930a. "Bozhestvenna komediia." *Zhyttia i revoliutsiia* 11–12: 85–103.

———. 1930b. "Cherhovyi blef M. Khvyl'ovoho." *Avanhard-Al'manakh* no. b (April), pp. 63–66.

———. 1930c. "Do Federatsiï radians'kykh pys'mennykiv." *Nova generatsiia* 4: 62–63.

———. 1930d. "Konstruktsiia mystetstv." *Avanhard-Al'manakh* no. b (April), p. 3.

———. 1930e. "Nove mystetstvo v protsesi rozvytku ukraïns'koï kul'tury." *Avanhard-Al'manakh* no. a (January), pp. 37–42.

———. 1930f. "Povist' pro hirke kokhannia poeta Tarasa Shevchenka." *Nova generatsiia* 5: 8–17.

———. 1930g. "Povist' pro hirke kokhannia poeta Tarasa Shevchenka." *Zhyttia i revoliutsiia* 6: 6–28.

———. 1930h. *Zhanna batal'ionerka*. Kharkiv-Kyiv: Knyhospilka.

———. 1930i. *Zruinovanyi polon. Misiats' z rushnytseiu*. Kharkiv-Odesa.

———. 1931a. "Pisnia kolhospnykiv (Z poemy 'Zyma 1930 roku')." *Hlobus* 9-10: 129.

———. 1931b. "Bez polemiky." *Literaturna hazeta* 8 (February 28): 1.

———. 1931c. "Zbory v sel'budi (Uryvok z poemy 'Zyma 1930 roku')." *Zhyttia i revoliutsiia* 7: 55–65.

———. 1931d. *Bozhestvenna komedii. Pamflety.* Kharkiv-Kyiv: LiM.

———. 1931e. *Dveri v den'. Roman.* 2nd ed. Kharkiv-Kyiv: LiM.

———. 1931f. *Noveli nashoho chasu. Proza.* Vol. 1. Kharkiv-Kyiv: LiM.

———. 1933a. "Proletars'ka tvorchist' kvitne buinym kvitom." *Hlobus* 7–8: 5.

———. 1933b. *Zyma 1930 roku. Frahmentarni maliunky, vykonani virshamy ta prozoiu.* Kharkiv-Kyiv: LiM.

———. 1968. *Dveri v den': Vybrane.* Ed. and intro. Aron Abramovych Trostianets'kyi. Kyiv.

———. 1982. "Zhanna batal'ionerka." *Suchasnist'* 1–2: 38–81; 3: 8–48; 4–5: 11–35; 6: 11–31.

——— and Dmytro Buz'ko. 1927. "Starym Dniprom v ostannii raz." *Nova generatsiia* 1: 21–35.

——— and Myroslav Irchan [Andrii Babiuk]. 1922j. "Lystuvannia z EM [*sic*] Irchanom." *Katafalk iskusstva* no. 1 (13 December), p. 2.

Shliakhy rozvytku suchasnoï literatury. Dysput. 1925. Kyiv: Kul'tkomisiia mistskomu UAN.

Shpol, Iuliian [Iul'ian; Mykhailo Ialovyi]. 1923a. *Vèrkhy.* Kyiv-Moscow-Berlin: Gol'fshtrom.

———. 1923b. "Misto." In Shpol 1923a, pp. 42–48.

———. 1923c. "V zalizni puta." In Shpol 1923a, pp. 13–14.

———. 1923d. "Fistul'no tonkoiu nytkoiu." In Shpol 1923a, p. 8.

———. 1923e. "Pershi khorobri." *Chervonyi shliakh* 9: 11–19.

———. 1929. *Zoloti lyseniata.* Kharkiv: Knyhospilka.

———. 1930. "Do ob'iednannia AsKK (Komunkul't) iz Hartom." In Leites and Iashek, eds. 1930, 2: 141–45.

Shums'kyi, Oleksander. 1927. "Ideolohichna borot'ba v ukraïns'komu kul'turnomu protsesi." *Bil'shovyk Ukraïny* 2: 11–25.

Shymans'kyi, O. 1930. "Plenum TsK 'Pluha.'" *Pluh* 1: 78–79.

"Shyroke zasidannia ideolohichnoho biuro Aspanfut (Komunkul'tovtsiv)." 1924. *Bil'shovyk* 5 (6 January): 6.

"Skhema tsentrkomunkul'ta okremoï Respubliky." 1924. *Honh komunkul'ta* no. 1 (May), p. 17.

Skrypnyk, Leonid. 1927. *Poradnyk fotohrafa.* Kharkiv: DVU.

——— [M. Lans'kyi]. 1927a. "Livyi roman." *Nova generatsiia* 2: 34–38.

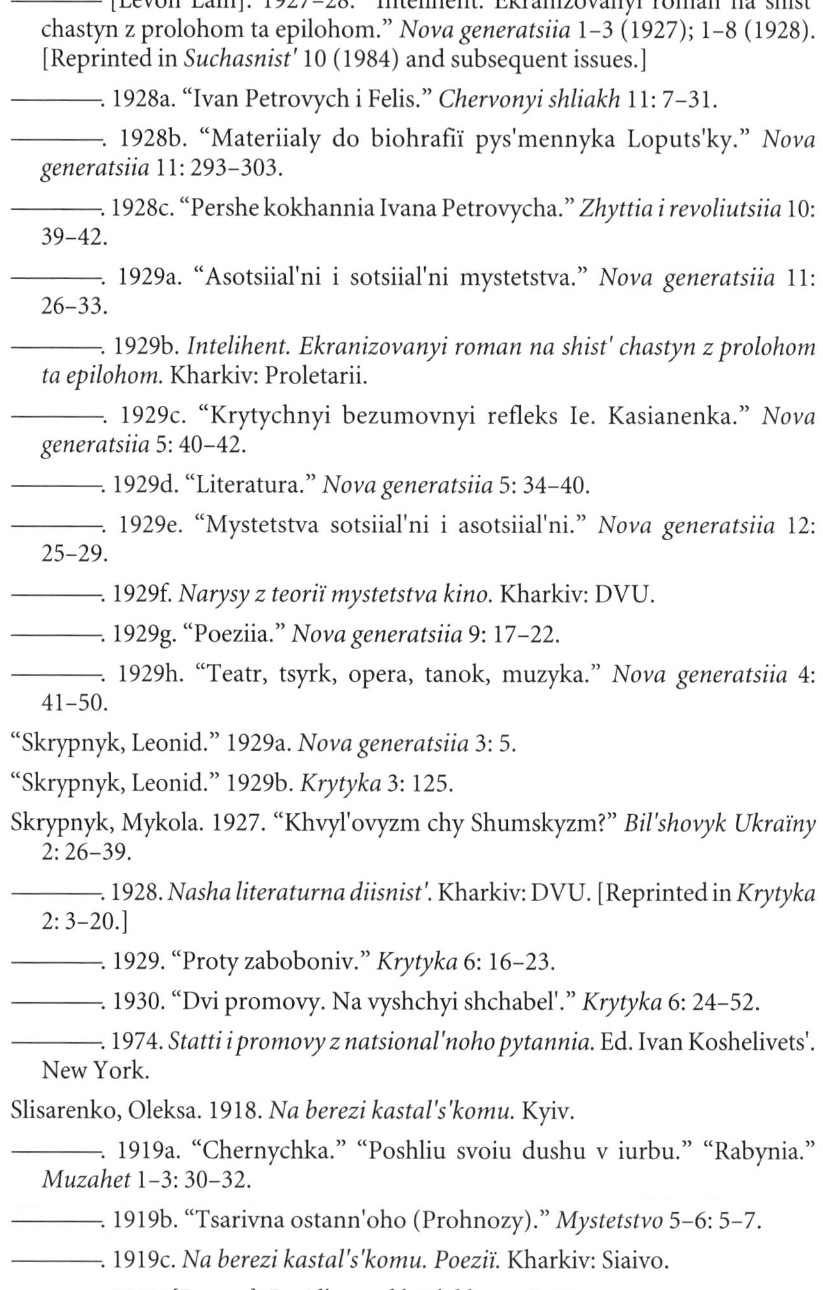

——— [Levon Lain]. 1927–28. "Intelihent. Ekranizovanyi roman na shist' chastyn z prolohom ta epilohom." *Nova generatsiia* 1–3 (1927); 1–8 (1928). [Reprinted in *Suchasnist'* 10 (1984) and subsequent issues.]

———. 1928a. "Ivan Petrovych i Felis." *Chervonyi shliakh* 11: 7–31.

———. 1928b. "Materiialy do biohrafiï pys'mennyka Loputs'ky." *Nova generatsiia* 11: 293–303.

———. 1928c. "Pershe kokhannia Ivana Petrovycha." *Zhyttia i revoliutsiia* 10: 39–42.

———. 1929a. "Asotsiial'ni i sotsiial'ni mystetstva." *Nova generatsiia* 11: 26–33.

———. 1929b. *Intelihent. Ekranizovanyi roman na shist' chastyn z prolohom ta epilohom.* Kharkiv: Proletarii.

———. 1929c. "Krytychnyi bezumovnyi refleks Ie. Kasianenka." *Nova generatsiia* 5: 40–42.

———. 1929d. "Literatura." *Nova generatsiia* 5: 34–40.

———. 1929e. "Mystetstva sotsiial'ni i asotsiial'ni." *Nova generatsiia* 12: 25–29.

———. 1929f. *Narysy z teoriï mystetstva kino.* Kharkiv: DVU.

———. 1929g. "Poeziia." *Nova generatsiia* 9: 17–22.

———. 1929h. "Teatr, tsyrk, opera, tanok, muzyka." *Nova generatsiia* 4: 41–50.

"Skrypnyk, Leonid." 1929a. *Nova generatsiia* 3: 5.

"Skrypnyk, Leonid." 1929b. *Krytyka* 3: 125.

Skrypnyk, Mykola. 1927. "Khvyl'ovyzm chy Shumskyzm?" *Bil'shovyk Ukraïny* 2: 26–39.

———. 1928. *Nasha literaturna diisnist'.* Kharkiv: DVU. [Reprinted in *Krytyka* 2: 3–20.]

———. 1929. "Proty zaboboniv." *Krytyka* 6: 16–23.

———. 1930. "Dvi promovy. Na vyshchyi shchabel'." *Krytyka* 6: 24–52.

———. 1974. *Statti i promovy z natsional'noho pytannia.* Ed. Ivan Koshelivets'. New York.

Slisarenko, Oleksa. 1918. *Na berezi kastal's'komu.* Kyiv.

———. 1919a. "Chernychka." "Poshliu svoiu dushu v iurbu." "Rabynia." *Muzahet* 1–3: 30–32.

———. 1919b. "Tsarivna ostann'oho (Prohnozy)." *Mystetstvo* 5–6: 5–7.

———. 1919c. *Na berezi kastal's'komu. Poeziï.* Kharkiv: Siaivo.

———. 1920. [Poems]. In *Al'manakh tr'okh,* pp. 9–18.

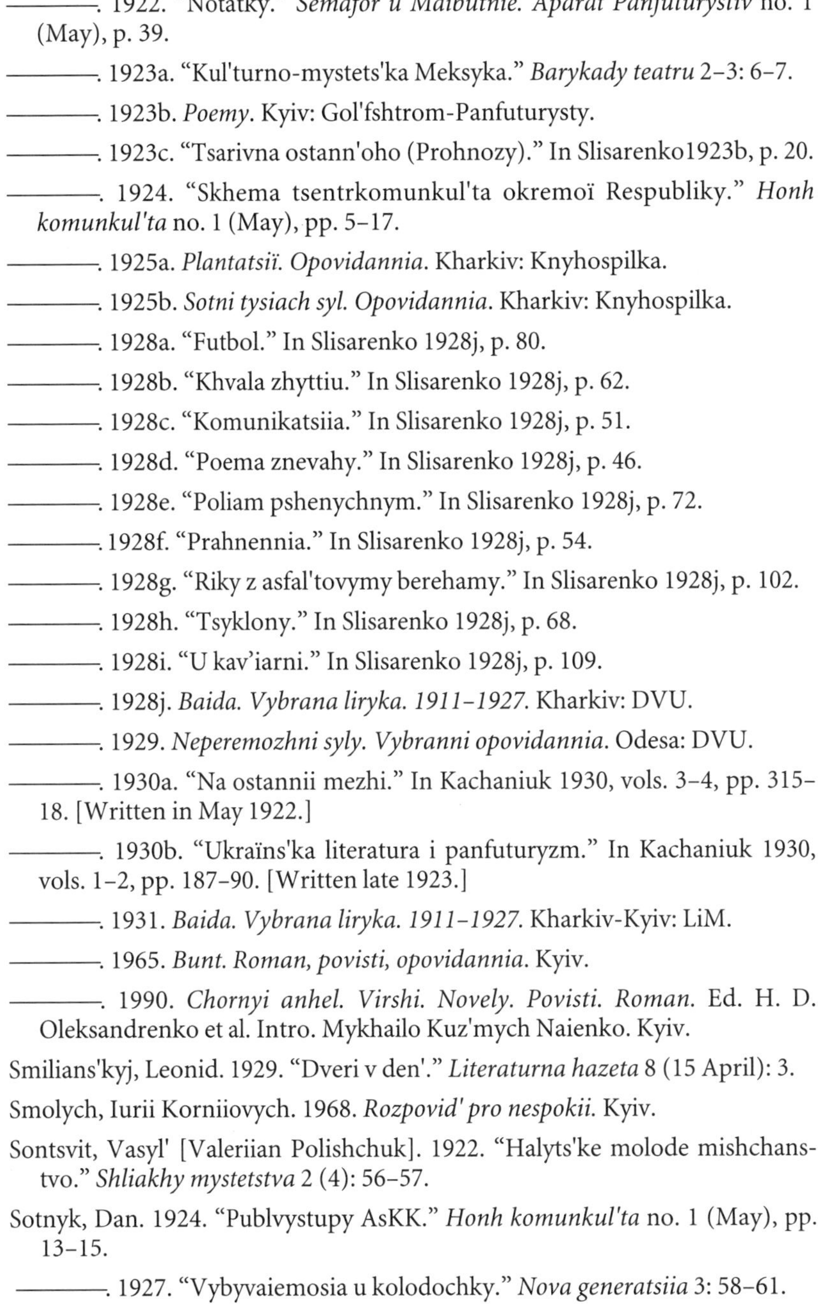

———. 1922. "Notatky." *Semafor u Maibutnie. Aparat Panfuturystiv* no. 1 (May), p. 39.

———. 1923a. "Kul'turno-mystets'ka Meksyka." *Barykady teatru* 2–3: 6–7.

———. 1923b. *Poemy*. Kyiv: Gol'fshtrom-Panfuturysty.

———. 1923c. "Tsarivna ostann'oho (Prohnozy)." In Slisarenko1923b, p. 20.

———. 1924. "Skhema tsentrkomunkul'ta okremoï Respubliky." *Honh komunkul'ta* no. 1 (May), pp. 5–17.

———. 1925a. *Plantatsiï. Opovidannia*. Kharkiv: Knyhospilka.

———. 1925b. *Sotni tysiach syl. Opovidannia*. Kharkiv: Knyhospilka.

———. 1928a. "Futbol." In Slisarenko 1928j, p. 80.

———. 1928b. "Khvala zhyttiu." In Slisarenko 1928j, p. 62.

———. 1928c. "Komunikatsiia." In Slisarenko 1928j, p. 51.

———. 1928d. "Poema znevahy." In Slisarenko 1928j, p. 46.

———. 1928e. "Poliam pshenychnym." In Slisarenko 1928j, p. 72.

———. 1928f. "Prahnennia." In Slisarenko 1928j, p. 54.

———. 1928g. "Riky z asfal'tovymy berehamy." In Slisarenko 1928j, p. 102.

———. 1928h. "Tsyklony." In Slisarenko 1928j, p. 68.

———. 1928i. "U kav'iarni." In Slisarenko 1928j, p. 109.

———. 1928j. *Baida. Vybrana liryka. 1911–1927*. Kharkiv: DVU.

———. 1929. *Neperemozhni syly. Vybranni opovidannia*. Odesa: DVU.

———. 1930a. "Na ostannii mezhi." In Kachaniuk 1930, vols. 3–4, pp. 315–18. [Written in May 1922.]

———. 1930b. "Ukraïns'ka literatura i panfuturyzm." In Kachaniuk 1930, vols. 1–2, pp. 187–90. [Written late 1923.]

———. 1931. *Baida. Vybrana liryka. 1911–1927*. Kharkiv-Kyiv: LiM.

———. 1965. *Bunt. Roman, povisti, opovidannia*. Kyiv.

———. 1990. *Chornyi anhel. Virshi. Novely. Povisti. Roman*. Ed. H. D. Oleksandrenko et al. Intro. Mykhailo Kuz'mych Naienko. Kyiv.

Smilians'kyj, Leonid. 1929. "Dveri v den'." *Literaturna hazeta* 8 (15 April): 3.

Smolych, Iurii Korniiovych. 1968. *Rozpovid' pro nespokii*. Kyiv.

Sontsvit, Vasyl' [Valeriian Polishchuk]. 1922. "Halyts'ke molode mishchanstvo." *Shliakhy mystetstva* 2 (4): 56–57.

Sotnyk, Dan. 1924. "Publvystupy AsKK." *Honh komunkul'ta* no. 1 (May), pp. 13–15.

———. 1927. "Vybyvaiemosia u kolodochky." *Nova generatsiia* 3: 58–61.

Sriblians'kyi, Mykyta [Mykyta Shapoval]. 1909. "Pro domo sua." *Ukraïns'ka khata* 7–8: 413–31.

———. 1910. "Poet i iurba: do kharakterystyky 'kul'tu Shevchenka.'" *Ukraïns'ka khata* 3: 201–206.

———. 1911. "Testimonium pauperitatis." *Ukraïns'ka khata* 9: 405–416.

———. 1912. "Borot'ba za indyvidual'nist'." *Ukraïns'ka khata* 2: 96–108; 3–4: 170–85.

———. 1913a. "Z hromads'koho zhyttia." *Ukraïns'ka khata* 9: 564–73.

———. 1913b. "Zakonoproekt iepyskopa Nykona." *Ukraïns'ka khata* 12: 768–78.

———. 1913c. Review of "Semenko. *Prélude. Liryka.* Kyiv 913 [*sic*], stor. 40. Ts. 20 k." *Ukraïns'ka khata* 7–8: 506.

———. 1914. "Etiud pro futuryzm." *Ukraïns'ka khata* 6: 449–65.

———. 1924. *Etiud pro futuryzm.* Kam'ianets' na Podilliu–Odesa [Kalisz, tabor internovanykh]: Chornomor.

"Statement by the International Faction of Constructivists." 1974. In Bann 1974b, p. 68.

Starynkevych, L. 1929a. Review of "Geo Shkurupii. Dlia druziv poetiv suchasnykiv vichnosty. DVU, 1929 r. 172 st." *Chervonyi shliakh* 11–12: 186–90.

———. 1929b. Review of "Leonid Skrypnyk. *Intelihent. Ekranizovanyi roman na shist' chastyn z prolohom ta epilohom.* Vyd-vo 'Proletarii.' Kharkiv 1929, 146 stor. 1 krb. 35 kop." *Krytyka* 6: 160–62.

Stephan, Halina. 1981. *"Lef" and the Left Front of the Arts.* Munich.

Stepniak, M. 1928. Review of "A. Slisarenko. *Dusha mastera. Rasskazy.* Avtorizovannyi perevod s ukrainskogo G. V. Prokhorova, M.V. Vishnevskoi i Blitsa, pod red. prof. M. P. Samarina. Izd. 'Ukrainskii rabochii,' 1928. Tir. 3160. Str. 332." *Chervonyi shliakh* 11: 279.

Strikha, Edvard [Kost' Burevii]. 1929a. "Odvertyi lyst do 'Novoï generatsiï,' M. Semenka i inshykh khutorystiv [*sic*]." *Literaturnyi iarmarok* 8: 321–23.

———. 1929b. "ZozendrOpiia [*sic*]." *Avanhard* 3: 126–33.

———. 1955. *Parodezy. Zozendropiia. Avtoekzekutsiia.* Ed. Iurii Sherekh. New York.

Sukhyno-Khomenko, V. 1930a. "Literaturna sytuatsiia na Radians'kii Ukraïni." *Zakhidna Ukraïna* 1.

———. 1930b. "Na prolitfronti bez zmin." *Hart* 3: 152–76.

Sulyma, Mykola. 1923. *Istoriia ukraïns'koho pys'menstva. (Konspekt).* Kharkiv: DVU.

Sulyma, Mykola Matviiovych. 1987. "Bilia dzherel. Mykhail' Semenko—redaktor VUFKU." *Kul'tura i zhyttia* 51 (20 December): 4.

———. 1989. "Mykhail' Semenko." In Kryzhanivs'kyi 1989, p. 284–304.

———. 1992. "Nepovtorne mahichne nime kino." *Suchasnist'* 12: 6–7.

Susovski, Marijan, ed. 1991. *Ukrajinska Avangarda, 1910–1930.* Zagreb: Muzej suvremene umjetnosti.

T.S. 1927. Review of *"Nova generatsiia* ch. 1, zhovten' 1927 r. Zhurnal livoï formatsiï mystetstva. DVU." *Pluzhanyn* 11–12: 87–89.

Tereshchenko, Marko [Mark Terewxenko]. 1922a. "Mynule i suchasne mystetsva diistva." *Semafor u Maibutnie. Aparat Panfuturystiv* no. 1 (May), pp. 43–45.

———. 1922b. "Mystetstvo diisvta (Budova i metody roboty)." *Semafor u Maibutnie. Aparat Panfuturystiv* no. 1 (May), pp. 37–38.

———. 1922c. *Budova i metody roboty mystetstva diisvta* . Kyiv: Hol'fshtrom.

——— [M.T.?]. 1923. Review of Sulyma 1923. *Bil'shovyk* 1 (1 January): 3.

———. 1966. *Krylate vidlunnia. Vybranne.* Kyiv.

Timofeev, L. 1929. Review of "Nova generatsiia—zhurnal livoï formatsiï mistetstv [*sic*]. DVU. 1928, N°N° 1–12 (ianvar'-dekabr')." *Na literaturnom postu* 9: 66–68.

Tisdall, Caroline and Angelo Bozzolla. 1978. *Futurism.* New York and Toronto.

Tkacz, Virlana. 1988. "Les Kurbas and the Actors of the Berezil Artistic Association in Kiev." *Theatre History Studies* 8: 137–55.

Tovarets', Ipolit. 1930. "Znakhabnila poshliatyna." *Avanhard-Al'manakh* no. a (January), pp. 93– 95.

Tovkachevs'kyi, Andrii. 1911a. "Kuda [*sic*] my pryishly." *Ukraïns'ka khata* 11–12: 567–72.

———. 1911b. "Literatura i nashi 'narodnyky.'" *Ukraïns'ka khata* 9: 417–33.

———. 1912. "Budynok na pisku, abo 'sobiranie Rusi' Petrom Struve." *Ukraïns'ka khata* 2: 111–27.

Trenin, Vladimir Vladimirovich. 1928. "Trevozhnyi signal druziam." *Novyi lef* 8: 30–36.

Tret'iakov, Serhii. 1930. "Kino p'iatyrichtsi." *Avanhard-Al'manakh* no. b (April): 79–81.

Trirog, M. [Mykhail' Semenko]. 1922. "Chto takoie destruktsiia." *Katafalk iskusstva* no. 1 (13 December), p. 2.

Trostianets'kyi, Aron Abramovych. 1968a. Introduction to Shkurupii 1968.

———. 1968b. *Shliakhom borot'by ta shukan'.* Kyiv: Naukova dumka.

Tryroh, M. [Mykhail' Semenko]. 1919. "Prozopisni. (Spirali)." *Mystetstvo* 4: 15–19.

———. 1922a. "Orhanizatsiinyi pryntsyp i mystetstvo slova." *Semafor u Maibutnie. Aparat Panfuturystiv* no. 1 (May), p. 13. [Reprinted in Semenko 1979–1982, vol. 2, pp. 138–45.]

———. 1922b. Review of "Deklamator slovo. Kyiv: Slovo, 1923." *Bil'shovyk* 65 (28 December): 3.

Tsebro, Anatol' [Mykhail' Semenko]. 1922. "Futuryzm v ukraïns'kii poeziï (1914–1922)." *Semafor u Maibutnie. Aparat Panfuturystiv* no. 1 (May), p. 40–43. [Reprinted in Semenko 1979–1982, vol. 2, pp. 166–75.]

Tychyna, Pavlo. 1918. *Soniashni kliarnety*. Kyiv.

———. 1983–1990. *Zibrannia tvoriv u dvanadtsiaty tomakh*. 12 vols. Ed. O. T. Honchar et al. Intro. Leonid Mykolaiovych Novychenko. Kyiv.

Tyverets', B. [Dmytro Zahul]. 1924. "Spad liryzmu v suchasnii ukraïns'kii poezii." *Chervonyi shliakh* 1–2: 141–66.

"U Komunkul'tovtsiv." 1924. *Bil'shovyk* 23 March (67): 5.

"U Kyïv AsKK." 1924. *Bil'shovyk* 2 September (198): 4.

Utechin, Sergej V. 1958. "Bolsheviks and Their Allies after 1917: The Ideological Pattern." *Soviet Studies* 2 (October): 115–19.

"Vahr" [Vasyl' Chumak]. 1919. Review of Muzahet in *Mystetstvo* 4: 44–45.

Val'den, Hervart. [Walden, Herwarth]. 1928. "Mystetstvo v Evropi." *Nova generatsiia* 9: 170–173.

Van Norman Baer, Nancy. 1991. "Design and Movement in the Theatre of the Russian Avant-Garde." In *Theatre in Revolution: Russian Avant-Garde Stage Design, 1913–1935*, ed. Nancy Van Norman Baer, pp. 35–59. New York.

"Vede." 1924. "Do dyskusiï pro konsolidatsiiu revoliutsiinykh mystest'kykh orhanizatsii." *Bil'shovyk* 276 (4 November): 6.

Vertov, Dziga. 1929. "'Liudyna z kino-aparatom,' absoliutnyi kinopys i radio-oko. (Zaiava avtora)." *Nova generatsiia* 1: 61.

"Vidpovidi chytacham. T. Supako, m. Dnipropetrovs'ke." 1928. *Nova generatsiia* 3: 239.

"Vid redaktsiï." 1918. *Universal'nyi zhurnal* 1 (October): 2.

"Vid redaktsiï." 1928a. *Nova generatsiia* 7: 61–62.

"Vid redaktsiï." 1928b. *Literaturna hazeta* 12 (21 June): 6.

"Vid Sekretariatu VUSPP." 1931. *Chervonyi shliakh* 1–2: 157.

"Vidozva Initsiiatyvnoho biuro zhovtnevoho bloku mystetstv." 1923. *Bil'shovyk* 253 (November 7): 9. [Also in *Barykady teatru* 1: 8.]

Vlyz'ko, Oleksa. 1928. "Marksyzm, shcho pidliahaie sprostuvanniu." *Nova generatsiia* 12: 418–21.

———. 1929. "Liryka Favsta." *Literaturnyi iarmarok* 2 (January): 8–9.

———. 1930a. "Poïzdy idut' na Berlin. Istoriia zakordonnoho pashportu." *Avanhard-Al'manakh* no. a (January), pp. 3–15.

———. 1930b. *Poïzdy idut' na Berlin*. Kharkiv-Kyiv: LiM.

———. 1931. "Do redaktsiï 'Literaturnoï hazety.'" *Literaturna hazeta* 8 (February 28): 4.

Voinilovych, S. 1929a. "Teoriia ekstruktsiï." *Nova generatsiia* 7: 22–32; 8: 33–41; 9: 22-26; and 11: 34–37.

———. 1929b. "Zasidannia Doslidcho-ideolohichnoho biura VUARKK, 7-ho veresnia ts.r; : Dopovidach—S. Voinilovych: "Pro teoriiu ekstruktsiï." 1929. *Nova generatsiia* 7: 61–65.

Volobuiev, Mykhailo. 1962. "Do problemy ukraïns'koï ekonomiky." In *Dokumenty Ukraïns'koho komunizmu*, pp. 132–250. New York: Proloh. [Originally published in 1928.]

Volok, Mykyta. [Valeriian Polishchuk]. 1920. Review of "O. Slisarenko, M. Liubchenko, M. Semenko, *Al'manakh tr'okh*. Kyiv: Vyd. T–va Ukr. Pys'mennykiv, 1920." *Grono*, pp. 91–93.

Voronyi, Mykola. [M. Y–ko]. 1913. Review of "M. Semenko. *Prélude. Liryka*. Kyiv 913 [*sic*], stor. 40. Ts. 20 k." *Literaturno-naukovyi visnyk* 6: 571–74.

———. 1929. *Poeziï*. Kharkiv: Rukh.

Vyshnia, Ostap. 1929–1930. *Usmishky*. 2 Vols. Kharkiv: DVU.

"Vystup Komunkul't-Aspanfut v Medinstytuti." 1924. *Bil'shovyk* 63 (March 18): 6.

"Vystup Komunkul'tovtsiv (Aspanfut) v robitnychomu klubi metalistiv." 1924. *Bil'shovyk* 88 (April 18): 4.

Weisstein, Ulrich. 1973a. "Expressionism in Literature." *Dictionary of the History of Ideas*. Vol. 2, pp. 206–209. New York.

——— ed. 1973b. *Expressionism as an International Literary Phenomenon. A Comparative History of Literatures in European Languages*. Paris.

Wellek, René and Austin Warren. 1956. *Theory of Literature*. New York.

"What Panfuturism Wants." 1930. In Leites and Iashek 1930, vol. 2, pp. 126–27. [Originally published in *Semafor u Maibutnie: Aparat panfuturystiv* no. 1 (May 1922), p. 12.]

"Z redzhurnalu." 1923. *Barykady teatru* 2–3: 1.

"Za hehemoniiu proletars'koï literatury (Rezoliutsiia komunistychnoï fraktsiï VUSPP)." 1930. *Krytyka* 6: 26.

"Zahal'ni zbory AsKK." 1924. *Bil'shovyk* 198 (2 September): 4.

Zahul, Dmytro. 1918. *Z dalekykh hir*. Kyiv.

——— [Iu.S.?]. 1923. "Mystetstvo v Kyievi." *Chervonyi shliakh* 4–5: 255.

——— [B. Tyverets']. 1924. "Spad liryzmu v suchasnii ukraïns'kii poeziï." *Chervonyi shliakh* 1–2: 141–66.

"Zaiava M. Irchana." 1924. *Bil'shovyk* 43 (21 February).

Zatons'kyi, Volodymyr et al. ed. [N.d.] *Budivnytstvo Radians'koï Ukraïny. Zbirnyk. Protsesy ideino-tvorchoï konsolidatsiï pys'mennyts'kykh syl Radians'koï Ukraïny (1917-1932).* Pt. 1: "Za Lenins'ku natsional'nu polityku." Kharkiv: DVU.

Zatvornytskyi, Hlib. 1924a. "Elektrifikatsiia golov (Agmas, kak apparat organizatsii byta)." *Honh komunkul'ta* no. 1 (May), pp. 8–9.

———. 1924b. "Komunkul't." *Barykady teatru* 4–5: 16.

"Zbirnyky 'Komunkul't.'" 1924. *Bil'shovyk* 127 (5 June): 6.

Zerov, Mykola Kostiantynovych. 1919. Review of "O. Slisarenko, *Na berezi Kastal's'komu. Poeziï.* Kharkiv: Siaivo, 1919." *Knyhar* 25–26: 1769–71.

———. 1925. "Z suchasnoï ukraïns'koï prozy." *Zhyttia i revoliutsiia* 5: 32–38.

———. 1989. "Ot rannikh dnei." *Raduga* 5: 104–109.

Zhorzh. 1924. "'Instsenirovka' AsPF [Aspanfut] chy nedostoina polityka 'Hartu'?" *Honh Komunkul'ta* no. 1 (May), p. 16.

"Zhovten' i my." 1927. *Nova generatsiia* 2: 27–30.

Zhukova, Varvara [Kost' Burevii {Burevoi}]. 1930. "Fashyzm i futuryzm." *Prolitfront* 3: 205–228.

Zhurba, Halyna. 1934. "Ale to buv Kyïv, Kyïv!..." *Nazustrich. Dvotyzhnevyk. Literatura. Mystetstvo. Nauka. Hromads'ke Zhyttia* (Lviv) 4 (15 February): 2.

———. 1962. "Vid 'Ukraïns'koï khaty' do 'Muzahetu.'" *Slovo. Zbirnyk* (New York) 1: 434–73.

Zolotoverkhyi, Ivan. 1961. *Stanovlennia ukraïns'koï radians'koï kul'tury.* Kyiv.

"Zukhvalyi zamakh ukraïns'koï kontrevoliutsiï." 1929. *Hart* 12: 177–82.

Index*

* Dates have been provided where possible for people. Authors have been listed under their primary name of publication or reference in critical literature. Pseudonyms and actual names are cross-referenced. Literary collections, journals, almanacs, etc., have been listed separately. For individual works of literature, consult under the author's name.

Text: Typeset at the Ukrainian Research Institute using Aldus PageMaker® 6.0, in 11 and 9 pt Minion. Printed by Thomson-Shore Printers, Inc. This book has been printed on long-lived acid-free paper.
Cover Design: Jennie Bush, Designworks.

Ukrainian Research Institute
HARVARD UNIVERSITY
Selected Publications

The Ukrainian Language in the First Half of the Twentieth Century (1900–1914). Its State and Status. George Shevelov. Harvard Series in Ukrainian Studies. Clothbound, ISBN 0-916458-30-X.

The Poet as Mythmaker. A Study of Symbolic Meaning in Taras Ševčenko. George Grabowicz. Harvard Series in Ukrainian Studies. Clothbound, ISBN 0-674-67852-4.

Alexander A. Potebnja's Psycholinguistic Theory of Literature. A Metacritical Inquiry. John Fizer. Harvard Series in Ukrainian Studies Clothbound, ISBN 0-916458-16-4.

The Great Soviet Peasant War. Bolsheviks and Peasants, 1917–1933. Andrea Graziosi. Harvard Papers in Ukrainian Studies. Booklet, ISBN 0-916458-83-0.

To receive a free catalogue of all Ukrainian Research Institute publications (including the journal *Harvard Ukrainian Studies*) please write, fax, or call to:

URI Publications
1583 Massachusetts Avenue
Cambridge, MA 02138
USA
tel. 617-495-3692 *fax.* 617-495-8097

e-mail:
huri@fas.harvard.edu
on-line catalog:
http://www.sabre.org/huri (follow the publications path)